OXFORD WORLD'S CLASSICS

SELECTED LETTERS

The future Catherine the Second (or Great) was born Princess Sophia Augusta Fredericka of Anhalt-Zerbst in the Prussian port city of Stettin (now Szczecin, Poland). In 1744 she took the name Catherine on her engagement to Grand Duke Peter, heir to the Russian throne. After her husband was deposed in 1762, she became the empress and reigned till her death in 1796. A reformer on the domestic scene and an ardent proponent of an expansive Russian foreign policy abroad, she was an active legislator and military commander and prided herself on her close management of a vast, multi-ethnic empire that enjoyed considerable commercial and industrial growth over the period. After putting down an extensive peasant rebellion in 1773–4, Catherine implemented an important set of administrative reforms but necessarily stopped short of dismantling serfdom, the basis of the Russian political economy. Even as an absolute ruler, she owed her security on the throne to her ability to balance oligarchic factions. She waged two victorious wars against the Ottomans, annexing Crimea in 1783; she made Russia a leading diplomatic presence in Europe, combating French animosity early in her reign, mediating in European conflicts, and colluding with Austria and Prussia in repeated partitions of Poland. A voracious reader of contemporary literature and philosophical writings, the empress courted the intellectual elite of Europe and used her prestige to project abroad Russia's image as a civilized and culturally distinguished land, marked by values of tolerance. At its peak in the 1780s, her reign saw the adoption of free press laws, and she patronized writers of secular literature, overseeing the flourishing of the theatre and the Academy of Sciences. Active herself as a playwright, amateur historian, and philologist, Catherine was a tireless epistolary writer for the sake of recreation as well as business.

ANDREW KAHN is Professor of Russian Literature at the University of Oxford and Fellow of St Edmund Hall, Oxford. He has edited several volumes for Oxford World's Classics, including Pushkin's *The Queen of Spades and Other Stories* and Montesquieu's *Persian Letters*, and for Oxford University Press is the author of *Pushkin's Lyric Intelligence* (2008) and co-author of *A History of Russian Literature* (2018).

KELSEY RUBIN-DETLEV is Assistant Professor of Slavic Languages and Literatures at the University of Southern California. She was previously the Foote Junior Research Fellow in Russian at The Queen's College, Oxford.

T0043733

OXFORD WORLD'S CLASSICS

CATHERINE THE GREAT

Selected Letters

Translated with an Introduction and Notes by
ANDREW KAHN AND KELSEY RUBIN-DETLEV

OXFORD
UNIVERSITY PRESS

OXFORD
UNIVERSITY PRESS

Great Clarendon Street, Oxford, OX2 6DP,
United Kingdom

Oxford University Press is a department of the University of Oxford.
It furthers the University's objective of excellence in research, scholarship,
and education by publishing worldwide. Oxford is a registered trade mark of
Oxford University Press in the UK and in certain other countries

Published in the United States of America by Oxford University Press
198 Madison Avenue, New York, NY 10016, United States of America

British Library Cataloguing in Publication Data

Data available

Library of Congress Control Number: 2018944466

ISBN 978–0–19–873646–2

Printed in Great Britain by
Clays Ltd, Elcograf S.p.A.

CONTENTS

INTRODUCTION

CATHERINE THE GREAT has fascinated the public from her reign as Empress of Russia (1762–96) to the present. Her charisma, her momentous times, and the story of her life have made her the inexhaustible subject of numerous biographies, documentaries, exhibitions, plays, novels, and satirical cartoons, and she has been impersonated on stage and screen by the likes of Mae West (in a 1944 Broadway play called *Catherine was Great*), Marlene Dietrich, and Catherine Zeta-Jones. Catherine was active as legislator, commander-in-chief, and diplomat during tumultuous times, starting with the Seven Years War (1756–63) and continuing through the disastrous yet transformative years of the French Revolution. Catherine was also a woman of no mean literary ambition and activity. She lived in a great age of letter-writing and stands out as one of its most accomplished practitioners. It is impossible to understand the course of her reign, the enigmas of her personal life (sometimes depicted as luridly oversexed), and the complexities of her achievements without knowledge of her correspondence, a correspondence remarkable for its magnitude and quality of writing. Of great historical interest, it also showcases the art of the letter, reflecting the intellectual ferment of the High Enlightenment and her skill in the genre.

The daughter of a minor German prince in Prussian employ, the adolescent Princess Sophia Augusta Fredericka of Anhalt-Zerbst left for Russia in 1744 to conclude an arranged dynastic marriage with her cousin, Karl Peter Ulrich of Holstein-Gottorf (Emperor Peter III from 1761), who, as a grandson of Peter the Great, had been named heir to the Russian throne by his aunt, Empress Elizabeth Petrovna. After her acceptance of the Orthodox faith upon her engagement, the young grand duchess became Ekaterina (Catherine) Alekseevna, the name chosen for her by Elizabeth in honour of her own mother, Empress Catherine I. Married at the age of 16, the new Catherine learned to bide her time in an unhappy marriage and navigate the hostile court environment, becoming in some ways a self-made woman. Catherine's sharp intelligence helped her to manoeuvre through the pitfalls of court intrigue—the subject of some of the earliest correspondence in this anthology (Letters 4–8)—and prepared her dramatic ascent through the coup d'état that overthrew her husband, Peter III, in June 1762 (Letters 9–12). After consolidating her position on the throne in the 1760s, she made serious attempts at modernizing Russian institutions and governance structures, while little more than a decade into her reign she oversaw the repression of a major peasant and Cossack uprising, the Pugachev Rebellion, which threatened the entire Russian state (the subject of many vivid letters). Peter the Great had established Russia's diplomatic and military presence by disabling Sweden's northern empire. Fifty years later, Catherine succeeded in the south by conquering Ottoman lands, then annexing Crimea, and eventually participating in the complete removal of the state of Poland from the map of Europe. Russia in her reign became a formidable power in the world political arena. Pitted against her, or in sometimes partial alliances, were Prussia, the Austrian Empire, and France. In the 1790s, when the French Revolution threatened to undo a legacy of continental stability and enlightened absolutism, she faced this new challenge head-on, proudly reviewing her accomplishments and asserting their lasting significance for Russia and for Europe as a whole (Letters 184, 186–7).

The industry and strategic vigour with which Catherine applied herself to administering her empire and managing complex sets of personal relations are reflected in her correspondence. The letters in this anthology are presented chronologically, and we have grouped them into six sections in order to show the fundamental preoccupations that emerge from one period to the next. The book aims to introduce readers to an impressive writer, whose communications with fellow rulers, generals, statesmen, and court figures, as well as with friends and influential European thinkers, constitute a primary historical record of her reign, a showcase of political correspondence, a form of autobiography, and a literary delight.

Catherine's Correspondents

Letters played an essential role in Catherine's daily life, and the time she spent on writing to a correspondent was itself a mark of esteem, as she hints to Marie-Thérèse Geoffrin, a leading figure in intellectual circles:

Since in your letter of 9 May you praise me so, Madam, for my eight pages of writing and for my punctuality in replying to you, you shall praise me even more for this one, which I am sending you on the very day on which yours was delivered to me. (Letter 18)

The burden of Catherine's workload meant that many official exchanges were routine and managed by secretaries, but Catherine monitored them very closely and herself regularly conducted the most important correspondences with monarchs like Frederick the Great of Prussia and Gustav III of Sweden, as well as Russian and European diplomats, generals, aristocrats, and doctors. All through the correspondence there are glimpses of tasks Catherine set herself as ruler, writer, commander, lover, and friend. Current research shows that Catherine wrote in her own hand to at least 220 people, and that number more than doubles if we include letters written in the hand of her secretaries. Although a circle of correspondents numbering more than 400 may seem considerable, it was surprisingly small by contemporary standards: Voltaire, for instance, had over 1,800 correspondents. It reflects Catherine's position: the dignity of a royal personage did not allow her to address just anyone in her own hand. An autograph letter from the empress was an honour that Catherine dispensed with care.

Catherine was the head of the extensive governmental correspondence network that connected her with her subordinates across her empire and abroad. There is no question that the very act of writing and reading letters mattered to Catherine as a civilized pursuit, and she took aesthetic pleasure in well-written, entertaining missives. Immediate practical concerns, however, are rarely left entirely behind, and the flexibility of the genre allowed her to mix business and pleasure in various degrees. She is comparable with other eighteenth-century enlightened monarchs in making letters a vehicle of public policy and pragmatic matters. Catherine stands out for writing so many epistles of substance and on such a variety of occasions and topics, and for her creativity in making her correspondences serve multiple purposes at once. We therefore find her letters to her literary correspondents doubling as foreign policy statements intended to be read by her fellow monarchs (Letters 184, 189), or a thank-you letter reinvented as a programmatic statement of allegiance to Enlightenment values (Letter 169).

Each correspondence has its own aims, conventions, and motifs, tailored to the addressee and to Catherine's reasons for maintaining the epistolary relationship. A multiplicity of separate networks came together on Catherine's desk: military command structures (letters to Petr Panin, Aleksei Orlov, and Alexander Bibikov), diplomatic networks (Dmitry Golitsyn and Semën Vorontsov), administrative institutions staffed by governors and judges, ecclesiastical hierarchies, and Catherine's immediate advisors at court (Nikita Panin). Much of Catherine's amorous correspondence also overlaps with her administrative correspondence: one of her favourites, Petr Zavadovsky, was initially her secretary, and after their affair he remained an important official in her government. Conversely, Grigory Potemkin was trained for government as a direct result of his intimacy with Catherine. The official importance of the Potemkin correspondence has ensured its survival, whereas many of

Catherine's other relations have left little or no epistolary trace, except for a few notes of business or flirtation.

The most exclusive group to which Catherine belonged was the web of familial and political ties that linked Europe's heads of state. Although most inter-state interactions occurred through official diplomats stationed at foreign courts, monarchs were also expected to correspond in their own hand with their allies and close family members. Catherine's official correspondence follows these diplomatic bonds: an ally of Prussia from 1764 until 1781, she wrote a few times a year to Frederick the Great; then linked to Austria, she corresponded with Joseph II until his death in 1790, then with his successors, Leopold II and Francis II. These exchanges were to a certain extent mere formalities, designed to provide assurances of the durability of the alliance, while the real details were worked out by diplomats behind the scenes. But monarchs could also make strong gestures by writing out their policy objectives in their own hand, showing thereby the importance they ascribed to the matters concerned (Letters 197, 202). The rhetoric of these letters expressed the concept (and often biological reality) of the monarchies of Europe as one large family or brotherhood: epistolary etiquette required kings and queens to address one another as 'Brother' and 'Sister'. Regardless of Catherine's personal distaste for Gustav III of Sweden, she was obliged to address him as 'My dear Brother and Cousin', reflecting their shared status as rulers as well as their blood tie as first cousins. Unlike most commoners, Catherine had to consider much of her familial correspondence a semi-public affair; while inter-monarchical correspondence was not read by the broader public, it was always composed in consultation with the ministry of foreign affairs. Catherine's correspondence with Gustav plays at escaping this rule, since Gustav initiated a 'clandestine' correspondence that passed not through the usual ministerial channels but rather through Catherine's postmaster in St Petersburg, Friedrich von Eck. Nonetheless, Catherine kept the exchange resolutely apolitical, despite Gustav's efforts to the contrary; it was also an open secret, as Catherine made eminently clear when she occasionally alluded to reading the letters to her favourites. Catherine did, of course, have genuine familial correspondences with her very closest relatives: her son Paul, his wife, Maria Fedorovna, and, eventually, short notes to her grandchildren. But her relations with her son and daughter-in-law were often chilly, and concerns of state were never far from the surface. Catherine used her letters to give lessons in ruling the empire or to discuss official matters for which Paul and Maria's cooperation was required (Letter 205).

Letters were a primary instrument of governance in the early modern state. They furnished the newly centralized administration with a constant flow of information and conveyed orders outwards to representatives of state power at home and abroad.[1] Catherine's personal instructions to her subordinates ranged from the very minute—such as specifying the use of particular sums of money—to the most general, sometimes expounding the principles behind state action (Letters 52, 92). A key characteristic of her administrative correspondence was her tendency to pepper her orders and instructions with friendly and playful messages that sought to win affection and loyalty by personalizing her power.

The conjunction of the personal and the political stands out very clearly in Catherine's correspondence with her most important subordinate, sometime lover, and possibly secret husband, Grigory Potemkin. During their passionate love affair in 1774–6, Catherine wrote almost daily, and some days more than once, to Potemkin. To none of her other correspondents (with perhaps the exception of Friedrich Melchior Grimm) did she expose herself so unabashedly, and never again did she break out of an imperial reserve entirely. From summer 1776 onwards, Potemkin was no longer Catherine's lover, but he remained her most trusted advisor, and they continued to write frequently. The shift in emotional tonality can be traced in her forms of address for him: 'Grishenka' and 'my golden pheasant' became 'friend of my heart' and 'Prince', her trustworthy confidant and her respectful (and much rewarded) counsel and agent. From this time until Potemkin's death in 1791, affairs of state became the primary preoccupation of the correspondence, often including detailed information about diplomatic negotiations, military plans, and personnel. In her letters, Catherine kept tabs on the many issues coming together in a decision-making process. The business of waging war and maintaining an active foreign policy was not only a matter of logistical planning. It also involved flattering friends as well as deceiving foes; keeping subordinates on board could be challenging because, even within her own team, gigantic egos vied for perks and rewards within the patronage system that Catherine used lavishly but with discretion. Potemkin's letters to her were intended to advise, inform, soothe, maintain his own position, and sometimes let off steam, his elaborate Russian a commanding vehicle for sentiment. Catherine's replies always retained a personal touch, staying true to her wish to

---

[1] Gary Schneider, *The Culture of Epistolarity: Vernacular Letters and Letter Writing in Early Modern England, 1500–1700* (Newark: University of Delaware Press, 2005), 37–41.

'preserve something truly human' about the statesman (Letter 12). Potemkin may be campaigning, supervising the navy, founding cities, or, rather absurdly, he may be next door and prostrated by gloom in a draughty palace, but Catherine can still tell him what a new favourite said or what her son did. As in her other most intimate correspondence, that with Grimm, Catherine reveals a taste for ordinary day-to-day living, so that even a local trip becomes an absorbing account.

The personal and the political again come together in Catherine's management and advertisement of life at her court, a theme that occupies much space in her correspondence. By enlivening her letters with news of engagements, marriages, and births, Catherine gave her correspondents a sense of proximity and loyalty to her inner circle. Her closest group of friends consisted primarily of favoured courtiers, but they are perhaps the worst represented in Catherine's surviving correspondence, since she had little need to exchange letters with individuals whom she met regularly under the rigidly structured conditions of the court. The traditional function of a royal household was to represent monarchical authority for the public, and Catherine's letters show her orchestrating large-scale festivities at Europe's most luxurious court—visitors thought it even more profligate than Versailles—and publicizing them abroad.[2] From an allegorical pageant for a visiting Prussian prince (Letter 56), to multi-day peace celebrations re-creating conquered Ottoman territory as a fairground (Letters 101, 106), and gambling with diamonds (Letter 122)—Catherine inventively and insistently narrated her imperial power through the activities of her court.

However, among the best-known of all Catherine's correspondents are the foreign individuals who did not belong to the world of state and diplomacy. Initially, these were the pre-eminent figures of the Enlightenment, the *philosophes*, a group of intellectuals, artists, and writers who had by then achieved prominence or even dominance in France and included d'Alembert, Marmontel, Diderot, and the sculptor Étienne-Maurice Falconet. Through affiliations conducted by letter and sometimes personal acquaintance, Catherine fulfilled an ambition to engage with them and their ideas. But with an eye on her own and her country's standing in Europe, she also wanted to benefit from their connections with influential court circles as well as their power over public opinion. This French epistolary network had largely disintegrated by the end of the 1770s, with Voltaire and Geoffrin in the grave and the

---

[2] T. C. W. Blanning, *The Culture of Power and the Power of Culture: Old Regime Europe, 1660–1789* (Oxford: Oxford University Press, 2002), 7.

other members ailing, ageing, or (in the case of d'Alembert and Falconet) no longer on particularly good terms with a Russian empress who had proved less than docile to their requests. Catherine then took the opportunity to develop her own cultural network in the 1780s and 1790s. The sole focus on the French *philosophes* was replaced by a more geographically diverse approach to culture. The German-born but Paris-based man of letters and Enlightenment busybody Friedrich Melchior Grimm became the key intermediary for Catherine's patronage abroad, corresponding on her behalf with writers, artists, and musicians in Italy, France, and Germany. In Germany, Catherine's cultural correspondence grew from the sole early exchange with an old family friend living near Hamburg, Johanna Bielke, to include writers from the blossoming German Enlightenment (Elisa von der Recke, Johann Georg Zimmermann, and others). Curiously, the correspondence with a Belgian prince in Austrian service, Charles-Joseph de Ligne, was in a sense the clearest continuation of Catherine's earlier French ties. A great admirer of Voltaire and proponent of elite French Enlightenment culture, de Ligne frequented the salons of all of Europe, including Catherine's, and made known her image, to which he gave an especially gendered spin, calling her 'Catherine le Grand' (intentionally using the masculine form of 'the Great'). Lasting until her death and rich in literary allusions, Catherine's exchanges with Grimm and de Ligne offered her a forum in which she displayed her belief that she was one of the last surviving representatives of the European Enlightenment.

Over time individual correspondences developed their own rhythms and style. In the case of Potemkin, changes in the letters' tone, frequency, and content followed shifts in the personal relations between the two correspondents. In other cases, an exchange could take on a life of its own. Although they met only for two extended periods in 1773–4 and 1776–7, Catherine wrote to Grimm her most revealing and most vivaciously literary letters. The correspondence began (Letter 86) as an overt continuation on paper of their sociable chats during Grimm's visit to St Petersburg in the entourage of Landgravine Karolina Henrietta of Hesse-Darmstadt, but it was also an additional strand in her web of exchanges with the *philosophes*. Catherine emphasized their shared contacts in French intellectual and German princely circles, and she sought to use Grimm to reinforce those ties. But on Grimm's second visit to Russia he officially entered her service and became her primary cultural agent abroad. This close cultural collaboration lent the exchange an increasingly confidential and political tone, to the point that the correspondents could no longer risk their letters being spied on by the governments of the countries (Prussia, France) they passed through on the way from St Petersburg to Paris. From the spring of 1781, to ensure greater privacy, Catherine and Grimm began sending their letters at approximately three-month intervals, having them carried by a courier whom Catherine dispatched specifically for this purpose. Catherine's letters accordingly began to resemble entries in a personal diary, written over many weeks before being sent off; they became the space in which Catherine most freely let loose her delights and vexations, but also where she indulged in her most fanciful literary experiments and constantly reimagined her own image in a humorous mode. Catherine frequently calls Grimm her 'Whipping-Boy', since he more than any other correspondent 'endures' the full force of all her moods and all her epistolary verve. Their running jokes throughout the exchange include abundant bodily motifs, including his 'bowel obstructions' and a shared association of storms and headaches with the increased imaginative creativity that the letters represented for each (Letter 103).

The correspondence between Catherine and the Prince de Ligne began in a rather similar manner, as the continuation of their social interactions during his visit to her court in 1780; the comedy and mockery of pseudo-learning typical of her gatherings at the Hermitage become the primary tone of their correspondence. Catherine put a great deal of effort into her letters to de Ligne, always parrying his witty sallies and matching his literary references. Another notable exchange is with Princess Ekaterina Dashkova, an early supporter who conspired to put her on the throne. Keen to encourage discretion at a dangerous moment in 1761, Catherine provides an object lesson in cloaking vulnerability in moralizing precept. She writes to Dashkova that 'To put oneself gleefully at the mercy of one's enemies and inferiors is nothing less than abject,' and in the same letter notes that independence is a privilege 'that every reasonable person ought to be keen to preserve because there are thousands and thousands of instances in life when one feels this has a practical usefulness' (Letter 8). Catherine's other epistolary relationships have their own character: showy rhetoric and classical allusion in the letters to Voltaire; an emphasis on gardening and the affairs of Britain and Denmark in the letters to Bielke; the interweaving of ambitious plans for the empire with playfulness and 'sentimental metaphysics' in the letters to Potemkin (Letter 83).

A final important but silent participant in Catherine's correspondences is the so-called Black Cabinet, the official intelligence service that existed in every European state to spy on correspondences passing through the post. As empress, Catherine herself was a regular reader of

intercepted correspondence, and her knowledge of surveillance mech-
anisms allowed her to make clever use of such systems. The postal
officials who spy on her letters' contents figure repeatedly in the early
stages of her correspondence with Grimm as mock addressees. At other
times, Catherine wrote specifically to be read by the Black Cabinets of
other states. She later claimed to have brought about the fall of the
French foreign minister, Choiseul, by writing to Voltaire and having her
letters read by the French Black Cabinet: her repeated insistence on the
strength and wealth of Russia and her frequent sideswipes at Choiseul
are all intended for that shadowy audience of her letters (Letter 43, for
instance). A further outstanding example of Catherine's awareness of
surveillance can be found in her letter to Zimmermann of 26 January
1791 (Letter 184). Facing a threat of military action from Prussia and
Great Britain, she decided to turn a reply to the German doctor into
a message of defiance for the Prussians. She intentionally sent the letter
to his home in the British territory of Hanover via the Berlin mail, in
hopes that the Prussian government would spy on its contents. As
Catherine told her secretary, she wanted 'to prove to the Prussians that
we are not afraid of them, and they will think twice before trying anything'.[3] She was thus highly aware of the criss-crossing paths that her
letters took to reach her correspondents all across Europe, and she
enjoyed finding ways of making the most of that geography.

Style and Content

People of high birth tended to learn letter-writing from their tutors and
would never admit to using the epistolary manuals in fashion at the
time, which were designed to help the inexperienced to write appropriate letters in common social situations: letters of congratulations, letters requesting favours or thanking someone for them, letters of
condolence, and so forth. Catherine was no exception. Rather, she was
an avid reader from her youth and had ample access to numerous works
of literature in epistolary form, including Richardson's novels and
Montesquieu's *Persian Letters*, as well as the letters of the ancients, like
Cicero. Catherine's style reflects most of all the sources from which she
learned to write letters: as a young girl, she practised penmanship by
copying models from the correspondence of the seventeenth-century
French courtier and man of letters Roger de Bussy-Rabutin, and a few

---

[3] *Dnevnik A. V. Khrapovitskago, 1782–1793* ['Diary of A. V. Khrapovitsky'], ed. Nikolai
Barsukov (St Petersburg: A. F. Bazunov, 1874), 356 (our translation).

years later she began her course of self-improvement by reading the most admired of all seventeenth-century letter writers, Madame de Sévigné, whose letters were in the public domain from 1725. These models of personal correspondence taught a mixed aesthetic of the 'gallant letter' practised in seventeenth-century French salon culture. Their style aimed to entertain through variety, liveliness, and affection without overemphasizing strong emotions. It encouraged Catherine's combination of folksy proverbs with more elevated quotations from classical tragedy; her emphasis on laughter and charm; and her chains of free associations that seek to surprise her reader.

In the eighteenth century, as today, the most memorable letters cultivate a personal voice, such as those of Lady Mary Wortley Montagu, Voltaire, Diderot, and later Jane Austen. Private letters on intimate themes or topics of personal interest were supposed to approximate conversation, loosely following trains of thought for a chatty exchange seemingly between equals. It is part of Catherine's art that she can manage to strike a purely sociable note without allowing her correspondents to forget her actual power. Catherine's letters do not straightforwardly and consistently follow the typical eighteenth-century evolution towards greater intimacy and emotional effusion, but rather display a conversational and intentionally witty voice designed to amuse and delight her aristocratic and literary circles. Although she speaks frequently of the heart and tenderness in her love letters, her notions of the emotions are entirely in keeping with neoclassical literary fashions and her preference for comedy over tragedy, and she had no sympathy whatsoever for sentimental literature.

Yet learning did not crowd out feeling, and calculation did not necessarily stifle spontaneity. Catherine's love letters very clearly reject the sentimental in favour of a more gallant style. Catherine escaped the gendered stereotypes of her century: she in no way emulated the modesty expected of women in their amorous correspondence, but neither did she write as a libertine. Rather, although her early letters to Zakhar Chernyshev represent an apprenticeship in heavy use of clichés drawn from novels and theatre (Letter 3), her mature love letters express the full force of her affection through exceptional zest and rapid oscillations between voices. In her letters to Potemkin, she parodies in quick succession the styles of the Russian peasant woman's lament, the neoclassical poet's allegories, and a mystical dream narrative. This level of control did not exclude forceful expressions of emotion, as in the letters to Potemkin that veer from scribbled billets-doux to exasperated reproaches, or in the grief-stricken letter she wrote to Grimm after the death of Alexander Lanskoy (Letter 151).

As in the case of many a legendary figure, Catherine's emotional life and attachments have been treated in popular culture as sensationally lascivious. To this day, Catherine is seen primarily through the prism of her sex life. The distortion, a reflection of a historical gender bias and male construction of kingship models, began to appear in representations of Catherine from the very moment of her coup d'état. It only intensified during the years of the French Revolution, when Catherine, like Marie Antoinette, became a target for crudely satirical and sexually explicit cartoons, all the more derogatory because she was now an older woman. Writers and caricaturists picked up the theme of her supposed voracity and depravity as a woman with vast ambitions as a ruler, and this anxiety about a woman in a supposedly masculine position of power culminated in the still rampant rumour regarding her unnatural death while copulating with a horse (in fact, she died naturally of a stroke). It is no surprise that, in a world of dynastic marriages where royal lines mattered, Catherine's love life should have attracted scrutiny. From the moment she arrived on the throne, foreign diplomats carefully observed the waxing and waning fortunes of her favourites because they hoped to profit from the sexual politics of court life. Her letters offer an antidote to this fascination with the imperial bedroom. Her own approach to gender was highly pragmatic and in keeping with the androgynous nature of her power as empress. In official ceremonial in Russia, she was expected to embody the typically male role of military defender of the Fatherland, as well as the feminine role of the 'Little Mother' of the nation. In her letters, she moves easily between feminine and masculine poses to suit the situation and her correspondent. When grand duchess, she sometimes wrote clandestine letters in a masculine persona as a security measure, hoping to confound unwanted readers (Letter 5). As empress, she could gossip about the Queen of Denmark's clothes with Johanna Bielke (Letter 51) or, a few days later, dispatch a lengthy instruction in military and public relations strategy to her subordinate (Letter 52). She could display herself as a doting mother in hopes of convincing d'Alembert to come to Russia (Letter 13), but she could just as easily set aside all traces of her gender and write in the typically masculine mode of the neoclassical panegyric (Letter 138). Contrasting with the overbearing weight of her femininity in popular views of her, it is this flexibility of gender performance that comes through most clearly in Catherine's correspondence.

For all her consistency of voice, Catherine was expert in modulating her tone and manner to suit diverse correspondents and circumstances. There was a practical imperative to do so: since letter-writing served a variety of purposes, she adapted her style across the spectrum from the pragmatic tone used in letters about state business to letters displaying the free play of intellect that approximate conversation. The letters Catherine wrote as a commander give evidence of military discipline and knowledge of what was happening on the ground: firm without anger when necessary, or, when irritation was unavoidable, resolutely pragmatic about finding a solution. Catherine had the literary skill necessary for such versatility, since she was an experienced author. She compiled histories and political theory and wrote memoirs, satirical journalism, history, children's literature, and some two dozen works for the theatre. Her letters, however, capture best what is most characteristic about Catherine the Great—her powers of observation, her strategic thinking, her sense of fun, her psychological insight, her chilling determination, and her powerful sense of deep feeling. Eighteenth-century practice required that one match the content and tone of one's letters to the addressee. Catherine therefore established with each of her primary correspondents a tone and a set of allusions particular to that exchange alone. Mutual flattery was part of the epistolary courtship between Voltaire and Catherine, just as restrained irony steadied the volatile competition between her and Frederick the Great. Consider the charm laced with irony she uses in writing about the south of Russia:

I have learned that Your Majesty is very fond of fruit, and that is why I am taking the liberty of sending you some watermelons from Astrakhan and Tsaritsyn and some grapes from the first of those locations, which I have just received. They are very highly regarded...(Letter 15)

When are grapes not merely grapes? In 1763, Frederick was desperate to conclude an alliance with Russia to prevent the Russians from joining up again with the Austrians, and because he had no other possible allies at the time. Although Catherine wanted Frederick's help to put her former lover Stanislas Poniatowski on the Polish throne, she also wanted to remain unfettered by alliances for the time being. Panin and his Northern System had not yet prevailed in Russian court politics, and Catherine was still negotiating between factions and possible foreign policy initiatives. She temporized, and Frederick's letter of 8 September to which Catherine is responding was an attempt to force her hand by insisting that the Austrians were aware of her plans for Poland and intended to oppose them. The grapes are an act of pseudo-politeness because they are a far cry from the signed treaty that Frederick wanted to receive instead.

Catherine's adaptability also allowed her to cut corners for great effect (as in the brusque dismissal of d'Alembert in Letter 71) or beat a correspondent at his own game by adapting to her interlocutor. The French sculptor Étienne-Maurice Falconet had a reputation for being contentious, prominently displayed in his debate with Diderot (not published until the twentieth century) on the judgment of posterity as a value. Catherine was determined to show that she was his very match, not only because she was, in point of fact, his employer but rather as a connoisseur of art with views on how and why images speak to posterity about the genius of great individuals. 'Send me your debate on posterity,' she writes in Letter 29, 'I shall tell you sincerely what I find fault with, provided the question has been treated in a manner that is not beyond my ken'; and she ultimately weighs in on their debate despite her initial protest ('I am unable to adjudicate', she demurs in Letter 34). Yet even in her bossier messages she leavens the brusque tone with doses of admiration and playfulness in reminding them both of the work of art she has commissioned: 'My respects to Peter the Great fully clothed. He has a visage, an energy, an expression, and a study has been made of the head of his charger' (Letter 29).

Survival at court required an acute understanding of human psychology: seeing through the masks of others, playing to their weaknesses, and hiding one's own designs were essential for getting ahead in a world where self-interested rivalries between courtiers were concealed under a veneer of etiquette and civility.[4] Catherine was very familiar with the seventeenth-century French tradition of character portraits, which pervaded every genre from the comedies of Molière to the maxims of La Bruyère and La Rochefoucauld, as well as letters and memoirs written at the court of Louis XIV. Catherine's mastery of court life can be seen in the striking portraits of Empress Elizabeth and Ivan Shuvalov in her letters to Sir Charles Hanbury-Williams (Letters 4 and 5), and she still exercised the art of staging and describing court scenes in her very last days (Letter 205). Some letters contain brief pen portraits of her addressees or third parties, revealing her astuteness in summing up the characters of intimates, as well as strategic allies and potential enemies such as her first cousin and fellow enlightened despot Gustav III of Sweden. In Letter 146 to Potemkin, she can scarcely conceal her mischievous delight at an injury Gustav has suffered in an accident, a blow to his vanity more than anything else. Her ability to maintain an

---

[4] Norbert Elias, *The Court Society*, trans. Edmund Jephcott (New York: Pantheon, 1983), 105–6.

apparently affectionate (though occasionally patronizing) correspondence with Gustav demonstrates her awareness that diplomatic negotiations require emotional intelligence, and that assuaging the vanity of human wishes is often a good way to retain loyalty.

Catherine's longest-standing favourites, Grigory Orlov and Grigory Potemkin, receive the most serious and penetrating character analyses in her correspondence, in part because they contributed the most to her own personal formation. Catherine knew well Orlov's impulsiveness and passion, the two traits that had made him and his brother Aleksei precisely the men needed to sweep her onto the throne in 1762 (Letter 144). Relying on Potemkin as a sounding-board and a predominant source of information and support throughout the mature years of her reign, Catherine admired his creativity verging on eccentricity, his strong leadership, his utter devotion to her, and his striving for perfection. Her eulogy of 1791 touchingly ponders whether the latter quality might have brought about his death, asserting that, over the almost two decades she had known him, Potemkin had so completely cured himself of all his faults that he had nothing left to do in life except to die (Letter 196). She was somewhat less perspicacious in her evaluations of her later favourites, as is evident in her praise of Platon Zubov, an unscrupulously venal character who greatly damaged her reputation in her final years. One might, however, see this wilful blindness as a result of court necessity: Catherine was forced to choose her favourites rather hastily in order to quell the intrigues that swirled whenever there was a vacancy—an atmosphere that sometimes wrong-footed her.

Of course, letter-writing is also a form of self-portraiture and sometimes psychological preparedness. Catherine's letters thus record her path to achieving fame and power amid the intellectual and political ferment of the second half of the eighteenth century. Educated by experience and well acquainted with failure and grief, by 1762 Catherine had matured enough to be caught up by her own destiny. The fatalistic pose at the beginning of Letter 11, in which Catherine portrays herself as swept along by others, is dramatically at odds with the histrionic player who rose energetically to the acclamation of the crowd, as she proudly tells Stanislas Poniatowski. In person, Catherine cut an elegant figure, and she devoted much attention to her image. Her imperial portraiture and iconography are substantial, and the correspondence was a related verbal vehicle for communicating her personal qualities of wit, sensibility, intelligence, and practicality, all of which she saw as essential in persuading her interlocutors of her stature, the importance of Russia on the world stage, and its place in European civilization. The self-portraits that Catherine repeatedly paints for her correspondents trace the evolution of how she wanted to be seen: from a beginning politician, determined to maintain her independence and integrity even under threat (Letter 8), to the hard-working but accessible new empress (Letter 16), to a mature woman confident in her ability to instruct the next generation (Letter 139), and finally to one of the most prominent people of the age, looking back over the legacy she would leave to posterity (Letters 174, 186). Through the many different topics her letters treated—court politics, domestic matters, foreign policy, and ideas— these attributes of perspicacity, brisk empathy, and humour consistently surface and mark out the individual voice of a ruler who took pride in writing as an art. Where other epistolary writers might enter into explicit philosophical discourse, Catherine conveyed her messages through carefully crafted manipulations of tone (jovial banter, polite society chatter, haughty declarations of principle, and heartfelt expressions of sentiment and moral support). She was also capable of imagining herself in the thick of battle, and a number of letters included here have the consistency of historical narrative, nowhere more compelling than in her own account of the coup that put her on the throne (Letter 11).

By holding up a mirror to the personalities and events of her court, as well as to her own attitudes, the letters complement her active interest in historical thought. Considered far more noble and more worthwhile reading than novels or other literary genres, eighteenth-century history writing was transformed by authors such as Voltaire, David Hume, and Edward Gibbon (all of whom Catherine read). The heroism of kings was still admired as a virtue, but personal glory was not to be sought for its own sake, since philosopher kings were expected to work to improve society, now regarded as the primary goal and motivator of history. Catherine saw herself as precisely such a heroic ruler guiding her nation's development, and her letters reflect her efforts to assume that mantle, as well as her more general interest in history. An admirer of Plutarch, Catherine enjoyed historical parallels and repeatedly cited the eighteenth century's pantheon of key rulers, including Marcus Aurelius, Caesar, Alexander the Great, and Henri IV and Louis XIV of France. She accumulated an extensive library of Russian chronicles and was one of the first to possess a copy of Russia's most famous medieval epic, the *Lay of Igor's Campaign*, rediscovered in the eighteenth century. This fascination with the Middle Ages and with the Russian national character were very much in keeping with the trends of the late eighteenth century, leading towards Romanticism (Letters 148, 203). In her correspondences with Voltaire and de Ligne, for example, Catherine transformed her conquest of formerly Ottoman territories into a revival of Greek and Byzantine antiquity or, alternatively, a latter-day crusade (Letters 57, 65, 157). But Catherine's most serious historical project was her growing understanding of Russia's past, culminating in her *Notes Concerning Russian History* (1787–94). While Catherine modestly presented her work as a mere textbook for her grandsons, and herself as an 'ignorant child', in her letters she highlighted with pride her methodical approach and her insistence on returning to the original sources.

It would be a mistake to construe Catherine's aims as exclusively or even primarily instrumental. For Catherine, as for many of her contemporaries, correspondence could be a form of sociability, a concept that was perhaps the great eighteenth-century preoccupation, explored by moral philosophers like Adam Smith and David Hume. In her Hermitage, part of the Winter Palace in St Petersburg, Catherine organized society gatherings for her close associates, including courtiers, favourites, and privileged foreign diplomats; her humorous rules set the scene with such injunctions as, 'Leave all ranks outside, likewise hats, and particularly swords,' and 'Others should join in any innocent fun that someone thinks up.'[5] Catherine reproduced this tone in her letters to intellectual figures and in all the letters by which she sought to win the personal allegiance and friendship of her correspondents. The letters to Dashkova and de Ligne, for example, portray her interactions with this group and give us a sense of the pride Catherine took in her sociable entertaining at court. Catherine enjoyed being a trendsetter in this domain as in so many others. Light-hearted, clever, and comparatively unbuttoned, the letters to de Ligne, among others, display a sensitive eye for landscape and cultural intelligence.

Catherine's use of Enlightenment thinking was accordingly multipurpose: a substantial element of pure intellectual enjoyment accompanied shrewd manipulation of ideas for practical ends. No letter better represents this feature than Catherine's first ever missive to a European intellectual figure: writing to d'Alembert on 13 November 1762, she strings together the Enlightenment discourses of stoical indifference to worldly goods, love for the greater good of humanity, the values of friendship and gratitude, and the power of education (Letter 13). Her wry postscript highlights the intention behind her skilled pastiche of the French *philosophes*' style: to make d'Alembert appear hypocritical

---

[5] Eng. trans. of Catherine's Russian-language rules from *The Memoirs of Catherine the Great*, trans. Mark Cruse and Hilde Hoogenboom (New York: Modern Library, 2006), unpaginated.

in declining her invitation to come to Russia as a teacher to her son Paul. Enlightenment sociability and intellectual activity were sources of personal enjoyment for Catherine, but also elements of an image she sought to project. It was a new form of courtly representation, in which the empress's cultivation and enlightened manner represented publicly Russia's new participation in European culture.

There was no firm boundary between the personal and the royal in Catherine's mind, and letters that begin in the realm of the sociable often shade into purposeful messages. Catherine believed that ideas had power. This feature stands out especially clearly in the correspondence with Voltaire. By mixing political matters, personal confidences, and philosophical topics, their rhetorically elaborate exchange appealed to Catherine as a pragmatist interested in bright ideas and flattered Voltaire as an ideas man interested in pragmatic solutions. It was not for nothing that this famous deist, a proponent of the idea of God as a watchmaker, found in Catherine a buyer of timepieces he manufactured at Ferney. Catherine's letters to Voltaire grew out of and fed into his other writings. In her first letter to him, she credited him as the main inspiration for her intellectual interests (Letter 14), but the correspondence took off only two years later, when Catherine thanked Voltaire for the dedication of his *Philosophy of History* (1765), a radical work of historiography that debunked ancient history and equated mythology and the story of the Bible (Letter 20). To promote her image as enlightened ruler, Catherine juxtaposes in Letter 22 her own actions with those of Voltaire in his campaigns for religious toleration. She highlights his recent success in obtaining the posthumous rehabilitation of Jean Calas, a Protestant who had been tortured and broken on the wheel in Toulouse, on suspicion of having killed his son for wanting to convert to Catholicism. Voltaire had launched a massive press campaign in favour of Calas and his family, and Catherine hoped to use those same publicity skills for her own projects. Catherine effectively adapted her style to Voltaire's in perpetuating the game of pseudonyms that had commenced their correspondence and in exerting his ironic wit against the ravages of religious fanaticism. She played to Voltaire's pet ideas in presenting her elected Legislative Commission as a triumph of religious toleration, displaying her pride in bringing together a broader cross-section of Russia's diverse population than ever before. Thanking him for his public declarations in her favour, Catherine requested a complete set of his writings, thus bringing their productive interactions full circle (Letter 37).

Catherine keenly followed the latest trends in European thought. While still grand duchess, she courted great danger by reading seditious books (a practice alluded to at the end of Letter 21). In her maturity, she secured a great publicity coup by purchasing the libraries of both Diderot and Voltaire, sending a message of her solidarity with the European Enlightenment and principles of intellectual liberty. Diderot was allowed to retain the use of his collection and received a pension in effect to serve as Catherine's librarian; in the case of Voltaire, the purchase was effected after his death through Grimm's negotiations with Voltaire's heir, his niece Madame Denis, and the library transported overland and by sea, with great fanfare, to St Petersburg. Catherine chose her allies among the thinkers she esteemed, forging a personal connection ('I learned of your illness, and I trembled for your life. Your recovery has assuaged my anxiety,' she writes to d'Alembert in Letter 21) justified by their common philosophical purpose. In d'Alembert's case, the basis of their bond was a hatred of fanaticism or religious intolerance. Those principles were not matters to be kept private, since they formed an indelible part of the image she cultivated abroad. Demonstrations of friendship gestured to the egalitarian values of intellectuals who liked to think of themselves as belonging to a Republic of Letters, another name for the work of the Enlightenment. Throughout her exchanges with d'Alembert, she contrasts her own admiration for him, evidence of her status as a civilized northern monarch, with the persecution the *Encyclopédistes* faced in France. She leaves the conversation open, staunchly reminding him of their shared opposition to superstition and keeping him informed about her legislative writings. But once d'Alembert compromised their friendship by blatantly doing the bidding of the French court, she ended the correspondence abruptly (Letter 71).

Catherine carefully meditated how to present her ideas, notably true in relation to the political theories of her century. Numerous Enlightenment thinkers turned their attention to devising the best means of governing the state, and all eyes were on Catherine as a ruler with a unique opportunity to implement these ideas. In her letters, Catherine flatters the French *philosophes* by acknowledging her debt to them, but she also makes it crystal clear that she intends to think for herself in applying new ideas to Russia. She conveys this message through her self-characterization as a bee (Letter 20) and as a 'bumbling mind' or 'awkward character' (Letters 96, 179) who selects and reworks ideas in accordance with her own will, or, as she would have put it, her understanding of conditions on the ground in Russia. Catherine declared throughout her reign the importance of the legislator in organizing government structure, as well as the need for sound legislation as the basis for state power. Her letters trace some of her readings on law, from Montesquieu's *Spirit of the Laws* (1748) to her later discovery of English law in William Blackstone's *Commentaries on the Laws of England* (1765–9), and they show her persistent interest in legal reform well beyond her famous *Instruction to the Commission for the Composition of a New Law Code* (1767). She defended to the end of her life the principles enunciated there, beginning with her belief that Russia belongs in Europe, and she presents her many enactments of the 1770s and 1780s as implementing these concepts.

A continuing source of pleasure for the modern reader is Catherine's skill as an ironist and humorist. It was not for nothing that this author of stage-worthy comedies ably projected an aura of good cheer. Her favourite literary references in the correspondence reflect her education steeped in French culture and particularly French comedies: Pont-de-Veyle's *The Sleep-Walker* (1739) and Molière's *George Dandin* (1668) are two of the most frequent. Humorous deflection was also a defence mechanism learned in a courtly world, allowing her to neutralize potential threats through charm. The tropes of theatrical buffoonery, as well as the eighteenth-century tradition of 'persiflage' or 'mockery', pervade her sense of humour, ranging from the beating she promises to give the Ottomans and the Poles, which she traces to Italian farces (Letter 44), to her renaming of Gustav III as the Shakespearean comic character Sir John Falstaff, alluding to his bravado despite his inglorious exploits like falling off a horse in front of his amassed troops (Letter 170). The fast pace of Catherine's letters accommodated multiple messages and shifts in tone, as the tragedy of war mixed with an aesthetic taste for the ridiculous.

Her humour is closely related to another stylistic feature she learned from reading authors like Voltaire: irony. Catherine enjoyed comic inversions and ironic quips against herself and others. Aimed at herself, Catherine's ironic phrasing allowed her to brag with apparent modesty (her legislation is 'accused of being a magnificent work' in Letter 104, for instance): favourite devices include the use of negative verbs to express positive opinions and other forms of ostensible self-denigration, such as her summation of her achievements in nineteen years of reign with the question 'Haven't we been idle?' (Letter 139). Aimed at others, Catherine's irony is, unsurprisingly, far less gentle and complacent: her letters to Gustav shine with such mockery. In some letters, the full context of the correspondence is key in unlocking irony, while the tone of others guides the reader into the gap between her real thoughts and her utterances. Abject insincerity marked her prostration before the Empress Elizabeth when she had to save her own neck (Letter 7).

Catherine's final letter to Frederick the Great ironically turns back on him the tools of flattery he had used for almost two decades in attempting to manipulate her (Letter 138). Desperate not to lose his ally, in his last letter to Catherine Frederick praised her in a known eighteenth-century satirical mode, the 'dialogue of the dead', in which he imagined meeting the late Russian emperor Peter the Great in the Elysian Fields and recounting to him all of Catherine's legislative, diplomatic, and military accomplishments. In her reply, Catherine reiterated her unceasing 'friendship' for him—at the very moment when she was concluding the secret Russo-Austrian alliance of May 1781. Whereas she normally wrote with more restraint, here she let loose classical parallels which were all the more meaningless since they were an ironic cover for her decision to reverse her allegiances in Germany. Earlier on in the exchange, her civility barely veils her competitiveness with Frederick, as in Letter 36. Proud of her legislative accomplishments, she pre-empts the snide criticism she expected him to make of her that the *Instruction* contains 'nothing new' because it is overtly a reworking of a number of well-known Enlightenment texts. Instead of waiting for him, she gets in first by mocking herself with reference to an animal fable. She then goes on to score points by praising the Russian language as an ideal idiom. Her prowess as a writer of Russian is an advantage she lords over a king who refused to learn to write properly in German, the language of his native land.

The fast pace of letters accommodated multiple messages and shifts in tone. Sarcasm could also be an essential tool in scotching unhelpful rumours—not uncommon on the subject of the cost of wars and the threat of taxation. 'People say that the money boxes in the cellars under my apartments are empty, but, then again, the money boxes are not exactly kept in the cellars beneath my apartments,' she says to Zimmermann (Letter 184). Letter 177 to Potemkin shows how well Catherine uses such incidental detail. Much concerned about an unhelpful rapprochement between Prussia and England, and the possibility that the Austrians would reach a deal with the Ottomans, leaving Russia to fight alone, she concludes with a mention of summer rains and the abundance of grain. This is more than polite chit-chat about the weather because rising prices and any hint of famine would be damaging both to the war effort against the Ottomans and to Russia's image abroad.

Reputation and Reception

Numbering over 6,000 and written in French, Russian, and German, Catherine's letters offer remarkable insight into the life, mind, and world of an essential figure in the history of eighteenth-century Europe. A monarch, a Russian, and moreover a woman, she could not but attract attention for her cultural and political ambitions expressed in artfully constructed letters. Her very first letter to a European cultural figure— that of 13 November 1762 to d'Alembert—was immediately published in journals and as a separate pamphlet. It was held up as a model of style, or at least as a striking curiosity, appearing in translation in an English epistolary manual as early as 1763.[6] Her letters to Voltaire enjoyed particular renown: they were allotted a separate volume in the first posthumous edition of Voltaire's complete works (published at Kehl in 1784–9), their separation from the chronological sequence of Voltaire's other correspondence signalling their prestige (only Frederick II of Prussia and d'Alembert were likewise honoured). Catherine would have preferred that they be published only after her death, so that she could avoid possible accusations of vanity; when the editors of Voltaire's works printed them anyway, she demanded a number of cuts to remove politically dangerous passages from the text. She generally limited the public circulation of her letters, exhorting all her correspondents not to publish her letters in her lifetime. While this choice curtailed the public renown she could win from them immediately, it was not false modesty. Hiding the text from the public did not conceal the existence of her epistolary exchanges, and a certain amount of mystery added to their appeal. The semi-privacy of her letters gave them an aura of prestige that all the better flattered the elite, influential correspondents whose support Catherine most desired. Although Grimm published none of Catherine's letters, his status as Catherine's favourite correspondent and cultural agent attracted a great deal of public attention and many solicitations from writers and artists eager for patronage. Allowing her letters to circulate only orally or occasionally in manuscript gave Catherine greater control over who read her letters and how they would be interpreted, since she could more carefully tailor her texts to specific readers. Within Russia, where Catherine had absolute control over the press, none but the most official of her letters were published, since the empress had to appear to the masses as the symbolic embodiment of the nation, not as a private person writing sometimes irreverent letters to the likes of Voltaire. However, Catherine did intend many of her letters to be discovered by posterity. Her self-portraits like the one for Gabriel

---

[6] George Seymour, *The Instructive Letter-Writer, and Entertaining Companion: Containing Letters on the Most Interesting Subjects, in an Elegant and Easy Style* (London: G. Kearsley, 1763), 227–8.

Sénac de Meilhan (Letter 186) were meant to be the raw materials for histories written about her by future generations. She often can be seen thinking ahead to later perceptions of her actions and of her letters, though often in humorous terms, as in Letter 59 where she mentions 'future antiquaries' puzzling over the clock from Ferney that she proposed to install in Constantinople (a project never to be realized, however).

The subsequent fate of Catherine's letters depended more than anything on political conditions in Russia. They have never been collected in a single edition. In the years immediately following her death, Catherine's son Paul tried hard to destroy her legacy, and her letters remained unpublished and undiscussed. After Paul's assassination in 1801, however, his son (and Catherine's most beloved grandson) Alexander I proclaimed himself the continuator of Catherine's enlightened reign. Translations and editions quickly acquainted Russian readers with all the letters already known in the West, including those to Voltaire and Johann Georg Zimmermann, as well as some of her Russian-language business correspondence. The palpable authority of the writer, and the fact that most of the addressees treasured the letters they received from her, ensured that many thousands were preserved. The letters were immediately celebrated by notable Russian writers like Nikolai Karamzin as proof of Russia's cultural achievements on the European stage.

However, Alexander's brother and successor Nicholas I, born only months before Catherine's death, rejected Catherine's legacy during his long reign (1825–1855), and Catherine's letters again largely disappeared from view. The pendulum swung back again under his far more liberal successor Alexander II: from the 1860s until the Russian Revolution, the vast majority of Catherine's surviving letters were finally published, albeit in numerous now obscure journals dedicated to recovering and celebrating Russian history. Catherine's fortunes ebbed once more in the Soviet Union: a foreigner and a monarch committed to a hierarchical social structure, she was regarded with official hatred and portrayed as a blood-thirsty, hypocritical villain. No serious study or edition of her works could be produced. In the West, however, the letters to Voltaire finally received scholarly treatment in Theodore Besterman's magisterial definitive edition of Voltaire's complete correspondence.

In recent decades, interest in Catherine has again blossomed in Russia and the West, with new editions of several individual correspondences finally reaching the bookshelves. The ongoing rediscovery of her letters continues to improve our understanding of this remarkable and complex figure of the European Enlightenment. While diverse in matter and style, the letters paint a unified portrait of an independent-minded, resilient, and hard-working woman deeply involved in the political and cultural developments of her age. Her letters provide a wealth of glimpses into one of the most glittering courts of the century, into a society where centuries of tradition and 'backwardness' confronted on a daily basis the alien influences of *ancien régime* Europe, and into the revolutionary transformations that at that very time were troubling and destroying the Europe that Catherine and her nation were seeking to join.

NOTE ON THE TEXT AND TRANSLATION

THERE is no single scholarly edition of the correspondence of Catherine the Great. The majority of her letters have been published, largely in nineteenth-century Russian journals; only a few of the best-known correspondences, such as the exchanges with Voltaire, de Ligne, Potemkin, and most recently Grimm have enjoyed modern scholarly editions. Fewer still English translations can be cited: the recent and impressive *Love and Conquest: Personal Correspondence of Catherine the Great and Prince Grigory Potemkin*, translated by Douglas Smith (DeKalb, IL: Northern Illinois University Press, 2005); the much less satisfactory *Voltaire and Catherine the Great: Selected Correspondence*, translated with commentary, notes, and introduction by Antony Lentin (Cambridge: Oriental Research Partners, 1974); and three very old editions—*Correspondence of Catherine the Great when Grand-Duchess, with Sir Charles Hanbury-Williams*, edited and translated by Giles Fox-Strangways, 6th Earl of Ilchester, and Elizabeth Langford-Brooke (London: T. Butterworth, 1928); 'Letters and Notes of the Empress Catherine to the Princess Daschkaw', in the second volume of *Memoirs of the Princess Daschkaw*, edited by Martha Bradford, 2 vols (London: Henry Colburn, 1840), 59–112; and a translation of the letters to de Ligne based on faulty texts in *The Prince de Ligne: His Memoirs, Letters, and Miscellaneous Papers*, translated by Katharine Prescott Wormeley, 2 vols (New York: Brentano's, 1899).

There is no definitive inventory of all of Catherine's letters. A figure of 11,000 published documents bearing her signature has been compiled, of which approximately 6,000 items can conservatively be classified as letters in the modern sense (and not just bureaucratic notes or rescripts). Many are in her hand, although, again, a precise count of those penned by her or written by her secretaries is lacking. This *Selected Letters*, representing perhaps 4 per cent of the total, provides a representative cross-section of Catherine's performance as a letter-writer in all the spheres of her activities. The criteria for selection from a wealth of writing are intrinsic interest, thematic continuity within sections and over time, readability and accessibility, and fame of the addressees. We have translated using the best available published editions. For a full list of source editions, see the Select Bibliography (p. xxxiv). Each letter is translated in full, except for the letters to Friedrich Melchior Grimm written from 9 July 1781 onwards. Beginning in spring 1781, Catherine's letters to him took on the form of diaries written in multiple sittings over up to three months. Since the complete letters to Grimm would have occupied inordinate space in our anthology, we have opted instead to translate between one and three complete instalments of each selected letter.

The diversity of editorial choices made in the various source editions requires a certain amount of standardization when assembling an anthology. Catherine typically did not use paragraphs; she wrote in a long block of text, only occasionally jumping to the next line for a new topic or new addition to a letter written over multiple days. Many editors, however, have created paragraphs following their own notions of the logical structure of the text. To unify the texts and improve readability, we have inserted paragraph breaks and altered previous editors' paragraphing as necessary. Similarly, Catherine followed the general practice of her contemporaries in using far less punctuation than modern standards require; she regularly joined strings of sentences with no more than commas, without necessarily implying a straightforward logical connection between syntactical units. Later editors have often added punctuation—typically semicolons, but also sentence breaks—at will. We sometimes disagree with their readings of Catherine's meaning and have translated accordingly. Again in the interest of readability, we have punctuated our translation in accordance with modern English standards. Similarly, we did not feel it was necessary to follow pedantically the spacing of the original manuscript in the closers or subscriptions to the letters.

Catherine's letters are written in French, Russian, and German, and she frequently included short passages in languages other than the primary language of a letter. We have translated all the text into English, indicating passages in other languages with explanatory notes. Only foreign interjections or expressions of no more than a few words have been left in the original to give the reader a sense of the multilingual experience of reading Catherine's original letters. These include use of the French 'Adieu' ('Farewell') in her Russian-language letters to Potemkin, or Catherine's occasionally boastful and intentionally exotic use of Russian words in Cyrillic script in letters to Grimm.

Catherine used French for the vast majority of her foreign correspondences and for some letters to Russians. The primary original language of the letters in this collection is French. Russian is the original language of the letters to Empress Elizabeth, the Senate, Nikita Panin, Aleksei Orlov, Alexander Bibikov, Petr Panin, and most but not all of the letters to Grigory Potemkin (Letters 7, 9, 31, 33, 52, 78–81, 83–5, 87, 89, 91–3, 95, 97, 102, 107, 110, 112, 114, 142, 146, 147, 149, 150,

161–6, 168, 171–3, 176–8, 181–2, 194). German is the original language of the letter to Elisa von der Recke (Letter 169).

Catherine's letters pose a variety of stylistic and syntactic challenges for the translator. In more informal contexts, she followed the dictates of early modern epistolary taste and sought to imitate the spoken language, complete with its ellipses and not infrequent confusions. At the same time, she consciously mixed different registers to surprise and amuse her readers, ranging within the same letter from amorous baby-talk to mock biblical style, from the ideologically charged language of Enlightenment reason to the officialese of the absolute monarch's decree. Her letters are rich in proverbs, private jokes, and associative leaps that—in their allusive omissions or ebullient verbosity—every now and then leave even the best-informed modern reader in the dark. We have therefore sought to reproduce the vivacity of Catherine's linguistic play while easing the task of the reader: we remain as close as possible to the original, but smooth out occasional solecisms, fill in some words that remained implied in her text, split excessively lengthy or convoluted sentences, and replace her idiomatic expressions with equivalents more familiar to the modern reader. Catherine's more formal letters pose a different set of difficulties: in both French and Russian, official style demanded exceptionally long sentences packed with subordinate clauses, bureaucratic terminology, and diplomatic blandishments (many of which often bore as little concrete meaning then as they do today). We retain the length and rigidity of many such periodic sentences, dividing only when the sense would not be otherwise sufficiently clear. Our overall aim is to produce readable modern English while conveying to the reader Catherine's assertive, often ironic voice in a variety of styles.

Eighteenth-century spellings of personal and place names could be erratic. We use the standard modern English forms of names whenever identifiable; diacritics are omitted in Polish. For Russian names and terms, we use English equivalents for members of the royal family (like Alexander rather than Aleksandr, Constantine rather than Konstantin; the Emperor Paul I) and otherwise retain transliterations of Russian proper names (like Petr, Pavel, and Ekaterina). Catherine's spelling of her own name was variable: we translate the Russian 'Ekaterina' as Catherine, but otherwise reproduce the spelling of her signature used in the source edition. We have adopted a modified Library of Congress transliteration system without diacritics. We replace '-ii' or '-i' with '-y' in surnames, such as Bariatinsky and Betskoy; we use '-y' in first names like Grigory and Dmitry, but not in names more familiar to English readers with an '-i', such as Andrei and Nikolai. We employ

Maria rather than Mariia and Natalia rather than Natal'ia. We omit the soft sign from the ends of names but retain it mid-word: Igor but Grigor'evich.

We have adopted the English forms of Russian and German titles and forms of address; for French people, we have retained 'Abbé', 'Chevalier', 'Duc', 'Madame', 'Mademoiselle', 'Marquis(e)', and 'Monsieur', as appropriate. In French, Catherine generally added a particle 'de' to any noble surname, regardless of national origin; we retain it only for French names.

Catherine uses two measurements of distance: the Russian 'verst', which is equivalent to 1.0668 km or 0.6629 miles, and the 'toise', a unit of 2 yards in length, used in pre-Revolutionary France.

Unless a note is provided on the text of a letter, biographical information about all people mentioned can be found in the Biographical Register. All editorial notes are marked with asterisks and can be found at the end of the book.

Until 1918, Russia used the Julian (Old Style) calendar, whereas the rest of Europe had switched to our current Gregorian (New Style) calendar by the mid-eighteenth century. Catherine typically dates her letters using the Julian calendar, which was then eleven days behind the Gregorian. All dates in the present anthology are Julian unless indicated otherwise by the initials '(NS)'. With some variations, Catherine generally wrote the location and date on the top right in more informal letters, and on the bottom left in more formal missives. We leave the dateline where it is in the source edition; if its placement on the page is not indicated, we place it at the top right.

SELECT BIBLIOGRAPHY

Source Editions

Amburger, Erik, 'Katharina II. und Graf Gyllenborg: Zwei Jugendbriefe der Prinzessin Sophie von Zerbst', *Zeitschrift für Osteuropäische Geschichte*, 7 (1933), 87–98.

Bartenev, P. I. (ed.), *Arkhiv kniazia Vorontsova*, 40 vols (Moscow: Tip. A. I. Mamontova and others, 1870–95), vol. 28.

Bartenev, P. I. (ed.), 'Liubovnyia zapisochki vysokoi osoby XVIII veka', *Russkii Arkhiv*, 6 (1881), 390–403.

Beer, Adolf (ed.), *Leopold II., Franz II. und Catharina: Ihre Correspondenz* (Leipzig: Duncker & Humblot, 1874).

Bodemann, Eduard (ed.), *Der Briefwechsel zwischen der Kaiserin Katharina II. von Russland und Johann Georg Zimmermann* (Hanover and Leipzig: Hahn, 1906).

Catherine the Great and Friedrich Melchior Grimm, *Une correspondance privée, artistique et politique au siècle des Lumières*, ed. S. Ia. Karp (Ferney-Voltaire and Moscow: Centre international d'étude du XVIIIe siècle / Monuments de la pensée historique, 2016), vol. 1.

'Chetyre pis'ma imperatritsy Ekateriny II-i k kniagine A. P. Cherkasskoy (urozhd. Levshinoi)', *Russkii Arkhiv*, 3 (1870), 529–40.

'Correspondance avec Catherine II', in Charles Henry (ed.), *Œuvres et correspondances inédites de d'Alembert* (Paris: Perrin, 1887), 193–261.

Goriainov, S. M. (ed.), *Correspondance de Catherine Alexéievna, grande-duchesse de Russie, et de Sir Charles H. Williams, ambassadeur d'Angleterre, 1756 et 1757* (Moscow: Société impériale d'histoire et d'antiquités russes, 1909).

'Imperatritsa Ekaterina II: Istoricheskie materialy, khraniashchiesia v Biblioteke dvortsa goroda', *Russkaia Starina*, 9 (1874), 277–300.

'Lettres et billets de l'impératrice Catherine II à la princesse Dachkova', in Princess Dashkova, *Mon histoire: Mémoires d'une femme de lettres russe à l'époque des Lumières*, ed. Alexandre Woronzoff-Dashkoff, Catherine Le Gouis, and Catherine Woronzoff-Dashkoff (Paris and Montreal: L'Harmattan, 1999), 227–54.

Ligne, Prince Charles-Joseph de, *Correspondances russes*, ed. Alexandre Stroev and Jeroom Vercruysse, 2 vols (Paris: Honoré Champion, 2013).

Lopatin, V. S. (ed.), *Ekaterina II i G. A. Potemkin: Lichnaia perepiska, 1769–1791* (Moscow: Nauka, 1997).

Marmontel, Jean-François, *Correspondance*, ed. John Renwick, 2 vols (Clermont-Ferrand: Institut d'études du Massif Central, 1974), vol. 1.

Pis'ma i zapiski imperatritsy Ekateriny Vtoroi k grafu Nikite Ivanovichu Paninu (Moscow: V Universitetskoi tipografii, 1863).

Proschwitz, Gunnar von (ed.), *Catherine II et Gustave III: Une correspondance retrouvée* (Stockholm: Nationalmuseum, 1998).

Pypin, A. N. (ed.), *Sochineniia imperatritsy Ekateriny II na osnovanii podlinnykh rukopisei*, 12 vols (St Petersburg: Tip. Imp. Akademii Nauk, 1901–7), vols 11, 12.

Rakint, V., 'Briefe Katharinas II. und des Stanislaus August an Elisa von der Recke', *Zeitschrift für Osteuropäische Geschichte*, 9 (new ser. 5) (1935), 222–30, 403–10.

Sbornik imperatorskago russkago istoricheskago obshchestva, 148 vols (St Petersburg: Imp. Akademiia Nauk, 1867–1916), vols 1, 6, 7, 10, 13, 15, 17, 20, 23, 27, 42.

Voltaire, *Correspondence and Related Documents*, ed. Theodore Besterman, 2nd edn, 51 vols (Geneva, Banbury, and Oxford: Voltaire Foundation, 1968–77), available online at *Electronic Enlightenment* <http://www.e-enlightenment.com/index.html>.

Biographies and Scholarly Studies of Catherine

Alexander, John T., *Catherine the Great: Life and Legend* (New York and Oxford: Oxford University Press, 1989).

Dixon, Simon, *Catherine the Great* (London: Profile, 2009).

Greenleaf, Monika, 'Performing Autobiography: The Multiple Memoirs of Catherine the Great (1756–96)', *Russian Review*, 63 (2004), 407–26.

Griffiths, David M., 'Catherine II: The Republican Empress', *Jahrbücher für Geschichte Osteuropas*, new ser., 21 (1973), 323–44.

Levitt, Marcus C., 'Catherine the Great', in *Russian Women Writers*, ed. Christine Tomei, vol. 1 (New York: Garland, 1999), 3–27.

McBurney, Erin, 'Picturing the Greek Project: Catherine II's Iconography of Conquest and Culture', *Russian Literature*, 75 (2014), 415–43.

Madariaga, Isabel de, *Russia in the Age of Catherine the Great* (London: Weidenfeld and Nicolson, 1981).

Madariaga, Isabel de, *Catherine the Great: A Short History* (New Haven and London: Yale University Press, 1990).

The Memoirs of Catherine the Great, trans. Mark Cruse and Hilde Hoogenboom (New York: Modern Library, 2006).

O'Malley, Lurana Donnels, *The Dramatic Works of Catherine the Great: Theatre and Politics in Eighteenth-Century Russia* (Aldershot: Ashgate, 2006).

Proskurina, Vera, *Creating the Empress: Politics and Poetry in the Age of Catherine II* (Boston: Academic Studies Press, 2011).

Sebag Montefiore, Simon, *Prince of Princes: the Life of Potemkin* (London: Weidenfeld and Nicholson, 2000).

Wolff, Larry, *Inventing Eastern Europe: The Map of Civilization on the Mind of the Enlightenment* (Stanford, CA: Stanford University Press, 1994).

Wortman, Richard S., *Scenarios of Power: Myth and Ceremony in Russian Monarchy*, 2 vols (Princeton: Princeton University Press, 1995–2000).

Eighteenth-Century Letter-Writing

Altman, Janet Gurkin, *Epistolarity: Approaches to a Form* (Columbus: Ohio State University Press, 1982).

Altman, Janet Gurkin, 'The Letter Book as a Literary Institution, 1539–1789: Toward a Cultural History of Published Correspondences in France', *Yale French Studies*, 71 (1986), 17–62.

Bannet, Eve Tavor, *Empire of Letters: Letter Manuals and Transatlantic Correspondence, 1680–1820* (Cambridge: Cambridge University Press, 2005).

Brant, Clare, *Eighteenth-Century Letters and British Culture* (Basingstoke: Palgrave Macmillan, 2006).

Caplan, Jay, *Postal Culture in Europe, 1500–1800* (Oxford: Voltaire Foundation, 2016).

Goldsmith, Elizabeth C., 'Authority, Authenticity, and the Publication of Letters by Women', in *Writing the Female Voice: Essays on Epistolary Literature*, ed. Elizabeth C. Goldsmith (Boston: Northeastern University Press, 1989), 46–59.

Melançon, Benoît, 'Letters, Diary, and Autobiography in Eighteenth-Century France', in *Representations of the Self from the Renaissance to Romanticism*, ed. Patrick Coleman, Jayne Lewis, and Jill Kowalik (Cambridge: Cambridge University Press, 2000), 151–70.

Sternberg, Giora, 'Epistolary Ceremonial: Corresponding Status at the Time of Louis XIV', *Past and Present*, 204 (2009), 33–88.

Whyman, Susan E., *The Pen and the People: English Letter Writers, 1660–1800* (Oxford: Oxford University Press, 2009).

Further Reading in Oxford World's Classics

Burke, Edmund, *Reflections on the Revolution in France*, ed. L. G. Mitchell.

Diderot, Denis, *Jacques the Fatalist*, trans. and ed. David Coward.

Montesquieu, *Persian Letters*, trans. Margaret Mauldon, ed. Andrew Kahn.

Voltaire, *Candide and Other Stories*, trans. and ed. Roger Pearson.

Voltaire, *A Pocket Philosophical Dictionary*, trans. John Fletcher, ed. Nicholas Cronk.

A CHRONOLOGY OF
CATHERINE THE GREAT

All dates are Old Style.

21 April 1729	The future Catherine the Great born Princess Sophia Augusta Fredericka of Anhalt-Zerbst in Stettin (now Szczecin, Poland).
28 June 1744	Renamed Grand Duchess Catherine Alekseevna on converting to Russian Orthodoxy ahead of her marriage (21 August 1745) to the heir to the Russian throne, Peter Fedorovich.
20 September 1754	Birth of Catherine's son, the future Emperor Paul.
Summer 1755–8	Affair with the Polish count Stanislas Poniatowski, then secretary to the British ambassador in Russia Sir Charles Hanbury-Williams.
1756–63	Seven Years War.
Spring 1758	Catherine implicated in the fall from favour of the Russian Chancellor, A. P. Bestuzhev-Riumin, and accused of a treasonable correspondence with General S. F. Apraksin. Catherine burns all her papers. In two dramatic encounters with Empress Elizabeth, Catherine offers to return home to her parents, but instead the empress is convinced of her innocence and pardons her.
1760/61–72	Affair with Grigory Orlov.
25 December 1761	Death of Empress Elizabeth. Accession of Catherine's husband Peter III. Withdrawal of Russia from the Seven Years War. Restoration of all Russian conquests to Prussia.
28 June 1762	Catherine assumes the Russian throne in a coup d'état and is proclaimed empress.
31 March 1764	Russia enters an alliance with Prussia.
26 August 1764	Stanislas Poniatowski's election as King of Poland at Catherine's instigation.
Spring 1767	Travels down the Volga to Kazan.
July 1767	Publication of her *Instruction to the Commission for the Composition of a New Law Code*; opening of the elected Legislative Commission in Moscow.
1766–8	Russia seeks to win greater influence in Poland by demanding greater freedom of religion for non-Catholics (including the Orthodox) in Poland. Invasion of Poland resisted by a series of associations between nobles called 'confederations', most famously the Bar Confederation.
October 1768	First Russo-Turkish War begins: the pretext for Ottoman action is an incursion by a group of Cossacks into Ottoman territory in pursuit of Polish confederates.

24–6 June 1770	Russian naval victory against the Ottomans at Chesme.
3 June 1771	The Russian army occupies Crimea, which in 1774 would become an officially independent khanate in Russia's sphere of influence.
5 August 1772	Russia, Austria, and Prussia sign the First Partition of Poland.
September 1772	Paul reaches majority, causing a court crisis over the following year owing to expectations that he might challenge his mother's hold on power. Catherine deprives him of his foreign territory and possible power base in Holstein (14 July 1773), arranges his marriage (29 September 1773) to Wilhelmina of Hesse-Darmstadt (Natalia Alekseevna), and removes him from the supervision of his former tutor and potential political ally, Nikita Panin.
Autumn 1773– spring 1774	Denis Diderot and Friedrich Melchior Grimm visit St Petersburg (respectively 27 September 1773–22 February 1774 and 6 September 1773–19 April 1774).
September 1773– September 1774	Pugachev Rebellion, a popular uprising led by the Cossack pretender Emel'ian Pugachev.
February– March 1774	Grigory Potemkin becomes Catherine's lover and possibly, secretly, her husband.
10 July 1774	Treaty of Küçük Kaynarca ends the First Russo-Turkish War.
10 January 1775	Execution of Pugachev in Moscow. Catherine enters the capital on 25 January.
5 November 1775	Promulgation of the Statute for the Administration of the Provinces of the Russian Empire.
June 1776	End of the affair between Catherine and Potemkin, who remains Catherine's most important advisor and deputy.
September 1776–18 July 1777	Grimm's second visit to St Petersburg.
June–July 1777	Gustav III of Sweden visits St Petersburg.
12 December 1777	Birth of Catherine's first grandson, the future Emperor Alexander I.
19/30 May 1778	Death of Voltaire; Catherine purchases Voltaire's library in December 1778.
2 May 1779	Peace of Teschen ends the War of the Bavarian Succession; Russia becomes a guarantor of the Peace of Westphalia, thereby enshrining its diplomatic influence in Europe.
March 1780	Declaration of Armed Neutrality, asserting the right of neutral nations to maritime trade, free of vexations by the belligerents in the American War of Independence, and again affirming Russian diplomatic influence.
May 1781	Secret alliance with Joseph II by an exchange of autograph letters, reorientating Russian foreign policy southwards.

8 April 1783	Annexation of Crimea by Russia.
June 1783	Catherine meets Gustav III at Fredrikshamn (now Hamina, Finland). His presumed friendship with Catherine does not procure him the permission he expects to attack Denmark.
25 June 1784	Death of Catherine's beloved favourite Alexander Lanskoy; during her grieving, she throws herself into the compilation of a *Comparative Dictionary of All Languages and Dialects* (2 vols, 1787–9).
21 April 1785	Promulgation of Catherine's Charters to the Towns and the Nobility.
1785–6	Catherine writes a trilogy of anti-Masonic plays, *The Deceiver*, *The Deceived*, and *The Siberian Shaman*.
19 April 1786	Premiere of the comic opera *Fevey*, composed by Vasily Pashkevich to a libretto by Catherine, her first in the genre.
January–July 1787	Journey to Crimea.
1787–94	Publication of the *Notes Concerning Russian History* in six parts (left incomplete).
August 1787	Second Russo-Turkish War begins.
June 1788	Russo-Swedish War begins: the immediate cause was Gustav III's ultimatum to Russia demanding, among other things, the return of Russian Finland and a return of lands taken from the Ottoman Empire.
3 July 1789 (OS) / 14 July 1789 (NS)	The fall of the Bastille marks the start of the French Revolution.
6 July 1789	Platon Zubov becomes Catherine's last favourite.
3 August 1790	Treaty of Värälä ends the Russo-Swedish War and re-establishes the territorial status quo ante.
March 1791	Britain threatens to send a fleet to the Baltic unless the Russian conquest of Ochakov is reversed. Russia, aware of her power as a trading partner, stands firm and the Pitt government backs down.
5 October 1791	Death of Potemkin.
29 December 1791	Treaty of Iassy (today Iași) ends the Second Russo-Turkish War.
10 January 1793 (OS) / 21 January 1793 (NS)	Execution of Louis XVI.
12 January 1793	Second Partition of Poland signed by Russia and Prussia.
Spring 1793	Visit of the Count d'Artois to Russia; Catherine sends him to Britain to plan an invasion of France, which founders on the British refusal to finance the military campaign.

5 October 1793 (OS) / 16 October 1793 (NS)	Execution of Marie Antoinette.
March–October 1794	Kosciuszko Uprising in Poland against the partition of the country between Russia and Prussia; brought to an end by the brutal Russian capture of Warsaw.
7 February 1795	Treaty between Russia and Britain against France.
13 October 1795	Third Partition of Poland between Russia, Prussia, and Austria, ending the political existence of Poland.
11 September 1796	Failure of negotiations for a marriage between Gustav IV Adolf of Sweden and Catherine's granddaughter Alexandra Pavlovna.
6 November 1796	Catherine dies of a stroke.

SELECTED LETTERS

PART I

MASTERING THE COURT
(1743–1762)

Between 1744, when the 14-year-old Sophia Augusta Fredericka of Anhalt-Zerbst arrived in Russia, and 1762, when she usurped the Russian throne, the future Catherine the Great underwent a remarkable transformation from the passive object of international politics to the world's most powerful woman and an intellectual capable of holding her own in correspondence with Europe's men and women of letters.

During these politically turbulent eighteen years, Catherine learned to navigate court politics and began to meddle, sometimes dangerously, in diplomacy. Her father, Christian August of Anhalt-Zerbst, was a military officer in the service of Frederick II (the Great) of Prussia, and Catherine met the king on her way to Russia with her mother, Johanna Elisabeth. During her stay in Russia, Johanna Elisabeth's intercepted correspondence proved to the Russian Empress Elizabeth that the former was attempting to interfere politically on behalf of Prussia. Although Catherine's marriage to the heir to the Russian throne, the future Peter III, was not jeopardized, her mother's actions contributed to the suspicions of treasonous Prussian sympathies that hung over Catherine for the whole of her time as grand duchess. Catherine assumed that rank upon her engagement to Peter and her conversion from Lutheranism to Russian Orthodoxy on 28 June 1744; Catherine's father opposed this conversion out of religious conviction, but the political ambitions of Catherine, her mother, and Frederick the Great overruled him (Letter 2). Peter and Catherine were then married on 21 August 1745.

The marriage was deeply unhappy and went unconsummated for nine years; only once both Catherine and her husband were encouraged to take lovers did Catherine produce the requisite heir, her son Paul, in 1754. Like almost all other royal consorts, Catherine had no political agency whatsoever until she had successfully given birth to an heir. Closely watched at all times, Catherine was not allowed to correspond privately, even with her family, but following Paul's birth, she soon became involved in court politics to an unprecedented degree. In 1755, she took a new lover, the Polish aristocrat Stanislas Poniatowski, to whom she was introduced by the English ambassador, Sir Charles Hanbury-Williams. As the Seven Years War brewed in the West, Hanbury-Williams sought, through Catherine, Russian support for the new Anglo-Prussian alliance; he not only subsidized her expenses, but also helped her to navigate court politics in a detailed secret correspondence (Letters 4–6). However, in January 1757, Russia acceded to the Treaty of Versailles, an alliance between Austria and France, conclusively marking Russia's entrance into the Seven Years War on their side, in opposition to Britain and Prussia. Catherine thus ended up on the wrong side of the political battle that raged over this decision at the Russian court.

This difficult situation was compounded by the failing health in 1756–7 of the Empress Elizabeth. Many Russians and foreign diplomats began to look to Catherine as the true leader of the country after Elizabeth's death, since Catherine's husband, Peter, was widely recognized as the weaker of the pair. Hanbury-Williams was among those who encouraged Catherine to think about claiming power, and Catherine's possible ascendancy brought her the support of her former opponent, Chancellor Aleksei Bestuzhev-Riumin, Russia's head of foreign affairs. However, their collusion soon became suspicious to Empress Elizabeth, and in February 1758 she had Bestuzhev-Riumin arrested on suspicion of treason. Compromised along with him, Catherine burned all her papers (thus depriving future generations of much important information about these years in her life). To clear her name, Catherine took the initiative and requested two interviews with the empress (Letter 7 thanks the empress for the second of them). In these meetings, Elizabeth confronted Catherine with three letters to General Stepan Apraksin, which Catherine had written without the approval of the Russian government; Catherine affirmed the innocence of the letters' contents, but offered to go home to Germany if she had forfeited the empress's affections. Catherine's performance on both occasions was convincing, and Elizabeth retained her at court.

Nonetheless, Catherine's position grew ever more tenuous and subject to local and international gossip, as her husband's affair with Elizaveta Vorontsova and his boorish antics became increasingly conspicuous (Letter 8). Upon Elizabeth's death in December 1761, Catherine acceded to the throne at his side as empress consort with no effective power. As Catherine had long since predicted (Letter 6), her husband immediately made peace with Prussia and prepared a new campaign in defence of his native territory of Holstein, provoking discontent in the military. Owing to his unpopularity and Catherine's ambition, Peter's reign lasted only six months: on 28 June 1762, with the support of her lover, Grigory Orlov, as well as his brother Aleksei and Catherine's close friend Ekaterina Dashkova, Catherine claimed the Russian throne for herself, refusing the urgings of some that she should reign only as regent for Paul. Her husband died in mysterious circumstances several days later. Letter 11 is essentially the only extant account of the coup from her own perspective. In international affairs, Catherine refused to re-enter the war on either side, and she waited to conclude an alliance with Frederick until 1764, after the end of the Seven Years War. Catherine's journey to political empowerment was now complete, but it remained for her to solidify her position and to learn to rule the vast and under-developed empire now under her dominion.

Alongside this political maturation, Catherine grew immensely as an intellectual. She had filled the lonely hours of her isolation as grand duchess with reading, partaking of the ancients (Plato and Tacitus, to the latter of whom she took a visceral dislike) as well as the moderns (Pierre Bayle, Voltaire, Montesquieu, d'Alembert, and much history writing). Her surviving notes include extracts from this reading, as well as reflections on the specificities that distinguished Russia's situation from that assumed by Western philosophers.

Importantly, it was also during this period that Catherine began to cultivate her skills as a writer of letters. Letter-writing was an important part of an eighteenth-century lady's education, and early letters show the 14-year-old Princess Sophia learning to write politely under her mother's watchful eye, as mother and daughter both corresponded with a family friend, the Swedish Count Gyllenborg (Letter 1). Her correspondences with Hanbury-Williams and Ekaterina Dashkova show her developing the arts of character description, political manipulation by letter, and self-presentation as a bold, steadfast, and heroic individual.[1] She also tried her hand at love letters (Letter 3): according to Catherine's memoirs, in 1751, she engaged in what she called 'a regular and very sentimental correspondence' with a courtier, Zakhar Chernyshev. She asserted that the affair was never consummated, but this was nonetheless her first experiment in the genre of the love letter. Dramatizing her passion in novelistic scenes and extravagant expressions of affection, these early letters exhibit an artificiality and conventionality that contrast with her exuberance and creativity in the later exchange with Potemkin. At other times, though, letters became a matter of life and

---

[1] *The Memoirs of Catherine the Great*, trans. Mark Cruse and Hilde Hoogenboom (New York: Modern Library, 2006), p. 105.

death, as in the letter to Elizabeth (Letter 7) and in her correspondence with Poniatowski shortly after her coup. In the wake of Catherine's coup, Poniatowski hoped to rush back to Russia and claim his place (and possibly a throne) at Catherine's side. Catherine wrote to restrain him, as she had no intention of bringing about her own ruin and his by introducing a Polish Catholic emperor (Letters 10, 11). She promised him instead the Polish throne, which she helped to obtain for him in 1764. In Russia, Catherine intended to rule alone, and her letters would be a key instrument in that effort.

1. *Sophia Augusta Fredericka of Anhalt-Zerbst to Count Henning Adolf Gyllenborg*

This is one of the earliest known letters by the future Catherine the Great, but it already exhibits the confidence and intellectual play that characterize her mature correspondence. Meanwhile, her somewhat obscure allusions to in-jokes shared in salon conversation suggest the importance she already attaches to sociability.

Sir, I learned with great pleasure of your arrival at Kassel. I hope that the rest of your journey will match this beginning—I have little doubt it will. As Providence is just, it cannot but arrange everything according to your merit, Sir. Whatever people tell me about women being slaves, thus far I have enjoyed my liberty so much that I cannot imagine this is the case. I also believe as you do that, in a certain sense, all men are born slaves, since it is not in their power to make their own destiny. In another, more comic sense, I maintain that women are freer than men, since it is not their business to swear oaths to any masters: people are generally more willing to believe that women, rather than men, are in good faith. But I see that all this leads us astray from our subject, and that it is impossible to argue a lost cause. The end of your letter sounds as if it comes straight out of a leather-bound manual. You know all that I might say about it better than I do, so I shall give up the fight. It remains for me only to tell you about the flutterer* (that means frivolous person), whose story would be too long to tell, and to assure you that I am with much esteem

    Sir,
Your most devoted friend and servant,

                                Sophie AFP AZerbst
                       at Hamburg, this 9/20 November 1743

PS Greetings from all the leather-bound heretic brothers and flutterers.

2. *Sophia Augusta Fredericka of Anhalt-Zerbst to her father, Christian August of Anhalt-Zerbst*

This official letter in French was doubtless written under the supervision of Catherine's superiors at the Russian court. Asking her father's permission for her already resolved conversion to Orthodoxy in order to marry the heir to the Russian throne, the future correspondent of Voltaire reveals that flexibility in matters of religion could be a political necessity as much as a daring philosophical position in the eighteenth century. The weakness she mentions in the postscript was caused by a life-threatening case of pleurisy, which struck her less than two weeks after her arrival in Russia.

Sire.

I take the liberty of writing to Your Highness to request your consent for Her Imperial Majesty's intentions concerning me. I can assure you that your will shall always be mine and that no one could ever make me neglect what I owe you.

Withal, Sire, I most humbly beg you to keep me in your good graces and grant me your blessing.

As I find almost no difference between the Greek and Lutheran faiths, I have decided (upon examining Your Highness's gracious instructions) to convert, and I shall send you my profession of faith at the first opportunity. I flatter myself that Your Highness will be satisfied with it, as I shall remain for the rest of my life, with profound respect, Sire, Your Highness's most humble and most obedient daughter and servant,

> Sophie A. F. Pr. of A. Z.
> at Zerbst,* 14 (3) May 1744

PS I most humbly beg Y. H. to convey my respects to my uncle and to tell him that I shall write to him by the next post. My hand is still terribly weak and will not allow me to do so today.

3. *To Zakhar Chernyshev*

Like the other notes exchanged during Catherine's flirtation with Zakhar Chernyshev, this letter was carried by one of Catherine's ladies-in-waiting, Princess Anna Alekseevna Matiushkina (née Gagarina) (1716–1804), here called 'our friend'.

[1751]

Although our friend often tells me that showing too much tenderness is not the way to be loved, I cannot help myself and must express my worry. It has been four days since I last heard from you. I know that I asked you not to write very often, but I have been told that you are jealous and angry. Just imagine what a state that puts me in! Could my eyes, which sought only yours, have possibly offended you? They must not yet have completed their journey, or they were getting ready to look at you. Believe me, dear friend: my eyes have never sinned for anyone but you. Just look how dear you are to me: I love even your jealousy. Is it true that your friendship diminishes just as much as mine grows? Be honest. What a day tomorrow is for me! Will it be as I hope? No, you have never been loved as I love you. Restless, I take up a book. I want to read, but you come and interrupt me at every line. I throw away the book and lie down on the sofa. I try to sleep, but I stay there for two hours without shutting an eye. In sum, I am a bit calmer only when I write to you. I am tempted to unbind my arm and bleed myself again—maybe that would amuse me. Does all this babble not bore you? I am ashamed of all that I write to you—forget what you have read if you don't like it.

4. *To Sir Charles Hanbury-Williams*

This letter reveals the dangerous diplomatic game that Catherine was playing in 1756: two years later, in 1758, she was denounced for pro-Prussian interactions like the one she describes with General Stepan Apraksin. The satirical portrait of Elizabeth that fills most of the letter reflects the sense of expectation with which Catherine and the rest of the court followed Elizabeth's failing health, ready to jockey for power when she died. Shuvalov's 'affections' are, of course, diplomatic ones.

Friday [6 September 1756]

Apraksin spoke to me yesterday about his departure. I said to him, 'I do not like war. There is nothing so good as peace.' He answered me, 'If the King of Prussia attacks me, I shall fight. If not, I shall not move against him.' It seemed to me as though he let that slip, for he caught himself and wanted to cover up those words with other verbiage.

This will make you laugh: the person whose coughs you were counting yesterday speaks of nothing in her inner chambers but of going to command the army herself. One of her maids said to her the other day, 'How can that be? You are a lady.' She replied, 'My father certainly went to war. Do you think me more inept?' The other replied, 'But he was a man, and you are not.' She was well-nigh angry and persisted in saying that she wanted to go to war herself. It is said that the good lady, far from being in a state to undertake such a venture, cannot climb her stairs without getting out of breath. The trapdoors that have been put in all over the place convincingly prove it. The flatteries that currently succeed best with her are that she surpasses her father in activity, action, and merit. And she believes it all so thoroughly that she is beginning to say so herself. Yesterday's exertions caused terrible pains in the lower abdomen along with the old ailments. She told me so herself as she left the hall, and my news for today has been confirmed. The hetman [Kirill Razumovsky] will tell you yet other things. I refer you to him. They say, among other things, that Petr Shuvalov's affections have changed.

5. *To Sir Charles Hanbury-Williams*

Catherine's intriguing courted danger for her and her allies. Letters could be a vital tactical tool in managing court friendships, as this letter documents in its narration of clandestine exchanges. A letter written to a single addressee could have, as we see here, multiple intended readers, including the person who transmitted it. Lev Naryshkin frequently carried messages between Catherine and Hanbury-Williams, here also delivering a missive to Elizabeth's favourite, Ivan Shuvalov. Ivan's cousin, Alexander Shuvalov, was the head of the grand ducal court and able to mediate between the grand ducal couple and the Empress Elizabeth. By turning to the Shuvalov clan, Catherine sought their help in keeping her other friends at court. These included Kirill Razumovsky, whom Catherine refers to by his title of hetman of the Zaporozhian Host; Catherine hopes to prevent him from being ordered to return to this official post in Ukraine, which would have deprived her of a necessary supporter. Catherine's lover and Hanbury-Williams's secretary, Stanislas Poniatowski, was recalled to his home country of Poland in early 1756, so much of the correspondence with Hanbury-Williams at this time revolves around efforts to bring him back to Russia as the official Polish envoy. The structure of this letter is complex because it contains a copy of Ivan Shuvalov's note, and because the text of the letter to Shuvalov is included at the end, in the form of a draft that Catherine had sent previously to Hanbury-Williams to keep him abreast of her plans.

Friday morning [15 November 1756]

My whole fine speech for Alexander Shuvalov, so prudently arranged, so skilfully deduced, so eloquently pronounced, so nobly sustained—in a word, the pinnacle of my wisdom—might have been a waste of breath owing to the extreme stupidity of the person in question, as I had foreseen—were it not for my letter to Ivan Ivanovich. Imagine a man who was to be hanged receiving his pardon at the very instant when he thought his death certain. Such was the state in which Ivan Ivanovich found himself upon reading that heaven-sent letter. Naryshkin thought he was going to have a heart attack, he was so beside himself. He bolted the doors shut to keep Ivan Ivanovich from committing some indiscretion. Finally, flinging himself into a small private chapel and there beating his head against the ground and his hands against his chest, Ivan Ivanovich remained in divine ecstasy for over half an hour. Naryshkin let him pour out his gratitude to the all-merciful God, without letting him out of his sight. He came back, started reading and rereading my letter; he then kissed the messenger's hand and finally wrote the following, after tearing up a dozen or so sheets of paper. 'I shall repay all your trust with eternal gratitude. I am most distressed that the letter which you sent me is a bit obscure at the end, when you speak of what set us at odds. *The same cause can reconcile us.* Explain yourself, Sir,* whether it is the same cause that provoked our quarrel or something similar. And rest assured that I will not fail to prove to you my constant attachment.'

He then showed great impatience to know everything; he spoke of the hetman and promised to do him service. He read my letter over and over again and, finally, after an hour and a half of solitude with Naryshkin, appeared in his antechamber. People spoke to him, but he did not reply. They asked what was wrong, and he complained that he had been writing all afternoon—which was not true. As I had my letter back, and he had to have his note back, I wrote under his words, 'I do not have time to tell you more. Do not be hasty in your judgments. All will be explained in good time.' I did this so that he would neither mistake the hetman for what he is not, nor fall back on old ideas. In any case, I shall not act without your approval. I spoke forcefully to Alexander Shuvalov about the hetman, and he has my conversation in writing—I refer you to it.

Yesterday in the afternoon I received a letter from the chancellor [Aleksei Bestuzhev-Riumin] in his own hand, a sign that the matter was important. He told me that he is distressed to see that I take him for a swindler; that if I no longer wish to trust him, I shall reduce him to planting cabbages on his estates; and that he cared more for my interests than for his soul; that if he tended to his soul as much as he did to my interests, he would think himself a veritable prophet Elijah in heaven. Here is my reply. I would not bore you with it if I did not think it would make you laugh.

'I know the prerogatives of your position. I believe you are sincere with me, and my own sincerity is too great not to tell you plainly that I do not find you so sincere with friends whose affection for me is just as true. If I distress you by presenting you with the naked truth, it would be much worse if I were reduced to dissembling. I am naturally incapable of this, and had not suspected that it could be required of me. Temper, then, your cruelty towards my friends, whom you are reducing to poverty, or promise not to make me compromise my sincerity. One must live and let others live.'

I was delighted yesterday that you were feeling a bit better; I hope to learn that this continues.

Since I am running the risk of wearying you on the subject of obtaining permission for Count Poniatowski's stay, I would have you know that the chancellor dictated the following three points to Prasse* as a reply to what had been declared to him: (1) that the court was sending Count Poniatowski here because, upon the recommendation he had received from us, they supposed they would thereby be doing something agreeable; (2) that, since he had been here, he was more capable than a new envoy of serving his master; (3) that, given the nobility and grandeur of his family, they supposed they would make a friendly gesture towards this court and prevent a numerous and necessary family from stirring. This is better put in Russian and passable.

Recently the empress was speaking with the chancellor and said, 'The court is going to think that I am the one in love with Poniatowski.' She added, but very gently, 'So why is he being sent as envoy?', and immediately ordered that a nice house be prepared for him.

Bernardi* told me I know not what, which you said is to be conveyed to the chancellor; I answered, 'Very well.' But it is very bad to write such a long document* to a sick man, and especially on the part of someone who has such extreme concern for his health.

Here is how I am thinking of writing to Ivan Ivanovich:*

You will be astonished, but rejoice: this paper will be like the Peace of Westphalia, which serves as the basis of all that has been done since. Here is, in essence, what I said to Alexander Shuvalov and of which he is to inform no one but you. You are the target at which I am aiming. I have seen his tears and heard his words. I have likewise learned of your own speeches regarding your current woes and uncertain fears. These steps seemed sincere to me; I found that my trust ought to match your advances to me. I thought about it for three days, and I resolved to give you proof of my sincerity. What follows below will even better convince you. Alexander Ivanovich tells me, 'You impute to us everything bad that happens. Yet the person whom you believe is your best friend, and not us, has done and continues to do you wrong.' He adds, 'In time you will see that we, not they, are the ones faithful to you.' I am basing myself on those words, and you will see that I am sincere from the following disclosure. Alexander Ivanovich doubtless has the chancellor in mind, and here is the truth of the matter. For four years, as though oblivious to his former offences, I gave him my trust and all the friendship of which I was capable. He has repaid me with nothing but deceptions and even betrayals. I could enumerate twenty for you. For just one, I hereby abandon him and cast myself into your arms. Have nothing to do with him if you want me to be wholly yours. I ask you for everything at present and promise you everything for the future.

Here is a sentence that is for you alone and about which Alexander Ivanovich knows nothing. Remember what put us at one another's throats. The same cause can reconcile us forever. I once knew you to have honourable sentiments. They will appreciate the generosity of my action.'*

6. *To Sir Charles Hanbury-Williams*

Although Catherine cautiously remains vague about some political specifics, this letter offers a vivid depiction of the wit, vigilance, and sense of spectacle that were necessary for effective manoeuvring at court. In the second half of the letter, Catherine furnishes somewhat allusive indications of what might happen in the event of an 'expiration', her euphemistic term for the death of Empress Elizabeth; she in fact foretells events quite exactly.

Monday morning [18 November 1756]

I spoke with Petr Shuvalov yesterday at court. I positioned myself so everyone could see that he was the one speaking to me. He harangued me for a good half an hour. I gave him free rein and listened. In the end I was forced to say something to him. My reply was, 'I shall see whether your protestations are sincere by the actions they produce.' He replied pompously, well and truly grandstanding. He spoke for another half an hour and finally said (he was apparently carried away by his passion for talking and no longer knew what he was saying) that for me he would subdue even his passions. I took him at his word: 'I shall give you a riddle to solve, to see if you are speaking the truth.' He replied, 'And what is it?' 'Ah, since it is a riddle, it is up to you to guess it. Think about it. Which passion might you overcome in order to satisfy me?' He mused and said, 'Are you speaking of the hetman?' 'Sir, I shall name no one, but since you say it, I shall not contradict you.' He was a bit disconcerted and said, 'In making peace with you, permit me not to abandon someone who was one of the first to approach me. Allow me to inform him so that he can play a role.' He wanted to go into detail and recount the matter to me, but I interrupted him, saying, 'So then, is this how you keep your promise to overcome your passions for me, even though this is the first thing I have desired?' 'Ah, well,' said he, 'that is true, and you will see that I can do anything if you wish it.' I replied, 'I shall see, and the reply that I have given you so many times this evening cannot offend you, since you assure me that it will turn out to your advantage.'

Trubetskoy told me that on Thursday they discussed acceding to the Treaty of Versailles, that Austria was working tirelessly to drag us into it, and that the College of Foreign Affairs has been ordered to draw up a plan for accession, which, however, had not yet been done.

Ivan Ivanovich, speaking with Naryshkin, told him that he would try to put me personally on good terms with the empress and that he would serve the hetman. He was overjoyed to hear that I had not taken badly his refusal regarding the hetman's departure.

Presently I shall go ahead and reply to what you ask about the intentions of Their Imperial Highnesses regarding His Prussian Majesty in the event of an 'expiration'. Here is what I know of it, Sir. In his taste for the military, the grand duke is irredeemably Prussian, and it runs so deep that it has become a passion ingrained in his temperament. As for my lady the grand duchess, since it has not yet been decided whether she will have much authority at that time, it is almost pointless to speak of her. But we shall satisfy your curiosity. I would have you know that she will never advise anything except what she believes to be for the glory and in the interest of Russia, for which she has a passion as strong as a Spartan's for Lacedaemon.* But she also knows how very much the nation needs to be well managed internally.

I am very sorry that I did not have the pleasure of seeing you yesterday, but since your health was concerned, I sacrifice for it my wish to see you.

When do you expect Count Poniatowski? Forgive the poor scribbling.

7. *To Empress Elizabeth of Russia*

Under suspicion of treasonous Prussian sympathies and the desire to undermine Empress Elizabeth's authority at the start of the Seven Years War, Catherine thanks the empress for their second interview. Her rhetorical act of submission here, reiterating her professed willingness to return home to Germany, helped her to win back the empress's sympathies and retain her position at the Russian court.

Most gracious Majesty,

Conscious of the many ineffable acts of kindness shown to me by Your Imperial Majesty, I am unable to depart without prostrating myself at the feet of Your Imperial Majesty with a tribute of my utterly unfeigned gratitude made from a sincere heart. May it indeed please the Lord God to show Your Imperial Majesty just how fully I feel the most sincere reverence, gratitude, and veneration for Your Imperial Majesty. There is not an hour when I do not beseech the Lord on my knees for the continuation of Your Imperial Majesty's inestimable health. Indeed, anything else would be unthinkable for as long as I draw breath. No sooner do I recall the superior kindnesses I have been afforded to hear from the lips of Your Imperial Majesty—and may they be blessed for eternity—than tears of joy stream from my eyes. How fortunate I should consider myself if I were permitted before my departure to convey in speech to Your Imperial Majesty my most abject gratitude, prostrating myself at the feet of Your Imperial Majesty; and for all the rest of my life through obedience, love, and sincerity from the depths of my heart to prove that I am even in the slightest degree worthy of a glance from Your Imperial Majesty. All my desires are directed to that end in order to achieve what is for me an ineffable blessing of seeing the gaze of Your Imperial Majesty and prostrating myself at the feet of Your Imperial Majesty with the greatest gratitude and with sincerity that was once sorrowful, but which is now, by Your Imperial Majesty's exalted grace, from a heart filled with joy. May the Lord God bless Your Imperial Majesty. May the Almighty grant that I might be able to express the deep reverence with which I am forever, most gracious Ruler, the most devoted, the most abject slave of Your Imperial Majesty,

Catherine, Grand Duchess
29 May 1758

8. *To Princess Ekaterina Dashkova*

Princess Dashkova, then Catherine's closest female friend despite being the sister of Peter's mistress, later commented positively on Catherine's determination to keep up appearances before and during Peter III's brief reign. Although phrased abstractly or, as Catherine terms it, 'metaphysically', the letter makes clear her underlying sense of self-worth and her combination of ambition and resolve to navigate court politics.

[1761–1762?]

I have often made mistakes by following my own inclination. But thus far I have never suffered the misfortune of following poor advice. That followed by Monsieur [Peter III]…in this case—this is just about at the limit. To put oneself gleefully at the mercy of one's enemies and inferiors is nothing less than abject. If my friends are unable to risk seeing me, I would prefer to deprive myself of the pleasure of seeing them rather than reward their zeal so poorly. I shall feel the gratitude I owe them no less. Despite the obstacles, I shall always show that there is a certain independence that every reasonable person ought to be keen to preserve because there are thousands and thousands of instances in life when one feels this has a practical usefulness, quite aside from the fact that a Prometheus* of this type by his very nature inspires respect. If my reasoning is becoming metaphysical to the point of opacity, it is because my principles lie deep, superior to any base conduct but also founded on a knowledge of the human mind and heart.

Do forgive, my dear Princess, this gibberish, and burn it once read. Rest assured that when I tell you with great clarity that I love you, I am following entirely naturally the impulse of my own heart.

My greetings to the Prince.*

9. *To the Senate*

This official order was issued in the evening on the day of the coup, when Catherine had been proclaimed empress and sovereign by the Imperial Guards regiments. She had secured her hold on the capital city of St Petersburg by appearing on a balcony at the Winter Palace, in the company of her son, to a cheering crowd, but she also made clear her intention not to reign as regent for the young Paul. Departing for Peterhof at the head of her troops to arrest her deposed husband, Catherine boldly assumed the typically male role of the military leader in full control of the nation.

28 June 1762

Senators, Sirs! I now proceed together with the troops to affirm and secure the throne, and I entrust you as my supreme government to guard the Fatherland, the people, and my son. It is decreed that Counts Skavronsky, Sheremetev, General-in-Chief Korf,* and Lieutenant Colonel Ushakov will remain present with the army and that they, together with Privy Counsellor Nepliuev, will stay in the palace with my son.

Catherine

10. *To Stanislas Poniatowski*

In the wake of Catherine's coup, rumours swirled about possible marriage plans: Grigory Orlov and Stanislas Poniatowski were both viewed as possible husbands and co-rulers for the new empress. Catherine knew that Poniatowski wished to rush to her side, driven by love and ambition. She had no intention of sharing power and knew that the mere suspicion she would give Russia a Polish and Catholic ruler could destroy them both. She sent this letter and the next to Poniatowski via the Austrian ambassador in St Petersburg: she could not risk sending them by Russian means, since the mere fact that she was corresponding with her Polish ex-lover would have raised suspicions among the population.

this 2 July 1762

I beg you urgently not to hasten here on any account since your visit in the present circumstances would be perilous for you and very harmful to me. The revolution that has just come about to my advantage is miraculous. It is quite incredible, the unanimous support with which this thing has happened. I am overwhelmed by things to do and cannot give you a complete account. I shall seek for my entire life to do nothing other than serve and revere you and your entire family. But the situation here at the moment is critical and decisive. I have not slept for the past three nights and have eaten only twice in four days. Farewell, and be well.

Caterine

11. *To Stanislas Poniatowski*

This is a unique perspective on the coup of 28 June 1762. The letter is private in the sense that Catherine writes confidentially to a man she has loved and whom she hopes will be her collaborator when he reaches the Polish throne. But it is also public, as Catherine could hardly expect the contents of her letter to go unknown to the Austrian ambassador and government. Catherine offers the official version of Peter III's death from 'haemorrhoids'; she hints at the inner struggles that surrounded her coup, but she does so mainly as a signal to Poniatowski that he must not, under any circumstances, come to St Petersburg.

2 August 1762

I am sending at once Count Keyserlingk as ambassador to Poland, in order to make you king upon the death of the present one, and in the event that he proves unsuccessful on your behalf, I would like it to be Prince Adam.*

All minds here are still in a state of agitation. For fear of exacerbating the situation, I beseech you to refrain from coming.

My accession to the throne was six months in the making. Pierre III had lost what little intelligence he had. He was heading for a collision with everything. He wished to break the Guards; he transferred them to the countryside for that purpose; he was going to replace them with troops from Holstein meant to remain in the city. He wished to change the state religion, to marry L.W., and to lock me up. On the day of the celebration of the peace, after making offensive remarks to me publicly during a meal, he ordered my arrest that very evening. My uncle, Prince George,* had the order retracted.

From that day on, I lent an ear to the proposals that had been made to me ever since the empress's death. The plan was to capture him in his room and to lock him up, like Princess Anne and her children.* Off he went to Oranienbaum.* We were confident of the support of a large number of captains in the Guards regiments. The three Orlov brothers were the most intimately involved in the plan, and Osten remembers seeing the eldest of them following me everywhere* and making a fool of himself a thousand times over. His passion for me was public, and he did everything with that in mind. These are people who are extremely determined and much loved by the rank and file, since they had served among the Guards. I am beholden to them more than anyone else; all of Petersburg can testify to this.

The Guards had been mentally prepared. By the end, thirty to forty officers were privy to the secret, as were nearly 10,000 ordinary soldiers. There was not a single traitor for three weeks because there were four factions who were kept separate and whose leaders came together to implement the plan. The actual secret was in the hands of the three brothers. [Nikita] Panin wanted the succession to be decided in favour of my son; the others never gave their agreement to this.

I was at Peterhof. Peter III was living and drinking at Oranienbaum. There was an understanding that, if betrayed, we would not wait for him to return. Instead we would assemble the Guards and make a proclamation for me. It was enthusiasm for me that produced the same effect as a betrayal. A rumour swept the troops on the 27th that I had been arrested. The soldiers began to make a move; one of our officers calmed them. A soldier went to a captain named Passek, the chief of one of the factions, and told him that I was certainly lost. He assures him that he has news of me. This soldier, still alarmed about me, goes off to see another officer and tells him the same thing. The latter was not in on the secret. Frightened to hear that an officer had sent this soldier away without arresting him, he went to see a major, and the latter ordered the arrest of Passek. Soon the entire regiment was agitated. A report was dispatched overnight to Oranienbaum. Here you have panic breaking out among our conspirators. They decided first of all to send the second of the Orlov brothers to me in order to accompany me into town, while the remaining two were to go about spreading the word that I was going to arrive. The hetman, Volkonsky, and Panin were in on the secret.

At six in the morning on the 28th, I was sleeping peacefully at Peterhof. I had spent a terribly worrying day, being aware of all that was going on. Aleksei Orlov enters my room and tells me with great calm: 'It is time for you to get up; everything is ready for your proclamation.' I asked him for details; he said to me: 'Passek has been arrested.' Hesitating not a moment longer, I dressed as quickly as possible, without doing my toilette, and took my seat in the carriage he had brought. Another officer disguised as a valet was at the carriage door; a third came to meet me some versts from Peterhof. Five versts from the city I met the elder Orlov with the younger Prince [Fedor] Bariatinsky. The latter offered me his seat in the chaise, since my horses were exhausted. And so, we went and got out at the Izmailovsky Regiment. There were no more than a dozen men and a drummer who began to beat the alarm. Then the soldiers arrived, kissing me, embracing me about my feet, and kissing my hands and my cloak, calling me their saviour. Two of them hustled under the arms a priest with a cross—there and then they set about swearing an oath to me. Once that was done, I was invited to get into a carriage. The priest with the cross walked in front; we proceeded to the Semënovsky Regiment, which came to meet us, shouting *vivat*. We proceeded to the Church of Kazan, where I alighted. The Preobrazhensky Regiment arrives, shouting *vivat*, and addresses me: 'We wish to beg your pardon for arriving last. Our officers stopped us, but here are four of them, whom we arrested and brought here to prove our zeal to you. We had the same wish as our comrades.' The Horse Guard arrives. They were in a paroxysm of joy, the likes of which I have never seen before, weeping, shouting for the deliverance of the fatherland. This scene took place between the hetman's gardens and the

Church of Kazan. The Horse Guard was in formation, the officers at their head. Since I was aware that my uncle, to whom Peter III had given this regiment, was utterly execrated by them, I sent guards on foot to entreat him to remain in his house, fearing that some accident might befall his person. All for naught—his regiment had sent a detachment to arrest him; his house was pillaged, and he was abused.

I went to the new Winter Palace,* where the Synod and Senate were assembled. A manifesto and the oath were prepared urgently. From there I went down and did a walk about the troops. There were more than 14,000 men of the Guards and regiments from the countryside. As soon as they saw me, there were cries of joy, repeated by the numberless people.

I proceeded to the old Winter Palace in order to take the necessary measures and to bring it all to completion. At that point, we conferred, and it was decided to go, with me at the head, to Peterhof, where Peter III was supposed to dine. There were sentries posted on all the highways and informers were brought to us almost continuously.

I sent Admiral Talyzin to Kronstadt. Chancellor Vorontsov arrived, having been sent to reproach me for my departure. He was taken to the church to take the oath. Prince Trubetskoy and Count [Alexander] Shuvalov arrived in order to secure the regiments and kill me. They did not resist when conducted to take the oath of loyalty.

After dispatching all our messengers and taking every precaution, around ten o'clock in the evening, I donned the uniform of the Guards, having had myself proclaimed a colonel to ineffable acclaim. I mounted my horse, and we left behind no more than a few men from each regiment to look after my son, who remained behind in the city. I then departed at the head of the troops, and we marched all night to Peterhof. We reached a small monastery en route. Vice-Chancellor Golitsyn* arrived there with a very flattering letter from Peter III. (I forgot to say that as we were leaving the city, three soldiers from the Guards came to me; they had been sent from Peterhof to distribute a manifesto among the people, and they told me, 'You see, Peter III charged us with this. We are handing it over to you and are very pleased to have the opportunity to join forces with our comrades.') A second letter followed upon the first, delivered by General Mikhail Izmailov, who threw himself at my feet and said: 'Do you take me for a gentleman?' I said to him that I do, yes. 'Well then,' he said, 'there is a pleasure in being in the company of intelligent people. The emperor is prepared to renounce the throne. I shall bring him to you after he makes his completely voluntary abdication. I shall easily avoid civil war in my country.' I entrusted him with the job; off he went to do it. At Oranienbaum, of his own free will, Peter III abdicated, surrounded by 1,590 Holsteiners. He came with Elizaveta Vorontsova, Gudovich, and Izmailov to Peterhof, where for his personal safety I gave him six officers and several soldiers.

As it was the 29th, St Peter's Day, it was necessary as per custom to dine at midday. Because such a large crowd was being catered for, the soldiers were convinced that Peter III had been brought here by Prince Trubetskoy, the field marshal, and that the latter was attempting to make peace between the two of us. There they were, accosting all and sundry, including the hetman, the Orlovs, and several others, with the information that it had been three hours since they last saw me, and they were panic-stricken that the old fox Trubetskoy would trick me 'by making a fake peace between your husband and yourself, and you would be lost and ourselves with you—but we will tear them to pieces.' Those were their words. I called on Trubetskoy and said to him, 'I ask you, please, to take a seat in your carriage, while I on foot walk among these troops.' I gave him an account of what was happening. He departed for the city, all flustered. And, as for me, I was received with unprecedented acclamations.—After this, I sent the deposed emperor away under the command of Aleksei Orlov, in the care of four officers and a detachment of men selected for their gentle character. They took him to stay at Ropsha, a place exceedingly out of the way and highly agreeable, so that comfortable and suitable rooms could be prepared at Schlüsselburg and so that there could be enough time to provide horses in a postal relay for him. But the good Lord settled it differently. Fear induced in him an attack of indigestion that lasted three days and that passed on the fourth. On that day he drank excessively, since he had everything he might have wanted apart from his liberty. (In fact, he requested only his mistress, his dog, his blackamoor, and his violin, but, fearing scandal and additional unrest among his guards, I sent him only the last three of these things.) A haemorrhoidal colic and brain seizures overcame him. He spent two days in this state, followed by severe weakness. Despite all the efforts of the doctors, he gave up the ghost while asking for a Lutheran priest. I feared that the officers had poisoned him. I had him opened up, but it is quite proven that not the smallest trace was found. His stomach was very healthy, but it was inflammation in his gut and a fit of apoplexy that carried him off. His heart was of a remarkable tininess and completely atrophied.

After he left Peterhof, I was advised to travel straight to the city. I anticipated that the troops would be alarmed at this. Under the pretext of learning the likely time they would be ready to be en route after three tiring days, I had a rumour planted. They replied: 'Towards ten in the evening, but only if she comes with us.' I then left with them and at the halfway point retired to Kurakin's country house, where I collapsed fully dressed onto the bed. An officer removed my boots. I slept for two and a half hours, whereupon we resumed our journey. Near Catherinehof I got on my mount again at the head of the Preobrazhensky regiments. A regiment of Hussars marched in front, then my escort, consisting of the Horse Guard; then immediately in front of me was my entire court. Behind me marched the regiments of the Guards according to seniority, and then three local regiments.

I entered the city to endless ovations and then went to the Summer Palace where the court, the Synod, my son, and everyone affiliated with the court awaited me. I went to Mass; then a *Te Deum* was sung; then I was congratulated. As for myself, having practically neither drunk, nor eaten, nor slept since six in the morning on Friday until Sunday afternoon, well, that evening I went to bed and fell asleep. Hardly had I done so when, at midnight, Captain Passek enters my room, wakes me, and says, 'Our men are completely drunk; a hussar in the same state has gone before them and shouted, "To arms! Thirty thousand Prussians are coming! They wish to take away our Mother!" Thereupon they immediately grabbed their weapons and have come here to enquire about the state of your health. They claimed it was three hours since you had last been seen and that they would go home calmly, provided that they had seen for themselves that you are well. They heeded neither their commanders nor even the Orlov brothers.' Once again I was up on my feet, and—so as not to alarm my guard from the court, which consisted of a battalion—I made my way first to them and told them the reason why I was going out at such an hour. I got into my carriage with two officers and went to see the others; I told them that I was fine, that they must be off to sleep and allow me to have some rest too, that I was merely going to bed after three sleepless nights, and that I wished them in future to heed their officers. They answered that those accursed Prussians had caused them great panic, that they all wished to die for me. I said to them: 'Yes well, I thank you, but leave now and go to bed.' Upon which they wished me a good evening and good health, and off they went like lambs to their lodging, all the while looking back at my carriage as they retired. The next day they sent their apologies and greatly regretted having wakened me, to the effect that 'if each of us should wish to see you all the time, then we'll harm your health and interests.'

It would require an entire book to describe the conduct of each of the commanders. The Orlovs were brilliant owing to their skill in managing minds, their prudent boldness, their ability with big things and small details, their presence of mind, and the authority that their conduct conferred on them. They have a great deal of good sense and abundant courage. Patriots to the point of fanaticism and thoroughly honourable people, passionately attached to my person, themselves friends as no other brothers have ever been, there are five of them, but only three were here. Captain Passek distinguished himself by his self-restraint, remaining under arrest for twelve hours even when the soldiers opened both windows and doors for him: he thus avoided throwing his regiment into panic before my arrival, even as he expected at any moment to be taken to Oranienbaum for interrogation. The order did not arrive until after I had. Princess Dashkova, the younger sister of Elizaveta Vorontsova, although she would like to take all the credit, because she was familiar with several of the main players, was in bad odour because of her family connection and at the age of 19 hardly made an impression on anyone. Yet she is still persuaded that everything intended for me passed through her, despite the fact that everyone had been in communication with me for the past six months and even before she had any inkling of their names. It is true that she has a strong character, but she combines with her great ostentation a meddlesome temperament and is greatly hated by our commanders. It was only careless people who kept her abreast of what they knew, which were small details. It is said, however, that I. I. Shuvalov, the lowest and most cowardly of men, wrote to Voltaire that a woman of 19 years of age had changed the government of this empire. I ask you to disabuse this great writer. It was essential to hide from the princess all the other channels of communication for five months before letting her know the least little thing, and for the last four weeks she has been privy to as little as possible. The strong character of Prince Bariatinsky deserves praise for having hidden this secret from his dear brother, the adjutant of the former emperor, not because the latter was to be feared, but because he would have been useless. In the Horse Guard, an officer named Khitrovo, aged 22 years old, and a low-ranking officer of 17, named Potemkin,* organized everything with discernment, courage, and energy.

Here you have our story, more or less. Everything came about, I will admit to you, under my careful direction, and at the last minute I threw cold water upon it because the depart for the country hindered its implementation and because for fifteen days the situation had been more than ripe for action. The former emperor, when he learned of the tumult in the city, was hindered by the young women in his retinue from heeding the advice of the old Field Marshal Münnich, who advised him either to flee to Kronstadt or to make off with a few people to the army. But when he did go in a galley to Kronstadt, the city already belonged to us thanks to the able action of Admiral Talyzin in disarming General Devier, who was already there on the emperor's behalf when the former arrived. An officer of the harbour threatened, on his own initiative, to fire with guns at the galley of the unhappy prince. In the end, the good Lord directed everything to the conclusion that He deemed fit, and this whole thing was more a miracle than a foreseen and arranged deed because such a large set of fortunate combinations could only have been coordinated by the hand of God.

I received your letter. A regular correspondence would be subject to a thousand inconveniences, and I have twenty thousand things about which I need to be cautious and do not have the time to write dangerous *billets doux*.

I am quite hemmed in…I am unable to tell you everything, but it is true.

I shall do everything I can for you and your family—of that be absolutely persuaded.

I have a thousand proprieties to follow and a thousand delicate things to handle, and besides all that I feel the full weight of government.

Be aware that everything happened according the principle of hatred against foreigners and that Peter III himself passed as such.

Farewell, in this world there are situations that are thoroughly strange.

12. *To Princess Ekaterina Dashkova*

The formalities of court life instilled in Catherine a keen awareness of the authority she needed to project and how it was bound to impinge on her friendship with the 19-year-old Dashkova. Drawing a line under old confidentiality, including memories of Catherine's public humiliation at court, and desiring to minimize Dashkova's role in the coup, Catherine assumes a continued loyalty based on feeling and deference owed her. This letter probably describes Catherine's arrival in Moscow for her coronation on 22 September 1762; at the ceremony, Dashkova was obliged to assume an inferior seat owing to her rank (her husband was a junior officer).

You have not yet written me a letter that afforded me greater pleasure than the one I have just received. I wanted to keep my word. I was bound by my promise to return the notebooks to you and to hand them to you alone. Your esteem means too much to me not to be treated with the utmost delicacy. You agree that I should be less strict about my son, and I accept that. I cannot deny that I was deeply touched by the public demonstrations of love that I received the other day from an enormous crowd. I observed how at a certain moment the acclamation turned into a roar. In the end, never could amour-propre have received more sincere flattery if, that is, it can rightly be called flattery. I note that I am not the only one to have seen it this way, since you, too, were aware. I often attended the late empress on similar occasions. But all in all I have never seen anything quite like it. Your coterie should be simply overjoyed. For at the least this was not some small expression of a few good wishes, but much more than that....Do thank your truly adorable spouse for showing the affection he bears me, and tell him what I have just said. I know that it will afford him much pleasure. I forgive your display of feeling. Do not make a crime out of it. Madame Des Houlières* says,

> I am charmed to have been born neither Greek nor Roman,
> So as to preserve something truly human about me.

It is a great sign of goodness of heart, this show of feeling that your mind manages to control. You must not let yourself be given over to chagrin and to melancholy; this would be weakness. Adieu, I love you with all my heart and would never belittle the dominion I have over you. Eliminate these things from your mind....

PART II
THE CULTURE OF LETTERS
(1762–1768)

In her first years on the throne, Catherine set out the legislative initiatives and domestic policies that were to serve as ideals for her reign until the 1790s. Her engagement with ideas about governance and rule of law, and her keen sense of the image of Russia she hoped to cultivate abroad, found a rich source and outlet in the correspondences she maintained, starting in these years. Overall, from beginning to end Catherine remained a cautious reformer and diplomatic risk-taker.

This was the only extended span in Catherine's reign when foreign affairs were in the background. The end of the Seven Years War in 1763 shortly followed her accession. Foreign policy was largely directed by Nikita Panin, a career diplomat senior in the College of Foreign Affairs, whose policies promoted stability. Russia entered into an alliance with Prussia in 1764, welcomed by Frederick the Great, who preferred to have Russia with him rather than with Austria. The accord permitted Russia and Prussia to settle problems in Poland and Sweden to their advantage and without antagonism. The alliance had immediate diplomatic impact: exercising a right to meddle in Polish affairs unwillingly granted to Russia in 1717, and relying on Frederick's support, the Russians used bribery and force to ensure the election of Stanislas August Poniatowski, once Catherine's lover, as King of Poland on 26 August 1764. Panin's eventual goal was to create a northern system incorporating Britain, Sweden, Poland, and Denmark as a rival block to the French, Spanish, and Austrian axis. Panin cultivated a pro-Russian party in Sweden, aimed at frustrating the restoration there of absolute monarchy. Although the British wanted to maintain advantageous commercial relations with Russia, negotiations failed because they were mindful of their interests in the Levant and refused to accept Catherine's condition that Britain assist Russia in the event of conflict with the Ottoman Empire. These policies were determined to stabilize the present situation but also reflected longer-term strategic goals and pressures—for one thing,

Poland's position would remain a recurrent challenge—one that Catherine would begin to confront later in the decade.

Domestic affairs took priority. The defining activity and accomplishment of Catherine's first years on the throne was setting in motion the reform of law in Russia, which had last been codified in 1649 and had no real tradition of modern teaching. In convening, in 1767, a Legislative Commission made up of elected delegates from all ranks of society except privately owned serfs, Catherine set herself a challenge. On the one hand, she wished to establish the principles according to which she felt a modern enlightened absolute ruler (and not a despot) should govern or be seen to govern. On the other hand, she was careful not to incite the delegates to assert themselves politically. Her advisors' responses to her first drafts of the *Instruction to the Commission for the Composition of a New Law Code* convinced her that serfdom could not yet be abolished in Russia, and she could not risk losing the support of her primary power base in the nobility. By presenting the Legislative Commission with an *Instruction* drafted by her, she kept control of the agenda. The *Instruction* was not a law-book but rather a statement of principles on which the future code should be based. Drawing on her wide reading of eighteenth-century political literature and jurisprudence, Catherine was overt about the sources of her *Instruction*: she wanted everyone to know that she was promulgating a digest of the latest political philosophy as a guiding document for legal reform. Yet, while borrowing from the West, she insisted on Russia's independent path and strengths (Letter 36). Some specificities were political: the *Instruction* revealed her thinking about the character of Russia as more European than Asiatic, and her belief that, given its size and diversity, Russia required the firm hand of an absolute monarch, whose power would be regulated by the rule of law and standards of justice. Others were cultural: at a time when the Russian language was rapidly evolving under Western influences, Catherine promoted Russian as a worthy rival for any European tongue as a literary language. She demonstrated this ambition by publishing her *Instruction* in Russian with parallel text in three other languages: French as the international language of literature and diplomacy, and German and Latin as the languages of jurisprudence. Read aloud to all members of the Legislative Commission and distributed in more than forty different editions, the *Instruction* signalled to the gentry at home and intellectuals abroad her determination to rule Russia as a progressive monarch in an Age of Reason. Catherine later gloated that the translation of her *Instruction* had been banned in Paris, which demonstrated the narrow-mindedness and foolishness of the French officials who treated an enlightened but manifestly pro-monarchical work as politically dangerous (Letter 60).

How much of that plan could be pragmatically implemented for the general good of her people was an ambition she continued to test, and be tested by, to the end of her reign. The Legislative Commission was prorogued without having produced the desired code, but the instructions given to the delegates by their constituencies, as well as the digests of existing laws and the records of debates produced by the Commission, provided invaluable information for Catherine as she went about writing her principles into law later in her reign. The legislative project dovetailed with the intellectual networking she did in the period through her letters. Immediately after taking the throne, Catherine sought to implement her Enlightenment ambitions for Russia by recruiting the best and brightest from Europe. She began in 1762 with the former co-editor of the *Encyclopédie*, the mathematician d'Alembert. Although he declined her invitation to come to Russia as tutor to her son Paul, he maintained an intermittent correspondence with her for several years. Her letters to d'Alembert and to the salon hostess associated with the *Encyclopédistes*, Marie-Thérèse Geoffrin, refer to the *Instruction* as her 'notes' and testify to her ambitions to put into practice through legislation and education the principles that d'Alembert and others theorized (Letters 17–19, 21). Then, in a great publicity coup, Catherine showed her solidarity with the European Enlightenment and principles of intellectual liberty by purchasing the library of the other editor of the *Encyclopédie*, Denis Diderot, allowing him to retain it and even paying him a salary to maintain it until his death. But she found the greatest enthusiast for her legislative projects in Voltaire. After difficult experiences with Frederick II, and uncertain whether Catherine would retain her crown, Voltaire hesitated to engage the empress directly until 1765. Nonetheless, her first note of September 1763 already introduced key themes and struck the tone for their lively exchange: lightly irreverent references to religion, Russia's might, Peter the Great as a mediating symbol of a Europeanizing Russia, and Catherine's desire to continue profiting (both intellectually and politically) from the productions of Voltaire's pen (Letter 14). However, once their correspondence got under way, Voltaire continually encouraged her ambitions as a legislator, and in return she called on him to publicize her *Instruction* as a model of enlightened government (Letter 23). She also for the first time advertised in her letters one of her many journeys across her empire. She set off on an expedition down the Volga in April 1767, proudly stopping in the 'Asiatic' city of Kazan to survey the diversity of the Russian Empire before arriving in Moscow to open her Legislative Commission. Voyages like this one exhibited publicly her desire to get to know her nation, but also to impose her power on the ground.

Catherine used the trip down the Volga for another grand gesture of patronage of the arts: as they sailed along, she and her courtiers translated into Russian a book recently banned in Paris for preaching religious toleration, Jean-François Marmontel's novel *Bélisaire* (1767). Drawing on the legend that Emperor Justinian had ordered the great Roman general Belisarius' eyes put out and forced him to become a beggar, Marmontel's version achieved cult status among the *philosophes*, and the episode was read as a parable about the ingratitude rulers show to their loyal servants. Publicizing this 'mirror for princes' gave Catherine a chance for a pointed exhibition of her enlightened rule and to affront her diplomatic adversaries, the French. She herself translated the ninth chapter, which focused specifically on the duties of the sovereign (Letters 31, 32, 38).

In a later letter of 17 November 1777 to Friedrich Melchior Grimm, Catherine wrote, 'I love unploughed lands—believe me, these are the best lands. I have told you a thousand times that I am fit for Russia alone.' European connections were of importance to Catherine for their intellectual richness, but also as a way to legitimate the foundations of her rule and her vision for Russia. Consistently throughout her reign the discourse of modernization associated with Peter the Great is appropriated as a project of cultural advancement or Enlightenment. As a foreign princess and convert to Orthodoxy, she understood that her own priorities and self-interest were served by establishing some continuity between Peter the Great's ambitions for his country and her own. To that end, she commissioned from the French artist and friend of Denis Diderot, Étienne-Maurice Falconet, a magnificent equestrian statue that came to be known as the Bronze Horseman. Positioned near the Winter Palace in St Petersburg, the statue of the Emperor Peter, arm boldly outstretched, dominates the view and seemingly embodies Russia's destiny.

13. *To Jean Le Rond d'Alembert*

Sounded out in September 1762 by Catherine's intermediary Jean-Michel Auda (d. 1773; a Frenchman from Nice, known in Russia as d'Odar), d'Alembert rejected her overtures in a letter of elaborate courtesy. A homebody who had spurned invitations from Frederick the Great, d'Alembert deflected the invitation by pleading ill health, asserting that his practice of philosophy required a life of retirement among friends.

Monsieur d'Alembert, I have just read the reply that you wrote to Monsieur d'Odar in which you refuse to uproot yourself in order to contribute to the education of my son. Philosopher that you are, I understand that you do not find it difficult to cast scorn on what one calls worldly honours and greatness. In your eyes, all this comes to very little, and I readily subscribe to your view. If we put matters on this footing, then I would have to regard the conduct of Queen Christina* as entirely trivial, she who has been praised so often—and so often, more rightly, faulted. But it seems to me that if you are born or called to contribute to the happiness and even the instruction of an entire people— to give this up is to refuse to do the good closest to your heart. Your philosophy is founded on humanity. Permit me to say to you that not to lend oneself to its service, when one can, is to miss one's vocation. I know you to be such a man of virtue that vanity cannot explain your refusal. I know that the cause is nothing other than your love of the quiet needed to cultivate literature and friendship. But what is getting in your way? Come with all your friends. I promise you and them, too, all the pleasures and comforts within my control, and perhaps you will find here even greater liberty and calm than you have at home. You have not given in to the remonstrances of the King of Prussia and to the debt of gratitude you owe him. That prince has no son. I confess that the education of this son is very dear to my heart and that you are so essential in this respect that I am perhaps putting too much pressure on you. Pardon my tactlessness in making my case and rest assured that esteem for you motivates my self-interest.

Moscow, 13 November 1762

PS Throughout this letter I have referred only to sentiments that I have found in your works. You would not wish to contradict yourself.

14. *To Voltaire*

This is the second of two notes sent to Voltaire but ostensibly addressed to François-Pierre Pictet, a Swiss secretary at Catherine's court and an acquaintance of Voltaire's from Geneva. Catherine attempts to set the terms for a correspondence, including non-publication of their missives. In the end, though, the cautious Voltaire declined to correspond, by responding to Pictet rather than to Catherine directly; Catherine's second attempt in 1765 was more successful and launched a lively exchange that lasted until Voltaire's death in 1778 (see Letter 20).

[September 1763]

Under the verses on the portrait of Peter the Great, which Monsieur de Voltaire sent to me through Monsieur de Balk, I have written: *God willing*.

I committed a mortal sin when I received the letter addressed to the Giant [Pictet]: I was so eager to read it that I ignored a stack of petitions and made several people wait for their good fortune. I did not even feel remorse. There is not a single casuist in my vast dominions, and I had never before been vexed by that fact. But seeing that I needed to be brought back to my duty, I found that there were no better means than to give in to the whirlwind that was carrying me away and to take up my pen to beg Monsieur de V. very seriously not to praise me any more until I have earned it. His reputation and mine are at stake. He will say that it is up to me alone to make myself worthy, although Russia is of such an immensity that a year is but a day, as a thousand years are with the Lord.* That is my excuse for not yet having done all the good that I should have.

I shall answer Jean-Jacques Rousseau's prophecy* by belying him most impolitely, I hope, for as long as I live. That is my intention; the results are yet to be seen. I would almost wish to say after that, 'Pray to God for me.'

I have also received with much gratitude the second volume of Peter the Great.* If I had been what I am now when it was started, I would have furnished you with many more materials. That great man's genius truly does not cease to amaze. I am going to go ahead and have his original letters printed, which I have ordered to be collected from all over. He paints his own portrait in them. The finest thing about his character was that, no matter how choleric he was, the truth always and infallibly had the upper hand with him, and for that alone I think he would deserve a statue.

As this will not be admired nor therefore published, I shall add most artlessly that the patterned paper was a pleasure to touch. This is the first time in my life that I regret not writing verses, so that I might answer yours. I shall be reduced, therefore, to saying in prose that I am very greatly obliged to the Author. From the moment that I could manage my own time until 1746, I read only novels. His works fell into my hands by chance: I could not stop reading them, and I no longer wanted anything to do with any book that was not as well written and from which one could not benefit as much. But where could they be found? So I started over again, and I tried to find books that at least would instruct me in all that his works had given me the liveliest desire to know. Meanwhile, I always returned to the original motivation behind my taste and my dearest entertainment, and, without doubt, if I have any knowledge it is to him alone that I owe it. But since out of respect he forbids me to be told that he kissed my note, then decorum demands that I leave him ignorant of my enthusiasm for his works. I am currently reading the *General History*.* I should like to know almost every page by heart, in anticipation of the works of the great Corneille,* for which I hope the credit note has been dispatched.

15. *To Frederick II of Prussia*

As the Seven Years War drew to a close, Frederick sought an alliance with Russia while warily watching Catherine's every move. In this letter, Catherine's humorous opening and high moral tone allow her to state all the more clearly her demands and expectations for the impending alliance—most importantly, control over the Baltic states and the placement of her candidate, Stanislas Poniatowski, on the Polish throne.

My dear Brother, I have learned that Your Majesty is very fond of fruit, and that is why I am taking the liberty of sending you some watermelons from Astrakhan and Tsaritsyn [now Volgograd] and some grapes from the first of those locations, which I have just received. They are very highly regarded, but I fear that there has been constant rainfall since spring in those provinces, which may have made them not as good this year as previously. Your Majesty may find it extraordinary that I should answer with a shipment of fruit your letter of 6 August, in which you inform me that you are sending the plan for a treaty, and that of 8 September, in which you are so good as to share with me equally important intelligence. Things big and small often come from the same source: my watermelons derive from the same principles as our planned alliance and Your Majesty's intelligence, that is, from the sincere friendship that I wish to maintain with Your Majesty, which makes me seize eagerly upon occasions to pay you my attentions. Your Majesty is too enlightened to be deceived: you do me justice in believing that the first of my motives is to make peace in Europe last as long as I can. I have no doubt that the Saxons will do all they can to read something bad into all my actions, particularly in Constantinople. But it seems apparent that they will not succeed: my intentions are too clear and too disinterested for the truth not to become apparent in time, and to convince the whole world that I have no goal but the happiness of my subjects and living in peace and good understanding with all my neighbours. Therefore, as quietly as possible, and with Your Majesty's help, we shall create a King of Poland when the time comes. Since my troops have left Lithuania to return to their quarters, one assumes that all protests will cease. I would not be at all surprised if the court at Vienna kept an extremely inquisitive eye on my every move: the nature of things at the present moment cannot but bring about such mistrust, especially by comparison with the past. I shall not say anything to Your Majesty about the business of Courland* because I consider it finished. But I cannot stop without assuring you that I am with the highest regard,

My dear Brother,
Your Majesty's good Sister,

Caterine
at St Petersburg, this 27 September OS 1763

16. *To Marie-Thérèse Rodet Geoffrin*

The salon hostess Madame Geoffrin numbered this letter as her fourth from Catherine. Catherine here tries to make her life appear as similar as possible to her correspondent's: by portraying herself as a 'friend' on an equal footing with Geoffrin and her circle, Catherine replicated the tone of the salon and projected the image of an enlightened monarch sharing the style and values of Parisian cultivated society.

this 6 November 1764

Once again I want no more of this scraping and bowing: between friends this is never the done thing. Since you are so good as to love me, you will adopt, if you please, the tone of friendship and cease regarding me as a Persian sultan of yore. Consider, Madam, that in this world there is nothing baser than grandeur. When I enter a room one would think that I was the head of Medusa: everyone becomes petrified, and each takes on an artificial manner. I often shriek like a hawk against these affectations. I admit that this is not the right way to make them stop, for the more I rail, the less people feel at ease, so I do also resort to other expedients. For instance, were you to visit my room, I would say: 'Madam, please be seated, let us chat at leisure.' You would have an armchair opposite me, a table between us, and then we would chatter about this and that for a long while—it is my forte. I am surprised that you credit me with wit; I've been told that among you French you do not believe anyone has any if they have never been to Paris. You contrive to make these efforts on my behalf out of friendship; I feel that very keenly and am not at all sure how I merited all the praise you lavish on me. I never believed that at a distance of nine hundred leagues from here anyone paid me the slightest attention. But since it is your pleasure, and you wanted to know from Nastasia* how I spend my day, I shall tell you better than she could because she is not always at my side. Do not be scandalized if you find in it differences with Parisian mores.

I rise regularly at six o'clock in the morning and read and write all alone until eight, when matters of business are read to me. Each person wishing to speak with me enters, one by one, one after the other, and this lasts until eleven o'clock and sometimes later, whereupon I dress. On Sundays and holidays I attend Mass; on other days I step into my antechamber where a number of people are usually waiting for me. We chat for about half or three-quarters of an hour, then sit down to eat—after which *the naughty General* comes to instruct me.* He takes up a book; I take up my knots.* Unless the delivery of stacks of letters or other nuisances interrupt us, our reading lasts until five thirty. Then I go to the theatre, or I play at cards, or I chat with anybody who comes along until supper, which finishes before eleven o'clock when I go to bed and repeat this all over again the next day as regularly as a sheet of music. Now, do not be so peevish with the General whom you scold so. It is true that he is terribly busy, not only with his duties, but also with a number of new institutions and projects. We call him the toyshop for children. He oversees the Foundling Home, the Academy of Fine Arts, and the upbringing of young ladies. He often pesters me about letting him go to Paris once all of these enterprises are well in hand. If he continues to insist, why then he will be all yours. I have no wish to be a hindrance to anyone. May I trust you to understand, Madam? Write to me however and as often as you would like. At least you will have no cause to complain about the brevity of this letter. But, Madam, you must not praise me for my style, for that embarrasses me. I would like to do better, but then the necessary ease escapes me. Besides, I have little opportunity to write in French, so if you were to learn Russian that would suit me greatly, as in that language I constantly have a quill in my hand. Lazy people say I am very active, but in my view I have always done too little when I think about everything that remains for me to do. I often find myself at a loss and weak in the head, and that's when I resort to simple common sense, which is a fairly certain method for settling a matter satisfactorily. I call this acting mathematically, the simplest solutions being acknowledged as the best. You see, Madam, your compliments have led me into such a labyrinth that perhaps your friendship will be able to forgive the gallimaufry into which I have strayed. I embrace you and return the embrace that you sent me in your letter, which gave me much pleasure. Scold me thoroughly for such a lengthy document; the General deems that I thoroughly deserve it—so don't pick another row with him over this as well.

17. *To Marie-Thérèse Rodet Geoffrin*

This letter offers a particularly dazzling display of Catherine's skill for epistolary role play. Catherine's combination of intellectual flair with a whiff of power, as well as the rapidly changing vivacity of the style, cater to the tastes of the Parisian elites who would have heard this letter read aloud in Geoffrin's salon.

at St Petersburg, this 28 March 1765

I recall very well, Madam, the seat that I gave you across from me, with the little table between us; you have not lost it. Never mind what they say about how everything changes overnight at court: I am not a woman who recants, as perhaps you have been told. The way you fill the seat by your letter of 1 March makes me very sorry that I cannot have that pleasure in reality and makes me desire that you should fill that arm-chair often, as long as it does not inconvenience you. Well yes, Madam, that is quite true, point by point: there is quite a match between our daily routines, and we would keep very good house together. And then I would also benefit from your advice, and I would say my bit, some-times erroneously, perhaps, which would make you scold as is your wont. But, since I flatter myself that I heed reason, I would often yield. I never sulk. I beg you, never again say that your letters are long. You have such fine sense of tact you must have understood long ago that I devour your letters and that I take an equal pleasure in reading and rereading them from beginning to end. They are charming—if I were a man, I would say ravishing, and what I say is true. All that would be far more expressive in Russian, but since you do not want to learn it and refuse point-blank to do so, we must speak of it no more. I am, Madam, at the point in your letter where you deal with my personal qualities. I shall go ahead and speak to you of them, at the risk of being scolded. Last year I commanded a flotilla of twenty-I-know-not-how-many ves-sels: I was the first to laugh over it, yet it went very well. This year I shall go ahead and command an army of 45,000 men at least, and then we shall have a carousel.* I asked those whom I thought most capable of telling me the truth whether or not the idea was ridiculous; they answered that only my performance could decide the matter. I shall go ahead and take the risk. Now tell me whether it takes much praise to make me presumptuous.

The last point of your letter so redounds with true friendship, and you show in it so much concern for my true glory, Madam, that I am very keenly touched. I see that you love me quite sincerely, and my gratitude matches how touched I am. The letter has reached me very opportunely, as I have something to say in reply. For the past two months I have been spending three hours every morning working on the laws of this empire. It is an enormous task. But over there where you are, people have false notions about Russia. You yourself, Madam, are so well informed and so enlightened, and yet you think that children do not inherit unless the sovereign grants them their fathers' property. That is not the case. Every child inherits from his father without the sovereign meddling; if there is no child, then it is the father's nearest relatives; if there are none, then the nearest branches take their place; and if there is none such, and if the owner has left no will, then the property belongs to the crown, which is something that can almost never happen. Our laws are very clear about that. But it is true that things could be confiscated too easily before my reign: this is something that I have already abolished in many cases and something about which the legislation shall be completely changed. It is still true that our laws no longer suit us, but it is also true that their meaning has become distorted only in the past forty years because misguided efforts obscured them. But, at any rate, Providence willing, I hope to put everything in a more natural state, one ratified by humanity and founded on public and private utility. The name of Montesquieu, uttered in your letter, drew a sigh from me. If he were alive, I would spare no ... But no, he would refuse me just as*. ... His *Spirit of the Laws* is the breviary of kings, if they have any common sense. I am very glad, Madam, that no prejudice prevents you from calling the King of Prussia, my ally, a great ruler. He has every right to it, for it is a pleasure to have dealings with him. He often writes me fine letters that deserve to be published, but that will not happen any time soon. No one has him in their thrall, and he does not pay any petty, deceitful souls or flattering politicians to tell him their fanatical views. Many other people consider their next steps based on these views, and for that reason they must take false steps.

There you have it, Madam: a good deal of this and that, all of which is to say that I find yours most agreeable, that I am talking to my friend who loves me, who scolds and praises me, and who claims that she does not flatter. She is a lady who loved my Mother, of whom the General [Ivan Betskoy] speaks so well and is echoed by everyone who knows her, and who paints her heart and mind so well in her letters that one would have to be dim-witted not to love such an excellent character. Madam, I hope that I shall never write another manifesto on such an occasion,* and you shall have the General whenever he pleases, for he is *free* and *very free* to do as he sees fit, and I do not mean to get in the way of anyone at all. I embrace you, Madam.

18. *To Marie-Thérèse Rodet Geoffrin*

Catherine advertises the full extent of her ambitions as she prepared to summon the Legislative Commission of 1767: to unite the diverse peoples of the empire under a single system that would account for Enlightenment values, such as toleration and the creation of a middle class, while maintaining the exceptional luxury and power of the Russian autocracy.

at St Petersburg, this 18 June 1765

Since in your letter of 9 May you praise me so, Madam, for my eight pages of writing and for my punctuality in replying to you, you will praise me even more for this one, which I am sending you on the very day on which yours was delivered to me. For, neither tomorrow nor perhaps in the next fortnight shall I have the time to write to you. To explain that to you, my good friend, I would have you know that since the beginning of this month I have been leading the life of a Kalmyk.* Now, the life of a Kalmyk consists of moving around continuously, since they have large herds that they graze wherever they can find grass. Although I am not taking herds to graze, I have not had, nor shall I have, three days in a fixed abode this whole month. I began by boarding a yacht—have a sailor explain to you what that is!—, and I spent three whole days sailing 90 versts with my Baltic fleet. Then I set foot on land and visited, as a jaunt, almost all my country houses; that took all of six days. Tomorrow I am off to the camp that is being set up a few miles from this city. I have already been to see the camp incognito, and I was thoroughly punished for it, for, taking a road not much in use, my carriages got lost in the woods, and I was forced to return 30 huge versts on horseback. Thank God it is never night here in the months of May and June! The tumultuous life I lead would be enough to make the ladies of Paris faint. You see that I am sprightly as a bird, yet Count Orlov,* of whom you will have heard, chastises me because in winter no one can make me rise from my armchair: he and the doctors think that the eternal armchair is harmful to my health. Well, well, Madam, are you not thoroughly informed now? Does it amuse you, and has your letter not been well answered? I have lost control of my pen; I am writing to my good friend, and she will forgive my chatter. We are both leaning our elbows on the little table, and we are chatting. But I do not like it when you are afraid: I have always been told that fear is good for nothing. I want you to be at ease with me. I do not want your head to be turned either, for I worry mine, too, will be turned, and your praise is most capable of having that effect, which would be good for nothing. With all due respect, I think that the King of Prussia and I would not make a good couple at all. I laughed a lot at the idea, it is very funny. I have always thought and I still think that the King of Prussia would in my position do far greater things than I, for he would have greater powers than he currently possesses. Everyone can act reasonably only according to their powers. And then he has good laws. Why should he change them? And, to a degree, he cannot. Madam, I do not like your St Theresa at all; this is the fault of your former ambassador to Empress Elizabeth, the Marquis de l'Hôpital. He told me one day that I was as excitable as she, since I was then much livelier and younger than I am now. At that moment my French politeness failed, and I retorted, 'Would you prefer to be excitable or drivelling?' He has never forgiven me for that, but nor do I think he has ever boasted of it. You reminded me of that pitiful anecdote by telling me about your patroness and, what is more, you compare me again to that saint: I am terribly afraid that the marquis spoke the truth. His reputation must be well established where you are, and you must know whether or not he has good judgment. But in the end, no matter what, I know well that I know how to love, that I love people who are good and of merit, and that you, my good friend, have a very distinguished place in my heart and mind. I can read your writing very well. Your letters are charming, the crossings-out do not obscure them, and the pleasure I take in reading them would not have allowed me even to notice the crossings-out if you had not mentioned them. So please do not trouble yourself to make fair copies any more. I would not even notice, and it would be a waste of effort. The big diamond, Madam, from which you turned away in order to read my letter, is very ugly: it is yellow and spotted, and I shall buy no more. I shall whisper in your ear that I do not care for diamonds much either, and yet I would prefer people to say after my death that I acquired them rather than frittered them away. Since you make such a fuss over my last letter, I shall think it fine. But, Madam, the copy you are sending me will not go to the archives: that would be a sure way to have it lost or burned, since before my reign it was the excellent custom to build them of wood. Madam, do not scold me: I shall have people of every class in my empire. The considerable merit that I see in your class makes me wish that my grand-nephews might have such good friends at home.* However, as hard as they and I try, we shall never have good friends like the one I have in Paris. Such merit is rare everywhere: that is why I love it well, and I would throw all the diamonds in the world into the river to have her here with me. Listen, my good friend, sixty-four pages on the laws are ready. The rest will come as it may—I shall send this notebook to Monsieur d'Alembert. I have got that off my chest, and henceforth I shall not say a single word for the rest of my life. Everyone who has seen it has said unanimously that it is the *ne plus ultra** of humankind, but it seems to me that there is still much to critique. I did not want anyone to help me: I was afraid that if more than one person worked on it, they would grasp at different threads, whereas only one, thoroughly followed through, was necessary.

Madam, you are really twisting my arm in forcing me to tell the General, 'You shall go on such-and-such a day.' I must gather my strength to utter that terrible and dreadful order. For the moment I cannot yet resolve to do it, but, if he asks me, I give you my word that I shall not refuse him. I beg you, Madam, to greet Monsieur d'Alembert on my behalf; if German roads are like your letters, they must be very agreeable.* One would be very tempted to use them frequently, and yet I am very sorry that Monsieur d'Alembert's last journey was detrimental to his health. No one wishes more than I that his health should be good enough for him to continue his work for the edification of humankind.

Truly, Madam, your grandmother was a woman of much merit, and your description of her is charming, as is her granddaughter. Farewell, my good friend. I love you very much and embrace you likewise.

19. *To Jean Le Rond d'Alembert*

In 1764, d'Alembert was inducted into the St Petersburg Academy of Sciences and continued to correspond with Catherine. Here Catherine responds to d'Alembert's 'On the Destruction of the Jesuits in France' (1765), a reaction to the expulsion of the Society of Jesus from France the year before. D'Alembert was much less of a crusader against religion than Voltaire, but he looked down on theology and resented the attacks of ecclesiastics on the philosophes. Catherine proved lenient toward the Jesuits, but she endorsed d'Alembert's maxim (which she cites in her letter) that 'Only with wise toleration (which religion and good policy both admit) can one prevent all these frivolous disputes from being detrimental to the tranquillity of the state and the unity of the citizens.'[1]

this 27 June 1765

I was truly moved, Sir, by the salutary force of reason that prevails in the book you sent me. By the grace of God, may reason triumph everywhere. It is surprising that since the beginning of the world, reason alone has met with failure most of the time. However, regarding this issue, the maxims on page 121 should serve everywhere as a rule, since they are the easiest and most natural one could follow. Despite the intelligence and subtleties attributed to the Order of Jesuits, it seems to me that the most grievous fault they have committed—one that no organization should commit—is not to have established themselves on the basis of principles impervious to all reasoned arguments. No matter what people say, the truth is invincible. Illusions do fall apart, and all the disputes that arise from them become absurd. What has made the entire world go mad is that those who should have been able to instruct the world have not done so for their own various motives. Sir, it is for you, more than anyone else, to lend your genius to reason so that it might pierce the shadows impeding it from the progress it deserves. I still remember the Catechism that you have undertaken and which you are afraid to complete.* Alas, Sir, if the idiotic persecutions of fanatics make you afraid, the least you can do is to entrust me with a copy. I give you my word that while nobody will ever know I had it from you, I shall still use it on behalf of reason with all the civic and political caution of which I am capable. The trust you place in me in your letter of 15 April emboldens me in making this request. However busy I should find myself, and whatever my duties are, they will never prevent me from reading your letters and writings with the greatest pleasure. I read the most recent pieces in the noisy company of the 33,000 men in whose camp I have been staying for the past eight days. This could scarcely be of any interest to you, and I inform you only as evidence that I am always receptive at any time to the enlightenment you are so good as to give me. I greatly anticipate what you have promised me with the utmost

[1] Jean Le Rond d'Alembert, *Sur la destruction des Jésuites en France, par un auteur désintéressé* (1765), 121 (our translation).

impatience. I have long been meaning to write, since I owed you some manner of response. I wished to attach herewith a certain notebook, but it took some time to add a dose of reason, and it remains unfinished. I will be happy with it if you approve of it. You will see in it how I have pillaged for the benefit of my empire the President Montesquieu, who remains unnamed. If from the other world he can see me working, I hope he will forgive an act of plagiarism committed for the benefit of thirty million people. He loved humanity too much to be a stickler about it. His book is my breviary.

There you have, Sir, an example of the fate awaiting the books of men of genius. They serve the welfare of the human species.

This is the fate of your own. Perhaps I write to you like a fanatic. Yet my fanaticism detests persecution and is inspired with enthusiasm by works in which genius guides reason. Carry on writing, I shall attempt to implement. I remain, with the consideration due to your talent, ever

Catherine

20. *To Voltaire*

Catherine expresses her delight that Voltaire has finally agreed to correspond with her directly by replying to her letter thanking him for the dedication of his 'Philosophy of History' (1765). Catherine perpetuates his game of pseudonyms in that work, which he presented as published by the nephew of the fictional Father Bazin. Meanwhile, she furnishes him with material to present her positively in subsequent works. In her view, as she puts it here, the French government ought to profit from the instruction of 'the inferior sort' (meaning individuals of lower rank in society, like many 'philosophes'), but, in Russia, Enlightenment must come from above.

this 22 August 1765

Sir, since, thanks be to God, Father Bazin's nephew has been found, I hope you will allow me to write to you a second time so that he might receive in his solitude the little attached packet, a testimony of my gratitude for the sweet things he has said to me. I would be very glad to see both of you attend my carousel, even if you had to disguise yourselves as unknown knights. You would have all the time you need: the constant rain that has been falling for several weeks has forced me to postpone the festivities until the month of June next year.

In all good faith, Sir, I think more highly of your writings than of all the exploits of Alexander, and your letters give me more pleasure than all that prince's show of courtesy could do.

In this you have yet more northern naivety. Truly we understand nothing of many things that come to us from the south. We are very surprised, on the one hand, to read works that are a credit to human-kind and, on the other, to see them put to so little use.

My emblem is a bee that, flying from plant to plant, gathers her honey to bring it to her hive, and its inscription is: *The Useful.* Where you are, the inferior sort of people offers instruction, and it would be easy for the superior sort to profit from it; over here, it is quite the opposite: we are not so well supplied.

The fondness that Bazin's nephew has for my late mother gives me a new degree of regard for him. I find him a most amiable young man, and I beg him to continue to show me the same sentiments. Such an acquaintance is very good and very useful to have. I hope, Sir, that you will rest assured that you have a share in my esteem for the nephew and that all I say to him is for you as well.

Caterine

PS Some Capuchin monks who are tolerated in Moscow (for toleration is universal in this empire—only the Jesuits are not allowed)* stub-bornly refused this winter to bury a Frenchman who had died suddenly, on the pretext that he had not received the sacraments. Abraham Chaumeix composed a deposition against them to prove to them that they had to bury a dead man, but neither the deposition nor two orders from the government could induce the Fathers to obey. In the end, they were told to choose between crossing the border or burying the Frenchman. They left, and I sent from here some more docile Augustinians, who, seeing that the matter was in earnest, did all that was required. So there you have Abraham Chaumeix growing reasonable in Russia and pro-testing against persecution. If he were to acquire wit, he could make even the greatest sceptics believe in miracles. But all the miracles in the world cannot wash away the stain he bears for having prevented the printing of the *Encyclopédie.*

21. *To Jean Le Rond d'Alembert*

Working away at her 'Instruction', Catherine implicitly contrasts herself with the King of France, Louis XV, who showed no interest in reform and during whose reign the 'philosophes' faced persecution. Catherine also juxtaposes French 'fanatics' (the Catholic clergy in France who sought to repress the 'philosophes') with those whom she calls the Russian 'fanatics', the Old Believers (who under Catherine were able to practise their religion freely).

at St Petersburg, 21 November 1765

Sir, I learned of your illness, and I trembled for your life. Your recovery has assuaged my anxiety. I could not believe that dejection about an injustice played a part in your illness. What you have rebuffed goes far beyond the trouble they cause you at present. I pity those whose fanaticism and persecution leads them to discredit themselves so. In France there must be a true surplus of great men if the government no longer feels obliged to protect men whose genius is admired in the most distant countries. It is, you say, of some consolation that your ruler is unaware of this. I find that for him it is nothing of the kind. Clearly the excessive scruples of his entourage deprive him of this knowledge. It is undoubtedly owing to the climate here in the north that we have less refined feelings. Sovereigns are not permitted to be unaware of distinguished thinkers, who have a right to rewards. They are obliged to encourage people's talents—otherwise they would be suspected of having none of their own. It aggrieves all those who are thirsty for knowledge that these illnesses have taken away your desire to finish the moral Catechism that you had undertaken. There are, however, ways and means over which neither persecution nor fanaticism have power. Truth, reason, and human genius demand this of you. My own notes would almost not dare appear without this so-long desired catechism. They are the work of a schoolchild. They grow voluminous and are already more than a hundred pages long. Sometimes I think they are good, sometimes inadequate. What pleases me best is the sense of goodwill that dominates. We shall see what objections the fanatics will have. We have some of our own fanatics who immolate themselves in order to be saved (if your own did this they would not persecute anyone any more).

I did not expect the purchase of Diderot's library would bring me such a lot of compliments. I am happy to have given you pleasure, Sir. It would have been cruel to separate a learned man from his books. There were many occasions when I feared lest my own books be confiscated, so I used to make it a rule never to speak about what I was reading. My own experience* prevents me from inflicting this grief on another. Rest assured of my continued affection and the interest I take in what concerns you.

Catherine

22. *To Voltaire*

Catherine presents herself as an ally in Voltaire's fight for religious toleration, emblematized by his successful campaign to obtain the posthumous rehabilitation of the Protestant Jean Calas, executed for supposedly killing his son to prevent him from becoming a Catholic.

at St Petersburg, this 28 November 1765

Sir, I am as hard-headed as my name is unpoetic. I shall reply in bad prose to your pretty verses. I have never written any, but I admire yours no less for that. They have so spoiled me that I can hardly abide any others. I shall retreat into my great beehive—one cannot work at multiple trades at once. Mine takes up a lot of time, and I find that, despite what you say about my very fine name, my mind is so intractable and so inflexible that the name Catherine was given to me very justly. It harmonizes with the harmony of my genius. It was the late Emp. Elizabeth, to whom I owe much, who called me this out of tenderness and respect for her mother.*

I would never have believed that the purchase of a library could attract so many compliments. I've had so many of them on Monsieur Diderot's, but admit it—you to whom humanity is indebted for the support you have given to innocence and virtue in the person of the Calas family—it would have been cruel and unjust to sever a scholar from his books. And, I beg you, keep d'Alembert from being too touchy about being refused the pension that he is owed. It is a trivial error that he should hold in contempt; he has sacrificed far more than that very modest pension.* The refusal has been harder on those who persecute him, and they suffer more than he.

The Metropolitan of Novgorod, Dimitry, is neither a persecutor nor a fanatic: there is not one principle in Alexis's pastoral letter* that he would not accept, preach, or publish whenever it was useful or necessary. He detests the notion of the secular and ecclesiastical powers and has more than once given examples of it, which I could cite for you, if I were not afraid of boring you. I shall put them on a separate sheet so that you can burn it* if you do not want to read it.

Toleration has been established here: it is the law of the land, and persecution is forbidden. It is true that we have fanatics who, in the absence of persecution, burn themselves of their own accord. But if the fanatics in other countries did the same, this would not do much harm. The world would be only more peaceful, and Calas would not have been broken on the wheel. There you have, Sir, the sentiments that we owe to the founder of this city [Peter the Great], whom you and I both admire.

I am very sorry that your health is not as brilliant as your wit; the latter is contagious. Do not complain of your age, and live as many years as Methuselah, even if you would then have to have a saint's day in the calendar despite having refused me that honour.* Since I do not believe that I have the right to have hymns sung to me, I shall not exchange my name for that of the envious and jealous Juno. I am not presumptuous enough to take that of Minerva;* I do not want the name of Venus, since that good lady has too many peccadilloes chalked up to her name. I am not Ceres either: the harvest was very bad in Russia this year. Mine at least makes me hope that my patroness* will intercede where she is, and, all in all, I think it the best for me, but, assuring you of the interest I take in all that concerns you, I shall spare you the useless repetition.

The pastoral letter reminds me of the honest Antoine Vadé and his speech.*

23. *To Voltaire*

Belief in religious toleration was the primary point of agreement between Voltaire and Catherine, so Catherine in this letter portrays their various efforts as intertwined: her inclusion of this principle in her 'Instruction' marked its consecration at the highest levels of government power. She expected Voltaire to publicize this accomplishment further to boost both their images all across Europe.

at St Petersburg, this 9 July 1766

Sir, the light of the Northern Star is but the aurora borealis.

The munificence distributed several hundred miles away, which you are pleased to mention, is not mine. The Calas family owe what they received to their friends; Monsieur Diderot, the sale of his library to his, just as the Calas and Sirven* families owe you everything. It is nothing to give to one's neighbour a little bit of what one has in great excess, but to be the advocate of humankind and the defender of oppressed innocence— that is to become immortal. Those two causes garner for you the veneration that is owed to such miracles. You have battled the joint enemies of man: superstition, fanaticism, ignorance, chicanery, bad judges, and the portion of power that lies in the hands of each. It takes a good many virtues and qualities to overcome such obstacles. You have shown that you possess them: you have conquered. You desire, Sir, modest assistance for the Sirvens. Can I refuse it? Will you praise me for this action? Is there anything to praise? On that basis, I confess that I would prefer that my credit note remain unknown. However, if you think that my name, as unpoetic as it is, could help those victims of the spirit of persecution, I shall trust in your foresight, and you may name me, just as long as that in itself will not harm them. I have my reasons for thinking it will.

The Bishop of Rostov's misadventure has been discussed publicly, and, Sir, you are at liberty to pass on the memorandum as an authentic document that you have from an incontrovertible source.*

I read most attentively the publication that accompanied your letter. It is very difficult to adopt in practice the principles that it contains: unfortunately, the majority will be opposed to them for a long time to come. It is, however, possible to wear down and blunt the opinions that bring about the destruction of human beings. Here is, word for word, what I have introduced on the subject, among other things, into an instruction for a committee that will rework our laws: 'In a great empire whose dominion extends over as many diverse peoples as there are different beliefs among men, the error most harmful to the peace and tranquillity of its citizens would be intolerance toward their different religions. Indeed, only wise toleration, admitted equall by Orthodoxy and by good policy, can bring all those lost sheep back to the true faith. Persecution is inflammatory, but toleration mollifies: it renders minds less obstinate by suppressing disputes that are inconsistent with peace in the state and unity among the citizens.'*

There follows a summary of the chapter in the *Spirit of the Laws* about magic, etc., which would be too long to recount here. All is said that can be said, on the one hand, to protect the citizens from the ills that can be caused by such accusations, without, on the other hand, disturbing peaceable beliefs or scandalizing the conscience of believers. I thought that the only practical way to introduce the cries of reason was to place them on the foundation of civic peace, the need and utility of which are felt continually by every individual.

Little Count [Andrei] Shuvalov is back in his homeland and has told me of the interest that you professed to take in all that concerns me. I conclude by attesting to you my gratitude for it.

24. *To Jean Le Rond d'Alembert*

Catherine's references to climate in this letter allude to Montesquieu's ideas about the connection between the geography or physical environment of a nation and its political and cultural shape. In adapting Montesquieu's text to Russia, Catherine sought to disprove his claim that Russia was a despotic state, held in a condition of backwardness by its harsh climate.

Sir, my main activities over the past two years boil down to copying and appreciating Montesquieu's principles. I have been applying myself to understanding him, and I erase today what yesterday I thought was good. Far from being an interruption, your letters always bring me the same pleasure. I received the short text in which you replied to my vague question.* This is practically the reply I had been anticipating. I find it very fair. It is impossible to speak by letter and at so great a distance as one would do in a conversation.

I learned of Madame Geoffrin's journey only after her departure from Paris. I have not suggested to her that she come here—nor shall I ever propose it. There are two reasons: one, the severity of the climate; the second is that I know all too well that this first reason would be the impediment.

It is true that Monsieur Euler and his sons were not deterred by such a brutal climate. They arrived just recently; I hope they will not freeze. Their genius and their zeal for the sciences will warm up my Academy,* and their names will remain eternally dear to all of our fellow citizens who love and benefit from measures of such use in the education of the human species.

Is it true that your government does not at all like philosophy? I have heard it said, moreover, that if you wish to seem important in France you must speak very ill of philosophers. Your mild and blissful climate opens up the intelligence. Our severe and dull climate does not allow the understanding to penetrate very far. We allow our learned men to get on quietly with their scientific work, and we do not burn anybody here. Therefore, we are not as fortunate or as clever as you, which is why few people settle here, whereas other countries teem with beautiful minds and affluence pervades even the countryside.

For fear of testing your patience I shall finish by reassuring you of the continued esteem that I have always borne you.

this 31 August 1766

25. *To Voltaire*

Catherine proclaims her wish to play a central role in the epistolary network that joined the Enlightenment's intellectual leaders. She expected Voltaire to publicize the slogan she formulates here: 'Woe be to the persecutors.'

at St Petersburg, this 9 January 1767

Sir, I have just received your letter of 22 December, in which you give me a definite place among the stars. I do not know whether such places are worth the trouble of setting one's sights on them. I would not want to be placed by anyone, except by you and the worthy friends you mention, in the ranks of beings that humankind has worshipped for so long. Indeed, however small one's pride, it is impossible on reflection to wish to see oneself the equal of onions, cats, calves, donkey skins, oxen, snakes, crocodiles, beasts of all kinds, etc., etc., etc. After such an enumeration, what man would want temples built to him? I beg you, leave me on Earth: here I shall be in a better position to receive your letters and those of your friends, the d'Alemberts and the Diderots. Here I shall witness the deep feeling with which you take an interest in all that concerns the guiding lights of our century, in whose number you have such a perfect claim to be.

Woe be to the persecutors—they deserve to be ranked among the deities listed above. That is their true place.

Apart from that, Sir, be persuaded that your approval is a great encouragement to me.

The article I shared with you concerning toleration will not fully see the light until the end of the summer.

I remember having written to you in my last what I thought of the publication of the documents concerning the Archbishop of Novgorod. That clergyman has recently given further proof of the sentiments you know him to possess. A man who had translated a book brought it to him; he told him that he advised him not to publish it because, he said, it contained principles establishing the two powers, secular and ecclesiastical.

Rest assured that, no matter what titles you assume, they will never harm in my eyes the regard due to him who pleads with the full extent of his genius the cause of humanity. The attached printed declaration* will allow you to judge, Sir, whether justice is on our side.

26. *To Jean Le Rond d'Alembert*

Writing as one author to another, the empress thanks d'Alembert for a copy of the fifth volume of his anthology 'Literary, Historical, and Philosophical Miscellany' (1753–67). Catherine, in return, suggests that d'Alembert learn more about her educational policies, which included the creation of the Moscow Foundling Hospital and the

Smolnyi Institute for Noble Girls in St Petersburg in 1764, as well as a redesigned curriculum for the Army Cadet Corps in 1766, also in St Petersburg. Curious to see new parts of a vast empire, Catherine now felt sufficiently secure on the throne to leave the capital. The Volga expedition set off in April 1767, shortly before the opening of the Legislative Commission.

at St Petersburg, this 3 February 1767

Sir, I have just received the volume of *Literary Miscellany* that you were kind enough to send me. I am most obliged. I do not believe that I am fit to give a critique of anything that comes from your pen, although that is what you ask of me in your letter of 15 December. What I am working on no longer resembles what I wanted to send you. I have erased, torn up, and burned at least the half, and Lord knows what will become of the rest. But in the final analysis it will be necessary to make up my mind before the deadline I have set myself.

Tomorrow I shall leave here for Moscow. From there I shall undertake one more long journey. I shall go down the Volga as far as Kazan; I shall return to Moscow in the month of June, when work will begin on the new law code based on the principles that I have established*—principles that will not be disavowed, I trust, by those who care about humanity. I shall return here in November or December—everything calls me back and in particular the educational establishments for girls and boys that I have opened in three different places. Monsieur Falconet has already spoken of them to Monsieur Diderot, perhaps.

Rest assured, Sir, that wherever I happen to find myself, esteem, respect for you, and the desire to have news from you will always accompany me.

27. *To Étienne-Maurice Falconet*

In Moscow, in advance of her Volga tour and the subsequent opening of her Legislative Commission, Catherine wrote her first letter to the newly arrived Falconet, clearly calculated to amaze and charm the sculptor with her friendly tone. As she mentions at the end, Catherine gave him the special privilege of reading the letters she had received from her intellectual allies, d'Alembert and Voltaire—thus offering proof that they all belonged to the same social and cultural world. The letters also provided her new correspondent with models for how to write to an empress.

at Moscow, this 18 February 1767

Yesterday I read in the article 'Religious Order'* in the *Encyclopédie* that your king St Louis said that if he could divide his person in two, he would do so, and give one of his halves to the Order of Preachers, and the other to the Order of Friars Minor.* You can see that this would not leave much of the good king for his kingdom. I have misspoken in saying 'good king'. One should have said 'simple man', for only a simpleton could produce such fantasies, whereas a good king would do better to give his whole self to his kingdom without sharing halves out with religious mendicants. What is more, if only he had spoken like Chimène in *Le Cid*,* designating two halves of herself and keeping a third, then one might have suspected that it was an error and that he in secret retained something for his kingdom. But not at all; he says definitively that there are two halves only, and he has made a settlement of them. For this generosity he has been rewarded, canonized, and named the best of kings. All the virtues are attributed him, and he is held up as a model to all those who might emulate him. I grant that nothing is more deserving of praise than gratitude. On this point, do accept my compliments. It is a fine thing to encourage merit this way by using all means possible to elevate the soul.

I who speak to you have only two eyes. I am unable to relinquish the use of the one needed to look after my affairs, but with the other from a distance I am ogling that intelligent beast which occupies the middle of your workshop, and I greatly fear that you might endow it with too much brain. Do you know, I simply think that you are not capable of making brutes. I wager that your horse will speak, and that if one does not understand what he says it will be because, accustomed as we are to hearing horses neigh, we shall take his speech for neighing. When you read this you will say:

1. How can she see all of this from one hundred leagues?
2. Oh, just let me get on with it!
3. I have plenty of brutes to pick and choose from and will be shown as many as I like.

Here is my response:

1. My vision has been augmented by the letter on the blind* that I return to you with my thanks.
2. You have only yourself to blame, and the next time do not ask me to give my opinion.
3. You don't need anybody's explanation on this score.

Farewell, Sir, stay well. Go on, guess who is writing to you. If you do reply, don't be ill at ease. Do not feel in the least constrained by formalities and, above all, do not pad out the letter with epithets for which

I have no use. You will have seen examples of these in the letters of Monsieur d'Alembert. Return to me Monsieur de Voltaire's letters when you have finished with them.

28. *To Voltaire*

In this letter, Catherine presents her tour of the provinces as just one of her many modes of inquiry into Russian geography, history, and language—an interest that only grew over the years. She already considered this knowledge essential to reforming the nation effectively.

at Moscow, 26 March 1767

Sir, I have received your letter of 24 February, in which you advise me to perform a miracle and change the climate of this country. This city was once very accustomed to seeing miracles, or rather the good people often took the most ordinary things for effects of the marvellous. I read in the preface to Tsar Ivan Vasil'evich's council* that when this Tsar had made his public confession, a miracle took place: the sun appeared at midday, and its light fell on him and on all the gathered Fathers. Note that the prince, after having made a general confession aloud, ended up reproaching the clergy in very sharp terms for all his failings, and enjoined the council to correct both him and his clergy, too. At present things have changed: Peter the Great brought in so many formalities for certifying a miracle, and the Synod fulfils them so strictly, that I am afraid to announce before you arrive the one for which you hold me responsible. Nonetheless, I shall do everything in my power to obtain better air for the city of Petersburg. For the past three years, we have been draining the marshes that surround it with canals and cutting down the pine forests that cover it to the south. Already at present there are three large plots of land occupied by settlers, where a man previously could not pass without having water up to his waist, and last autumn the inhabitants sowed their first grain.

Since you seem, Sir, to take an interest in what I am doing, I attach to this letter the least poor French translation of the manifesto that I signed on 14 December last year* and that was so badly mangled in the Dutch newspapers that no one quite knows what it was supposed to mean. In Russian, it is a respected document: our language's richness and forceful expressions made it so, and it was all the more toilsome to translate it. In the month of June, the great assembly will begin its sessions and will tell us what we lack, after which we shall work on laws of which humanity, I hope, will not disapprove. From now until that time, I shall go on a tour of various provinces along the Volga, and perhaps, at the moment when you least expect it, you will receive a letter dated from some paltry village in Asia. There, as everywhere, I shall be filled with esteem and regard for the lord of the castle of Ferney.

PS Count [Andrei Petrovich] Shuvalov showed me a letter in which you asked him, Sir, for news of two works sent to the Economic Society of Petersburg. I know that, of the dozen essays that have been submitted to resolve their question, there is one in French that was sent via Schaffhausen.* If you could indicate to me the mottos* of the letters that interest you, I shall have the society asked whether they have received them.

29. *To Étienne-Maurice Falconet*

Catherine takes as the theme of her letter the article 'Joli' ('Pretty') in the 'Encyclopédie', which discusses an opposition frequent in eighteenth-century aesthetic theory: the distinction between the pretty, pink fantasies of the 'galant' and Rococo styles, on the one hand, and the austere beauty of neoclassical notions of the Sublime, on the other. The paragraph that Catherine claims could turn her head contains a mention of Russia: 'That northern empire, which in our time has been lifted from its former barbarism by the care and genius of the greatest of its kings—could it tear from our hands both the crown of the Graces and the girdle of Venus?'[1] Although France was typically associated with the pretty, Catherine naturally wanted to see Russia excel in both the pretty and the Sublime.

Moscow, this 28 March 1767

I shall begin the present letter, Monsieur, by responding to your questions, and then I shall say what I may.

Your judgment on the subject of the Chevalier de Jaucourt and his article 'Russia'* is fair. Read the article 'Pretty'. There is a paragraph that would turn my head if it were not already turned.

As you would like me to give my views to Miss Collot, you may tell her that she can do anything she likes with her work. I shall consent with pleasure, especially after I read that sentence: *So, then, my friends, create pleasures!**

---

[1] *Encyclopédie, ou Dictionnaire raisonné des sciences, des arts et des métiers*, ed. Denis Diderot and Jean Le Rond d'Alembert, 17 vols (Paris: Briasson, David, Le Breton, Durand, 1751–72), viii. 871 (our translation).

Send me your debate on posterity.* I shall tell you sincerely what I find fault with, provided the question has been treated in a manner that is not beyond my ken. I would be tempted to assume that there was nothing to correct, were it not that I have seen spelled out in writing that Monsieur Falconet has no ambition to make his Peter the Great a master-piece; that he was not born into this world for that purpose; that he will not do it; that others would do better to cast aside their delusions, etc. But here then is a singular case of stubbornness. Myself, I believe that the climate has begun to have an effect on you. By nature the French are more flexible, more pliant, and if I have to put it in a word, more pleased with themselves, and there is nothing but the northern air that could render anyone so little obliging. I would say that you are being purely malicious if I did not know that you promise to do your best. Well then, do your best, we shall all be happy and will never pick a fight over words.

I am delighted to see from what you call your 'folly'* that you have by nature a rose-coloured imagination. Forgive me the expression. I have not liked the colour, since you told me that Greuze's *The Paralysed Man*,* because it was not like this, met with little success in France. Yet I find that its tint is pink, but in the sublime sense of beautiful rather than pleasingly pretty. In order to make sense of this babble, I refer you to the article 'Pretty', where you will find that we are condemned to be deprived of the latter, which is one of those things that belongs exclu-sively to the inhabitants of the south. I do not know whether the Inquisition is also in that group of things. A mischievous joker would say that one must truly live and let live.

Keep the book that belongs to me for as long as you like. The *Encyclopédie* is quite sufficient. I am unable to stop reading this book. It is an inexhaustible source of excellent things in which one finds, how-ever, occasional gross blunders. But one should not be surprised, for what contradictions and vexations have they not endured? It is cer-tainly the case that they displayed great courage and an invincible wish to serve and to instruct the people who have persecuted them and upbraided them and who shouted at them: 'No more education, we do not wish to know anything.'

My respects to Peter the Great fully clothed.* He has a visage, an energy, an expression, and a study has been made of the head of his charger. That is what you have told me, and that is what I am very sorry not to be there to see. You say nothing of the arm that he extends over his empire. Count Orlov says that it is this arm that he thinks is the hardest and most delicate thing to fashion, and that only you are able to find the right expression for this arm. You see, when he said this he had no idea that you had renounced the idea of creating a masterpiece. Do not start saying again that I am difficult and above all do not stop because of what I say because I can put things badly. Follow your own course. Adieu, Monsieur Falconet, stay well and rest assured that I am very eager to see both you and your work in Petersburg. That location is enjoying what seems like the beginning of spring; here it is like horrible autumn. I shall leave here at the end of the month of April and travel to Petersburg via Kazan.

30. *To Frederick II of Prussia*

Royal marriages and births were occasions when political ties could be reinforced by familial ones: as Frederick's ally, Catherine agrees to be the godmother of the future Duchess of York and Albany, Frederika Charlotte Ulrika Catherina (1767–1820), daughter of Frederick's nephew, the future Frederick William II of Prussia. At the same time, Catherine responds gracefully and wittily to Frederick's flatteries regarding her 'Instruction'.

at Kazan, this 27 May 1767

My dear Brother, the happy occasion of the birth of the princess of whom the Princess of Prussia has just been delivered, as Your Majesty was so good as to inform me by your letter of 12 May, is one upon which I seize eagerly, not only to congratulate Your Majesty thereupon, but also to protest to you that nothing can happen either to you or to Your House in which I do not take a sincere interest. As a result of the feelings of friendship that Your Majesty knows me to have possessed for a long time, I gladly accept the title of the young princess's godmother in accordance with the desires of the Prince of Prussia and his wife, and it is with all the more pleasure since I see reborn in them the same dispositions towards me, which I care so much for in Your Majesty. I cannot, however, refrain from pitying the young princess, my goddaughter, because she will bear a name as unpoetic as mine. To all the flattering things that you think it good to add on the subject of the new laws that I am going ahead and trying to establish in Russia, I can answer you only with a metaphor, one that is perhaps scarcely noble but very true: namely, that when one's coat has grown too short and tight, one usually makes a new one. The Gospel says that a patched coat is good for nothing.* That is the situation in Russia. If the new laws are better than the old ones, it will also be because those who come last have the advantage of experience and insights over their predecessors. In all this, therefore, I have no share but that, by chance, of my fortunate situation: I call on Your Majesty's enlightened judgment, as I am with the highest esteem and most distinguished regard,

My dear Brother,

Your Majesty's good Sister and faithful Ally,

Caterine

31. *To Nikita Panin*

Catherine describes her chance encounter at the Monastery of the Virgin with Nefed Nikitich Kudriavtsev (1676–1774), an elderly relative of her minister; he was once the vice-governor of Kazan and was to die at the hands of insurgents during the Pugachev Rebellion (1773–4). She consciously echoes the premise of Marmontel's novel 'Bélisaire', in which the Emperor Justinian comes to recognize his former ingratitude towards the elderly, blind, and beggared, but ever loyal, general Belisarius. The magnanimous Catherine rewarded Kudriavtsev with a snuffbox after their encounter, as a gesture of thanks for his gift of fine horses (Letter 33).

from Kazan
29 May 1767

Nikita Ivanovich! Yesterday evening I received your letter of 24 May, and owing to the stubbornness of Mr Elagin a messenger was not dispatched to you yesterday. I have yet to fix the date of my departure from here: we are thoroughly happy here and truly at home. Tell your brother that yesterday I visited the local convent, where your grandfather, Kudriavtsev, met me at the gates and was so overjoyed that he could barely speak. I stopped and began to talk to him, and he told me how weak he was and almost blind, and since he kept moving his head closer in order to see me—well, I moved much closer to him, and he seemed very pleased with that. He can no longer walk or dress but is led about. Please greet my son with a bow from me, and I wish you both good health.

Catherine

32. *To Voltaire*

The two brand new works by Voltaire to which Catherine responds in this letter both contained quotations from her earlier letters; the 'Letter on Panegyrics', in particular,

*offered extensive extracts as material for a panegyric of her. Her plea that her letters
be kept out of print in their lifetime is in earnest: she was keenly aware of the fine
line between positive advertising and excessive self-promotion.*

at Kazan, this 29 May 1767

I had threatened you with a letter from some paltry village in Asia, and
today I am keeping my word to you.

It seems to me that the authors of the *Anecdote on Bélisaire* and of the
Letter on Panegyrics are close relatives of Bazin's nephew. But, Sir, would
it not be better to postpone writing any panegyrics about people until
after their death, for fear that sooner or later they might belie them,
given the inconsistency and ineptitude of all things human? I do not
know that people have cared much for panegyrics of Louis XIV since
the Revocation of the Edict of Nantes. The refugees,* at least, were not
inclined to lend them much weight.

I beg you, Sir, to bring your influence to bear on the scholar of the
canton of Uri so that he does not waste his time writing a panegyric of
me until I am dead.* In the end, the laws that people are talking so much
about have not been made yet, and who can say whether they will be
good or not? Truly, it is posterity, and not we, who will be in a position
to settle this question. Just think, I beg you: the laws must work for Asia
and for Europe. What differences of climate, peoples, habits, even ideas!
Here I am in Asia, since I wanted to see it with my own eyes. In this city,
there are twenty diverse peoples who do not resemble one another at
all, yet a coat must be made to fit them all. There may well be some
general principles, but what about the details? And what details they
are! I would almost say that there is a world here to be created, unified,
preserved, etc. I could go on endlessly, and yet in any case this is already
too much. If it all does not work out, the scraps of letters that I found
quoted in the latter publication will look like ostentation and God-
knows-what both to the impartial and to those who envy me. And then,
my letters were prompted by esteem alone and could not be fit to print.
It is true that I was very flattered and honoured to see what feelings
prompted this from the author of the *Letter on Panegyrics*, but Bélisaire
says that such a moment is precisely the most dangerous one for the
likes of me.* Since Bélisaire is right about everything, doubtless he is
not wrong about this either. The translation of this latter book is finished and will be printed. To try out the translation, it was read to two
people who were not familiar with the original. One exclaimed, 'May
my eyes be poked out, as long as I become Bélisaire! That would be
reward enough!' The other said, 'If that happened, I would envy you.'

In conclusion, Sir, allow me to express my gratitude for all the signs of friendship that you show me, but, if possible, keep my scribbling out of print.

33. *To Nikita Panin*

In this letter, Catherine handles legal matters large and small: sorting out a case regarding the business difficulties of a certain English merchant in Arkhangelsk by the name of Home, she continues to meditate on the possibility of creating a uniform legal code for a large and diverse empire.

from Kazan
31 May 1767

Nikita Ivanovich! Yesterday I received from you via courier your letter with all the details about the business regarding Home, and one of two things will undoubtedly happen: either he will find a place for himself or he will deserve the gallows. I now understand the entire business better than I did last year in Tsarskoe Selo, but still I do not see the light about his paying the terrible sum that he owes the Treasury, since it is doubtful whether the first 50,000 in debts to the bank were actually paid out. I do not believe that this whole factory cost 100,000, and he's not the only one in the business; about his other factories, etc. there is almost no point in speaking, since they are even worse than this one.

The grand duke's letter made me very happy, especially because he writes so affectionately. I still forgot to instruct you that you should continue to have him write under your dictation, since he expressed a wish for it in his last letter. We are all well; today we shall have a masked ball, and tomorrow, or the day after, from here I shall travel to Simbirsk, which I consider to be already on the way back, and I shall not dawdle there any longer than it will take to unload the carriage from the ships. Count Zakhar Chernyshev and Count Grigory Grigor'evich Orlov have put off their trip to Tsaritsyn and are going only to Saratov, which I believe will make their journey 300 versts longer than my own. It is impossible to leave here: there are so many different things that deserve my attention, one can collect enough ideas* here for ten years. This is a separate empire, and it is only here that one can see how immense an undertaking our laws are, and just how ill-suited the current ones are to the state of the empire in general.* They have endlessly tormented the people, whose condition till now has inclined towards extinction rather than increase; same thing with respect to property. Farewell, I wish you good health.

Catherine

I am returning the three parcels to you, but am keeping the one about Home. Old man Kudriavtsev* has given me as a gift a very lovely team of horses, and I have sent him a golden snuffbox.

34. *To Étienne-Maurice Falconet*

Denis Diderot's 'Salon of 1765' contained extensive comments on Falconet, stimulating a vigorous exchange between the two men, which continued after Falconet arrived in St Petersburg in October 1766. The philosopher and the artist debated the specific merits of certain artists and writers, largely from classical antiquity. But their main subject was the timelessness of taste and the value of posterity, and their considerations included the question whether the judgment of posterity was valid as a reward or justification, especially for those left unrewarded in their lifetime. The two men planned an edition of these 'letters on posterity', and Catherine's letter was to be included, but ultimately the exchange was published only in the twentieth century.

7 June 1767
from a corner of Asia

I am unable to adjudicate. Each of you is strongly inclined to stick with his respective opinion, and even if I were to say everything I want, it would be in vain. For each of you would protest, and the dispute would start all over again. If you had said, 'Tell us your opinion,' I would have known how to respond, but you tell me, 'Decide.' If I declare myself for Monsieur Diderot, then Monsieur Falconet, given his state of mind, will not be convinced. If I find that the latter is right, then the other one's logic will contradict me. Let us give this some thought. Do you not argue like theologians? One says clearly, 'I have posterity in my sights, and I pursue it'; the other, 'I do not disdain posterity. However, to be precise, it is not for posterity that I take pains. I want to do well, and it is the approval of my contemporaries that I seek.' And so! Well, Monsieur Falconet, it is for your contemporaries that you have placed your name at Saint-Roch.* Let us erase this name, Monsieur Diderot. Now that contemporaries have seen it, perhaps someone will put the name of another there instead of your own. Monsieur Falconet, may we have an answer, please, to this proposal? If you insert a *but*, you will have a hard time making a case. You have found that your contemporaries often are mistaken, and that this is also true of posterity. Your soul, proud and true, craves the approval of a small number of connoisseurs, and why should they come from your own century? What have those who will succeed them done to you to make you not want to please them? Could it be because you do not know them? Is it true that one should only be agreeable to those one knows? Would you punch a stranger? And why would you show so little consideration to our grandsons? But your Peter the Great will prove to posterity not only your goodwill towards your contemporaries, but indeed your attraction to posterity as well. You are not content to stop with a horse made from clay, but are casting a statue in metal, averring proudly, 'I do well because one should not execute a task badly.' But, despite yourself, this horse escapes your fingers as they work the clay, and races headlong towards posterity, which will certainly appreciate its perfection better than contemporaries. Make a note of where you were in this great creation of yours when you received this missive. Upon my return I shall see whether this last phrase has made you retrace your steps. Farewell, Monsieur Falconet, stay well; I shall soon return.

It is a real pleasure to read a dispute free from bitterness and yet, nonetheless, full of equal parts of heatedness and pleasantness. I return your book to you, many thanks.

35. *To Étienne-Maurice Falconet*

Catherine corresponded with Diderot through Falconet, here answering a long letter to the sculptor (but intended for Catherine's eyes) in which 'the Philosopher', as she calls him, explained his reasons for not travelling to Russia. Catherine had not shown much interest in Diderot's proposal to produce for her a monumental, philosophically inspired French dictionary, but had been eager to see Diderot in Russia. Diderot was reluctant, most especially not wanting to leave his mistress, Sophie Volland—hence Catherine's promise of discretion.

at Moscow, 12 October 1767

You do me wrong by not remembering that I know how to feel. When one renders me such evident marks of respect as you have just done by entrusting me with the Philosopher's letter, I fully appreciate what it means and what I owe you. In a word—rest assured of my gratitude and my discretion. All the same, I am sorry to have neither the Philosopher nor his work, no matter what he says. I do not know what he could have seen in the letter from Mr Betskoy, but I know for sure that I never rejected his work. I would like my sculptor to correct my philosopher on this mistaken notion. But why should you have become conceited? I do not believe it: someone who has a good head on their shoulders could not have their head turned. And I assure you that to the best of my knowledge your head numbers among the good ones. Well then, people say that I can do as I wish in Russia, and I have written and signed a statement that the sovereign should only wish what conduces to good. It is my wish that your head not be turned, and I would prohibit it from turning—were it not that this ban might look excessively despotic. That good head of yours mustn't be turned. Wouldn't that be an evil rather than the good we both desire? For now, be happy with these explanations until I return. In the month of January, we shall resume this lovely conversation at length, and once I have seen the great emperor and his intelligent beast we shall have more to discuss and decide on.

In his letter the Philosopher says, 'It is I who am wanted, not my work.' But by what contradiction would I not want his work, when I offered the *Encyclopédistes* the chance to have their book printed here? And now, moreover, a certain number of people have gathered in Moscow to translate as best they can the articles of this dictionary into Russian, and there is already a volume on sale and another being printed. I already had great respect for Monsieur Diderot, and I esteem him even more after reading the twenty pages. His effort in making a sincere confession was heroic. He will come when he is able and will always be welcome. I would not have the heart to advise him to do what would make him or *others* unhappy. I believe that Prince [Dmitry] Golitsyn has been sufficiently briefed on the purchase of the different collections that your friend offers. It is not the works of Greuze that I relinquish, but him personally and his better half.* I was unaware that Van Loo* existed until Mr Betskoy received a letter on the subject from Prince Golitsyn, but if he produces only portraits then we could do very well without him at the Academy.

The difficulty that Prince Golitsyn has in translating from French into Russian stems from the fact that, like most of our gentlemen, he is ignorant of his own language—but it is a language that, I believe, has no equal for richness. I wouldn't dare to cite my own work, the great *Instruction* for the composition of the laws. Ask Russians—it contains not a single foreign word even though the material is not the simplest, and I do hope that nobody will confuse one word for another.

Farewell, Monsieur Falconet; rest assured that I shall hasten to return to St Petersburg, mainly for the sake of your work, and that I anticipate the pleasure of having a chance to chat with you about many things. But since you confide in me the secrets of your best friends, tell me your true opinion about Monsieur de La Rivière. Just between us, I hope he does not put on airs, since as it happens I may have no need of him. Could you give a little thought to what he's all about? But if such a task is not congenial to you, you can blame only the friendly tone that you have assumed with me. I give you my trust in return for yours. And like me you should feel it deeply—and not be put out.

36. *To Frederick II of Prussia*

Sending a copy of her 'Instruction' to Frederick, Catherine calls on one of her favourite literary genres, the fable. The story of a bird who dressed up in peacock's feathers only to have them humiliatingly torn away can be traced to ancient Greece. In selecting a crow as the guilty bird, Catherine seems to be drawing on the German version of the tale, offered, for instance, by Gotthold Ephraim Lessing in his 'Fables' (1759). Catherine's choice to send a German translation to Frederick was a jab at his disdain for and ineptitude in writing in his native language—he preferred to read and write in French. By contrast, Catherine flaunts her mastery of her nation's language and her belief in its ability to become one of the great literary languages of Europe.

at Moscow, this 17 October 1767

My dear Brother, in complying with Your Majesty's wishes, today I have had delivered to your representative, Count Solms, the German translation of my *Instruction* for reforming the laws of Russia. Your Majesty will find nothing new in it, nothing that you do not know: you will see that I have acted like the crow in the fable, who made himself a coat of peacock feathers. There is nothing of my own in the document except the arrangement of the material and here and there a line, a word. If one gathered together all that I have added, I do not think it would be more than two or three pages. Most of it is taken from President Montesquieu's *Spirit of the Laws* and from Marquis Beccaria's treatise *On Crimes and Punishments*.

Your Majesty will perhaps find it extraordinary that, after this admission, I am sending you a German translation, whereas the French would seem more natural. Here is the reason why. Since the Russian original was watered down, corrected, and adapted to possibilities and local conditions, it was easier—so as not to make Your Majesty wait—to complete the German translation already begun, rather than to have a French half-copy, half-translation, since we did not have anyone who understood Russian and French perfectly. However, the latter translation, too, will be started shortly. I must warn Your Majesty of two things. One, that you will perhaps find various passages that seem odd to you: I beg you to recall that I often had to adapt myself to present circumstances to avoid blocking the path towards a more favourable future. The other, that the Russian language is much more energetic and richer in expressions than the German and in inversions than the French. That is proven by the fact that in the translation we were often forced to paraphrase things that had been said in a single word in Russian, and to divide what was a single stroke of the pen, so to speak. Those who have criticized the latter language for lacking vocabulary were either mistaken or did not know the language.

It would be a most touching mark of Your Majesty's friendship if you found it good to communicate to me your views on the document's flaws: they could not but light my way on a path that is as new as it is difficult for me, and my humbleness in reforming it would show Your Majesty how infinitely I value both your friendship and your enlightenment, being always with the highest regard,

My dear Brother,

Your Majesty's good Sister, Friend, and Ally,

Caterine

37. *To Voltaire*

Asking for a copy of Voltaire's complete works (using his pseudonym, 'Father Bazin's Nephew'), Catherine also thanks Voltaire for his 'Historical and Critical Essay on the Discord of the Churches of Poland' (1767), which sought to justify Catherine's armed intervention in Poland as a defence of religious toleration. It too was published under a pseudonym, this time 'Joseph Bourdillon, Professor of Public Law'.

[*c*.22 December 1767]

Sir, the two essays sent to the Economic Society of Petersburg that are of interest to you have arrived at their destination, but they will not be read until after my return, since most members are absent.

Catherine II is already much indebted to Father Bazin's nephew for all the flattering things he ascribes to her. If she knew where he lived, she would appeal to him and urgently entreat him to increase her debt by sending her everything—every single line—that has ever come from the respectable pen of his uncle and from his own. For, however greedy we are here at the sixtieth parallel for his creations, some will inevitably escape us, a loss that we feel very keenly. Sir, I do not know the Father's nephew, but if you manage to dig him up and to persuade him to send all his writings, new and old, quite complete, you would add to my gratitude.

It will perhaps seem strange to you that I should appeal to you so often with all kinds of commissions. You will say, 'She has but one means, she uses it all the time, and, unfortunately, it falls on me.' But, Sir, not everyone is gifted with an inexhaustible imagination and the gaiety of a 20-year-old. It is easier to admire talents than to imitate them: this is a universal truth recognized from south to north. But, unfortunately, the same cannot be said of the idea that the north is so perfectly correct as Monsieur Bourdillon, professor in Basel, has just proven it to be. Admittedly, one might say that he is not correct, but I defy honest people to prove it, even using the customary formalities of the Inquisition, whose manual I have read.* As I read, I reflected how astounding it is that there could have been people who had so little reason on their side: I think this has caused more than one establishment to crumble. By 'reason', I mean sound reason, since those other people undoubtedly must have had their own, and it drove them into a frenzy of iniquity and injustice. May God shield us all from that sort of reason. You may well deduce, Sir, that at the moment we are warding off the misfortune of establishing something like it in Russia.

I must give the nation its due: it is excellent soil in which good seed sprouts quickly, but we also need axioms that are indisputably recognized as true. Any others will meet with resistance. When the French translation of the principles that are to form the basis of our laws has been completed, I shall take the liberty of sending it to you, and you will see that, thanks to such axioms, this document has won the approval of those for whom it was composed. I shall venture to foretell the greatest success in this important work, since I have seen the ardour that everyone brings to its drafting. I think that you would enjoy being in an assembly where the Orthodox sits next to the heretic and the Muslim, and all three listen peaceably to the voice of an idolater, and all four often confer in order to render their views amenable to all. They have so thoroughly forgotten the custom of mutually grilling one another that, if someone were so ill-advised as to propose to a deputy that he should boil his neighbour to please the Supreme Being, I can answer for everyone that not a single one would fail to answer, 'He is a man like me, and, according to the first paragraph of H. I. M.'s *Instruction*, we should do one another as much good as possible, but no evil.' On my honour, I assure you that I am not getting ahead of myself and that everything is literally as I tell you it is. If necessary, I could have 640 signatures to attest to this truth, with a bishop's at the top. In the south, they might say, 'What times, what customs!'* But the north will be like the moon and take its own path. Rest assured, Sir, of the esteem and particular and inalterable regard that I have for you, your writings, and your fine deeds.

38. *To Jean-François Marmontel*

The empress took evident pride in the achievement of this collective translation of Marmontel's 'Bélisaire', a seminal work of the period, and her circumstantial description also makes clear her belief in the wise use of leisure time. Accustomed to being the dedicatee of literary works, here Catherine takes pleasure in being the donor. She is also delighted to point out that, whereas the French Catholic author- ities at the Sorbonne had banned the work, the Russian translation was dedicated to an Orthodox clergyman.

Sir, when *Bélisaire* arrived in Russia, he happened to discover that a dozen persons had been planning to journey down the Volga from the city of Tver,* all the way to Simbirsk,* which makes a distance of 1,300 versts, in the units of distance used in this country. They were so charmed by reading this book that they decided to employ their leisure hours in translating *Bélisaire* into the language of this country. Eleven of them shared out the chapters by drawing lots. The twelfth, who came too late, was commissioned to compose a dedication from the translators to the Bishop of Tver* whom the group deemed worthy to be named at the head of *Bélisaire*. Apart from his fine qualities of mind and heart, he has just excelled himself with a sermon in which moral teachings reached a level of purity equalled by that of this excellent book. Far from disapproving of this dedication, the bishop has given clear evidence of his joy in receiving it and that he gloried in it. Our translation has just been printed. However flawed it may be, those who worked on it find it impossible to dispense with offering a copy to you, Sir. Receive it as proof of the esteem we have conceived for *Bélisaire* and for its author. It is this esteem that prompted us to undertake something at which the majority of us had never tried our hands. One might reproach our translation for its divergent styles, a fact that we cannot disavow, but we deem it appropriate to change nothing in it, since it is none other than that very diversity of style that induced these people to translate *Bélisaire*. Each chapter is a separate work based on a belief in the purest morality and not on persecution and fanaticism.

Our pleasure and respect are equal in declaring ourselves:

The author of the Dedication from the Translators to the Bishop— Count [Andrei Petrovich] Shuvalov

    The translator of the Preface and of Chapters I and IV—I. Elagin

    Of the Second Chapter—Z. G. Chernyshev

    Of the Third Chapter—S. Koz'min

    Of the Fifth—Count Grigory Orlov

    —— VI. X. XI. XII—I. Volkov*

    —— VII. VIII. Chapters—A. Naryshkin*

    —— IX—Catherine

    —— XIII—A. Bibikov

    —— XIV—S. P. Meshchersky*

    —— XV—Count V. Orlov

    —— XVI—Grigory Kozitsky

at St Petersburg, 11 September 1768

PART III

PHILOSOPHY AT WAR
(1768–1774)

In the years of the First Russo-Turkish War (1768–74), Voltaire developed in his letters and public writings an image of Catherine as a 'legislatrix, warrior, philosopher',[1] a multifaceted and even universal ruler. The concept captures the multiplicity of Catherine's activities during this campaign, which she pursued without losing sight of her cultural aims and while continuing to plan for the legislative initiatives she was to launch immediately after the return of peace. The war dominated her foreign policy decisions but also made demands on how she handled her image abroad. Catherine continued to furnish Voltaire with material for his pro-toleration (and pro-Catherine) campaigns (Letters 42, 70). To reinforce Voltaire's image of her as the leader of a new alliance of enlightened rulers, able to take on the Ottomans even without allies, Catherine, moreover, emphasized not only Russia's victories at war, but also her ongoing civilian undertakings in keeping with the recommendations of Enlightenment philosophers, such as the colonization of Russia's southern provinces and the encouragement of agriculture and the grain trade (Letter 43).

This was a territorial war, fought to expand Russia's access through Crimea to the Mediterranean and to enhance trading arrangements during a period of industrial expansion. But the *casus belli* was a pushback by a Polish group of nobles, who formed the Bar Confederation to oppose Russia's intervention in 1768 in defence of dissenters from Catholicism. Through her correspondence, most especially with Voltaire—famed as an apostle of tolerance—but also with Frederick the Great and others, Catherine positioned Russia as a defender of religious rights. At the end of September 1768, pressed by European powers like France to take advantage of Russia's apparently precarious engagement in Poland, the Ottoman Empire sided with the Bar Confederation and used a skirmish

[1] Voltaire, letter to Catherine, 26 February 1769 (NS).

on the border with Poland as an excuse to declare war on Russia. Neither the Russians nor the Turks were entirely prepared for this escalation into fully fledged war, but the conflict played out in some of Russia's most famous sea battles, and in an inconclusive land campaign— the back-and-forth across the Danube is a recurring topic in Catherine's letters of these years. Closely followed and managed by Catherine, the campaign tested and eventually established Russia's capability as a naval power. While Catherine characteristically confronted major challenges pragmatically with the aim of stabilizing her rule, she rarely missed an opportunity to make statements of principle, some-times touching on theories of natural justice, and also giving precise instructions on how to destabilize the enemy (Letter 52). Undermined by her ally Frederick II, who launched a diplomatic offensive to pre-vent Russia from conquering new lands, Catherine resolved not only to fight the Ottomans alone, but also to promote her victories as those of civilization over barbarity and ignorance. Voltaire at first quite enthusiastically embraced this point of view, advertising her suc-cesses in exactly those terms and even recommending that her armies adopt Greek-style chariots to give their conquests more of a classical feel. Declining the suggestion but relishing the play of classical imagery that lent her war an aura of historical grandeur, Catherine's correspondence regularly blended the pursuits of war and peace in a cultured conversational tone, designed to demonstrate her confi-dence of success (Letter 42). Her cultural accomplishments, such as patronage of a Russian translation of the *Aeneid*, announced Russia's claim to influence in the lands where classical antiquity flourished (Letter 45).

Catherine sought to make Voltaire a hub of pro-Russian news in Europe by allowing him to print information from her letters in news-papers and to communicate insider information through personal channels. She insisted that her letters were the only reliable source of news, but she also requested reports from him about the publicity her navy's exploits in the Mediterranean were earning in Europe. The vic-tories of 1770 culminated in the Battle of Chesme, in which the Ottomans lost their entire fleet and approximately 11,000 men on the night of 25–6 June. The amazement expressed by European powers gave her evident pleasure. While Voltaire praised the undertaking as the 'most astonishing ever conceived', saying in a letter of 2 January 1770 that 'Hannibal's scarcely came close to it', the Russian fleet's successful first appearance in the eastern Mediterranean presented a formidable chal-lenge to the maritime balance of power (treated at length in Letter 52).

Both the Polish and Ottoman conflicts ended successfully for Catherine. The prospect of Russian territorial gains against the Ottoman Empire induced her neighbours, Austria and Prussia, to seek enlargements of their own. When Frederick the Great's brother Henry visited St Petersburg in 1770–1, he proposed to Catherine a partition of Poland between the three powers. The Russians decisively defeated the Bar Confederation in summer 1772, and the treaty granting substantial swaths of Poland to each power was signed in August that year. It took another two years and several rounds of negotiation for Catherine to obtain from the Ottoman Empire terms of peace that she found satisfactory, but the Treaty of Küçük Kaynarca, signed 10 July 1774, brought her remarkable territorial gains, shipping rights on the Black Sea, and Crimea's independence from the Ottoman Empire as a protectorate of Russia.

The period also saw momentous change in Catherine's personal life as well as on the home front. Her relationship with Grigory Orlov, the father of her unacknowledged son, unravelled in 1772. Despite their common interests—he was an admirer of Rousseau and held progressive views on land reform—Orlov had a roving eye; Catherine paid him off generously, but he was nonetheless affronted and remained possessive of Catherine even as she began her love affair with the charismatic Grigory Potemkin in early 1774. Their liaison dates to the last days of February, when Potemkin rapidly entered Catherine's inner circle. Catherine's notes to her new lover show the couple and Catherine's courtiers working out the conditions and significance of a fresh relationship, which was to prove decisive for Catherine's reign and her empire (Letter 78). The letters also lay bare the highly volatile nature of the passionate phase of what would prove to be Catherine's most enduring attachment.

She had no such trust and affection for her son and legitimate heir, Paul. Differences in temperament were one factor, but Catherine remained on guard against a weak character who was easily manipulated by factions at court with their own designs. When he came of age in 1772, a drunken group of soldiers intent on proclaiming him emperor hardly constituted a threat, but Catherine understood that sedition could spread like wildfire. To keep her son busy, settle his status at court, and, most importantly, ensure the line of succession, Catherine arranged for his marriage in September 1773 to Princess Wilhelmina of Hesse-Darmstadt, who upon her conversion to Orthodoxy became Grand Duchess Natalia Alekseevna. It was further cause for alarm that Paul's name was mentioned during the Pugachev Rebellion of 1773–4.

A pretender who claimed to be the Emperor Peter III, Emel'ian Pugachev caused serious unrest among the Cossacks, industrial and state peasants, and privately owned serfs across a wide region of the southern Urals. The rebellion proved more difficult to suppress than expected and even threatened Moscow. In victory, Catherine's retribution fell short of her opposition to capital punishment, yet she also instructed her army to carry out the rebuilding of devastated industry and settlements in the Ural region. As another consequence of the unrest, land reform and the abolition of serfdom became much harder to address.

Pugachev, the Turks, and the Poles were not the only enemy. Smallpox was one of the most feared illnesses of the eighteenth century, causing countless deaths and disfigurements. Early in the century, the practice of inoculation had been imported from the Middle East and enthusiastically embraced by Enlightenment thinkers, but was mistrusted by the Church. In having herself and her son inoculated by the English doctor Thomas Dimsdale in 1768, Catherine sought to show herself more forward looking than many European leaders, including Louis XV of France, who died of the disease in 1774 (Letter 40). During his visit, Dimsdale set up an inoculation hospital in St Petersburg, and in the same year Catherine opened a public facility for vaccinating people from all levels of society. Her convergences, at least in theory, with Western attitudes to corporal punishment, justice, and social welfare fed into her correspondence, particularly with Voltaire. It also paved the way for the visit of the *philosophe* Denis Diderot to St Petersburg in 1774, when the tension between theoretical blueprints for an ideal state and pragmatic decisions bubbled to the surface in their animated conversations (Letter 76).

39. *To Frederick II of Prussia*

At the end of September 1768, pressed by European powers like France to take advantage of Russia's apparently precarious state of engagement in Poland, the Ottoman Empire used a skirmish on the border with Poland as an excuse to declare war on Russia. After a silence of over a year, Catherine now needed her ally's support: she sent not only diplomats, but also a friendly letter in hopes of engaging Frederick to help, which he was very unwilling to do. Honouring his treaty obligations, he grudgingly provided a subsidy, but did all he could to put an end to the war as quickly as possible and without Russian gains.

at St Petersburg, this 14 November 1768

My dear Brother, the letter that Your Majesty was pleased to send to me on 27 September through the chamberlain Count Vorontsov* gave me the purest satisfaction, as I found it filled with precious assurances of your friendship and with the sentiments and actions of a faithful and constant ally. However much I desired to attest to Your Majesty both my gratitude and the reciprocity of my sentiments, and to entreat you to lend credence to all that Count Chernyshev* has told you on my behalf, I did not dare to answer you earlier, as much because I was forbidden to exert myself in the least during my inoculation for smallpox as because, having learned from Count Chernyshev that Your Majesty disapproved of this action (which doubtless would have influenced my decision, if I had not learned it too late), I wanted to let the critical moment pass and myself give Your Majesty the news that all danger for me personally had ceased and that this time my temerity had turned out well. Then again, I had scarcely recovered when I was forced to make arrangements for the war that the Porte means to wage on me in order to please those who envy me* and without really knowing why. I delayed my thanks, but there was no delay in my feeling what I owe to Your Majesty for all the obliging things that you are so good as to say to me about my various enterprises. Certainly nothing gives me more pleasure than the sincere interest that I see Your Majesty taking in the well-being of my empire. Until now I have tried to do good. At the moment I am being forced to do evil—for that is what all wars are, or so the philosophers tell us. The only one that can be tolerated, I believe, is the one I shall go ahead and wage. I have been attacked, and I am defending myself. That is also what I have been doing until now in Poland. Owing to our break with the Porte, things look quite different in that country now, relative to when Your Majesty's letter was written, and thus I can only thank Your Majesty for having communicated to me your opinion on the situation at that time, and similarly for the overtures that Count Solms has made to my ministers concerning the war and Your Majesty's concern about it. For myself, I am convinced that I have done nothing in Poland that is not in the essential and permanent interest of the Republic and its neighbours. Therefore, I believe firmly that the justice of my cause will lead Providence to turn everything to the great detriment of my present enemies and that they will repent of the offence they have given me owing to the manipulations of those who envy me. I consider myself assured of the loyalty of Your Majesty's alliance. Both by personal sentiment and as a principle of state, I shall be attentive to seize every occasion to assess each event in such a way as to render the bond of our alliance indissoluble. Consequently, my ministry will make known to Your Majesty by your representative the measures that I have taken, both to defend myself against my enemy and to pacify Poland, having no doubt that Your Majesty will cooperate in everything because of the trust, the high regard, the friendship, and the particular esteem with which I am,

My dear Brother,

Your Majesty's good Sister and faithful Friend and Ally,

Caterine

40. *To Frederick II of Prussia*

In Frederick's conventional note of congratulations on her recovery after her inoculation for smallpox, he did not praise her enlightened action, but rather reproached her for endangering herself personally. His scolding gave Catherine a further chance to exhibit her enlightened use of reason in her reply. In 1775, Frederick finally followed her advice and invited English practitioners to teach inoculation in Prussia.

at St Petersburg, this 5 December 1768

My dear Brother, I saw from the letter that Your Majesty was pleased to write to me on 26 November not only how much of an interest you take in all my affairs, but even that your friendship for me makes you think my inoculation was rash. I am going to spell out for Your Majesty what led me to do it, and I hope that you will agree that I did nothing out of order. As a child I was brought up to have a horrible fear of smallpox; at a more reasonable age, I have had a thousand difficulties in mastering that fear: if the least malaise came over me, I thought it was the afore-mentioned illness. Last spring and summer, when the disease wreaked great havoc here, I fled from house to house, and I banished myself from the city for five whole months, not wanting to put myself or my son at risk. The turpitude of the situation so struck me that I considered it weakness not to seek to escape it. I was advised to have my son inoculated. 'But,' said I, 'how would I have the nerve to do it if I did not start with myself, and how would I introduce inoculation if I did not preach by example?' I set about studying the subject, quite resolved to adopt only the least dangerous course of action. The following reflection made up my mind: 'Any reasonable man, on seeing two dangerous paths before him, chooses the one that is the least so, all things being otherwise equal.' It would be cowardice not to follow the same rule in things of the greatest importance: 'To remain for one's whole life in real danger, along with several thousand men; or to prefer a lesser danger that lasts only a short time and to save many people?' I thought that I was choosing the safest option: the moment has passed, and I am out of danger. My only regret in all this is that I gave Your Majesty some apprehension, as you are so good as to protest to me. I had hoped you would learn of the whole trifle only once it was over, for to tell the truth I found that the mountain had given birth to a mouse* and that it was a peril not worth speaking of. One could not say the same of natural small-pox. But to fulfil my duty as a loyal ally and to return Your Majesty's friendship, I dare to entreat you most earnestly not to put all the people you hold dear at risk of this natural danger, but rather to employ the protection that has been so good for me. And I dare to assure you that if the inoculator is experienced, there is no danger. Baron Dimsdale, whom I brought from England, has had 6,000 patients, and not one has ever died, except for one little child who had not yet been given smallpox. Not one of his patients keeps to his bed. In a word, one is ill as pleasur-ably as can be. He inoculates from the age of 3 to the most advanced age. Your Majesty will forgive me for going into all this detail: I have done it as much to exonerate myself in your mind from the suspicion of imprudence as to make you see how little danger I was in. But above all my desire to return the friendship that Your Majesty professes has rendered my letter longer than I would have wished, in order not to bore you. Besides, I am with the highest regard and sincerest friendship,

My dear Brother,

Your Majesty's good Sister and faithful Ally,

Caterine

41. *To Voltaire*

Catherine here makes a grand gesture of patronage through a seemingly modest, very common type of eighteenth-century letter: the apology for not writing sooner. The letter, accompanied by a snuffbox made by Catherine herself and decorated with her portrait, a rich fur, the translation of her 'Instruction', and the manuscript journal of her inoculation, were all delivered to Voltaire by a Russian prince, Fedor Kozlovsky, with the pomp of a foreign embassy. This grand gesture thanked Voltaire for his propagandistic efforts on Catherine's behalf and encouraged him to continue his support for her as the war with the Ottoman Empire heated up.

Sir, I suppose you must think me a bit flighty. I begged you about a year ago to send me all that has ever been written by the author whose works I love most to read. Last May I received the parcel I desired, accompanied by the bust of the most illustrious man of our century, around whose neck I found a chivalric order of a colour as vibrant as the imagination of the man represented in plaster.* I had never before seen the fleece suspended on the ribbon. I could not find it in any book nor in any annals, and therefore I guessed that it was a courtesy of my good friend, Father Bazin's nephew. May God preserve his health for many years. I felt equal satisfaction upon receiving each of the parcels: for the past six months they have been the finest ornaments in my apartments and the object of my daily study, but up to now I have neither acknowledged their receipt nor thanked you for them. My line of reasoning was as follows:

A poorly scribbled bit of paper covered with bad French is a pointless thank-you for such a man. I must pay him my compliments by some action that he might like. Various deeds presented themselves, but the details would be too lengthy to give. In the end, I thought it best to make of myself an example that might be useful to mankind. I remembered that, happily, I had not yet had smallpox. I sent to England for an inoculator; the famous Doctor Dimsdale was bold enough to come to Russia. Of the 6,000 people he has inoculated, only one little 3-year-old child who had not yet had smallpox has died. This truly skilled man inoculated me on 1 October 1768. After the operation, I was quite astounded to discover that the mountain had given birth to a mouse. I said, 'It's hardly worth shouting about it and keeping people from saving their lives with such a trifle.' It seems to me that the shouters have nothing better to do, or that they are thoroughly foolish, or thoroughly ignorant, or thoroughly mean. But let us pay no mind to those overgrown children, who do not know what they are saying and who talk just for the sake of talking.* I did not keep to my bed for a single second, and I saw people daily. I am going ahead and having my only son inoculated right away. The Grand Master of the Artillery, Count Orlov, a hero like the ancient Romans of the golden age of the Republic, who has both their courage and their magnanimity, was unsure whether he had had the illness. He is presently in the hands of our Englishman, and the day after the operation he went hunting in a severe snowstorm. Several courtiers have followed his example, and many others are preparing for it. Besides that, there are inoculations happening now in Petersburg in three schools and in a hospital established under Mr Dimsdale's oversight. There you have, Sir, the news from the North Pole. I hope it is not uninteresting to you. New writings are rarer, but a French translation has just appeared of the Russian *Instruction* given to the deputies who are to compose the project for our Code. There has not been time to print it, so I hasten to send you the manuscript so that you can better see our starting point. I hope there is not a single line of which an honest man would not approve.

I would very much like to send you verses in return for yours, but he who lacks the brains to write good ones had better work with his hands. I have put that into practice and made a snuffbox, which I beg you to accept. It bears the imprint of the person who has the most regard for you: I need not name her, for you will recognize her easily.

I had forgotten, Sir, to tell you that I added to the small or non-existent quantity of medicine that is given during inoculation three or four excellent remedies that I advise any man of good sense not to forget on such an occasion. It is to have the *Scotswoman*, *Candide*, *The Artless Man*, *The Man with Forty Crowns*, and *The Princess of Babylon** read to one. It is impossible to feel the least pain after that. Count [Andrei] Shuvalov is moreover an excellent reader and did not leave my side during my illness.

PS The enclosed letter was written three weeks ago. It was awaiting the manuscript.* They took so long to transcribe and correct it that I had time to receive your letter, Sir, of 15 November. If I could wage war on the Turks as easily as I introduced inoculation, you would soon risk being summoned to meet me, as you promised, in a place that has supposedly ruined everyone who conquered it [Constantinople]. That is enough to make anyone tempted give it up. I do not know if Mustafa has any wit, but I have reason to believe that he says, 'Muhammad, close your eyes,'* when he wants to wage unjust and unprovoked war on his neighbours. If we are declared successful in this war, I shall owe much to those who envy me: they will have proven my glory in a field of which I had not even been thinking.

Too bad for Mustafa if he does not like either theatre or poetry. He will be quite caught out if I manage to bring his Turks to the same show that Paoli's troupe is performing so well. I do not know whether the latter speaks French, but he knows how to fight for his homeland and his independence.

As for the news from around here, I can tell you, Sir, that just about everyone wants to be inoculated, that there is a bishop who is going to undergo the operation, and that we have inoculated here more people in a month than were inoculated in Vienna in eight.

I could never, Sir, give you enough proof of my gratitude for all the obliging things that you are pleased to tell me, but above all for the keen interest you take in all that concerns me. Rest assured that I feel the full worth of your esteem and that there is no one who has more regard for you than

Caterine
at St Petersburg, this December 1768*

I take up my pen once more to beg you to use against the north wind and the coolness of the Alps (which they say sometimes bother you) the fur I send here. Farewell, Sir, when you make your entry into Constantinople, I shall take care to meet you with a fine Greek costume lined with the richest spoils of Siberia. Such an outfit is far more comfortable and more sensible than those tattered clothes that all Europeans wear and in which no sculptor is willing or able to dress his statues for fear that they will appear both ridiculous and pathetic.

this 17 December 1768

42. *To Voltaire*

Catherine responds to Voltaire's thank-you letter in verse and prose, in which he told her: 'Beat the Turks, and I shall die happy.' Imagining Catherine as the leader of a new alliance of enlightened rulers chasing the supposedly barbarous Ottomans from Europe, he expressed his surprise that no other nations were rushing to join forces with Russia.

at St Petersburg, 15 April 1769

I have received, Sir, your fine letter of 26 February. I shall do my best to follow your advice: if Mustafa does not get thrashed, it will assuredly be neither your fault, nor mine, nor that of my army. My soldiers go to war against the Turks as though they were going to a wedding. Since the other powers of Europe have lost the urge to make common cause against the barbarians, Russia alone will gather these laurels, and our concentration on thoroughly beating our enemies will not be diverted by the subterfuges of concerted campaigns in which often only the enemies win out. If you could see all the predicaments that poor Mustafa faces as a result of the rash step that he was forced to take, against the advice of his Divan and of the most reasonable people, there would be times when you would be unable to refrain from pitying him as a man—and as a man for whom things are going very badly.

Nothing better proves to me how sincerely you share in all my concerns, Sir, than what you tell me about the recently invented chariots. Our military men, however, resemble those of all nations: untested novelties strike them as dubious.

I am very glad, Sir, that my *Instruction* has your approval. I doubt it has that of the Holy Father and of the Mufti. The cardinals ought to elect the latter as pope: they are now on such good terms with him. It will be up to the ultramontanist cardinals to propose it to the conclave.*

I beg you, Sir, to rest assured that I take infinite pleasure in all that comes from you. I cannot thank you enough for what you sent me, including Mr Huber's paintings—it is a real gift.* I would be very sorry to lose out on future publications. I think they should be sent to Holland by means of some merchant, and from there they can be sent to me either by post or on other occasions, which are not rare in that country.

Live, Sir, and rejoice when my brave warriors beat the Turks. I think you know that Azov, at the mouth of the Tanais [now the Don], is already occupied by my troops. The last peace treaty stipulated that both sides would leave that position deserted. You will have seen in the newspapers that we have already sent the Tatars packing in three different places when they wanted to pillage Ukraine. This time they left as ragged as they were when they left Crimea: I say ragged because the prisoners taken were wearing rags, not clothing. If they have not succeeded as they had wished here, then they have been compensated in Poland, if only by their allies, the protégés of the papal nuncio.

We are very good here at making what is called bisque porcelain. I do not know, Sir, how I could have told you that your bust was made of plaster. A French lady would say that it was a gaffe of unparalleled boorishness, but, since I have not the honour of being Welche,* I will say that it was absentmindedness worthy of Mustafa.

Just as I was finishing these lines, I received your letter, Sir, of 1 April. The advice that you gave to the young Gallatin* is a new and most flattering mark of your friendship for me. Truthfulness requires me to tell you that if the young man still needs to study at a university, his parents would do better to send him there rather than to Riga, where I fear he will not find anything comparable to German universities. But if he needs to learn only German, Riga is as suitable as Leipzig itself, and then you will kindly direct him, Sir, to the governor-general of Livonia, Mr Browne, who resides in Riga, to whom I shall write on this subject. We shall look after him, if he still wishes to settle in Russia; otherwise he will be quite at liberty to do as he pleases, and even to come and attend your entry into Constantinople. You have promised to come and find me there, once I arrive, of course. In the meantime, I shall try to study a fine Greek compliment, which I shall recite to you. Two years ago, when I was in Kazan, I learned a number of Tatar and Arabic phrases, which greatly pleased the inhabitants of that city, who for the most part are of that nation. They are good Muslims, very rich, who since my departure have been building a magnificent mosque of stone. I am very sorry that your health does not correspond to my wishes: if my armies' successes can help to restore it, I shall not fail to tell you of all good things that happen to us. Up to now, thank God, I have nothing but very good news from all sides. We are sending all the Turks, Tatars, and especially Polish insurgents away thoroughly trounced.

I hope shortly to have news of something more decisive than skirmishes between light troops, and I am with most particular esteem

Caterine

43. *To Voltaire*

Catherine contrasts Voltaire's support with the anti-Russian policies of her bugbear, the French secretary of foreign affairs, Étienne-François de Choiseul. To disprove reports circulating in France that Russia lacked the resources to continue the war, Catherine compares herself to the 'good king' Henri IV of France, who was reputed to have promised that none of his subjects would be too poor to afford 'a chicken in his pot'.

at Peterhof, this 14 July 1769

Sir, I received on 20 June your letter of 27 May. I am delighted to learn that spring is restoring your health. Although you say out of politeness that my letters are helping, I nonetheless dare not ascribe that property to them. Be glad, for otherwise you might well receive them so often that they would end up boring you.

Not all your compatriots, Sir, think about me as you do. I know some who like to persuade themselves that I cannot do anything right, who torture their wits to convince others, and woe be to their hangers-on if they dare to think otherwise than has been drummed into them. It is in my good nature to think that it is an advantage they give me over themselves: he who knows things only from the words of his own flatterers knows them poorly, sees in a false light, and acts accordingly.* Since, in any case, my glory depends not on them, but rather on my principles and my actions, I can console myself for not having their approval. As a good Christian, I pardon them, and I pity those who envy me.

You tell me, Sir, that you think as I do about various things I have done and that you take an interest in them. Well, Sir, I would have you know, since you take pleasure in it, that my fine colony of Saratov totals 27,000 souls;* that, despite the newsmonger of Cologne, they have nothing to fear from Tatar or Turkish incursions, etc.; that each region has churches of their rite; that they cultivate their fields in peace; that they will pay no taxes for thirty years; that in any case our taxes are so modest that there is not a peasant in Russia who has not a chicken to eat when he likes, and lately there are provinces where they prefer turkeys to chickens; that the export of wheat, permitted under certain restrictions to guard against abuses and not hinder trade, has made the price of wheat rise,* which suits the farmers so well that cultivation grows from year to year; that the population has similarly grown by a tenth in many provinces in the past seven years. We are at war, it is true, but Russia has been in that trade for a good long while, and we emerge from each war more prosperous than we went into it. Our laws are proceeding apace: they are gradually being worked on. It is true that they have become matters of secondary importance, but they will not lose out for all that. The laws will be tolerant: they will not persecute, not kill, nor burn anyone. God keep us from a story like that of the Chevalier de La Barre: any judges who dared undertake such proceedings would be sent to the madhouse. Peter the Great thought it good to lock up the madmen of Moscow in a building that was once a monastery.* Although the war has diversified my labours, as you observed, nonetheless my various establishments will not suffer. Since the start of the war I have formed two new ventures: I am building Azov and Taganrog, where a port was begun and ruined by Peter I. There you have two jewels which I am having set and which might well not be to Mustafa's taste. They say that the poor man does nothing but cry: his friends got him into this war against his will and reluctantly. His troops started by pillaging and burning their own country: over a thousand people were killed as the janissaries left the capital, and the emperor's* envoy, his wife, and his daughters beaten, robbed, dragged by their hair, etc., before the eyes of the sultan and his vizier. The government is so weak and poorly organized that no one dared to put a stop to such disorder. And that is the terrible phantom with which people want to frighten me.

You will have learned, Sir, that, in accordance with your wishes, the Turks were beaten on 19 and 21 April. We took ten flags, three horsetails,* the pasha's commander's baton, and a few cannons; two Turkish camps and somewhere around 50,000 ducats fell into the hands of our soldiers. It seems to me that this is a fairly acceptable opening gambit. When they brought me the horsetails, someone in the room exclaimed: 'Really, they won't say that was bought at the market!'

My military men claim, Sir, that, now that cannons have been invented, Solomon's twelve thousand chariots are of little use alongside a good artillery battery. They add that the chariots, the horses, and the drivers would be as good as dead if we tried to use them in this day and age to drive those chariots. What you tell me of them, Sir, is new proof of your friendship, which I feel most fully and for which I must offer you many thanks.

One might say that the human spirit is always the same: the absurdities of past crusades have not prevented the clergy of Podolia from preaching a crusade against me on the papal nuncio's cue, and those madmen, the confederates as they call themselves, have taken up the cross in one hand and, with the other, have entered into league with the Turks, from whom they have taken two provinces. Why? In order to prevent a quarter of the nation from enjoying the rights of citizens. And that is why they are burning and sacking their own country. The pope's blessing promises them paradise. As a result, the Venetians and the emperor would be excommunicated, I think, if they took up arms against those very Turks who are today defending the crusaders against someone who has not touched the Roman faith for good or for ill. You will see too, Sir, that the pope will be the one to oppose the supper at Sofia that you suggest.*

Please strike Philippopolis from the list of cities. The Ottoman troops who passed through this spring reduced it to ashes because people tried to keep them from pillaging it. I am not too sure whether or not the Jesuits took part in all the misdeeds of their comrades. It seems to me that I have given them no cause, and even when they had been chased from the realms of Portugal, Spain, and France, I took pity on them as men and as unfortunate men, who are for the most part innocent, I believe. Accordingly, I have said and said again to whomever would listen that if there were any willing to marry and settle in Russia, they could rest assured of the government's full protection. I still feel the same way: it seems to me that for someone who has no place to lay his head, those propositions are as welcoming as they are respectable. I hope as you do, Sir, that all this wickedness will cease, that my enemies and enviers will have done me far less harm than they had hoped, and that all their little tricks will come back to shame them. I am sorry to hear of what befell the young Gallatin.* I beg you to let me know, Sir, if you make up your mind to send him here or to Riga so that I can fulfil my promises to your protégés. The poor opinion you have of universities confirms the opinion I had of them: all such institutions were founded in quite unphilosophical times, and it would be a task worthy of a man of genius to prescribe a reform on which one could model such schools in future.*

Farewell, Sir; rest assured of the most particular regard I have for you.

Caterine

PS Here, Sir, is the latest from my army. On 19 June, our light troops sent back to the far bank of the Dniester 20,000 Turks who had tried to cross, and the army crossed the river two days later without the enemy showing himself. On the 28th, 29th, and 30th, the light troops came to blows, and our army advanced on all three days. On 1 July, 10,000 Turks and 20,000–30,000 Tatars attacked them. We fought them off as we continued to advance. On the 2nd, 70,000 Turks renewed their attack but were pushed back from one hill to the next, so that they fled and took refuge behind the cannons of Khotin. On that same night, the corps that had been posted opposite the fortress on the far bank of the river under the orders of Lieutenant-General Rennenkampff began bombarding the city. Prince [Alexander Mikhailovich] Golitsyn camped 2 versts from the Turkish entrenchment. The Turkish corps fled. The next day we turned the bombardment into a blockade. Our light troops are sending patrols beyond the Pruth.*

44. *To Voltaire*

Catherine's gaiety in the first paragraph of this letter is belied by the final sentence of the second: failed attempts at taking the Ottoman fortress of Khotin (in present-day Ukraine) had caused the recall of the Russian commander, Alexander Golitsyn, and, even after the Russians took Khotin on 10 September 1769, other Ottoman strongholds, like Bender, remained a menace.

at St Petersburg, this 25 September 1769

Sir, I told you the other day all about the taking of Khotin and how the army of the victorious and witty Mustafa was annihilated. The present letter will not be full of murderous deeds, which you like no more than I do. Before answering your two letters, Sir, I shall say only that the news from Azov and Taganrog speaks of nothing but balls, dinners, and suppers given by the generals and commanders: ever since those fortresses have been occupied, there has been no more talk of enemies there. Yet in the month of June the Turks sent some ships with troops to make a raid on the coast; the vessels put in at Kaffa [now Feodosia] in Crimea, and there the troops revolted against their pasha, killed him along with the commissary of supplies, rushed back to the boats, and went off God-knows-where. If my enemies had grand designs, I congratulate them on it, but it may be that they counted their chickens before they hatched. I would have lived a hundred years without ever starting a war, but since, thanks to kind attentions of my enemies and enviers, I am forced to wage one, I shall most certainly leave nothing undone in order to pull through nicely. Most Italian farces end with beatings, and that of the Turks crusading alongside the nuncio and his disciples might well end the same way.

Nothing could be more flattering than the journey you wish to undertake to come and meet me, Sir. I would respond poorly to the friendship you show me, if I did not now ignore the personal satisfaction I would find in seeing you and instead heed only the worry I feel when I think of the risks you would run on such a long and difficult journey. I am aware of how delicate your health is. I admire your courage, but I would be inconsolable if by some misfortune the journey were to weaken your health. Neither I nor the whole of Europe would forgive me if ever the epitaph that you were pleased to compose and that you so cheerfully sent to me were used:* I would be accused of having put you at risk. Besides, Sir, it is quite possible that if things remain as they are at present, my presence will be required in the southern provinces of my empire, which would double the length of your route and the discomforts inevitable over such distances.

Furthermore, Sir, rest assured of the perfect regard with which I am

Caterine

45. *To Voltaire*

A number of Frenchmen volunteered to serve on the side of the Polish confederates; Catherine's threat of sending any Frenchmen captured to Siberia became a recurring theme in her letters to Voltaire, probably in hopes of passing the message to the French government (see Letters 70, 71).

at St Petersburg, this 9 November 1769

Sir, I am very sorry to see from your obliging letter of 17 October that you were distressed by a thousand false news reports about us. However, it is very true that there has never been an example of a campaign more successful than ours. Raising the blockade of Khotin for lack of provisions was the only event they could find to our disadvantage. And what was the result? The total defeat of the horde that Mustafa had sent against us. The envious and our enemies then had one recourse—to spread false news and doubts about our successes. That's what the *Gazette of France* and that of Cologne excel in. They will keep going in the same vein,

I think, and I shall scoff at them as long as the outcome favours me. The only pain I feel is for yours over the false reports. I have shared with you everything worthy of some attention, knowing that you are so good as to take such an interest. I don't know whether my letters have reached you.

A colonel who has served against the Corsicans is, I believe, more capable than any other of joining up with the Turks.* But since he will apparently be without official recognition, and since this is not exactly an honourable path, were he to fall into our hands as a prisoner he might well meet up with his comrades—somewhere.* He will still be unworthy of returning to your chateau, since he has resisted the voice of reason and has listened only to that of passion, fanaticism, or madness—which all boils down to the same thing.

It is not the Grand Master of the Artillery, Count Orlov, who presides at the Academy: it is his younger brother [Vladimir], whose only occupation is study. There are five brothers: it would be difficult to name the one with the most merit, or to find a family more united by friendship. The Grand Master is the second. Two of his brothers [Aleksei and Fedor] are currently in Italy. When I showed the Grand Master the part of your letter where you tell me, Sir, that you suspect him of not much liking French verses, he answered that he did not have enough French to understand them. And I believe that is true, for he very much likes poetry in his own language, and not long ago he dug up a young man who is translating the *Aeneid* in verse* with surprising success and almost literally. Count Orlov likes beautiful things, so how could he not enjoy your verses? I hope, Sir, that you will soon give me news of my navy. I believe it has passed Gibraltar. We shall have to see what it does: that navy is a new sight in the Mediterranean. Wise Europe will judge only by the outcome. Luck is needed before friends and flatterers can be found. Up to now, thank God, we have not been short on luck. I confess, Sir, that it is always most agreeable and satisfying for me to see how you share in what happens to me. Be persuaded that I feel perfectly the worth of your friendship: I beg you to continue it and to rest assured of mine.

Caterine

46. *To Alexandra Levshina*

Catherine took a personal interest in the progress of her educational establishments, as seen here in a letter to a pupil at the Smolnyi Institute for Noble Girls. Writing sometimes in childish language, Catherine teases Levshina about her letter-writing,

*her beauty, and her charm, suggesting that after a simple walk in the Summer Garden
in St Petersburg, Levshina and her classmates had induced all the young men of the
city to write amorous verses about them.*

[*c*.1770]

Here, Miss, is my response to your two letters. Let it be said in passing
that the first is written in such a minute hand that, if you continue to
perfect this manner of writing, you will put me to an expense—six
months from now I shall be obliged to buy spectacles in order to read
your letters. Well, whether I am with or without spectacles they will
afford me equal delight. Do tell Madame de Lafont for me, if you
please, how fluently that tall white missy, with a dusky complexion and
the nose of a parakeet, who used to produce such a store of vowels when
I arrived at and left the convent, writes as spontaneously as she fills her
letters with good cheer. I like it a lot when a beautiful nature follows its
course without affectation or contrivance, and I find that dusky Levushka*
with her impulsiveness and her daring flashes of wit is exactly to my
taste. Continue, Miss, continue. Three years hence I shall come and
abduct you from the convent, and you will shout, resist, and weep
in vain. In spite of yourself, you will see this Tsarskoe Selo* of which
you have such a low opinion, and despite your temper, you will be
obliged to conclude, because you love the truth, that the place is beautiful, incomparably more beautiful than the Summer Garden of which
the white class was the finest ornament on the day some peahens went
for a stroll and turned the head of the entire city. But just look what these
Misses have done! Since that day the city has been inundated with
squiggly things—not, however, those which devour the leaves of trees
and cause such terrible damage here in my garden—but rather the ones
poets produce when they have before them objects that enliven their
imagination. I shall come to town one day to see how Madame de Lafont
arranges all the nooks and crannies of the bourgeois abode you told me
about. I hope that your brood will continue not mewling. You can see
that owing to your efforts I employ your school's vocabulary, or at least
your very own. Do not be afraid that Mr Betskoy insists on teaching
you how to swim. At his age it is a kind of exercise that requires strength
and skill. It is typical to make more of a fuss than is actually necessary.
I advise you to take him at his word, and his embarrassment in fulfilling
his promise will exceed your own. You shall see how he will reply to you,
'Excellent, excellent, Mademoiselle,' and he will then put off the outing
till another day. You will have to ask him why he has placed a sofa in
the Turkish style in my room in the Winter Palace. He usually puts

everything he likes in my rooms; the only thing I put there myself is your face as done by Miss Molchanova.* That is a much-loved furnishing, which will never leave the place I have given it. Or would it be better to say the one that you have given it yourself? If that seems enigmatic then ask your superiors for an explanation: they will surely know it. I find the serenade that Prince Orlov gave you very well conceived. He likes to please you; he has known you from birth and feels limitless fondness for you. He loves what is good for his country, and your education conduces to that good. Also, he has a particular affection for you. Do you know why? Because you are lovable. Well, there we are! My letter is already quite long. Still, I have more to tell you: greet the little brown children, pet the blue marmots, hug the grey sisters, and throw your arms around the neck of the white pelerines,* my oldest friends. Make a very deep curtsey to Madame de Lafont, and in doing this show on your face all the sentiments which she has inspired in you so successfully and which have met with such applause. This can only give her pleasure because it represents her efforts. And do tell all the men or women who find something objectionable in my calling you peahens above that peahens are the most beautiful of all possible hens.

47. *To Voltaire*

The first ever arrival of a Russian fleet in the Mediterranean marked a major turning point in European politics. Supported by the British, who wanted to get back at France, Catherine sent her ships on a mission to raise an uprising among the Christians in Greece and to fight the Ottomans by sea: it was a grandiose plan that made Russian power and ambitions impossible to ignore.

this 19 January 1770

Sir, I am very touched that you share my satisfaction at the arrival of our vessels at Port Mahon.* There they are, closer to the enemy than to their own homes, yet they must have made the journey joyfully despite the storms and the lateness of the season. You see, as is their custom when the occasion merits, the sailors have composed some songs that speak only of conquest and of forcing Mustafa to beg humble pardon. I cannot deny the construction of vessels at Azov, about which you are informed. The sultan had forbidden people to believe that my navy could arrive in the Mediterranean. He said that it was a rumour spread by infidels to frighten the servants of Muhammad. The Sublime Porte, for all its sublimity, did not foresee that one. I am not at all surprised by the ignorance of the governor of Rumelia,* ambassador to France, who had never heard even the names of Greece or Athens. What more can one expect from stevedores transformed into pashas, viziers, etc., who often do not know how to read and who receive the full science of government from the fatwa of the Grand Turk. They do not have even a single man who is really up to date on the flow of current affairs. I have met Christian and Most Christian ambassadors* who, although of better birth, were no better informed than the Turkish representative about whom you told me, Sir.

I repeat: wise Europe will approve my projects only if they succeed. You are so good as to compare the Mediterranean expedition (which is unjustly attributed to me—I shall refrain from naming the author until it has succeeded) to Hannibal's undertaking. But the Carthaginians had to deal with a colossus in his full strength, whereas we find ourselves face to face with a weak phantom, whose every limb slackens when touched.

The Georgians are indeed up in arms against the Turks and are refusing them the annual tribute of recruits for the seraglio. Heraclius, the most powerful of their princes, is a man of intelligence and courage. Previously he contributed to the conquest of India under the famous Nader Shah. I have the anecdote from the very mouth of Heraclius' father, who died here in Petersburg in 1762. My troops crossed the Caucasus this autumn and joined up with the Georgians. Here and there little clashes with the Turks occurred, reports of which, I believe, were printed in the newspapers. Spring will reveal the rest. Meanwhile, we are continuing to fortify our positions in Moldavia and Wallachia, and we are working to clear the near bank of the Danube.

But, best of all, within the empire we are so little affected by the war that we cannot remember a carnival at which people were more universally inventive in their amusements than this year. I do not know whether it is the same in Constantinople: perhaps they are inventing resources in order to continue the war. I do not envy them that joy, but I am pleased to have no need of it. Too bad for those who like to deceive themselves:* they easily find flatterers who will pull the wool over their eyes for money. I showed Count Shuvalov the clause in your letter, Sir, that concerns him. He told me that he had meticulously answered all your letters. Perhaps they have got lost.

Please allow me to thank you for all the flattering things in verse and in prose contained in your letters. I would gladly have given you news today, but I have none of interest. Since, Sir, my assiduity in writing does not burden you, rest assured that I shall continue it throughout the year 1770. I hope that it will be a happy one for you and that your health will be fortified just as Azov and Taganrog are already. I beg you to be persuaded of my friendship and appreciation.

Caterine

48. *To Voltaire*

Amid heavy fighting around present-day Romania, a new menace presented itself: bubonic plague. Catherine denies the contagion in her report to Voltaire, both out of concern for Russia's image and because her own officers on the ground were concealing the true nature of the threat. In reality, the plague contracted by Russian troops from the Ottomans in the winter of 1769–70 was spreading northwards from Moldavia, leading to the Moscow Plague Riot of September 1771.

at St Petersburg, this 31 March 1770

Sir, I received three days ago your letter of 10 March. I hope that this letter finds your health completely restored and that you reach a greater age than Methuselah. I do not know whether there were exactly twelve months in that honest man's years, but I want there to be thirteen in yours, as there are in the year of the English Civil List.*

You will see from the enclosed page, Sir, what our summer and winter campaigns were like. I have no doubt that people are spouting a thousand falsehoods about them—a weak and unjust cause must resort to leaving no stone unturned. Since the *Gazettes* of Paris and Cologne had ascribed so many lost battles to us and the outcome belied them, they have taken it into their heads to make my army die of the plague. Don't you find that funny? It looks as though in the spring the plague-stricken will rise from the dead in order to fight. The truth is that none of our soldiers have had the plague.

You find, Sir, the paintings that I bought in Geneva expensive. I was tempted more than once to ask your opinion before the deal was done, but excessive tact, perhaps, held me back. I had assurances from Paris that Monsieur Tronchin* was an honest man, and then one must agree that the price of paintings is pretty much a price set on a whim. I have one that always gives me great pleasure when I see it: it is the one you sent me a year ago. That Monsieur Huber had third parties promise me several, but it seems he does only one a year. Up to now I have only two. Yet the subjects he chooses are so appealing that I want my collection to be complete.* I cannot but be most touched by your friendship,

Sir. You want to arm all Christendom to help me. I care a great deal for the King of Prussia's friendship, but I hope that I shall not need the 50,000 men that you would like him to give me against Mustafa. Since you think exaggerated the number of 300,000 men, at whose head it is claimed the sultan himself will march, I must tell you about the Turkish armament last year, which will make you see him for the phantom he is. In the month of October, Mustafa thought it opportune to declare war on Russia—he was no more prepared for it than we. When he learned that we would defend ourselves vigorously, he was surprised, for he had been led to hope for many things that did not happen. Then he ordered that 1,100,000 men from the various provinces of his empire come to Adrianople [now Edirne, Turkey] in order to take Kiev, spend the winter in Moscow, and crush Russia. Moldavia alone was ordered to provide a million bushels of grain for the innumerable Muslim army. The hospodar* replied that Moldavia did not harvest so much in a fertile year, and that it was impossible for him to do it, but he received a second command to execute the orders that had been given, and he was promised money for it. The army's artillery train was proportionate to that multitude: it was to consist of 600 pieces of cannon, which were allocated from the arsenals. But when it came to making them move, most of them were ditched, and only about sixty pieces marched. Finally, in the month of March, over 600,000 men were in Adrianople. But since they lacked everything, desertion started to set in. Yet the vizier crossed the Danube with 400,000 men; there were 180,000 on 28 August near Khotin. You know the rest, but you perhaps do not know that the vizier was the seventh to cross back over the Danube bridge and that he had not even 5,000 men when he retreated to Babadag.* That was all that remained of that prodigious army. Those who had not perished had fled, resolved to return home. Please note that, when coming and going, they pillaged their own provinces and burned the places where they encountered resistance. What I am telling you is so true that I have even understated rather than exaggerated things, for fear that they would seem the stuff of fables.

All that I know of my navy is that one part has left Mahon and the other is about to leave England, where they wintered. I think you will have news of them before I do; however, I shall not fail to inform you in due course of the news I receive with all the more alacrity, since you wish it.

Work on the Code has been a bit delayed by all these deeds of war; it has become a secondary priority. It must be hoped that the time will come when it will reassume priority among my occupations. You entreat me, Sir, to bring the war and the laws to completion as soon as possible so that you can bring news of it to Peter the Great in the next world. Permit me to say to you that this is not the way to make me finish any time soon. It is my turn to entreat you most seriously to postpone that jaunt for as long as can be: do not aggrieve your friends in this world for love of those who are in the next. If over there or up there everyone can choose to spend his time in such company as he likes, I shall arrive with a daily routine all ready, arranged for my satisfaction. I hope well in advance that you will already now grant me a quarter of an hour's conversation a day; Henri IV will join in, Sully too, and no Mustafa.*

I am very glad, Sir, that you are pleased with our Russians who come to visit you; those who return home from abroad without having been to Ferney forever regret it. In general, our nation has the most fortunate proclivities in the world: there is nothing easier than giving them a taste for what is good and reasonable. I do not know why mistakes have often been made in the choice of methods. I would willingly put the government at fault for going about it clumsily. When this nation becomes better known in Europe, people will recover from the many errors and prejudices that they have about Russia.

I always see with great pleasure your remembrance of my mother, who died very young to my great regret.

If our friends the Venetians so wished, nothing could be easier than to send Mustafa, as you desire, to spend carnival in the year 1771 with Candide in their damp city.*

I am delighted to learn that Count [Andrei] Shuvalov is back in your good graces. It would have been stunning if he had not answered you, for most certainly he is one of the most meticulous and most diligent men I know. I do not think I am deceived in predicting that the fatherland can expect great services of him. His capacities are far beyond his age: he is not yet 30. Rest assured, Sir, of all the sentiments which you know me to possess and of the distinguished esteem which I shall not cease to have for you.

Caterine

49. *To Voltaire*

The Catholic Church opposed Catherine's intervention in Poland, which she presented as a struggle for religious toleration. Frederick II saw Poland as a way to distract Catherine from the east; Voltaire enjoyed skewering his usual target, the Catholic Church, whenever possible. Here Catherine jokes about the Church with her attention squarely on the Turks, since, as she saw it, only the Ottoman war could bring her the glory of major conquests against the centuries-old enemy of Christendom.

at my country house of Tsarskoe Selo, this 6 June 1770

Sir, I hasten to reply to your letter of 18 May, which I received yesterday evening, for I see that you are suffering. The tribulations that Mustafa's adherents are giving out that my army has sustained, like the loss of Wallachia, are tall tales. I have had no greater anguish than seeing that you feared them to be true. Thanks be to God—none of that happened. A week ago I received further news that a small Turkish unit had crossed the Danube on rafts near Isaccea* to reconnoitre our positions, but they were so well greeted that they went back with far more haste than they came. Our soldiers pulled over 300 drowned corpses, not counting those killed and wounded, from a stream that the Turks had attempted to swim across.

I told you by the last post the news that I had received from the Peloponnese, which seems fairly satisfying for a first start. I hope that through your intercession the Holy Virgin will not abandon the faithful. Those poor devils, the followers of Mustafa, have no other means of making the cart go but by inventing endless battles disadvantageous to Russia; however, they will not manage in this way to repair overall decay of the Turkish monarchy. The phantom is crumbling: they themselves may have given it an untimely shock, perhaps. That is what comes of not knowing with whom you are dealing. King Ali of Egypt managed to take advantage of the situation: they say that Christians and Muslims are equally satisfied with him, for King Ali is tolerant and just. Politicking when they ought to be making a profit, the Venetians are like the animal in the fable who died of hunger between two bales of hay.* Sleep soundly, Sir: your favourite's affairs (I boldly assume that title, given what you tell me and the friendship that you never cease to show for me) are rattling along very respectably. She herself is pleased with them and does not fear the Turks, either on land or at sea. For lack of sailors they have sent out on their ships the gardeners of the seraglio or the bostanjis.*

Brother Ganganelli is too clever to be really upset in the depths of his heart by my progress. We have nothing against one another: I have taken neither Avignon nor Benevento* from him. My cause is ultimately that of Christendom. Brother Rezzonico* was the only one to be blinded by his piety; Clement XIV seems to me to be more enlightened. I believe, Sir, that the Capuchins have the same rights as the Franciscans. You can become pope. I even think it must be done for the good of the Church, and here is why: the two heads of the

Greek and Roman Churches will not only be in direct correspondence, but they will even be bound by ties of friendship, something which has never happened until now. I can already foresee in advance the great good it will do Christendom. I declare to you that I shall be firm, but not harsh.

Farewell, Sir, be well and rest assured that nothing could add to how touched I am by all the signs of friendship that you show me, nor could anything equal my esteem for them.

Caterine

50. *To Étienne-Maurice Falconet*

Joking about her improvements to the gardens at Tsarskoe Selo, Catherine compares herself to a character in Antoine de Fériol de Pont-de-Veyle's play 'Le Somnambule' (1739)—a baron obsessed with his unrealistic plan for a garden. Russian troops had occupied Azov from March 1769; Catherine dreamed of one day cultivating Crimea, which, if annexed, would be the most luxurious garden in her empire.

[14 June 1770]

I am returning to you Monsieur Collin's letter.* The imprint of the gemstone is very handsome. Could you please let me know the cost of the gem? And then we shall see. I shall ask Mr Betskoy to whom he gave the medals, which I sent to your friend. Not only is the empress tanned, but she has once again become as light as a doe, and everyone complains that they can barely keep up with her on foot. She potters around in her garden in the morning; in the afternoon she plays the role of the baron and his plan from that comedy. Anglomania has swept over all the landowners of Ingermanlandia.* Farewell, Monsieur Falconet; I salute Peter the Great and I think very highly of the gifted artist in whose hands he is to be found.

PS In the little parcel attached here you will find some wild grapes from Azov. I am sure you have never seen any from that country before.

51. *To Johanna Bielke*

Instead of the triumphant war news and declarations of religious open-mindedness that Catherine was sending abroad to Voltaire, this letter turns international affairs into homey gossip, suitable for chatter with a family friend and maternal figure.

Exploitation of natural resources, military strength, and the maxims of governance give way to jewellery, fashion, and the language of good sense.

I am delighted, Madam, that you liked the rock I sent you and especially that it made you happy. It is a jewel from Finland, where, in the past two years, quarries of the finest possible marble of every colour have been opened. We are very shortly going to use it for various buildings, both inside and outside. Augustus said that he had found Rome built of bricks and that he would leave it built of marble; and, for myself, I shall say that I found Petersburg almost made of wood and that I will leave buildings adorned with marble.* For, despite the war and the Welches, we are building. A Turkish prisoner said to Field Marshal Prince Golitsyn a few days ago, 'For the good of both empires, you should send one of us home to bring word that in Petersburg you are building, having fun, and not suffering at all from the war, whereas for us all is in disarray. We think that it is the same here, and I see quite the contrary.' These words show well that common sense can be found in all nations. Heaven grant that the passions should heed it. Do you know, Madam, that I do not like one little bit the nonchalance, the inattentive manner, and the apparently universal boredom of the son of the Prince-Bishop?* Underneath all that there may well be a great deal of ambition and not knowing one's place, and if that is his temper, his father's house will ruin him, while his mother's love will make nothing of him.—No, Madam, I cannot get over the leather breeches, heavy boots, and little coat: granted, such a postilion's outfit is very light, but also a bit too uncovered for a woman.* God grant that her temper be not so meddlesome as her mother's. Cabals should never be the domain of kings and queens: they cannot become leaders of one faction of their subjects without renouncing the others. Such a role cannot therefore befit them. Farewell, Madam, be well and continue your friendship for me, and never doubt of mine.

Catherine
at Peterhof, this 13 July 1770
To Lady Bielke at Hamburg*

52. *To Aleksei Grigor'evich Orlov*

The letter is one of the most trenchant foreign policy documents of Catherine's reign. Its immediate concerns are: first, the integration of newly recruited Danish officers, led by Admiral Ivan Nikolaevich Harf, into a squadron led by Admiral Grigory

Spiridov in the Mediterranean; and, second, Aleksei Orlov's mission to stir Orthodox Christians in Greece to revolt against Ottoman rule. Catherine presents to Orlov a principled strategy, based on a theory of natural justice governing international relations. She also deploys Christian rhetoric, evoking the strong cultural and religious ties between Russia and the Byzantine Empire as the source of Russian Orthodoxy. She implies a notion of Europe as a Christian republic that includes Russia: Catherine is inviting the Greeks to rejoin Europe after three centuries of Ottoman rule. This strategy of mobilizing public sentiment about religion for political ends under the guise of Russia's dedication to religious toleration will be a consistent argument in Catherine's defence of her expansionist agenda in Crimea and Poland. Orlov's initial landings in the Peloponnese failed, as did the planned uprising, but he was much rewarded for the Battle of Chesme.

By the grace of God, We Catherine II, Empress and Autocrat of All Russia, etc., etc., etc.

To our lieutenant-general Count Orlov

In the past few days a new convoy of land forces has set out from our port at Revel [Tallinn] to join you. When they embark on the vessels their precise number will be made up of a detachment of 523 guardsmen from the Preobrazhensky Regiment and 2,167 men from different infantry regiments. We have entrusted their transportation and escort to their destination to Rear Admiral Harf, who was recruited from the Danes to our service specifically for this and because of his excellent skill and experience in the navy.

You will see the orders he received when he set sail from the copy attached herewith, which will among other things make clear to you that Rear Admiral Harf has been ordered to put at your disposal the English transport vessels under his control as part of the army; and you will also see authentic documents proving that they have been contracted into our service and precisely the conditions thereof.

Since we are sending the same orders regarding the transport ships to our Admiral Spiridov today, the next command will depend on you and the very same Admiral Spiridov: that is, whether to escort them back home with the compensation stipulated in their contract and under some sort of protection to a safe haven; or whether to keep them there in our service until further notice, to be employed in some manner according to the circumstances of your position, about which we cannot and do not wish to determine any decisive measures. By the same token you will see from the above-indicated instruction that we have herewith entrusted command over a small squadron armed to protect the transport to Rear Admiral Harf. We have decreed that even after their fleets join forces, and he has been made subordinate to Admiral Spiridov in accordance with the rules of service and by virtue of the authority of his rank, he will retain command. On this occasion, our decree arises from the internal composition of Harf's squadron. On all these ships, alongside our own men, we will be summoning into our service this rear admiral, the Danish officers who are undoubtedly recognized in their own homeland as being among the best, as well as a certain number of Danish sailors to supplement our insufficient numbers. The sea journey this squadron will complete to reach your shores might bring about a fusion of peoples necessary for the mission, despite their different languages and somewhat disparate rules of service. For this reason, then, we decree that it will be most useful, to promote cooperation between these people, that the order and command of this squadron, having been determined conclusively, be enacted without misunderstandings and problems among people who are still unaccustomed to our ways of doing things; whereby the failure to implement our mutual responsibilities shall be pre-empted, something that could easily occur when a single squadron is once again fragmented among different new commanders. Understanding as you do the need for such precaution, you will of course not fail to reconcile this with all the measures that have been undertaken in this regard by you in the service of Ourselves and the nation. And you will carry out these measures, when the occasion arises, such that the ships of Harf's squadron remain in the same division both when they are part of the main fleet and when they are on separate expeditions; and that they are always used under the command of their current commanders. For, on the one hand, this is what the service to Ourselves requires; while, on the other hand, We are certain that Rear Admiral Harf, zealous and meticulous in the execution of everything entrusted to him, will strive to justify in our eyes the reputation of a brave and skilful officer, which he has acquired for himself in the service of others.

Hopeful as we are that the hand of the Almighty will protect our righteous use of force, we fully expect that this new transport, designated to reinforce the operations that you have undertaken and that have made so propitious and glorious a commencement in the very depths of the enemy's territory, will soon arrive safely; and that owing to this and to your own successes, which are increasing daily, it will be capable of inflicting even graver blows on our perfidious enemy.

All of Europe is amazed by our great feat, and in curiosity turns its gaze on you who brought it about. All who are dispassionate rejoice in our successes and wish for them to be expanded and solidified; by contrast there are the powers who, envious of the glory and elevation of our empire, and raging against us for this reason, are hourly growing more vexed in their furious hatred; their intrigues and plotting intensify in spite of everything. We can safely presuppose that they will exhaust all possible underhanded means in assessing our activities anywhere and everywhere, most especially where you are, since it is the weakest point, given its distance from Us, and the one where they stand the greatest chance of achieving some success. In response to this, prudence and reason of state require us to undertake in a timely fashion all the measures and precautions that can blunt the sting of malice and reduce their actions to nothing or at the very least lessen them and possibly cause them shame before the world.

For all these reasons and for your guidance, We would like here to reveal to you Our overall private thoughts and considerations on what we consider necessary and suitable to protect Our undertaking against hostile plots in the present situation, in the first instance, and until circumstances present us with entirely new and clearer prospects.

Rulers and kingdoms must manage their relationships with one another on the basis of mutually accepted rules of natural law. It is by these lights that the world considers and judges all the actions of royal courts. A court sure of public recognition may confidently expect that the opposing side would not dare—at least not obviously and openly—to act against it because of the risk of raising the indignation and mistrust of every part of the Christian republic, and thereby providing their rivals with greater advantage and the chance of achieving their goals.

To our particular and heartfelt delight, we are assured that all of the dispassionate powers of the Christian republic suppose justice to be on our side; and that such widespread assurance constrains our enemies, against their will and inclination, to mask their true views. At present the fact is that the glory and interest of our Fatherland requires that such a positive view of us be preserved and confirmed in the public sphere. With this goal in mind, it is essential that all our undertakings and measures be truly kept within the limits of justice and selflessness. This is especially the case with the things that are currently taking place under your brave and patriotic direction in Greece. They must somehow be publicly declared to be so (though not directly at Our instigation) and thus be firmly and generally recognized as such.

To obtain this goal there is one method, but it is thoroughly reliable and seemingly not open to doubt and complication. It is only necessary that in gathering under your leadership various Greek peoples you forge out of them as quickly as possible some visible entity unified for the purpose of a joint victory. To the world they should look like a new, complete army. Having been assembled with such a public declaration (which must be distributed as widely as possible), thereby establishing its political existence, this army must then call out to the whole Christian republic in terms like the following, for instance:

'Having by the will of God been subjected to the onerous yoke of the evil son of Hagar, the numerous Greek peoples, no longer able to bear tortures, persecution, despoliation, and the violence of their tyrant which grew more unbearable by the day and which threatened with certain and final annihilation not only them but Christianity itself, in dire straits in their own lands were at last forced to rise up against such barbarity and to cast off the shackles of enslavement. The illegal and perfidious war begun by the Turks against the Russian Empire marked the moment, on the one hand, when their pitiful condition, caused by the barbarians' ferocious hatred of the religion they share with the Russians, deteriorated hourly; but, on the other hand, it also gave the Greeks a long-sought chance of liberation. Now, having summoned to their aid Christ the Saviour, against whom the Muhammadan disgrace pronounces so much evil and blasphemy, and united as they are among themselves by a sacred vow of alliance, they have taken up arms and intend to defend their faith and liberty to their very last drop of blood. In this manner, by coming together into a whole and constituting a new member of the Christian republic, they beseech and appeal to all rulers and lands, conjuring them by the wounds and blood of the Saviour of one and all, to acknowledge them as having this status and insofar as possible to supply them with all kinds of aid and protection. For their own part they will in every possible manner always seek to deserve the support that might, in any case, be of equal use to all of Christianity by creating a new bulwark against the arrogance, greed, and treachery of the Ottoman Porte. And, moreover, now that they have tasted the fruits of precious freedom and as they restore to themselves the freedom of the Christian confession, they would prefer to fall in battle rather than see themselves once again subjected to the bonds of slavery. They leave it to the divine Last Judgment to avenge them on those who, having forgotten their Christianity, by some unexpected motives of vanity or greed would aid against them the implacable enemy of the Christian race.'

The usefulness of such a formal gesture is palpable, and we certainly expect that you will apply all means and force to sustain it in the name of and in association with the Greek peoples. For in this way your own mission will acquire a new and thoroughly flattering guise wherefrom We can expect, not without cause, that We shall have greater capacities to force the Porte to concede a stable and glorious peace.

In conclusion, We shall say briefly but with particular pleasure that we are utterly satisfied by the initial orders you have given. For they have already begun to bring about important results in facilitating our military preparation. Having complete confidence in your judgment, and in your proven love for the Fatherland, and anticipating further success from your leadership and activity on the ground (and may the Heavenly Power guide and strengthen you in them), We remain well disposed toward you in all Our Imperial favour.

Given at Peterhof, 19 July 1770
Catherine

53. *To Voltaire*

This letter begins and ends with a major Russian victory against the Ottoman Empire. On 21 July 1770, at Kagul (in present-day Moldova), Russian troops, commanded by Petr Rumiantsev, defeated a significantly more numerous Ottoman force and pushed them back to the Danube; Rumiantsev was promoted to field marshal for this crucial victory. On 26 July, Prince Nikolai Repnin took the fortress of Izmail in Odessa; returned to the Ottomans at the end of the war, it was taken again by storm in 1790, before being relinquished once more.

this 9/20 August 1770

Sir, you tell me in your letter of 20 July that the fear I cause you is a form of exercise and that my victories are a form of relaxation. Here is a little dose of the latter for you. I have just received a courier informing me of what happened after the Battle of Kagul. My troops advanced on the Danube and took up a position on the edge of the river across from Isaccea. The vizier* and the agha of the janissaries fled to the other side, but the rest of his entourage were killed, drowned, and dispersed when they tried to follow. The vizier had the bridge removed. Almost 2,000 janissaries were taken prisoner on this occasion; twenty pieces of cannon, 5,000 horses, immense spoils, and a great quantity of provisions of all kinds fell into our hands. The Tatars immediately sent a plea to Field Marshal Count Rumiantsev that he might allow them to cross into Crimea. They were informed of his demand for tribute, whereupon he sent a sizeable detachment to the left, towards Izmail, to coax them into acquiescing. We have known for a long time that they dreamed of joining us and were simply avoiding being accused of perfidy. A few mirzas or leaders of hordes also had qualms because they shared the religion of the Turks. Even so, they would frequently sigh and say among themselves that the Tatars of Kazan, their brothers and relatives, lived happily without war or oppression. Please note that the latter are build-ing a very fine stone mosque.

The news from Greece and even that from Constantinople confirms the rumours of three defeats suffered by the Turkish navy.

You do not want peace, Sir. Do not worry, up to now it has not been spoken of. I agree with you that peace is a good thing; when it reigned, I thought it the *ne plus ultra* of happiness. Now that I have been at war for almost two years, I see that one can get used to anything. War really does have some pretty good moments too. I find it has a great fault, which is that at war one does not love one's neighbour as oneself. I was used to thinking it impolite to hurt people. Today, however, I can con-sole myself a bit by saying to Mustafa, 'George Dandin, you asked for it.'* And with that thought, my mind is easy, more or less as before. I have never disliked great events, but I have never been tempted by conquest. Nonetheless, I do not foresee the time of peace to be very near. It is amusing that the Turks are led to believe that we cannot sus-tain the war for long. If those people were not blinded by passion, how could they have forgotten that Peter the Great sustained a war for thirty years, sometimes against the Turks themselves, then against the Swedes, the Poles, and the Persians,* without the empire ending up on its last legs? On the contrary, Russia has always emerged from each of its wars more prosperous than at the start; it was war that truly set industry on its feet. Each of our wars gave birth to some new resource that invigor-ated commerce and exchange.

It will be difficult for the Venetians, Sir, to achieve great things; they finesse things too much. They reason when they ought to act. I agree, Sir, that for a long time they will not meet with a more favourable occa-sion to recover what they have lost.

If the so-called Christian princes who have sided with the Turks are jealous of our successes in this war, they have only themselves to blame. Why did they act against me without foreseeing how it would end? For those who agree that order and discipline are preferable to disorder and disobedience, this was easy to predict. If their hopes were founded on my supposed financial disarray, they were again pitifully deceived. I have said it before: Peter the Great had smaller revenues and fewer troops than I. The deal that has been negotiated on my behalf in Holland is a trifle that serves merely to ease exchange rates.

Your peace plan, Sir, seems a bit like the lion's share in the fable:* you keep everything for your favourite. The Spartan legions should not be excluded from that peace of yours; we shall talk about the Isthmian Games* later. Just as I was finishing this letter, I received news of the taking of Izmail: here are some rather exceptional circumstances.

Before crossing the Danube in a little boat, the vizier harangued his troops. He told them that they could see for themselves that Heaven was so angry at the Muslims and so much in favour of the Russians that they could no longer hold out. He said that he, the vizier, found himself obliged to cross to the other side of the river and that he would send them all the boats he could find to save them. But, in the event that he could not fulfil his promise, and if Russian troops happened to attack, he advised them not to resist at all, but rather to lay down their arms. He assured them that the Empress of Russia would have them treated humanely and that all they had been led to believe about the Russians until now had been invented by the enemies of the two empires. After that, my troops appeared before Izmail; the Turks left, and those who remained laid down their arms. The city's capitulation was completed in half an hour. We took forty-eight pieces of cannon and sizeable stores of every kind. From 21 to 27 July (since the Battle of Kagul, that is), we count almost 8,000 prisoners, and in the last year we have taken almost 500 pieces of cannon from the enemy. Count Rumiantsev has sent a detachment to the right, towards your Braila, which will be taken as you intend it to be, and another to the left, which is to seize Kiliya.* Well, Sir, are you satisfied? I beg you to be as well satisfied with my friendship as I am with yours.

Caterine

54. *To Voltaire*

Catherine here records, for one of the century's most famous historians, a dramatic account of one of the most glorious military successes of her reign: the victory in the naval battle of 24–6 June 1770 that took place off Chesme, a town on the western coast of Anatolia. The Ottomans lost nearly their entire fleet, while the Russians demonstrated decisively their strength in the Mediterranean. Catherine was immensely proud of this victory, which took place only two days before the anniversary of her coup and under the command of one of the men who helped to put her on the throne, Aleksei Orlov.

at St Petersburg, this 16/27 September 1770

Sir, I have so many things to tell you today! I do not know where to start. My navy, under the command not of my admirals but of Count

Aleksei Orlov, after beating the enemy navy, has incinerated it in the
Port of Chesme in Asia, formerly Klazomenai. I received direct news
of it three days ago. Almost a hundred vessels of all kinds were reduced
to ash. I hardly dare tell you the number of Muslims who died there: it
is said to be up to 20,000. A general council of war had put an end to
the discord between the two admirals by passing command to the army
general who was aboard the fleet and was in any case their senior in
service. Everyone approved unanimously of this result, and from that
moment on, harmony was restored. I have always said that those heroes
were born for great events. The Turkish navy had been pursued from
Nafplio,* where it had already been harassed twice on the way to Chios.*
Count Orlov knew that reinforcements had left Constantinople, so he
thought he would pre-empt their joining forces by attacking the enemy
without delay. When he arrived in the strait of Chios, he saw that they
had already joined up. He found himself with nine men-of-war, in the
presence of sixteen Ottoman ships of the line; the numbers of frigates
and other boats were even more unequal. He did not hesitate and found
that all were unanimous in their determination to vanquish or perish.
The battle was joined. Count Orlov kept to the centre; Admiral Spiridov,
with Count Fedor Orlov on board, commanded the van, and Rear Admiral
Elphinston the rear. The Turkish battle order was such that one of their
wings was up against a rocky island and the other near the shallows, so
that they could not manoeuvre. For several hours the fire was fierce on
both sides. The vessels came so close to one another that musket fire was
added to that of the cannons. Admiral Spiridov's ships had to deal with
three warships and a Turkish xebec.* He captured the Kapudan-Pasha's
ship, which was carrying ninety guns. He threw so many grenades and
combustible material onto it that the vessel caught fire, spreading to
ours. Both ships exploded just moments after Admiral Spiridov, Count
Fedor Orlov, and about ninety other people had disembarked. When, in
the heat of battle, Count Aleksei saw the flagships explode, he thought
that his brother had perished. He then understood that he was mortal. He
fainted, but, when he recovered moments later, he ordered all sails raised,
and he rushed with his ship into the enemies' midst. At the moment of
victory, an officer brought him news that his brother and the admiral
were alive. He says that he has no words to describe what he felt at that
moment, the happiest of his life, when, victorious, he was reunited with
the brother whom he had thought dead. In disorder and disarray, the
rest of the Turkish navy fled for cover in the port of Chesme. The next
day was spent preparing fireships and bombarding the enemy in the
port, to which the latter replied. But during the night the fireships were

released and did their duty so well that the Turkish fleet was consumed in under six hours. The earth and the waves shook, they say, from so many exploding enemy vessels: it was felt as far away as Smyrna [now İzmir], which is 12 miles from Chesme. During the fire in the port, we dragged away a sixty-gun Turkish vessel that had been upwind and so had not been consumed. After the fire we also seized a battery that the Turks had abandoned. The Turkish vessel called the *Rhodes* was given to the Russian captain who had boarded the flagship, and this is how he survived: when his ship exploded, he was thrown into the air, then fell into the sea, and was pulled out by our rowboats. Apart from getting a bit wet he suffered no harm, which may sound like a fairy tale but is nonetheless true.

War is an ugly thing, Sir. Count Orlov tells me that the day after the burning of the enemy fleet, he was horrified to see that the water in the port of Chesme, which is not very large, was stained with blood, for so many Turks had perished there.

Another anecdote: when the two ships exploded, some of the crew members who had fallen into the water caught hold of debris they had found. Even in that condition, when they came across their enemies, they tried to fight or drown one another. This letter, Sir, is a response to yours of 28 August, in which your concerns about us were already starting to be allayed. I hope that now you have no more; it seems to me that business is going fairly well for me.

As for taking Constantinople, I do not think it will happen so soon. Nonetheless, they say that in this world one should despair of nothing. I am beginning to think that it is up to Mustafa more than anyone else. That prince has gone about things so well up till now that, if he persists in the stubbornness his friends have instilled in him, he will expose his empire to great dangers. He has forgotten his role—he is the aggressor.

Farewell, Sir, be well. If battles won can please you, you should be well satisfied with us. Rest assured of the esteem and regard I bear for you.

Caterine

Prince Kozlovsky, who visited you, perished on the *Eustace* when it exploded.

55. *To Voltaire*

The events on which Catherine lightly touches promise imperial acquisitions: the unrest in Crimea prepared its independence as a Russian protectorate, formalized in the Treaty of Küçük Kaynarca in 1774; this was a first step towards the annexation of Crimea by Russia in 1783. Meanwhile, Frederick the Great's brother, Prince Henry of Prussia, visited St Petersburg with a scheme for the two powers to acquire territories in Poland.

[November 1770]

I have scarcely any news to send you today. I shall simply answer your letter of 2 October to tell you that Lieutenant-General Berg, whose unit is holding the stretch between Taganrog and the Dnieper, almost took prisoner the Khan of Crimea, who wanted to move from Ochakov to Perekop, where men had been sent to meet him. The rest of his equipment has been taken and his men killed, dispersed, or taken prisoner. He himself has fled to Ochakov. He can unquestionably be counted as a prince who has been well and truly robbed, for some of his subjects (the three hordes of Belgorod and Budzhak, who live between the Dniester and the Danube, and that of Yedisan, which is settled between the Dniester, the Dnieper, Ochakov, and Bender)* have declared themselves in favour of Russia. Crimea remains his, but divisions are rife. A large segment is leaning towards us, the other towards peace, and no one wants to fight because they see that their greatest supporters, the Turks, have got themselves into no state to save them. It is said that Mustafa is thinking quite seriously of withdrawing to Adrianople. He wants to take personal command next year. At present that prince is still deluding himself with the pleasant thought that we shall be unable to sustain the war for another two campaigns. The poor man does not know that at the beginning of this century, when Russia was less wealthy and when, so to speak, we were not so well aware of our resources, we nonetheless were at war for thirty years in a row. He may do as he pleases: the choice between war and peace is his.

I like peace, but I do not dislike the great events of war. You will agree that this campaign is one of the finest that can be had; it is some consolation for my pain at seeing that in Paris they have carriages, precious centrepieces, newfangled choruses both charming and noisy, and that your German dancers dance better than my Italians. I know too that they are dying of hunger there. In Russia, everything is rattling along as usual. There are provinces where people are almost unaware that we have been at war for two years. No one lacks anything anywhere; we sing the *Te Deum*, we dance, and we rejoice. I am very touched, Sir, by your courtesies and those of Monsieur d'Alembert. My armies have entered their winter quarters. They cannot go as fast as you wish because in twenty-four hours one has to rest once and eat twice. Next year we shall see what there is to be done. In the meantime, I am most agreeably kept busy by the presence of Prince Henry of Prussia, whose merit most assuredly matches his great reputation. It seems to me that he does not entirely dislike it here. Farewell, Sir, live as many years as Methuselah and rest assured of my friendship.

56. *To Voltaire*

Catherine and Voltaire were taken with the air of adventure and myth that came with southern and oriental conquest, which evoked the great conquerors of antiquity. The neoclassical aesthetic that governed court entertainments like the one Catherine narrates here made her and her contemporaries especially attuned to such historical reminiscences. Her pointedly arch self-portrayal in most of the letter contrasts with the blunt language of military discipline applied to the adventurer Naum Choglokov, although his abortive plan to usurp the throne of the mountain kingdom of Georgia has a mythic quality.

at St Petersburg, this 4/15 December 1770

Sir, repetitions get boring. I have informed you so often that such and such a city has been taken and that the Turks have been beaten. To be entertaining, they say, you need variety. Well then! I would have you know that your dear Braila was besieged, that an assault was made, that the assault was repulsed and the siege lifted. Count Rumiantsev got angry: he sent Major-General Glebov with reinforcements back towards Braila a second time. You might perhaps think that the Turks, encouraged by the lifting of the siege, would have defended themselves like lions. Not in the least. When my troops drew near a second time, they abandoned their position, cannons, and the stores that were there. Mr Glebov entered and occupied it.* Another detachment went to re-occupy Wallachia; the day before yesterday I received news that Bucharest, the capital of the principality, was taken on 15 November, after a skirmish with the Turkish garrison. But, since you wished the Danube to be crossed, you will be truly amused that this was when Field Marshal Count Rumiantsev sent a few hundred chasseurs and light troops to the other side of the Danube. They left Izmail in boats and seized on 10 November the fort at Tulcea, which is 15 versts from Isaccea, where the vizier had his camp. They dispatched the garrison to the next world, took away several prisoners and thirteen pieces of artillery, nailed the rest shut, and returned safely to Kiliya. When the vizier learned of this little escapade, he dismantled his military base and decamped with his entourage to Babadag. That is where we stand at the moment, and if it so pleases Mustafa, we shall keep going, although for the sake of humanity it would be high time for that lord to hear reason. Mr Tottleben has gone to attack Poti on the Black Sea: he says nothing good of Mithridates' successors, but then again he finds the climate in ancient Iberia* to be the finest in the world. The latest letters from Italy say that my third squadron is at Mahon. If the sultan does not change his mind, I shall send him another half-dozen—you would think he enjoyed it! The current English ailment cannot be cured save by a war: they are too rich and disunited, and a war will impoverish them and bind them together in spirit. Therefore, the nation wants one, but the court is cross with no one but the governors of Buenos Aires. You see, Sir, that I am replying to several of your letters by the present one. The festivities occasioned by Prince Henry of Prussia's stay have somewhat impeded my exactitude in answering you; he is leaving today for Moscow. I gave him several such celebrations, which he seemed to enjoy. I have to tell you about the very last one. It was a masquerade, at which there were 3,600 people. At supper time, Apollo, the Four Seasons, and the Twelve Months of the Year entered: they were children between the ages of 8 and 10, taken from the educational institutions for nobles of both sexes that I have established. Apollo gave a little speech inviting the company to make their way to the salon that the Seasons had prepared; then he ordered his retinue to present their gifts to their chosen recipients. The children did their very best to carry out all they were to say and do. You will find attached their little compliments, which are, it is true, mere child's play. The 120 people who were to dine in the Hall of the Seasons made their way there: it was an oval containing twelve alcoves, in each of which there was a table for ten people. Each alcove represented a month of the year, and the space was decorated accordingly. Above the alcoves, a gallery had been constructed all the way around, on which there were, besides the crowd of masks, four orchestras. Once we were seated at the tables, the Four Seasons, who had followed Apollo, began to dance a ballet with their retinue. Then Diana and her nymphs arrived. When the ballet ended, the music Traetta had composed for the hall was heard, and the masks entered.

After supper, Apollo arrived to entreat the company to make their way to the theatricals he had prepared. In an apartment adjacent to the hall, a stage had been erected on which the same children performed a little comedy, *The Oracle*.* After that, the assembly enjoyed dancing so much that we retired only at five in the morning. The whole celebration had been prepared in such secrecy that no one knew that there would be anything more than a masquerade. Twenty apartments were filled with masks; the hall of the seasons was 19 toises* long and was quite well proportioned.

I think that Ali Bey cannot but find it advantageous to continue the war: they say that the Turks and the Christians are very satisfied with him and that he is tolerant, brave, and just. Do you not find it curious that all of Europe has been caught up in the frenzy of seeing the plague everywhere, with precautions taken as a result, whereas it is only in Constantinople that it has never ceased? I too have taken my precautions: everyone is perfumed to the point of suffocation, and yet it is quite doubtful that the plague has crossed the Danube.

I have ordered that a word be had with the family of Mr Choglokov about the payment of the bills that you sent me; when I have their reply, I shall forward it to you, Sir. The young man's poor conduct in Georgia, where he had asked to go, his disobedience with regard to his general, and his intrigues against Mr Tottleben have cast him into a labyrinth from which he will have some trouble emerging. He is currently awaiting judgment before a war council in Kazan. You know what such a council can be like in matters of military disobedience and machinations against a general. Timepieces made at Ferney will not fail to sell here: they need only come, and we shall avail ourselves of them. Farewell, Sir, be well and continue your friendship for me: there is no one who knows its worth better than I.

Caterine

57. *To Voltaire*

As a third year of fighting began, Catherine points out to Voltaire the French government's ongoing support of the Ottomans against Russia. Fascinated with the Middle Ages ever since she read medieval romances such as 'Tirant lo Blanch' (1490) as a teenager, Catherine transposes Russian exploits into the world of the Crusades, highlighting the irony of the military and diplomatic affiliation between Catholic France and the Muslim Ottoman Empire.

at St Petersburg, this 14/3 March 1771*

Sir, as I was reading your Encyclopedia,* I kept repeating what I have said a thousand times: that no one wrote like this before you, and that it is very doubtful whether after you anyone will ever equal you. I was in the middle of such reflections when your last two letters of 22 January and 8 February reached me.

You may well guess, Sir, how pleased I was to receive them. Your verses and your prose will never be surpassed: I consider them the *ne plus ultra*, and I shall stick to that. When one has read you, one would like to reread you, and one loses one's taste for any other reading.

Since you approve of the celebration I gave for Prince Henry,* I'll allow myself to think it was a success. I had given him an earlier one in the countryside in which candle ends and rockets were involved, but no one was hurt: precautions were well taken, since the horrible things that happened in Paris* have made us prudent. Besides that, I do not recall having seen a livelier carnival for a long time; from the month of October until the month of February, there was nothing but celebrations, dancing, and shows. I do not know whether it was the last campaign that made it seem so to me, or whether joy really reigned among us. I have learned that things are not like this everywhere, even where people have been enjoying uninterrupted, sweet peace for eight years. I hope this is not due to their Christian sympathy for the woes of the infidels. That sentiment would be unworthy of the descendants of the first Crusaders. Not long ago you had in France a new St Bernard who was preaching a moral crusade against the likes of us, although I do not believe that he himself really knew to what end. But that St Bernard was mistaken in his prophecies just like the first one was: nothing of what he predicted has come true.* He only embittered people; if that was his goal, we must confess he succeeded. Yet such a goal seems quite petty. Sir, you are such a good Catholic. Persuade those of your creed that the Greek Church under Catherine II bears no ill will towards the Latin Church, nor towards any that can be found under the cover of the clouds filled with water. The Greek Church knows only how to defend itself. Confess it, Sir: this war has made our warriors excel. Count Aleksei Orlov is constantly accomplishing feats that make people talk of him. He has just sent eighty-six Algerian and Salé* prisoners to the Grand Master of Malta, asking him to exchange them for Christian slaves in Algiers. It has been quite a while since any Knight of St John of Jerusalem* has delivered so many Christians from the hands of the infidels. Have you read, Sir, the count's letter to the European consuls at Smyrna, who interceded with him in hopes that he would spare the city after the defeat of the Turkish fleet? You speak to me of how he sent back a Turkish vessel bearing the goods and the servants of one of the pashas. Here are the facts. A few days after the naval battle at Chesme, a treasurer of the Porte was returning on a vessel from Cairo with his wives, his children, and all his belongings, and was headed for Constantinople. He received along the way the false news that the Turkish navy had defeated ours; he rushed to land to be the first to bear the news to the sultan, and in anticipation galloped at breakneck speed to Istanbul. One of our ships brought his vessel to Count Orlov, who strictly forbade anyone to enter the women's cabin or to touch the vessel's cargo. He had the youngest of the Turk's daughters, 6 years of age, brought to him: he gave her the gift of a diamond ring and a few furs and sent her back with her whole family and their belongings to Constantinople. That is more or less what has been printed in the newspapers, but what has not yet been printed is that when Count Rumiantsev sent an officer to the vizier's camp, the officer was brought first to the vizier's Kiaya-bey. After the initial compliments, the Kiaya said to him, 'Are any of the Counts Orlov with Marshal Rumiantsev's army?' The officer told him no. The Turk asked him eagerly: 'Where are they, then?' The Major said that two were serving in the navy, and that the other three were in Petersburg. 'Well then,' said the Turk, 'I would have you know that I hold their names in veneration and that we are all astonished by what we see. They have shown their generosity to me above all. I am the Turk who owes them his wives, his children, and his goods. I can never repay them, but if in my life I can be of service to them, I shall think it my good fortune.' He added many other protestations and said, among other things, that the vizier knew of his gratitude and approved of it. He spoke with tears in his eyes. There you have Turks touched to the point of tears by the generosity of Russians of the Greek Church. A painting of Count Orlov's deed might one day hang in my gallery as a pendant to that of Scipio.*

Now that my neighbour, the King of China, has called for his subjects to remove some unjust barriers, they have been trading with mine like a charm. They exchanged 3 million roubles' worth of goods in the first four months after trade resumed. My neighbour's palace manufactories are busy making tapestries for me, whereas my neighbour has asked for wheat and sheep.

You speak to me often of your age, Sir, but no matter what it is, your works are always the same. Take as proof that Encyclopedia, which is full of new things: one need only read it to see that your genius is in full force. With you, the mishaps ascribed to old age turn out to be prejudices. I am very curious to see the work of your clockmakers.* If you were to establish a colony at Astrakhan, I would look for a pretext to go and see you there. Speaking of Astrakhan, I can tell you that the climate in Taganrog is incomparably finer and healthier than that of Astrakhan.

Everyone who has been there says that they cannot praise the place enough. On that topic, like the old lady in *Candide*, I am going to go ahead and tell you an anecdote.* When Peter the Great first took Azov, he wanted to have a port on the sea, and he chose Taganrog. The port was built, after which he hesitated for a long time whether to build Petersburg on the Baltic or at Taganrog, but in the end the circumstances of the time drew him to the Baltic. We did not win out as far as the climate is concerned: there is almost no winter at all there, whereas ours is very long.

Do the Welches, Sir, who praise Mustafa's genius also praise his prowess? In this war, I know of no such deeds except having the heads of a few viziers chopped off. He could not restrain the populace of Constantinople, who before his very eyes beat up the ambassadors of the main European powers, while mine was in the Seven Towers (the Viennese internuncio died of his bruises). If those are marks of genius, I pray to Heaven that I be spared it and that it be saved entirely for Mustafa and the Chevalier de Tott, his supporter. The latter will be strangled one day: the vizier Mehmed certainly was, even though he saved the sultan's life and was his son-in-law.

Peace is not as near as the public papers have claimed: a third campaign is inevitable, and Mr Ali Bey will have gained time to secure his place. In the end, if he fails, he can go and spend carnival at Venice with your exiles, who went to spend the winter in the countryside.

I beg you, Sir, to send me the letter in verse that you mentioned writing to the young King of Denmark:* I do not wish to miss a line of what you write. Gauge from that how much pleasure I take in reading your writings, how highly I think of them, and what friendship and esteem I have for the holy Hermit of Ferney who calls me his favourite. You see that I am giving myself airs over it.

58. *To Voltaire*

In this letter, Catherine responds to a request and two works by Voltaire. Voltaire idealized China as the realm of an enlightened and highly cultured poet–monarch, and so he asked for clarification of Catherine's repeated ploy of contrasting herself as a European monarch with her uncouth eastern neighbour. After a display of perfect Enlightenment cultivation, Catherine then responds to the article 'Lois' ('Laws') for the 'Questions on the Encyclopédie' (9 vols, 1770–2), in which Voltaire praised her Legislative Commission and the 'Instruction' of 1767. He sent the as yet unpublished article to Catherine on 19 February (NS); on 27 February (NS), he sent his

'Epistle to the Empress of Russia' (1771), in which he celebrated Catherine as a civilizing conqueror-monarch.

this 7/26 March 1771*

Sir, I received your two letters of 19 and 27 February at almost the same time. You wish me to tell you a little something of the coarseness and foolishness of the Chinese, which I mentioned in one of my letters. We are, as you know, neighbours: our borders are peopled on both sides by herding, Tatar, and pagan peoples. Those tribes have a great propensity for brigandage: they kidnap (often in retribution) one another's herds and even people. Their occasional quarrels are settled by commissaries sent to the borderlands. My Lords the Chinese are such great quibblers that they never stop trifling. We have seen them more than once, after negotiations were exhausted, demand the bones of the dead—not to honour them, but just to quibble. They offered such trifles as pretexts to break off trade for ten years. I say pretexts because the real reason was that His Chinese Majesty had given to one of his ministers a monopoly on trade with Russia. The Chinese and the Russians complained of it equally, and since all trade that naturally occurs is very hard to impede, the two nations exchanged their goods wherever there was no established customs house and set necessity above the risks. Mr Minister harassed the Chinese border provinces and did no trading. When we wrote to them from here about how things stood, we received in reply stacks of very long-winded and poorly constructed prose, in which not the least trace of the philosophical spirit or politeness could be discerned. From start to finish the reply was nothing but a tissue of ignorance and barbarity. We told them that we did not care to adopt their style, for in both Europe and Asia that style was considered impolite. I know that one might reply that the Tatars who conquered China are not as good as the ancient Chinese. I would like to believe it, but it nonetheless proves that the conquerors did not adopt the politeness of the conquered, and the latter run the risk of being dragged down by the prevailing customs.

I now come to the article 'Laws', which you were so good as to share with me, and which is so flattering for me. Certainly, Sir, if it were not for the war that the sultan unjustly declared on me, much of what you say would have been done. But at the moment, so far, we cannot do much more than make plans for the different branches of the great tree of legislation, according to my principles which have been printed and which you know. We are too busy fighting, and that is too great a distraction for us to apply ourselves suitably to that huge enterprise at the present moment.

I prefer, Sir, your verses to a detachment of auxiliary troops, who could turn and flee at a crucial moment. Your verses will delight posterity, who will but echo your contemporaries. The latest you sent imprint themselves on one's memory, and the fire in them is astounding: they inspire me to prophecy. You will live two hundred years. One readily hopes for what one wishes: please fulfil my prophecy, as it is the first I have ever made.

Caterine

59. *To Voltaire*

Catherine contrasts her own military success and optimism with the political chaos in France. The Parisian high court, called the 'parlement', had been suspended at the end of 1770 as part of efforts by the chancellor, René Nicolas de Maupeou, to supplant the chief minister, Choiseul. In April 1771, Maupeou created a new judicial body with reduced authority. Behind Catherine's gloating over this blatant political vacillation is her personal satisfaction at the disgrace of Choiseul, a powerful anti-Russian figure in the French government.

this 20/31 May 1771

Sir, the northern powers are surely much indebted to you for the fine epistles that you have addressed to them.* I find mine admirable and am sure that each of my young colleagues will say the same for his. I am very sorry that I can give you nothing but poor prose in return: I have never in my life been able to write verses or play music, but in no way do I lack the sentiment of admiration for the productions of genius.

Your description of the pre-eminent people in the universe would provoke the envy of others for the present state of the Welches. It seems to me that they are currently making a great fuss without really knowing why unless they are just following fashion. (The latter sometimes is said to substitute for reason in Paris.) They want a *parlement*. They get one. The court has exiled the members of the old one. No one contests the king's power to exile those who have incurred his disgrace. Those members, it must be admitted, had grown irksome and were a source of anarchy in the state. It seems that the whole uproar cannot lead to anything, and that there are far more big words than there are principles founded on good authority in all the writings of the party opposing the court. It is also true that it is hard to judge how things stand when looking from as far away as I am.

Apparently the Turks do not lay much store by Master de Tott's cannons, since they have finally released my resident minister,* who, if one may believe what the Porte's ministers say, should be at this instant on Austrian territory. Have the Turks ever before in history released in the middle of a war the representative of a power whom they had offended by such an infringement of human rights? It looks like Count Rumiantsev and Count Orlov have taught them a bit about how to live. Here we have one step towards peace, but that does not mean that peace has been made. The opening of the campaign has been very advantageous for us, as you have been told, Sir. Major-General Weismann has crossed the Danube twice, the first time with 700 men and the second with 2,000. He defeated a corps of 6,000 Turks and seized Isaccea, where he burned the enemy stores, the bridge that they had started to build, and the galleys, frigates, and boats that he could not take with him. He took much plunder and many prisoners, besides fifty-one bronze cannons, half of which he nailed shut. Then he came back to this side of the river unchallenged, even though the vizier and 60,000 men are at Babadag, which is only a six-hour march from Isaccea. If peace is not made this year, do not forget to order a clock from your manufactory, which we shall then put in St Sophia,* where it will provide future antiquaries with a topic for a few scholarly dissertations. I do not doubt the quality of the craftsmanship of the clocks you are sending me. I would be grateful if you could tell me to whom they have been sent. Rest assured of the sentiments which you know I possess, and be well, at least until your flock* begins to pray for you, for then there is no doubt that their prayers, which have been ignored, will be fulfilled on your behalf and that you will become fresh as a rose once again.

Caterine

60. *To Voltaire*

Pleased with her armies' successes, Catherine not only imagines her conquests as contributions to geographical knowledge, but also contemplates the possibility of taking Constantinople, evoking the Emperor Constantine (d. 337). These ideas would take a more serious form in Catherine's Greek project of the 1780s, when she envisaged refounding the Byzantine Empire under her own grandson, named Constantine for that purpose.

this 22 July/3 August 1771*

Sir, I can give no better answer to your two letters of 19 June and 6 July than to tell you that Taman and three other little towns, namely Temryuk, Achai, and Achuevo,* located on a large island that forms the other side of the strait from the Sea of Azov into the Black Sea, surrendered to my troops in the first days of July. Over two hundred thousand Tatars living on the islands and on the mainland followed their example.

Admiral Seniavin, who had left the canal with his flotilla, assailed fourteen enemy ships by way of a little jaunt, but a fog saved them from his clutches. Haven't we gathered a lot of material for correcting geographical maps? During this war we have heard of a lot of places, the names of which had never been heard before and which had been described as wilderness by geographers. Have I not also explored enough for four?* You may say that one does not need much wit to seize deserted towns: so this may be why, as you say, I am not unbearably proud. On the topic of pride, I want to make my full confession to you. I have had great successes in this war, and I have very naturally rejoiced at them. I said to myself, 'Russia will become well known because of this war. People will see that it is a courageous and indefatigable nation and that it has men of eminent merit who have all the qualities that make heroes. People will see that it does not lack resources and that its resources have not been used up, but rather that it can defend itself and fight a war with ease and vigour when unjustly attacked.' Full of such ideas, I have never thought of Catherine, who at 42 years of age, will not grow any more in body or in mind—but who, by the natural order of things, must remain and will remain as she is. Accordingly, where then could pride come from? Are things going well for her? She says, 'What could be better!' If they were going less well, I would put all my faculties to work to put them back on the best track possible, as I understand it. This is my sole ambition. What I tell you is true. I shall go further: I shall tell you that, to spare human blood, I sincerely wish for peace, but that peace is still very far off, even though the Turks desire it ardently, for quite different reasons. Those people do not know how to make peace. I desire equally that the Polish quarrels, having no foundation in reason, be quelled: I am dealing there with fools who, rather than contribute to a common peace, are each of them capriciously and thoughtlessly sabotaging it.

My ambassador* has made a public declaration that ought to open their eyes and restore them to reason if they are capable of it, but I would bet that they will let things go to the last extremity before they can bring themselves to make a wise and suitable decision. Nowhere but in Poland have Descartes's vortices* ever existed. There, every brain is a vortex constantly spinning around itself and stopping only occasionally by chance, never by reason or judgment.

I have not yet received either your *questions*＊ or your watches from Ferney. I have no doubt that your manufacturers' work will be brought to perfection because it is under your supervision, Sir. I flatter myself that the carillon they will make for St Sophia, when we have it, will be their masterpiece. Only I would not like them to put Constantine and his mother, St Helena,* on it, for as head of the Greek Church I do not wish to see people like them occupy the very place that is often given to roosters and cuckoos. Each of them is equally out of place, to be frank, but at least the latter show the time, whereas I really know not what one might expect from the former on a carillon. Do not scold your settlers for having sent me too many watches. The expense will not ruin me. It would be very unfortunate for me indeed if I were reduced to not having to hand such little sums whenever I need them. I beg you not to judge my finances by those of the ruined countries of Europe: you would do me wrong. Although we have been at war for three years, building and everything else continues as in peacetime. For two years no new tax has been imposed. The war currently has its own fixed budget, decided upon once and for all, which in no way disturbs the other parts; if we take one or two more Kaffas* the war will have been paid for. I shall be pleased with myself every time I have your approbation.

I also had my *Instruction* for the law code brought to me a few weeks ago,* for then I thought we were closer to peace than we are, and I found that I was right when I wrote it. I must admit that the law code, for which many materials have already been and are still being prepared, will still give me quite a bit of difficulty before it reaches the degree of perfection I would like to see it attain. But no matter, it must be done.

Although Taganrog has the sea to the south and highlands to the north, your projects for that location cannot be realized until peace has guaranteed its surroundings against any threats by land or by sea. For until Crimea was taken, it formed the border with the Tatar lands. Perhaps shortly the Khan of Crimea himself will be brought to me here: I have just learned that he did not cross the sea with the Turks, but rather is still wandering about in the mountains of Crimea with a very small entourage, more or less like the Scottish pretender after the defeat at

Culloden.* If he comes, we shall work at reviving his spirits this winter, and I shall take my revenge on him by making him dance, and he will go to the French theatre. Farewell, Sir, continue your friendship for me and rest assured of the sentiments that I have for you.

I was about to close this letter when I received yours of 10 July, in which you inform me of the adventure that befell my *Instruction* in France. I knew that story, but with the sequel that it happened on the orders of the Duc de Choiseul. I confess that I laughed when I read it in the newspapers, and I found that my revenge had already been taken.

According to the police reports, the fire that took place in St Petersburg consumed in total 140 houses, of which about twenty were built of stone; all the rest were nothing but wooden huts. High winds caught the fire .the next day and made it seem supernatural, but there is no doubt that wind and excessive heat caused all the damage, which will soon be repaired. We build here with greater celerity than in any country in Europe. The fire of 1762 was twice as big and consumed a large neighbourhood built of wood. It was rebuilt in brick within less than three years. You will permit me to reiterate my thanks for all the friendship you profess for me.

61. *To Voltaire*

Having received Voltaire's somewhat deviously over-large shipment of watches and graciously paid for them nonetheless, Catherine used historical and literary parallels to put a good face on less than perfect news from the Danube. Comparing Russian events to those in Alsace during the War of the Austrian Succession (1740–8), she also contrasts the French and the Russians by associating the former with inferior light genres of literature (comic opera and parody) and the latter with the higher, solemn genre of tragedy.

this 4/15 September 1771

Sir, the *Questions on the Encyclopédie* have arrived, accompanied by the watches from Ferney. I must tell you that there were more watches than were listed on the invoices. It is possible that one of the invoices got lost, but as every watch had its price attached, it was easy to find out the total sum. I have ordered that it be remitted to you, since I do not know how else it could reliably come into the hands of the manufacturers. I hope, Sir, that you will forgive me for the trouble I am causing you, and please be so kind as to receive my thanks for both parcels. You had promised me a clock that I did not find in the package. I am currently reading the *Questions* and cannot put them down. In response to your question, whether it is 'true that at the very moment when my troops were entering Perekop, there was action on the Danube to the disadvantage of the Turks?', I must tell you that this summer there has been only one single battle on this side of the Danube, in which Lieutenant-General Prince Repnin and his detachment defeated a Turkish detachment. The latter had advanced once the commander of Giurgiu [now in Romania] had returned the post to the enemy, more or less in the way that Lauterbourg went to the Austrians when de Noailles was commanding the French army* after the death of Emperor Charles VI. When Prince Repnin fell ill,* Lieutenant-General Essen* wanted to take back Giurgiu, but his assault was repulsed. Nonetheless, despite what the newspapers say, Bucharest is still in our hands, along with all the posts on the bank of the Danube from Giurgiu to the Black Sea. I do not at all envy your homeland the exploits of which you inform me. If the fine arms of the excellent ballerina at the Paris Opéra, and the Opéra-Comique that will draw *universal* admiration, can console France for the extirpation of its *parlements* and for its new taxes after eight years of peace, we shall have to concede that they have thereby rendered essential services to the government. But when they have collected those taxes, will the king's coffers be filled and the state freed? You tell me, Sir, that your navy is preparing to sail from Paris to Saint-Cloud:* I shall trade you news for news. Mine went from Azov to Feodosia and to Constantinople. Certain people are quite melancholy over the loss of Crimea. One ought to send them some comic opera to cheer them up, and the Polish mutineers should receive puppets instead of the multitude of French officers who are being sent to their ruin there. Those captured by my troops will be able to attend performances of Mr Sumarokov's dramas in Tobolsk, where there are some very good actors.

Farewell, Sir; let us fight the evil people who will not rest, and let us beat them, since they bring it upon themselves. Love me, and be well.

62. *To Voltaire*

By casting her account of the Moscow Plague Riots of 1771 as one in a series of supplements and corrections to Voltaire's 'Questions on the Encyclopédie', Catherine places in an Enlightenment framework a tale of superstition, violence, and bubonic plague (which she refuses to name) that would seem more appropriate to the Middle Ages.

at St Petersburg, this 6/17 October 1771

Sir, I have to provide you with a little supplement to the article
'Fanaticism'. It might have also suited the article 'Contradictions', which
I read with the greatest satisfaction in the book of *Questions on the
Encyclopédie*. Here is what it's about. There are illnesses in Moscow—
spotted fevers, malignant fevers, hot fevers with and without spots—and
they are carrying off many people despite all the precautions we have
taken. The Grand Master, Count [Grigory] Orlov, asked me as a favour
to allow him to go in person to see what the most appropriate arrangements were for ending these woes. To this fine and zealous act on his
part I consented, but not without feeling the keenest anguish at the
danger he would face. He had been on his way scarcely twenty-four
hours when Marshal Saltykov* wrote to me about the following disaster, which happened in Moscow between 15 and 16 September OS.
The archbishop of the city, named Ambrose and a man of intelligence
and merit, learned that for several days great crowds of people had
massed in front of an image they claimed could cure the sick (they were
dying at the Holy Virgin's feet) and that they were bringing a lot of
money there. He ordered his seal placed on the money box, so that it
could then be used for charity—a use of funds to which every bishop
has a perfect right in his diocese. It is to be supposed that his intention
was to remove the icon, as had happened more than once, and that
sealing the box was simply a first step. Indeed, such a great crowd of
people gathered together during an epidemic could only spread the
disease. But here is what happened.

A segment of the populace raised an outcry: 'The archbishop wants
to steal the Holy Virgin's treasure! He must be killed!' Another faction
took the side of the archbishop. After an exchange of words, they came
to blows. The police tried to separate them, but the ordinary police
were insufficient, since Moscow is a whole world, not a city. The maddest faction dashed towards the Kremlin. They broke down the doors
of the monastery where the archbishop resides, pillaged it, and got
drunk in the cellars in which many merchants keep their wines. After
failing to find the person they were pursuing, some went to the Donskoi
Monastery, as it is known, dragged out the old man, and savagely mas-
sacred him. The other faction stayed behind to grapple over their share
of the spoils. Finally, Lieutenant-General Eropkin arrived with about
thirty soldiers and forced them to make a hasty retreat; the most rebel-
lious were taken. Truly this famous eighteenth century has little to be
proud of. Look how wise we have grown. But you hardly need to be told

this sort of thing: you know mankind too well to be surprised by the contradictions and eccentricities of which they are capable. It is enough to read your *Questions on the Encyclopédie* in order to be convinced of the deep knowledge you have of the human heart and mind. I owe you a thousand thanks, Sir, for the various places in the book where you were so good as to mention me. I am very often astonished to find my name at the end of a sentence where I least expected it. I hope that by now you will have received the credit note to pay the manufacturers who sent me their watches. The news of a naval battle at Lemnos is false. Count Aleksei. Orlov was still at Paros on 24 July, and the Turkish navy dares not venture with its fine ragamuffins beyond the Dardanelles. Your letter about the battle is one of a kind. I am touched, as I should be, by all the marks of friendship that you are pleased to give me, and I am exceedingly obliged to you for your charming letters.

In the *Questions on the Encyclopédie*, which are so full of things as excellent as they are new, in the article 'Public Economy', page 61 of the fifth part, I found, Sir, these words: 'Give Siberia and the Kamchatka together, which make up four times the territory of Germany, a Cyrus for a sovereign, a Solon for a legislator, a Duc de Sully or a Colbert for a finance minister, a Duc de Choiseul for a minister of war and peace, an Anson for an admiral,* and they will still die of hunger with all their genius.' I grant you all the land in Siberia and the Kamchatka above the 63rd parallel, but on the other hand I shall plead before you the cause of all the land that lies between the 63rd and the 45th parallels. It lacks a population proportionate to its extent, and wines as well; yet it is not only arable, but even very fertile: wheat grows so abundantly there that, besides what the inhabitants consume, there are immense distilleries for liquor, and there is still enough left to take some to Arkhangelsk, by land in winter and by river in the summer. From there grain is sent to foreign countries, and perhaps there is more than one place where people have eaten it while saying that wheat never ripens in Siberia. Domesticated animals, game, and fish can be found in great quantities in those climes, and there are some excellent species that are unknown to the other nations of Europe. Overall Nature's produce is extraordinarily rich in Siberia, as can be attested by the large number of iron, copper, gold, and silver mines, and the quarries of all colours of agate, jasper, crystal, marble, talc, etc., which one finds there. There are entire districts covered with a remarkable density of cedars, as beautiful as those of Mount Lebanon, and in wild fruit trees of many different species. If you are curious, Sir, to see the produce of Siberia, I shall send you collections of various species that are common only in Siberia and rare everywhere else.

But there is one thing, I think, that proves the world is a bit older than our nurses tell us—it is that one finds in northern Siberia, several toises underground, the bones of elephants that have not lived in those regions for a very long time. Rather than concede the antiquity of our globe, scholars have said that they were made of fossilized ivory. Well, they can say what they like: fossils do not grow in the form of quite complete elephants. Having thus pleaded before you the cause of Siberia, I leave you to pass judgment on my case, and I shall withdraw while reiterating my assurances of my highest regards and sincerest friendship and esteem.

Caterine

63. *To Voltaire*

Catherine turns a delay in payment for the watches from Ferney into a chance to attack the French government's devious smear that Russia lacked the resources to sustain the Ottoman war. She draws a parallel with her benefactions to Denis Diderot in the 1760s: she had promised to pay Diderot a salary as custodian of his own library, which she had purchased from him and left to him for the duration of his life, but his second yearly payment did not arrive. She therefore sent him in 1766 his salary for the following fifty years (he lived less than twenty more).

this 28 November/9 December 1771

Sir, I am distressed to see by your letter of 12 September that the money for the watch manufacturers has not yet been remitted to you, and moreover that the poor people are in need of it. I do not know to what I should attribute this delay, which aggrieves me greatly. I hope that the credit note has not been purloined like the one I once sent to Monsieur Diderot which got lost in the post between Paris and the French border. All the other post stations had the packet noted down in their registers. Someone* thought they could thereby convince people that I had no money. But what can such petty ruses accomplish? They can only reveal small-mindedness and bitterness. Neither of these can bring esteem or respect. I have ordered Master Frederiks, my banker, to take precautions.

My navy has taken so many stores from the Turks at Chalcis, Volos, Kavala, Makria Miti, Lokroi,* and several other places, not counting what they took at sea, that I would venture to believe that they will have fewer shortages than some people suppose. I am quite willing to believe that they will need more provisions than initially calculated, given the number of Albanians who have joined my troops. But the dispatches that the last courier brought me from there a week ago speak of no lack of rations for the moment.

The illnesses in Moscow have nearly ended, thanks to the precautions taken and to the cold. Count Orlov has already left Moscow and is in quarantine on his estates.

Deeply touched by the marks of friendship that you give me, I hope that you do not doubt the extent of my gratitude.

Caterine

64. *To Voltaire*

Catherine was very proud of her Smolnyi Institute for Noble Girls. Performing amateur theatricals was an important part of education and social entertainment in the eighteenth century, as it taught declamation and grace, as well as a thorough knowledge of fashionable literature. In response to Catherine's request in this letter, Voltaire promised to edit a collection of plays for the girls, a task he never completed.

this 30 January/1 February 1772*

Sir, you ask me for a copy of the pamphlet about the assassination attempt by the Reverend Fathers Poignardini, confederates* for the love of God, but no account of that foul scene has been printed here. I have ordered that your protégé Mr Poliansky be given money to travel to Italy. I hope that he will have received it by now, and the same for your settlers, whom I have said should be paid the 247 roubles that were missing from the bill that was formerly paid them.

In one of your letters, among other fine things that your friendship for me dictates to you, you wish me more entertainments. I am going to go ahead and tell you about a sort of entertainment which interests me greatly and on which I beg you to advise me. You know, since nothing escapes you, that 500 young ladies are being raised in a community that was formerly reserved for 300 wives of Our Lord. These young ladies, I must admit, have exceeded our expectations; their progress is astounding, and there is a general view that they are growing as amiable as they are full of knowledge useful to society. To all of that they add irreproachable morals, without, however, the finicky imperiousness of recluses. During the past two winters, we have started having them perform tragedies and comedies; they acquit themselves better than our professionals. Yet I confess that only a very few plays are suitable for them because their mother superior would like to avoid having them perform any that might arouse the passions too early. It is said that there is too much love in most French plays, and even the best authors have often been hindered by this national taste or character. To have new plays written would be impossible, since one cannot pay authors by the page to produce good ones. Only genius can do that. Bad or insipid plays would ruin our taste—what is to be done? I know not. I appeal to you. Should we select scenes? That is far less interesting than continuous plays, in my opinion. No one will better be able to decide the matter than you—assist me, I beg you, with your advice. I was about to finish this letter when I received yours of 14 January. I see with regret that I have not answered four of your letters; the last is written with so much vivacity and warmth that it seems you grow younger with each year that passes. I hope that your health is restored in the course of the present one.

Several of our officers, whom you have been so kind as to receive at Ferney, have returned thoroughly enchanted with you and your welcome. Truly, Sir, you give me most touching evidence of your friendship; you extend it even to all the young people who are keen to see you. I fear that they might abuse your kindness. That said, you might reply that I do not know what I want, since I shall also tell you that I scolded Count Fedor Orlov, who spent fourteen hours in Geneva, for not going to see you. To tell the truth, misguided shame prevented him: he claims that he does not speak French as fluently as he would like. I answered that a primary mover in the Battle of Chesme can be excused for not knowing French grammar perfectly; that the interest that Monsieur de Voltaire is so good as to take in all that concerns Russia, as well as the friendship that he professes for me, leads me to suppose that, while he may not like carnage, perhaps he would not have regretted hearing the details of the capture of the Morea and of the two memorable days of 24 and 26 June 1770 from the mouth of a general officer as amiable as he is brave. He would have forgiven him for not speaking perfectly a foreign language of which many natives are growing ignorant, if one were to judge by so many works that appear daily in print. I held up to him as an example the author of the tragedy of the Siege of Calais, who has just been made an academician,* although in truth the two acts of his play that I slogged my way through were not written in the French language to which your writings have accustomed me.

You are surprised at my purchases of paintings: it would perhaps be better if I bought fewer, but lost opportunities cannot be recovered. Moreover, my money is not mixed up with that of the state, and, with a bit of management, a big state can sort out anything—I speak from experience. I would bet that France is penniless, not because they lack money, but rather because they lack or have lacked orderliness. I have just realized that my letter is getting too long. I shall close by asking you to continue your friendship for me and to be convinced that if there is no peace treaty, I shall do all I can to give you the pleasure of seeing Mustafa even better provided for than previously. I hope that all good Christians will rejoice with us and that in one way or another those who do not will harken to reason thanks to proofs as convincing as two plus two equals four.

65. *To Voltaire*

Catherine displays the sharper side of her wit by threatening Siberia for Frenchmen caught fighting for the Confederates in Poland and quoting the refrain from 'Candide' to mock the French who claimed that Russia lacked resources. Catherine jokingly compares herself, an avid collector of paintings, to the Byzantine Empress Theodora (c.815–c.868), who is said to have risked punishment by her iconoclastic husband, Emperor Theophilos (813–842), for venerating icons. Her irreverent comment about icons at the end of the letter was censored in the first edition of her correspondence with Voltaire.

this 30 March 1772

Sir, I received one after the other your two letters of 12 February and 6 March. I did not reply because I had clumsily hurt my right hand, which kept me from writing for over three weeks—I could scarcely sign my name. Your last letter left me truly alarmed at the state you were in. I hope that the present letter will find you recovered. Monsieur Darta's ode is not the work of a sick man.* If men could become wise, you would long since have made them so. Oh, how I love your works! There is nothing better in my opinion. If those madmen, the so-called Confederates, were beings endowed with reason, you would have persuaded them long ago. But I know of a remedy that will cure them. I also have one for those fops who, although their government will not admit it, are leaving Paris to come and tutor brigands. This remedy is to be found in Siberia—and they will get it when they are there. These are not the secrets of a charlatan: they are effective. If the war continues, there will be hardly anything left for us to take besides Byzantium, and truly I am beginning to think that this is not impossible. But one must be wise and say, with those who are so, that peace is better than the finest war in the world. That all depends on Lord Mustafa. I am ready for both the former and the latter, and although people may tell you that Russia is on tenterhooks, do not believe a word of it. We have not yet touched a thousand resources that other powers have exhausted in times of peace. In the past three years we have not imposed any new taxes, not that it could not be done, but because we have all we need, and more.

I know that the songsters of Paris have given out that I had conscripted every eighth man: that is a blatant lie and defies common sense. Apparently where you are there are people who like to be deceived: they must be allowed that pleasure because all is for the best in the best of all possible worlds, according to Doctor Pangloss. All Monsieur Tronchin's actions towards me and of which you tell me are impeccable.* I am like Empress Theodora: I like images, but they have to be well painted. She kissed them, but I do not: she almost came to harm because of it. I have received the letter from your clockmakers.

I am sending you nuts containing the seed of the tree called the Siberian cedar. You can have them planted in the ground—they are not at all delicate. If you want more than are contained in this packet, I shall send you some.

Please accept my thanks for all the friendship you attest to me, and rest assured of all my sentiments.

Caterine

66. *To Voltaire*

Continuing to vaunt before Voltaire her enlightened theories of education, Catherine applies the theatrical metaphor to the war. Shahin Giray was later the last Khan of Crimea under Russian protection. His adoption of elite Russian culture stands for the new dominion that Russia was acquiring over that southern territory. In his reply to this letter, Voltaire pointed out Catherine's deliberate omission to mention the fact that she was concluding with Prussia and Austria the First Partition of Poland, which in 1772 began the process of erasing the country from the map.

this 3 April OS 1772

Sir, your letter of 12 March gave me great satisfaction. Nothing could be more fortunate for our school than what you propose. Our young ladies perform tragedies and comedies. Last year they gave us *Zaïre*, and this year during carnival they put on *Semira*, a Russian tragedy and the best by Mr Sumarokov of whom you will have heard.* Ah! Sir, I would be infinitely obliged to you if you would undertake for those dear children the work that you call an amusement and which would cost anyone else so much effort. You will give me thereby a most touching mark of that friendship which I hold in such esteem. Moreover, the young ladies, I must admit, are declared charming by all who see them. Some are already fourteen or fifteen years old. I am certain that they would secure your approval if you saw them. More than once I have been tempted to send you some of the little notes I have received from them and which most assuredly were not written by their teachers, for they are very childish. But already now one can see, alongside their innocence, the pleasantness and gaiety of their wit in every line. I do not know whether this battalion of girls, as you call them, will yield Amazons, but we are very far from wanting to make nuns or scrawny creatures of them by making them wail in church at night, as they do at St Cyr.* On the contrary, we are raising them to be the delight of the families they enter: we want them to be neither prudes nor coquettes, but rather amiable and capable of raising their own children and caring for their homes. Here is how we go about assigning roles for the plays: we tell them that such-and-such a play will be performed, and we ask them who wants to play which role. It often happens that a whole roomful of them learns the same role, after which the one who does it best is chosen. Those who play men's roles in comedies wear a sort of long tail-coat, which we call 'the fashion in that country'. In tragedies, it is easy to dress our heroes as befits both the play and their station. The old men are the most difficult and the least well performed roles. A big wig and a stick cannot put wrinkles on adolescence: those roles have been performed a bit stiffly up to now. We had a charming coxcomb this carnival, a most original Blaise,* an admirable Lady Croupillac,* two soubrettes and a Lawyer Patelin* who were ravishing, and a most intelligent Jasmin.*

I do not know what Mustafa thinks about comedies, but over the past few years he has offered to the world the spectacle of his defeats without being able to make up his mind to change roles. We have here the Kalga Sultan, the brother of the most independent Khan of Crimea by the grace of God and the arms of Russia. This young Tatar prince has a gentle spirit as well as wit; he writes Arabic verse; he never misses a play and enjoys them; he goes to my school on Sunday afternoons, when people are allowed to enter for two hours to watch the young ladies dance. You will say that this is like taking the wolf to the sheepfold, but fear not. Here is how we go about it. There is a very large hall, in which a double balustrade has been placed: the children dance inside, and the company is lined up around the balustrades. It is the only occasion when relatives can see our young ladies, who are not allowed to leave the house for twelve years.

Fear not, Sir, your Parisians in Krakow will not do me much harm: they are performing a bad farce that will end like an Italian comedy.*

It is to be feared that the unhappy news from Denmark* will not be the only such instance there.

I think I have answered all your questions, Sir. Send me as soon as you can satisfactory news of your health, and rest assured that I am always the same

Caterine

67. *To Johanna Bielke*

Catherine announces an imminent peace congress at Focşani (now in Romania), with an (ultimately justified) hint that she neither expects nor particularly desires it to be successful. In discussing the situation in Denmark with Bielke (who lived on territory that had been until recently Danish), Catherine shows a certain sympathy for Queen Caroline Matilda: Catherine, too, had taken lovers when faced with a husband whom she described as mentally deficient.

at Tsarskoe Selo, this 28 April OS 1772

Madam, you shall be served according to your tastes. You do not wish to wait any longer for peace: my two ambassadors, the Grand Master Count Orlov and Mr Obreskov, left this week for the congress, and the Turkish ambassadors are also on their way. But since there can be no certainty about anything before it exists, I shall not tell you it is a done deal. But if the Turks do not do it, I shall say that the Devil has got into them, given their condition and given what we can still capture in order to compel them.

The situation in Denmark is horrific: how can they behead those poor people?* Does their zeal to punish stem from their master's inability to lead? If he were different, would all this have happened? When the plaintiffs are the judges, one's hair stands on end. It lacks all common sense; all the guilty parties similarly lack common sense. It is a terrible thing to have to deal with deranged minds. I know what it is like, since I have been in the same situation.

I pity the fate of your peach and apricot trees very much, and I share your woes on the matter. I sympathize entirely because I too suffer from Plantomania: I could never live in a place where I could not plant or build. Otherwise even the most beautiful place in the world bores me. I am here for that very purpose: I often drive my gardeners mad, and more than one German gardener has said to me in his life, 'But, my God! Whatever will come of it?'* I have found that most gardeners were nothing but pedants stuck in their routine; they are scandalized by the deviations from that routine which I frequently suggest to them. And when I see that the routine is stronger than I, I use the first docile assistant gardener ready to hand, and I ditch the master of the art. It's none too pleasant for him, I admit, but my garden is mine, and I want to like it. No one laughs so much at my Plantomania as Count [Grigory] Orlov does: he spies on me, he imitates me, he mocks me, he criticizes me, but as he was leaving, he ended up commending his garden to me for the summer, and now this year it is I who shall pull pranks there after my fashion. His estate is very near this one; I am very proud that he has recognized my gardening merit. I have never enjoyed any comedy as much as the one in which there is a baron and his plan;* I recognized myself in it and said at each scene: that's me, that's me, there I am precisely. But that's enough playing at my own expense. Love me despite my faults and rest assured that you do not love an ingrate.

Catherine

68. *To Voltaire*

Catherine gives the information in her letter to Johanna Bielke (see Letter 67) a Voltairean twist. She adds a promise to defeat the Polish Bar Confederation once and for all: after their failed attempt on King Stanislas Poniatowski's life in November 1771, they were on the defensive. Their refuge in the monastery at Częstochowa fell a month after this letter was written, and the Confederation was soon disbanded.

at Peterhof, this 6 July 1772

Sir, I see with pleasure from your letter of 29 May that my cedar nuts reached you. You will sow them at Ferney; I did the same this spring at Tsarskoe Selo. That name might strike you as a bit hard to pronounce, yet I find it an exquisite place because I plant and sow there. After all, the Baroness of Thunder-ten-tronckh thought her castle to be the most beautiful of all possible castles.* My cedars are already a pinkie-finger tall. How are yours doing? I am currently mad about English gardens: curving lines, gentle slopes, ponds in the shape of lakes, archipelagos on dry land. And I have a profound disdain for straight lines and parallel paths; I hate fountains that torture water to make it run against its nature; statues have been relegated to galleries, vestibules, etc. In a word, Anglomania holds sway in my Plantomania. Amid these occupations, I calmly await the peace treaty. My ambassadors have been at Iassy for six weeks, and the armistice for the Danube, Crimea, Georgia, and the Black Sea was signed on 19 May OS at Giurgiu. The Turkish plenipotentiaries are on their way. Since they have no horses that side of the Danube, their carriages are being drawn by the descendants of the god Apis.* After each campaign, I have offered peace to those gentlemen, but apparently they no longer feel safe behind Mount Haemus,* since this time they have parleyed in earnest. We shall see if they are sensible enough to make peace in time. The regulars of the Madonna of Częstochowa will hide under the habit of St Francis, where they will have all the time they need to meditate on the great miracle worked by that Lady's intercession. Your imprisoned coxcombs* will go home to recount self-importantly in the salons of Paris how Russians are barbarians who do not know how to fight a war. My school, which is not barbaric, recommends itself to your attentions. I beg you not to forget us. For myself, I promise to do my best to continue proving wrong those who, contrary to your opinion, have maintained for four years that I would succumb. Rest assured that I am very touched by all the proofs of friendship that you give me. My friendship and my esteem for you, Sir, will end only with my life.

Caterine

69. *To Voltaire*

On 28 August 1772 (NS), Voltaire wrote to Catherine with a query about a red bird that the Russians supposedly had agreed to adorn with a diamond necklace and send to the Ottomans every year. Catherine was all too pleased to debunk this myth about a purported article of the Treaty of the Pruth, which ended the conflict between Peter the Great and the Ottoman Empire (1710–11) on terms not very advantageous to the Russians. The enquiry also gave Catherine the chance to display in the supplementary note she appends her own and her Academy of Sciences' participation in the community of professional and amateur scientists that we think of as the Enlightenment Republic of Letters.

this 3 October 1772

Sir, to satisfy your curiosity about the white heron with fire-coloured feathers (of which I had never heard before), as soon as I received your letter of 28 August, I sent to the Academy of Sciences to ask about the bird. The Academy answered me that they had no bird whose plumage resembled that about which I was asking, save the red goose, a painting of which I am sending you. The attached note contains what the Academy knows about the bird. So you see that the ridiculous tale that is circulating about a supposed article of the Treaty of the Pruth, according to which the bird had to be sent each year with a diamond necklace to the Grand Turk, simply does not hold up. The Treaty of the Pruth contains no such article. All conquests made since 1698 were returned, all the fortresses demolished, etc. Your Baron Pellenberg* has arrived, but it will be hard to give him a position here as long as he is in the Spanish service. I defy him to serve at the same time two masters whose states are located at the two extremities of Europe. The proximity between California and Kamchatka will never make us look like neighbours anywhere except on globes one foot in diameter. Preserve your friendship for me and be well.

Caterine

Note: The flamingo, in Russian *Krasnoi gus*, that is, red goose. This bird was sent to the Academy in 1769 from Ufa, a small town in the province of Orenburg, by Mr Pallas, a professor who is being paid by the Academy to travel and take part in the natural history of the empire. It was found on the River Emba, which flows into the Caspian Sea. In the twenty-eighth part of his *Travels*, Mr Pallas* speaks thus: 'The red geese that one sees on the Emba are in all respects identical to the flamingos of the Mediterranean Sea and of the East Indies.'

An extended description of this bird can be found in the *Reasoned and Universal Dictionary of Animals*, by Monsieur Brisson, volume 2, page 179,* and, in his *Ornithology*, volume 6, page 532.*

70. *To Voltaire*

In October 1772, d'Alembert wrote to Catherine, requesting that she free the French noblemen taken prisoner by the Russians in Poland. Catherine immediately suspected that he was writing at the behest of the French government and rebuffed him (see Letter 71). Sending to Voltaire a copy of her reply of 20 November, she counterbalances her denunciation of his misguided 'philosophy' with an anecdote illustrating the effectiveness of her policy of toleration. She asks implicitly: who is the true 'philosophe' here?

this 22 November 1772

Sir, I received your letter of 2 September when I was answering a fine, long letter that Monsieur d'Alembert wrote to me after five or six years of silence. In it, he demands in the name of philosophers and philosophy the Frenchmen taken prisoner in various parts of Poland; the attached note contains my reply. I am sorry that calumny has led the philosophers into error. Mr Mustafa is recovering from his own errors. He is having his Reis Effendi* work in very good faith at Bucharest towards the re-establishment of peace. After that, he can resume the pilgrimages to Mecca that Lord Ali Bey had slightly disrupted by taking up arms. I do not know how far the Turks go in their reverence for their saints, but I am an eyewitness to the fact that they have them, and here is how. During my journey on the Volga, I disembarked from my galley at 70 versts downstream from the city of Kazan, in order to see the ruins of the ancient city of Bolgar, which Tamerlane had built for his son.* Indeed, I found seven or eight stone houses and just as many very solidly built minarets still in existence. I drew close to a hovel, near which forty or so Tatars were standing. The governor of the province told me that this place was a sacred site for those people and that those I saw had come on a pilgrimage. I wanted to know what their worship consisted of and to that end addressed a Tatar whose physiognomy seemed thoughtful. He gestured that he could not understand Russian, and he ran off to call a man standing a few steps away. That man approached, and I asked him who he was. He was an imam who spoke our language fairly well, and he told me that the hovel had been occupied by a man who led a holy life, and that people came from very far away to pray at his tomb nearby. What he told me made me conclude that it was pretty much equivalent to our cult of saints. Our clergy had been hindering their pilgrimages; in fact, previously they wanted to claim that such large assemblies of Tatars were harmful to the state. But I took the opposite view: I prefer to see them worship there rather than go to Mecca. I forbade any impediment, and they are very grateful for it. We have had good proof of it during the present war.

It is the King of Sweden who will offer you a shorter route to come here* if he seizes Norway, as people have been saying. This political escapade might draw all the other powers into the war.

If France has no money, Spain has enough, and one must admit that there is nothing more convenient than when someone else pays for us. Farewell, Sir, preserve your friendship for me. I wish you with all my heart the years of the Englishman Jenkins, who lived to be 169 years old.* A fine age!

I shall send you shortly a French translation of two Russian comedies.* A fair copy is being made.

71. *To Jean Le Rond d'Alembert*

France was not directly involved in the partition of Poland, but a number of French officers from Lorraine fought on the side of the Polish rebels and were captured. Undeterred by Catherine's refusal to heed his first request for their release, d'Alembert wrote to the empress again at the end of December 1772. In his plea, he claimed that granting his request would be a gesture of support for the 'philosophes', equivalent to her previous marks of support. But he also made the rhetorical mistake of revealing that he was receiving his information from the French government, from a source 'so exalted' and 'so apparently sure'. Unable to disguise her exasperation after more politely declining his request in November, Catherine here turns d'Alembert's own reasoning against him and then brusquely dismisses him, ending their correspondence.

[late 1772/early 1773]

Monsieur d'Alembert, I have received a second letter in your hand on the subject of the French prisoners. It contained word for word the same thing as the first. This second one was followed by a third, which I suppose was a reply to my own. By this last letter you seek to induce me, as much by the solidity of your reasoning as by the force of your eloquence and the harmony and beauty of your style, to release the French prisoners who are in my empire.

But, Sir, allow me to attest to you my astonishment at seeing you so eager to deliver from what is captivity only in name a bunch of rabble-rousers who fanned the flames of discord wherever they happened to be. I promise you that once peace has been established, I shall repeat to your compatriots the words that you tell me, 'Go, be free, return to France and render thanks to philosophy.' I shall add this, 'Philosophy will teach you not to be wicked just for the fun of it.' Thousands of Turkish and Polish prisoners, victims and dupes of those whose inter-ests you represent, could complain of having been abandoned by humanity; whereas so many paths are being tried to return the French to their homeland which, besides, has never acknowledged these gentlemen and their genteel deeds.

I ask you: would it be just to give an advantage to those who have caused evil and to leave at a disadvantage those who were used as a toy?

True humanity, as I understand it, pleads more for the latter than the former. But do rest assured, Sir, that in response to your entreaty I shall set both groups free—in due course. I say 'in response to your entreaty' because if you plead for the cause, it logically follows that you were also making a case for the effects. You might, therefore, add the names of the Turkish prisoners to those of the French on your tombstone.* That said, I hope that for the good of philosophy it will be a long time before you shall have the need for an epitaph.

I am, Sir, very touched by all the compliments you shower on me. I pray that you will be persuaded of the continuation of the sentiments that you know I have long borne you and your friends.

72. *To Voltaire*

The correspondence with Voltaire waned after 1772: Catherine sent only three letters to him in 1773. Here she continues her strategy of smoothing over their political disagreement about Poland by adopting the tone and topics of discussion in the Republic of Letters: experimental science and the philosophy of history.

at St Petersburg, this 3 March 1773

Sir, I hope that nothing remains of your anger of 1 December at the Imperial Majesties of the Greek and Roman Churches.* I would have tried to allay it immediately if you had not sent me a memorandum by that Monsieur Aubry* for whom you are seeking an associate's diploma from the Academy of St Petersburg. You thereby put me in negotiations with all kinds of scholars, and the resulting congress was no more successful than the one at Focşani, although it did not give rise to such nasty gossip. I scarcely managed to get the attached reply to Monsieur Aubry. It seems to me that our academicians' observations are a bit bad-tempered. I think they could simply have said, 'Until now we had never thought about what you suggest, although it was before our eyes every day. But we are sending you what we found in our library, and since the empress asked us for a reply, ergo, we have given one, such as it is.' Prince [Grigory] Orlov, who likes experimental physics and who is naturally gifted with particular perspicacity in such matters, has performed perhaps the most curious of all experiments on ice. Here it is: in the autumn he had a ditch dug for the foundation of an archway. In the subsequent winter, during the deepest freeze, he had the foundation filled bit by bit with water, so that the water would turn to ice.

When it was filled to a suitable height, the foundation was carefully shielded from the sun's rays. In the spring, on top of it they built out of bricks a very solid arched door, which has been there for four years and will remain, I believe, until someone knocks it down. It is worth noting that the ground on which the arch was built is marshy and that the ice replaces the piling that would have had to be used if it were not there. The experiment with the bomb filled with water and then frozen was performed in my presence, and it exploded in less than an hour with a great bang. When you heard that ice can lift houses out of the ground, it should have been added that it happens to poorly built wooden shacks, but never to stone houses. It is true that thin garden walls on unstable foundations have been gradually pulled out of the ground and overturned by ice. Similarly, when ice can cling to pilings, they rise up after a while.

If the Turks continue following the good advice of their so-called friends, you can be sure that your wish to meet on the Bosphorus is very close to coming true. That might be excellent timing to help with your convalescence, for I hope that you have got rid of that awful constant fever which you told me about and which I would never have suspected given the gaiety that pervades your letters. I am currently reading the works of Algarotti. He claims that all the arts and all the sciences were born in Greece.* Tell me, please, is that really true? They still have wit, for sure, and a most free one, but they are so downtrodden that they have lost their nerve altogether. Nonetheless, given time, I am beginning to think that they could be toughened up again, as attested by the recent victory at Patras, which was obtained over the Turks after the end of the second armistice. Count Aleksei [Orlov] tells me that there were some who conducted themselves admirably there. Something similar happened on the coast of Egypt, the details of which I do not yet have, and a Greek captain was in command too. Your Baron Pellenberg is with the army. Mr Poliansky is secretary of the Academy of Fine Arts; he has not drowned even though he frequently crosses the Neva in a carriage, but there is no danger in that here during the winter. I received a second and third letter from Monsieur d'Alembert on the same subject: he has spared no eloquence and has set himself the task of convincing me to free his compatriots. But does one feel human compassion only for compatriots? Why does he not plead also for the Turkish and Polish prisoners, who are the dupes and the victims of the French? The Turks and Poles are more unfortunate than the French. It is true that your men are not in Paris—but then why did they leave in the first place? No one forced them. I would like to answer that I need them to introduce fine manners into my provinces. I am very glad to learn that my two comedies did not seem all bad to you. I await impatiently the new work that you promise me,* but even more so your recovery. Rest assured, Sir, that I am extremely touched by all the obliging and flattering things you say to me. I sincerely wish you longevity, and I am ever with friendship and all the sentiments you know me to have

Caterine

73. *To Prince Dmitry Golitsyn*

Diderot finally set out for Russia from Paris in June 1773, stopping first in The Hague, where he visited his friend Prince Golitsyn and stayed at the Russian embassy. Catherine's sharp treatment of d'Alembert was known; the empress is concerned to accord Diderot a congenial reception. In the event, he arrived on 27 September and met with Catherine regularly until his departure in late February 1774.

[late May/early June 1773]

Prince Golitsyn, Sir, I have received your two letters from The Hague dated 10 April. I shall say nothing about the one about the pictures, and simply say *spasibo*.* I read your letter to the vice-chancellor on the subject written about in the second, which is of great interest to me. Impatience gets the better of me here. I must clarify with you several preliminary points on the issue. The newspapers have announced the departure of the person in question for the month of July. According to your first letter of the month of February, I must not write until after they have left. They will spend some time as the guest of our neighbours—about a month, I suppose. That then takes us to the month of August or September. Will it not be risky to travel here in that season by sea? Of course I shall send my 'golden squadron', that is to say, the yachts I use myself and of whose reliability in fetching them I feel confident. Nonetheless, the lateness of the season will give me concern. I also have to say, quite apart, that I would much prefer if this person came during a season when it would be possible to enjoy the delights of my assorted country houses in my company. One is always more constrained in the city. On that score, I admit that in the autumn and winter I hibernate like a marmot and that I am more energetic and distinguished in summer and spring than at the end of the year. Well, then, it follows that I would like to know—it might be difficult for you to guess why—first, whether I must wait for the departure to Sweden before I write to the king. Second, whether it has been conclusively decided that the preliminary journey to Sweden will take place in July. In any case, we shall do our best to receive such a distinguished person and to demonstrate to them how much pleasure their arrival gives us. Which will indeed be very true and sincere.

74. *To Gustav III of Sweden*

The stiff tone betrays the mistrust between Catherine and her 'brother and cousin' (brother in the sense of fellow monarch; first cousin by blood). Nonetheless, a marriage between the king's brother Charles of Södermanland and Louise (1761–1829), the younger sister of Wilhelmina of Hesse-Darmstadt, the bride whom Catherine had selected for her own son, would have been an important diplomatic tie between the two countries. In the event, Charles married another of Catherine and Gustav's cousins, Hedwig Elisabeth Charlotte of Schleswig-Holstein-Gottorf (1759–1818).

My dear Brother and Cousin, touched to the quick by the amiable and confidential manner in which Your Majesty was pleased to discuss with me, in your letter from Gripsholm dated 22 August, the overtures that the king, your uncle, made to Your Majesty's Queen Mother* concerning a marriage to be contracted between the Duke of Södermanland and the youngest of the princesses of Hesse-Darmstadt, I feel great satisfaction that this proposition has in principle received Your Majesty's approbation.

I would respond poorly to the sincerity and trust with which you speak if I did not admit to you that I have given the King of Prussia a hint of my desire for such a union. Your Majesty did not mistake the motive that guided me: it is the keen and pure interest that I take in all that concerns your house; it is the joining of my closest relatives that I desire; it is to tighten more and more the bonds of blood that unite us anyway; it is finally to reinforce as much as possible and by all possible means the tranquillity in the north, and its happiness, which Providence has entrusted to our hands. When I first ordered that the King of Prussia be informed of my idea, I did not know Your Majesty's designs on the Princess of Holstein, your cousin and mine. Or, to express myself more precisely, I had heard that marriage spoken of only vaguely several years ago. Now that I know the state of affairs from the friendly account that Your Majesty has found it good to give me of them, I can only applaud the choice that you are contemplating, and assuredly when my uncle, the Prince-Bishop of Lübeck,* speaks to me of it, I will not advise him against it.

As for Princess Louise of Hesse-Darmstadt, by Your Majesty's own desire I could not and dared not enter into any overtures with her mother.* Since that respectable princess, whom I love and esteem in every regard, is absolutely ignorant of all that concerns this matter, and so am I as to what she thinks of it, all I can tell Your Majesty with full knowledge of the facts is that the Princess has a most agreeable face, that her heart is good, that she has much wit and vivacity, and that she is truly charming. Otherwise I shall leave to Your Majesty's judicious decision all that you will find it good to do on this occasion, and I cannot but be extremely moved by the friendly, open, and sincere manner in which you have been so good as to speak to me about it. Doubtless I shall never neglect any circumstances in which I could give you proof of the reciprocity of my feelings and of my conduct towards Your Majesty, as I am with the highest consideration and the most distinguished esteem,

My dear Brother and Cousin,

Your Majesty's good Sister, Friend, Cousin, and Neighbour,

Caterine
at St Petersburg, this 29 [August] OS 1773

75. *To Étienne-Maurice Falconet*

Dissatisfied with the now old-fashioned baroque architecture of her palaces (most notably Bartolomeo Rastrelli's Winter Palace in St Petersburg and the Catherine Palace at Tsarskoe Selo), Catherine looked to update her surroundings in the new neo-classical style. In response to this letter, Falconet and his friend Charles-Nicolas Cochin contacted the artist Charles-Louis Clérisseau (1721–1820), famous for his influential views of classical architecture. Catherine rejected his overly ambitious plan for a gigantic palace, which led to a dispute over payment. Nonetheless, Catherine purchased Clérisseau's collection of drawings in 1780. It was an Englishman of Scottish descent, Charles Cameron (1745–1812), who travelled to Russia in 1779 and built the proposed Roman structure (a bathhouse) and several other neoclassical structures and interiors.

[2 September 1773]

Monsieur Falconet, your books of classical costumes have given me the idea of asking you kindly to write to Cochin* or another of your acquaintances capable of executing what I am about to describe. I would like to have done a drawing of an antique house, the interior of which is laid out in the classical manner. All the rooms are to be decorated in the same manner as appropriate to their different uses, and all the furniture designed to match the costumes. The house will be neither too large nor too small, the façade, the overall shape, etc. I have the wherewithal to have a Greek rhapsody or equivalent Roman one built in my garden at Tsarskoe Selo as long as it is not too large. Above all, I love to distraction the dining room, and the couches with pillows ringing the table. I would love all of that. I entreat you to help me satisfy this fantasy. Have no fear about my paying.

76. *To Voltaire*

Catherine discusses with Voltaire three important individuals at her court in 1773–4: Denis Diderot, Friedrich Melchior Grimm, and Wilhelmina of Hesse-Darmstadt, now Grand Duchess Natalia Alekseevna.

this 7 January 1774

Sir, the philosopher Diderot, still in shaky health, will remain with us until the month of February, when he will return to his homeland. Grimm, too, is thinking of leaving around that time. I see them very often, and we have unending conversations. They will be able to tell you, Sir, how highly I think of Henri IV and of the author of the *Henriade** and so many other writings by which you have rendered our century illustrious. I do not know if they are very bored in Petersburg, but, for myself, I could talk with them for my whole life without growing weary. Diderot, I find, has an inexhaustible imagination, and I rank him among the most extraordinary men ever to have lived. If, as you tell me, he does not like Mustafa, at least I am certain that he wishes him no harm: his goodness of heart would not permit him to do so, despite his mental energy and an inclination I perceive to tip the scales in my favour. Oh, well, Sir! You will have to console yourself for the failure of your planned crusade by realizing that the good souls you had to deal with did not, it has to be said, have Diderot's energy.

As head of the Greek Church, I cannot see you err without calling you back in good faith. You would have liked to have seen the grand duchess rebaptized in the Church of St Sophia. Rebaptized, you say! Oh, Sir! The Greek Church does not rebaptize: it regards as authentic any baptism administered in the other Christian communions. The grand duchess, after pronouncing her Orthodox creed in the Russian language, was received into the Greek Church by a mere sign of the cross with odoriferous oil. It was administered to her with great ceremony, a rite which we, just like you, call confirmation, which is when a name is given. In this matter we are stingier than you, who give them by the dozens, whereas here each person has no more names than he needs, that is, just one. Now that you have been set straight on this important point, I shall continue my reply to your letter of 1 November. You will know by now, Sir, that a detachment of my army crossed the Danube in October, beat a very considerable Turkish corps, and took prisoner the three-tailed pasha who was commanding it. This event could have had consequences, but the fact is—and this is something which perhaps will not please you—that it did not. And Mustafa and I find ourselves more or less in the situation we were in about six months ago, except that he has had an asthma attack and I have not. It may be that the sultan has a superior mind, but nevertheless we have beaten him these past five years, despite the advice of Monsieur de Saint-Priest and the instructions of the Chevalier Tott. The latter can be dressed in ermine caftans and can produce cannon and drill artillerymen until he drops dead, but the Turkish artillery will not improve or be better served as a result. Those are all childish follies to which people attach much more weight than they deserve. I have read someplace that this turn of mind comes naturally to the Welches.* Farewell, Sir, be well and rest assured that no one thinks more highly of your friendship than I.

77. *To Gustav III of Sweden*

Catherine and her advisors worked very carefully to perfect the phrasing of this delicate diplomatic letter. At his majority in 1772, her son Paul came into possession of a territory he had inherited from his father, the Duchy of Holstein in northern Germany. It was a threat to her throne to allow her son to keep a foreign power base of his own, and she convinced him in 1773 to cede Holstein to Denmark in exchange for two other territories, Oldenburg and Delmenhorst. These were then given to Catherine's maternal uncle, Friedrich August of Schleswig-Holstein-Gottorf. As the son of another of Catherine's uncles, the then deceased Adolf Frederick (1710–1771), Gustav was concerned for the claims of his own bloodline to familial territories.

My dear Brother and Cousin, the frank tone in which Your Majesty speaks to me for the second time in your letter about my settlements and those of my son, both with the court of Denmark and in favour of the cadet branch of the House of Holstein, cannot be other than extremely agreeable to me. It is also the tone that I most like to see in a king who is my close relative, and the only one that matches my sentiments, for it comes naturally to me.

I therefore cannot adopt any other tone in my reply to Your Majesty's communication. You are aware that the possible exchange of Holstein, which I have settled upon with the King of Denmark, is what the late king, your father, had agreed with the same court. He was probably moved by the same motive as I am, which is to pluck an apple of discord in the north.

My son, upon reaching the age of maturity and reflection, felt the solidity of these diplomatic aims and consummated the deed. His feelings of tenderness for his family, which I happily saw increasing, also drew his attention to the younger branch of our house. He could not but be moved upon seeing how much less favoured by Providence it is than the three elder branches, which have been called to fill the three northern thrones. It was by a pure impulse of affection and by his own free will that he wished to diminish this disadvantage by transferring to them, as an exchange of hereditary states, the possession that he was to inherit.

Just as I could not but approve of my son's act of generosity and applaud the sentiment that dictated it, I similarly cannot find anything objectionable in Your Majesty's proposal to retain your rights and those of your branch with regard to the head of the Roman Empire. I am far from thinking that you might in any way attack the eminent right of sovereignty so nobly used by my son. In my eyes, this is thoughtfulness for your family's interests whose many claims are dear to me as well.

It is in this spirit that I like to discuss with Your Majesty matters that might concern them, and, on this occasion, I am satisfying no less my sincere desire to maintain the most perfect harmony between us and within our house than that to prove the sentiments of high regard and friendship with which I am,

My dear Brother and Cousin,

Your Majesty's good Sister, Cousin, and Neighbour,

Catherine
Tsarskoe Selo, this 10 February 1774

78. *To Grigory Potemkin*

While away fighting against the Ottoman Empire, Potemkin received in December 1773 an entirely unexpected and extraordinarily friendly letter from Catherine, written, as Catherine ambiguously put it, to give him 'confirmation of her thoughts about him'. After setting his military affairs in order, Potemkin arrived at Catherine's court at Tsarskoe Selo, for what he expected to be a temporary visit, on 4 February 1774.

[26 February 1774]

I thank you for the visit. I don't understand what kept you. Can it be that my words gave you a reason not to come? I complained that

I wanted to go to sleep only so that everything would go quiet sooner and so I could see you sooner. You were scared by this, and, so as not to find me in bed, did not even come. I ask you not to lose your nerve. We, you know, are on the ready. No sooner had I gone to bed and all the others had left, than I got up once again, dressed, and went to the entrance of the library in order to wait for you. I stood in a draught for two whole hours, and it was nearly eleven o'clock when I sorrowfully returned to my bed where, thanks to you, I spent a fifth sleepless night. Tonight, once again, I am wracking my brains to understand why you changed the previous plan you'd willingly conceived. Tonight I am thinking of going to the Convent* if the performance there is not cancelled. And then, no matter what, I want to see you, and I need to do so. The person you call the apothecary* visited me. He screwed up his face a great deal, but to no effect. Not a single tear flowed. He wanted to prove to me how unbridled my actions are with you and ended by saying that he would persuade you to return to the army for the sake of my own glory. I agreed with this. All of these people outwardly use all means possible to preach moral lessons at me, which I hear out, but inwardly they, and especially the prince [Grigory Orlov], do not dislike you. I admitted to nothing; nor did I deny anything which might have led them to complain that I had lied. In a word, I have an awful lot to tell you, especially in the vein of what I told you between noon and two in the afternoon yesterday. But I'm not sure whether you are in the same frame of mind as yesterday, since so often your words fail to match your actions, as has been the case over the past day. I say this because you repeated that you would come and didn't. You cannot be angry about my complaining. Farewell, may God be with you. I think about you constantly. Oh goodness, what a long letter I've scribbled. Guilty—I momentarily forgot that you don't like long letters. No more of those in the future.

79. *To Grigory Potemkin*

Catherine advises Potemkin to tread carefully and not to take sides in the struggle for influence between the two main groupings at court, which centred on the Orlov brothers and Nikita Panin, respectively.

[28 February 1774]

Grishenka isn't my beloved because he is so sweet. I slept well but am not feeling up to much. My chest hurts as does my head, and, to be honest, I just do not know whether I shall appear today or not. But if I do go out then it will be because I love you more than you love me. I can prove that just as two and two make four. I will come out to see you. After all, not everyone has as much self-control as you do. And indeed, not everyone is so smart, handsome, and pleasant. I am not surprised that all of St Petersburg has credited an innumerable number of women to your balance sheet. I venture there is nobody in the whole world who is so skilled in consorting with them. I think that in every respect you are out of the ordinary; in fact, you utterly stand out from all others. I ask you not to do only one thing: do not undermine or attempt to harm Prince Orlov in my estimation. For I would regard this as ungrateful on your part. Previously and right up until your arrival, there was no one whom he praised more or, as far as I can see, whom he loved more than you. And while he has his faults, it would be unbecoming for either you or me to take stock of them and tell everyone about them. He loves you, and since they are my friends, I will not part with them. There's a lesson in morality for you. If you are clever you will heed it: it would not be clever to contradict this for the reason that it is the honest truth.

If I am to remain reasonable when you are with me, then I would do well to close my eyes. Otherwise I shall have to say in earnest the thing I always ridiculed, 'my gaze is captivated by you'. This expression I used to consider stupid, unreal, and unnatural, but I now see that this can happen. Once my eyes are fixed on you, not even a penny's worth of reason penetrates my mind, and I become Lord only knows how stupid. And it takes me about three days, when there is an opportunity of not meeting you, before I can restore my mind and recover my memory. If I didn't, you would quickly be bored with me—that would be inevitable. Today I am furious with myself and thoroughly chewed myself out and have made every effort to be more intelligent. Should I somehow muster any strength and resolve, it will be what I absorb from you—you set the very best example. You are smart, you are resolute and firm in your chosen decisions. Proof of this is the very fact that for so many years, as you say, you have been trying to get my attention—not that I myself noticed this, but others have told me.

Farewell, my dear. It is only three days until our assignation. But that will be the first week of Lent, days of repentance and prayer on which seeing you will be completely impossible since it would be in every respect deplorable. I have to fast. Ugh! I do not even want to think about it and am on the verge of tears at the very thought. Adieu, Sir, please do write today, would you, to say how you are, whether you had a good rest or not, and whether you still have a fever. Is it high? Panin will tell you, 'Allow

me to advise, Sir, that you take quinine, quinine, and more quinine!'
How jolly it would be if you and I were able to sit together and converse.
If we loved one another less we would be cleverer and more cheerful.
You see, I am a very convivial person when my mind is free, even more
so when my heart is, too. My joy, you will not believe it, but for the sake
of good conversation it would be better if love played less of a role.

Write, would you, to let me know whether you laughed when you read
this letter. For I myself rocked with laughter when I read what I had
written. What a lot of rubbish I've scribbled, a veritable fever and rant.
All the same, off it goes—one way or t'other you might be amused.

80. *To Grigory Potemkin*

*The need for discretion caused Catherine some inhibition as their romantic liaison
progressed. Nonetheless, Potemkin's rise was quickly cemented with official gestures.
On 1 March, she promoted Potemkin to general-adjutant; other appointments and
honours rapidly followed.*

[St Petersburg, 1 March 1774]

My little dove, my dear Grishenka, although you left early, this was my
worst night—to the point that I felt such a disturbance of the blood
that I wished to send for the doctor to bleed me, but towards morning
dozed off and was calmer. Do not ask who is in my thoughts, but know
once and for all that you are there forever. I say 'forever', but with time
will you want it to stay there forever or will you want to scratch it out
yourself? The great affection I bear you terrifies me. Well, all right,
I shall find a way to be fiery, as you like to say, but this I shall try to
conceal even from you. But you cannot forbid me to feel. This morning
in accordance with your wishes I shall sign the document prepared in
fulfilment of the promise made yesterday. Arrange it with Strekalov so
that we might be alone when you thank me, and then I'll let you into the
Diamond Chamber.* Otherwise where could we hide our mutual feeling on this occasion from curious onlookers? Farewell, little dove.

81. *To Alexander Bibikov*

*Catherine authorized Bibikov in the campaign against Pugachev to establish a tem-
porary local department of the state security organ, called the Secret Department,*

to interrogate captured rebels. Unnerved by Pugachev's claim to be the Emperor Peter III, Catherine was on guard against any possibility of collusion with a court faction. From 1762 onwards, Catherine issued several official orders limiting the use of torture. She reiterates that principle here, although torture was used with her permission on other occasions in repressing Pugachev.

Alexander Il'ich, your letters of 2 March have reached my hands, and the response I am obliged to make is to regret how extensively the villains have spread out. I am extremely concerned that they might penetrate into Siberia. And matters in the district of Ekaterinburg are comparable—not of a kind to make me cheerful. Please, you should order the Secret Department to be cautious in investigating and punishing people. In my view, the soldiers Aitugan and Sangulov were flogged unjustly. And why for that matter is it thought necessary to flog during interrogation? Under my supervision, the Secret Department in twelve years has not flogged a single person during interrogation, yet it has got to the bottom of every case, and we always found out more than we wanted to know. The entire city wishes to designate your friend Potemkin as a lieutenant colonel of the Preobrazhensky Regiment. The entire city often lies through and through. On this occasion I shall not leave the city guilty of a falsehood. There is a distinct possibility that this is what will happen. Why did I think it necessary to write about this? To amuse. If you were here I would not tell you. But the business will have been concluded even before you receive this letter. Just leave it: I am the first to tell you this and have been assured that you are not opposed. Who has assured me, however, I shall not say. I would have appointed Gagarin to the post of lieutenant colonel immediately, were it not for the misgiving I have that promotion among your troops might become as commonplace as we find in Count Rumiantsev's army. On which note, I remain well disposed to you and hope that the matter with which you have been entrusted will come to a swift conclusion.

Catherine
15 March 1774

82. *To Voltaire*

Catherine had avoided mentioning the Pugachev Rebellion to Voltaire throughout 1773; when she finally did so in a letter of 19 January 1774, she referred to Pugachev dismissively as a 'highway robber' and minimized the risk that he posed to her reign.

Voltaire had been well aware of the uprising from news reports, and in his letter of 2 March (NS) he suggested that the French were orchestrating it as they had the Ottoman war on Russia, through advisors such as François de Tott. Diderot, meanwhile, left St Petersburg to spend the spring with the Russian ambassador in The Hague, Dmitry Golitsyn.

this 15 March 1774

Sir, only the newspapers are making a lot of noise about the brigand Pugachev, who most certainly has neither direct nor indirect relations with Monsieur de Tott. I think as highly of the cannons cast by the latter as I do of the former's undertakings. Mr Pugachev and Monsieur de Tott nonetheless have one thing in common: one of them gets nearer every day to a hempen rope, while the other risks a silken cord. Diderot has left to return to Paris. Our conversations were very frequent; his visit gave me great pleasure. His is a most extraordinary mind, the likes of which one does not meet with often. He was sad to leave us: he said that returning to be with his family was the strongest mark of affection that he could give them. I shall let him know of your desire to see him; he will stop for some time in The Hague. This letter is a reply to yours, Sir, of 2 March NS. At the moment I have nothing interesting to tell you, but I shall never grow tired of reiterating to you the sentiments of esteem, friendship, and regard that you have inspired in me for so long.

Caterine

83. *To Grigory Potemkin*

Catherine mocks her courtiers' growing realization of the unique status that Potemkin had already acquired in her affections and at court. She concurs entirely with their assessment that Potemkin is entirely different from the previous favourite, Alexander Vasil'chikov, with whom she had been very unhappy.

[after 19 March 1774]

Sweetheart, I bet you really did think that I would not write to you today. You deign to be wrong. I awoke at five o'clock and it is now almost seven and—time to write to him. However, if I am to be honest (now please listen to what sort of truth it is), I do not love you and do not wish to see you any more. You will not believe it, my joy, but I cannot stand you. As if I could not do without him at all! Yesterday I chattered away until midnight, and then sent him packing. Do not be angry! It is not as if I couldn't do without him! The nicest thing about the conversation was that I learned what they say between themselves, 'No', they say, 'he isn't like Vasil'chikov, she knows him some other way.' And there is indeed someone she knows. And nobody is surprised. Instead, they have taken the matter as though they had long been expecting that it was to be so. But no, everything is going to be another way entirely. From my little finger down to my very heels and from them to the last hair on my head, I have promulgated a general prohibition on showing you the least caress today. And love is shut up in my heart behind ten locks. It is awful how cramped it feels. It just barely fits and at any moment and in any place it might just break out. Well, think about it yourself, you are an intelligent man. Would it be possible to contain more madness than there is in this many lines? A river of nonsense words has flowed from my head. What it is like for you to have to deal with such a deranged mind, I have no idea. O, Mr Potemkin, what damned miracle have you wrought in so upsetting a head that until this moment had passed for one of the best in Europe?*

Well it is time, it really is high time to get my mind in order. It is shameful, terrible, a sin for Catherine II to allow a mad passion to reign over her. Through such unreasonableness you will become hateful even to him. I often start repeating this last maxim to myself, and I think it is the only one that can bring me back to the true path. And this will not be one of the least proofs of your great power over me. It is time to stop, or else I shall scribble out an entire sentimental metaphysics, which in the end will make you laugh, but no other good can come of it. Well then, my ravings—go then to the lands, to those happy shores where abides my hero. Perhaps you will not find him at home any more, and you will be brought back to me—in which case I shall throw you right into the fire, and Grishen'ka will not see this madness, in which, however, God knows that there is a great deal of love. But it would be much better for him not to know about this. Farewell, Giaour, Muscovite, Cossack. I do not love you.

84. *To Grigory Potemkin*

The Demidov family had accumulated substantial wealth in mining and metalworking since the 1750s, when these industries were transferred from the state to private ownership. The Pugachev Rebellion severely disrupted the industrial base of the Urals, destroying several of the Demidovs' factories and many others. The empress is keen to make sure credit is available to stabilize the running of the forges and furnaces.

[before 21 April 1774]

My turtledove, I attach herewith a letter to Count Aleksei Grigor'evich Orlov. If there are spelling errors I ask you to make corrections as necessary* and return it to me. To those who object to the promotion of the seigneurs Demidov as Councillors of the Mining College*—an area in which they, it has to be said, are quite knowledgeable and can be of use—you can say that the Senate often exercises its right to raise even moneylenders to the ranks of the nobility. And therefore, I consider that I too as befits my power may reward bankrupt people from whom (thanks to their competent management of factories) my trade and tax accounts have received sustained and substantial income. They are no worse than that idiot general Mr Bilstein* on whose behalf the entire city lobbied. But it is the custom here to see everything in the worst light. Well, I am accustomed to it and don't care a fig. I have known for a long time that people who think they can satisfy everyone just because they have innocent intentions are making a mistake. My dear spinning top, do not be cross that I have written out in a letter what you would not have allowed me to say or hear aloud if we were together. It is normal for everyone to try to justify themselves, perhaps most especially me, since I am subjected hourly to innumerable reproaches and criticisms from the clever and the stupid alike. Which is why, when my ears are jammed full of it, my mind obsesses about this and my thoughts are not as cheerful as they would naturally be if I had managed to please everyone.

When you have the time please write to me about Bibikov, Prince Golitsyn, Freiman, Mansurov, and Reinsdorp.*

Now I shall speak about something that, perhaps, will be more pleasant for both of us. Namely, Ivan Chernyshev lied to you when he told you that I am not able to love at a distance,* since I love you even when I do not see you. But it seems to me that I see you very rarely even though in fact it is not infrequent. Chalk that up to passion: if you do not love someone then you never hunger to see them. Farewell, my sweet.

85. *To Grigory Potemkin*

On her birthday, 21 April, Catherine lists off the chivalric orders she has awarded Potemkin: the Polish Order of the White Eagle (granted by her former favourite, Stanislas Poniatowski), the Russian Orders of St Anne and St Alexander Nevsky (which were both worn on red ribbons), and the Order of St George. Catherine had founded the last-named in 1769 to reward military bravery; its ribbon had (and still has) black and orange stripes; its motto is 'For service and bravery'.

[22 April 1774]

Greetings, dearest, and congratulations on the White Eagle and the two red ribbons and the scrap of striped cloth, which is, as it happens, dearer to me than the others since it is my own handiwork. It was possible to demand it as rightfully belonging to merit and bravery. It is our wish that we not be humiliated in future. Let us draw a veil over flaws and mistakes, rather than put them on public display, which would be most unpleasant. And, really, that would be unbecoming with a friend, much less with one's wife. Well, there's a reproach for you—but it is, mind you, entirely tender. I woke up cheerful, and in this I was much helped by yesterday evening and your own cheerfulness and pleasure. I like it terrifically when you are jolly. I wonder how many fittings today will bring. Adieu, my jewel. You often lack common sense, but you are always most delightful.*

You forgot to write and speak to me about Reinsdorp.

86. *To Friedrich Melchior Grimm*

This is Catherine's first letter to Friedrich Melchior Grimm, which she presents as a continuation of their jovial exchanges at court. Catherine jokes about the postal officials who will spy on the letter's contents on behalf of the governments in the territories it will pass through before reaching its destination: conscious of that secondary readership, Catherine here expresses in her chatter nothing of political significance, despite her intimate tone and apparently confessional mode. Later, however, politics occupied an ever-growing place in the exchange.

this 25 April 1774 OS

Mr Grimm, I received yesterday your letter dated from Riga on 19/30 April. If you played the cry-baby with Mr Riedesel, at least you were not the only one: he made me cry a good deal too. The landgravine was an exceptional woman: how she knew how to die!* When my turn comes, I shall try to imitate her, and I shall banish as she did all cry-babies from my sight. When the moment comes, I want only those who have souls of stone and who are laughers by trade.

You say to me, 'How can I leave your empire?' How can I reply, save by Molière's phrase, 'Monsieur George Dandin, you asked for it.' Well then, it's for you to decide whether to come back. I congratulate you on the great joy you took in celebrating my 46th birthday* in Courland. I hate that day like the plague. What a fine present it gives me—every time the gift of one more year, something I could well do without! Tell the truth—an empress who was but fifteen years old all her life would be a charming thing.

But farewell, Mr Grimm, this letter is beginning to resemble the chatter after eight o'clock at Tsarskoe Selo, and the fools who will read it before you do might find it indecent that two serious personages like ourselves should write such letters. You know what consideration everyone owes to one's neighbours, and especially that which Mr Thomas* enjoys. Well then, out of consideration for fools more foolish than our friend Tom, I shall end, wishing you good health and a good journey. I am sending my letter by the means you indicated to prove to you my punctiliousness.

Orenburg has been liberated, and, as I prophesied, this farce will end with beatings and hangings, for which, however, I am not developing a taste. I have, however, suffered a real loss. General Bibikov died after thirteen days of a hot and bilious fever 200 versts this side of Orenburg. By the way, how are you? Diderot has written to me—and what's more from The Hague—to ask the state of your health. I can see from here that when you read this letter you will enjoy more than one purging of the spleen, and no eccentric will be spared.* I know quite well the reason: the path of the planets and the succession of things in this world will have brought about that moment. Admit that you were not expecting this ending.

87. *To Grigory Potemkin*

[after 8 May 1774]

My sweet little dove, what was it you were pleased to groan about as you lay on the bed? I was not eavesdropping behind the partition when I overheard this. Your *okh!* reached my ears from across all the corridors and rooms all the way to my divan. Please tell us what this *okh!* means? And *Jesus Maria* meant that I love you a great deal.

88. *To Gustav III of Sweden*

Catherine informs her cousin Gustav of the death of the elder son of their uncle Georg Ludwig of Schleswig-Holstein-Gottorf, Wilhelm August (1753–1774). The younger brother, Peter Friedrich Ludwig, left Russia soon after his brother's death and later ruled the family territories of Lübeck and Oldenburg. This letter exemplifies

the formal terms in which familial events and emotional bonds among royalty were
codified in official epistolary rituals.

at Peterhof, this 14 July 1774

My dear Brother and Cousin, I am convinced ahead of time that Your Majesty will share with me the grief and pain caused me by the unexpected death of Prince Wilhelm August of Holstein, the elder son of the late Prince Georg Ludwig, our uncle, of which, with great regret, I inform You by the present letter. Extraordinarily unfortunate in its circumstances, the loss is all the more distressing to me because, since the death of the late duke my uncle, as Your Majesty is not unaware, I had had the greatest care taken in the education of the two princes he left behind. I must say to their credit that they met my expectations perfectly. It was with the greatest satisfaction that we saw their return last autumn from Italy, where they had completed their studies. Their successes befitted their pedigree.

The elder prince, by taste and inclination, desired to learn the science of naval service, and, to test whether his health would permit him to follow his penchant, he had asked that, while his younger brother went on his first campaign in Bulgaria, he might spend the fine season with my squadrons exercising in the Baltic. I consented that he might indeed embark on one of them towards the end of June. It was there that it pleased Providence, whose workings are inscrutable, to allow the prince's career to end in a most deplorable manner. For, despite all the precautions taken every time he wished to climb on the masts and rigging, where he was accompanied by officers and sailors, he fell into the sea on the 3rd of this month within sight of the port of Revel. Despite the divers sent from the vessel, the *Ezekiel*, and the efforts made by the entire crew, not only could the prince's life not be saved, but even his body has not yet been found.

With a heart heavy over the sad event that is the subject of this letter, I wish for Your Majesty's prosperity and preservation, remaining always with very high regards and most particular friendship,

My dear Brother and Cousin,

Your Majesty's good Sister, Cousin, and Neighbour,

Caterine

89. *To Grigory Potemkin*

When the news of Pugachev's ravaging of Kazan reached St Petersburg, Nikita Panin
pressured Catherine into appointing his brother Petr Panin to take charge of the

operations. Although she conceded very substantial powers over the military forces and civilian populations in these areas, better news about a government victory over Pugachev at Kazan gave her the strength to place some limits on Panin's authority. She insisted that legal norms not be violated and refused to give him authority over Mikhail Volkonsky, the governor of Moscow. Her reservations about empowering Panin speak to the political worries posed by the practical surrender of absolute control.

[29 July 1774]

You will see, my dove, from all the bits and pieces enclosed with this note that Count Panin has deigned to make his brother the ruler with unlimited sovereignty of the best part of the empire: that is, the provincial government of Moscow, Nizhny Novgorod, Kazan, and Orenburg, with others *sous-entendus*. And you will see that if I sign off on this, then not only will Prince Volkonsky be annoyed and feel ridiculed, but I myself will be without the slightest protection and, for fear of Pugachev, I shall praise before the entire world and elevate higher than all other mortals in the empire its chief liar and my personal antagonist. He who knows best holds all the cards: read the enclosed please and admit that the arrogance of these people is towering. I herewith enclose Bibikov's instructions for a *confrontatie*.* And I also like the point where it is said that he [Petr Panin] can execute and pardon all people, however, whenever, and wherever.

90. *To Friedrich Melchior Grimm*

In a triumphant mood over the highly advantageous conclusion of the Ottoman war, Catherine writes a vivacious letter that continues setting the tone and motifs of the ensuing correspondence. The metaphors of madness and muddling stand for the energetic and entertaining letters she wants to see in future, while she shows her trust in Grimm by taking the risk of gently mocking Frederick the Great, whom she calls the physician of Sans-Souci.

at St Petersburg, this 3 August, a day reserved for a *Te Deum*, whether you like it or not, for the peace treaty. This is the second on the occasion, and I have two more to listen to—once the two embassies have exchanged ratifications, that of my good friend Mr Abdülhamid and my own. Now, this peace treaty came upon us quite unexpectedly; it is a good and honest one, and everyone is pleased with it, including me. And you too, are you not?

I had the honour of receiving your no. 4 this morning, which is only eight pages long. I thank you—it is, with all due respect, the maddest of all your scribblings. However long they might be, all the same I gladly read them two or three times, since they are very amusing if not very sensible. I have such a prodigious number of things to tell you that I cannot tell you a single one from beginning to end. I am not Diderot: I cannot comprehend at the same time the many subjects he does, nor scribble as quickly. I would need an enormous ream of paper and time, and I have a *Te Deum* on my hands and three quarters of an hour (not counting the obstacles that will come at me) to devote to you. Besides, Mr Thomas and his darling daughter are in my room and demand a thousand attentions from me.

Now then, to begin properly, I shall tell you that I cannot have committed all the wrongs you say I have because I lack the capabilities you attribute to me. Perhaps I am a good person; I am usually gentle, but my position forces me to be uncompromising in seeking whatever I want—that's the sum total of who I am, no more no less. But enough about me.

The doctor from Sans-Souci who sent you to Carlsbad pleased me greatly with his cure. My courage does not yet extend to curing others: up to now I have been curing and treating only my own illnesses. I understand nothing about bowel obstructions, and I would bet that the doctors are wronging the reputation of your bowels and that one day, may God delay it as long as possible, they will find your bowels healthy. Regarding the return and non-return,* of which you speak to me so much, I have written you a special missive about it, to which I refer you.

I had reached this point when there arrived a very large dispatch, which I had to read and which told me that the Marquis Pugachev, as Voltaire calls him, has been beaten for what I believe is the eighth or ninth time: he kept not a single cannon. That made me set aside my letter, and then came the *Te Deum*, and then a typical day, and then a court reception day and eleven hours in between. From that you can see that at nine in the evening I shall be less witty and have a mind less querulous than this morning, when it was entertainingly wound up. Nonetheless, there is no need to despair completely of your good genius, which normally gets more out of people than others can manage. You have a talent for elaboration and the capacity to bring out into the open what is inside the head of your interlocutor. You are going to protest, but it is true and very true.

On that note, what are you going to do in the entourage of the Duc d'Orléans?* This association will not be to your advantage, for he has been exiled. Amen. I am no longer bruising my fingers: since you left

I have not made a single knot.* I am currently knitting a bedspread for my friend Thomas, which General Potemkin threatens to steal from him. Ah! what a good head that man has! He played a bigger role than anyone in the peace treaty, and his good head is devilishly amusing. Mr Heretic, when you go and join the devils, you will see how amusing they really are. You are going to get there faster if you keep writing letters eight pages long when you are at Carlsbad to take the waters.* That was a very bad thing to do, and I ought to scold you at least as much as Madame Geoffrin scolds Burigny, but I shall leave that to your chief physician of Sans-Souci. But, as you might not know what a chief physician is, I shall tell you that it is the title to which all Asclepiuses* aspire, and which I have not yet given to a single one, not because I think them totally inept, but perhaps nearly so.

My compliments on Prince Henry's letter, and, as poorly constructed and poorly scribbled as this one is, I hope that it might be conducive to your good health. Farewell.

91. *To Grigory Potemkin*

Rumours circulated about an affair between Count Andrei Razumovsky and Grand Duchess Natalia Alekseevna. The grand duke disbelieved his mother's revelations and supported his wife and Razumovsky, his close friend. Catherine's relations with the heir, never warm, continued to deteriorate.

[before 23 September 1774]

I think, my soul, that if the grand duke is blind and cannot be made to see sense about Razumovsky in any other way, then perhaps Panin should persuade him to send Razumovsky to sea in order to diminish the hateful rumours that are circulating around the city. Make use as you see fit of the parcel that is attached.

92. *To Petr Panin*

On 15 September 1774, Pugachev's own supporters captured him and delivered him up to government officials. As Panin mopped up fringe unrest, Catherine took no time to gloat. Panin is authorized to repair local administration and granted powers to pre-empt famine, resettle families, and restore commerce, even as the letter looks ahead to a form of due process and trial for Pugachev.

Count Petr Panin, I learned from your letter of 22 September from Penza* and from the documents sent with it that at last the monster Pugachev is in your hands; that he has been handed over by his accomplices; and that until the very end they rampaged furiously. But nonetheless I render thanks to the Lord that this awful history has now been cut short despite the damage it has done to the reputation of the empire— not to mention the terrible internal destruction, disorder, and countless misdeeds of that mob's ferocity and its inhumanity. In the eyes of all Europe, this has sent us right back to the barbaric times of at least two or three hundred years ago—to my deepest regret and to the increase of my heart's deepest wound over the suffering of the people. As per my previous instructions, so now once again I confirm to you that it remains my firm intention that the villain and his key accomplices be transported to Moscow in such a secure manner that they will never be able to escape— on this point I rely completely on you to make sure that no aspect will be overlooked. Looking to the speedy resolution of this business in Moscow, and if possible even before my arrival there, it is my wish that as per the enclosed note you collect the most reliable information and testimony, as much as you possibly can, and have it sent to me. In my last letter I wrote that you should take up to 10,000 roubles and distribute them as charity in the first instance to people ruined by Pugachev. Since you will now have more time following the end of this rabble's outrages, I ask you to have a keen eye and show special consideration for the needs of victims in those places entrusted to you. And if you find it necessary and required, then use up to 300,000 roubles to relieve the wailing and lamentation of those who have been ruined and are suffering deprivation brought on by the wrath of God in the provinces and *uezds*.* I hereby authorize you to do so, but do let me know how much you spend. After bringing Pugachev and his accomplices to their knees, a multitude of thoughts suddenly arise. Among which the first noteworthy one is the treachery of the Bashkirs, who were in no way oppressed yet nevertheless who take every opportunity to declare themselves to be villains. The second are the raids of the Kirghiz.* How to pacify both of them will be at your discretion in future, too, but now it is all the more necessary to take advantage of the present misfortune in order to stymie the Kirghiz from harming our commerce with India and Bukhara.* The third thing I have learned from past and current events is that a large number of fugitives are hiding around the Irgiz River* and the tributaries that merge with it, that Schismatics* and robbers live there, and that for several years bandits have been coming out of there. In order to stop the mayhem caused by the wildness of these locations, I think the first order of business when you have time, allowing for the condition of the provinces under your control as governor, is that you should have these areas surveyed, too, and in time brought under tighter control by founding small cities and installing administrators and clergy. Now is the most advantageous time to make these arrangements because a large number of soldiers have been brought into the region. Finally, with great pleasure I accept your devoted and sensible conduct in the crucial business that has been entrusted to you, as I do the congratulations sent on the anniversary of my coronation. I remain of goodwill towards you.

Catherine

3 October 1774

93. *To Grigory Potemkin*

Information had reached Catherine in a letter from Pavel Sergeevich Potemkin, a political rival of Petr Panin in charge of investigating the Pugachev Rebellion in Kazan, that Panin had exaggerated his subordinate Alexander Suvorov's involvement in the capture of Pugachev. Seeing this as another attempt by Panin to undermine him, Pavel Potemkin had tried to resign, but Catherine kept him on to continue balancing out the influence of the Panins. How to handle generals and their expectations of reward at the end of a campaign was a perpetual problem, as was Grigory Potemkin's hypochondria.

[10–12 October 1774]

My little dove, Pavel is right: Suvorov had no greater involvement in this than Thomas, but rather arrived at the end of the fight and after the villain had been captured. I hope that all of Pavel's disagreements and discontentedness will be at an end once he receives my order to go to Moscow. Return to me please the letters of Petr Ivanovich [Panin]. I must draft a reply and settle some of his demands. But, my dear, I love you most tenderly, and hope that the pills have expunged all your ailments. I only ask that you show restraint in taking them—sup on bouillon and drink tea without milk.

94. *To Voltaire*

With the threat from Pugachev now past, Catherine finally offered Voltaire her account of the uprising. But she quickly shifts attention away from Pugachev's impending execution to more humorous matters. On 6 October 1774 (NS), Voltaire retracted a recommendation letter that he had felt obliged to give a Frenchman, perhaps Jean

Germain Dumesnil (1740–1798), who claimed that his godfather had advised him to become the legislator of the Russian Empire. Voltaire was right to be wary: Catherine responded with her usual dismissiveness towards such adventurers.

this 2 November 1774

I shall gladly satisfy, Sir, your curiosity about Pugachev. It will be all the easier for me to do so, since he was caught a month ago, or, to speak more exactly, he was tied up and put under guard by his own followers in the desolate plain between the Volga and the River Yaik, where they had been chased by troops sent to attack them on all sides. There, deprived of food and means of replenishing their supplies, and moreover disgusted by his cruelties and hoping to obtain pardon for themselves, his companions handed him over to the commander of Yaik fortress, who sent him to Simbirsk to General Count [Petr] Panin, and from there he is currently on his way to Moscow. Hauled before General Panin for his first interrogation, he ingenuously admitted that he was a Don Cossack, named the place of his birth, said he was married to the daughter of a Don Cossack, that his wife was alive, that he had three children, that he had married another during the unrest, that his brothers and nephews were serving in the First Army, that he had himself served in the first two campaigns against the Porte. Since General Panin has many Don Cossacks with him, and since that nation's troops have never taken the brigand's bait, all this was soon verified by Pugachev's compatriots. He does not know how to read or write, but he is an extremely bold and determined man. Up to now there has been no sign that he was the agent of any external power or intelligence, nor that he was following the inspiration of anyone at all. One must suppose that Mr Pugachev is a master brigand rather than the valet of any living soul. I think that, after Tamerlane, hardly anyone has destroyed more of the human race. First he mercilessly hanged without any type of trial all noble families, men, women, and children, all the officers, and all the soldiers whom he could attack. He and his band did not pass by any place without pillaging and ransacking it. Even those who sought to preempt his outrages and win his favour by receiving him well were not safe from pillage and murder. But what shows the extent to which the man flatters himself is that he dares to conceive some hope that I might pardon him. Or he says that with his courage he might, by his future services, obliterate his past crimes. If I were the only one whom he had offended, his reasoning might have been sound, and I would have pardoned him; but the cause is that of the empire, which has its laws.

For this reason, Sir, Dumesnil, the lawyer of whom I have never heard despite the opinions of his godfather, would be too late if he were to come to concoct laws for us. Even Monsieur de La Rivière, who six years ago assumed that we went on all fours and who most politely troubled himself to come from Martinique to raise us onto our hind legs, came too late. As for kissing the hands of priests, about which you ask, I can tell you that it is a custom in the Greek Church, which, I believe, was established at almost the same time as the Church. In the past ten or twelve years, priests have begun to pull back their hands, some out of politeness, others out of humility. Therefore, do not get yourself too much up in arms about an old custom that is disappearing. I also do not know whether you would find much cause to scold me for conforming since the age of 14 to an established custom. In any case, I would not be the only one to deserve this. If you come here and if you become a priest, I shall ask your blessing and when you give it to me, I shall willingly kiss the hand that has traced so many truths and good and beautiful things. But, so that you know where to find me, I warn you that this winter I am off to Moscow. Farewell, be well.

95. *To Grigory Potemkin*

[8 December 1774]

My sweetest sweet, your letter gave me great joy, all the more so because Leo of Catania* told me that you were unwell and led me to conclude that you were morose. My mind, taking flight as usual, had found a niggle that I might perhaps have upset you. And I thought that my letter might have been to blame. Of course it struck you as being gruff. And I was planning to write to you a second time because of my feelings, and these feelings are indeed full of tenderness for you, my dear little lord. I am sorry, peerless soul, that you are ailing. In future, do not run up the staircase barefoot, and if you want to get over your cold as soon as possible then sniff a bit of snuff.* You will feel better instantly. Adieu, my love, my heart,* my husband who is dear, glorious, sweet, and everything darling, pleasant, and intelligent that you can imagine.

96. *To Friedrich Melchior Grimm*

Pugachev was executed on 10 January 1775; Catherine was careful not to be present in Moscow for the execution, entering the city on 25 January. In this letter, she

moves on quickly from a subject that threatened her image as an enlightened mon-
arch. Reworking a frequent theme in the correspondence, Catherine brags about her
ability to reinvent the sources of her thinking, reworking for her own purposes the
lessons of her childhood tutors and of the 'Encyclopédistes', but also rejecting the
ideas of others, like the Physiocrats (then referred to as the Economists).

Reply to no. 9,* this 21 December 1774

A few days from now, the farce of the Marquis Pugachev will be over. His trial has reached sentencing, for which some formalities had to be observed. His trial lasted three months, and it kept everyone busy from morning until evening. By the time you receive this sheet, you can be certain that you will not hear that man spoken of again.

One would think that the close friendship and harmony that reigns between my beloved brother Abdul and myself was making you waste away. So there! That is what you deserve to be told for giving me the lovely epithet of 'homewrecker'. I would have you know once and for all, Sir, that I have never wrecked a home in my life: there have always been far more people who wanted to meddle with mine than I with theirs. Sometimes I have been called on to patch things up in someone else's, and then I have, as is customary in such cases, done all that I could to do good under the circumstances. Yet, on my honour, it is difficult to patch things up. Our Saviour himself said so 1,750 years ago or thereabouts.* I have far better cause to quote this passage than do others, whose name I shall spare the postal clerks from having to read. These others, I say, take as their witness Heaven, which they suppose empty or quite nearly so. But let us lay aside such subtle matters and speak of something else.

You will be able to reconcile the two different stories regarding Prince Henry's journey when you find out that he wanted to come and celebrate the peace treaty here in accordance with his former promise; that the trip to Moscow intervened; and that he meant to go there. But since the city was affected by a great fire last summer, it would have been difficult to lodge him agreeably near the court and even more difficult to provide him with ease and entertainments at his disposal there, especially as there is no habitable country house near Moscow for the summer. When these considerations were presented to the prince, he agreed to delay his journey until the court returned from Moscow, an opportunity of which I advise you to avail yourself, if you still intend to come back.* Do not go and wail over this expression as you did at the recollection of the bowing and scraping.

Why should your young monarch,* with all the virtues that compose his motto, fear bulldogs? His role is to go his way and let them bark as he passes by. For myself, I can do without the other three *ists*,* but I confess to you that I cannot go a single day without the *Encyclopédie*: despite all its faults, it is a necessary and excellent piece. Miss Cardel and Mr Wagner had to deal with a bumbling mind who turned everything she was told the wrong way round. Mr Wagner wanted tests* of another kind, and the bumbling mind said to herself: 'To be something in this world, one must have the qualities required for that something. Let us look seriously into our little heart: do we have them? If not, let us train them up.' Is there anything *pedestrian* or *Lutheran* about that? In faith, no. Martin Luther was a boor who never learned that.

I was informed through Berlin of what you wrote about the young man.* There are nonetheless two good things about him: he is not mean, and he is not proud. He wants to remain in Moscow, and I shall not dissuade him from doing so. His sister* is almost always ill, but how can she not be? Everything is excessive with that lady. If we go for a walk, it is for 20 versts; if we dance, it is twenty contra dances and as many minuets, not counting the allemandes. To keep our apartments from getting too hot, we make no fire at all. If the others are rubbing their faces with ice, the whole body right away becomes part of the face. In sum, we are far from the middle way. For fear of villains, we mistrust the whole world and listen to neither good nor bad advice. In a word, graciousness, prudence, and wisdom have yet to be seen, and God knows what will happen, since we listen to no one and have our own mind made up for ourselves. Can you imagine that after a year and a half and more, we cannot yet speak a word of the language?* We want to be taught, but we do not apply ourselves for one moment a day. Always spinning like a top, we cannot endure this or that, we owe more than twice what we have, and yet we have what hardly anyone in Europe has. But mum's the word! One must never despair of young people. One must not grumble too long either: one must not aggrieve the *ists* or non-*ists*, nor *pedestrians* nor obstructed bowels!

You have a very exact memory of things. That recapitulation of Prince Dolgorukov's arrival on my feast day* does your memory proud. I congratulate you on it and thank you for all the obliging things that you say to me, and namely about the armistice that was granted for the two lines that had the misfortune of displeasing you.

Here is a bit of news for you. There is a new illness that is called Legislomania, a severe attack of which, they say, the Empress of Russia is suffering for the second time. During the first, she merely laid down principles. This time, the job is in earnest. Oh! The poor woman will die of it, or else bring it off. Now, is that not a masterful will against which no obstacle can persist?

You will tell me that a reputed minister like the Marquis Felino could not be a knave and that as a result I can buy his paintings* without having them inspected. But since I have seen some reputed ministers who were nonetheless knaves, I should very much like you to have those paintings examined by someone who understands them, without, however, sharing my sententiae with anyone, much less with Mr Felino, who has very politely offered me his paintings. I should also very much like to have the catalogue.

Monsieur Pont-de-Veyle's collection of plays has not yet reached me. As for the author of the *Philosophical History of the Commerce of the Indies*, I shall task Count Munich with rereading the article on Russia* and putting his comments in writing. Have a good evening, Mr Baron.*

PART IV

DOMESTIC AFFAIRS
(1775–1780)

With the Russo-Turkish War and the Pugachev Rebellion behind her, Catherine took pride in asserting her undeniable place as a diplomatic powerhouse in Europe. This involved symbolic displays such as the magnificent celebrations of the Treaty of Küçük Kaynarca. Catherine herself designed the festivities to represent the integration of the new territories into Russia: the lands were recreated as a fairground on Khodynka Field, to the north-west of Moscow, on 21–3 July 1775 (Letters 101, 106).

Her dominant position could be seen in her relations with Gustav III of Sweden. Since at least 1774, Gustav had been angling for an invitation to St Petersburg in hopes of improving relations between the two countries: he feared (unfoundedly) that Catherine was plotting to overturn militarily the revolution he had instigated in 1772, which had made him an absolute monarch. The visit finally took place in June 1777 (Letter 117). Continuing his efforts to bring about a rapprochement between Sweden and Russia, Gustav wrote to Catherine upon his return home, requesting permission to begin a supposedly clandestine correspondence. Stripped of the usual etiquette, the exchange avoided diplomatic channels and instead passed through the hands of Friedrich Matthias von Eck, the postal director in St Petersburg (Letter 119). She enjoyed the opportunity to write freely and occasionally to mock her cousin, and she thwarted all Gustav's attempts to profit politically from their ostensibly intimate correspondence, since she limited their discussions to social and familial chatter.

Catherine also made clear her ascendancy in real diplomacy. There were tense moments, particularly in 1778, when the international situation was troubled by the War of the Bavarian Succession, the American Revolutionary War, and a dispute between Russia and the Ottoman Empire over Crimea. The War of the Bavarian Succession offered an important opportunity for Catherine to wield her clout. Russia was responsible both for initiating the negotiations between Austria and Prussia and for mediating alongside France, resulting in the Peace of Teschen (13 May 1779 NS). Making Russia a guarantor of the Peace of Westphalia, the treaty visibly demonstrated and legally enshrined Russia's new status as an arbiter within the European balance of power (Letter 135).

However, during these years Catherine turned her attention largely to internal reforms. The crucial achievement lay in the Statute for the Administration of the Provinces of the Russian Empire, promulgated in November 1775, which completely restructured the administration and judiciary in the Russian provinces. Its system of local courts and administration remained in place until the abolition of serfdom in 1861, and its administrative division of territory was preserved, essentially, until the Bolshevik revolution in 1917. Planning further reforms, Catherine shifted her attention to an English model, claiming to have been reading since 1774 Sir William Blackstone's *Commentaries on the Laws of England* (1765–9) (Letter 125). She also continued to think about education reform, asking her Parisian friends for help (Letter 100). The Statute for the Administration of the Provinces charged local governments with creating primary schools in all sizeable towns, and Catherine's reflections during this period developed subsequently into the Russian Statute of Higher Education of 1786.

Relative outward peace left Catherine time to attend to her rapidly changing private life. Catherine's initial warm feelings for her daughter-in-law, Natalia Alekseevna, quickly changed into exasperation at the couple's financial excesses and the grand duchess's recalcitrance (Letter 102). In summer 1775, Natalia finally became pregnant with a possible heir to the throne, but it was suspected the child was really Andrei Razumovsky's. In the event, a deformity prevented her from giving birth normally, and both she and her child died on 15 April 1776. Catherine quickly arranged Paul's remarriage, to Sophia Dorothea of Württemberg, the future Grand Duchess Maria Fedorovna. Sophia, who had been too young in 1773, had always been Catherine's first choice. Delighted with her new daughter-in-law, Catherine noted the striking similarities between herself and the young bride: they were both born in Stettin, they were both christened Sophia, and they were even taught by the same writing master (Letter 116). Maria Fedorovna turned out to be a robust mother, giving birth to ten children, all but one of whom survived to adulthood. Catherine was overjoyed at the birth of her first grandson, Alexander, on 12 December 1777 (Letter 121). In her letters, Catherine proudly showed off her innovations in the art of grandmothering. Her emphasis on leaving the child as free as possible and building his physical strength is in tune with the general developments of educational theory in the eighteenth century: one of her sources is undoubtedly John Locke's *Some Thoughts Concerning Education* (1693) (Letter 130).

Being a grandmother or nearly so did not prevent Catherine from pursuing her own sometimes stormy love life. From the summer of 1775, business matters rather than passionate feeling became a source of mutual interest in the correspondence between Catherine and Potemkin, with occasional moments of intimacy (Letter 107). Often trading recriminations and regrets rather than caresses, Catherine could also be candid about her fears of letting down her guard, wary that personal vulnerability could undermine her royal dignity (Letter 97). The winter of 1775–6 brought tensions to a head as Catherine became smitten with Petr Zavadovsky and recast her relationship with Potemkin, rewarding him with gifts, the title of Prince in March 1776, and new status as her unquestioned first deputy (Letter 115). After a brief affair with Semën Zorich, in 1778–9 Catherine took as her lover Ivan Rimsky-Korsakov, whom she amorously likened to the famous military commander Pyrrhus, King of Epirus (318/19–272 BC) (Letter 126). Finally, in March 1780, she found a more satisfying relationship with Alexander Lanskoy, to whom she was introduced by Potemkin (Letter 136).

Catherine's cultural networks were in transition during these years. During Friedrich Melchior Grimm's second visit from September 1776 to July 1777, he officially entered Russian service, receiving, from then on, an annual salary of 2,000 roubles (Letter 118). He was instrumental in building Catherine's status as a patron. For example, he was the intermediary for the precious Chesme Inkstand, a major artistic commission managed by Grimm. Completed in 1778 by Barnabé Augustin de Mailly, the inkstand commemorated the victory at Chesme, and in 1783 it finally took up its intended home in the chapterhouse of the Order of St George, the most prestigious military decoration in Russia, founded by Catherine in 1769 (Letter 103). Similarly, with Grimm's help, in September 1778 she commissioned from Christopher Unterberger a reproduction of the Vatican loggias by Raphael and his studio; the Raphael loggias can still be seen in the Hermitage Museum in St Petersburg today (Letter 125). Most famously, at Catherine's request, Grimm purchased Voltaire's library from his somewhat unwilling heirs, and it still finds a home in St Petersburg today, in accordance with Catherine's wishes (Letter 126). Given the prestige of the figures involved, the transaction was given the air of an exchange of gifts rather than a mere purchase (Letter 132).

In the meantime, Catherine hesitated about whether or not to allow her letters to Voltaire to be printed: modesty required that she not appear to seek publicity for the letters, while at the same time she wanted to retain the right to censor passages in which she too harshly mocked the Church, the French, and the Austrians. They ultimately appeared in the first posthumous edition of Voltaire's works, published at Kehl, Germany, in 1784–9, but Catherine and Grimm imposed post hoc cuts to eliminate the worrisome passages. The general editor was the playwright Pierre-Augustin Caron de Beaumarchais (1732–1799); his machinations to ensure the publication of Catherine's letters rather disrupted her admiration for his play, *The Barber of Seville* (1775), which she repeatedly expressed during this period (Letters 118, 126).

97. *To Grigory Potemkin*

[1775]

Something was written on this piece of paper. Well, it must have been scolding, since your superiority to me yesterday was manifest in the following: you blustered with all your heart, whereas I was tender with a grieving heart and searched with a lantern for the exhausted tenderness of your love. But I was unable to find it before evening.

But what has transpired? O, God! It took my cleverness to make right what my sincerity had ruined. The scolding the other day came about because I attempted sincerely, cordially, and frankly, without premeditation or cunning, to declare to you thoughts that nobody could possibly think detrimental to anyone. On the contrary, they were actually to your advantage. But yesterday in the evening I did act with deliberate cunning. I confess that I deliberately did not send for you until nine o'clock to see whether you would come to me, and when I saw that you were not coming, I sent for news of your health. You arrived and were incensed. I pretended not to notice. And, more adroit than you in every respect, I allayed your anger and your blustering and was pleased to see that you were pleased to be rid of them. You will say that you requested from me a tender letter and that instead I recapitulate the scolding. But just wait a bit, allow the distress in your heart to subside. Tenderness finds a place wherever you make room for it. My kind of tenderness is fussy;

she bustles in wherever she is not kicked out. And even if you do kick her out—even then the feeling lingers, like a demon, seeking out a place to occupy. When my tenderness sees that sincerity has failed to win the day, she immediately dons the mantle of guile. You see how crafty tenderness is. She'll gladly take on any appearance as long as she can get to you. If you punch her, she'll bounce back and immediately cross over to the other side to occupy a better position—a vantage point closer not to her enemy, but to the friend of her heart. And who is he? His name is Grishen'ka. She overcomes his anger. She forgives him for wrongly distorting her words. She ascribes to his words an extenuating sense; she allows the hot-tempered ones to go by unheard; she does not take the insults to heart or tries to forget them. In a word, our tenderness is the sincerest and most extreme love. But go ahead and get angry if you can, and, if you can find a way, make us forget how to be sincere. You'll profit greatly from it. Think again, flare up again, but, please, reciprocate just a bit, and we will both be satisfied.

98. *To Johanna Bielke*

Catherine enjoyed tallying up the accomplishments of her reign, and she took her first return to Moscow since the Legislative Commission of 1767 as an opportunity to do so.

at 7 versts from Moscow, in a village that belongs to
the Prince of Georgia,
this 25 January 1775

Madam, I was on the road when I received your letter of 13 January, which I shall go ahead and answer as soon as I have told you that today I am making my public entry into Moscow, as is customary after peace treaties or for public ceremonies. The peace celebrations will be a fine example of the latter.

I made the journey here from Petersburg in fifty-six hours. I stopped at Novgorod, and also twenty-four hours at the halfway point, twenty hours to catch my breath, thirteen at Tver, and I have been resting here for the past three days. On the road I saw a newly built city and two more that have been erected, and I was surprised to see how, despite war, plague, and several fires, this road and its inhabitants have prospered in the eight years since I last saw these places. Before, you used to see little children in nothing but a shirt running around barefoot on the snow in the villages; now there is not a single one who does not have a suit of clothes, a fur, and boots. Although made of wood as before, the dwellings have grown larger, and most of the houses are now two storeys high. I saw schools in several places, which pleased me, and two seminaries, where there are a thousand priests' sons and where they teach, besides the national language, Greek, Latin, German, and French. I am truly happy about all that; another ten years like these, and I guarantee you that the changes will be evident to anyone who has not sworn to be blind.

My consent to the coadjutor's marriage* was sent already from Petersburg. I have always said that the Faculty meddled in prophecy without understanding a thing, and I am very glad that the Comte d'Artois has belied them.*

So you are piqued by the treaty between the House of Austria and Protector of the Roman faith, and the enemy of Christendom.* But despite their formal denials of the treaty, it exists nonetheless: we shall see its results shortly. I fear very much that my prophecies regarding America will come true sooner and better than those of the Parisian Faculty of Doctors.

Farewell, Madam, rest well assured of the invariable continuity of my friendship, and keep on loving me a little.

Catherine

99. *To Friedrich Melchior Grimm*

An exchange of New Year's wishes was an essential aspect of maintaining epistolary relationships in the eighteenth century. Catherine describes her lodgings in Moscow, the temporary Prechistensky Palace, constructed to house the court after the ravages of the 1771 Plague and the accompanying fires left no suitable imperial residence in the city.

from right in the middle of Moscow
this 30 January 1775

Mr Philosopher, I hereby declare to you my deepest gratitude for the wishes that you were pleased to waft through the air to me on New Year's Eve. Their reverberations got here yesterday. So you promise never again to fill up more than four pages with writing: do what is most convenient for you, Mr Philosopher, and for your very famous bowel obstruction. But please permit the Greek calendar to remain in its current state and to borrow nothing from the Latins. In the end, I think it a matter of indifference which way of counting one adopts, for in point of fact no part of the world has a really accurate way, and you will change another ten times, whereas we shall have the pleasure of having summer or spring in the winter months.*

Do you know (you who know everything) that I am delighted to be here and that everyone here, great and small, is delighted to see me? This city is a phoenix that will be reborn of its ashes. I find the populace very noticeably diminished: the reason is the plague that doubtless carried off over 100,000 people in Moscow. But let us not speak of that. You want to have the floor plan of the house I occupy, and I shall send it, but getting one's bearings in this labyrinth is like trying to drink the sea dry. I was here for two hours before I managed to recognize the way to my study without opening the wrong door—this house is a triumph of exits. I have never seen so many doors in my life. I have already had half a dozen condemned, and I still have twice as many as I need. But, to speak fairly, I would have you know that by having built a great hall, two immense galleries, and half a dozen state rooms, I have managed to join together three very large stone houses. I occupy one that the vice-chancellor's brother* has lent me; my son occupies another which I bought; and a third, which I also purchased, is for those who must indispensably be housed at court. The rest of my entourage have set up camp in ten or twelve houses that I have rented. Well now, all of that makes up a labyrinth of which I have no hope of giving you an accurate idea. But that is enough for today: there you have three pages in exchange for your four. Have a good evening.

100. *To Friedrich Melchior Grimm*

Catherine focuses in this letter on education, inter alia mentioning a book that she came to admire greatly: 'Emilie's Conversations' (1774), a work on women's education by Grimm's companion, Louise d'Épinay. Both Grimm and Diderot responded to her call for an outline of an education system, with an 'Essay on Studies in Russia' and a 'Plan of a University', respectively.

at Moscow, this 27 February 1775

Since your no. 13 was presented to me under the title of a mere addendum, I thought it would be good to consult the archives and see what was to be done in such a case. But since no examples of a similar incident were discovered, I thought it would be sufficient to respond on a separate sheet, and, at that, not before no. 14 arrived. Thanks be to God, it did not tarry—I received it today in due and proper form, and here is my reply.

Your Olympie* is an original to be reckoned with. I esteem her greatly without having the honour of knowing her. It never entered the late Marquis Pugachev's mind to propose that I conquer China: I am not sure he was even aware that God had made such a place. So you are writing to me about prunes—one must admit that you talk an awful lot about them. I am sorry that I have not received them, but I thank you for them as though I had them already, since I consider them a mark of your attentions, Sir. You see that today I have not forgotten the word 'Sir'. Miss Cardel would doubtless have scolded me for such forgetfulness, for the deceased lady constantly repeated that the word ' "Sir" never broke anyone's jaw'. I believe she got that maxim from some comedy. Among other knowledge, she knew all the comedies and tragedies imaginable like the back of her hand, and for all that Miss Cardel was very amusing.

But, by the way, listen: do not go playing so terrible a trick on me as to go giving out copies of my chatter with Diderot. I greatly esteem Monsieur de Castries, but he is a mortal, and my memorandum would pass from hand to hand until it reached the printers.* And I fear print like fire. Therefore, no matter what you might say, or my friend Prince Henry either, no copies, please, for a living soul, and tell Diderot, to whom I send my greetings, not to give out any and to deposit my replies in our shared library.

But listen for a moment, Mr Philosophers-who-are-not-a-faction, you would be charming and adorable people if you had the charity to draw up a plan of study for young people from their ABCs through university, inclusive. You will tell me that it is indiscreet to ask you for that, but they say that one needs three kinds of schools. And I, who have neither studied nor been to Paris, have neither knowledge nor wit and therefore do not know what should be learned, nor even what can be learned, or where to get all that—if not from you. I do not yet have the book that you have been so kind as to send through Prince Dolgorukov from Emilie's mother.* But I am very much struggling to get an idea of a university and its management, of a secondary school and its management, of a primary school and its management. While I wait for you to accede or not to my entreaty, I know what I shall go ahead and do: I shall go flip through the *Encyclopédie*. Oh, most assuredly I shall grab everything by the ears, whether I need it or not.

I find in the extract of Prince Henry's letter the full weight of his sound judgment. But nonetheless I must argue against him: my replies are not worth all that your geniuses are kind enough to claim. You see them as Diderot sees paintings and books, and as Father Malebranche saw all in God.* Have a good evening. That is, in faith, quite enough for this evening; all the rest another time. Farewell, *Sir*.

101. *To Friedrich Melchior Grimm*

Against a comic domestic background of her family of dogs, Catherine presents herself as a creator, making order out of chaos after the Pugachev Rebellion and recreating an entire conquered region by designing magnificent celebrations for the Treaty of Küçük Kaynarca.

Reply to no. 16 of 16 March, this 7 April 1775, at Moscow

Sitting between three doors and three windows, a Tuesday in Holy Week.* Forgive me, but I am making my devotions: I began them yesterday by attending the concocting of the holy oils. Now, since it is a balm and even a holy balm, if you like, I shall send you some, Sir, to cure you of various ills, including that of the bowel obstruction. At least I greatly wish it would perform that miracle, but you would need one mustard-seed of faith, something that I have no hope of finding in a heretic de-faithed by Luther.

Oh, please, why are you making so much fuss about the fact that I wrote on the road and when I disembarked here? It was really the right time for replying: I had all the time I needed to write you at least long if not good replies. But on that topic, I thank you a thousand times for your prunes from Tours, a basket of which I have received and which I have been eating while walking about in my room. You will think that too utterly boorish, but that is because you Parisians are sticklers when it comes to all trivialities. So there, you have been scolded in advance for what you might say one day. Go on and scribble—scribble my portrait, so be it. I shall not get any angrier than I was at Tsarskoe Selo. You at least will not say that I am lazy, for I have already scrawled out four manifestos since I've been here. One of them, accompanied by forty-seven points and depriving me of 1.5 million roubles in revenues, will be a landmark in many respects, which it would take tremendously long to tell you about in detail. Another manifesto provides 1.5 million at 1 per cent interest over ten years for the families ruined by the late marquis [Pugachev], etc. All that would be too long to detail for you. I prefer to tell you that Miss Mimi and Mr Thomas are lying there like good friends behind me on my bed. The young lady comes to me from Prince Repnin, who is madly in love with her and who, in order to give her a good home during his embassy, entrusted her to me. You will agree that he is splendidly good at finding positions for people, and our Mimi is living in perfect harmony with the Thomas family, whom everyone has been seeking out ever since their multiplication has made it possible to give them away.

You were mistaken, Sir, in supposing that your letter would not make me laugh, for I burst out laughing several times, and the point regarding Jules and his calendar* had that effect the whole way through. Since you speak of the peace celebrations, listen a bit to what I am going to go ahead and tell you, and do not believe a word of the ridiculous things that the newspapers tell you. A plan had been made that resembled every other celebration: Temple of Janus, Temple of Bacchus, Temple of the Devil and of his Grandmother, and allegories that were unbearable and stupid because they were gigantic and were great exertions of genius in order to lack all common sense. Very angry with all these grand and fine plans and wanting none of them, I had Mr Bazhenov, my architect, called before me one fine morning, and I said to him: 'My friend, 3 versts from the city, there is a meadow: imagine that the meadow is the Black Sea. You can get there from the city by two roads: well, one of the roads will be the Don, the other the Dnieper. At the mouth of the former you shall build a banqueting hall, which you shall call Azov; at the mouth of the other you shall build a theatre, which you shall name Kinburn. You shall use sand to sketch out the Crimean Peninsula, on which you shall place Kerch and Yeni-Kale as ballrooms. To the left of the Don you shall place buffets with wine and meat for the people. Across from Crimea you shall have illuminations representing the joy of the two empires at the return of peace. Beyond the Danube you shall have fireworks, and in the space that is supposed to be the Black Sea you shall place and shall scatter illuminated boats and vessels. You shall adorn the banks of the streams acting as paths with landscapes, windmills, trees, and illuminated houses, and there you shall have a celebration that lacks imagination, but perhaps will be as fine as many others, and much more natural.' Enchanted by the idea, the man seized on it instantly, and so we have the preparations under way for the celebration. I forgot to tell you that to the right of the Don there will be a fairground baptized 'Taganrog'. Tell me, you professional criticizer, do you think that is unclassy? It is true that having the sea on dry land does not exactly show good sense, but forgive us that fault and all the rest becomes quite bearable. The open space and the night will make it all pleasant, I hope, or at least as much so as all those lousy temples to divinities which bore and exasperate me. And in any case I dare anyone to imitate us.

Farewell, Sir, that is enough for today. I do not have a high opinion of Van Loo's drawing* and shall not buy it. I shall await your description of Huber's paintings, and I thank you in advance for it, as for all the signs of devotion that you are so good as to give me. I have received from Ferney, from a supposed 18-year-old boy, the tragedy of Peter the Cruel with notes, in which Nonnotte, Fréron, and their ilk are hung out to dry* as usual and in which many rogues are praised, I think, *pro forma*.

102. *To Grigory Potemkin*

Exasperated by the grand ducal couple's excesses, Catherine may be shifting the blame to her daughter-in-law. Andrei Razumovsky might have been able to influence Paul as his closest friend, but, notorious for his own extravagance and his affair with the grand duchess, he was unlikely to be much help.

[after 21 April 1775]

The grand duke has been to see me and said that he feared that I might have heard something and become very angry. He came himself to tell me that he and the grand duchess are in debt yet again. I told him how unpleasant it was to hear this and that I wanted him to 'cut his cloth to suit his figure' and to desist from wanton expenditure. He told me that her debt arose from this and that—to which I offered the response that she had an allowance (and this is in fact the case) like nobody else in Europe; and that moreover her maintenance went entirely on her dresses and whims. Everything else—her servants, her table, and her carriage—is taken care of for them. And what is more, she was already supplied with a wardrobe and everything else, to last three years. It would be no bad thing to buy and order less of all this rubbish and rags and to put their house in order. He said that the cost of moving between establishments had become high. To which I offered the response that I am the one moving them and that I had paid twice as much for them as for myself. On this point he wished to assure me that they would bear the cost that had passed to me. In short, he requests more than 20,000, and I fear this will not be the end of it, ever. Ask Andrei Razumovsky to get a grip on this profligacy, for it is truly tedious and thankless to pay their debts—and pointless, too. If you were to add this sum to what I had already given—why then, more than 50,000 have gone on them in a year, and they are still in need. As for a thank you and their gratitude—not a penny.

103. *To Friedrich Melchior Grimm*

She continues to treat her dogs as people and introduces the motif of the Chesme Inkstand. The German proverb that she cites—'wisdom comes with time' ('kommt Zeit, kommt Rat')—was one of her favourites and is frequently repeated in the correspondence with Grimm.

> Reply to no. 17 at Kolomenskoe, this 29 April 1775,
> at 7 versts from Moscow

Kolomenskoe is to Tsarskoe Selo what a bad little play might be to a tragedy by Monsieur de La Harpe. You see that I have chosen modestly, for Tsarskoe Selo is not the finest country house in the universe. Tell the truth—no one has ever started a letter with the date.* That custom was born here, in my head, and it is up to you to take it for a stroke of genius. I have not lost hope of having genius, since the doctor, the one who is so famous that—my word—I always forget his name, has become an idol venerated by the economic *nonsense*.* And *nonsense* here means a cult. Do you understand, Sir?

There you have a preamble to a letter to which one might in good conscience say 'bravo', since it promises much gaiety. Yet I do not have a fever, but the fact of the matter is that today is quite blustery: that gives one imagination, or a headache. Try to have the work begun on the famous inkstand during a storm, and you will see that it will become a masterpiece of imagination or even of madness. Just yesterday I gave orders for you to be paid 36,000 *livres tournois*,* which you will be so good as to use to commission the inkstand as you see fit.

But how can I write? Has Tom Anderson not just come and asked to be covered up? He has taken a seat in an armchair across from me. I have my left arm and he his right paw on an open casement, which one might have mistaken for the door to a church if it were not on the third floor. From this casement, Sir Anderson can gaze, first, on the Moscow River, which meanders and forms some twenty bends within sight. He is anxious and is barking; it is because of a boat coming up the river—no, no, it is, besides the boat, some twenty horses who are swimming across the river to go and graze in the green meadows full of flowers which compose the far bank, which extend up to a hillock covered in freshly ploughed fields, and which belong to the three villages there before my eyes. On the left there is a little monastery built of brick and surrounded by a small copse, and then some bends in the river and some country houses that reach all the way to the capital, which can be seen in the distance. The right side offers to Mr Tom's contemplation some hills covered in thick forests, amid which one can see bell towers, stone churches, and also some snow in the hollows of the hills. Mr Anderson is apparently tired of contemplating such a beautiful vista, for there he is curling up in his blanket and going to sleep. If my description has made your eyelids heavy, Sir, you may do the same. If, in order to alleviate your boredom, you are curious to know the current state of the Anderson breed, here it is. It is led by the head of the breed, Sir Tom Anderson, his wife Duchess Anderson, their children, young Duchess Anderson and Mr Anderson. As for Tom Tomson, he has settled in Moscow under the tutelage of Prince Volkonsky, the governor-general of the city. Besides these, whose reputation is well established, there are also four or five young people of infinite promise who are being raised in the best houses of Moscow and Petersburg, such as, for example, those of Prince Orlov, the Naryshkins, and Prince Tiufiakin.* Sir Tom Anderson's second marriage was to Miss Mimi, who has since that time taken the name of Mimi Anderson, but up to now there have been no descendants. Besides these legitimate marriages (for one must tell people's faults as well as their virtues when writing their history), Mr Tom has had several illegitimate liaisons: the grand duchess has several pretty little doggies who have driven him to distraction, but up to now no bastard children have made an appearance, and it seems that there are none. No matter what they say, it is but calumny.

Your idea for a historiographer of the Order of St George is a very good one, but there is still so much to be done that the chapter and commanderies and secretariat probably will come only after the inkstand. Make it so fine that the desire to place it somewhere will speed up the construction; little things have often set great ones in motion. The paintings belonging to Her Imperial Majesty, made by Huber, will be most welcome, but why have you not begun to describe them, even though you have been promising this by every post since I have been here? Listen, Philosopher, without your descriptions I shall perhaps understand nothing at all about your paintings. I beg you at least to send them around the time I return to Petersburg, where those paintings will await me, since I am afraid to have them brought here. Your prunes were eaten during Lent. I am currently reading your *Emilie's Conversations*, and I cannot put them down. As soon as I can part with them, I shall have them translated into Russian.* Not only is the book charming, but it is also of all sorts of use for anyone interested in the education of children. Alas! if, rather than wracking their brains to write nonsense, authors would write only such things, there would be fewer useless things in the world.

There seems to be improvement in the young person's state of health,* but that improvement is mingled with a thousand frailties. Perhaps spring will fix it all, but her health is deteriorating visibly. I shall take *ad notam** what you tell me about the dowager duchess of Saxony-Weimar: wisdom comes with time, as they say at Wetzlar.* Please do not talk to me about my birthday. I have just turned a full 46 years old, and I have heard people talk about the same thing forty-six times in my life, and therefore I have had it all drilled into my head. I do not like that day: you always get another year added on, and there is no common sense in that. Farewell, be well in spite of the bowel obstruction, and rest assured of my gratitude for all the marks of devotion that you give me.

I forgot to tell you that Vicomte Laval-Montmorency was here* and that, although he is perhaps not the greatest genius in the world, he is nonetheless the first Frenchman whose manners I did not find unbearable. I am very pleased with him, and therefore I distinguished him as much as I could, for he is a Montmorency, and it is nice to hear that name. I would like him to be made a marshal of France; I think he understands war just as well as they.

104. *To Friedrich Melchior Grimm*

Narrating the purchase of the estate near Moscow that she named Tsaritsyno, Catherine toys with a profusion of textual forms: commentaries, narrations, descriptions, public proclamations, dialogues, and letters.

Notice

I feel inclined to respond today. Sir, I received your no. 19 just as I was getting into my carriage to come here.

Commentary on the word 'here'.

One fine day, tired of roaming the vales and meadows of Kolomenskoe and bored of the constant choice between either getting her feet wet or clambering like a roebuck, the Imperial Majesty got on the highway that leads from Moscow to Kashira, a city that can be found in the world if not on the map. That highway took her to an enormous pond, which was connected to an even larger pond; but the second pond, with its deliciously varied vistas, did not belong to said Majesty, and rather to a certain Prince Kantemir,* her neighbour. Adjacent to the second pond was a third pond that formed a prodigious number of bays, and so, going from pond to pond, sometimes in the carriage and sometimes on foot, the ramblers found themselves 7 huge versts from Kolomenskoe and began to covet their neighbour's property. He was an old man of seventy years and more, who cared not a bit for the waters, the woods, and the fine vistas that thrilled the ramblers; he spent his life playing cards or fulminating over his losses. Now, prudently and with all possible tact, the whole court, headed by its mistress, set about conniving to get the lay of the land with His Illustrious Highness, to find out whether he was winning or losing, whether he would sell his estate, whether he cared for it, whether he went there often, whether he needed money, who his friends were, who might approach him. We told him, 'Do not just defer to us. We do not want to steal someone else's property. We are willing to buy, but it would not be a crime to refuse us. As you please, Sir, we are a bit covetous, but we can do without it.' My courtiers are all in a flurry. One comes to say: 'He refused me: he is not selling.' Very well, so much the better! Another reports: 'He has no need of money: he is fortunate.' A third: 'He says, "I cannot sell. I have neither heirs nor anyone else: my estate belongs to the Crown, and I leave it to her."' Aha, a fifth one arrives: this one tells us that Kantemir had said, 'In faith, I declare that my estate shall be sold to none but the Crown.' Ah! Prettily said! And now an envoy-extraordinary is dispatched to find out whether he likes the estate. 'Not at all,' says he, 'and to prove it, you see that I reside elsewhere. It came to me from my brother,* and I never go there. It can suit none but the empress.' 'What do you want for it, Sir?', asks the envoy, bowing. '20,000 roubles.' 'Sir, I have been authorized to give you 25,000.' Commentaries are always long! Once the purchasing contract had been closed, something had to be built, and a fortnight later, thanks to our wooden buildings, I have come to take up residence here today. Oof! What a commentary! But 'here' is not the name of my acquisition: I have named it Tsaritsyno Selo. This beautiful place, which everyone agrees is an earthly paradise, was called 'Black Mud', Chernaia Griaz.

Now let us return to that no. 19, which almost made me die of laughter, first of all for its opening about new pens, and then for all the other fine things it contains. For myself, my manservants give me two new pens a day, which I believe I have the right to use up. But when they have been spoilt, I hardly dare to ask for more. Instead I turn them one way and then another as best I can. Another interesting anecdote: I have never yet seen a new pen without smiling at it and without being sorely tempted to use it.

I have already given orders that as soon as the great Huber's paintings arrive in Petersburg, they should be sent right away to Tsarskoe Selo. And another order has been given there that they should be unpacked, framed, and locked up in a room without a living soul seeing them before I arrive. And I shall give you a candid description of the effect that they have on me at first sight, since you seem curious about the occasion. I find that I owe you thanks for the copies of Mr Huber's letters: his is a mind in torment, as Falconet the Difficult would say of that great man. His letters are truly eccentric, or rather are written by an eccentric, and you know we have no aversion to those. Miss Mimi is not on the right path for you to be able to hide behind her during the viewing of the paintings: she is quite seriously indisposed. After the natural history of birds of prey, you should enlist Huber* as historiographer of the Thomas family. In so doing, you would relieve me of a great burden, for you can well see that this task keeps me very busy, and in good conscience I think myself obliged to work at it. I am sorry that Huber does not feel tempted by your proposal that he do a dramatic painting of the Patriarch. I laughed too to see that it was I who was supposed to persuade the latter to let himself be painted. Apparently Huber does not know that Voltaire did not even answer me when I spoke to him about these paintings.

As regards the forty-seven ineptitudes of Miss Cardel's pupil, I would have you know that such trifles were seven years in the making* and were kept in the drawer in anticipation of the moment when they should appear. We also have another trifle containing a few dozen articles in a different style, which are not without merit and which we ourselves accused of being a magnificent work when we reread them.* We are keeping the latter trifle for the autumn, and we shall go about it so imperceptibly that you will have trouble distinguishing from where you are between what is happening and what is not. I advise you to acquire a good telescope: such a thing would be useful, for example, for making out things on the moon. Do keep your terracotta medallion: no one is thinking of taking it from you.

Since Monsieur de Juigné, your agent and that of the King of France, has not yet arrived, I can tell you nothing of your prunes, etc., but I thank you for them in advance. I am very glad of that loyal knight's reputation, but I still have a *scripile:** is he susceptible to prejudices? And the judgments made by all the bad minds who preceded him and by all those who directed them—will they not influence the loyal knight? That is a question. It might produce a conversation like Diderot's with the wife of Marshal *** on piety, and the result would be the same.* As I think I have answered all your jeremiads by bits and bobs in my previous letters, I shall say no more of them herein, but rest assured that your letters give me great pleasure and that I choke with laughter when reading them.

this 30 June 1775

105. *To Johanna Bielke*

This missive speaks volumes about how Catherine recycled and rewrote material. Written on the same day as Letter 104, this letter offers a variation on its legislative theme, as Catherine brags again about her soon-to-be-promulgated Statute for the Administration of the Provinces of the Russian Empire. Catherine concludes by borrowing from a different letter: her account of the peace celebrations written almost two months earlier (Letter 101). In between, she discusses more recent news relevant to Bielke, who lived on the border with Denmark: George III's sister who died on 10 May 1775 (NS) was Queen Caroline Matilda of Denmark. The Siege of Boston began in April 1775, marking the start of the American War of Independence.

Madam, In my opinion, all you have read in the newspapers about things done to relieve the people are nothing but silliness, when compared to the huge creation of which you will hear something said in two or three months. Now that is a piece of work and a magnificent piece of work.

  The King of England is an excellent citizen, a good husband, a good father, a good brother. A man like that never thinks it a stroke of good fortune to lose a worthless sister: I would bet that he was more upset by her loss than by the defeat of his troops in America. You know that those excellent citizens are very bored and that they often there-fore…But no, I shall not finish. I hope with all my heart that my friends, the English, can make it up with their colonies, but so many of my prophecies have come true that I fear I shall see America separate from Europe in my lifetime.

Our peace celebrations will begin ten days from now. I wanted no Temples to Minerva, nor Temples of Janus, nor Temples of the Devil and of his Grandmother. But we shall have the Black Sea and Russia's acquisitions represented on dry land, and, since an engraving is being made of it, I shall send it to you. I dare anyone to imitate it. Farewell, Madam, rest assured of my friendship, and maintain yours for me.

at Moscow, this 30 June 1775

106. *To Friedrich Melchior Grimm*

The much anticipated celebrations of the Treaty of Küçük Kaynarca finally take place.

Reply to no. 20, at Moscow, this 22 July 1775

In the august manner of kings, I forbid you to die either from gratitude-induced suffocation or from the joy that my letters give you, for either one or the other of those deaths would defy common sense, as the late Miss Cardel would say. Besides, those ways of dying are out of fashion. Gratitude is rare, and the joys of this world, according to Mr Wagner, are not worth the trouble. Now, you are well aware that all Paris would disapprove of unfashionable deaths. So may God save you from them, no matter what. Although you have accepted the gift of the holy oil fried in my presence, I am not able to send it to you, for it has begun to stink, with all due respect to it.* General Potemkin had a fine flask of it, which he has recently had thrown in the river because the odour had grown unbearable.

Ah well, shush! I shall not breathe a single little word more about your dear Luther, nor shall I invent words that are on the tip of everyone's pen when they are scribbling, since you so strongly espouse the cause of that fat lout. Platon, the Archbishop of Moscow, made us all dissolve into tears on the day of the peace celebrations. In his sermon, he addressed to Field Marshal Rumiantsev a passage that was so beautiful, so eloquent, so nicely apt, so true, so appropriate, that the field marshal himself and the entire church (which was crammed like an egg) could not hold back their tears, and neither could I, just like the others.* What then is all that racket you are making about the ukases* and the hosts of declarations that I published in the month of March? All that is as old as Herod and almost forgotten: only the effect felt from them is still brand new, and people are amazed by it like a cow by a new gate—a noble simile drawn from your darling's *Table Talk*.* If anyone else comes and asks you, 'So how does she do it? So from where does she draw her resources? Where does she get all that she gives? All that she hands over? All that she lends at 1 per cent, after six years of war?', tell them that if I get angry, I shall do something much worse than that, even without possessing the philosopher's stone. Wait a little while, and you will see fine things that no one expects, and then I shall allow you to harrumph like the proudest mayor in all of Germany.

But, on that note, I have to tell you how I looked after Marshal Rumiantsev on the day of the peace treaty. He received (1) a diploma on which all his victories and conquests and the conclusion of the treaty are laid out in full; then, (2) a commander's baton adorned with diamonds; (3) a superb sword; (4) a hat with a crown of laurels; and, as a plume in it, (5) an olive branch in diamonds and enamel; (6) the order and star of St Andrew in diamonds; (7) 5,000 peasants; (8) 100,000 roubles; (9) a silver service for forty people; (10) a collection of paintings.

If you knew what these peace celebrations are like, you would swoon with pleasure. We had a delectable one yesterday. I say yesterday because, owing to an illness that I came down with the day after the first, all the ruckus was put off until yesterday. But since you were born curious, I must tell you what was wrong with me. Here is an exact account of it. On 11 July, at three in the afternoon, I came down with diarrhoea, which I tried to get rid of with four glasses of Spa water. When I had drunk them, they gave me a fever. I summoned Rogerson, who scolded me and made me take salt three times with Seltzer water; that had no effect until the next morning. On Sunday, dysentery made itself known with a large increase in the fever, so that, seeing that the fever and excessive dysentery had lasted forty-two hours, the doctor took advantage of a moment of respite and had me bled, which put me in the clear but left me very weak. Thus delayed for eight days, the celebrations recommenced yesterday—*ma** what celebrations!

I am sending you the engraving of the setting, but it is impossible to describe for you how beautiful the view was, how many people there were, how delightful the hills on which all those buildings have been placed. In a word, there has never been a finer festival; no accidents have troubled even for a moment our joy and contentment. Everyone agreed it was a truly charming celebration. Tomorrow everything will end with a masquerade and fireworks in the same place. But it is an exceptional place. Imagine it—100,000 people, neither hurried nor harried. Effortlessly each can have his carriage when and where he wants it and come and go as usual. You are neither hot nor cold, and you have everything that might entertain you, if you wish. But in order to understand the engraving, you must know that Kinburn is a theatre, Kerch and Yeni-Kale three large halls, Azov the dining room, and the feasts, fountains, and shows for the people have been set up where the Nogai Tatars have their camp.

Have I not scribbled enough for today? You see that Monsieur Laurent, who was my writing master and who still lived at Stettin as of three years ago, did not get paid for nothing, even if he was a dumb simpleton. Neither Monsieur de Juigné nor the fruit pastilles have yet arrived, and I promise you that the latter will be eaten up just like the prunes.

The young man* quarrelled impertinently with General Potemkin, but the latter gave him such a dressing down that he begged his pardon. The former was so humbled before him that he might have whipped him without offending him. But I confess that I would like to be free of this rascal who has neither wit nor good behaviour. Farewell, be well and rest assured of my continuing esteem and friendship, as well as my gratitude for all the devotion which you are so good as to show me.

107. *To Grigory Potemkin*

As a working couple, Catherine and Potemkin sometimes found that their numerous official duties got in the way. They had dined together the day before, but on the day this letter was written, Potemkin was busy receiving the Church leadership and other dignitaries. Catherine teases Potemkin about hosting Aleksei Longinovich Shcherbachev (d. 1802), the head of the Russian postal service and therefore the supervisor of its coach drivers, but not his beloved empress.

[2 August 1775]

Doll, either you are being aloof or you are angry because I haven't seen a line from you. That's enough, my soul, I shall punish you and give you a kiss—so take that! It seems to me that you have become accustomed to being without me. It's almost a whole twenty-four hours that I haven't seen you, while Shcherbachev and all those other riffraff who are not worth so much as my finger and who don't love you as much—*they* are admitted into your presence, indeed have wiped away all thought of me. Well, all right, I shall become the leader of the coach drivers* at your side, and that way I will obtain access to Your Excellency.

108. *To Friedrich Melchior Grimm*

The big news of the day—the miracle to which Catherine alludes—is Grand Duchess Natalia Alekseevna's pregnancy. Catherine and Grimm jokingly attribute it to Catherine's pilgrimage in May–June 1775 to the most revered Russian Orthodox monastery, the Trinity Lavra of St Sergius, north-east of Moscow.

at Tsaritsyno, this 27 August 1775

I had the honour of receiving this morning your no. 22, written, as you declare, with no pretext. You will agree that I have a pretext for answering you. First of all, to go in order point by point, I must tell you that all the Andersons, large and small, are in fabulous health, as is Miss Mimi. At six o'clock this morning I had the pleasure of seeing them when they were all out for a walk. They were sorely aggrieved for a few moments, for, while I was crossing a reservoir on a raft, they reached the woods and, unable to come to me, they began to whine, to squeal, and even to yowl until I sent the raft back so that they could follow me. Look, there you have another painting that could be a pendant to that of the surroundings at Kolomenskoe, especially if you put behind the Thomas family a steep bank covered in a very large wood, with H. M. and her manservant on the raft crossing the reservoir. In front of her, a lowland with bushes, where you will put a pheasantry. On the right, a large pool of water ending in an embankment, on which there are some very large willows, through which one can discern a still much larger pond. One of its banks is very steep and occupied by several little villages, and the other slopes gently and offers you a view of fields, pastures, clumps of trees, and solitary trees. To the left of the raft there is a muddy stream covered by trees, which rise up like an amphitheatre. Well, imagine all that, and you will be at Tsaritsyno, which is something else entirely from Kolomenskoe, which no one wants to look at any more. Just see what this world is like: not long ago the view at Kolomenskoe was ravishing, and now we prefer this bit of land that was dug up, bought, and built on in a fortnight, and where we have been living for about six weeks, whether you like it or not. Since it was the grand duchess's name day yesterday, we had a comic opera in the woods. Annette and Lubin sang and built their cottage, to the great astonishment of the peasants in the area, who, I believe, had lived until now in perfect ignorance that there was such a thing as comic opera in the world.* No sooner said than done: you wished that my pilgrimage to Trinity Lavra might produce a miracle and that Heaven might do for a young princess what it once did for Sarah and old Elizabeth. Your wish has been fulfilled: the young princess is in her third month, and her health perfectly restored. This event will hasten my return to Petersburg, and I shall go there on the first sleighs.

I believe you will have taken pleasure in Prince Orlov's appearance in Paris,* since you seem to take an interest in the people who come from over here. I have reason to believe that his stay will last until the marriage of Madame Clotilde,* since the whole royal family have expressed their desire for it. He speaks with infinite praise of the welcome and the distinctions he has been given, and I confess that it pleases me. But if he stays until the end of his arguments with Diderot, it will be a long time before he sees his homeland again. I shall tell you no more of the peace celebrations of which you speak, since I got everything off my chest on that subject in my previous letters. But you will be so good, Sir, as to receive my thanks for the interest you took in them. I would have wanted to see your illuminations and the rockets in your hovel. Did you sing alleluia at the top of your lungs or in a whisper? If you see Prince Orlov again in Paris, tell him, I beg you, that the Duke of Braganza has gone to Constantinople to witness Prince Repnin's audiences and his entrance. I have a high opinion of the famous inkstand* that was begun during a storm. Storms and high winds that come in the morning, when one has not yet broken one's fast, are especially conducive to great strokes of imagination; I very much like that you find this idea to be nearly inspired. What do you know? Perhaps one day I shall prophesy during a tempest. If that happens, I shall send you the text so that you can comment on it before anyone else. Farewell.

109. *To Voltaire*

In this draft letter, Catherine responds somewhat sarcastically to Voltaire's letter of 18 October 1775 (NS), which contained a series of apologies for asking Catherine to patronize various French adventurers and preferment-seekers. In previous letters, Voltaire suggested candidates to become Russian vice-consul in Cádiz and consul in Marseilles. In a previous letter, he had sent her a portrait of himself ('writing in front of [Catherine's] portrait') by Pierre-Martin Barat (1736–1787), whom Catherine calls the 'painter from Lyons'.

[November 1775]

Sir, by your letter of 18 October I see that my engraving of the peace celebrations has reached you and that you are pleased with the idea. The darkness of the night and the boats helped to create the illusion of a sea on dry land. In any case, Sir, the celebrations have taken up all our time.

I just gave my empire a set of regulations for the administration of the provinces, which contains 215 printed pages in quarto and which, it is said, is in no way inferior to the *Instruction* for the law code. I prefer this one: it is the product of five months' work all on my own. I have ordered that it be translated, and then I shall send it to you.

I have not received the picture by the painter from Lyons.

Your consuls and vice-consuls could not be hired either because the positions are not vacant, or because they had been promised or given away, or because I have no consuls in those locations.

Please allow me to have a moment's fun at the expense of one of your protégés* who, I believe, was once in the service of the Comte d'Artois and whose name I have forgotten. He recently went to the Turkish ambassador, offering his services and proposing to don the turban. The ambassador had a reply sent that, for those purposes, he need only go to Constantinople, where he would present him to the Porte, but that a peaceable minister does not proselytize. Unfortunately, his bosses learned of the affair, and they took it ill that, while in Russian uniform, he should go and offer his services to another power. They had his uniform confiscated. He went and complained to the Marquis de Juigné, but since the latter did not decide the case in his favour either, he really has no choice but to go follow the Beylerbey of Rumelia* to Constantinople. As for Baron Pellenberg,* they say that he swigs wine no more sparingly than a German cleric does, and, when he has been drinking, he wants everyone to acknowledge him as your nephew. In any case, Sir, rest assured that nothing can change the sentiments that you know me to have for you, as well as the infinite regard that I have for your friendship. Be well and live, if that is possible, as long as your writings will remain in the memory of mankind.

110. *To Grigory Potemkin*

[early 1776]

Despite all the tenderness I have lavished on you, there is not a single respect in which I have made an inch of progress. One cannot oblige anyone to show tenderness; to demand it is unbecoming; and to fake is a sign of cravenness. Be good enough to behave in a way that keeps me pleased with you. You know my character and my heart, you know my good and bad features, you are smart, and I leave it to you to fashion your behaviour in a manner that is appropriate. You torment yourself in vain, you feel anguish in vain. Only reason true and proper will lead you out of this worrying situation. Unless you avoid extremes you will undermine your health for no good reason.

111. *To Grigory Potemkin*

This highly theatrical letter coaches the volatile Potemkin in anger management and asks him not to exacerbate a difficult situation with public displays of jealousy. Playing on the multiple meanings of the French term 'esprit' ('mind', 'soul', 'imagination', 'intelligence', 'judgment'), Catherine explores the connections and contradictions between reason and sensibility, strategy and feeling, self-interest and love.

[February–March 1776]

To hear you speak sometimes, one would think that I am a monster of imperfections, and especially that of being a gross fool. You say that I am monstrously hypocritical. If I am upset, if I weep, you say, it is not because I am sensitive, but for an entirely different reason, and therefore that is all to be disregarded, and I am to be treated condescendingly. That is a truly gentle approach that always wins me over. However, this intelligence of mine, no matter how wicked and nasty it is, knows no other way to love except by making those whom it loves happy. This is why my mind finds it impossible to fall out for a moment with my beloved and not feel despair. It finds it even harder to be continually busy carping at the loved one about this and that all day long—just the opposite since my intelligence is busy identifying the virtues and merits of my beloved. I love the marvellous things I see in you. Come on, tell me: how would you feel if I were to complain to you all the time about the faults of all your acquaintances, of all those you esteem or who work for you most often. What if I were to make you responsible for the silly things that they do? Would your patience hold out? What if, noticing that you were irritated, I were to become enraged, stand up and storm out, slamming the doors behind me, and then later avoid you, not even look at you, and even feign being colder towards you than was actually the case; and what if I were then to add threats to all this? Would all this mean that I was putting on airs? Finally if after all this your head was raging and your blood boiling, it would not be very surprising if the two of us were not in our right mind, did not understand one another, and talked across one another, would it?*

For Christ's sake, find a way to make sure that we never have a row. Our rows are always the result of some irrelevant nonsense. We fight about power, but not about love. Now that is the truth for you. I know what you will say. So do not even bother to utter it. That's right, that way I won't have to answer, since for my part I have of course decided not to get upset. If you wish to make me happy, speak to me about yourself, and I shall never be angry.*

112. *To Grigory Potemkin*

Catherine burned the majority of Potemkin's love letters. This pair of vows survived. Written as declarations and affirmations, they were sent on two different occasions, both probably in February–March 1776. The 'duet' suggests that a new foundation was being laid for a relationship in which Potemkin's influence and position as a statesman at Catherine's court would be unassailable.

[February–March 1776]

In the hand of G. A. Potemkin	*In the hand of Catherine the Great*
My priceless soul,	I know.
You know that I am completely yours,	I know, I understand.
And that you are my one and only.	The truth.
Till death I shall be faithful to you,	Without a doubt.
And your interests are as my own necessities.	I believe it.
Both for this reason,	
And equally because it is my desire,	
Serving you pleases me more than anything,	Long since proven.
As does your readiness to use my abilities.	
Whatever you shall do for me,	Joyously, but what?
Truly you will never regret it and will see	I would be glad to, with all my heart,

In the hand of G. A. Potemkin	*In the hand of Catherine the Great*
The use.	but I am too dull to understand. Say it more clearly!

[February–March 1776]

In the hand of G. A. Potemkin	*In the hand of Catherine the Great*
Permit me, my little dove, to say how I think this clash will end. Do not be surprised that I am perturbed by the matter of our love. Over and above your thousand kindnesses to me you have placed me in your own heart. I wish to be there, alone and more important than all my predecessors for the reason that nobody ever loved you so much; and since I am a creation made by your own hands, I thus wish that you would arrange for my tranquillity, that you would be joyful when doing me good; that you would devise everything to comfort me and in so doing you should find respite from the important labours you perform according to your high calling.	I permit it. The sooner the better.
	Rest easy.
	One hand washes the other. Firmly and strongly.
	As you are now and will be in future. I see and I believe it.
	I would be glad to, with all my heart. The first of all my pleasures. That will happen of itself. Let our thoughts subside, so that our feelings can act freely; they are tender and will seek out the best path for themselves. Here ends our row.
Amen.	Amen.

113. *To Grigory Potemkin*

Catherine and Potemkin's private pact could not curtail the gossip mill or end Potemkin's touchiness. Court watchers concluded that Zavadovsky's rise inevitably spelled the end of Potemkin's influence (in the event, Zavadovsky himself fell from grace rapidly, lasting only a year). In the meantime, Catherine continued the work of reconciling Potemkin to a new reality in which her independent private life co-existed with their partnership as an essential part of her reign.

[May 1776]

You have put a dagger in my heart for an action that was basically praiseworthy by saying that such a deed on my part has diminished the love you bear me. My word! As if your love for me were reliable. There is no reason for you to say such a thing, since I have done nothing at all that could possibly offend you—nor shall I, nor do I have any intention of doing so, despite everything that your lively and sensitive spirit could lead you to imagine with your usual ardour. No matter what you say, I am not worried about you. I know full well that as a rule you make little show of esteem and respect for me in the things you say. But in reality you feel a great deal in your soul and in your heart for me. I repent not one jot having written that letter, but I am acutely distressed by the effect it has had on you, and I foresee that you will punish me suitably by raising this matter over and over again with all manners of curses. As usual, I shall endure this with resignation, courage, and patience. Well, get on with it. There is only one thing that I could not tolerate, and that would be if you were to cease to love me for real.

114. *To Grigory Potemkin*

[May 1776]

Be patient when you read my answer—after all, I am not bored when I read your letters. Here is the reply to your first line: I wish that God may forgive you not only for your vain despair and fury, but for the unfairness as well that you have shown me for reasons that you adduce and that cannot but be pleasing to me. But, if possible, let us please try to forget all unpleasantness. Catherine has never been unfeeling. Even now she is attached to you with all her heart and soul. She never told you otherwise and always tolerates insults and injuries. Read her letter from yesterday, and you will find her as you would like her to be always. I do not understand why you call yourself unloved and nasty and claim that I am gracious to everyone apart from yourself. Forgive me, but those are three lies. Up to now you have always been first in my graces. Nasty and unloved you can hardly be. The word 'loathing' rips out not only your soul but mine as well. I was not born for hate. Hate cannot live in my soul. Never have I ever felt it nor have I had the honour to be acquainted with it.*

I believe that you love me, although all too often in your conversations there is not a trace of love. I believe it because I am discriminating and fair. Indeed, when I see that people are not following common sense I do not judge them by their words in such moments. You thought it good to write in the past tense, think it good to say 'I was, it was'. But my actions every day try to turn us towards the present. Who wants your well-being and calm more than I? Now I hear that you were contented with the past, while at the time it seemed too little to you. But God will forgive you; I am not complaining, I give you the benefit of the doubt and shall say to you something you have not yet heard: that is, that although you have insulted me and vexed me endlessly, nonetheless I cannot in any way hate you. Rather, I think that in the time since I started writing this letter, I have begun to see you again in your right mind and with an accurate memory, and that everything is practically as it used to be. If only you remain firm in this state, and should you remain steadfast then truly, dear friend, my soul, you will not regret it. You know the tenderness of my heart.

115. *To Grigory Potemkin*

At the end of May, Zavadovsky was publicly recognized as Catherine's favourite and awarded a substantial number of serfs, to which further gifts were added on the anniversary of Catherine's coup on 28 June. To ease Potemkin's sense of being slighted by Zavadovsky's rise, Catherine granted him the Anichkov Palace in St Petersburg, with 100,000 roubles for its décor. Potemkin retained a bedroom in the Winter Palace, but Catherine's use of the language of friendship sends a firm message.

[after 7 June 1776]

Listen, my friend, your letter would require lengthy discussions if I wanted to respond to it in detail. I have selected two essential points. The first is Anichkov House. In Moscow the asking price was 400,000 roubles. This is an enormous sum and I have no idea where to find it, but Elagin has only to ask what the price is; perhaps it will turn out to be cheaper. The house is not fit for living in and is on the brink of collapsing; a wall on one entire side has caved in. Maintenance and repair will, I believe, not be insignificant. The second point concerns friendship. Dare I assert that there is not a more faithful friend than myself?

But what does it take to be a friend? It always seemed to me that mutual trust was essential; for my part it was complete. It remains to be seen which way the balance leans, and in whose interest … etc.; but that's enough discussion. I do not propose either to argue or to embitter. I know how to appreciate, and I know the value of things.

116. *To Friedrich Melchior Grimm*

When Grand Duchess Natalia Alekseevna died in childbirth, Catherine swiftly arranged for Paul to travel to Berlin with Prince Henry of Prussia to collect his new bride, Sophia Dorothea of Württemberg, the future Grand Duchess Maria Fedorovna.

Reply to no. 32. Now, if you number them badly, it is not my fault.
at Peterhof, this 29 June 1776

I am very glad that my letter informing you of the sad event, which we must try to forget because it cannot be remedied, reached you just when you were wanting to know how things went. Put your mind at rest as to my health: it is good. When I saw that the vessel had capsized, I lost no time. I righted it, and I immediately put some irons in the fire to repair the damage. And thereby I managed to dispel the profound grief that had overwhelmed us. I began by suggesting travel, comings and goings, and then I said, 'But since the dead are dead, we must think of the living.* Since we thought we would be happy but lost that faith, should we despair of regaining it? Let us move on—in a word, let us look for another.' 'But who?' 'Oh, I have one ready to hand.' 'What, already?' 'Yes, yes, and a real jewel, even.' And wouldn't you know, curiosity gets going: 'Who is it? And what is she like? Is she a brunette or a blonde, little or tall?' 'Sweet, pretty, charming, a jewel.' A jewel. A jewel is gratifying. It makes us smile. One thing leads to another, and we call on a certain third party, someone so nimble that he leaves people swearing behind him, and who recently arrived, just in time to console and distract. There he is, set up as an intermediary and negotiator. A courier dispatched, a courier returned, a journey arranged, an interview afforded, and all that with unheard-of speed. Now the lumps in throats are beginning to loosen. They are sad, but busy with the need to arrange a trip that is indispensable for health and for taking minds off things. Give us a portrait in the meantime; a portrait is quite innocent. Not many are liked: a painting has no impact. The first courier brings one. What good is that? It might make a disagreeable impression. Well, then, it is better to leave it in the box. There it lies, all wrapped up, right where it was put on its arrival, on my table next to my inkstand. But is it pretty? That depends on your tastes, but, for myself, I find it quite suits mine. At last it was looked at and immediately put in a pocket and then looked at again. And at last he attended to and hastened the travel arrangements, and there they are on their way. And you will receive this letter already having witnessed the rest: *basta*.*

I think I have written to you several times since the month of April, but I do not know exactly how many times. I guess, then, that my letters will have reached you somewhere on the road and that they will have told you that I was doing well, once I had rested from the extreme fatigue I endured during the five most awful days and nights a human has ever endured. Come on, get yourself well and properly on the road. The path will be well trodden: you will find not a single bramble or thorn between Berlin and Petersburg. If you get there on 24 July NS, you will not be expecting the sight God has destined for you.* How few long faces there will be! I still think that you are destined by Providence to be a regular at weddings. Come no matter what, I shall give you balls and celebrations. In faith, philosophy shall leap and bound, or else it will have some explaining to do. Before I even knew it, ever since 1767 I have always felt an overwhelming inclination for this young lady. Reason, which, as you know, leads instinct astray, made me prefer the first because the excessive youth of the second prohibited this arrangement at the time. And look, at the very moment when I might have lost her forever, a most unfortunate event brings me back to my overwhelming inclination. What is all this? You will go on and reason in your manner: you will chalk it up to chance. Not at all—I am an enthusiast, I am. I cannot be satisfied with that explanation—I need something vaster.

Sir Tom greets you. He puts no obstacles in the way of your journey. On that note, I must tell you that your big, foolish, lanky fellow has gone off to herd geese on a pension of 10,000 roubles, but on the condition that I neither see nor hear of him again. Riedesel gave him the good news.* I do not really know why he came here.

What will you go and do in Stettin? You will not find anyone alive, except perhaps Monsieur Laurent alone, a decrepit old man who was but a simpleton when he was young.* But if you cannot lose the itch, I would have you know that I was born in Greifenheim's house on St Mary's Square; that I lived and was raised in the wing of the castle that is on the left when you enter the castle's large courtyard; and that I occupied three vaulted chambers on the top floor, next to the church which formed the corner. The bell tower was adjacent to my bedroom, and that is where Miss Cardel indoctrinated me and where Mr Wagner taught me his tests.* That is also where, two or three times a day, I bounded all the way along the corridor to go and see my mother, who occupied the other end. But I do not see anything very interesting in all that, unless you think that the location is a good one or that it has an influence on making decent empresses. In that case, you should suggest to the King of Prussia that he set up a nursery for growing that sort of thing, and whoever likes may boldly take possession of them. Farewell, be well.

117. *To Gustav III of Sweden*

When Gustav III finally visited St Petersburg in June 1777, Catherine duly entertained her cousin, although their friendship was far from heartfelt on her side. Here she takes the opportunity of Gustav's departure to arrange for her current favourite, Semën Zorich, to be decorated with the Swedish Orders of the Sword and Seraphim.

My dear Brother and Cousin, I cannot see Your Majesty depart without professing the deep regret with which I am left upon your departure. I beg you to be persuaded that I shall recall as a most pleasant memory the short time that you were so kind as to spend in my realms and all the marks of friendship that you were pleased to give me. All that concerns you will always be of infinite interest to me. It occurred to me that your precious health might run a certain risk at sea in the current cold and damp weather. To ward it off as best I can, I have charged my aide-de-camp, Colonel Zorich, with the task of bearing to Your Majesty a black fox fur, the finest that our land can provide. At the same time, he will have the honour of returning to you the insignia of the Order of the Sword, with which Your Majesty entrusted me so that I might decorate whomever I would.

My dear Brother, I cannot in good conscience invest anyone with them, as I do not know the statutes of that military order. I shall be so bold as to beseech you yourself to be so good as to invest with them such of my subjects as you deem worthy, and to rest assured that it is with the highest regard and the most particular esteem and friendship that I am,

My dear Brother and Cousin,

Your Majesty's good Sister, Cousin, and Neighbour,

Caterine
at Peterhof, this 5 July 1777

118. *To Friedrich Melchior Grimm*

Upon his departure from St Petersburg in July 1777, Grimm visited Gustav III in Stockholm, before travelling on to Stettin and Berlin. His correspondence with Catherine resumed in livelier style than ever. Catherine keeps Grimm up to date on the court jokes concerning the escapades of her black servant, Azor (see his 'fête' described in Letter 122).

at Tsarskoe Selo, this 24 August 1777

This morning your no. 3, dated from Stockholm on 19 August, was delivered. I received it just as I had finished thinking up a little operation, very easy and not complicated at all, which should fill the bank's coffers with 20 million roubles and not withdraw a single penny from circulation. Now, you should know that I got up with a terrible headache and that the wind was very high. Thus, after this terrible birth, my head felt completely relieved. So I had been ill with constipation of the imagination.

But what good is it to tell you that? You will say that it is a tour de force, or that it is a boast. That is up to you, but I shall keep going as I am, and my operation will be a good one. After that, my most dear brother, friend, and neighbour Abdülhamid can be as bad-tempered as he likes. For myself, I am quite at ease, and I shall answer your documents right away because I have a smidgen of a suspicion that you share Lord Azor's temper: you want to be answered right away. But about Azor, I think you know that he wrote to his mother, who is in Guadeloupe. His letter was sent there, and yesterday he received the reply. His mother said that whites assume that blacks are scarcely more than beasts. Azor wants to answer her that, in Russia, blacks can attain the highest ranks and that there are some who are generals, and he is accompanying his letter with his strong-box, which you know about, I think. Besides that, he wants his mother and his sister Pauline to come and join him. I am sick with fear that he means to make them ladies-in-waiting at court, but he is somewhat mortified by the fact that in the letter it is said that they are in the service of a poor woman, whereas he had begun to tell everyone that he was an African gentleman.

Do you know the news of the day? While you have been amusing yourself with critiquing the addresses on my letters, which end with *God Knows Where*,* Euler has predicted the end of the world for the month of July next year. Expressly for that purpose, he is bringing over two comets, which will do something or other to Saturn, which in turn will come to destroy us. Now, the grand duchess has told me to believe none of it, since the prophecies of the Gospel and the Apocalypse have not yet been fulfilled, and namely the Antichrist has not come yet, nor have all beliefs been united. For myself, I answer all this as would the Barber of Seville. I tell one, 'God bless you', and the other, 'Go to bed',* and keep going as I am. What do you think of it? We must let the world chatter, and we must let especially the cities of Moscow and Petersburg gawk and reason left and right like the political tinkers* and search for hidden reasons why I came here from Peterhof. In fact, it takes just a bit of good sense to see that it would have been foolish to bring a few thousand people to a big garden 40 versts from the city when it is raining. What for? In order to send them back, soaking wet, another 40 versts from Oranienbaum to the city. Be cheerful, I preach it to you once again, and stay cheerful. Believe me, there is nothing better than that. Paisiello's opera will not take place until the month of September.* In the meantime, he goes for walks here, and they say that he is mad about my garden, which grows more beautiful by the day. A path is being made to the Grand Caprice, which looks superb to me, but *up to now* it is only so in *my imagination*, for the trees have not been planted there yet, and there are only two rows of grass.

Prince Belosel'sky has told me about all your feats of prowess and those of the King of Sweden.* I am very glad that the circumstances, conjunctures, conjectures, etc., were not forgotten, but when you mention that multitude, never forget that the staircase in the theatre is too narrow, for I have noticed that good minds are always most struck by that.

Nothing but follies in these four and a half pages! About follies, the Duchess of Kingston has come here on her own yacht under the French flag. That is what makes a good mind. Wit is not what she is lacking, by God. She finds me most amiable, but since she is a bit deaf, and I cannot raise my voice very loud, she will hardly benefit from it.

Just look at this imperceptible chain of ideas. And look at that: a fancy has taken me to talk to you about the dowager Queen of Sweden. Well, well, how did you end up at dinner at Svartsjö?* Belosel'sky told me what I already knew about the so-called reigning queen.* Since I am talking about queens, I have to tell you that if the one in Portugal* were to act logically, she would have the Marquis of Pombal's head cut off. Take the time to read the speech by the procurator general of Portugal on the day of the queen's proclamation, and you will see whether I am wrong. Ay, ay, ay! I am sorry for the queen, my sister: the whole multitude of my brothers and sisters concerns me, and I want them all to have enough intelligence, reason, and glory for four.

Remember what Piron said.* Why, pray tell, do you pretend like this to be mortified by the caresses you receive from my family of brothers and sisters? And why these professions of humility that reek of Luther the Hypocrite? Lift up your head: I shall set tests* for you, and you will see that the family is not wrong to give you its best treatment. That is how I see the matter. You will say this reeks of the august manner of kings, but I would myself assert that this is the most reasonable sentence in this entire gigantic document. May Heaven bless your journey, but what in the Devil's name are you going to do in Stettin? Crusades are no longer in fashion. Farewell, be well.

Do you see precision and depth, magnanimity, noble pride, and sublime goodness in this letter too? Should you say yes, I shall say that your imagination is playing up. Good evening.

119. *To Gustav III of Sweden*

Catherine agrees to Gustav's proposal of a purportedly clandestine correspondence. 'Counts Chef and Pa' are the chief ministers respectively of Sweden and Russia, Ulrik Scheffer and Nikita Panin. Catherine pretends that the ministers will punish their sovereigns when they discover the exchange, or at least that they will lecture their masters on the diplomatic dangers of such a correspondence.

at Tsarskoe Selo, this 7/18 September 1777

I owe many thanks to Mr Eck's new correspondent for being so good as to remember me and to profess friendship for me. I fear only one thing in this lovely little correspondence arrangement that you have dreamt up (I say 'you' because you have renounced all ceremonial): it is that when Counts Chef and Pa become aware of it, they will arm themselves with a fistful of rods and will whip us. Or at least they will talk to us so much about circumstances, conjunctures, and conjectures that one of us will swoon with boredom. But enough musings: I am as touched as can be by the sentiments that you are pleased to reiterate to me. Rest assured of my gratitude.

It gives me joy to hear from all sides that you are pleased with your voyage. May the angel Gabriel have you in his holy and worthy keeping. Farewell.

I would bet that it was Grimm who made your mouth water at the thought of using Mr Eck as an intermediary. It seems to me that we are quite tempted by the extraordinary, you and I. I think this may be the first time that two crowned heads have written to one another furtively. I laughed until my sides ached when I received your letter, and you see how I have responded. Farewell once more. I kiss you cordially, like a good relation.

120. *To Gustav III of Sweden*

Mock horror about clandestine letters aside, Catherine mentions for the first time an important episode that will later recur. At a masked ball at Peterhof to celebrate the Feast of Sts Peter and Paul (29 June 1777), Grimm, Gustav, and Catherine joked that the real aim of the French Encyclopédistes was to overthrow the monarchical system. Although during the French Revolution this episode assumed a more sinister aspect, at the time Gustav and Catherine did not feel threatened by the French writers, and their joke served to exhibit their sense of pride at participating in the sophisticated intellectual culture of their day.

at St Petersburg, this 12 October 1777

The Lord of Drottningholm's* letter of 21 September/2 October fully convinced me that he runs no risk in continuing this fine correspondence. The formidable words inscribed in that letter, 'I fear not the rod', have become for me articles of faith that keep my mouth shut. The same cannot be said of the phrases that follow, with which I am not at all happy, even though they appear to be a continuation of what went before: 'We are two liberated schoolchildren, whose mentors will have a good deal of difficulty in admonishing them, especially if we get up to mischief together.' Why those 'we's? In no way do I approve of those 'we's, nor of that 'especially'; the 'together' could also shock the ears of prudes and gossips when this correspondence is printed. For that matter the decidedly mutinous tone that dominates it cannot possibly square with the deportment that I learned from my late governess* and reminds me that all the risks of a correspondence in which mischief is spoken of could very well fall on me. However, since one must speak the truth, I shall admit to you that the part that pleases me infinitely is the friendship that you profess for me and that every phrase of your letter reprises.

I have another predicament on my hands when writing to you like this. You see, I cannot call you 'Sir', and 'you' is not always terribly polite, so you might be shocked by it in spite of yourself (both your ears being accustomed to the most refined expressions of honour and to titles and blandishments invented to flatter them).

Look, here we have a ready-made happy medium. Listen, dearest Brother, you have a frighteningly good memory: you remember even the malicious words spoken about the *Encyclopédistes* by the masked figures on the stairs at Peterhof. And then there are the 'circumstances and the conjunctures',* etc., and the notorious 'it will come',* which you have used this time a bit peculiarly, but I forgive you because I know from experience that so many different things are said about the likes of us. As a result, the likes of us find it very difficult to estimate our own worth accurately. By the way, if this seems arcane to you, I shall exclaim with Shah Baham (glorious be his memory): 'I understand myself quite well'. I hope with all my heart that your injured thumb has healed and that you can once again sign four hundred boring documents a day as joyously as can be. Doubt not the friendship with which I return your Russian salutation on your right cheek.

121. *To Friedrich Melchior Grimm*

The birth of Catherine's first grandson, Alexander, ensured the succession and gave her a new generation on whom to focus her hopes and attentions in place of her own disappointing son. The choice of the name Alexander was a significant one: it evoked not only St Alexander Nevsky, but also Alexander the Great, the conqueror of Asia Minor. The latter eponym represented Russia's imperial ambitions, particularly the Greek project aiming to liberate Orthodox Greece and overthrow the Ottoman Empire.

at St Petersburg, this 14 December 1777

Do you know Mr Alexander? Do you often go to Versailles? Do you or do you not know the assistants to Mr Alexander's assistants? At least those of the Mr Alexander who is talked about so much in *The Ingénu*.* But I bet you do not know Mr Alexander at all—at least not the one I am going to go ahead and tell you about. He is not at all Alexander the Great, but rather a very little Alexander who was just born on the 12th of this month at ten and three quarters hours in the morning. All that is to say that the grand duchess has just given birth to a son who, in honour of St Alexander Nevsky, was given the pompous name of Alexandre and whom I call Mr Alexander because, if he takes it upon himself to live, without fail in time his assistants will have assistants. Just look what the farsighted prophecies and the gossiping of grandmothers are like. Is that not proof of astounding and outstanding perspicacity? But, my God, what will come of the young man?* I take comfort in Bayle and in Tristram Shandy's father, who was of the opinion that the name had an influence on the thing.* Zounds, this is an illustrious one: there have been matadors* who bore it—let us hope all the aces have not been used up in that pack. Do you think family examples make a difference, or what? Sometimes there is an embarrassment of riches. According to the Gospel of the venerable Pastor Wagner, examples do nothing; nature does everything. But where can one find that? Is nature really the secret of good constitutions? We seem to have one of those, as long as the body mass does not consume volatile spirits: the flesh and bones can drive the mind off course.* I shall send it all to the dowager Queen of Sweden,* who will make better sense of it than I. Too bad fairies are out of fashion: they used to endow children for you with everything you wanted. Myself, I would have given them fine presents and would have whispered in their ears: 'My ladies, some nature, a smidgen of nature, and experience will more or less do the rest.' Farewell. Be well.

I received your postscript about the fine things that Thiers is bringing me, but he has not yet arrived. Are you pleased with the eulogy of Madame Geoffrin?* I find it well said, but nothing sticks in the mind. I know quite well what is lacking: that author is not my author. Our minds do not match. God knows that all young people want more than they can do, and I like heads that work of their own accord, without effort and without getting all wound up.* When one gets old, I think one gets too demanding, and that is what has happened to me.

122. *To Friedrich Melchior Grimm*

Catherine employed Azor, her black servant, to organize a fête as part of the extended celebrations of the birth of her first grandson and the second in line for the throne, the future Alexander I. The name Azor comes from the popular comic opera 'Zémire and Azor' (1771), with music by André Grétry and libretto by Jean-François Marmontel; a version of 'Beauty and the Beast', the opera recounts how the Persian Prince Azor frees himself from a fairy's enchantment and becomes an ideal ruler by earning the love of a virtuous and self-sacrificing young girl, Zémire. The setting of the fête echoes Azor's enchanted and opulently furnished palace; sudden scene changes and resplendent wall inscriptions also draw on the play's décor. To supplement her description, Catherine provided Grimm with a copy of the printed manifesto distributed by her servant Azor in the theatre, and she copied out in her own hand the instructional 'notice' that her guests found on the diamond-bedecked gambling tables.

this 14 February 1778

Mister Whipping-Boy, I must write to you because I have a headache.
Do not expect a great deal of imagination on this day, or numerous
words tumbling over one another, like the water from a broken dyke.
No, indeed, it will be just a simple account of Lord Azor's fête. And so,
by way of introduction, I must have you recall how I told you that we
were up to our ears in fêtes and masquerades and that we were trund-
ling through the city from house to house, like a rat in an attic. Now
a poor little day of rest comes along, Tuesday, 13 February, on which
everyone, dazed with music and overwhelmed by dancing and fatigue,
thought they could each have a respite in their own rooms. Would you
believe it, but the Devil, that enemy of repose, came and meddled.
What did he do? He inspired the African lord gentleman to choose
a day at the opera when the boxes were almost empty and the stalls
fairly sparse. This lord came decked out in his national costume and
presented thirty or so of the most esteemed individuals with the
attached manifesto. This lovely writ, in which no one understood
a thing, set all minds in motion: 'What is this? What will come of it?
I can guess … I can't guess.' Everyone imagined, everyone wracked
their brains, and everyone laughed. 'In the meantime, I wish you
a pleasant time preparing for the fête,' said Azor. Halfway through the
opera, according to the African lord's desire, all the guests went to the
designated location and were obliged to climb a small and quite narrow
spiral staircase—not exactly to the attic, however, but rather to a certain mezzanine where all was redolent with Asian ambrosia. There,
three large velvet-carpeted tables were set up for macao.* On each there
had been placed a little box and a little gold spoon (I am going into
detail for the benefit of those who will want to emulate Lord Azor),
accompanied by the attached notice. The company hastened to fulfil
their host's intentions. 'Nothing could be livelier than these games',
said the men. 'Nothing more entertaining', said the women, 'it is pretty
to play for diamonds. It is like in the *Thousand and One Nights*: gold and
jewels roll.' Everyone was mighty witty. The pea soups* said that the
novelty of it all could not be more entertaining; others said nothing but
played a nine.* In the end, this lovely game lasted an hour and a half
until supper, and the boxes were not yet empty. It was decided to share
out what remained, after which everyone descended the staircase by
which they had ascended. It led to an apartment all of mirrors: walls,
ceiling, everywhere covered in them. Opposite the staircase there was
a large casement window, the curtains of which opened suddenly to

reveal a large 'A',* a yard in height and a hand in width, made of the largest crown diamonds. Under that immense 'A' stood about twenty pages dressed in gold hessian with blue satin sashes. They were there to serve at table, and they fit well in the window beneath the 'A' of diamonds. The tables were placed along the walls to the right and left and were pushed up against the mirrors, so that the guests were sitting across from the mirrors. But how can I describe for you the centrepiece placed in front of the mirrors? All the treasures from the four cupboards you know about were there, covering the most beautiful pieces from the Breteuil dessert service.* The design and all the arrangements were literally a marvel. I ordered that a sketch be made for an engraving. I shall send it to you. On entering the room, literally everyone was dazzled by the beauty and richness of the spectacle, and more than half an hour went by before we managed to get the guests settled and seated at the tables. The enthusiasm lasted the whole supper, after which it was necessary to go back upstairs for a few moments.

I forgot to tell you that when we entered, we passed through the room, which was completely empty: it was entirely arranged for supper while we were playing the game with diamonds. Another omission: across from the large 'A' in the casement, there was in a niche another large 'A' in the same shape made of pearls. Farewell. That is enough for today.

Manifesto

Francisque Azor has had the honour of demonstrating more than once, in the presence of witnesses, that he is an African gentleman. He does not know whether it is out of envy or otherwise that many have cast doubt upon the above-stated fact that he has enunciated. But that is not the matter in question today: he has finally resolved to declare before the public that he is the representative of his homeland, the home of gold, silver, gemstones, and monsters—in a word, of the large part of the terrestrial globe called Africa. He will do more: he offers to prove this fact to anyone to whom he gives the present writ, in person or by proxy, as long as they are so kind as to make their way, when leaving the theatre on this Tuesday, 13 February 1778, into the empress's apartments, this writ in hand. Enlightened people will agree that, as the lord representative, he could not choose a better moment to make his declaration, since the earth, the heavens, the waves, and beings of all natures have been set in motion at every possible moment, one after the other, over the past few days, in order to render this a brilliant time. He concludes by wishing that, after the game and supper, sweet sleep might come over his guests' tired eyes.

Notice

The lord representative has laid out on each table a box full of diamonds, not for sale, but so that during the game of macao, he might pay for each nine with a one-carat stone.

123. *To Friedrich Melchior Grimm*

In February 1778, the 'Patriarch' Voltaire made a triumphal entry into Paris after an absence from the capital of over twenty-five years. Catherine promised Grimm a recommendation letter that he could carry to the Patriarch, but Voltaire never received it, since he died on 30 May 1778 (NS).

at St Petersburg, this 2, 3, and 4 March 1778, at various moments

Come, come, Baron,* I must speak with you. The wind is high today, and here are two of your letters, nos. 14 and 15, asking for a reply. It is true that there are two from the King of Prussia, three from the King of Sweden, two from Voltaire, three times as many from God knows whom, all older and delivered before yours. They do not entertain me because I have to write letters in reply, whereas with you I chat and never write (make a note of that, for it is new). I prefer to be entertained and let my hand, my pen, and my mind go wherever they would like to go.* Come along! Go on and bombard me, bombard me with letters—you would do well, for it entertains me. I read and reread your documents, and I say, 'How he understands me! Oh heavens! He is the only one who understands me well.' If I ever proclaim a day of prayer, it will be to call upon Heaven to give the understanding of a Master Baron to those who fail to understand me. I shall add a litany specially in order to obtain for several others your talent of elaborating. After everything I have laid out above, go on and produce jeremiads like the ones contained in your no. 14, about the purported possibility that I should not find a quarter of an hour to produce epistles for you.

As for Mr Alexander, he is not talked of any more at all. It is quite as though he were not here: not a whit of worry since he came into the world. May God bless his mind as well as his body: he is a prince who is in good health—and that's that. You tell me that he has the choice of imitating either the hero or the saint of the same name.* It seems you are unaware that the saint was a man of heroic qualities: he possessed courage, steadfastness, and acumen, which raised him above his contemporaries who were appanage princes like him. He made the Tatars respect him; the Republic of Novgorod submitted to him out of respect for his virtues; he whipped the Swedes thoroughly; and the title of grand duke was bestowed on him owing to his reputation. Well then, I am of the opinion that Mr Alexander is not free to choose, but rather he need only follow his nose in choosing one or the other; and in any case, he cannot fail to be a handsome boy. There is but one thing that I fear for him: I shall tell you one day in person—a word to those with good noses. Your fairies' reasoning flatters me too much for me to answer them. My heart tells me that not my first grandson, but rather the second will resemble me (and if that comes true, I shall write his life and deeds in advance). He will have nothing in common with my good brother or share his days of fasting and penitence.* But what are you thinking when you believe that he wants to imbue people with audacity? He is on the right course to be taken down a peg or two. He is a good citizen,* and that's that. You know my profound veneration for that word: as soon as it has been uttered, one must fall silent. As for Franklin, he was bound to turn out this way,* since nature deprived his master of the ability to sniff out a friend who might have been dear to his heart. Now that's surprising, isn't it? This is proof of what was said before. But, for God's sake, advise the 80-year-old elder* to stay put in Paris—whatever would he do here? He would catch his death of cold, or die from old age or an accident here or on the road.* His visit would be as bad as the one by the K. of S.* Remember what a good scare that gave me? You can, among other reasons, make it clear to him that Kate looks good only from afar.* I laughed a lot at that Kate.

But on that note, in Holland a medal has been struck on which the Queen Emp. and the Emp. of Russia are in a carriage together, with the K. of Prussia* on the coachman's box. They are asked where they are going, and they answer, 'Wherever it pleases the coachman to take us.' I found that very funny; it lacks only truth or the music for a French comic opera. The first would give it some sting; the second would make it an utter platitude. Since Dorat's punchlines are like the aforementioned music, I shall place his works next to those of Monsieur de La Harpe in the corner from which I never take any books. Leave Dona

Maria* and her armful of relics where she is: we shall have to talk as much about one as about the other, but what will happen to my Duke of Braganza? Tell me that one day.

The twelfth and final page of your no. 14 is pure chatter, and I shall not answer it. There are certain points on which, once you start, you can never stop. In informing you of it, I am rendering you a friendly service.

Regarding the death of the man who sharpened your pens and the mourning clothes that you might don for him, it has occurred to me that I might talk to you about the national costume that my good brother and neighbour is going to introduce, and which, I am told, is made up half-breeches and a half-mantle, black and bright red.* I think it will be pretty, that sort of prettiness that you say some people dispute.* But, my God, why are you always so busy speculating about my doings and dealings?* The Sèvres service that I have ordered is for the universe's leading nail-biter, for my dear and beloved Prince Potemkin, and I said the service was for me so the work would be finer. I advise you to work at composing funeral orations: the sublimity of the one you wrote me for Lekain gave me the idea. I am sending you a missive for the Lord Patriarch, with which I hope you will be able to appear before him in complete safety. But do not show him any of my letters: our style is good for none but ourselves and the postal clerks, who are nonetheless often a bit caught out, since they understand nothing or understand things differently from how we do.

My Lord Chatham is a brawler.* Be on your guard, just as I am with regard to my *marabouts* who are mustering an infinite army of true believers.* For myself, I would like them all to appear on the same day, at the same hour, on the same field, in accordance with the summons that the Supreme Caliph Abdülhamid, my most dear brother, has sent them. As for Germany's indigestion, to put an end to it, we shall require some time and some shufflers,* all speaking through their noses, repeating and digesting every word and syllable and above all signing less quickly than the most high and most powerful Lord Charles Theodore.* But what say you of *that one there*? Until now it had been thought that when two people were happy to have ended their quarrels, others had no business meddling. Now one might sing the song: 'My good man, you are not the master of the house when we are here.'* Good day and good evening. You will need the patience of God's chosen people during the Babylonian captivity in order to read these eight pages of chattering.

this 24 March

The missive for Master Patriarch delayed this one until today: here it is.

But if only you knew what a big sixteen-year test we have undertaken! Yes, you can well say it: this is a test which not many people would think of and not everyone can do, for lack of materials or other sources. Our results are so impressive that retelling them might get boring. Bide your time, and you will soon hear something of it. This is but a prelude, which we call a test; it is a little bitty example of acting and refraining, of saying, writing, and being silent; it is snuff to be taken by a good nose.*

124. *To Gustav III of Sweden*

After almost twelve years of a childless marriage, Gustav's wife, Sophia Magdalena, was finally pregnant. But, fomented by Gustav's own mother, Louisa Ulrika, rumours were circulating that the child was not Gustav's. Informed of the situation by Gustav, Catherine is reminded of her own predicament as grand duchess, when after nine years of childlessness she was encouraged by Empress Elizabeth to take a lover and produce an heir. In her memoirs, Catherine left much room for doubt as to whether her heir Paul's biological father was Peter III or the selected lover, Sergei Vasil'evich Saltykov (b. 1726).

From Prince Potemkin's estate called
Osinovyia roshchi or Eschenbaum*
at 23 versts from Petersburg
in the direction of Finland and therefore
closer to you
this 29 May 1778

I received, dearest Brother, your three letters of 8, 22, and 25 May one after the other. In your distress at the lateness of my letters I discern signs of the friendship that you profess for me on every occasion and that it is a pleasure to reciprocate with my own.

Prince Menshikov was most fortunate to have managed to gain your approval. He conveyed, dearest Brother, what you bade him say. In the first place, I am delighted that my wishes have been granted and that finally you will have heirs. Rest assured that, as a good relative and friend, I share in your joy. I would have wished it without bitterness, and especially that no one had brought up what, it seems to me, needs no bringing up. But, as you say, dearest Brother, who in this world has not endured calumny? No one has more cause to disdain it than I. I complained of it once, and I was told to console myself by reading the article 'Schomberg' in Bayle's *Dictionary* in order to see just how far it can go.*

Since I am not very thoroughly acquainted with the place, it seems to me that the only advice I could have given you in reply to your request, dearest Brother, would have been: do not take the matter so much to heart, avoid publicity, and let it all slip quite naturally into complete oblivion. I shall certainly not be the one to disclose or to misuse what you confide in me under the seal of friendship. I know the full worth of your trust in me: I would repay you poorly for it if I did not provide the good offices that you ask of me in relation to your uncle the king, if the opportunity arises.* Rest assured, dearest Brother, that nothing could give me greater satisfaction than to be able to contribute to your well-being and happiness.

I pity Count Hamilton* for having such a clumsy dentist.

I had forgotten to tell you that Prince Menshikov showed me your new outfit: I think it grows quite easy on the eyes.*

I see with pleasure, dearest Brother, that Prince Iusupov has merited your attention. He is a Tatar peppered with Greek and Latin and who has solid and commendable qualities.

In a few days it will have been a year since I had the satisfaction of making your acquaintance. I beg you to remember it with the same interest and friendship with which I am invariably.*

125. *To Friedrich Melchior Grimm*

Despite the frustrating diplomatic situation, Catherine's peace-time domestic and cultural life was bustling. She also still had time to speculate about future grandchildren and to play with her pets.

at Peterhof, this 8 June 1778

I had scarcely had time to answer your no. 17, when, lo and behold, here comes an enormous document named no. 18. When I saw that, I said, 'My Lady Document, it will be enough just to read you today; the reply will come later.' But, tell me please, what is the big deal about that 2 May, that 21 April, Old Style, New Style? It is all one. And, moreover, the day of my birth was so long ago that all those who were present are dead and buried—my wet nurse died last year. I was as afraid of her as I am of fire and of visits from kings and renowned personages: when-

ever she saw me, she grabbed hold of my head and kissed and re-kissed
me to the point of stifling me. With all that she stank of smoking
tobacco, which her honourable husband employed amply. (But wait
a moment, now I am being prevented from writing.) I am taking up my
pen again. Let us babble a bit. Since we were talking about wet nurses,
do you know why I am afraid of visits from kings? It is because they are
ordinarily boring, insipid characters, and you have to hold your body
straight and rigid. Famous personages, too, keep my nature in check.
Around them I want to be witty enough for four. Sometimes I find that
being witty enough for four consists of listening, and since I like to
chat, being silent bores me. Look, *that* is the spitting image of her! I bet
that you will go into ecstasies over this babbling page, since I have
noticed that you like precisely those of my letters of which I think nothing and of which Miss Cardel would say that they lack all common
sense. But I wish to babble today. You say to me: '*What goodness!*' Reply:
'That may be so.' A dialogue between a German baron and myself. The
Germ. baron: 'What a mixture of greatness, sentiment, and character,
of gaiety and of that goodness, etc.' Me: 'Greatness! Remember who
I am. Sentiments! I am a woman. Character! Zounds, this world has
made sure to build me a bit of that. Gaiety! That is my strong point.
That goodness! Goodness of heart always creeps in everywhere.
Badness of heart also makes itself felt everywhere. I have never seen
a written page without being able to say whether its author has a good
or a bad heart. Any candidate for a bishopric who preaches before me is
chosen not according to his eloquence or his erudition, but according
to how much goodness of heart we have discovered in his narration. He
can do what he likes, but it cannot escape us, for it would always sneak
in, insensibly and willy-nilly, everywhere high and low. Thus we have
a collection of bishops the likes of which can rarely be found anywhere
else. And we have to select them from a state which is contrary to
nature: the state of a monk. But St Alexander Nevsky became one too,
and St Alexander Nevsky had heroic virtues that will one day make me
write a panegyric of him because I have never yet been satisfied with
the one I have heard delivered on his feast day. I shall have my panegyric
recited when Mr Alexander is of an age to take part without it being
a panegyric of him. I care not whether he has any sisters, but he needs
a younger brother, and I shall write that one's history. I am assuming,
of course, that he will have the acumen of Caesar and the capacities of
Alexander, for if he is a poor sire, I shall exclaim: 'Give me a third, etc.'
The girls will all be most unhappily married, for there is nothing
unhappier and more unbearable than a pr. of R.* They will not be able

to adapt to anything: everything will look shabby to them. They will be acerbic, bad-tempered, critical, beautiful, thoughtless, and superior to prejudice, etiquette, and gossip. They will doubtless attract buyers, but there will be countless quirks, and worst of all will be Miss Catherine: her name will give her more quirks than her sisters.* With all that, it might be that they will be sought after. I would be tempted to fix everything by naming them all after the Virgin Mary, even if there were ten of them.* In my opinion that would make them all stand up straight; they would all mind their figures and their complexions; they would each eat enough for four; they would be prudent in their choice of books and would eventually attain the title of excellent citizens wherever they ended up. But, my God, what twaddle this is! What stuff people write! There are some curiously furnished heads out there.*

When in future you speak of my dogs, of the Raphael loggias, of Bibiena, and Blackstone,* you will be so good as to include in the catalogue a certain Angora tomcat that Prince Potemkin gave me as a thank-you for the Sèvres service. It is a tomcat, the most tomcat of all tomcats; cheerful, clever, not at all stubborn, and precisely as you could wish a velvet-pawed tomcat to be. About that tomcat, I must tell you how astonished Prince Henry was one day when Prince Potemkin let a monkey loose in the room and I started to play with it rather than continue the fine conversation we had started. He opened his eyes wide, but do as he might, the monkey's tricks won out. I have received two letters from the Lord Patriarch of Paris. I am off this evening to Tsarskoe Selo, where I shall finish this one.

at Tsarskoe Selo, this 11 June

Yesterday I had no ordinary headache. Nonetheless I went to Mass because it was Sunday, and then instead of dining I slept for three hours, after which I dressed up pretty and reviewed a regiment of grenadiers and then I walked all the way around the pond, still squealing about my headache. Today it is better, but I have no more wit than a pin.*

I have been very angry for the past four days. This is what has been written to me: 'As for Engl., it is only too true that they have managed to ruin the happiest and most flourishing of all States. When one remembers the brilliant situation in which the kingdom was nineteen years ago, and then the one in which it finds itself today, it makes one's heart bleed. The constitution and government that were thought the best in Europe and that are the worst: a government that dares not punish the guilty. All its deliberations, its arrangements, even its plans are public. Factions slow everything down or make everything difficult', etc. That makes one grit one's teeth, and all is lost if that is what they think on the ground there. For myself, I say, 'Brats behave this way, but George II and his predecessors behaved differently. So it is not the form, but rather the actors who are at fault.' But here is another devil of a postscript that has arrived. First of all, the petition full of the confederated priest's lies is something to be thrown into the fire: all that priest needed do in order to be rehabilitated was address himself to his king.* I shall have nothing more to do with those gallows-birds, the robbers and the robbed. The truth is that a coffer filled with 15,000 ducats was handed over to a bishop, and since the priest complains of everyone, everyone will also have to be heard in order to decide his case. However, I have no right to judge him, for I am not his judge.

I care not at all for Monsieur Du Busquet or Du Buscher's so-called Giulio Romano cartoons, nor for your subscriptions to views of Greece, nor for any poems:* I shall buy them when they are for sale. Farewell, Baron: the aforementioned good citizens, enemies of their fatherland, have put me in a bad temper. By overthrowing what they ought to worship, they might well overturn the stool of their vile, sullen, oafish, etc., etc., etc., oracle. All possible insults to him and to them, and much friendship and esteem for German barons.

126. *To Friedrich Melchior Grimm*

When Voltaire died in Paris on 30 May 1778 (NS), Church authorities refused him the right to be buried on hallowed ground, and his nephew arranged a rapid, nearly clandestine burial. Catherine contrasts this funeral with the public acclamations that had greeted Voltaire upon his arrival in Paris and the theatrical crowning of his bust on the stage of the Comédie Française exactly two months before. Meanwhile, there have been developments in Catherine's personal life: a new favourite, Ivan Rimsky-Korsakov, whom she calls Pyrrhus, King of Epirus.

at Tsarskoe Selo, this 21 June 1778

Alas! I need not spell out for you all the sorrow I felt upon reading your no. 19. Until then I had hoped that the news of Voltaire's death had been false, but you have made me certain of it. I instantly felt a wave of total discouragement and the greatest disdain for all things of this world. The month of May dealt me mortal blows: I lost two men whom I had never seen, who cared for me and whom I honoured—Voltaire and Lord Chatham. No equal, and certainly no superior, will replace them for a very, very long time (and perhaps never, especially the former). I want

to scream. But is it possible that one can so supremely honour and dis-
honour, be reasonable and be raving mad, as where you are? A few weeks
ago they publicly honoured a man whom today they dare not bury—and
what a man! The best of the nation, on whom they should well and duly
pride themselves. Why did you not seize his body yourself, and do it in
my name? You should have sent it to me, and—zounds! That's when for
the first time in your life, you lost your head. I promise you that he would
have had the most precious tomb possible. But although I do not have
his body, at least he will not lack a monument here. When I get to town
this autumn, I shall gather up the letters that the great man wrote to me,
and I shall send them to you. I have a large number of them, but, if it is
possible, buy his library and all that remains of his papers, including my
letters. For myself, I shall gladly pay his heirs lavishly, for I think they do
not know the worth of any of that. It would also give me great pleasure
if you could get me from the Cramers not only the most complete edition of his works, but also even the most minor pamphlets that came
from his pen.* I shall make a salon in which his books will find a home.

It is true that the Moroccan ambassador has left Livorno on one of
my merchant ships.* Your postscript sent with the Dutch horse-drawn
barge has reached me: I do not have much of a taste for projects and
undertakings of that sort. Russian ports are open to all traders and
that's that. I fear monopolies within a radius of a hundred miles: I do
not like to regulate everything, much less to impede it. Undertakings of
that sort are risky: there is always trouble with such companies. I am
like Basile in *The Barber of Seville*: I have my little maxims that I stick
to and which I use with variations when I apply them.* The pig's breakfast* in the Levant will be revealed for what it is soon or never at all; as
for the Bavarian one, I think it is indigestible. No, no, Baron: it is not
just the inside of the palace at Tsarskoe Selo, but also the façade on the
side of the Kagul obelisk that will be knocked down from top to bottom:
that façade will be made attractive but nothing else. I have no greater
aims ever since hearing Mademoiselle Bertin's judgment that only the
pretty leads to immortality.* That Mademoiselle Bertin's family is
a most distinguished one. Her brother is Prince Potemkin's cook, and
I bow to him every time I see him, saying, 'Monsieur Bertin,* all my
cooks, every last one of them, are but kitchen boys by comparison to
you.' And so Monsieur Bertin loves me the way he loves bread. I am at
present reading what Baron Dalberg has to say,* and his mind is in
harmony with mine. But, by the way, the notorious inkstand has
arrived:* I have seen it, and it has received by acclamation the epithet
of 'charming'. Only the mast that acts as a cover does not suit: it hides

it, overloads it, and ruins it. I had it removed. All the rest, each part separately and all together, is charming. God bless our inkstand and all those who put it together, made it, and helped with it.* I also received the medallion of Franklin—now that is a big head! I shall send you that of Pyrrhus, King of Epirus, and you will say, 'Now that is a fine head, a Greek physiognomy and Greek proportions.' It is one of those figures about which our sculptors know nothing: I can prove that many positions that Falconet and others think are not in nature are in fact there when nature is so perfect. Oh, Sir, that thing is a fine thing: you will thank me for it one day. Farewell, be well.

127. *To Gustav III of Sweden*

Marking the one-year anniversary of Gustav's departure from Russia and respond-ing to a letter about his visit to Denmark, Catherine feigns to find the king amiable, although she in fact found him an excessive stickler for etiquette. Immediately upon his departure from Russia in 1777, Gustav had suggested a further meeting at the border town of Fredrikshamn (now Hamina, Finland), which Russia had acquired from Sweden in 1743. Catherine demurred and the encounter did not take place until 1783.

I have just received, dearest Brother, your charming letter of 28 June from Maltesholm, near Kristianstad in Scania.* I found that you were gay as a chaffinch, and I exclaimed, 'A cheerful and personable king is such an amiable thing!' Let it be said in passing and without offending anyone that I find that we Medusa heads petrify everyone who comes near us anyway. If, to top it off, we are glum, frosty, and stiff, we make people want to defenestrate us, and only fear holds them back. Well, my dear champion, you are not at all a salt statue, good and stiff, like Lot's wife: you go looking for adventures, visiting princes, princesses, kings, kingdoms, soldiers, warriors, etc. You talk about all that in the plural to brighten up your tale: you tell me of your journey in the most agreeable way in the world. You quote your governess and comic operas just like me. How could you think I could forget or hate you? I would have you know once and for all that you are not odious.

I am very sorry to hear of the piteous state in which you found your brother-in-law.* I had long since been warned of it, yet they say that here and there he has good moments and even witticisms, but that is not much good. You will have found Prince Ferdinand to be a character of quite another sort.*

You were not mistaken, dearest Brother: I am indeed at Peterhof, and as soon as I arrived, I looked around for the Count of Gotland. He is not present this year, and he is literally missed. We have already said many times that 'on St Peter's Day this year the black domino (the one you want me to recall) would not have got wet, for it would not have left the house.' The weather was diabolical that day,* but nonetheless there were lots of masks. The illumination stayed on the ground, that is, there were only lanterns on the ground.

I do not know why they are dawdling over my house at Fredrikshamn. I have already twice told Count Bruce to build it, and he is not naturally a dawdler, but I shall reheat his memory.

Farewell, dearest Brother, be well and rest assured that I return most affectionately all the marks of friendship that you give me.

This 5th day of July 1778, on which a year ago you unfortunately left, I attended the ordination of a bishop and am dead tired. Writing to you seems to me like resting. Come on now, may your queen give us a fine boy with the same sense of humour as his Papa: I would be very glad of it because I like beautiful boys and cheerful people.

128. *To Gustav III of Sweden*

Circling back on old themes, such as the Peterhof masquerade with Grimm on the Feast of Sts Peter and Paul in 1777 (see Letter 120), Catherine directs the correspondence with Gustav towards a new apolitical point of commonality: the tending and education of children. Catherine presents herself with seeming nonchalance as a model grandmother to the infant Alexander, obliging her correspondent to request her advice on raising the future Gustav IV Adolf of Sweden, born on 1 November 1778 (NS).

at Peterhof, this 13 July 1778

By the present, dearest Brother, I announce to you the arrival of your letter from Drottningholm of 9 July. I found it more worried and less cheerful than the previous one, and I said to myself, 'Ha! I know that feeling well. He has returned home, and one has fewer worries when one is not at home.' I am thoroughly convinced that, with wisdom and prudence, you can dispel yours. But, from my experience of many situations in my life, I recognize truly how much one suffers while wisdom and prudence are doing their work.

I am very glad about the queen's pregnancy. Rest assured that no one, after Papa King, will be more delighted than I at the birth of a crown prince. I hope that he will be as healthy as Mr Alexander, who knows nothing of vests nor stockings nor caps, who bathes up to three times a day in cold water, and who most of the time wears just a very short shirt. If you want more details about that, let me know, and I shall send them to you in writing. He is a big, tall boy who is marvellously healthy: he fears neither draughts nor evening vapours nor anything else.

If the storm had brought you here safe and sound, I would have thanked the storm heartily and would not have called it vexing. If we drown one day, you and me, dearest Brother, it will not be our fault, for we are like ducks on water. But that will not happen too soon, I think: I believe it is written somewhere that I shall see you again one day. I have a sort of inner conviction about it.

I have already informed you, dearest Brother, of how we spent the holidays this year. Your plumes would have remained intact, and you would have escaped the *Encyclopédiste*'s elbows, for he is no longer here.

Prince Belosel'sky, rather than go through Sweden, headed to Berlin, where an apoplectic stroke has left him on his deathbed.

Farewell, dearest Brother, be well, and have fun while all of Europe goes off to fight, despite the unbearable heat we have this summer.

129. *To Gustav III of Sweden*

Admirers of Voltaire, Catherine and Gustav would have read the story of his burial, as well as Madame de Boufflers's verses on the subject, in the June 1778 issue of the 'Literary Correspondence', a manuscript periodical, formerly edited by Grimm and addressed exclusively to the 'enlightened' princes and princesses of Europe. Marie-Françoise-Catherine de Beauvau-Craon, Marquise de Boufflers (1711–1786), was a close associate of Voltaire during his years at the court of Lorraine at Lunéville, and her witty poetry circulated widely in eighteenth-century France.

at Tsarskoe Selo, this 18 August 1778

I have, dearest Brother, your letters of 1, 2, and 7 August to answer. I am very glad that one of my epistles contributed to the success of your portrait, and I thank you most sincerely for all the signs of friendship you give me; it will always be a real pleasure for me to return them. You are lightsome as a feather, but when you decide to saddle your horse to travel to Fredrikshamn, I hope that you will be so good as to give me notice, so that my speed might at least match yours. Our bigwigs, the keepers of circumstances, conjunctures, and conjectures, must have nothing to complain about on either side. Each has his little reputation to maintain. I do not want yours to accuse me of impoliteness, nor mine of lack of decorum. As for the political tinkers,* we shall let them reason away, and the historians too may scribble this way and that: I care no more for them ever since the death of Voltaire. Now that was someone who was delightful and inimitably cheerful. I scolded Grimm for failing to claim his body in my name when Monsignor de Beaumont refused to bury him.* I think you know, dearest Brother, Madame de Boufflers's verses on the subject, which begin, 'God does well all that He does—La Fontaine has said so', and which end, 'His divine genius can be refused a tomb, but not an altar.'

Well, yes, they are fighting in Germany, and in my opinion the winners of a battle are those who advance. When Field Marshal Rumiantsev won the battles of Larga and Kagul within a fortnight, on the first reception day at court, your envoy Mr Ribbing cut through the crowd and ran over to Countess Bruce, the field marshal's sister, to tell her, 'Madam, I congratulate you on having a right proper brother.'* That made everyone laugh, and that burst of laughter prevents me from telling you that you too have two uncles who are *right proper* men, if there ever were any.*

I would very much like to know where you got the verses that ended your letter in order to mollify me after you spoke ill of women in general. But come, come, I hold no grudges—you have never spoken so much ill of women as I have thought of men. Baron Nolken gave me your letter, dearest Brother: he will have told you how I received him, and I confess that it was a pleasure to see him again, since he came from where you are and from you.

I am delighted by the queen's good health. I think that the grand duchess is again three months pregnant; it would not be at all bad if they went on taking turns at making babies.

Here I am now at your third letter, dearest Brother. But listen then, on my honour, it is written in a spidery scrawl. I read it three times and still could barely decipher its contents. I am very sorry to hear of your worries: gloomy thoughts are good for nothing. If my letters could dispel them, I would gladly write to you every day. When I become a fairy or a witch, I shall write 'gaiety' on my wand, and I shall endow everyone around you, even the antique maids of honour at court, with that delightful quality. I do not know if you recall what I told you once at table at Peterhof about antique maids of honour.

You will have Mr Alexander's routine in full detail. He is in marvellously good health and is the spitting image of his mother. That will add further to your knowledge on the subject, and your Senate will not fail to find you to be the best-informed prince in the universe on this matter. I hope that they will be grateful to me for having made a small contribution to this, but no matter what they say, rest assured that it will always be great merriment for me to profess the reciprocity of my friendship for you on all occasions.

130. *To Gustav III of Sweden*

Catherine sends her cousin a doll in a basket to illustrate her detailed instructions on how to care for an infant.

Mr Alexander was born on 12 December 1777, so in winter. At his birth, I took him in my arms, and, after he was washed, I took him to another room, where I put him on a large square piece of cloth. He was wrapped up very lightly, and I would not suffer him to be swaddled in any way except as the attached doll is. That done, Mr Alexander was put in a basket like the doll; this was so that there would be no temptation for his nurses to rock him. As for the basket, it was placed behind a screen on a settee. Thus provided for, Mr Alexander was handed over to General Benkendorf's widow; he was given as a wet nurse the wife of an assistant gardener at Tsarskoe Selo. After his baptism, he was moved from his noble mother's apartments to those which had been assigned to him. It is a large room, in the middle of which there is a sky or canopy with a back, placed on four pillars and attached to the ceiling, with curtains all around reaching all the way to the ground. These curtains and canopy, under which there is Mr Alexander's bed, are surrounded by a railing high enough to lean on; the wet nurse's bed is behind the bedstead. The room is large so that the air is better; the canopy is in the middle of the room, facing the windows, so that air can circulate more freely around the canopy and curtains. The railing prevents too many people from getting close to the child's bed all at once. Not too many people were allowed even to be in the room around him, and only a couple of candles were lit in the evening so that the air would not be stuffy in the least. Mr Alexander's bed (since he knows neither rocking nor cradles) is made of iron without curtains. He lies on a mattress covered with leather, which is covered with his bed sheet; he has a pillow, and his English blanket is very light. All loud cooing has been avoided, but, then again, people have always spoken aloud in his room and even when he was asleep. No kind of noise in the corridors above or below his room is forbidden. Cannons are even fired from the Admiralty fortifications across from his window, which has made it so that he is afraid of nothing. Great care has been taken that the thermometers in his room never rise above 14 or 15 degrees. Every morning when his room is swept, in winter as in summer, he is carried into another apartment, and the windows are opened in his bedroom to refresh the air in the room. In winter, when the room has been reheated, Mr Alexander is carried back to his apartment. Ever since he was born, he has become accustomed to being washed every day, when he is well, in a basin of water. At first the water was lukewarm; now it is cold, just brought in the evening before. He likes it so much that wherever he sees water he wants to get in, and in the heat of the summer he was bathed two or three times in his basin of cold water. He was accustomed not to have his every cry or whimper appeased by the wet nurse's breast, to be awake at certain times, to be fed, etc., at other times. Once the spring air was bearable, Mr Alexander's cap was removed, and he was taken into the fresh air. Bit by bit he became accustomed to sitting on grass and sand alike, even to sleep for a few hours there in the shade when it is nice out. Then he is laid out on a pillow, and he rests like that marvellously well. He has never yet worn or endured stockings on his legs, and he is not dressed in any piece of clothing that restricts his body in any way. When he was four months old, so that he would be carried less, I gave him a rug of about four square cubits, which is spread out in his room. One or two of his nurses sit there on the floor, and Mr Alexander is laid on his belly: it is a joy to see him wallow there. He gets on all fours and goes backwards when he cannot go forward. His favourite outfit is his very short shirt and a very loose little knit vest. When he goes out, a little light dress of hessian or taffeta is put over it. He knows no chills; he is big, fat, healthy, and very cheerful. He likes very much to jump about and hardly ever screams. He just grew his first tooth without illness. He is almost nine months old.

this 2 September 1778, at St Petersburg

131. *To Gustav III of Sweden*

Dispatching to Sweden her letter of 2 September (see Letter 130) with its accompanying doll, Catherine slips in a few diplomatic jabs. According to the Peace of Westphalia (1648), France and Sweden were required to act as guarantors of the constitution of the Holy Roman Empire. The War of the Bavarian Succession

*threatened that political order, so Catherine reminds Gustav of his obligation to help
her to put an end to a war in which she had no desire to participate, despite her alliance with Prussia. At the same time, she was putting strong pressure on Austria to
agree to her joint mediation with France, an acceptance which arrived in St
Petersburg only a few days after this letter was written.*

at St Petersburg, this 18 September 1778

One piece of news in exchange for another, dearest Brother: by your
letter of 28 August/8 September you inform me that the Estates of
Sweden have been summoned for very peaceable purposes. I shall give
credence to that, and, in return, by this letter I shall inform you that
you will receive a beautiful doll, dressed and put to bed exactly as Mr
Alexander was at the moment of his birth. I beg you most earnestly to
forbid your natural vivacity to touch, disturb, or rumple the smallest
part of it with your royal hands. But, if you think it appropriate to look
after or arrange your child in the same way, you will be so good as to
hand the doll over to a prudent lady, for whom every part will be
a model. I add to it the attached text that I have written in accordance
with your wishes: if all that can help your child to be healthy, rest
assured that I shall be truly glad of it. But you are going at quite a rate:
you are already thinking about a wedding between two children who are
not yet born. I warn you that I want the grand duchess to give birth to
a boy, but any girl she brings into the world will be a prude. Everyone
will come to court her, but she will marry only by inclination, and God
knows whom she will like. The Germans say: time brings wisdom.*

One must concede that your dear uncles go on superb marches.*
But, by the by, you guarantors of the Peace of Westphalia ought to work
on allaying these quarrels, which will cost so much innocent blood, and
ought to support all steps leading in that direction. In the meantime, be
well, dearest Brother, and rest assured that I return most sincerely all
the marks of friendship that you show me.

132. *To Friedrich Melchior Grimm*

*Still lamenting the deaths of Pitt the Elder, 1st Earl of Chatham, and especially of
Voltaire, Catherine made arrangements to acquire Voltaire's library. Catherine
feared trickery on the part of Voltaire's niece, Marie-Louise Denis, and her brother,
Alexandre Jean Mignot, Abbé de Sellières. Aware that the author's death made
a posthumous publication of his correspondence quite likely, she was especially concerned to regain control of the letters she had exchanged with him.*

Reply to no. 22, at St Petersburg, this 1 October 1778

It has been a very long time since I stopped heeding two things with regard to my actions, and I in no way take them into account in all that I do: the first is the gratitude of men; the second is history. I do good to do good, and then that's that. This is what revived me from the discouragement and indifference to the things of this world that I felt upon hearing the news of Voltaire's death. Besides, he was my teacher: it was he, or rather his works, that formed my wit and my mind. I have said it to you more than once, I think: I am his student. When I was younger, I liked to please him: anything I did had to be worthy of being told to him for me to be pleased with it, and so he was immediately informed. He became so accustomed to this that he scolded me when I left him without news and when he found out by other means. My scrupulousness in this matter had diminished in the past few years, given the rapidity of the events that preceded and followed the peace treaty and the immense labour that I had undertaken, which made me lose the habit of writing letters. I feel less of an inclination to write them and find it less easy to do so.

I am much obliged to you for the perseverance that you think I have in cultivating, arranging, messing around, etc. I admit it, everything is moving along as before, but Voltaire is no more, and England is without Lord Chatham. You recognize the English nation in what they have done to honour Lord Chatham's memory and in the reward that they have given to his descendants, but I could not read of one or the other without indignation. They seemed to me to be insults from his enemies. What, the corrupt parliament who rejoiced at his death has buried him and given his children a pension! That is like the tyrant, the Roman emperor who said that the body of a dead enemy smelled fragrant.* Well, why did they not honour him when he could be of use to his fatherland? Why did they not pursue his ideas and plans with acclamations? His last oration in Parliament contained precisely what I had guessed that he thought two years ago.* If my ambassador had been Baron Grimm, I would have scolded him for not demanding Voltaire's body in my name, since it was left without a tomb in his fatherland. But we must do justice to all: Prince Bariatinsky must not be scolded any more than Father Mignot for not sending it to me all wrapped up.

I am very glad to know the reason for your silence, for I was really beginning to think that my credit with you was faltering and that some German prince had expelled me from your memory, given the passion that I know you to have for them. I said to myself: he is on the tracks of some rare genius, just as we have seen him to have been. As for the sorrows that friendship causes you, be assured that I share in them sincerely,* just as in all that concerns you.

Your account of the purchase of Voltaire's library is delicious. God grant that Madame Denis should remain firm in her resolutions and that He bless you in your behaviour, given the history of the so-called purchase of the library of Ferney. First, I have ordered that you be sent a letter of credit for 30,000 roubles; second, here is my letter to Madame Denis; third, the snuffbox with my portrait will be crafted and will accompany, fourth, the diamonds; and, fifth, the fur will head straight for your place, so that you can exchange all that for the aforementioned library. But, above all, make sure that my letters are in it and that nothing really interesting has been purloined. But so that you can complete the *Memoranda Illustrating The History Of The Great Men*, it is good for you to know the following characteristic deed. Corberon came a few days ago to see Mr [Ivan] Shuvalov and told him that Father Mignot and company had written to him and had had others write to him. He had been asked to entreat Mr Shuvalov to beg the Empress of Russia not to deprive them of their uncle's library, which she was buying from Madame Denis and which was the only property that remained them from their uncle. Mr Shuvalov answered that he could not undertake such a foolish entreaty, that Madame Denis was free to sell and the empress had a right to buy whatever she liked, and that this was neither the first nor the last thing of the sort that she would buy. I told him to add that it was illogical to want to keep in the country something for which citizens could be deprived of burial.* Take care, therefore, that the library not be snatched from you nor swapped in the cradle: it would seem that the dear nephew would like nothing better than to see his uncle's library burnt on the Place de Grève.* I am looking for Voltaire's letters, a large number of which Falconet, who, N.B., left here without taking leave of me, might well have taken away with him, since he begged me to give them to him to read and never returned them, if memory serves. Once they have been found, I shall make a packet of them and send it to you. Up to now only ninety-two have been dug up.*

The notorious inkstand adorns my Hermitage along with the two busts of Voltaire: I prefer the bust without a wig. You know my aversion to wigs, and especially to busts with wigs: it always seems to me that the wig has been put there as a joke. I have had delivered to the Chevalier de La Teyssonnière the packet that you sent me for him. Prince Potemkin has become fond of this officer and enjoys conversing with him, especially on his frequent trips: he takes him into his carriage and finds it entertaining to listen to him tell of his travels and campaigns. I see with pleasure that you are happy with my prince-bishop.* Farewell.

133. *To Friedrich Melchior Grimm*

Planning to reconstruct Voltaire's manor at Ferney in her own gardens at Tsarskoe Selo, Catherine purchased a model of the house, as well as floor plans and even fabric samples. The reconstructed manor was never built, but the planning materials are still preserved in the Hermitage and in Voltaire's Library in St Petersburg.

this 17, 18, or 19 October 1778

Scarcely had my letter of 1 October (which, incidentally, was finished only today) been put in the post, when I remembered that there were heaps of things I had forgotten to tell you, and namely that you should subscribe for one hundred copies of the new edition of Voltaire's works. Give me one hundred complete copies of my teacher's works, so that I can deposit them everywhere. I want them to serve as an example; I want them to be studied and learned by heart; I want minds to be fed on them. It will educate citizens, geniuses, heroes, and authors; it will nurture a hundred thousand talents which would otherwise be lost in the darkness of night, ignorance, etc. Look what a tirade has got going here: who would have guessed it when I took up the pen, and who can predict with what this page will end?

Please let me have the façade of the manor at Ferney and, if possible, the interior plan of the arrangement of the rooms. For, either the park at Tsarskoe Selo will not exist, or the manor at Ferney will come and occupy it. I also must know which rooms in the manor face north, and which south, east, and west. It is also essential to know whether one can see Lake Geneva from the windows of the house and from which side; the same goes for the Jura Mountains. Another question: is there an avenue leading to the house, and on which side? Look here, do you like the idea? And why should you not like it? It is true that it is not new. We have a C. called N. F.* Let us see whether you recall that you received a letter from me from there: I even think that you have a description of the furniture and that I told you about the master of the house, who was not at all where he should be, for he naturally should be in the Academy of Sciences.*

I do not approve at all of the bookseller Panckoucke's idea to print first what is new in Voltaire's works: I would like to see the whole thing arranged chronologically, according to the years in which they were written.* I am a pedant who likes to see the progress of the author's mind in his works, and, believe me, such an arrangement is of far greater consequence than is commonly believed. The more you think about it, the more you will find that I am right. I could write you an entire dissertation on the subject: it would include the unripe, the ripe, and the overripe, and the convincing argument would be the progress of ideas, but, my God, all that requires very profound *studia*. One need not say everything, for sometimes saying everything sounds mad, even if they may perhaps be wise things when they come from good sources and are said at an opportune *hora*.* Look, that is sublime, that is. But *basta*, it is growing too mad.

The maker of the notorious inkstand* has not yet arrived. I think that there is a pencil drawing like yours here, which came from Rome and belongs to Major-General Zavadovsky. Count Vorontsov sent it to him,* and it is a very fine thing. Mr Shuvalov told me that in Rome they had no trouble making portraits of me, that they boldly took up a medal or medallion of Alexander, and that they very boldly drew my portrait from it too.* I am very proud of that, and since that time I have been telling everyone: 'I look like Alexander, but I am twenty years older than he.' I know not whether Joseph II looks like the Prince-Bishop of Lübeck, but it is proven that he does not want peace.

As I was finishing my reply to no. 22, here comes no. 23, entitled, 'Continuation of no. 22', immediately followed by a postscript. But just look what this world is like. Just as you were telling me about Martin Luther's floating, living, and weaving* in order to prove to me the high degree of favour in which I remain with you, here I was believing myself not only fallen, but even denigrated by the arrival of some prince, a great genius. As for the Barber of Seville, Miss Cardel, and Mr Wagner, I beg you to hold them in high honour: they are people who go with any sauce, and Basile is one of the foolish rogues who have most amused me in this world. When one day I meet Caesar,* I shall recommend that play to him.

When Monsieur de Vergennes spoke to you about the purchase of Voltaire's library, it seems that he knew nothing of the Chevalier Corberon's negotiations.* Under Louis XV, I would have thereby understood that it was being dealt with by the Comte de Broglio's department, but at present I am quite disorientated and suspect only Mignot and company.* I lack only a fur and a few of Voltaire's letters before it can all leave together and addressed to you. As for the letters, there are about a hundred, but we keep recovering them every day. It is true that they are never to be printed, and, on mature consideration,

I am not sure whether they can be, and that is for three reasons. First, because I shall be accused of vanity for having handed over letters to be printed that are brimming with flattering epithets for me. Second, because there is an abundance of biting jokes at the expense of the two-faced man's mum. Third, because the *piccolo bambino* is treated even worse.* But then, if they take the ones that are left—not much will be left. If they had found either drafts, or copies of his letters among his papers, fine then, but I do not want to provide them, and it would be better if they remained deposited in the manor at Ferney, near Tsarskoe Selo, in Monsieur de Voltaire's library. I very much approve of what you have suggested that I do for Wagnière: if he wanted to remain librarian of his master's library, it would be entirely up to him, and he could follow it next spring, or as convenient for him. But, if he cannot or does not want to, you will give him for his trouble at least as much as his master left him, or more, as you deem fit.

Monsieur Bertin, when interrogated about his supposed brother-hood—sweating and changing colours, but unfalteringly serving at table—declared flat-out, 'Indeed not.' Therefore, you were very right to keep silent when you found yourself near the feathers, or rather covered in the feathers, panaches, etc., of Mademoiselle Bertin, who lays people very low, for, as would have been reasonable, you would not have managed to escape her very just indignation. In any case, Monsieur Bertin is now my head cook.*

Infatuated, infatuated! You know quite well that the term is inappropriate when one is speaking of Pyrrhus, King of Epirus, the downfall of painters and the despair of sculptors. It is admiration, Sir: it is the enthusiasm inspired by the masterpieces of nature. Pretty things fall and shatter like idols before the Arc of the Lord, before the marks of greatness. When Pyrrhus takes up a violin, the dogs listen; when he sings, the birds come to listen, as they did for Orpheus. Pyrrhus has never made a gesture or a movement that was not either noble or gracious. He is radiant like the sun: he spreads his brilliance all around him. None of that is effeminate, but virile and as you would like someone to be. In a word, he is Pyrrhus, King of Epirus. All is in harmony: there is not one piece detached from the rest. Such is the effect of the precious gifts that nature has amassed in his beauty. Art has nothing to do with it, and affectation is ten thousand miles away. It is true that the Cardinal de Bernis has let me have from Rome a copy of the trial of Anne Boleyn, but I confess that I was not after that trial, but rather the classical authors, Greek and Latin, who have not yet been printed.* They say that in that library there are things that no one knows about.

As for the postscript that contains nothing but the *summa summa-rum** of the bills for the inkstand, I acknowledge its receipt, but I shall not answer in order to save pen and paper. Farewell.

134. *To Gustav III of Sweden*

Poetic and mock epitaphs were fashionable in the eighteenth century, both as a form of published literature and as an entertainment in sociable settings. Here Catherine perpetuates the sense of friendly ties between Stockholm and St Petersburg by circulating such a mock epitaph for one of her courtiers, Lev Naryshkin. About a year before this letter was written, Catherine penned her own, rather more serious epitaph: 'Here lies Catherine the Second [...]. Eighteen years of boredom and solitude made her read many books. When she came to the Russian throne, she wanted to do good and sought to procure happiness, liberty, and property for her subjects. She forgave easily and hated no one. Indulgent, easy-going, of a cheerful disposition, with a republican soul and a good heart, she had friends. Work was easy for her, and she liked good company and the arts.'[1]

this 5 February 1779

I have entrusted this letter to Major-General [Alexander] Stroganov, dearest Brother. He has orders to tell you what you have known for a very long time, namely how much I shared in your joy at the birth of the crown prince.* I would have wished it to be without any bitterness. I see in the details that you thought it good to make known to me new evidence of your trust, by which I am very touched. I wish an end to all these squabbles that will satisfy all sides, and may they never arise again.

The grand duchess will shortly be giving us a second tot:* male or female, he will be cared for according to the same routine as his elder brother.

I hope, my dear, that you have no doubts about the sincerity with which I return your profession of friendship. Farewell, be well.

To give you a moment's amusement, since you know the protagonist, I am taking the liberty of sending you the attached inscription. I beg you to share it with Count Scheffer as a state secret that should not be printed.

---

[1] *Sbornik imperatorskago russkago istoricheskago obshchestva*, 148 vols (St Petersburg: Imp. Akademiia Nauk, 1867–1916), xxiii. 77 (our translation).

For the information of posterity

Inscription (a)
to be placed on the first stone laid in the foundation of the
country house of Grand Equerry Leon Naryshkin
This is the home
of Sir Leon Naryshkin, Grand Equerry.
No dashing steed has ever had cause to complain of him
for he has never mounted one.
In his youth, Lady Nature promised to make him handsome.
No one knows why she did not keep her word.
When he was to be married off, he married her of whom
he was thinking the least.
He loved wine, women, and dress, yet
no one ever saw him drunk, in love, or well-combed.
He shaved himself for fear that the barber would cut him,
so the grander the festivities, the more
razor-marks could be seen on his face.
He looked everywhere for adventures and found none
anywhere.
His friends said that he was most respectful on first acquaintance
and irritable afterwards.
He danced a lot and was agile and light every
time his corpulence did not
divert his left leg in order to follow the right.
He was rich and never had a penny in his pocket.
He liked going to market, where he readily
bought what he did not need.
Of all his possessions he loved most the one hundred fathoms
you see before you.
He liked to spike them with empty bottles,
new ones every year. They could be reached by
winding paths planted with shrubs
lined by ponds and streams
that were dry when there
was no rain.
Despite that, he spent most of the summer
on the highway.
'Be joyful and make others joyful' was his motto.
Joy was his element.
His peals of laughter followed close on his heels.

He himself attests that all of this is true to the letter.

(a) This was to have been an epitaph, but since he is too afraid of death, it had to be made an inscription.

135. *To Gustav III of Sweden*

Catherine is nonchalant about her great diplomatic triumph, the Peace of Teschen, as well as her latest personal joy, the birth of her second grandson, Constantine. Meanwhile, in Sweden, the Estates met in 1778–9 to discuss reforms, which included a resolution proclaiming religious freedom for foreigners in the realm. In a later letter to Grimm of May 1781, Catherine described and even sketched the toddler Alexander's outfit, which she mentions here: a jumpsuit that closed easily in the back and that resembled a Russian caftan.

at Tsarskoe Selo, this 14 June 1779

I thought you so busy with your Diet, etc., dearest Brother, that it seemed to me that it would have been commendable of me not to write to you, but I cannot resist thanking you for the fine things you say to me in your letter of 11 June NS about those that have just happened out there in the world. As for the Congress of Teschen, one did not need to be a great magician to carry it off successfully, so I am not in the least puffed up by my role of co-mediator. Everyone most sincerely wanted peace, and it can truthfully be said that *the circumstances, conjunctures, and conjectures* were at that moment in perfect agreement on the matter.

On that of Lord Constantine, nothing can be said except that, when he came into the world,* I did not think he would live three days, and yet there he is, still alive after six weeks. Whether he lives or no, I must agree with you that you and I have not left our children and grandchildren bereft of resounding names. But tell me, will you: where in the world will we fish out more names if we end up with a dozen? It is sad that, as old as the world is, it does not abound as many such names as one would like.

I am delighted with what you tell me of the crown prince: I think I have contributed a bit, and I congratulate myself on it. Let male and female gossips chatter, persevere, and you will silence them on the matter of decorum.

I am sending you an outfit like the one I had put on Mr Alexander after his first birthday: he is thereby dressed and undressed in a jiffy without having his arms twisted and without any laces. He has not yet known any other outfit, and now he is wearing shoes and stockings with it because he runs all over the place. I refer you to what Mr Nolcken will say of him. He is a strong, robust child who is afraid of nothing and who is becoming charming because no one contradicts him except on things that would cause him or other people harm. And when we prevent him from doing something, he is told the reason why he should not do it. For example, if he wants to play with a pin, he is told, 'You will prick yourself', and the point is pressed against the speaker's hand or that of the child. He is already so used to it that I have seen him testing all kinds of pointy things to see if they would prick him. Since his temper is not embittered by continual contradiction, he is always cheerful, and you can do anything you like with him because he is so trusting of what he is told. This cheerful temper is nurtured as much as possible by giving him all possible opportunities to exercise it. He is acquainted with all possible toys: if he breaks them on purpose, they are taken away because he broke them; if he hits them, he does not see them again because he hit them. A book of engravings, chock-full of things that he had never seen, kept him very much entertained for several months: he always picked up the book himself and went over to someone to find out what it was he saw in it. Please note that he cannot yet speak, so we named for him the things that he pointed at or designated in his own way. When his attention was exhausted, he cast aside his book, and no one mentioned it again.

Forgive these minute details: I thought they might be of use to you, given the bad way in which I have seen so many poor tots treated. You have encouraged me to share my discoveries and principles on the subject.

In a few days I am off to Peterhof, the one where you would like to come and land. If you had succumbed to temptation, I would have had cause to assure you in person that at every opportunity I return with great pleasure the marks of friendship that you are so good as to give to your good Sister and Neighbour.

136. *To Grigory Potemkin*

Catherine wrote several letters in early 1780 about 'Cagliostro's spirits'—that is, about Potemkin arranging Catherine's new attachment to Alexander Lanskoy. At this very moment, Giuseppe Balsamo, alias the legendary Freemason and mystic Count Alessandro Cagliostro, was in St Petersburg, attempting to recruit followers

from among Catherine's nobility. Catherine the rationalist and enemy of all forms of
occultism refused to see Cagliostro, but here she uses imagery associated with his
practice of alchemy and necromancy to create an allegory of her hesitant desire for
new love.

[late February–early March 1780]

I am writing this note to tell you that the spirits of Cagliostro appeared
to me in a dream tonight, and they said, 'Every dream is a lie.' But they
wrote, 'In the chemical mixture that he is concocting for you, Prince
Potemkin is using all sorts of excellent and healthy herbs.'

The apparition gave the names and nicknames for all these herbs.
I could compile a separate catalogue (but I shall set this aside for
another time so that it doesn't spoil or complicate this whole matter).
'But,' added the little spirits whose height was one and a half inches
tall, 'there are two herbs, which grow on the same stem, that he does
not like or has neglected to include in his mixture; yet it is essential for
you and your happiness that they be part of it. These herbs are tender
and delicate; they have no other names, but the stem from which they
come has a name that is sacred to noble-born souls.' What these spirits
said I found stunning. I rushed to add a sprig of these herbs to your
alembic, since without them, the spirits assured me, the rest would boil
down to nothing. But even though I walked on tiptoe, I had scarcely got
close to the alembic when I found you in my way. You rebuffed me with
such force that I woke up with a start, my eyes bathed in tears because
it was precisely the herbs which could render the mixture good, healthy,
and pleasant for me, which could have created a good solution, that you
rejected and didn't want to hear about. When I woke up I remembered
my spirits and said, 'He really needs to know about this dream of mine.'
And so here you have it. If you do not find it amusing, all you need to
do is tell Cagliostro to rein in his spirits so that they stop appearing to
me. I could easily do without them.

PART V

EMPIRE

(1780–1787)

Having made a considerable mark on her 'unploughed land', in the 1780s Catherine was at the pinnacle of her imperial power. In her foreign policy, she was tireless in working to maintain a détente that would strengthen Russia within and without. The individual ambitions of dynastic houses in Sweden, Prussia, and Austria, as well as in Great Britain, would remain permanent and volatile challenges. Her first diplomatic triumph of the period was the policy of Armed Neutrality, proclaimed in February 1780 in response to vexations exerted by belligerent powers in the American Revolutionary War (particularly the British) on Russian ships. She declared that neutral nations should be allowed to trade unimpeded (Letter 137), and by 1783 she had succeeded in creating a European policy agreement of exceptional reach, with signatories including Denmark, Sweden, the Netherlands, Prussia, Austria, Portugal, and the Kingdom of the Two Sicilies. The ageing Frederick the Great had signed in 1781 as a last-ditch attempt to retain his alliance with Russia (Letter 138). But it was too late: at that very moment, in May 1781, Catherine rendered the Russo-Prussian alliance effectively defunct by concluding a secret alliance with Austria. The idea for this complete reorientation of Russian foreign policy arose during Joseph II's visit to Russia in May 1780, and it marked the definitive shift of Catherine's attention toward the so-called Greek project: a plan to eliminate the Ottoman Empire and to resurrect the Byzantine Empire in the lands of Greek antiquity and under the leadership of Catherine's second grandson, Constantine.

Even when Russia was not actively on the march, foreign policy dominated strategic interest. The first step was the annexation of Crimea, and, in July 1783, Potemkin led the Russians to occupy the territory and to receive its occupants' oath of allegiance to Russia, which the Ottoman Empire did not yet venture to oppose (Letter 147). As she was impatiently awaiting Potemkin's letter announcing that Crimea was hers, in June 1783 Catherine met Gustav III in person once more, this time in the small Finnish town of Fredrikshamn on the then border between Russia and Sweden (Letter 146). Each ruler had major policy objectives in agreeing to the encounter. Gustav wanted to form an alliance with Catherine and to win her approval for his plan to take Norway from Denmark by force; Catherine cleverly refused him by making a counter offer of an alliance between Russia, Sweden, and the very Denmark that Gustav hoped to attack. For her part, Catherine wanted to send the message to Gustav's ally, the Ottoman Empire, that they should not count on Sweden to defend them against the Russian annexation of Crimea, and in this she was successful.

With Crimea seemingly stable, Catherine then wished to exploit the cultural value of the region as an Edenic paradise and its association with Greek myth, which involved the promotion of the region as a trading emporium ripe for colonization (Letter 157). A remarkable episode in her reign was a historic journey to Crimea in 1787, the planning and execution of which is documented in her letters. The journey publicized the annexation as a success, and her entourage included well-connected figures like the diplomat–soldier and intellectual Prince Charles-Joseph de Ligne, with whom she had maintained a highly literary correspondence since his visit to St Petersburg in the winter of 1780 and who helped to spread news of the grandiose voyage in Europe. She met briefly again with Stanislas Poniatowski of Poland, but it was Emperor Joseph II whom she sought to impress as they travelled on a magnificent flotilla down the Dnieper. They paused to view Kherson, a showpiece as a town founded by Catherine and Potemkin in 1778 on land formerly belonging to the Khans of Crimea, and Sevastopol, where Catherine and Joseph reviewed Russia's new naval base and Black Sea fleet (Letter 159). Showing off her southern feats to the Austrian monarch was one way to flatter him into supporting her against the Ottoman Empire in future. The prime mover behind the Crimean spectacle, Prince Potemkin, was lavishly rewarded for his efforts and given the new title of 'Tavrichesky' ('of Tauris').

Her partnership with Potemkin was a mainstay of these years, and her letters to him reflect her skill at synchronizing intelligence as she briefs him on the European situation. Letters often show Catherine as a micro-manager, mastering multiple strategies and budgets as she allocates resources; her orders were frequently conveyed in these years through Potemkin, whose presence on the ground in the southern provinces made him indispensable in the management of empire. Their ambitions in foreign policy became increasingly bold in the 1780s and, to implement them, Catherine kept her eye on the workings of courts, psychological motives, and back channels of influence, ever alert to the complex balance of alliances the pacification of Crimea would require (Letter 146).

At home, Catherine's legislative endeavours culminated in a series of key enactments: the Police Ordinance of 1782, which provided a structure as well as moral guidelines for the police and separated out the jurisdictions of the police and the law courts; a decree of 1783 allowing the establishment of private printing presses for the first time in Russian history; and charters to the Nobility and the Towns of 1785, which laid out the rights and responsibilities of the gentry and townspeople, respectively, and regulated urban self-government.

Empire was about extending civilization and improving the welfare of subjects. Catherine attentively supervised and supported Potemkin's efforts to settle and develop Crimea and the other southern territories. At her request, her new literary correspondent in Germany, the doctor and writer Johann Georg Zimmermann, recruited twenty-three German doctors for Russian service mostly in that region (Letter 156). Health was, in general, a prime concern: in 1781, the English doctor Thomas Dimsdale returned to Russia to inoculate Catherine's grandsons Alexander and Constantine (Letter 140). Although Catherine was proud of the inoculation hospital in St Petersburg, it was slow to attract volunteers willing to undergo the procedure. She nonetheless continued her efforts, and a new quarantine and inoculation centre was established in 1783. She also pursued her interest in education, promulgating in 1786 the Russian Statute of National Education intended to set up schools throughout the Russian provinces.

Another domestic priority was to facilitate the flourishing of the arts—especially literature, to which, as a writer herself, Catherine attached great importance. In late 1782, Catherine appointed her old friend Ekaterina Dashkova director of the Academy of Sciences in St Petersburg, and the following year she also made her president of the new Russian Academy, which was to mirror the Académie française and create the authoritative dictionary of the Russian language (Letter 143). Despite initial hesitations, Dashkova devoted herself heart and soul to her tasks, and Catherine found that the best way to manage her unstoppable old friend was usually to indulge her plans.

As for Catherine herself, her continued commitment to the Age of Reason manifested itself in her trilogy of plays against mysticism and Freemasonry (*The Deceiver*, *The Deceived*, and *The Siberian Shaman*, 1785–6), and her lampoons of quacks and pseudo-scientists like Mesmer and Cagliostro in her letters (Letters 139, 160). Self-development through intellectual pursuit and civilized pleasures such as gardening, an enthusiasm shared with de Ligne into the 1790s, gave ballast to her duties and also provided comfort. The shift in her relationship with Potemkin had left Catherine eager for romance but also vulnerable— nowhere more apparent than in the devastation she felt at the sudden death of her favourite, Alexander Lanskoy, on 25 June 1784 (Letter 151). She sublimated her grief by renewing her research in languages, turning again to writing and, in collaboration with the scholar Peter Simon Pallas, compiling a *Comparative Dictionary of All Languages and Dialects* (2 vols, published 1787–9). This massive undertaking compared the words for essential terms like 'God', 'sun', and 'bread' in some 200 languages and had an element of linguistic imperialism (Letter 153); it also enabled her to score points in her semi-rivalrous friendship with Dashkova (Letter 155). Emboldened and delighted by her many achievements as a modernizer, commander, and cultural figure, Catherine no longer felt overshadowed by Peter the Great, the mythic reforming tsar. When the statue of the Bronze Horseman was unveiled in 1782 (Letter 142), four years after Falconet left Russia following a dispute over money, the statue was as much about her claims to immortality as her predecessor's.

137. *To Gustav III of Sweden*

Catherine cites two major diplomatic achievements of the year 1780. Her first meeting with Joseph II (who was travelling under the pseudonym of Count Falkenstein) in May 1780 brought about the Russian reversal of alliances from Prussia to Austria a year later. Similarly, the declaration of Armed Neutrality in February 1780 displayed Catherine's ability to orchestrate a large-scale, multi-state policy agreement.

at St Petersburg, this 22 April 1780

It would be a hard thing, dearest Brother, to forget you, but it is not only very common among us to be dilatory correspondents despite the world's best intentions, but, if I must be blunt, it is an illness that runs in the family and in our line of work.

The portrait of your charming little gentlemann,* of whom I hear a thousand good things and in whom I take an infinite interest, occupies the finest spot in the museum on my mezzanine. For a long time, I had him in my arms all the time, and I did nothing but look at him and show him to everyone. You see thereby that my gratitude, although it was not put into writing, existed nonetheless in my heart and mind.

What you were pleased to tell me of the coadjutor* confirms my opinion of him: he is one of the family and can be shown off without others finding fault with his deportment.

I am off in a few days, leaving pleasant Troezen.* I shall start by shutting myself up, starting tomorrow, to stay seventeen days at Tsarskoe Selo. I shall spend them gathering my wits, which have been scattered by eight months of hard work. After that, I shall mount my chariot to be borne, not through the air or pulled by griffins,* but as quickly as possible on the ground along the highway from Narva, Pskov, and Polotsk to Mogilev, where I am off to make the acquaintance of Count Falkenstein, a lord from a very good, ancient, and respectable house. The same fear that I felt before the arrival of the Count of Gotland* has me now in its grip again: well, we shall get by as best we can, since it is so easy to get on with people who are without affectation.

I beg you to pray for me, dearest Brother, in this predicament, since you are a great saint of the cult of the unaffected, and I entreat you to rest assured of all my sentiments.

Does Count Scheffer not find that my neutrality will bring about what many wars have not brought about?

138. *To Frederick II of Prussia*

In his last letter to Catherine, dated 23 April 1781 (NS), the ageing Frederick, hoping to retain his alliance with Russia, announced his impending accession to her League of Armed Neutrality. Catherine reassures him—just as the final details are being ironed out for the secret Russo-Austrian alliance of May 1781.

at Tsarskoe Selo, this 26 April 1781

My dear Brother, it is with satisfaction commensurate with our venerable and reliable friendship, long known to Your Majesty, that I received the letter that you were pleased to write to me on 22 April.* You thereby inform me of the approval which Your Majesty is so good as to give to the principles that the majority of the neutral powers have adopted and that you wish to solemnify by your formal accession to the treaty. I am firmly persuaded that Armed Neutrality cannot but acquire a new lustre when, among the names of the sovereigns who have recognized the principles of the treaty to be commensurate with those of equity and of the independence of states, the universe might count that of a great king whose dazzling virtues and heroic actions inspire among the nations just as great and deep a respect as does his power. Permit me, Your Majesty, to profess my gratitude for it. I am also most indebted to you for promising to recommend me well to Emperor Peter the First in the next world. However, it is no less in my interests to beseech Your Majesty to delay such an outing until the century following this one: then I shall have the time to accompany you and to witness your first interview with the illustrious personages of whom you do me the honour of speaking. Above all I would like to see Marcus Aurelius, Caesar, and Alexander fighting for precedence in coming before Your Majesty and turning the conversation to the Ancients, while blushing a bit at Your Majesty's deeds, which are the only ones they will envy. But in the end, in this world or the next, it will always be an honour for me to profess to Your Majesty on every occasion the very high regard and sincere friendship with which I shall never cease to be,

My dear Brother,

Your Majesty's good Sister and faithful Friend and Ally,

Catherine

139. *To Friedrich Melchior Grimm*

In spring 1781, instead of sending frequent letters by post, Grimm and Catherine began writing to each other at intervals of a few months so that their missives could be carried by Russian couriers traversing Europe. The text below constitutes two days' entries in a letter written from 8 July until 31 August 1781. In the first instalment, she tells the story of the visit by the Freemason and mystic Alessandro Cagliostro to St Petersburg in 1780. In the second, she gives an account of her reign and activities in thoroughly rational and even Voltairean terms of opposition to fanaticism and of enlightened, constructive leadership. Catherine enjoyed tallying up her achievements, and in this case the mock sums recall the famous 'Report to the King' published in 1781 by Jacques Necker, which revealed France's troubled financial situation to the reading public.

this 9 July

Since you speak to me of the charlatan Cagliostro, I, too, shall have to speak to you of him. He came here calling himself a colonel in Spanish service and a born Spaniard, letting it be known that he was a wizard, a master wizard, who could conjure spirits and who had them at his disposal. When I heard that, I said: 'That man was very wrong to come here. Nowhere will he be less successful than in Russia.' We do not burn wizards here, and in a reign of twenty years there has been but one single case in which it was claimed that there were wizards. When the Senate asked to see them, they were produced—and declared stupid and perfectly innocent. Mr Cagliostro, however, arrived at a very favourable moment for him, a moment when several Masonic lodges, besotted with the principles of Swedenborg, wanted to see spirits by any means possible. So they ran to Cagliostro, who said he possessed all the secrets of Dr Falk, the intimate friend of the Duc de Richelieu who once made him sacrifice to the black goat in the middle of Vienna.* But, unfortunately for him, he was not able to satisfy the curiosity of those who wanted to see and touch everything—when there was nothing to see or touch. Then Mr Cagliostro produced his marvellous healing secrets: he claimed to draw quicksilver from the foot of a gout-ridden man, and he was caught in the act of pouring a spoonful of quicksilver into the water in which he had had the gouty man placed. Then he produced dyes that dyed nothing and chemical reactions that did not react. After that he had a long and thorny quarrel with the Spanish chargé d'affaires, who disputed his title and his status as a Spaniard, and after that it was discovered that he hardly knew how to read and write. At last, riddled with debt, he took refuge in the cellar of Mr Elagin, the deposed or dispossessed Worshipful Master, where he drank as much champagne and English beer as he could. One day he apparently exceeded the usual limit: when as he rose from the table he grabbed the household secretary by the forelock; the latter gave him a slap; from one slap to the next some punches got mixed in. Weary of both Brother Cellar-Rat and of the excessive expenditure on wine and beer, and of the secretary's complaints, Mr Elagin politely persuaded him to leave in a kibitka* and not by air, as he had threatened to do. So that his creditors would not encumber this light equipage on its way, he gave him an old invalid to accompany him and my lady the countess to Mitau.* That is the story of Cagliostro, in which there is everything except anything marvellous. I never saw him either from afar or up close, nor was I at all tempted to see him, having no love of charlatans. I assure you that Rogerson spent as little time thinking about Cagliostro as he does about Noah's Ark, and perhaps less. Prince Orlov, contrary to his habit, cared not at all for Cagliostro: he even mocked those who out of mere curiosity were inclined to see him, and he contributed not a little to cooling the enthusiasm of the poor devil's shameful partisans. But since the most foolish and most ignorant charlatans have the right to make an impression in big cities, it is therefore to be supposed that Cagliostro will be right at home in Paris. I wish you a good journey and much enjoyment at Spa.

[...]

this 11 July

Many thanks for the jam that you sent me. Tell Sedaine that he is free to have his plays printed and to place my name at the top. But it will be a ticket to nowhere, since even passages of letters from lawyers in Chartres are being erased, even when one would never have guessed they were erasable.* But, my God, with all their goodwill, why are they so blissfully limping along in the tracks of their grandfather?* Truly, Lord Brother-in-Law does not do the same, and for that reason Lady Mother-in-Law has been so very soon forgotten too.* It is very useful for every young man to have in mind someone whose bent of mind he tries to follow. In my youth I always wanted to have everything in accordance with the mind and writings of Voltaire. Well, you know for yourself what came of it. As for Mr Alexander, he says, 'Yes, Grand-mamma will approve of it', and so he makes the knob of a walking stick into a soldier. Come on, shove into the mind of the good-willed grand-son the notion that he will be judged on how well he emulates his fore-fathers, and then let the young man go his way.*

I shall add Siberian furs to the golden medallions from my reign that have been prepared for Monsieur Buffon, and I would be very curious to know if he liked my bracelets found in Siberia.* I repeat my entreaty to obtain for me the bust of that illustrious man. I found the fragment of the Nabuchodonosorian tragedy most edifying: there are moments when one would like to see the Lord Ox's metamorphosis happen, or rather be renewed. I would immediately make into his devotees all those who believe in metamorphosis in the manner that Mr Grand Cham. explains it.* *Ma basta per lei:** one must first, I think, be prudent enough to publish an edict forbidding the consumption of roast beef, beef steaks, etc. From that you can see that I am thinking of how to preserve the species, even though you threaten that I shall never have a whit of their approval. I am delighted to know that Don Olavide is in Paris. In God's name, make sure he never returns to the lands of the Inquisition, and tell me whether he is demoralized by his experience or not, and what sort of life he leads in Paris. If I were in his shoes, I would thumb my nose at Mrs Inquisition, and she would never catch me again. I am very sorry that you do not think that I put the Inquisition and the Ox King on the same level.* I shall do more and add to the list plans for campaigns that lead only to useless expense; all that goes together. It is up to you to put my blunders over Tronchin's catalogue and the burnt cities of the Holy Roman Empire in the same category.* This year on 28 June, the factotum Mr Bezborodko came and brought me my report up until that day.* He is to add to it every year in the course of the year, and here is the laconic result:

In the past nineteen years:

Provincial governments erected according to the new model	29
Cities erected and built	144
Agreements and treaties concluded	30
Victories won	78
Memorable edicts containing laws or foundations	88
Edicts to ease the people's burden	123
	492

This is all state business, and no personal business has a place on this list, as you can see. Well, Sir, are you satisfied with us? Haven't we been idle?*

If Mr Haller is happy that he has been paid, I am too.* Mr Factotum must have acted and forgotten to tell me about it. Perhaps he will do the same for Gillet:* I shall go ahead and talk to him about it again. About the fire that reduced the Paris Opéra to ashes,* you tell me who was not burned, but you carefully avoid talking about those who were burned and whom your admirable firemen did not save, NB.

Leave the exchange rate be. One cannot always win. Mr Shuvalov is yelling about the exchange rate* because he has no other object on which to pour out his bile. Once it has gone low enough, it will climb again. All those people who do all that they can to make it go down then yell about the fact that it has gone down. Pope Braschi* owes me a reply that has been taking a good little while to come. If you become an angel of reconciliation at Spa, you are very skilful. But why did he not go to Prague?* But why did he never leave Dresden in the winter? That is what neither his friends nor his enemies can understand. I, who know everything without ever having learned anything,* I think that I know and can guess it, even though my teacher Voltaire forbids guessing because those who meddle with guesswork like to invent systems. And those who make systems want to force in everything, whether it fits or no and whether it rhymes or no,* and then love for oneself becomes love of one's system, which gives rise to stubbornness, intolerance, and persecution, which are drugs that my teacher says people should stay away from. I hope that with the help of the Lord this letter will draw more than one burst of laughter from your body, for never has a larger number of absurdities been found in such close proximity.

140. *To Gustav III of Sweden*

Having brought the English doctor Thomas Dimsdale back to Russia to inoculate her grandsons, Alexander and Constantine, Catherine encourages her cousin Gustav to do the same for his son. Gustav himself had been inoculated in 1769, but the practice did not become widespread in Sweden until the beginning of the nineteenth century.

Petersburg, this 15 December 1781

I could very well say, dearest Brother, that you seem to be judging me by your own experience when you ascribe my long silence to forgetfulness. But take comfort: I shall do you no wrong. I know that it is not so easy to forget one's neighbours, friends, and closest relatives. Since you tell me, dearest Brother, that you have been very busy this summer, I think that I did very well not to write to you.

I can very well believe that you had your reasons for taking the prince, your son, away from the ladies who were spoiling him. The same cannot be said of my grandsons. They are in perfect health, and their entourage is such that I can only hope to find their equal when it is time to hand my grandsons over to men.

I thank you, dearest Brother, for the joy that you say you felt at their recovery. They were inoculated this autumn by Baron Dimsdale, who about a dozen years ago performed the same operation on me, my son, and a few hundred other people here.* I confess that I am a bit surprised by the fear you show of inoculating the crown prince. Do you mean to leave him in constant danger of catching this terrible illness naturally, when it is in your power to diminish the sickness and its dangers? If you were in danger yourself, it was doubtless the fault of the method by which you were inoculated. You could very well, dearest Brother, send a good surgeon or doctor here to learn at the St Petersburg inoculation hospital Dimsdale's method of inoculating, which is incontrovertibly the best. And when he went home, he could convince you by inoculating children of lesser importance than the crown prince, and you would see, dearest Brother, that by this method it all becomes almost a trifle.

I shall not tell you about the sweetness of my grandsons, whom I love very, very much and who entertain me and keep me occupied most pleasantly. Once I start talking about them, I never stop. They are lively, raring to go, strong, and full of goodwill. The elder is learning to read and write on his own initiative, and he is a most determined questioner.

I see, dearest Brother, that you are making very early plans to send the prince, your son, travelling. If ever Russia were to be part of his tour, as you tell me it will, he will find the memory of the Count of Gotland's appearance etched in all our minds.

I shall not fail to inform my son of the invitation that you have made to him, dearest Brother, to pay you a visit. But truly, the kings and emperors of this century are behaving like good and loyal gentlemen who invite their neighbour to come and spend a few days on their estates. It is only the distances that are not exactly the same.

I shall not hide from you, dearest Brother, that I am not sure my daughter-in-law will have the resolve to cross the sea: she fears water like fire. While I await their reply, I thank you in my own name and in theirs for the very polite and friendly invitation that you have made them,* as well as for the obliging things that you say to me on the matter, and I beg you to rest assured of the persistence and reciprocity of my sentiments towards you.

Farewell, dearest Brother. Although you have not had any letters from me for a long time, here you have a good long one this time.

141. *To Grigory Potemkin*

After Prince Charles-Joseph de Ligne visited St Petersburg in 1780, he began corresponding with both Catherine and Potemkin; Potemkin acted as the intermediary who delivered de Ligne's letters to the empress. Here Catherine asks Potemkin to thank de Ligne for a copy of his 'Glance at Belœil' (1781), an essay on gardening in which de Ligne describes his own estate at Belœil and praises Catherine's at Tsarskoe Selo. Catherine and de Ligne shared a genuine love of gardening; the final two sentences of Catherine's note are a direct quotation from de Ligne's book.

[1782]

Mon Ami, when you thank him for his book, tell the Prince de Ligne that the description of Belœil enchanted me. I have always loved tempestuous minds and have scarcely read any other book that contains a bigger encyclopedia of mental operations than his. I sing his tune in saying that one should see and think of the beauty in everything.* Let no one complain.

142. *To Grigory Potemkin*

Potemkin left St Petersburg for the south shortly after the unveiling of Falconet's statue of Peter the Great on 7 August 1782. This letter keeps him up to date on family matters (especially the pregnancy of his niece, Countess Skavronskaia) and naval intelligence.

[12 September 1782]

My little master, I am sorry about the unpleasant companions, awful weather, bad roads, and poor horses that accompanied you to Pskov.* The fact that Gdov* is a bit prettier is nice enough, but I would like to expect better tidings from you. Yesterday, that is, on the 11th, I arrived in the city. In the entrance hall, I met Somers and enquired of him about the health of Countess Skavronskaia. He told me, and Rogerson confirmed this later, that she is much better and that she will be transferred today to the city.

Herewith I attach a letter to you from Alexander Dmitrievich Lanskoy, who is practically in tears because he has had not a line from you. Farewell, dear friend, be well, and return quickly and mirthfully to us.

It is said that the English were careless and lost a one-hundred-gun ship in the anchorage at Spithead, that the battle-hardened Admiral Kempenfelt* was drowned on it, and that out of nine hundred people only three hundred survived. They wanted to repair something and had moved the cannons across to one side and just at that moment the wind overturned and submerged the ship.

143. *To Princess Ekaterina Dashkova*

In December 1782, Catherine approached her old friend Ekaterina Dashkova at a ball and offered her the position of director of the Academy of Sciences in St Petersburg. Dashkova stayed up all night writing a letter in which she tried to decline the proposal. In this, her reply, Catherine refuses to take no for an answer, alluding to the events of her coup twenty years before. Catherine presents her choice as honouring her promise, given at the time, to recall always the ties which (as Dashkova repeatedly asserted) bound Dashkova's fate and fame to Catherine's (see Letter 12).

Monday, at eight o'clock in the morning

You are more of an early bird than I, since you provide me with a letter, my beautiful lady, at breakfast. I ought then to reply and thus begin the day more agreeably than usual. To begin with, since you are not refusing my proposal, I forgive you for the word 'incapacity', which you deigned to employ. I shall refrain from offering my gloss on this matter until the appropriate time and place. I knew that what you call my 'rights' is my gratitude, which dates from long ago. But I was

unaware that it was I and not Lady Nature, who had added gumption
to your character.

In any case be reassured that on any occasion when you think you
need it, it will be a pleasure for me to come to your assistance in deed
and in word.

144. *To Friedrich Melchior Grimm*

*These are the first two segments of a letter written between 19 and 29 April 1783.
Catherine follows her usual practice of commenting on Grimm's letters as she reads
them, adding her own thoughts and digressions at will. In the first segment, she discusses two of her current literary projects: first, her 'Notes Concerning Russian
History', which began appearing in serialized form in 1783 (later continued and
published as separate volumes in 1787–94). It was a digest of Russian history that
Catherine wrote to present her grandsons with past examples of wise Russian rulers
who rallied their people behind them. It was rapidly published in German translation
by the Berlin Enlightener Friedrich Nicolai, as part of the series of Catherine's
works entitled 'Library of Grand Dukes Alexander and Constantine'. The second
project is the 'Fairy-Tale of Tsarevich Fevey' (1783), which in 1786 she rewrote as
an opera libretto and had produced for her birthday celebrations. In the second segment, she mourns the death of her former favourite Grigory Orlov, who, since the
death of his young wife in 1781, had descended into mental illness.*

at Petersburg, this 19 April 1783, at seven o'clock in the morning, a day
on which they have taken away all my paperwork because I am leaving
for Tsarskoe Selo. Along the way I am opening the chapterhouse of St
George at Chesme* in the presence of the very formidable inkstand
that in the past made you gag so often.

You see that I have nothing better to do than to write to whipping-boys,
but God knows when this will be sent off. First I set about reading
your commentary on the forty-one pages, and I see that I have nothing
more urgent to do than to alert you that you are in danger of a flood of
paperwork worse than all those that have nearly drowned you.* You are
going to tremble in fear when you hear that the first age of the history of
Russia (that is, from the creation of the world to the year 862) is being
translated into German for you.* That alone comprises about forty
pages. It is part of the Alexander–Constantine library, so Whipping-Boy
must have it. Besides that, Mr Fevey will introduce himself to Your
Excellency, translated literally into French, as you wish him to be.
Perhaps the second age, at least twice as ample as the first, will be finished and translated before this document is dispatched. If that misfor-

tune occurs, you will have only one rather than two, since they will arrive together. The second age begins in the year 862 and ends in the middle of the twelfth century: all that was bungled up in three months' time or thereabouts. It will be an antidote to the rogues who degrade Russian history like Dr Le Clerc and Tutor Levesque,* who are fools (forgive me!), and boring and disgusting fools too. I beg your pardon in advance for all that clutter. Feel free to throw it in the fire and to do the same with the three last ages that will immediately follow the first two, for there will be five in all. You will say that Her Majesty is becoming a personage as boring as she is insipid. What can I do? Each person takes on the tone and the wit of his rank, and such is mine. Do you not also pity my tots that they have such fat morsels to digest? In the meantime, they have set about learning to write and to draw. Alexander's teachers say that he is making astonishing progress for his age, that other children flee their teachers, and that he finds that he never has enough time with them, but, for their part, they take great care to withdraw at the prescribed time. This winter we have discovered a peculiar desire of Mr Alexander's: one day he pulled into a corner one of my ladies, with whom he likes to play, and he urgently begged her tell him whom he resembled. She said that he seemed to have his mother's features. 'That is not', he said, 'what I am asking. My temper, my manners—whom do they resemble?' The lady told him: 'Well, in that you might very well resemble Grandmamma more than anyone else.' 'Ah!', he said, 'that is what I wanted to know', and he flung himself upon the lady's neck to kiss her for what she had said to him.

General Lanskoy is preparing a bundle of his own for you; it will fill up a corner of your apartment. [Richard] Brompton died without finishing the portrait he had begun. But you will see that Gen. Lanskoy's choice is not bad. God knows where he dug it up: he prowls all the studios every morning, and he has his own whipping-boys whom he puts to work like galley slaves. I think that in my gallery there are more than a half a dozen whom he drives mad every day. He calls one of them 'Bruder',* and each of the others has his own epithet, but I swear he does not know their names. I have never seen anyone who more readily calls people by names that one might have sworn were theirs. But in fact he hardly ever knows the name of any individual or individuals if he does not know them very well indeed.

at Tsarskoe Selo, this 20 April, at seven o'clock in the morning

The chapterhouse of St George set up house yesterday with a capital of 260,000 roubles, which my lord the Grand Master* took care to raise independently of the order's income. After that exploit, I came here, where I was awaited by the very sad news of the passing of Prince Orlov, who died in Moscow during the night of the 12th to the 13th of this month. Although I was quite prepared for this painful event, I confess to you that I feel the keenest affliction: I have lost in him a friend and the man to whom I owed the most and who rendered me the most essential services of anyone in the world. No matter that they tell me, and I tell myself, all that can be said on such occasions: fits of sobbing are my reply, and I have been suffering terribly from the moment I received the fatal news. Work alone can distract me, and, since I do not have my papers, I am writing to you for relief. Gen. Lanskoy is bending over backwards to help me to endure my pain—but all that just upsets me all the more. There is something remarkable in the passing of Prince Orlov: it is that Count Panin died fourteen or fifteen days before him,* and neither one knew of the other's death. Consistently of opposite opinions, and not at all fond of one another, those two men will be very surprised to see one another again in the next world. In truth, water and fire could hardly be more different. I spent many years caught between those two counsellors, and things nonetheless carried on, and carried on splendidly. But sometimes one had to do as Sir Alexander did with the Gordian knot,* and then views converged. The one had boldness of mind and the other mild prudence, and your most humble servant made a short gallop* between them: this lent a grace and an elegance to things that were not to be trifled with. You will say: 'How will you manage now?' To that I shall answer you, 'The best we can.' Each country always provides the necessary people, and since everything in the world is human, therefore humans can cope with it all too.* Prince Orlov's genius was very vast; his courage was, I believe, the *ne plus ultra* of courage. At the most decisive moment, there came into his mind precisely what was needed to turn a thing the way he wanted. And, when necessary, he was imbued just in time with such forceful eloquence that no one could resist it because it left everyone else uncertain, while he was the only one who was never uncertain. Despite those great qualities, he had little diligence for those things that seemed to him not to deserve it, and few things seemed to him to be worthy of that honour, or rather of that exertion, for diligence was an exertion for him. That made him seem more negligent and disdainful than he really was. Nature had spoiled him, and he grew lazy about everything he did not grasp instantly. Count Panin was naturally lazy, and he knew the art of passing that laziness off as deliberate prudence. His nature was neither as good nor as frank as Prince Orlov's, but he was worldlier and knew better how to hide his faults and vices, and he had large ones.

145. To Gustav III of Sweden

Catherine was a great promoter of a panacea invented in the 1720s by her former adversary and then ally at court, Aleksei Bestuzhev-Riumin: known as 'Bestuzhev drops' or, in France, as the 'General La Motte's Gold Tincture', it was a solution made with gold salts or iron chloride. In 1779, Catherine purchased the recipe and had it published the following year in the newspaper 'St Petersburg Messenger', hoping to popularize the Russian-made remedy. The argument that Catherine offers here for the drops' effectiveness reflects the empiricist attitudes of the Enlightenment. From the seventeenth century, the testimony of reliable witnesses was one of the primary forms of scientific proof, and, as a professed opponent of superstition and charlatanry, Catherine carefully presents herself as a witness to her chosen drug's scientific value.

at Tsarskoe Selo, this 21 April 1783

Rest assured, dearest Brother, that you are not wrong to say that you are convinced I share in your joys and your sorrows. I felt real pain at the bad news announced in your letter of 28 March.* I hope with all my heart that you can recoup such a significant loss* as soon as possible. But since you do me the honour of telling me in detail about the accident which carried off your second prince, permit me to recommend an effective remedy against convulsions, and especially those of teething children: Bestuzhev drops. I beg you not to believe the doctors and others who will tell you that they are General La Motte's drops. I have seen this remedy work miracles on such occasions in both the young and the old. Among others, I have seen an 11-day-old child who was, according to the doctors, on the point of death and who recovered thanks to this remedy in spite of their opinion; he is still alive and perfectly healthy. Two years ago, I saw here at Tsarskoe Selo a French dancer named Lefèvre who was brought low by that illness during a ballet rehearsal. The attack was so violent that eight men could scarcely hold him down: they wanted to bleed him. Instead, I gave him some of the drops in question. He had scarcely swallowed them when he came to. They were administered once more the same evening and the following morning. That evening he felt so well that he was able to dance the ballet in the play. I tell you only what I have seen with my own eyes. Moreover, it is the only effective remedy against pertussis of the stomach. If I told you all that I know of it, you would take me for a charlatan. I dare not send you any, dearest Brother, but if you would like some and if you ask me for some, and if the rumours of your upcoming trip to Finland come true, and if you were pleased to indicate, according to our ancient agreement, the place on the border where I might have the pleasure and the delight of seeing you again, I shall hand you myself one or several bottles of this excellent elixir.

Prince Golitsyn* is most fortunate to have won your approbation.

May Heaven preserve you from all future misfortunes. This year has been full of many events that have keenly affected me: I have lost several people whom I loved and esteemed, including General Bauer, Count Panin, and Prince Orlov. This best of all possible worlds makes us sigh so very much.*

Farewell, dearest Brother, be well and rest assured of my continued friendship.

146. *To Grigory Potemkin*

The preparation for annexing Crimea involved the exercise of both military and soft power. Shahin Giray, a Tatar Prince and the last Khan of the Crimea, requested the highest Russian order of chivalry, that of St Andrew, as a reward for ceding power to Russia. The motto of the order was 'For Faith and Fidelity'; Catherine had new insignia and an abbreviated motto designed to replace the usual Christian symbols for her new subject.

from Tsarskoe Selo, 5 June 1783

It is three days since I received from the King of Sweden a messenger with notification that he arrived safely in Åbo after twenty-two hours at sea; and yesterday he sent a second messenger with the information that during the inspection on horseback of his troops outside Tavastehus* his steed was startled by cannon fire, dashed off to the side, and His Majesty fell and shattered his left arm from the elbow to the shoulder. The messenger reports that the king was moved on a chair from there to Tavastehus Castle. He wrote himself using his right hand with a request that I agree to defer our meeting until the 20th of June; and to say that his physician encourages him to think that he will be able to be with me at that time with his arm in a sling. I replied with an expression of sympathy, dispatched a chamberlain for information about his health, and agreed to the postponement. Gosh, *mon Ami*, it's a clumsy hero who falls in this manner while executing manoeuvres in front of his troops.*

I received your letter, my dear friend, from 18 May. In order to satisfy the wish of the khan regarding the blue ribbon, and at the same time to maintain everything for which he and I are responsible, I have ordered the preparation of a blue ribbon to be worn across the shoulder with an oval medallion on which at the centre of its diamond surround there will be a word from the inscription of the Order of St Andrew: 'Fidelity'. There will also be a diamond star with the same inscription. He will have to be told that since he cannot wear a cross any more than I can give him one, for he is not a Christian, I am presenting him a blue ribbon with the inscription of the Order of St Andrew and as a privilege of that order the rank of lieutenant-general. I await eagerly news from you about the conclusion of the Crimean matter. Well, go on and take it before the Turks manage to show some resistance. I have ordered that the furs and things that you asked for be sent to you and Pavel Sergeevich as a gift.

The route that you suggest and that goes to Riga, up the Daugava,* and then along the Dnieper is not the most direct way to transport the licornes* to defend Sevastopol Bay against enemy vessels in Akhtiar harbour.* Of course you have other intentions in choosing that route. If you need them faster, then you should have them taken to Smolensk. From here to Riga it takes three weeks, and whether you can get through by going up the Daugava, Lord knows, but from there to the Dnieper will be by portage. However, I have still ordered that the licornes be sent.

Field Marshal Rumiantsev writes to me that he requires a general staff, engineers, and extraordinary funding. I ordered him to communicate his requests to you. He is anxious that the Turks might head him off. Since war has not yet been declared, it seems that everything will still be able to make it in time.

Adieu, mon Ami, be well.* After this campaign I shall change my generals and war commissaries.

Zorich was going to come here, but I sent to tell him that until he resolved the Zanovich business* I did not want to lay eyes on him. He then requested permission to go to Cesvaine,* which I granted.

147. *To Grigory Potemkin*

Potemkin's month-long silence had Catherine on tenterhooks regarding Crimea. Five days before she wrote this letter, Potemkin had finally written: 'Three days from now I will congratulate you on Crimea.' The news of his success arrived on 20 July.

from Tsarskoe Selo, 15 July 1783

You can imagine my state of anxiety, not having had a line from you in more than five weeks. Moreover, we have false rumours that I have no way to refute. I expected the conquest of Crimea to take place in mid-May at the latest, but it is now mid-July and I'm about as knowledgeable about it as the pope. Inevitably this creates all sorts of chatter, which I find thoroughly disagreeable. In any case I ask you in every possible way to keep me informed more often so that I can follow how things unfold; it is in the natural vivacity of my intelligence and mind to forge a thousand ideas that often torment me.*

All sorts of stories are reaching me also about the plague. You can calm down my spirit with more frequent communication. I am unable to say anything else, since neither I nor anyone else actually knows where you are. I am sending this to Kherson on the off-chance. Field Marshal Rumiantsev is as usual on the lookout for various unappetizing blunders.*

Adieu, mon Ami, stay well. When will your Crimean saga finally be over once and for all?*

148. *To Gustav III of Sweden*

Gift-giving was essential to international diplomacy. Here Catherine thanks Gustav for a substantial shipment of such gifts: materials for the 'Notes Concerning Russian History' that Catherine was then writing, toys for her grandsons, and the diamond cross of the Swedish Order of the Polar Star for her favourite, Alexander Lanskoy.

at Tsarskoe Selo, this 28 August 1783

I must thank you most sincerely, dearest Brother, for the Swedish books that you have been so good as to send me. I admired the catalogue that Your Majesty yourself made of them and that contains a concise summary of each of the books. I doubt that all your scholars together know more than you do about the history of Sweden, and henceforth I shall regard Your Majesty not as a king (such people, like all great lords, know everything without having learned a thing), but rather as a scholar of history, one of the worthiest academicians of my Academy.* Therefore, after the passages that I need have been translated, I shall have all these fine books, in their magnificent bindings and with the so very precious catalogue written in Your Majesty's hand, deposited in the Library of the Academy of St Petersburg, and it will not be one of the least precious items preserved there. I am also much indebted to Your Majesty for the permission that you have allowed me to grant to whomever I shall send to Uppsala to copy the Russian manuscript that is preserved there: I shall not fail to take advantage of it. I have ordered that someone be chosen specifically for this purpose and sent off. The anecdote of which you have informed me, dearest Brother, about copies of a chronicle being burnt leads me to believe that it was one of those that people kept in their houses and which fuelled chicanery and private quarrels. To curtail them, it was agreed by common consent to burn all those books in a single day and to regard those that survived as null and void. Thousands of copies escaped the conflagration, but they are no less interesting for all that: their antiquity can be recognized by certain letters of the alphabet that have not been used since the fourteenth century.*

I have no doubt that my grandsons will take great pleasure in receiving the toys that the crown prince has given them as gifts. These gifts evidently are the result of his conversations with his royal Papa: at least I seem to discern in them traces of his friendship for me, sentiments which he is evidently trying to inspire in his son, the prince. I cannot but be touched by them: I hope that mine will inherit my manner of thinking and the reciprocity of my friendly sentiments for Your Majesty, my closest relative, and for your royal family.

I am very sorry, dearest Brother, that your arm is giving you trouble.* I hope that the waters of Pisa and the air of Italy will help to fortify Your Majesty's health. Since I have heard that Your Majesty wished to have *kissel*, *shchi*, and *kvas*, and since those drinks are untransportable,* I am sending to Your Majesty along with the *drozhki** and other light vehicles of this country a man who can instruct the kitchen boys at the court of the Lord of Gripsholm in the great art of composing the aforementioned drinks. He has been furnished with all the precious ingredients that go into them, and within eight days the kitchen boys will excel unfailingly and without great expense in the great art of making them every day of the year, to the satisfaction of aficionados.

The general with the diamond cross is at Your Majesty's feet, and he is perfectly ignorant of how he deserved all your favours and goodness.

I very much hope, dearest Brother, that you will everywhere remain convinced of the unchanging sentiments which I profess to have for Your Majesty.

149. *To Grigory Potemkin*

In addition to his many other duties, Potemkin was also a valuable advisor on Church affairs: interested in religion from his youth, he was appointed assistant to the Procurator of the Holy Synod by Catherine in 1763.

Dear friend of my heart, I am in a state of extreme anxiety about you and so am sending a special courier to learn how you are. I hear from strangers that you are, it seems, somewhat better. With all my heart, I hope that's true and more than anything that you will make a complete recovery. I shall give you my opinion concerning business: should the Turks not declare war on us before 1 October, then the troops should be bivouacked in their winter quarters at that time. As to where precisely, however, I ask you to send me your opinion, provided you are strong enough to do so (which I sincerely hope is so with the help of God). Bohusz-Siestrzencewicz came here and delivered your letter, and I found him still much as you describe. Because of the death of our metropolitan in Kiev,* I shall transfer the Metropolitan of Rostov to Kiev. But to make sure that those in Novgorod, Moscow, and Pskov are not in black klobuks* when he dons his white one, I am thinking about attiring all three of them in white klobuks by giving them the title of metropolitan. And to the eparchies* in Rostov and Vladimir, currently vacant, I shall promote by rank as per the decision of the Synod.*

We are currently hearing from all over about French intrigues and scheming. This will all come to nothing, as long as you are well. The most important thing is that you be healthy. Farewell, my dear friend.*

150. *To Grigory Potemkin*

Catherine reports to Potemkin what she has heard from her representative in Sweden, Arkady Morkov, about Gustav's assertive foreign policy aims, abetted by the French. As Catherine mentions, there were substantial diplomatic ties between Russia and Denmark: Russia had signed a defensive alliance with Denmark in 1765 and a formal treaty of alliance following the exchange of Holstein in 1773, and Denmark had acceded to Catherine's policy of Armed Neutrality in 1780.

17 May 1784

Friend of my heart, I received your letter from Kremenchuk. I rejoice that in places this plague is drying up, and hope that thanks to your good orders it will be entirely eliminated in Kherson. From England and Denmark a great deal of detailed news is arriving about the escapades, bordering on lunacy, that the Swedish king has undertaken against Norway and even against the city of Copenhagen—so much that there can scarcely be any doubt or mistake. He cannot attack Denmark without becoming embroiled with us. And therefore in order to put a lid on his rash deeds as quickly as possible, I have ordered the General Staff to prepare 10,000 infantry, 3,000 cavalry, and forty pieces of field artillery for the military camp situated beyond the Neva, and ordered the provisioning store in Finland to provide forage for the same number sufficient for a whole year, while you will send here one or two regiments or between 1,000 and 2,000 Don Cossacks.

The Danes are preparing for any contingency. There will be enough naval firepower to quash all of Sweden, that is: five ships coming from Livorno, three from the city of Archangelsk, a further seven from Kronstadt, while the Danish will have six in the Øresund. I have commanded that the Swedish ambassador be told that these rumours are rife and that, while arguably they do not deserve to be credited, the Swedes must know, all the same, that it will be awkward for them to attack the Danes when the latter have an ally in Russia.

You saw that even what the Swedish king said to Morkov was in character. Let us now observe whether, after leaving France, he tones down this foolishness, or not. I reckon that he should not expect much aid from the Turks to come of that celebrated treaty of alliance about which he boasts.

We have had continuous freezes; the leaves on the birches are not larger than a silver penny; and the limes and oaks are not even thinking about putting out leaves. The grand duchess is pregnant once again and thinks she will give birth in November.

Let ships be built in Smolensk; how they will travel can always be worked out. Farewell, be well. I was pleased to hear that you are trying your hand at agricultural things, too. Success is undoubted, for when you apply yourself to things, they go swimmingly. *Adieu, mon Ami*, I love you a lot and rightly.*

151. *To Friedrich Melchior Grimm*

Catherine exuberantly recounts her activities as an enlightened ruler, a role that she viewed as intimately linked to her cultivated aesthetic tastes. After the secularization of Church estates in 1764 (much to Voltaire's delight), Catherine continued Peter the Great's policy of close state control over Church affairs, and in April 1784 she approved a new census and reform of the clergy. But her joy was brutally interrupted by the sudden death of her beloved favourite Alexander Lanskoy on 25 June 1784.

at Tsarskoe Selo, this 7 June 1784

I rose at half past six, and I wrote the following in a certain memorandum that I am writing and that we call 'materials': 'NB convents and religious communities are bad legatees: either they manage poorly, or they manage so excessively well that they become unjust.' This fine reflection immediately spawned the idea that I should write to you to tell you that I heard the astonishing Todi sing for the second time yesterday, and that I lost my head over this singer (who is, in my opinion, one of a kind). She proves to me that perfection has its incontestable rights and that the rights of perfection are such that they steal the souls of the wise and the ignorant. Now that I've told you this, can you tell me how and why the first and the second idea could go hand in hand and follow one another in my head? I see no analogy between them, unless they were conjoined by my desire to communicate to you both one and the other.

this 2 July

When I began this letter, I was living in happiness and joy, and my days passed so quickly that I knew not what became of them. It is no longer so: I have been plunged into the acutest pain, and my happiness is no more. I thought that I myself would die from the irreparable loss I suffered only a week ago—that of my best friend. I had hoped that he would become the helpmeet of my old age. He worked hard and benefited from it. He had come to share all my tastes. He was a young man whom I was cultivating; who was grateful, gentle, and honest; who shared my woes when I had them and rejoiced at my joys. In a word, I have the misfortune of telling you, through my sobbing, that General Lanskoy is no more. A malignant fever, joined with the quinsy, carried him off in five days to his grave, and my chambers, formerly so pleasant to me, have become a vacant cavern in which I can scarcely even drift like a shadow. A sore throat and a raging fever overcame me on the eve of his death. Nonetheless I am out of bed since yesterday, but so weak and sorely afflicted that at present I cannot see a human face without my sobs robbing me of speech. I can neither sleep nor eat, reading bores me, and it exceeds my strength to write. I do not know what will become of me, but I do know that in my whole life I have never been so miserable as I have been since my best, amiable friend thus abandoned me. I opened my drawer and found this page begun. I traced these lines, but now I can bear it no more.

152. *To Prince Charles-Joseph de Ligne*

Already planning to invite the Prince de Ligne back to Russia, Catherine imagines him inspecting the latest additions to her garden, including a copy of Jean-Antoine

Houdon's 'Voltaire Seated' installed in a grotto at Tsarskoe Selo. She also reminds him of the social gatherings in her Hermitage, which ranged from larger, more formal occasions, to the relaxed, salon-style atmosphere of her 'small Hermitage' parties.

at Tsarskoe Selo, 18 August 1784

Prince de Ligne, Sir, your letter of 17 April has not got lost. It did a tour of the Crimean Peninsula and the Caucasus. Prince Potemkin brought it to me in fine condition from there. But the letter arrived at a moment when I was busy studying universal grammar* and for that reason I excused myself from responding to the letters people wrote to me. I scarcely even speak any more except in monosyllables. On the other hand, I make the most wonderful and rare discoveries daily. I do feel obliged to keep them to myself, since experience has already taught me that when I share with others some of the finer points of my discoveries, people either turn away from me or reward me with malicious smiles.

If you should arrive here, my Prince, by balloon,* I shall reconcile myself to this lovely invention. Apprehensive that it may increase the risks of fire for the wooden buildings of which we have far too many in our lands, I have banned it. The balloon crash in Lyons etc. has not yet inspired trust among us in this new mode of transport. If you land at Tsarskoe Selo you will see Voltaire seated there in the middle of the handsomest Roman statuary, cast in bronze in Petersburg. NB Hercules and his club are missing.

Rest assured, my Prince, that it is not the testimonial you give for Louis XVI's new minister* that will harm him. But these gentlemen only view things through an excessively cautious lens and only listen through ear trumpets that confuse one sound for another.

As for you, my Prince, I know that your manner of seeing things is far from biased. Also, in truth, I am counting on you to think about me in an amiable way. I make it out as something of importance for me and still hope to have the pleasure of seeing you again some day in a large or medium or even in a very small group of friends.

Catherine

153. *To Friedrich Melchior Grimm*

As Catherine began to recover from her grief at Lanskoy's death, she turned again to writing. This time, after reading the Frenchman Antoine Court de Gébelin's 'The

Primitive World, Analysed and Compared with the Modern World' (9 vols, 1773–82),
particularly volume 2 on universal and comparative grammar, Catherine decided to
work with the scholar Peter Simon Pallas to compile a 'Comparative Dictionary of
All Languages and Dialects' (2 vols, 1787–9). As Catherine implies here, it had
a political as well as a scholarly agenda: to use etymology to trace Russia's imperial
reach and cultural prominence to the most ancient times.

at Petersburg, this 9 September 1784

I must answer three of your letters, the last of which, dated 11 (22)
August, requires a prompt reply.

I must admit that all this time I have been in no state to write to you
because I knew that it would cause us both to suffer. Count Fedor
Orlov and Prince Potemkin arrived eight days after I wrote you my
letter in July. Until that moment I could not stand human faces. These
two went about it the right way: they started wailing along with me,
and then I felt at ease with them. The way forward was hard, and my
excessive sensitivity had made it impossible for me to have other feelings apart from grief. The latter increased and was fuelled by each step
and each word. Yet do not go and think that, despite the horror of the
situation, I neglected even the smallest matter demanding my attention. In my most awful moments, I was asked to give orders on all
things, and I gave them well, methodically and intelligently. General
[Nikolai] Saltykov was particularly struck by this. More than two
months passed without any sort of relief. At last there came a few
interludes, at first calmer hours, and then days. As the season progressed and the weather grew damp, the apartments at Tsarskoe Selo
had to be heated. Mine started smoking, but with such violence that
on the evening of the fifth of September, no longer knowing where to
take shelter, I called for a carriage and went unexpectedly and unsus-
pected to town, where I disembarked at the Hermitage. Yesterday
I went to Mass for the first time, and consequently I saw everyone for
the first time as well, and everyone saw me. But, truly, it was such an
effort that, on returning to my chamber, I felt so weary that anyone
other than myself would have fainted, which is something that has
never happened to me in my life.

Now let us come to the principal points of your letter. The *Queen
of Golconda** has not arrived, as far as I know. When Emilie marries,*
give her 12,000 roubles on my behalf, and if you have no money from
me, draw up a promissory note for us. But let it not be put in the
newspapers.

Give Diderot's widow* 1,000 roubles: that makes five years' pension

in advance, at 200 *livres* a year. I shall respond to all the other points of
your letter another time. For the moment, you must pardon me. Truly,
I am making such an effort, since I have been weakened by God knows
how many various kinds of fevers that I have endured over the past two
and a half months. In the meantime, I have read half a dozen Russian
chronicles and three volumes of *The Primitive World*. Are you familiar
with that book? And I have had brought to me all the language dictionaries I could find, including a Finnish one, one of the language of the
Cheremis, and one of the Votyaks.* And my tables are covered with all
that. In addition, I have gathered copious knowledge of the ancient
Slavs, and I could at the drop of a hat prove that they were the ones who
gave names to most of the rivers, mountains, valleys, circles,* and
regions of France, Spain, Scotland, and other places.

Farewell for now. You are now, on the whole, as up to date as you wish
to be on all that concerns me.

I am most obliged to you for your offer to come here. But I advise you
to do no such thing, for you would either see me die, or I would see you
die, and that would only grieve the one who was left. As for purchases,
speak to me no more of them, and most of all not of a certain kind.*
I have long since ceased to buy for myself.

154. *To Johann Georg Zimmermann*

*Another source of solace for Catherine after Lanskoy's death was the Hanoverian
doctor Johann Georg Zimmermann's 'On Solitude' (4 vols, 1784–5), which combined Enlightenment critique of irrational Church practices with a pre-Romantic
interest in melancholy. Catherine rewarded Zimmermann with a golden portrait
medallion of herself, a diamond ring, and a flattering little note in January 1785. In
this reply to Zimmermann's letter of 29 March 1785 (NS), Catherine seeks to consolidate her new literary correspondence by presenting her own intellectual activity.
She also furnishes her new literary representative with a fine gift of medallions,
which could serve as conversation starters for him to advertise Russian exploits to his
friends, acquaintances, patients, and visitors.*

at Petersburg, this 9 May 1785

I have just received your charming letter, Sir, of 29 March. I am
delighted to see that mine dispersed the clouds that had surrounded
you. In a sense, it gave you the same assistance that I received from your
book: by showing me the thorns hidden in solitude, you drew me out of
my near-seclusion of almost nine months, which I had found difficult

to leave. You will hardly be able to guess what I did there, and since this was such a rare occurrence, I shall tell you. I drowned my woes in an unprecedented hodgepodge. I made a register of 200–300 root words in the Russian language. I had them translated into as many languages and tongues as I could find, already more than 200 in number. Every day I took one of the words, and I wrote it in all the languages I could gather. This taught me that Celtic resembles Ostyak;* that what means 'sky' in one language means 'cloud', 'fog', or 'vault', in others; and that the word 'God' in certain dialects signifies 'the most high' or 'the good', while in others it is 'the sun' or 'fire'. I grew weary of this hobby-horse once the book on solitude had been read through.* But since I would have been sorry to throw such a large mass of paper into the fire (the room, about ten fathoms long, in which I lived as a study in my Hermitage, was in any case quite warm enough), I invited Professor Pallas to come and visit me. After I had made an exact confession of this sin, we agreed that, by printing them, we would render these translations useful to those who would wish to busy themselves with other people's boredom. To this end we are awaiting nothing more than a few dialects of eastern Siberia. Whoever wishes may or may not discern here many different strokes of brilliance; that will depend on the respective mental dispositions of those who will busy themselves with it. It no longer concerns me at all. Perhaps it will produce some miracle almost as good as that which St Anthony, dressed by you,* worked on me. The two volumes of that excellent book that you promise me will be most welcome: I need not tell you how much I value it, as I flatter myself that you already know. Please note that all this is meant to be a reply to your letter and that I have now arrived at the place where you speak so touchingly and so much in harmony with my own thoughts about my Prince Orlov.* Yes, Sir, you describe just as he was that unrivalled and truly great man, so little understood by his contemporaries. You and I will miss him always. On two famous occasions his courage and his heroic virtues were displayed in their true light. I commemorated the latter, the Moscow plague of which you speak, with a triumphal arch at Tsarskoe Selo. Its inscription says simply that Orlov saved the city of Moscow from total ruin, which is as true as what it says on the medallion that you liked* and that I am sending you. It is accompanied by one for his brother, struck to mark the famous Battle of Chesme, which reduced the Sublime Porte's naval forces to total inaction for a long time. These two medallions are a rare example in a single family and are not poor proof of their virtues, glorious for the individuals and useful for their fatherland. Your friend Weikard is presently troubled by rheumatism of the hip: he has exhausted all remedies for it, but I, who am no doctor, shall perhaps cure it.* As for my health, it continues to be as you wish it to be. I cannot finish my letter without telling you how touched I am by all the agreeable and flattering things that I find in it.* I would have you know, please, that your view of things it is no way indifferent to me. This proves to you, moreover, the esteem in which it is held by

Catherine

155. *To Friedrich Melchior Grimm*

In these extracts from a long letter that Catherine wrote, diary-style, from 28 October until 23 November 1785, Catherine asserts her intellectual maturity. She speaks jokingly of the official 'Dictionary of the Russian Academy' (1789–94): she disagreed with the semi-etymological organization of the dictionary, preferring an easier-to-use alphabetical order, but she did not enforce her views in an authoritarian manner and left Dashkova and her staff to complete the work as they saw fit. At the end of the letter she addresses the problem of theory versus practice in government, discussing both Jacques Necker's 'On the Administration of Finances in France' (1784) and Diderot's then unpublished 'Observations on the Nakaz [the Russian name for Catherine's 'Instruction']' (1774). Critiquing the French government for talking too much and doing too little, she levels a rather similar accusation at Diderot, who wrote in the abstract, without understanding the realities of governance. She then defends her 1767 'Instruction' by insisting that its values had guided her later reforms without creating chaos of the sort that would soon menace France.

this 2 November

I am much obliged to you, and to Monsieur de Ségur as well, for preferring me to my dear neighbour Abdülhamid the Beheader. Zounds, whoever wishes can support him—when the time comes, we shall see. Once again, I beg you most insistently to leave my ignorance undisturbed. The Grand Equerry Naryshkin and I are professional ignoramuses, and we drive the Grand Chamberlain Shuvalov and Count Stroganov mad with our ignorance: they are both members of twenty-four academies at least, and namely of the Russian Academy.* Now, partly to put them in a rage and to show them that their Russian dictionary must be guided by the views of ignoramuses, we put together the *Vocabulary* in God knows how many languages, and that work is the work of *ignorantissimi bambinelli*.*

After treading many ways and byways this summer, I am still very ambulatory this autumn. For, since the day I returned to town, I have been getting up every morning at six, drinking a cup of coffee, and then fleeing to the Hermitage, and there, from six till nine, I am at it, turning and returning a hodgepodge I call an 'extract'. Then Sire Factotum and all the factotums come.* At eleven I return to my chambers to dress and to play with the cohort of grandsons and granddaughters. When I am dressed, I return to dine at the Hermitage. After dinner, I return to my apartments, and from there once again to the Hermitage, where I start off by giving hazelnuts to a white squirrel whom I tamed myself. Then I play several games of billiards. Then I go to see my cameos or engravings, or I wander among the paintings, after which I pay a visit to a charming monkey of mine who is so mad that I can never see him without laughing. At four I return to my chambers; I read or write until six. At six I go out into my antechamber, with which I am reconciled.* At eight I ascend to my mezzanine where a more select company joins me. At eleven I go to bed.* Now you can follow me step by step all winter, if you have the urge.

When the toy ambassadors were taken out of their box and brought to Tsarskoe Selo, I did it to keep my word, which I gave on the road, not only to show them Tsarskoe Selo in the greatest detail, but also to take them with me to see Pella's beautiful and agreeable location.* The dinners and suppers at the Naryshkins were also unavoidable. That is all very much in order, despite all the clamouring crib-biters.* I swear I know not what has become of Count Anhalt:* Factotum has your letter for him, but he knows no better than I where to send it. He may very well have crossed the Caucasus and gone to the court of King Heraclius in Georgia. I would not swear that the adventure hasn't tempted him and that he isn't now surrounded by the most beautiful of all possible Georgian ladies. Zelmira and her boor have returned from Vyborg. She claims that she has had nothing to complain about from him this summer. They have been back here for three weeks. Today she dined with me at noon. I did not, and shall not, give Zelmira her parents' letters* unless I think it necessary. Zelmira is young, inexperienced, and, it seems to me, weak of character. She is less timid, however, than she is put upon, and since they seem to be getting on well, I do not wish to reawaken a sleeping beast. But if their misunderstandings reawaken, I shall let loose the letters, and her parents may be certain that I shall not abandon her for as long as she remains within my realm. She was at Tsarskoe Selo this summer without her husband, and this autumn she spent six weeks with him at Vyborg of her own accord, in order to have her children inoculated.

There is a touching passage in your letter to which I cannot reply. I do not wish to burst into tears.* But why did Roman emperors, on the anniversary of their accession to the throne, bore Rome or their court with what they had done? Do you know that there is nothing as boring as such a recapitulation, and that I have never managed to read even one of all Mr Thomas's eloquent eulogies?* They belong to the genre of the boring, and my teacher, Voltaire, used to say that of all genres, the boring one was the worst. And so, that genre is no good. Permit me to stick to the one I have adopted and not to imitate those of others. I shall be very glad to see this Marquis de La Fayette, if he speaks in the manner of his cousin Ségur, who is never ill at ease, but whose health has been very precarious since he has been back here.

Those Belorussian rascals are fools: they just lost a big one,* but they have enough blockheads of the same metal to replace him.

I am very pleased with the good testimonial I have received from Monsieur de Ségur's valet in Paris, Versailles, and Saint-Cloud. I know nothing more of him than that he made some reed flutes that the grand equerry showed us. If he enjoyed the trip, then, truly, I am well pleased. The German translation of the notebooks on Russian history has been delivered to its master,* who wants to translate it into French himself.

[…]

this 8 November

Shchedrin began working on my bust for you* eight or ten days ago.

I have read the introduction to Mr Necker's book—I just finished it. Since esteem moves him, assure him that he has all of mine. One can see that he held the right post and filled it with passion; he admits it himself. I like the words: 'What I did, I would do again.'* One cannot speak thus without being good; one must be desperately so to have lost nothing after many trials. I am going to go and read the rest, and I shall speak to you of it again before the end of this missive.

Poor people. People without boots cannot stand people with boots.* They are too strong, too fat, too heavy, too reasoned, too argumentative, too full. All that is burdensome. Do more, prattle less: that too is a way that sometimes has hit home more often than all lofty chatter about oneself. There are indeed more people in the world who do not always wish to see their faces in the mirror. Well, he sits there and is bored and therefore he writes, but how does that help?* Who will look for people to match the painting? And where to find them? It is an art to make things go as well as possible, and better every day, with people of all sorts.*

[…]

this 23 November

I found in the catalogue of Diderot's library a notebook entitled: *Observations on H.I.M.'s Instruction to the Deputies for the Composition of*

Laws. This morsel is utter prattle in which one finds neither knowledge of things, nor prudence, nor foresight. In order for my *Instruction* to have been to Diderot's taste, it would have to have been capable of setting everything topsy-turvy. But I maintain that my *Instruction* was not just good, but even excellent and well tailored to the circumstances. For, in the eighteen years it has existed, not only has it done no harm, but rather all the good that has been done and that is recognized by everyone began with the principles established in that *Instruction.* Criticism is easy, but art is difficult. That is what one can say when reading the observations of a philosopher who, it seems, was prudent enough to live his whole life well supervised. He must have written that after he returned from here, for he never spoke to me of it.

156. *To Johann Georg Zimmermann*

Zimmermann discussed in his letters the terms of the employment of the German doctors he had recruited for Russian service. He was particularly concerned with providing for the two more prestigious recruits, a Doctor Meyer and a specialist in mining, Falkenberg. After responding to Zimmermann's queries, Catherine then discusses her latest dramatic works, a trilogy of anti-Masonic comedies which, with Zimmermann's help, were promptly published in German translation in Berlin. 'The Siberian Shaman' (1786) promotes the conviction of the 'Encyclopédie' that mystics are mere swindlers who oppose the progress of science and reason.

this 17 April 1786 OS
at St Petersburg

I received yesterday, Sir, your letter of 7 April NS. It informs me of the pains you have taken to obtain good doctors and surgeons for us. The two dozen that you promise us will be very useful. I cannot but approve the measures that you and my envoy Mr Gross have taken between you. The gentlemen you will have examined will not have to go through the College of Medicine's examination ceremonies, since I exempt them and give you my complete confidence. Fear not: Dr Meyer will not have much to do with the College of Medicine. All urgent cases, and namely all suspected cases of the plague, here fall under the jurisdiction of the provincial government. He will be most welcome, as will Master Falkenberg. The memorandum included with your letter, Sir, is evidence of your desire to further my aims. Some Swiss families are coming, and they may be useful. I am very glad that Mr Kalifalkzherston* amused you. All that you say about the play is most flattering for its author. Immediately after that comedy he produced another, entitled *The Deceived*. I do not remember too well whether I have sent you the translation: in any case, I include a second copy with this letter. A third is on the work-bench: it is *The Siberian Shaman*. The article 'Theosophist' in the *Encyclopédie* gave me the outline. You will have it in due course. The first two plays met with a prodigious success here: the pit wanted no other plays, and they brought in over—and well over—20,000 roubles for the impresarios. Farewell, rest assured of my most perfect esteem.

Catherine

157. *To Prince Charles-Joseph de Ligne*

As Catherine prepares to depart on her voyage to Crimea, she expresses her delight that de Ligne has accepted her invitation to join her on the trip.

at Petersburg, this 2 December 1786

Prince de Ligne, Sir, your letter of 15 November reached me a few days ago. It gave me true pleasure, and soon I shall have that of seeing you again. My departure from here to Tsarskoe Selo is fixed for 2 January, and from there I shall be en route on the 4th. If it pleases God, I shall arrive in Kiev on 25 January. I shall wait there for the ice to thaw on the Dnieper before embarking. This will be in April, more or less.

My itinerary bears no resemblance at all to the brilliant image of the sun which you employ. We are taking every possible precaution to resemble skies dense with clouds: each of the stars that will accompany me will be furnished with excellent and thick black furs. And since all the stars—my travel companions—would like their furs to be in the same style, the model we have is driving everyone to despair. I myself would prefer it to be just torn up or lost, so as not to hear any further talk about it. This bad mood will long have passed and the magnificent constellation of the Bear risen by the time your friends rejoice at seeing you again. I shall join the chorus. I hope the voyage down the Dnieper will go well and that it does not bore you. Medusa heads, which petrify people as soon as they appear, are not good company. I have always tried to avoid adding to their number.* You will find the grand equerry unrecognizable—not least because since his illness he has cultivated a hairstyle that gives him the look of a chorister. I suspect that he harbours a wish to conquer the Tritons of the Black Sea, for over the past summer he was very busy breaking in chargers that were more suitable for swimming than racing.* Reports indicate that he has travelled a great deal since you saw him last. Why, he has even attempted a trip to the other world. All this means that he has done well for himself and not even forgotten Chinese. At the moment there are two people who claim to have spent seven years in China. I recommend the other one to you* in advance and am convinced that you will not feel sorry at making his acquaintance. I hope, my Prince, that the journey will not cause your eye to smart,* and that quite soon I shall have the satisfaction of telling you in person the distinguished feelings I bear you. These are very different from those of Monsieur your father and the two tutors you have told me about.* I believe you have more than one manner, and the occasions on which I have had the pleasure of knowing you have inspired in me a very special esteem for you.

Catherine

158. *To Friedrich Melchior Grimm*

Busy with preparations for her journey to Crimea, Catherine took time out to express in a verbal portrait her infatuation with her new favourite, Alexander Dmitriev-Mamonov.

from Petersburg, this 17 December 1786

I received your nos. 76 and 77, one after the other, through Bacchus.* I find there is nothing to say in reply, as Mr Whipping-boy has arranged it all admirably well. If you take up the subject of Mr Redcoat, you will find someone to talk to; go on, you will hear him spoken of. Ten days from now we shall be leaving for Kiev, and when you receive this, we shall already be quite nearby it. Now, I confess that I would like to be there already, since a confluence of things just as I am departing has not left me a moment to myself or for what I would like to do. Among other things, Zelmira's affairs are in dire straits, and by all appearances in a few days I shall write to her father directly. For the past eight days, I have had a sort of fever whenever I think of her. After that, go ahead and say, if you can, that I take no interest in the fate of others. Farewell and good evening.

Metaphysical, physical, and moral portrait of the Redcoat

This red coat envelops a being who combines an *excellentissimo* heart with a great fund of gentility. We have more wit than most, an inexhaustible fund of gaiety, much originality in our way of grasping and rendering things, and an admirable education, since we are singularly well instructed in all that can make wit shine forth. We conceal our inclination for poetry as though it were murder; we have a passionate love of music. We grasp all things with rare ease; God only knows what we do not know by heart; we can declaim; we can chat; we have the manners of the best company; we are exceedingly polite; we can write in Russian and French as one rarely writes here, both for the style and for the hand. Our exterior matches our interior perfectly: our features are very regular; we have two superb black eyes with traced eyebrows, the likes of which one hardly ever sees; above middling height, a noble demeanour, an easy gait. In a word, we are just as solid inwardly as we are outwardly adroit, strong, and brilliant. I am convinced that if you were to meet this Redcoat, you would ask for his name, if you did not guess it instantly.

159. *To Friedrich Melchior Grimm*

This is an excerpt from a letter written from 24 April to 23 May 1787, during Catherine's legendary voyage to Crimea. In this instalment, she describes the humorous aspects of her second encounter with Joseph II of Austria, who was travelling once again incognito as Count Falkenstein. On 7 May, the two monarchs met near Kaidaki, a Ukrainian village on the Dnieper.

at Kherson, this 15 May

Since I wrote the last pages for you, I have received a letter from Papa Brunswick. The letter seems gentle and reasonable to me, so I dispatched it straight away to Koluvere to calm my protégée.*

On the seventh of this month, when I was on my galley below Kaidaki, I learned that Count Falkenstein was racing towards me at full tilt. I instantly disembarked and raced towards him too, and we raced so well that we met head-on in the middle of the fields. The first word he said to me was, 'We've caught out the politicians really well this time: no one will see our meeting.' He was with his ambassador, and I with the Prince de Ligne, the Redcoat,* and Countess Branicka. Their Majesties climbed into the same carriage and raced 30 versts non-stop to Kaidaki. But, after racing all alone across the fields, he was counting on dinner from me, just as I was counting on Field Marshal Prince Potemkin. And since the latter had opted to fast in order to save time and prepare to build a new city, we indeed found Prince Potemkin back from his expedition—but no dinner. However, since one is resourceful when in need, Prince Potemkin opted to become a chef himself, Prince

Nassau a kitchen boy, Great Crown Hetman Branicki a pastry chef. And so it happened that, since their coronations, the two Majesties have never been so grandly and so poorly served. Nonetheless we ate, we laughed, and we were satisfied with the dinner, such as it was. The next day we had a better dinner and the day after we went to Ekaterinograd,* where we laid the first stone of the city. From there, we were on the road for three days to reach this place, where we have been for four days. Today we launched three war vessels: they are the seventh, eighth, and ninth that have been built here. But what shall I tell you of all that we are doing and seeing here?

Kherson is not yet 8 years old, and it could pass for one of the most beautiful cities, both military and commercial, in the empire. All the houses are built of dimension stone. The city is at least 6 versts long; its location, its soil, and its climate are admirable. There are at least 10,000–12,000 inhabitants of all nationalities. One can obtain here everything one wants, like in Petersburg. In sum, the diligence of Prince Potemkin has turned this city and this land (where there was not a single hut at the time of the peace treaty) into a flourishing region and city. And with each passing year it will become much more so.

The day after tomorrow we shall set out for Crimea with Count Falkenstein. I shall have this letter sent from Sevastopol, and that *per la curiosità*.* We shall be back in fifteen days. Everyone is well, and namely the Comte de Ségur is so: you may assure his family of it. They claim here that Monsieur de Ségur's father* and Monsieur de Castries have been or will be fired as well. That *is called** cleaning house, or clearing out the house.

160. *To Johann Georg Zimmermann*

Returning from Crimea, Catherine turns her journey into a literary work and an opportunity for scientific observation, and touts her own plays as daring expressions of enlightened thought. In so doing she caters to the interests of her interlocutor, who was a strong opponent of the eighteenth-century fad of animal magnetism, a pseudo-science invented by Franz Mesmer and based on a belief in transferring energy between living beings. The Harmonic Society of United Friends of Strasbourg was one such organization who advertised supposed medical cures using this theory.

at Moscow, this 1 July 1787

I received on the road, Sir, your letter of 12 June. I arrived back here on 24 June OS and tomorrow or the day after tomorrow I shall leave here for

Petersburg. I do not know why people bother to speak overly favourably or overly critically about this journey. It was planned three years ago to dispel the bout of hypochondria that your book *On Solitude** thoroughly dispelled. I left in the winter to take advantage of the sledding. I waited for spring in Kiev, and it took a long time to come. I sailed down the Dnieper because, on a journey of 6,000 versts, travelling a few hundred very comfortably by boat is not something to sniff at. It has pleased everyone to turn all that into a fantastic, picturesque, heroi-comical journey and to lend it importance that I never imagined it would have. Now I am back, and I do not at all regret having undertaken and nearly completed this great journey without causing the least inconvenience to anyone among all who accompanied me. I have seen the most beautiful lands and most beautiful climates in the world. I saw everywhere a very large number of old people—which proves, in my opinion, that those climes, and namely that of Crimea, are not so dangerous as people believe. It is hot during the day and pretty cold once the sun goes down. I think that by drinking wine moderately and solely to fortify the stomach, which is weakened by frequent perspiration, and by covering up more in the evening than during the day, one can avoid the fevers of which people have previously complained. These are bilious fevers: it is very hot, which makes people impatient, and then the smallest thing rouses their bile. We all got angry at the smallest trifle, and the next minute we made light of our own anger. At Bakhchysarai, the former residence of the khans, there was a mosque across from my windows, where five times a day the imams called the people to prayer with great cries. I do not know whether Heaven is deaf to their prayer, but I know quite well that one would like to be so in order not to hear the racket they make in their mosque. One needs to be very accustomed to it to endure such mighty shouting. There are some among them who spin until they faint while shouting 'Alla hue'. They are nearly in a state of inspiration and are consequently not very far from the Shamans of Siberia and Germany. I do not know whether [Friedrich] Nicolai will be brave enough to reprint the *Shaman*, the *Deceived*, and the *Deceiver* in the middle of Berlin:* I think those plays are contraband, given the spirit of the present age. I saw your refutation of the Strasbourg 'magnetizers' in the Hamburg newspapers, as well as the mention you made of the Siberian Shaman in that refutation. I flatter myself that soon countries with such a definite taste for these charlatans will start importing them from Siberia. I can assure you in advance that they will be cheaper and will cause less damage than Cagliostro and his ilk. But there is more than one such fashionable windmill—and more than one Don Quixote, too, to construct them in order to tilt at them. Worst of all are political windmills and their champions: they breathe animosity everywhere. And when one looks at things closely, one cannot but agree that these chimaeras are produced by just a few heads who have invented them in the hope of accruing a lustre that they could scarcely have otherwise. I am in better health and am spending less than the newspapers from Holland have advertised, and I am full of esteem for you.

Catherine

161. *To Grigory Potemkin*

Leaving Potemkin behind in the southern provinces, Catherine briefly took stock of the trip's success. Her return itinerary was overland, and her arrival in Moscow coincided with the twenty-fifth anniversary of her reign. On Tuesday 29 June, during the feast of Sts Peter and Paul she appointed Platon Levshin Metropolitan of Moscow, the most senior position in the Russian Orthodox hierarchy.

My friend, Prince Grigory Alexandrovich, I was planning to write to you from Moscow. But I could not find your letters of 22 June from Kremenchuk* because somehow they had been mislaid, and I was in haste. At last, here in Tver where I arrived yesterday, I have now opened them. Forgive me, my friend, for such carelessness. I now have the following to say in response. First of all, I am entirely pleased with the state of mind and the mood in Kremenchuk following my departure, while your own feelings and thoughts are all the dearer to me because I love—truly, truly love—you and your devoted service, which comes from pure commitment—and you yourself are priceless. This is something I say and think daily.

We arrived in Moscow and then at our present location in good health, and since the rains followed us, we have not been in the least bothered by dust or heat. Without us Kremenchuk felt deserted to you, while without you we felt forlorn during our entire journey. Even more so in Moscow—as though our arms had been cut off.

On St Peter's Day in Moscow in the Cathedral of the Assumption* we consecrated Platon as metropolitan* and sewed onto his white klobuk a diamond cross a half-arshin* long and wide. Throughout he was like one of those peacocks you find in Kremenchuk.

During the terrible heat that assails you in the afternoons I beseech and entreat you to do me the kindness of looking after your health for the sake of God and ourselves, and of being as happy with me as I am with you. Farewell, my friend, may the Lord be with you. After lunch I shall go to Torzhok* and spend the night there.

Tver, 6 July 1787

I thank you for the four squadrons of regular Cossacks. Lord above, what a grand fellow you are, something that I preach to all.

162. *To Grigory Potemkin*

A short letter could quickly survey the entire European scene and sum up pithily a new set of problems on the horizon, with challenges and opportunities for Russia. Catherine was always keeping Potemkin on the qui vive and synchronizing their intelligence. Great Britain and Prussia's joint repression of unrest in the United Provinces was a step toward the Triple Alliance between those three countries, which formed in 1788 with the express goal of preventing Catherine from gaining territory and power during her second war against the Ottoman Empire (see Letter 165).

My dear friend Prince Grigory Alexandrovich, I received the other day your letter of 17 July and learned how much joy my letter from Tver caused you. The relationship between you and me, my friend, requires few words—you serve me, and I am grateful. The gist of it is right there. You have rapped the knuckles of your enemies through your devotion to me and by your zeal for the interests of the empire. I rejoice in your good health. Show some restraint, I beg you, when eating fruit. Thank God you are free of disease there and no one is ill.

Matters in Europe are getting into a tangle. The emperor is dispatching troops to the Netherlands. The Prussian king is arming against the Dutch. France, although bankrupt, is setting up camps. England is deploying its navy and providing funds to the Prince of Orange. Other powers are vigilant, but I take walks around the garden, which has grown lush and lovely. Farewell, may God be with you.

from Tsarskoe Selo, 27 July 1787

PART VI

EMBATTLED
(1787–1796)

The symbolic threat implied by the military displays and the joint presence of the allies Catherine and Joseph on the journey to Crimea provoked the Ottoman Empire to declare war promptly in August 1787. The war caught Catherine off guard (Letter 163), as she and Potemkin had been hoping to build their strength for another two years before commencing hostilities. Despite his initial feelings of inadequacy, Potemkin was made commander-in-chief of the Russian forces. With the Second Russo-Turkish War now under way, spreading pro-Russian war reports was again the order of the day, and the successful storming of Ochakov on 6 December 1788 offered necessary fodder for Catherine's efforts. Although Austria initially came to Catherine's aid, her friend and ally Joseph II died in February 1790. Faced with unrest in the Netherlands and Hungary, and the threat of war with Prussia, Joseph's brother and successor, Leopold II, withdrew from the Ottoman war in July 1790. Catherine was left fighting alone once more.

Her war effort in the south was hindered by multiple distractions in the north. Hoping that war would rally national unity and thereby put down noble opposition at home, Gustav sought military glory by attacking Russia. Assuming Russia would be too busy fighting the Ottoman Empire to put up much resistance, Gustav made a pretext out of a supposed insult to his dignity in a note from the Russian representative in Sweden, Andrei Razumovsky, to declare war. In an ultimatum on 12 June 1788, Gustav demanded Razumovsky's recall because a note the diplomat had addressed to the Swedish government, conveying Catherine's assurances of her peaceable intentions, had seemed to create a distinction between the king and his subjects (Letter 170). Ten days later, border skirmishes in Finland marked the start of the Russo-Swedish War, which lasted for two years (1788–90). The battles between the Russian and Swedish navies came within earshot of Catherine's palace at Tsarskoe Selo, offering her an unusual chance to display her military bravery. The war came to a rapid end on 3 August 1790, with a treaty signed in the small Finnish town of Värälä. Both sides were relieved to end the conflict with no territorial modifications (Letters 178–80).

Throughout the Ottoman war, Catherine also faced the enmity of the Triple Alliance between Prussia, Britain, and the United Provinces. The Prussians wanted to prevent Russia from making any territorial gains against the Ottomans, while hoping themselves to obtain Danzig and Thorn from Poland (Letter 181). These tensions came to a head in March 1791, when the British under the leadership of William Pitt the Younger resolved to issue an ultimatum to Catherine: make peace with the Ottomans with no territorial gains, or face a Prussian invasion on land and a British one by sea. Catherine again showed her nerve by refusing to give in; under public pressure within Britain, Pitt was forced to back down, and the ultimatum was never issued (Letter 189). The matter of Danzig and Thorn was part of a much larger Polish question that concluded in the elimination of Poland itself. Relying on Prussian support, the Poles, in collaboration with their king Stanislas Poniatowski, promulgated in May 1791 a new constitution which transformed the formerly weak (and therefore easily influenced) oligarchic system into a stronger hereditary monarchy. Strategically, Catherine could not accept a form of government that would allow Poland to escape her tutelage.

Signed on 29 December 1791, the Treaty of Iassy ended the southern war; the Ottoman Empire accepted that Crimea was now Russian territory and relinquished further territory, including Ochakov, for which the late Potemkin had fought. It also freed Catherine's hand in Poland. After political struggles at court, Russian troops entered Poland. In January 1793, the Second Partition of Poland between Russia and Prussia took effect; what remained of Poland was to be a Russian protectorate, and the Polish army was disarmed. However, a Polish military officer, Tadeusz Kosciuszko (1746–1817), led an uprising in March 1794 (Letter 202). To wipe out the last traces of unrest, in 1795–6 Austria, Prussia, and Russia partitioned what remained of Poland.

Behind these matters of realpolitik, France was the key political and ideological threat lurking throughout these years. The years immediately preceding the French Revolution saw a marked rapprochement between Russia and France, producing notably a commercial treaty with France in January 1787 that replaced former ties to Great Britain. Later that year, the French ambassador and member of Catherine's inner circle, Louis-Philippe, Comte de Ségur, attempted to proceed to a quadruple alliance joining France, Spain, Austria, and Russia, in opposition to the Triple Alliance of Prussia, Britain, and the United Provinces. But Catherine saw insufficient advantages in such a plan and, as unrest grew in France, Ségur's negotiations came to nothing (Letter 165). The French Revolution, beginning in 1789, completely changed the political landscape: Ségur returned to France and attracted Catherine's ire by supporting the Revolution, the violence and disorder of which she observed with growing horror. Her other foreign policy objectives meant that she could not devote large monetary or military resources to restoring the French monarchy. Catherine sporadically attempted through other channels to influence the course of events, but the growing chaos continually thwarted these efforts, and she focused primarily on what she saw as Jacobinism in Poland. She watched very carefully all developments in France: she knew, for instance, of the plan for the French royal family to flee the country on 20–1 June 1791 (NS). Louis XVI, his wife, and their children were recognized at Varennes and taken back to Paris; their flight further undermined what remained of the king's authority (Letter 188). Catherine lent verbal and some financial support to Louis XVI's brothers, but, at the end of 1791, many of the German princes of the Rhineland ordered the French émigrés on their territories to disperse, rendering Catherine's proposed émigré-led counter-revolutionary attack impossible. Her alliance with Sweden, signed in October 1791, was designed specifically to encourage Gustav III to make a military effort against France, but without committing Russian troops to the undertaking (Letter 197). But this plan too came to an end with Gustav's assassination on 29 March 1792 (NS) by a discontented nobleman at a masquerade ball. On 21 January 1793 (NS), Louis XVI was executed in Paris; Catherine was made physically ill by the news when she received it. Less than two weeks later, France declared war on Britain and several other European countries. Catherine promptly sent the Comte d'Artois to Britain, offering a Russian corps to join his proposed invasion of northern France. But she expected Britain to bear the cost of the campaign until they could claim reparations from France, which George III was unprepared to do (Letter 199).

Within this whirlwind of political events, Catherine did not cease to evolve intellectually. In the first part of this period and in her correspondences with Johann Georg Zimmermann and the Baltic German writer Elisa von der Recke, Catherine continued to declare her support for the German Enlightenment in its opposition to the anti-rational trends of Freemasonry. However, Catherine's correspondence with Zimmermann petered out in 1791 as he grew physically weaker and increasingly immersed in reactionary conspiracy theories regarding the

French Revolution's roots in the Enlightenment (Letter 193). In her correspondences with de Ligne and Grimm, meanwhile, she strove to make sense of the Revolutionary reinterpretation of the writers of the French Enlightenment whom they had all known and admired. Both of these correspondents played a certain political as well as a cultural role: de Ligne was Joseph II's representative in Potemkin's army at the start of the Second Russo-Turkish war, while Grimm became Catherine's informant on news from France as well as her agent for assisting French émigrés in distress. Finally, history became ever more important to Catherine as the Revolution forced her to question the conditions under which her legacy would be judged. She continued working on her *Notes Concerning Russian History*, and she invited the émigré Gabriel Sénac de Meilhan to visit Russia, which he did in spring 1791 on the pretext of writing a history of Russia (Letters 186, 187, 190). Sénac de Meilhan was one of the earliest theorists of the French Revolution and one of the first to recognize the importance of the so-called 'noble revolt' of 1787 as a cause. Since Catherine believed that a close alliance between the nobility and the monarchy was essential to restoring the pre-Revolutionary order in France, Sénac de Meilhan's theories were of substantial interest to her, and she had his book *On the Principles and Causes of the Revolution in France* (1790) reprinted in Russia.

On a personal level, these were dark years for the ageing Catherine. The man she most trusted in private and public affairs, Potemkin, died on 5 October 1791. Bereft, and ill served by Potemkin's inexperienced replacement, Platon Zubov, Catherine nonetheless remained entirely in control of the empire and continued to pursue ambitious plans. Hoping to free Russia from future threats from the north, Catherine sought to arrange a marriage between her eldest granddaughter, Alexandra, and the young King of Sweden, Gustav IV Adolf. Although Gustav was already engaged to a German princess, he travelled to Russia with his uncle, Charles, Duke of Södermanland, in August 1796. His infatuation with Alexandra notwithstanding, Gustav insisted that she convert to Lutheranism, which Catherine refused, and the betrothal fell through on 11 September (Letter 205). This diplomatic humiliation is thought to have caused the first in a series of strokes, the last of which killed Catherine on 6 November 1796. In her last days, she kept seeking further glory on all sides, defending the Caucasus against Persia and finally arranging to send Alexander Suvorov to combat Revolutionary France. Her death brought an end to all these plans, as her son Paul rushed to overturn her legacy.

163. *To Grigory Potemkin*

Crimea was the battleground for three empires: Austria, Russia, and the Ottomans. Assuming in the absence of confirmation that war with the Turks was inevitable after her vice-consul in Moldavia, Ivan Lavrent'evich Selunsky, was ordered by the Ottomans to leave, Catherine rehearses with Potemkin an old plan to go on the offensive by taking Ochakov. The Russians had been hoping to delay the war for another few years, but were wrong-footed by the speed of the Turkish declaration of war. In response, Catherine aimed to grant Potemkin as much control as possible in the early stages and to devise a defensive strategy that would allow them to play for time as Russian forces came up to full strength. Austria hoped to make conquests of its own while limiting Russian takings; they waited until February 1788 to declare war, but, as Catherine predicts, Joseph II sent the Prince de Ligne to represent him at Potemkin's military headquarters until the end of 1788 (Potemkin and de Ligne, two colossal egotists, got on each other's nerves). Catherine was, however, overoptimistic about the Poles, since negotiations to draw them in failed; she also proved wrong about the Swedes, since Gustav III, taking advantage of Russia's preoccupation with the Ottomans, declared war in summer 1788.

Dear friend of my heart, Prince Grigory Alexandrovich, I rejoice that you have recovered, although at the same time I deeply regret that cases of illness in Kherson are on the rise. People are saying here that not a single healthy person is left and that all are suffering from diarrhoea. Everyone in Kherson, and indeed in all the locations where there is diarrhoea, should have stocked up on rice. Nothing will ease these attacks of diarrhoea except rice. Remember that the Tatars, Turks, Persians, Italians, and all residents of warm places eat rice. Everybody will start buying it once it becomes cheap, but you could even feed the sick for free. In addition to this comestible you should order that a glass of fortified wine be given to each ailing person. Once these ideas occurred to me, I felt obliged to let you know about them and hope that they will not be useless. If it were at all possible I would send you in the post the rains we have here. From 10 July when I arrived here to today it has rained daily, and we have practically not had any clear and warm days since the Feast of Sts Peter and Paul.

All of the above I wrote immediately after receiving your letter of 14 August. But yesterday evening as I returned from the opera *Fevey** I received the news dispatched by Consul Selunsky on 11 and 14 August, from which it became apparent that the Moldavian Hospodar* himself has bidden him to inform me that war has been declared and that he and all Russians have been ordered to depart for Russia. In order not to make a mistake, I shall consider that this is the way things are*—that is, I shall consider war to have been declared unless I receive other news. Nonetheless, the expulsion of Selunsky could be sufficient on its own, since they tried to get him recalled and said that they would expel him. The rest sounds like the news we have had from Moldavia and Wallachia, which has sometimes been false, but this appears to have the imprimatur of truth.* And so my thoughts have turned solely to the question of armament, and since yesterday evening in my mind I have begun comparing my strength now in 1787 with the position in which I found myself when war was declared in November 1768. The last time we expected war would break out in a year's time, the regiments were billeted all over the entire empire, it was late autumn, no preparations had been started, revenues were much lower than now, the Tatars were under our nose and marauding tribes on the steppe got as far as Tor and Bakhmut, invading the region of Elizavetgrad* in January. The plan devised for the army turned our defensive strategy into an attack plan. Two armies were sent. One served to defend the empire, while the other progressed to Khotin. Once Moldavia and the area along the Danube had been taken in the first and second campaigns, the second army captured Bender and occupied Crimea. The navy was prepared in the Mediterranean and a small infantry party sent to Georgia.

Now our border is along the Bug River and the Kuban. Kherson has been built. Crimea is a region of the empire, and there is a sizeable navy in Sevastopol. There are troops in Tauris [Crimea], sizeable armies are already at the border, and they are stronger than the defensive and offensive forces of 1768. With God's help funds will suffice—for this I shall make every effort and hope to be successful. I am aware that it would have been much better if the peace had lasted about another two years so that the fortresses of Kherson and Sevastopol could have been completed and the army and navy brought into the condition we would have liked to see them in. But what's to be done if the bubble has burst early? I recall that when we concluded the Peace of Kaynarca,* wise men at the time doubted that the vizier and sultan would ratify it, and then we had their false predictions that the peace would not last more than two years. Instead, we were about to go into the fourteenth year. If the Turks have declared war, then I think that they have left their navy in Ochakov so as to hinder the ships built in Kherson from going to Sevastopol. If in fact this is not what they have done, I think that next year it will be harder for them to weigh anchor at the mouth of the Dnieper than it is at present.

I am relying on your fervent solicitude to make sure that the fleet and harbour at Sevastopol remain unmolested since a navy in harbour for the winter is always at risk. Yes, it is true that Sevastopol is not Chesme. I confess that one thing alone worries me, and that is disease. For God's own sake, I ask you please to take throughout your three provinces, in the army, and in the navy, all possible measures in good time so that this evil does not once again insinuate itself among us and weaken us. I know that in Constantinople the plague is unheard of at the moment. But since it is unstinting there, their troops spread it wherever they go. Send me (and this is for my eyes only) the plan for how you think you will conduct the war. This way I shall know and be able to measure you against your own intentions. Last year in 1786 a rescript was issued to you—inform me about everything in detail so that I might anticipate and lessen any damage and pre-empt actions and eventualities. It seems that the French now have a good excuse for denying all aid to the Turks, since war was declared despite their resolution to maintain the peace. We'll see what the emperor will do. According to our treaty he is obliged to declare war against the Turks within three months.

The Prussians and Swedes are blowhards, but the first, I believe, will not create a diversion, and the latter are hardly in a position to do so unless the Spanish provide money, which is scarcely likely. And can you do very much when fighting on foreign money? Count [Ivan] Saltykov has been told to make for the army. Farewell, my friend, be well. Everyone is well here, but war is sloshing around in my head like young beer in a barrel, and Sasha [Alexander Dmitriev-Mamonov] is taking every pain in attempting to calm my worried little head.

The Austrian Embassy has not yet had a messenger. Fitzherbert has departed; Ségur and de Ligne wanted to leave on Tuesday, but as soon as de Ligne hears about the war and receives permission from the emperor, he will in all likelihood gallop off to where you are. I suspect that you have no nails left on your fingers—you've chewed them all away.

Adieu, mon Ami.

24 August 1787

The real cause of the war is and will remain the Turks' desire to redo the treaties, both Kaynarca and the convention on Crimea, and then the commercial treaty as well. It may be that once war has been declared they will attempt to turn the whole business into a negotiation. They acted the same way in 1768. However, if my minister has been imprisoned in the Seven Towers, as happened last time, they will have to answer in exactly the same manner as before,* since the dignity of the Russian court will not allow us to listen to any offers of peace for as long as a minister of this power has not been repatriated to her.

A further idea has occurred to me: as soon as I have confirmation that we are at war, I shall send an order to Stackelberg that he initiate negotiations with the Poles about an alliance. If war is really declared, then it will be essential to include in the War Cabinet men who are able to shut up many others and who themselves have something useful to say. And for that purpose, I am thinking about appointing Count Valentin [Musin-]Pushkin, General Nikolai Saltykov, Count Bruce, Count [Alexander] Vorontsov, Count [Andrei] Shuvalov, Strekalov, and Zavadovsky. The last of these know all about our operations during the previous war. I am recalling the procurator general [Alexander Viazemsky] from the spa at Tsaritsyn [now Volgograd]. Apart from those named above, I have and can think of nobody else here.

164. *To Grigory Potemkin*

At the time of writing this letter, Catherine, who consistently notes how informa-tion arrives (see Letter 147 and her anxiety over disruptions), was unaware that the Russian fleet at Sevastopol had been severely damaged by a storm. Potemkin's letters betray his tendency to bouts of depression and hypochondria, and Catherine's standard response is to buck him up with cajoling and praise, and also by praising others such as Suvorov in order to stimulate Potemkin's jealous nature. The letter thinks through options in playing off the competing as well as mutual interests of rival states, yet it again displays her awareness that foreign policy depends on the internal politics of courts and governments. With false news reports in London announcing her death, Catherine's worries about plague in the south and Potemkin's health are part of a more general concern with ageing and mortality.

My dear friend, Prince Grigory Alexandrovich, after waiting seventeen days for letters from you, yesterday I suddenly received your missives of 13, 15, and 16 September about which you will shortly receive my decisions. I shall attach a list of them here as soon as I complete my answer to the letter in your own hand. I shall begin with the fact that it gives me no small pleasure to see that you give my letters their true value: they are and shall remain sincere friendly letters and nothing else. Your health genuinely worries me. I know how painstaking, how keen you are, striving with all your might. For God's own sake, and for my own, take greater care of yourself than you have been doing. Nothing terrifies me so much as your ill health. At this particular moment in time, my dear friend, you are not some little private person who just lives and does what he likes. You belong to the state, you belong to me. You have an obligation and I command you to look after your health. I lay this obligation upon you because the good, the defence, and the glory of the empire are entrusted to your care, and it is necessary to be physically and mentally fit in order to do the task you have at hand. After this maternal exhortation, which I entreat you to receive humbly and obediently, I shall continue.*

I learned from your autograph letter that Kinburn was besieged by the enemy and at that point had already withstood four days of cannon-fire and bombardment. With the help of God we shall not lose it, since every loss is unpleasant. But let us suppose it happens—not for the sake of being glum, but rather in order to attempt in some way to avenge ourselves and get our own back. The empire will remain the empire even without Kinburn. Is that all we have taken and lost? The best thing of all is that the Lord pours boldness into our soldiers there, and here too there is no despair. Public opinion lies to its advantage and takes cities, and concocts battles and actions at sea, and has Voinovich bombarding Constantinople. I listen to all of this in silence and keep my own council as I think: 'As long as my Prince is healthy, then everything will be fine and in order, even if something unpleasant pops up some-where.'

It is very good that you ordered wine and meat to be given to the besieged, this is very good. May the Lord help Major-General Reck and Commander Tuntsel'man* as well. The dedication of Alexander Vasil'evich Suvorov, which you depict so vividly, thoroughly delighted me. You know that there is nothing that gives me more pleasure than giving due credit to efforts, zeal, and ability. For Crimea and Kherson it would be good if it were possible to save Kinburn. At present we have to await news from the fleet.

Several Danish naval officers who have heard about the war wish to join our service. Prince Repnin wrote to me, offering his readiness to serve wherever and under whomever I should please. I answered that I view his dispositions with pleasure and shall not hesitate to avail myself of him wherever the opportunity should arise. Do write to let me know whether or not you need him; he writes to me from Sarepta,* where he has gone to take the waters at Tsaritsyn with Viazemsky. I sent for the latter as soon as I got the first news, but they had in the mean-time learned of the war from the Gorich brothers,* who had gone to Astrakhan, and Repnin wrote to me as noted above. I do not know why Count Ivan Petrovich Saltykov is dawdling. However, I shall give the order that he be asked in writing to go quickly.

A first conscription is currently being carried out, and I shall straightaway have a second done, and I reckon that the joint total will be not 60,000 but in fact 80,000. I hope this will be sufficient.

The emperor, as you will see from the papers already sent to you, is readying 120,000 for action, and he has promoted numerous generals, among whom there is de Ligne.

You write that we should make up to the English* and Prussians nicely. As soon as Pitt learned about the outbreak of war, he wrote to summon Semën Vorontsov. When he arrived he informed him that war had been declared and that it was being said in Constantinople and Vienna that their ambassador had stirred up the Turks, and he swore that their ambassador had no such instruction from the ministry of Great Britain. I believe this, but the foreign affairs of Great Britain are not currently conducted by the English administration and rather by a cunning king, as per the rules of Hanoverian ministers. It is owing to such good governance that His Majesty has already lost fifteen provinces. So it is no wonder if he gives his ambassador in Constantinople orders that contradict the interests of England. He is governed by petty personal passions and not by governmental and national interest.

As for the Prussians, so far their treatment has been nothing if not gentle, but they do not repay it with kindness, which could be owing to Hertzberg and not the king. Their troops have really entered Holland. Let us see what the French will say about this.* It seems they will intervene, or else incur scorn, which presumably they will not want to do. The French king has placed himself under custody and appointed a prime minister, on account of whom the ministers for the army and navy have resigned.*

I shall order a large fleet to be armed next year both in the Archipelago and in the Baltic. The French can say what they like. I am not accustomed to ordering my affairs and actions other than as consistent with the interests of my empire and my interests, and therefore the powers may be friends or enemies as they please.

I pray that God will grant you strength and health and will relieve hypochondria. It is no wonder that you have no rest since you do everything yourself. Tell me whom you need, and I shall send him. Why do not employ a general who could take care of the little details? This is why a field marshal is entitled to a full complement of generals so that the field marshal will not be tormented by trivia. I am confident that you will not fail, but in any case do not worry, and preserve your strength. God will help you and not forsake you, and the tsar will be your friend and bulwark. This 'wretched defensive position', to use your words, is obvious, and it is something I do not like. Try as soon as possible to transform it into an offensive one. Doing this will indeed make things easier for you and everyone. There will be fewer sick men, since they will not all be concentrated in the same place. And you are surprised that you have grown weak after writing me seven pages and much more! If you see that you can leave, then come to us: I shall always be very happy to see you.

When the manifesto declaring war was issued,* the grand duke and grand duchess wrote to me with requests. He would like to join the army as a volunteer, just as before in 1783, while she would like to travel with him. I answered them with a refusal. To her, I cited the letter to him, while to him I replied praising his good intentions but describing the current difficult and defensive position, along with the lateness of the season and the cares besetting both field marshals and which also increase illnesses and costs, along with the poor harvest and lack of provision. In response to this letter I received another letter from him with a second request, to which I replied that the excellent reasons described in my first letter compelled me to dissuade him from departing this year to be a volunteer in the army. After this letter, both were entirely contented to stay behind, letting it be known only that they had wanted to join. A week ago I received also from the Prince of Württemburg a letter with a request to assign him to the army. This I answered with a neat but polite refusal, which satisfied his sister and brother-in-law too.

Farewell, my friend, the order for conscription has been given. MacNob will be pardoned.* You write that Greig should be sent with the navy, and I shall send him. But would not the name of Aleksei Grigor'evich Orlov of Chesme not be more renowned? However, this is between us, since neither he nor I have said a word. I have written down what came to mind because of an abundance of ideas. The money will be sent. The artillery in both armies has also been increased. It has been ordered that the non-commissioned officers and cadets be allowed to graduate, and everything that is up to me has been fully implemented as per your letters and reports. I pray to God that He will restore you to health.

24 September 1787

Sasha [Dmitriev-Mamonov] is as clever and charming as can be.

165. *To Grigory Potemkin*

In late 1787, the Comte de Ségur and the Prince of Nassau-Siegen acted as inter-mediaries for Catherine's negotiations with France regarding a possible alliance.

Catherine saw clearly how much the French needed her support. In September 1787, France had exhibited its diplomatic weakness by failing to prevent the Prussians from interfering in the unrest that was then shaking the Netherlands. This did not help France's claim that it could help Catherine to manage the danger of Swedish aggression: well aware of France's precarious finances, Catherine doubted their pretensions to controlling Gustav III through subsidies. In the meantime, Catherine prepared for war. The Ottomans had already named their own Khan of Crimea, Shehbaz Giray, and, in response, Russian strategy focused on controlling Crimea and taking the key Ottoman fortress of Ochakov.

My friend, Prince Grigory Alexandrovich, I received today your letters of 1 November at the very moment I was planning to speak with Nassau. And now that he and I have talked things over, I have so much to write to you that I truly do not know where to begin. Ségur has here put forward that his court is prepared to enter into an alliance with us, as you should have already been able to see from the communications forwarded to you, including the answer that was made to him.

When we spoke, Nassau told me about the current inclinations of the French court and changes to their way of thinking. I accepted all this with a pleasant demeanour, and said that it was with pleasure that I observe how people are thinking differently from how they used to think. I thanked him for the diligence he had shown and for his good efforts, and I expressed my concern that the court might change its outlook yet again. To which he replied that if, when the first courier arrived, he perceived the slightest hesitation in the thinking of the French government, he would gallop back in order to apply all his strength to reinforcing that court's good intentions towards us. When he talked about a rapprochement through an alliance, I said that I would not hide from him that matters hung in a delicate balance in the consideration of our trade relations with England, and with respect, as well, to our great future arming of the navy, and that this was why we were accustomed to find shelter in English ports. On this point he offered French ones, but I said that the location of the former was more convenient. But the main reason this is being discussed is in order to explore with him the advantages and disadvantages associated with each outcome, and to show that I recognize and have already spotted the various advantages of a friendship with Louis XVI. We parted on very good terms, having said everything there was to say. They are in the process of arming themselves and will go to war, since they themselves feel they will lose face if they leave affairs in the Low Countries as they are.

Nassau told me that the French consider that they have the Swedish king in their pocket, but I told him that they would do well not to depend excessively on this man. His trip to Copenhagen (and to Berlin, it is said) demonstrates indeed that the King of Sweden would be in the pocket of anyone who gave him money, a fact that France's enemies could also sometimes use to their advantage. Well, here you have, my dear friend, an honest confession of what passed between Nassau and myself.

I return to your letters. First of all, thank you for them, and for writing to me with such sincerity and friendly candour; and for not failing to keep me informed in detail, despite all the troubles of your location and situation. Do not stop, however, informing me in detail about all the vexations and duties there. It is with excellent and heartfelt feeling that I receive all this, and I am remarkably satisfied with you. You have displayed to the world at this moment such a breadth and quality of knowledge and conduct as to confer honour on my selection and on yourself, and for that I love you twice as much. I see that Ochakov worries you. In granting you, herewith, complete control, I only ask that God bless your good undertakings.

And seeing from your letters the details of the service of Alexander Vasil'evich Suvorov, I have finally decided to confer on him for his faith and fidelity the Order of St Andrew,* which this messenger will bear you.

May the Lord help you to scourge the steppe beyond Ochakov and Bender and to attack and expel from our domains this new khan.

Ségur has letters from Choiseul to the effect that the vizier's position is already precarious. There are complaints about him because of the declaration of war and so up to now he has not acted.

That your duties do not release you to visit here even for a short while—I thoroughly regret it. I would gallop off to you myself if it were possible to do this without increasing all the fuss.

It is a matter of great comfort to me that your health is improving, since I love you truly and am very, very pleased with you.

I will give the order to build frigates equipped with heavy guns as per your design. I shall say no more about the loss of the ship *Mary Magdalene*.* What is done is done, and the same goes for other vessels that have been lost. I have given the order that an effort be made somehow to get Lombard.*

Concerning the Prince of Hesse-Philippsthal,* who is serving in the Horse Guards and wishes to be a volunteer, I shall say to you that I have already refused many and in general all such requests, no matter who the volunteer is, and for that reason I cannot grant permission. However, if you want it, I shall release him to the army and then make a contribution to the cost of his equipment. I have refused volunteers for various reasons, and in the final campaigns of the last war we established that no volunteers from anywhere would be accepted.

Farewell, my friend, may God be with you and may it never come into your head to think that you could ever be forgotten for a moment by me.

9 November 1787

Alexander Matveevich loves you as his very own soul.

Write out for me, would you, how the wounded and ill are and whether you sent my first letter to Suvorov?

166. *To Grigory Potemkin*

It was unusual for Rumiantsev to make requests for hardware direct to the empress, since, despite once being Potemkin's superior, he was now under Potemkin's command. Given the court gossip that closely followed any tensions between the two men, Catherine is double-checking, especially as Potemkin rejected the use of some of this weaponry in the First Russo-Turkish War. The fleet was being armed in the Baltic to sail from there to the Mediterranean, but in the event it was required to stay and fight against Sweden.

My friend, Prince Grigory Alexandrovich, after a twelve-day expectant wait for your letters, at last the messenger has arrived with your letters from the twelfth of this month. From your fine arrangements we must anticipate that the Tatars will not be more successful in their winter operations than the Turks in their autumn exercises and in the previous war, when they combined with the Tatars: whenever they encountered even the least resistance, they retreated immediately.

The fact that the emperor has not yet declared war on the Turks I ascribe to the intrigues of the Prussians and English. These courts are sowing the view that they have found a means to lure us to their side and to oblige us to dance to their tune despite the fact that they roused the Turks to declare war against us. It is impossible to manipulate Prussian politics by using Danzig, since at the height of our friendship we established and agreed that the status of Danzig was protected by a *casus foederis*. My predecessors and I have signed guarantees of the city's freedom and of its right to remain as it currently is, and the convention concerning the partition of Poland again confirmed this.*

Regarding the emperor, I shall also say this: he no more anticipated war than we did and is just as unprepared. Between now and March we should expect nothing from him, since the treaty stipulates that December, January, and February are to be excluded for the movement of troops. Yet it is widely known that significant preparations are ongoing there. I shall order that the ambassador here be reminded of this a bit more often, and you tell de Ligne. It is also true that in the previous war we fought on our own against the Turks, and fought successfully. But since we have a treaty and a prospect of receiving aid, it is appropriate at the present time to rely on it, since at the very least it is more promising than the favours and good intentions, or dispositions, of those courts whose malicious actions in declaring war we have experienced. The system with the Austrian court is your work; it has long been preferable with respect to southern matters and that border, since we have a mutual interest in the local situation of those countries. Panin himself, when he was not yet charmed blind by the Prussians, regarded any other ties as a *pis-aller* that did not compensate for the loss of the Austrian alliance when it came to the general foe, that is, the Turks. From many of your letters I could conceivably conclude that you hesitate to realize the plan you had sketched out and had already begun concerning the Turks and all that relates to them. But I must not allow myself these thoughts, and I chase them from my head, since I cannot imagine hesitation of this kind occupying your thoughts. For there will be neither glory, nor honour, nor reward in having undertaken and propounded warmly such a matter and then, without completing it, wilfully distorting it and starting another. You have conducted perfectly the defence of the borders. May God grant you health, my friend, so that you can successfully conduct the offensive actions too.

Preparation for arming the fleet is under way here. I have written to the Counts Orlov and received their reply to the effect that they are delaying their departure. I would have taken this for a refusal to accept the command—had they not written straightaway that they are coming here.* Their trip has been somewhat delayed by the death of the eldest son of Count Vladimir Grigor'evich. I think this is why they are staying for a while in Moscow. At the moment Admiral Greig proposes up to 5,000 regular troops to man the local fleet. During the last war, everyone was sent—from the guards, as well as from the Schlüsselberg regiment, the artillery, and the cuirassiers—with a total of 2,370 men of all ranks. I am now demanding advice from you: what to send? I think that Greig is asking for a lot and the cuirassiers are excessive. From what regiments should men be sent? Should they be sent in regiments or in battalions from different regiments? Moreover, in the outfitting of the troops an army general will be required to be on the fleet. He can go straight to Italy, and it is desirable that he be someone whose usefulness is certain. Advise me on whom to send.

With this courier you will receive an order dispatching Prince Yuri Vladimirovich Dolgorukov to the imperial army.

Field Marshal Rumiantsev writes: (1) About *chevaux de frise* and portable bridges and for that he is relying on our decision here. If there is a need for each of these, then I advise you to coordinate between yourselves and correct the extraordinary expenditure. (2) About the Cossacks who have yet to arrive. But I hope that you will have sent them or that they will have reached him even as he wrote. (3) About the artillery for the grenadier regiments. It is essential that the two of you confer and establish the quantity and calibre of cannons with which to equip these regiments and where to get them and the soldiers to man them. And, then, once the order on provisioning has been given to the right person, we must be thoroughly briefed. (4) About the old and infirm, and similarly about the underage. On this point, too, I ask that you reach an agreement about where and to whom they will be left.

With respect to building frigates on the Don, I have ordered the procurator general [Alexander Viazemsky] and Pushchin to confer with you on this, to agree how much you will need, and to attempt to resource you. Drop me a line to say whether it is true that the Turks and other enemies have been spreading the rumour that the ship *The Glory of Catherine* is in their hands, that it was captured at the mouth of the Danube, and that supposedly Voinovich abandoned the vessel on a lifeboat? Perhaps you should rename the ship* if we still have it. Anything can happen—I do not want the villains to boast that *The Glory of Catherine* is in their hands.

Farewell, my friend, may the Lord be with you. Be well and successful, and my thoughts are always with you.

23 November 1787

167. *To Johann Georg Zimmermann*

Catherine's public campaign against Masonic mysticism culminated in the West with Friedrich Nicolai's publication of her anti-Masonic trilogy in German translation. At the same time, with the start of the Second Russo-Turkish War, Catherine saw an opportunity to make Zimmermann her publicity agent, just as Voltaire had been during the previous war.

You will say, Sir, that I am responding very late to your letter of 4 September, but better late than never. To tell the truth, the past three months have been quite eventful. Shortly after I returned from Moscow, the Sublime Porte and its not-so-sublime advisors saw fit to declare war on me, as you know. So be it: so far no great harm has been done. If I manage to beat my enemies, I hope both sides will be better satisfied. And as it is my motto that when it comes to blows, it is better to deliver than to receive them, I have tried to make my arrangements accordingly. That done, I take up my pen to answer your letter. My journey to Tauris now seems a dream. My minister in Constantinople was simply told to give Tauris back, a little trifle that was very easy to say, but in which only two things were lacking: common sense, on the one hand, and the possibility of my agreeing, on the other. Besides, here we do not yet regard the loss of one or several provinces as a stroke of good fortune. States do not seem to be of the same nature as ditches, which grow wider as one removes earth from them. Granted, it is hard to recognize any traces of European manners in the Sublime Porte's manner of dealing with things.

But let us return to the journey of which you speak. I passed so quickly through Tauris, and had so many things to see and such good company, that I did not have time to reflect as I could and should have on seeing a region as rich in events as it is fertile. Nonetheless, I recall very well the Alma Valley and the Europeans I saw there, and with whom my illustrious travel companion spoke on my behalf,* while, dying of heat, I was thrilled to be silent for a moment. I must say that the new inhabitants of Crimea are easy to please, since a smile gave them such pleasure. If good cheer could spread happiness across a country, then that journey could have made many a happy person, for it is difficult to travel more cheerfully and in better company. It is Europeans who have said, written, and printed all the ill that has been said of the unhealthy air of Tauris. Those people, when they come to the province, are bored and do not follow the customs of the natives, who are very healthy, get old, and multiply considerably, especially the imams. The latter often make up more than half the population of a village from which they receive tithes. On the subject of imams, Nicolai of Berlin sent me the three comedies, the first pages of which you saw at Pyrmont,* Sir. They say that all the shamans of the new sects have gone to Switzerland:* we shall see whether the mountains will echo with the sound of the apostolate. Here, all projects have given way to just one: that of defending the unjustly attacked state. It is remarkable what base means our enviers use against us. They enjoy lying every time the post comes; they give money to the newspapermen and in the newspapers have us defeated regularly twice a week. They did the same during the last war, but events, and the peace treaty especially, proved who the liars and who the defeated were. If you are told that Kinburn and the island of Taman have been taken by the Turks, Taganrog and Azov attacked, and the Sevastopol fleet destroyed, do not believe a word of it. The fleet weathered a windstorm at the equinox: it even lost a ship and a frigate. The Turkish fleet lost twice that, and that is counting too modestly, as well. But, otherwise we have not lost a single inch of ground. Farewell, Sir, be well and rest assured of my esteem.

Catherine
at St Petersburg, this 3 December 1787

168. *To Grigory Potemkin*

Catherine ponders how to respond to news of the ongoing Swedish armament.

My dear friend, Prince Grigory Alexandrovich, yesterday your letter of 27 May reached my hands with news of the arrival of the Turkish fleet at Ochakov. Captain Lieutenant Sacken's brave deed* compels one to regret him greatly. I am minded to give his father a rent-free property and have ordered that his brothers be located so that I can find out what sort of reward to offer them.

Field Marshal Rumiantsev writes me that he will cross the Bug River to meet you and agree coordinated movements. While the power of Turkey is aimed at us, the Swedish king, who receives money from the Turks, has armed about twelve ships of war and is transferring troops to Finland. All these manoeuvres are directed, I reckon, at one end: to stop in this manner the fleet that is being prepared for the Mediterranean. But nonetheless, the fleet will maintain its course and, should it encounter obstacles in its path, then it will seek to destroy them. Our ideas are divided: the vice-chancellor says, 'Before leaving here, we should attack the Swedish navy, even if they don't provoke us,' while others say, 'When our fleet departs for the Mediterranean, that is when the Swedes will provoke us.' I think they will not provoke us, but will limit themselves to a demonstration of force. It remains to decide a single question: should we put up with this ploy? If you were here, I would make up my mind how to act in five minutes after talking it over with you. If I were to follow my own inclination, then I would order Greig's fleet and Chichagov's squadron to smash this demonstration to smithereens: it would be another forty years before the Swedes built any more ships.

But if we did this, we would have two wars rather than one, and that might bring about unforeseen consequences. And to forestall this possibility, as soon as the Swedish minister in Stockholm spoke to the Danish ambassador (who informed us of it), we wrote to elicit an explanation. In the meantime, write to me quickly with your opinion. I need it in order to put a check on my rambling thoughts. Twelve days or so will make no difference. Just let me know as soon as possible what you think, and, even if Greig were to set sail, we shall have twelve ships in addition to the Danish ones,* while Greig has a total of twenty-seven ships of war as well as frigates. When I look at this my hands itch— though not without pausing. To tell the truth, the destruction of Swedish naval power would give the Turks a cautionary example. Yet we do not want to prove the Swedish king right, since he has let it be known that he is arming out of a concern that we are preparing to attack him and that we supposedly transferred the Kalmyks and Tatars to the borders for that purpose. This is a pure fabrication, as you know for yourself.

The weather here is most horribly cold, and a storm over the past five days has been breaking the trees.

Farewell, my friend, we both have quite enough cares. But God is merciful. He knows how He will lead us out of this safely, God willing. Be well and happy.

4 June 1788

Another reason why we absolutely should not initiate hostilities is that, if he provokes us, then according to their constitution he will not be entitled to any help from the Swedish nation. But if we provoke them, then they have to give him help. For that reason, I propose to give him free rein to behave stupidly, waste money, and eat up his stores.

169. *To Elisa von der Recke*

Thanking Elisa von der Recke for her polemical works against the Freemasons, 'Information on the Infamous Cagliostro's Stay in Mitau in the Year 1779' (1787) and 'Something about the Apologia of the Senior Court Chaplain Johann August Starck' (1788), Catherine declares her continued support for the Berlin Enlightenment against the mystical movements running rife in Germany. The letter was immediately printed in the 'Berlin Monthly', the same journal in which Kant's famous essay 'What is Enlightenment?' had appeared four years before. In her subsequent letter, Catherine gently scolded von der Recke for this indiscretion. The 'deceivers' and the 'deceived' allude to Catherine's own plays by those names, which were being published in Berlin at precisely this time, while the neologism 'Isis-Templery' refers dismissively to Cagliostro's Egyptian Rite Freemasonry.

Mrs von der Recke, the second work that I received from you gave me as much pleasure as the first. Both bear the marks of a heart that feels the truth deeply and, at the same time, of an enlightened and capacious mind. Indeed, it is deplorable that at the end of the eighteenth century opinions recognized as false and contrary to reason already thousands of years ago are again spreading, even though they were rejected and despised as such by all intelligent people even in times when so many superstitions shameful to human understanding were still being contested. Nonetheless, even when a horde of deceivers has already regained the upper hand—and when the number of the deceived has similarly grown—it is nonetheless to be hoped that all these devotees of Isis-Templery, their superstition, and all the flights of fancy associated with it, are facing imminently a return to their previous state of decline. Particularly when pens as good as yours continue to tear away the veil of nonsense in which this secret mumbo-jumbo wraps itself, and to give to the citizens of the world such powerful arguments to the contrary. I hereby recommend you, Mrs von der Recke, to God's care and remain

  Your most affectionate

Catherina

Tsarskoe Selo, the [17] June 1788*

to Mrs von der Recke in Mitau

170. *To Friedrich Melchior Grimm*

In this excerpt from a letter begun on 19 April 1788, Catherine mordantly lays out her case against Gustav III of Sweden, whom she dubs 'Falstaff' after Shakespeare's comic coward. On 22 June, a day after Catherine wrote this message to Grimm, the Swedes responded to an attack by 'Cossacks' (probably Swedish soldiers in disguise) and fired the first shots against the Russians at Nyslott (also known as Savonlinna, in south-eastern Finland).

this 21 June

Sir John Falstaff, as he embarked for Finland, ordered Count Razumovsky to leave Stockholm for telling him in writing that I had no intention of attacking him and that I had no notions hostile to him *or to his nation*.* Falstaff's pretext was that naming his nation as separate from him wounded his honour and glory. He seems to wish to erase the word 'nation', which, as it happens, is used in grammatical treatises and dictionaries. For him there are no more nations: there are only kings. This makes him the most despotic king ever seen. As he embarked for Finland, he himself said that he was embarking on a perilous endeavour. One might ask him, 'And why, then, are you doing it?' In the meantime, I have received news that the Prince of Nassau and Paul Jones have fought in the Liman against sixty Turkish vessels; that they exploded three and chased away the others.* I do not yet have the details, but I know that we did not lose a single vessel.

Sir Falstaff is a bad relation and a bad neighbour. His outrage against me is unheard of. I have never failed him in anything and have showered him with courtesies. I fed his Finns for several years when they had a famine. He never complained of anything; so far as I know there were no complaints. H. M. is proving that he uses the authority that he usurped from his subjects to make hardships for his subjects and to encumber them with fighting their neighbours. Each king, each sovereign is the foremost individual in a nation, but a king alone is not a nation. Does naming the Swedish nation wrong him? What right does he have to arrogate that of judging the Russian minister? He expels him for naming the Swedish nation. Is there a law that forbids it? He goes from one insult to the next: he had his squadron ask three of our vessels for a salute, which is contrary to article 17 of the treaty of 1743, where it is stipulated that none be given. The note that the King of Sweden gave to all the courts is also very offensive and full of calumnies. It speaks of the fundamental laws of the Kingdom of Sweden: it seems that these are those made or dictated by Gustav III.* He complains in it of the principles and schemes of Count Razumovsky's predecessors. I could say as much of the Swedish envoys. I know that my subjects have no complaints about me; that I have no designs on their liberty; that I employ neither ruses, nor feints, nor duplicity with them; that I do not permit myself to undertake unjust wars; that I do not fear that foreigners might turn my subjects away from their fidelity, which is intimately tied as much to their well-being as to their essential and true interests. You are going say, 'That was quite a diatribe.' What can I do? It just poured out of my pen. Please note that the King of Sweden always seemed very satisfied with Count Razumovsky, and I believe I have a letter in which he recommended him to me.* And he has never complained about the said count, nor about any of his predecessors.

171. *To Grigory Potemkin*

Catherine is delighted at news of the Second Battle of the Liman, which took place on 17–18 June 1788 in the Black Sea. In the meantime, on the very day she wrote this letter to Potemkin, she signed a decree ordering her navy to attack Sweden.

My dear friend, this morning I received from Count Apraksin* the written dispatch, in which you inform me that the Almighty has granted us a victory, that the fleet of the Kapudan Pasha has been destroyed by our galleys; that six ships of the line have been burnt and two run aground, while thirty damaged vessels took refuge at their fortress; that the ships of the Kapudan Pasha and vice-admiral have been destroyed and more than 3,000 men have become our prisoners; and that General Suvorov's artillery has done much harm to the enemy. I rejoiced in all this thoroughly. Great is the mercy of God that He permitted us by some miracle to vanquish military ships with our frigates. You will receive a rescript containing rewards. I am giving Nassau 3,000 souls and Aleksiano* 600, and the crosses have been sent. You, my friend, I thank for your efforts and vigilance, and may God Himself come to your aid. We shall impatiently await details of all this, and I ask you to convey to all from me the most profound thanks.

With this you will receive news that is unamusing: the Swedes have attacked Nyslott where two regiments of Jaegers were stationed, but war has not been declared.* This is what is called banditry.* We are gathering our troops from all directions. The day after the holiday I shall travel to the city and live there in order to buck up the people, even though their spirits have not fallen. However, all the troops are on the march. He who laughs last, laughs best. Justice, reason, and truth are on our side.*

I have signed an order to Greig to seek out the Swedish navy and to try to attack and destroy it with the help of God. I would, my friend, like to be able to give you as soon as possible good news from here.

I know that that would give you as much joy as it would me. But on your victory I congratulate you with all my heart. May God grant that you take Ochakov without any losses, and be healthy. Now we cannot even think of sending even a single sailor from here. Is there any way in which you can put the Greek prisoners to use? Once we have had a chance to get our bearings here, then perhaps, if it is possible, we will send some. For our part, everything has already been done. Farewell, my friend, may God help us.

26 June 1788

I have promoted Count Apraksin to be Senior Lieutenant of the Preobrazhensky Regiment and given him a snuff-box and 500 gold pieces.

172. *To Grigory Potemkin*

Immediately after the British and Prussians forced Denmark to abandon its ally, Russia, at the end of September 1788, the Prussians brought their influence to bear in Poland. Hoping to win Danzig and Thorn, the Prussians made a public declaration against the proposed Russo-Polish alliance, offering an alliance of their own, which encouraged the Poles to seek to break free of Russia entirely. Catherine accordingly made plans to resist Prussia and here writes to consult Potemkin about them.

Dear friend of my heart, Prince Grigory Alexandrovich, while you are kept busy in front of Ochakov, this is what is happening here. The Prussian king has made two declarations: the one sent to Poland is against our alliance with the Poles, and, since I can see that matters might reach combustion point, I have given the order to put this on hold for the time being. The second is addressed to the Danish court, threatening to send to Holstein a force of 30,000 troops, should the Danish court in support of us make an incursion into Sweden. However, the reality is that the Danes have already made a start and taken captive a Swedish lieutenant-general, eight hundred men, and ten cannons. What answer the Danes have made to the Prussian king is still unknown.

The Prussian ambassador here sent to the vice-chancellor the afore-mentioned declaration made to the Danish court by the Prussian king, with an excerpt from the king's letters (not written in the best style). In effect, their intentions and the plan they have adopted become clearer by the day: not only to harm us in every possible way, but also to provoke us at an already difficult time. The business in the Netherlands has worked out for them. They have now immediately taken on the same dictatorial tone with the Danes and will accost us in the same manner. I am attempting in so far as possible not to give them an excuse to bother us. However, may it not go unnoticed that, without waiting for our reply to their proposed mediation (which the Swedish king had entrusted to six courts), they already made such an announcement to the Danes in his sole favour and to our detriment. This is despite the fact that the primary characteristic of a moderator should be objectivity. But here we see clearly and plainly that the opposite is the case: my ally is under threat of all-out attack for giving me aid, while my obligation to defend my ally is commensurate only with how much he aids me. I have prepared a letter on the subject for Count Nesselrode* and attach a copy herewith. I am sending it deliberately through the ordinary post. Let them open and read it on the off-chance that they might feel ashamed or give some thought to the matter, if only briefly. I do not anticipate anything more. But I think that if the Prussian king's harmful intentions regarding Russia and our ally come out into the open: (1) We shall turn the army of Field Marshal Count Rumiantsev, as was already foreseen in your master plan, against the Prussian king, and reinforce its musketeers as per the new eight-company military structure; (2) For the purpose of closing the borders and augmenting the active troops, we shall have a corps of up to 30,000 soldiers deployed in Lifland and Belorussia. In the formation thereof I herewith designate the newly established Estland Jaeger Corps and the infantry regiment that is currently in Riga, as well as the four cavalry regiments currently here and in Belorussia. By way of supplement to this, we still need from the army six regiments, and one of dragoons, as well as a thousand Don or Ural Cossacks. On the matter of this supplement, I place under your supervision the question of designating from where these regiments might be drawn most conveniently. Indeed, it is essential to redouble the effort so that they can arrive here, that is, in Belorussia and Lifland, by spring.

The army in Finland will remain as it is. I shall reinforce the guards.

Write to me, please, about this in detail and quickly so that I do not fumble anything important. Most importantly, make an effort to set up peace negotiations after the conquest of Ochakov. But do not forget that Bulgakov is still sitting in the Seven Towers.

Yesterday I received further the bad news that Admiral Greig has died, to the chagrin of all. He had been ill for three weeks with a fever and jaundice at the port of Revel on the hundred-gun ship *Rostislav*. I dispatched Rogerson to him two weeks ago when I heard that he had fallen so dangerously ill. But nothing was able to save him from the will of God. Spiridov* has already returned to Kronstadt with six ships, and all the others are now heading for their winter harbour. I feel so much afflicted by the death of the admiral that I cannot express it, and this loss at this time is a misfortune for the empire, since we do not have in the navy anyone of comparable skill and reputation to take his place.

Farewell, my dear friend. May God give you health, happiness, and good fortune. We await news from you, and may it please God that it be good.

19 October 1788

PS For the force that I intend to gather in Lifland and Belorussia, I'd like your advice about which of the full generals, lieutenant-generals, and major-generals to choose. How suitable would Prince Iury Vladimirovich Dolgorukov be for that? We would spare him the trip to the emperor's army, where someone else can be sent, regardless of rank, since the business here is more pressing.

173. *To Grigory Potemkin*

The multiple arenas in Catherine's foreign policy sphere demand simultaneous attention. This news round-up, beginning with triumph against the Ottomans and a conspicuous act of clemency, quickly moves on to the pressing question of Russia's strategic contest with Prussia and Great Britain. The letter attests Catherine's firm resolve to stand up to all her adversaries and insist on advantageous conditions for Russia before making peace.

My friend, Prince Grigory Alexandrovich, yesterday I received your letters of 17 November and from them I see that where you are, just like here, there is snow and freezing cold. I commend you entirely for trying to dress your men in winter clothing and footwear. I noted with pleasure that you captured Berezan.* I pray to God that Ochakov, too, will quickly surrender. Now that the Turkish fleet has departed, it would seem that there is no longer any point in their waiting around.

I grant freedom to the two-tailed Osman Pasha captured at Berezan and to all the others to whom you made a promise. Command that he be released with honour. From Constantinople the friends of the Kapudan Pasha are striving to free some Turkish naval captain held captive by us; you'll see this on the ukase written to you about this. In exchange for him, we should demand Lombard, who is going out of his mind and tried to cut his own throat. I very much hope to hear good news about Tekelli.*

Considerable hatred of us has arisen in Poland. And by contrast a great love for His Majesty the Prussian king. This, I reckon, will last until he decides to lead an invasion of his undefeated troops into Poland and occupy the better part of it. It is certainly not for me to prevent it, and I dare not even think it possible to contradict His Majesty the King of Prussia in thought, word, or deed. The entire universe must resign itself to His Most Exalted will.

You reiterate your advice that I should quickly make it up with the Swedish king, using His Majesty the King of Prussia to persuade the former to make peace. But if His Majesty the King of Prussia were thus inclined, then he would not have allowed the Swedish one to go to war. You can be confident that no matter how much I try to get close to this omnipotent dictator, no sooner will I have uttered anything at all, then my wish will surely be destroyed. And they saddle me with the most trivial conditions, such as: the surrender of Finland and perhaps of Lifland to Sweden; of Belorussia to Poland, and the region up to the Samara River to the Turks. And should I not assent to this, then I can have a war. Moreover, their style is so coarse and indeed even stupid, as to be unprecedented, whereas the style of the Turks is as sweet as can be relative to theirs.

I swear by the Almighty God that I am doing everything possible to put up with everything that these courts do, most especially the almighty Prussian court. But the Prussian court has got so big-headed that unless they bust open their own head, I see no honourable way to accommodate their wishes. Indeed, at present the court does not even know what it does or does not want.

At present the King of England is dying, and, should he die, then perhaps his son (who has been heeding Fox and the patriotic English party rather than the Hanoverians) might just manage to establish concord.* I know that the German League did not like Prussian actions in Denmark.

Allow me to tell you what I am beginning to think: that it would be far better to have no allies at all rather than to vacillate from one side to another like a reed during a storm. Besides, wartime is not the right period for establishing an alliance. I am not in favour of retribution, but whatever goes against the honour of my empire and its essential interests is harmful to it. I shall not give up province after province. Who will allow laws to be dictated to them? They will end up being shamed, for no one has yet succeeded in doing this to us. These people have forgotten themselves and with whom they are dealing. These idiots have put their hopes in the possibility that we will be accommodating!

Take Ochakov and conclude a peace with the Turks. Then you will see how they slink away like snow on the steppe after a thaw, and how they crawl away like water in steep places.* Farewell, God be with you. Be well and safe. I feel deep regret for Maximovich.*

27 November 1788

174. *To Johann Georg Zimmermann*

Catherine responds to two letters from Zimmermann: in the first, dated 14 November 1788 (NS), Zimmermann wrote a panegyric of Catherine in the form of a dialogue of the dead, on the pretext that in the afterlife he could speak 'freely' about her. In the second, he congratulated her on Potemkin's successful and rapid storming of the key and well-defended Ottoman fortress of Ochakov on 6 December 1788.

You, Sir, are surely the first doctor who has ever asked someone for permission to send them to the next world. Not only that—you even accompany them to the Elysian Fields. I could ask for nothing better than to go in such good company, on the condition, however, that I might choose my company, which could be exceptionally entertaining. Your harangue, I confess, would be very much to my taste, if I could be quite sure that it was not too flattering. Here is more or less what I would have to say in response. If my century has feared me, it was very wrong to do so. I have never wanted to cause terror in anyone. I would have wished to be loved and esteemed according to my deserts, and nothing more. I have always thought that I was subject to calumny because I was misunderstood. I have seen many people who were infinitely cleverer than I. I have never hated or envied anyone. My desire and my pleasure would have been to make people happy, but since one can be happy only in keeping with one's character or caprice or understanding, my wishes in this respect have often met with obstacles of which I could make no sense. My ambitions were certainly not evil, but perhaps I overdid it in believing men capable of becoming reasonable, just, and happy. The human race in general has a penchant for unreason and injustice and thus can hardly be happy. If people heeded reason and justice, the likes of me would not be needed. As for happiness, as I said, everyone understands it in his own way. I have held philosophy in high regard because my soul has always been remarkably republican: I admit that this temper of soul stands in remarkable contrast, perhaps, to the unlimited power of my position, but also no one in Russia will say that I have abused it. I love the arts out of pure enjoyment. As for my writings, I value them little. I have enjoyed trying my hand at different genres. It seems to me that all I have done is fairly mediocre, and therefore I have not ascribed any importance to it other than entertainment. As for my diplomatic conduct, I have sought to follow the plans that seemed most useful to my country and most tolerable to others. If I had known of better plans, I would have adopted them. Europe was wrong to fear my designs, from which, on the contrary, it could only have benefited. If I have been paid with ingratitude, at least no one will say that I have been ungrateful. I have often avenged myself on my enemies by doing them good or by forgiving them. Humanity in general has found in me an unfailing friend on all occasions.

Here ends the dialogue of the dead. Let us return to the living. Trousson returned to the army towards the end of the siege of Ochakov. Here is what I have dug up about him. He wrote me two letters to tell me that he had been forgotten, but it seemed to me that the Order of St Vladimir and the various gratifications he had received were proof to the contrary. It is possible that he has not been employed as he would have wished. Perhaps those who arrived later were employed for jobs that may have struck him as more prestigious or more to his taste. That is possible, but it is certain that until he left for the army, he remained employed here in Petersburg at the task assigned to him by the late Lieutenant-General Bauer, and it is not yet finished. The Dutch, who have aroused his envy, had their jobs in various corners of this immense empire. As they had a long way to travel and difficulties to overcome, they enjoyed, in proportion to their efforts and their ranks, different emoluments to which Captain Trousson did not seem to have the same right. I know of Monsieur Deluc, your friend of whom you told me and who takes the same interest as you do in the fate of this officer (for whom I shall try to do what befits me), from the letters on Switzerland, which he addressed to the Queen of England. I do not know if he is reader to Her Majesty in title or in fact, but, in the latter case, I hope with all my heart that he might succeed by his readings in diminishing, distracting, and calming the distress that must afflict the heart and mind of the queen, in view of the king's state of health.*

As for the Marquis Lucchesini, who you say recently entreated you 'to teach him to be worthy of my kindness'—you may tell him frankly, Sir, that he will certainly not do it by harming my interests. It is generally rather peculiar that the Marquis Lucchesini, a friend of the late king and one towards whom all those who did justice to that great king's virtues were favourably disposed, has chosen to begin his diplomatic career with the dirty job for which he has allowed himself to be used. It amounts to no less than the destruction of an edifice, in the construction of which the late king participated most directly. It is even more strange that the court at Berlin can be so deluded as to think that they can harm my interests and, in all things, display passionate partiality for my enemies and their most unjust cause, and yet at the same time try to persuade me that they are on the path to winning my friendship and even to obtaining an alliance with me. Those reasons are neither attractive nor convincing to me. The examples of Holland's submission to Prussian troops and of Denmark's compliance with Mr Elliot's threats* do not trace out a suitable path for Russia. There would be no honour for us in being the next to go. Here we have not yet forgotten that in the Seven Years War, despite the King of Prussia's superior genius, the wealth lavished on them by England, and the heroes who commanded the armies, the late king saw his very capital invaded. And it was Catherine II who, in 1762, had the honour of returning to that prince the Kingdom of Prussia and a good part of Pomerania, a province which Peter I gave to the house of Brandenburg.*

From your letter of 16 January, which I have just received, I see the joy that the taking of Ochakov caused you, Sir. Naturally, Field Marshal Prince Potemkin tried all other means before resorting to an assault. The most suitable time for the undertaking was undoubtedly when the ice-covered Liman rendered the seaside inaccessible to reinforcements for the besieged. Once the city was taken, there was time to take the necessary precautions for the future. But the impatience of hot-heads, of young people full of courage, of half-wits who cannot see past their noses, of three-quarters-wits with crooked reasoning, of enviers, and of open or concealed enemies, is surely the most inconvenient thing in such a situation. The field marshal's steadfastness and perseverance had very much to endure from that quarter. In my view, it does him the greatest honour that, among his other great and beautiful qualities, I have always known him to possess that of forgiving his enemies and of doing them good, and in this manner he always prevails over his antagonists. This time, in an hour and a half he defeated the Turks and those who had criticized him. Now they are saying that he could have taken Ochakov earlier. That is true, but never with less risk. This is not the first time that our sick have left hospital to go on the attack, a fact at which you express surprise. I have seen that same thing happen on all momentous occasions. There is great enthusiasm here for the public good. This summer, when the King of Sweden attacked us without warning, I sent word to the villages on the nearest estates to send recruits;

they were to decide for themselves how many each village would give. And what happened? One village of a thousand males sent 75 fine recruits and another sent 250 out of 4,000. A third, in Tsarskoe Selo, where there are 3,000 peasants, sent 400 horses with men and carts to transport army supplies; they served for the entire Finnish campaign. But this is not all. Upon hearing what was happening over by Sweden, the surrounding districts, and then all the others one after the next, offered by their own free will a battalion and a squadron per district. The city of Moscow alone would have sent up 10,000 men if I had let them. Our people are born warriors, and our recruits are easy to train. The nobility serves or has served: when truly necessary, no one has ever said 'no' to anything. Everyone runs to defend the state and the Fatherland—no effort is needed to make them join. Farewell, Sir, that is enough for today, be well.

this 29 January 1789

175. *To Johann Georg Zimmermann*

Written in two sittings two months apart, this letter reflects evolving diplomatic and military tensions. While Catherine lavished rewards on Potemkin and the other participants in the storming of Ochakov, Prussia tried to force Russia to back down without taking land from the Ottomans. In his letter of 18 April 1789 (NS), Zimmermann offered the services of an unnamed 'gentleman' with 'an often decisive influence on one side of the Berlin cabinet', which Catherine here somewhat aggressively declines. While she demurs with seeming modesty at the suggestion that she become Empress of the Greeks, she hints at her desire to see her grandson Constantine in that role.

at Tsarskoe Selo, this 23 May 1789

I received, Sir, your letter of 18 April three days ago. I see with pleasure that you are pleased with my response to your speech that imagined me in the Elysian Fields. Before I make that descent, I am going on many strolls here, where I have done nothing but build and plant for the past twenty-two years. I leave it to the Marquis Lucchesini and his companions to cause all the harm they can and do cause. I am very much in agreement with those or with him who believes that Frederick II never would have approved of conduct so contrary to his consistent position from 1762.* Today, the court at Berlin has adopted the political principles of Monsieur de Choiseul, whom Frederick II so much mocked. Everyone knows what good the Duc de Choiseul's policies did us: his chimerical fear of Russia's greatness was a cover-up for his passions, his hatred, his envy, and his duplicity. He wanted to harm me, and he merely revealed his own weakness and that of the Turks whom he brought into play. He always had the balance of Europe on the tip of his tongue—that metaphysical balance of Europe, which has always unbalanced all the powers that have leaned on the phrase. It serves to throw dust in the eyes of the multitude, and to mask vicious and incoherent aims and intentions when the latter have supplanted justice, the foundation of all states and the bond of human society. I believe and am convinced that the reputation of cabinets is just like that of individuals: he who sows discord left and right in his neighbours' houses can never inspire any confidence nor merit any reputation other than that of an incendiary. Duplicity is a poor road by which to march towards glory, and those who employ it cannot help but be duped by their own handiwork. But many people know how to do only two things in politics: to pour oil on the fire and to fish in troubled waters. And that is what has stirred up in every century those bloody spectacles called wars: princes who are either hot-headed or led by ministers of that character repent of them only when their subjects are the victims. I hope that soon your wishes will be fulfilled and that the Turks and His Swedish Majesty will be beaten on sea and on land. Then I hope that, to stay true to their roles, those who have fomented them, and who second and support them, will congratulate me on it. I have just learned that the King of England's journey has been postponed until another time.

The surgeons that you have hired will be paid, doubt not. I do not know why they do not address themselves to me rather than to you for it: when one puts 'in her own hands' in the address, every post office is required to deliver the packet to me 'in my own hands'. I approve very much of the gift that you have suggested to Mr Gross for the surgeon-major who has helped you to choose the people whom you have sent to us.

this 20 July

This letter, which had remained on my desk for two months for various reasons, witnessed the arrival of yours of 12 June, which was brought by courier. As best we understand, it seems that Selim III tends towards cruelty and inhumanity, and therefore it would be difficult for him to become your hero or mine. If he is featherbrained, it will be all the more natural for him to form ties with Gustav III. One will strangle his pashas, and the other liberty and truth in his speeches and writings, and each of them will find approvers and admirers, along with help and apologists in the tortuous politics that now grips the cabinets of several courts of Europe. They believe that they are setting out on a brilliant road, whereas, at root, they are preparing for themselves a vast field that will lead them sooner or later straight to their ruin. But those who envy me know no limits to their malevolence, and we shall have to see which of us laughs last. Prince Potemkin and his army fought perfectly well; it was quite just that they should be rewarded. General Kamensky is full of fire and zeal. If your gentleman prevents the court at Berlin from being unreasonable, he will render a very good service to humanity. He would have to try to render it less unjust, less besotted with supporting, approving, and fomenting Gustav III's injustices and Polish follies. Very far from consuming the Poles' next harvest, we are withdrawing all our storehouses from Poland. And once this has been done, I promise you that Poland will not see a single bushel of its wheat consumed by my army. Thereby Poland will lose millions, which they will miss and will not recover anywhere, since no one can consume more than they need or compensate Poland for this loss. Up to now in Finland there have been only skirmishes over small outposts, which recur every day: at the end of the campaign we shall say what the result is. Admiral Chichagov has gone in search of the Swedish navy, but if it has gone to hide its disrepair at Karlskrona, he will be quite obliged to return without having found it at sea. I shall send you the news that reaches me from north and south when it is worth it. I have never had the idea of becoming Empress of the Greeks or of Greece. I know how to limit myself. But I hope that the Greeks will become free and happy under a Christian prince of their creed and that they will cease to suffer under a terrible and inhuman yoke. This letter will go by courier.

I thank you for your wishes in my favour, and be assured of my esteem. Farewell.

176. *To Grigory Potemkin*

Catherine describes the Battle of Vyborg Bay. The Russian and Swedish navies had been fighting since May in the Gulf of Finland, sometimes within earshot of Catherine at Tsarskoe Selo. On 21 June, the Prince of Nassau-Siegen attacked the Swedish flotilla protecting the main Swedish fleet, which was positioned in Vyborg Bay. The Swedes managed to escape, but lost twelve ships in the process.

Well, friend of my heart, Prince Grigory Alexandrovich, there is plenty to write about. The Swedish king, with his fleet of warships and galleys, was blockaded from 27 May to 21 June, as I wrote you. During all that time, a west wind was blowing, a total headwind directly against our rowed ships. Meanwhile in Petersburg we succeeded in building gunboats to replace those lost by Slizov.* Finally, on the 20th there blew a fair wind for our galleys, and Prince Nassau took them into the Berezovye Islands* and engaged in a five-hour battle with the King of Sweden himself and his galleys. After that the Swedish king retreated and went off past Vyborg Bay, where he joined forces with his flotilla of warships and attempted with them to break through our fleet. What happened thanks to the power and wisdom of the Lord? The Swedes ignited three fireships and launched them with the strong north wind against five ships from the squadron under the command of Rear-Admiral Povalishin.* But the fireships became entangled in two of the Swedish ships, and all five Swedish ships blew up. Of ours not a single one! The Swedes took four hours to sail past Povalishin. You will see what he, and then Khanykov,* captured or sank from the list. I can't quite recall from memory. Chichagov, Kruse, and Pushkin* weighed anchor and gave chase. I ask you to read what they, too, captured and destroyed.* Nassau gave chase to the Swedish galley fleet and kept pace. One sixty-gun ship surrendered to him. Crown* was near Pitkäpaasi.* Even now he is still sending captured galleys one after another to Kronstadt.* One seventy-four- and another sixty-four-gun ship have been brought to Revel, and even now the hunt continues. In a word, we still haven't managed to gather all the details about this complete victory: there are up to 5,000 prisoners, up to 800 cannons, and we do not yet have the number of small vessels. As for the king—well, different things are being said. Some maintain that he escaped on a launch flanked by two supply ships. Others say that he was on his yacht, *Amphion*. When it sank, he supposedly got off and boarded a galley. When this galley was captured, he jumped ship onto a sloop; when this sloop was also captured, he escaped into a small boat, and this boat sailed off. His breakfast was taken captive: it consisted of six dry biscuits, a smoked goose, and two carafes of vodka. The king's brother departed to Sveaborg* on his own badly battered ship, ahead of which Chichagov is now cruising.

I congratulate you on the holiday today and on the victory. God has released us from this burden, and Chichagov has once again made you happy, as you see. Yesterday, on the anniversary of the Battle of Poltava, I held a prayer service here. On Sunday I shall travel to the city and conduct prayers in the naval church of St Nicholas the Wonderworker.*

Farewell, may God be with you. It is being said that after the first of July the Prussians will be on the march, about which I shall similarly inform you: they wish to go to Riga by passing through Courland, but the king has already long been in Breslau, and negotiations are still ongoing in Reichenbach.*

28 June 1790

Your cornet [Platon Zubov] was delighted by what you sent, and his behaviour remains as praiseworthy as ever.

177. *To Grigory Potemkin*

Catherine reacts to Potemkin's news that the Russians, led by Fedor Ushakov, have caused serious damage to the Ottoman fleet in the Kerch Strait, which separates Crimea from the Taman Peninsula. She is less pleased with Potemkin's other news, namely that the Prussians and Austrians have signed the Convention of Reichenbach (16 July 1790), which entailed an armistice between Austria and the Ottoman Empire and therefore the abandonment of Russia by its ally. However, as Catherine hints, she would soon be saved from the prospect of fighting a double war alone, since a peace treaty with Sweden was to be signed only a week after this letter was written.

Dear friend of my heart, Prince Grigory Alexandrovich, the victory over the Turkish fleet, which the Lord gave us as a gift, and about which you attached a short note when sending your letters of 13 July, brought me great rejoicing. I now live in anticipation of the more circumstantial description of this affair that you will forward. Meanwhile, this messenger will bring you information on happenings here. In a few days' time we shall find out whether the King of Sweden has initiated direct negotiations to conclude peace in earnest or as a ruse. If it is in fact true, as rumour has it, that there have been disturbances in Sweden, then I expect the peace to be concluded expeditiously. According to the prisoners taken captive at Vyborg, His Majesty is at present not exactly in their good books. I think that once the Turks learn that he is making peace, and that the Prussian is dawdling, and that the Poles are refusing to attack, then they can hardly fail to open their eyes. They cannot possibly expect to do better than reaching a peace settlement in which they forfeit no more than the land up to the Dniester area. The Swedish king, however, and indeed the Prussian, too, will fleece them of a fortune without bringing them so much as an ounce of benefit. Farewell, may the Lord be with you, write more often.

The English—or, it would be better to say, the King of England—blindly follow the commands of the Prussian. Should the Austrian court especially wish to make peace, we shall come out of it as we were in the previous war and be no worse off than up to this point. However, if the Prussians antagonize us, then the Austrian court will have to get involved. It is not likely that the matter will get that far, since the Prussian king's allies would reconsider if they went on to the offensive.

We had three days of summer until yesterday, when once again it was rainy. However, the grain and hay are everywhere quite abundant. Be well. Despite all the demands I am rather well.

Your cornet's pleasant and nice manner wards off many a spell of ennui.

27 July 1790

178. *To Grigory Potemkin*

Catherine announces to Potemkin the Treaty of Värälä.

My dear friend, Prince Grigory Alexandrovich, God has ordained that one paw will be extracted from a sticky spot. This very morning I received a messenger from Baron Igelström bringing a peace treaty signed by him and Baron Armfelt without mediation on 3 August. It was because of my personal insistence, if I dare say so, that they dropped the demand that we accept their intercession with the Turks to facilitate a peace treaty, and prrrr! they didn't get it. But I suspect that this peace will not entirely please the Prussian king. I now pray to God that He aid you to achieve the same with the Turks. Yesterday we celebrated the victory of the Black Sea fleet over the Turks with a service in the city at the Kazan Cathedral, and I do not remember the last time I was so merry. I ask you to convey my deep thanks to Rear-Admiral Ushakov and all his subordinates.* You see that with this I am hurrying to answer your letters from 20 July, and that I am hastening as much as possible to inform you of our not insignificant news.

For Christ's sake, send quickly a receipt from the pasha of Ochakov for the moneys sent to him by the Turks.* This way, the French will desist from tormenting the vice-chancellor [Ivan Osterman] about the transfer of these moneys. They have got it into their heads that we steal and withhold funds like they do.

Farewell, my friend, may God be with you.

from Tsarskoe Selo, 5 August 1790

Your cornet, so heartfelt in his affection, is happy beyond words about the peace, as he shall tell you himself.

179. *To Prince Charles-Joseph de Ligne*

Literature and politics mix in this response to a letter from the Prince de Ligne. The Prince had just read two publications of letters by enlightened monarchs: Catherine's correspondence with Voltaire, published in the first posthumous edition of Voltaire's complete works, and Frederick the Great's correspondence published in the first edition of his 'Posthumous Works' in 1788. Complimenting Catherine on her epistolary and military successes, de Ligne contrasted her 'good letters' with Frederick's, where the king appears as a 'witty person, somewhat ponderously harping on about philosophy and literature'.

Here, here, Sir: I am answering your letter from Starý Jičín, on the border with Silesia where you were awaiting ... 14 July.* And I am doing it with the same pen with which I informed Field Marshal Prince Potemkin-Tavrichesky that, in the open countryside between Värälä and Kauvala, on 3 August at five o'clock in the evening, a peace treaty was concluded with the King of Sweden. It was signed on my behalf by the Lieutenant-General Baron Igelström and on Gustav III's by Baron Armfelt, his plenipotentiary.

This is the history of how your letter reached me in the first place. The Princess of Clary* gives a letter from her father to my ambassador in Vienna, the latter in his diplomatic capacity sends it to the vice-chancellor who seals it in an enormous parcel of letters destined for me. Its sheer volume catches my attention when I receive it, then I see that it was addressed to Kronstadt. I open it, and it attests to the boredom that you are enduring. While you wait, why have you not made your enemy die of boredom too, like Belling* before the Peace of Teschen? You have been itching to come to blows with the enemies of Christians ... not with the allies of non-Christians; and out of spite you seized a pen and filled four sheets of paper as ample as that containing the peace treaty signed in the open countryside by two barons without any initial meeting or final congress. But how shall I respond to this enormous letter without producing one that—because it is even larger still—you will perhaps have neither the time nor the will to read because the boredom of waiting will most likely have passed by the time you receive it.

I am tempted to send you a commentary on your letter, now that I have written its history—one of those works that one reads at leisure, and this is where I shall begin. (But on the subject of commentaries, when shall I have yours on the campaigns of the Margrave of Baden-Baden? You promised me one.)* You pity me for having to fight on all fronts. I shall tell you once and for all that this is not the way to pay court to me—to pity me—since I have never wished to seem pitiful; and if I have much preferred to make people envy me, at least I have never felt a shred of envy for a living soul. Please now cross the King of Sweden off the list of those on the attack. Then, being less encumbered, I shall be in a better position to answer you. But I hope that our correspondence will not be printed as my poor letters to Voltaire unfortunately were—about which I am terribly cross. I write letters in my own hand to people who I believe love me and whom I hold in high regard. You know, it is impossible for me to chase intelligence and eloquence. For that reason I never write to go into print and nothing looks more idiotic to me than what I have written, if I happen to see it printed. When Voltaire feared that I had insufficient money to buy his watches at Ferney, he thought as much only from heeding the rumour spread by the Duc de Choiseul who wished in front of the entire world to make me look like a penniless spendthrift. In order to please him, that's what one had to say—and people did. When he arrived in Russia, Louis-Philippe Ségur must have found the embassy archive stuffed with documents which prove what I have just said. That was how people who did not like Russia or whose aims were opposed to mine were able to strut about with pride. When you thought I was parading around with my chin practically in the air, you were unaware that my late governess Miss Cardel often advised me to tuck my chin in. For she found when I was a child that there was something terribly pointy about it, and told me that by sticking it out I would clobber anyone who bumped into it. Miss Cardel was an intelligent girl who was always accusing me of having an awkward character. Baron Grimm must have a large collection of the sayings and deeds and maxims of Miss Cardel. I do not know what has happened to the awful bust in the Hermitage about which you ask for news. But what is certain is that it is no longer where you saw it, about which I am delighted since I never walked past it without having an attack of bile. It had an impertinent air about it. Well, you know, that's what bad painters and sculptors call a 'majestic air', and when you get right down to it that is how they cover up their foolish mistakes. I do think My Refuge* will put your chin right up in the air, since you say it is immune to all the oddities of the world and of liberty. If I were to tell you everything that I have to say about this liberty it would come to another complete volume. If this French fashion turns into an epidemic, I congratulate the Turks. With a single gesture, now that the Rights of Man have been established, they will forthwith conquer Europe, and will make this entire part of the world Muslim at sword-point as Pasha Köprülü did in Bosnia in less than a year.* It is said that since 14 July the confederates are constantly drunk.* Since there is no effect without a cause, there must also be a cause for so many thousands of men to be drunk every day in Paris. I think that Voltaire and his writings would have provided a diversion from the fanaticism of the current absurdness, which really can't continue. Voltaire disliked all fanaticism, and his writings had a great influence on the minds of his contemporaries.

The ignoramuses, both men and women, are precisely as you left them and still as incapable as they are known to be of writing the verses that you cited, despite the two good teachers who took such pains in order to teach them to get the measure of their thoughts. However, I much prefer Monsieur de Ségur's verses to his prose; he used the latter to attack the skilled workers of the National Assembly, who destroy and break everything, who confiscate but give nothing, who by all the rules and norms that existed until now lack good sense and who only create masterpieces of imprudence. The fable about the appendages of the human body wishing to lay down the law to the stomach* could never be better applied than in this situation. Do please write to me as much as you wish: your letters afford me great pleasure, and I shall always have time to reply to you. I have not read the great man's letters to his correspondents.* By some misfortune, with all due respect to the great man, when his immense writings were brought to me I fell upon seventeen pages full of proven falsehoods,* and once I saw this, I closed the book and have not touched the rest of it. Neither the hundred chariots nor the two troupes of actors astonish me, and I recall a certain shirt embroidered in ermine with ribbons under a white domino that I saw spread out and of which someone was very proud. This is what it means to lack everything until the age of forty. As a result one ends up showing off like a parvenu.* I share the grief that you and the entire Austrian monarchy must have felt at the loss of Marshal Laudon. Heroes are so rare: I would like to see them all assembled in paradise, that is, the ones who are already dead—it is my wish that those who are still alive shall long continue to add brilliance to their careers. There is no need to provide an account of the news from the Baltic; you already know it. After the memorable rout in Vyborg Bay when we captured many Swedish vessels and men, our flotilla of oarsmen suffered a rude setback, although nothing like so ruinous for us as the first battle must have been to the King of Sweden. Just as the peace treaty was being signed, the Prince of Nassau had once again surrounded the Swedish galleys. This summer there really was a reason for the Imperturbable One* to live up to her name. Now that things have turned out according to our wishes it will be necessary to agree terms, here and there. These are of the greatest necessity. Farewell, stay well.

Catherine

at Tsarskoe Selo, this 5 August 1790

180. *To Gustav III of Sweden*

Immediately after the signature of the Treaty of Värälä ending the Russo-Swedish War, Gustav wrote to Catherine, seeking not only to renew their previous friendly correspondence, but also to achieve an eventual alliance. In this reply, Catherine archly reminds Gustav of his guilt in starting the war.

My dear Brother and Cousin, yesterday morning I received news of the signing of the peace, which has happily been restored between Your Majesty and myself. I say happily because I have always considered peace to be the greatest happiness of humankind and because my wishes have invariably been to procure it for my subjects to enjoy.

When I awoke this morning, I was most pleasantly surprised by the letter that Your Majesty was pleased to send me and that is dated 15 August NS, the day after our plenipotentiaries signed the peace. You thereby indicate your desire to resume a sincere and unbreakable friendship with me. It will not be difficult for me personally to return Your Majesty's sentiments, which are equally in keeping with our blood ties and with the interests of our states. I shall even say that I would have wished that they had never been interrupted and that Gustav's perseverance regarding Catherine had taken precedence over the constancy with which Your Majesty tells me that you supported my enemies. As I look to the future, I entreat Your Majesty to rest assured that, for my part, the articles of the peace, the ratification of which I have the pleasure of signing today, will be fulfilled most exactly and that I shall neglect nothing that might contribute to consolidating good harmony, friendship, and peaceful neighbourliness, as I am with as much sincerity as high regard,

My dear Brother and Cousin,
Your Majesty's good Sister, Cousin, Neighbour, and Friend,

Catherine
at Tsarskoe Selo, this 6 August 1790

181. *To Grigory Potemkin*

Catherine and Potemkin trade war news, and music by Giuseppe Sarti (1729–1802), an Italian composer in Russian employ. His 'Te Deum', commissioned by Potemkin to celebrate the conquest of Ochakov, was performed on 30 August 1790—complete with scored cannon-fire—following the consecration of Holy Trinity Cathedral of the Alexander Nevsky Lavra in St Petersburg. Sarti also composed some of the music for Catherine's grand opera libretto 'The Beginning of Oleg's Reign' (1790). In it, Oleg of Novgorod (d. 912) successfully attacks Constantinople; the play therefore had evident political resonances with current events.

Friend of my heart, dear Prince Grigory Alexandrovich, today the ratifications of peace with the Swede are being exchanged in Värälä, and this courier has been dispatched to you to share with you the declarations that have been exchanged in Reichenbach and sent here.* They are in my opinion shameful. As far as we are concerned, I instruct you under no circumstances to send anyone to their stupid congress in Bucharest, but rather to try to conclude a separate peace for us with the Turks on the basis of the instruction given to you and signed by me.

The Prussian once again is conjuring the Poles to concede Danzig and Thorn, and this time, beguiling them at our cost, he cedes to them Belorussia and Kiev. He is the universal distributor of other people's property. A courteous reply of no substance will be made to Goltz's communication concerning the Reichenbach negotiation. Farewell, my friend, may God be with you.

9 August 1790

We have extracted one paw from the muck. Once we extricate the second, we shall sing a Hallelujah! *A propos*, Platon Alexandrovich has given me Sarti's choruses. Two are very good, but the 'We praise you, O Lord'—what a shame that it cannot be sung in church owing to the instruments—it is the most exquisite of all.

I thank you for what you sent. They can now prepare *Oleg* for the celebrations of the northern peace, in which we achieved the cessation of military actions and, consequently, spared men and money. The Swedes will smart from this for a long time, and His Majesty is becoming thoroughly unpopular with them. Rumour has it that the Prussian king has dismissed 120 of his officers in Silesia. So far nobody knows the actual reason. If you should find out, tell me. Hertzberg* is telling anyone willing to listen that he is overcome by chagrin. No one knows the reason, but it cannot be his master's affairs that are to blame, since they are going marvellously well. They have spent 25 million on arms, and a further several million on scheming, but what is 30 million for people who presume to impose their will on the entire world and who have an immense treasury in hard cash.*

182. *To Grigory Potemkin*

Managing subordinates is one of the major themes of this letter. On 28 June 1790, the anniversary of Catherine's accession, the Russian navy under the Prince of Nassau-Siegen attempted to attack the Swedish fleet off the coast of Finland; in the ensuing battle, they lost a total of sixty-four ships. The mortified Nassau-Siegen wrote to resign his command, but instead Catherine wrote a letter of consolation, exhorting him to pick up the pieces. She believed firmly that encouraging rather than punishing subordinates would allow her to get the best out of them.

My dear friend, Prince Grigory Alexandrovich, with these lines I am replying to your letters of 3, 16, and 18 August. As regards the unfortunate loss of part of the fleet, which you mentioned, well, here is an account of my conduct in reaction to this matter. As soon as Turchaninov reached me with the news, I more than anything sought to mitigate the misfortune and rectify it in any way possible in order to deprive the enemy of a chance to inflict even greater damage. And so, I made every possible effort to raise the spirits of those who could feel distressed. There were not many people available to select here, but in general I have always worked with what I have. And so, I wrote to Nassau, who had asked that I have him judged by a military court. I answered that I had already judged him in my own mind, since I remembered in how many battles he had defeated the enemies of the empire. I wrote that there is not a single general to whom such a misfortune could not happen in war; that there was nothing worse than despondence; and that only in misfortune could a resilient spirit be seen. Whereupon he was ordered to recover everything that could be recovered and to produce and provide me with a detailed description of the actual loss, as well as everything that needed to be done and found. And finally by virtue of these orders, within a month things reached the point where once again the Swedish navy's galleys were hemmed in and in such a position that they could all have been destroyed, a fact that contributed not insignificantly to the peace.

That you heard of the peace with great joy, I have no doubt at all, knowing your devotion and love for me and for our common interest. How pleasurable it is for me to hear from your own lips that you credit this to my invincible resolve. The Empress of All Russia cannot be otherwise when she has 16,000 versts at her back and sees the goodwill and enthusiasm of the people for this war. And now, since God has blessed us with this peace, I assure you that I shall neglect nothing in order to secure us on this side in the future. A good foundation has already been laid. General Stedingk has been sent here by the Swedish king, and I am sending von der Pahlen in the first instance.

I am certain that you will not, for your own part, miss this useful opportunity to reach a peace deal. Do the sultan and Turks not see that the Swedes have abandoned them? That the Prussians, despite having promised in a treaty last spring to attack us and the Viennese court, lied to them pure and simple? The Prussians will demand from the Turks compensation for the expenditures they made on arming. What else could idiots possibly expect? They will never secure a better peace than we offer, and, should they heed the Prussian king, then there will be no peace ever, since his appetite has no limit. I think that if you write all of this to them in your own style, you will open their eyes.

Where you are there is a heatwave and drought, and the rivers have run dry, whereas here it has been raining since the month of May, and even now not a day goes by without some rain. Throughout the entire summer it has been utterly unbearable, and we can barely even warm our hands. The speed with which you crossed from Ochakov to Bender was unprecedented. Is it any wonder that you feel weaker after such a sprint? Rest assured that I shall not leave those you recommended without favours and distinctions—namely your worthy cornet and Count Bezborodko, on whose behalf you enquire. I thank you for the splendid snuff-box and the thoroughly fine carpet that you sent. Each of these pleases me greatly, so you must, therefore, keep your word: you promised to be jolly if they pleased me, and I like it when you are jolly.

I have designated the eighth day of September for the celebration of the Swedish peace, and I shall try to the best of my intelligence to manage things. But often, my friend, I feel that there are many instances when I should like to have a word with you for a quarter of an hour. I am sending Igelström to Lifland with the regiments that served in the Finnish war. I am very sorry cases of illness are increasing among your men. The number of ill people we have had here since spring is incredible.

As far as concerns Field Marshal Rumiantsev and his presence in Moldavia under various pretexts, I think that it would be best to send him word that he might quite easily find that he will be taken captive by the Turks unless he leaves quickly.* But if this should fail to help, then send a convoy for him that would protect and get him out of there. Truth be told, I have protected him as much as possible on account of his former service and out of gratitude, and I do retain a memory of his personal service. My predecessors would have acted differently.

By now Bulgakov should already be in Warsaw. The peace with the Swedes has flustered vicious minds there, as everywhere else. We shall see what measures they take, but if God aids you to persuade the Turks, then our most implacable enemies will have been quelled. Farewell, my friend, may Christ be with you.

Tomorrow, on the feast day of St Alexander Nevsky, the knights* will transfer his remains to the cathedral of his monastery and consecrate the church in my presence. A table will be laid for the knights in the monastery, and at another table there will be the clergy in the company of the grand duchess and the other five orders, just as used to happen during the reign of the late Empress Elizabeth Petrovna. I remain with unfailing goodwill.

29 August 1790

Tomorrow, if the Lord grants health, during the meal in the Nevsky Monastery 'We praise you, O Lord', which you sent me, will be sung with instruments.* As a sign of my appreciation for the construction of the church, I have today rewarded the Metropolitan of Novgorod and Petersburg* with a medallion of the Virgin in emeralds, a very fine piece.

Since you write that you have been sleeping well since you found out about the peace with the Swedes, I shall on this point tell you what happened to me: since 1787 I kept having to have my dresses taken in, but in these three weeks they have started to become tight, so soon I shall have to let them out again. I have indeed become much more cheerful. The delightful nature and manners of your esteemed cornet have contributed to this greatly.

183. *To Prince Charles-Joseph de Ligne*

Late in the year, Catherine takes stock of the challenges posed by Russia's complex geopolitical position, while growing unrest in France feeds into her general worry about stability and a European order possibly spiralling out of control. This letter also caused a disruption in her correspondence with de Ligne: he allowed it to be leaked to the newspapers, risking serious diplomatic embarrassment for Catherine. He received a serious scolding and a few months' silence before she resumed correspondence as usual.

Prince de Ligne, Sir, have no fear, I shall never treat your letters as I do my neighbours'. Your letters always give me pleasure, while the others frequently bore me. Moreover, I hand them over very quickly to the profound scrutiny of my council, with whom I always agree—whenever they agree with me. Meanwhile, I gladly take care of replying to you myself. The newspapers from Peking report that my Chinese neighbour, whose little eyes you so respectfully mention, has been carrying out with a truly exemplary meticulousness the endless rituals to which he is subjected. As for my Persian neighbours, they slaughter one another regularly every month. They bear no small resemblance to the glaciers of the Arctic Sea that crash into one another, smashing one another to bits during storms. The Poles, in order to put the finishing touches to their liberty, are preparing to yield to the most arbitrary military despotism.* Their decision is all the more voluntary insofar as it is up to each person to accept or refuse the ringing coins that they will be given in return. Selim and his Divan* have decided that it is time to go back to school and will leave the care of badly messing up their affairs to their tutors. That is convenient to say the least.

In the meantime, we shall beat them and whip them, as is our laudable custom, on land and sea. You, you are making peace ... The two barons would like to consolidate the peace of Värälä with reciprocal embassies. England is arming, Spain negotiating. The King of Prussia [Frederick William II] has pretensions to dictatorship of a kind which his uncle [Frederick the Great] could not have entertained in 1762. France has 1,200 lawmakers whom no one obeys apart from the king. Holland would much prefer to profit from its commerce rather than squander on armaments, etc. But I forget myself, I was not going to speak to you of anyone other than my neighbours. Instead, I have done an entire tour of Europe and Asia. By bringing me your letter, to which this serves as a response, Count Starhemberg spared me the cost of postage,* whereby you have done my finances a good turn.* According to those better informed than myself, my finances are in a very poor state, since I have sustained two wars at the same time without coming up with so much as the smallest little tax, whether because I lacked the means to do so or perhaps because of ignorance. You are very lucky with your cousin: Count Starhemberg appears to be thoroughly likeable. I hope that he will return from his visit here contented and that he will find you healthier than when he left you. Farewell, my Prince, rest assured of my unchanging regard for you.

Catherine
at St Petersburg, this 6 November 1790

184. *To Johann Georg Zimmermann*

Three years into Catherine's war against the Ottomans, Prussia and Great Britain were nonetheless determined to force Catherine to back down without any territorial gains, and they threatened to attack Russia militarily if she did not. When she received a letter from Zimmermann petitioning for his friend August von Kotzebue to obtain an extended leave from Russian service, Catherine instead used her reply to send an indirect message to her opponents in Prussia. Posting the letter to Hanover through the Berlin mail, she hoped that the Prussian government would intercept it and learn that their opposition to her aims in the south was in vain.

Mr Zimmermann, I have just received your letter of 8 January NS and was pleased to see the sentiments for me that you profess in it. If, as you say, the events that have come one after another throughout the eighteenth century have been glorious for Russia, and if the envious have often been struck with astonishment, then one need seek no further cause than the very intrigues and machinations of the enemies of this empire. In wishing to cause it great harm, they have placed it under the necessity of developing means that no one suspected, since those most concerned nonetheless know little about Russia and even less about its resources. The wars that have been stirred up against us have done nothing other than harden our troops. They have pushed us so far forward that, after the Seven Years War, I had the honour of returning to the late King of Prussia his kingdom and part of Pomerania. And, after the first war with the Porte, I had that of returning to the Sublime Porte three provinces twice as large as the Kingdom of Prussia and incomparably better in soil and location, without counting Tauris and the islands of the Archipelago. Despite this, then as now, we were said to be without money, without troops, and without resources. Newspapermen were paid, then as today, to spout senseless projects that Russia is presumed to have and that, they say, would overturn all governments by intrigues, by money, or by force. Here they contradict themselves, for someone who has neither money nor force can neither give nor use them. Intrigues are the means of the weak, calumny that of the evil, and neither the one nor the other befits a great empire. Both are contrary to the candour, probity, and elevation of soul that one likes to see in those who are in a position to direct human destinies. And yet that is what people are brazen enough to do against us. God knows that I am not the one plotting intrigues, and my aims are neither base nor evil. But, accordingly, it is certain that no human power will make me do what is not in the interests of my empire nor in keeping with the dignity of the crown that I wear. Besides, it shall be as God wills. Some people's animosity against Russia goes so far that it even falls upon individuals. To hear them talk and write, one would think that we lack men for every purpose, including war. Yet it seems that our generals should have some right to their esteem, since they have served in so many wars, won so many battles, taken so many cities, beaten so many various troops from Europe and from Asia, conquered so very many provinces that just one of our soldiers has done and seen more than many entire generations before him. It should be granted at least that they have some experience, along with the sagacity necessary to overcome their enemies. Perhaps we are also believed to be without money because, when we take money from our coffers, we do it without any of those formalities that lend it weight. People say that the money boxes in the cellars under my apartments are empty, but, then again, the money boxes are not exactly kept in the cellars beneath my apartments, and so it is true, I believe, that those cellars are empty. People are right about that, but up to now, thank God, we have given money when it was needed. We have not imposed any taxes; our troops are always poised for war and know no other way to be. Besides, I am very peace-loving and wish to be at peace with all my neighbours. I have no intention of starting up with any of them, but if, however, I am attacked, I believe I have proven that I know how to defend myself. I think that one cannot have an easier time than with the ungrateful: a just cause is the first step on the way to glory. Do what one will, nothing in the world can mask unjust actions, much less presumption, even in eyes of contemporaries, much less of posterity. If I am attacked, if I fight alone or with my allies, you can be sure that I shall count solely on the support of Heaven's blessings, my just cause, and the zeal of my subjects, whose cause I uphold and who certainly will not yield to any orders except my own, which is founded on the interests and dignity of my empire. At any rate, it is to be hoped that, as you say, calm will follow all the insidious manoeuvrings of politics and the noises of combat. No one needs it more than the poor Turks, who are in dire straits and are being lured on by false promises for as long as possible. They will be caught and sunk for sure if the war lasts: people can be wilfully blind to their situation as much as they like, for he who does not find help within himself cannot find help in another. They can spend all imaginable wealth, but one cannot resuscitate a dead man. But that is enough of these fine things. I thank you for your New Year's wishes: I hope yours is as happy. The friend for whom you are concerned will have an extension of his leave of absence.* Farewell, be well.

this 26 January 1791

185. *To Friedrich Melchior Grimm*

In this extract of a letter written from 29 April until 19 May 1791, Catherine takes aim at the political chaos in Europe, drawing connections between British and Prussian animosity towards Russia and the Revolutionary upheavals in France.

at Tsarskoe Selo, this 2 May

Yesterday I came here at breakneck speed without a word of warning to anyone, and as I have nothing to do while awaiting the arrival of the heavy* baggage, I am resuming my epistle to the people of Grimma.* I do not like the honours that were paid to Mirabeau, and I do not understand the reason for them, unless it was to encourage villainy and all vices. Mirabeau deserves the respect of Sodom and Gomorrah. I have started to read the coalition's little brochure. When you send me the scene between Brother George and the Prussian minister, I shall send you its counterpart, which has Brother Gustav's employee with a certain someone he had to deal with* and which is a masterpiece of the genre. I have no doubt that your democrats are on the payroll of the Absolute and the Limited.* It is to be hoped that epilepsy will rid us one day of the *grandissimo* politician Hertzberg, before he has time to do all the evil that he is meditating.

I would like you never to be ill, and I thank you most sincerely for the plan that you propose to me: it has already been partly executed.* As for Mr Gustav Falstaff, who can answer for him? Nonetheless I think that he is no longer flexing muscle to get money, for he must expect to be abandoned. And if the English do not stick their noses into the Baltic, I think the other will not be tempted to start up again, but he is a villain on whom one can never count. It seems at the moment that the English are changing governments and perhaps changing policies, given the English nation's extreme aversion: they are writing on all the houses, 'No war with Russia'. But whether they come or not, we shall sing with you: 'Jean left as he came, eating his capital along with his income'.* But I beg you to lose no sleep over it, since there is no need.

I wish with all my heart that the plans to travel to the waters of Bourbonne and Frankfurt bring you relief. Mr Mashkov brought me Madame de Bueil's compliments.* I am delighted that she has not changed her name, and I beg you to give her my greeting. I hope that Katinka and Cateau have recovered from their inoculation. Inoculation does terrible things to those who would have died of non-inoculated smallpox. My third granddaughter* is unrecognizable: she was lovely as an angel before her inoculation, but at present all her features are swollen and she is anything but pretty at the moment. You will do what is appropriate for Katinka and Cateau—everything that you consider useful for them. Believe me, beauty is nowhere superfluous, and I've always had a *grandissimo* opinion of it. I have never been very beautiful, *ma** all beauty has a great claim to my appreciation. Godfather Alexander is taller than I am by the breadth of my hand, and he grows visibly every day. You could answer Katinka's question, 'What is an empress?', by saying that you will tell her when she is bigger, for at present she will not understand a thing. And if she insists, relate at great length what an empress is, and then she will see for herself that she does not under-stand a thing. That is what I have done with my little coxcombs, and it has always worked for me.

I shall not join in the quarrel over Taurician or Taurian, and if you wish to take it up with the Marshal Prince Potemkin—that is up to you.* For myself, as soon as any academic subject arises, I bundle myself in my ignoramus's mantle and am silent. I find it most convenient for us ignoramuses. There is only one thing being said about the present Duc de Richelieu: may he one day play in France the role of the cardinal of the same name, but without his faults. I like people of merit, and on that account I wish him well in every way, though I do not know him. I wrote him a fine chivalric letter when sending him the cross of St George. And, in spite of the National Assembly, I want him to remain the Duc de Richelieu and to help re-establish the monarchy. Do you hear, Whipping-Boy? Such is my will.* But there is a man whose escapades I cannot forgive: it is Ségur. Fie, he is as false as Judas, and I am not surprised at all that no one in France likes him. One must have a point of view in this world, and he who does not is to be disdained. What role will he play before the pope? The one he is playing before me. When he departed from here, we rubbed his nose in all the axioms of old French chivalry after making him concede that he was in despair over what was happening. And what did he do when he got to Paris?

186. *To Gabriel Sénac de Meilhan*

Catherine invited Sénac de Meilhan to Russia in hopes of guiding his plan to compose an appropriately positive French-language history of Russia, and perhaps also planning to use him as an agent against Revolutionary France. But he proved a severe disappointment.

[May 1791]
Wednesday morning

I am returning to you, Sir, the sheet of paper and a copy of the 'Comparison of the Church of St Peter, etc.', which you were so kind as to leave with me yesterday. Here is, more or less, my portrait. I have never thought that I had a creative mind. I have met a lot of people who, as I saw without envy or jealousy, were far more intelligent than I. It has always been very easy to guide me because to do so one needed only to present me always with ideas infinitely better and more solid than mine. Then I would be as docile as a lamb. The reason for this lay in the extreme desire that I have always had for the empire's good to be achieved. I have been fortunate enough to come across good and true principles, which have brought me great successes. I have had some misfortunes that resulted from errors that I had no part in and which perhaps occurred because my orders were not meticulously carried out. Despite my natural flexibility, I could be stubborn or firm (however one wishes to put it) when it seemed to me that it was necessary. I have never got in the way of anyone's views, but on occasion I have had views of my own. I do not like to argue because, in my experience, everyone always sticks to their own opinion anyway. Besides, I cannot raise my voice. I have never held a grudge because the place that Providence has assigned me makes it senseless for me to bear resentment against a private individual; I do not find the stakes equal, all things judiciously considered. In general, I like justice, but I am of the opinion that strict justice is not justice and that human weakness can endure only equity.* But in all cases I have preferred humaneness and indulgence for human nature over the rules of severity, which has often seemed to me to be misguided; in this I have been guided by my own heart, which I think to be gentle and good. Whenever old men preached severity to me, I confessed my weakness and burst into tears, and I have seen some of them come round to my opinion with tears in their eyes too. My nature is cheerful and frank, but I have lived through too much in this world to be ignorant of the fact that there are some churlish minds who do not like cheerfulness and that all minds cannot contain truth and frankness. Farewell for today.

187. *To Gabriel Sénac de Meilhan*

Catherine offers another self-portrait in response to flattering verses from Sénac de Meilhan. She recalls the Prince de Ligne and the Comte de Ségur's failed efforts to teach her to write poetry on the journey to Crimea; the only results were a French couplet and a short Russian poem that she sent to Potemkin.

Monsieur de Meilhan, you will say that an empress is a very poor cor-respondent, and you will speak the truth; nonetheless, it was not for lack of will to respond. Your first letter from Thursday is charming: that is what I wanted to tell you the very next day, but so many things prevented me from doing so that I would bore you if I even enumerated them. I did not know that you had the agreeable talent of writing such pretty impromptu verses as those that you included in your letter. If I had benefited from the lessons of the Prince de Ligne and of the for-mer Comte de Ségur, who were at great pains to teach me to write them, I would have answered you with a few stanzas. But one cannot be inocu-lated with talent as one is for smallpox. My ear seems to be impervious to harmony—I have had no more success with music than with poetry. I would want to be criticized all the time if all criticism were as pleasant and as favourable to me as that you give of my letter. Yet I must con-fess that criticisms from my greatest enemies, and even the harm that they have sought to do me, have often worked to my benefit. May this not seem a paradox to you—it is not. I have tried to fix what was criti-cized, when I thought it necessary, and I have disarmed my enemies by pitting truth and reason against passion and intrigues. You will accuse me of speaking often of myself, but you must blame yourself for eliciting it by arousing my pride. One day next week I shall entreat you to come and see me, and then you can tell me what you think you forgot. Besides, you are perfectly free to accept—or not to accept—titles and posts as suits you, and please be so good as to be persuaded that I am capable of appreciating your merit and your mind. I hope that by our third conversation you will be quite at ease with me. I thank you for the corrected comparison with St Peter's of Rome that you sent me. My printer will reprint the 'Principles and Causes', etc. etc., which you tell me in your second letter that you have sent him. Farewell, Sir, be well.

this 16 May, Friday

188. *To Friedrich Melchior Grimm*

In this opening section of a letter written between the beginning of June 1791 and the 7th, Catherine reveals her advance knowledge of the royal family's attempt to escape France on 20–1 June (NS). Catherine ironically borrows the utopian language of the French Revolutionaries in designating Paris as the 'abode of all imaginable human perfection and happiness'. She contrasts its chaos with the luxury and order of her own court, which she antiphrastically calls her 'hovel'.

at Tsarskoe Selo, this 1 June of the year of our Lord 1791

Mr Whipping-Boy, I think that it has been said on high that you and I were both created precisely to have pen in hand continuously so that we could write to one another endlessly and unceasingly. No sooner had an enormous document set out for the abode of all imaginable human perfection and happiness, when a most ample one reaches my hovel—from which the exalted allies* have not yet dragged me against my will, as you can quite well see by the dateline above. I do not know whether the present document will find you at the waters of Bourbonne or at Frankfurt, but wherever you have gone, I pray to the Almighty that He bless your steps. You would do very well to take with you, if it can be done, the King of the French, or even, if possible, to put him in your pocket as you leave Sodom and Gomorrah, so that he might reach at least the borders of his kingdom safe and sound. There you would hand him over to Monsieur de Bouillé himself or to another well-intentioned individual, so that he might preserve His Most Christian Majesty from all the misfortunes that seem to threaten him. And while we have not trembled even for a moment for ourselves, every day of our life over three years we have trembled for our great friend Louis XVI, for the queen his wife, and for his dear children, whom we would like to know were out of Paris. But pray tell, Whipping-Boy, how did it happen that they are left there abandoned and threatened with all possible misfortunes? We do not approve of this at all here, and I cannot bear it. They must get out of there, for it is not to be endured, and Charles I himself in England had not, I reckon, so much ignominy to withstand.*

You perhaps do not suspect that my response begins here to your letter begun on 19 (30) April, which you sent to Bacchus and which the latter received and brought to me the same day. For myself, I thought that I would find in this letter the secrets of at least ten or twelve states, and God knows what a racket was going on in my head already when I learned that Bacchus would come himself to bring a letter received by an express messenger. The Factotum had already assumed his air of most exalted mystery upon seeing the mysterious messenger who had gone himself to bring Bacchus the packet containing this famous secret. I thought that I would find at least a formal invitation from the husband or the wife to commit myself to working for their release and whatever else was swinging about on the Swedenborgish rainbow of ideas.* Here comes Bacchus riding in with very tired horses on a hot day. The Factotum, all sweaty, runs to meet him, and with a most preoccupied air and manner he sneakily shoves two very voluminous packets into my hand. Two is a lot and very heavy: one falls on the ground, the other I hold firmly. Now they have quickly been read, but they are very long and rambling. Here comes the whole baggage of children, all six* at once, to thwart me. All were sent off to eat: in the meantime, it has already got late, and finally one reads. Wherein, wherein lies the secret?*

189. *To Johann Georg Zimmermann*

Zimmermann was officially physician to George III in Hanover, a territory subject to the English ruler. Catherine once again addresses a message of defiance indirectly to an enemy government through him. But already at the end of March, Prime Minister William Pitt the Younger had backed down from his threat to send an English fleet into the Baltic to force Catherine to relinquish Ochakov. Nonetheless, her rhetoric holds a warning against any such endeavours in the future.

I am very glad, Sir, that so far our commerce of letters has not yet been disrupted, and, since the English fleet has not yet passed the Øresund, I can answer your letter of 24 May. I know the history of England well enough to know that the Parliament of Great Britain, or rather the majority, is always in the hands of the government and that, as long as it has the latter, there is no argument that can oppose its views. I am not unaware either that every government that wishes to retain its position would be very wise to adapt its projects to the general wishes of the nation, for if it acts otherwise it runs the risk of losing its majority and its position too. Besides, all my life I have set great store by the esteem of the English nation. Therefore, I thought I could flatter myself that I had the friendship of the court: I was thus predisposed until I was undeceived by Mr Ainslie's conduct and the excessive partiality for the Turks and against Russia that all the political employees of the English government have shown at the various courts. This prepossession is very strong, as it is on the verge of rendering null all the old principles that I have never seen anyone doubt, as though there existed between Russia and Great Britain immutable relations of interest between countries. A failure to recognize their relations can come only from personal hatred which is, I shall make bold to say, aimless and quite unchristian: that is called allowing oneself to be dragged along by other people's passions. Now, these so very passionate people are at present groaning under the weight of their own intrigues, and they would be very glad to get out from under them as soon as possible. But what an account they will have to render before God and posterity if owing to their inhuman caprices they spill yet more torrents of innocent blood. For whom? For the Turks' beautiful eyes? For the desert of Ochakov? For that ridiculous balance of power which a desert will supposedly tip? They would do much better to help the princes of Germany keep what was guaranteed to them by the Peace of Westphalia and, to that end, to come to an agreement with those who might have a say in the matter. This would be the duty of every prince who is part of the Constitution of Germany. This would be a just and honourable cause. The God of War is not in my heart: I have never attacked anyone, but I know how to defend myself. You alone think me so brave. As for my colleagues, they cannot have such a good opinion of me, since they always want to scare me. It shows a lack of judgment, if I dare say so, for how can I be afraid at the head of a nation who has defeated all its enemies for the past hundred years? I confront all these incivilities with justice and moderation, and, besides,

I fear God, dear Abner, and have no other fear.*

Come what may, I cannot act otherwise. In my opinion, justice, truth, and reason are an invulnerable shield. Farewell, be well.

at Tsarskoe Selo, this 6 June 1791

190. *To Gabriel Sénac de Meilhan*

In his planned dedicatory epistle for his history, Sénac de Meilhan insisted that Russia remained entirely unknown in France and that dispersed facts about the nation needed to be compiled and embellished. Catherine asserts, on the contrary, that the problem is misinformation rather than a dearth of information. In a last-ditch attempt at guiding Meilhan in the right direction, Catherine further expands on her philosophy of history and her view of the Russian national character.

It was not very difficult for me, Sir, to write down in four days, at your request, things that I know almost by heart and that I have been thinking about for a long time. But I admire your patience in reading six times the jumble I sent you, without being frightened by the pedantry that perhaps dominates it and that always comes with a naturally methodical mind. I have often faced reproaches for this, and, since I have never been good at knowing how to be witty, I have often limited myself to looking for why things are the way they are. And my zeal for the glory and the prosperity of the nation with which Providence deigned to entrust me has led me to discover different causes and intentions from those found by the other writers I have read. Moreover, my station requires of me extensive knowledge (at least that which thirty years on the throne has procured me) of the character of a nation whose territory extends across a third or a quarter of the known globe.

This nation did not obey petty magistrates, but rather followed leaders or princes whose display of ambition and personal qualities inspired them with the confidence they needed to succeed in their undertakings. This nation neither loved nor esteemed weak princes. Indeed, it scarcely tolerated them without impatience and without letting them know that they were unfit to rule. In fact, this nation embraced danger intrepidly as soon as it sensed the value. I am telling you all this in order that you appreciate more and more my manner of thinking and the spirit in which I would like history to be written. This is, in my opinion, how history becomes useful to posterity, and, if I daresay, this is how the ancients wrote it. I approve what you tell me of your intention to write an introduction, and everything that you propose to include seems to me highly appropriate. I confess again my decided taste for everything earlier than the reigns of the house of Peter I. Yet for each period one must never ignore the spirit of the age in which a reign happened, for the spirit of the age will explain many unexpected things. It has always been said that to judge a man well one must put oneself in his place. Now, the historian who, in writing history, fails to retrace the spirit of the age does so to the detriment of his history. Just as all men are men in this world, every age has its spirit and its direction. Could one not also say that in numerous instances the previous reigns paved the way for the next ones? If my expressions are not entirely French, you will forgive me once you understand me—and besides, my letters are not written for publication, and everyone explains himself more or less as he can. Moreover, I would like it if history never favoured a single reign. I know very well why one or another reign pleased foreign nations more or less, and why the natives had a different preference. Did not President Hénault fall into that trap when he sacrificed 1,200 years to the reign of Louis XIV? You know that no one utters the name of that truly great king with more respect than I. France became so illustrious under his reign that her splendour survives to the present day; only in the past two or three years has public opinion begun to forget that impression, which had lasted a hundred years. As regards my reign, since you oblige me to speak of it, I persist in what I told you, namely, that I do not like monuments to, or histories of, living sovereigns. Contemporaries are always more or less partial, either for or against. As each year of a thirty-year reign is truly the equivalent of an entire epoch, it is impossible not to please or displease this or that contemporary. Any successes I have had clashed with or compromised the glory, or vainglory, of individuals. What is certain is that I have never undertaken anything without being deeply persuaded that my action was in keeping with the good of my empire. What this empire has done for me is infinite:—I believed that all my individual faculties, when used constantly for the good of this empire, for its prosperity, and for its best interest, could scarcely suffice to pay back my debt. I have sought to procure the good of each individual wherever it did not contravene the public good. I think that every sovereign thinks thus and wishes to act in accordance with justice and reason. The question is rather who of us has misunderstood the definition of justice and reason. This is a matter which only posterity can judge, and that not before we are dead—every last one of us. It is to posterity that I appeal: I can tell it boldly what I found and what I shall leave. An account of my reign could be curious, but peace must be made, and then we shall see. It will be said that I have experienced much good

fortune and a few great misfortunes. But when it comes to good fortune
and misfortune I have, as for many other things, a category of my very
own. Each is nothing but a conflict between a number of accurate or false
measures. Good or evil heard, seen, or committed count for much in my
calculations. It follows that a history of a living person might offend
the proud and perhaps would comparatively demean others—something to which I would not like to contribute. Now, I sense that you
will accuse me of conceit, and undoubtedly I have my fair share. Who
does not? If you should outlive me, you may write what you like, but in
my lifetime write it if you want, but do not publish. Then I shall be able
to provide you with my account, and perhaps I shall compose it myself.

I have told you, and I repeat, Sir, you are very much entitled to write
wherever you wish, and I am very touched by what you tell me on this
topic. I have ordered a digest to be made of the catalogues of materials
that might be of use to you. If your elder son applies himself to learning
Russian, he may be of great help to you in this work. I have spoken with
the vice-chancellor [Ivan Osterman] and with Count Bezborodko about
his entry into government service, and they will not fail to speak with
you of it, and equally of his maintenance and of the residence you would
like him to inhabit. That which I wrote on the margins of your dedicatory
epistle, namely that too much has been printed about Russia, I gleaned
from various review journals printed in Germany. These journals complain that they have more than they need about Russia, but in France
a new pamphlet is preferred to such books. I think that the writings of
various professors of the Academy who have travelled around Russia
have been translated into French, but, since your countrymen do not
keep abreast of what is happening even in England, it is hardly surprising that they know no more of Russia. Doubtless it will be found to
have a foreign air, and with the most beautiful style in the world you
will have trouble inducing them to forgive that air. But are not the
French themselves beginning to have a foreign or strange air in their
own country? When your sentimental journey is finished, I hope that
you will kindly let me read it.* You want me to give you the solution to
a problem that has been occupying you for a long time, you say, and this
problem is: how could it possibly be that Charles IX, King of France,
wrote more elegantly than his poet Ronsard? Well, I shall tell you: it is
because it is the court that purifies a language, not authors. Even in
Constantinople, the language of the seraglio (which is nonetheless not
the most enlightened court in the world) offers the most elegant Turkish,
the best blend of Arabic and Persian, the most sophisticated language,
the most polite, the most flowery, the most ceremonious. But if there

were a court that started to flaunt the language of the marketplace by imitating its turns of phrase and its manners, then the nation's language would be lost, retrievable only in the good authors. I said nothing about the inscription from Tacitus, nor about the one you composed, because you ought to appreciate their suitability better than I. It is not for me to judge the individual, especially as I have no Latin, despite my good universal knowledge of languages,* of which I am very afraid I have caught only a few insights. Farewell, Sir, forgive the length.

this Monday, 16 June 1791

191. *To Prince Charles-Joseph de Ligne*

Catherine makes an impassioned plea against French Revolutionary ideology, attacking the dismantling of traditional notions of honour and mocking the Revolutionaries' belief that they were 'regenerating' the French nation to create citizens imbued with new civic virtues.

Prince de Ligne, Sir, if your last undated letter by its sheer size at first glance looked almost like a kite, then its contents in twenty separate paragraphs certainly gave it the appearance of a definitive treaty. You must forgive me for making such a mistake at a time when my mind is preoccupied with such things, having heard talk of nothing else these past ten to twelve months—not that the task has advanced by a jot the size of your thumb. But let us pass over to the contents of your enormous letter. The first point concerns gratitude. You aver that it is more than an impression: it is an engraving. You have found my weak spot there. I have always felt a distinct predilection for beautiful minds. Those with excellent memories who retain by heart that which has never been copied out but merely read aloud—why, I think you will punish them by not furnishing them any more material on which to exercise their talent!* My prophecies resemble those of the Sibyls,* whose own age I am now approaching; experience of the past afforded to those ladies some rights to divine the future. The beauty of the miniature portrait of Asia and Europe, which gave you such a great deal of pleasure, has not enjoyed universal acclaim. This is just how things are. Everyone has their taste, and the proverb says that on matters of taste and colour, one must not argue. This is why I have no wish to take it up with any living soul; for, if I thought I was right, I would not change my opinion either. Those who read between the lines in this portrait have perhaps given the words more meaning than they contained. Anybody who sought a morsel of encouragement believed they had found it, etc. etc. Oh, good Lord, what are you saying? How could one not adore a nation that says: 'Do not give anything up. We shall give you everything you need: take it.'* Ah, this is so lovely! If they add, 'We, too, do not want to give up anything', well, so be it. If we are not taking anything away, then what harm is there if these worthy men have spoken a few useless words in vain? I shall always love them better than your Belgians, forgive me! ... That superb light cavalry and a certain infantry that marches ahead joyously and grumbles impatiently about any move that does not abbreviate the path to victory—well, it is those people indeed who, working together, are able to lead matters to a positive outcome faster and with greater certainty than those bizarre pens inked with venom, who contrive to invest in each phrase all their ingenuity in order to foster troubles of which nobody has any need.

I do not share your view that nations deteriorate: my reason is that people are always people. What is absolutely clear, however, is this: if lawyers, judges, people who are inexperienced and rash, and people who are villains electrify a nation, in order to regenerate it, then they ruin it at the same time. Indeed, from all this and from other recent evidence that I have seen, I would say that the result is that, in order to behave well in this world, one must begin by having a good heart and a judicious mind. Without these, one accomplishes nothing of value, and one dances, as the song goes, clumsily, getting off on the wrong foot. Of the magic lanterns in Warsaw, I shall say nothing. They are clamouring for the Jesuits, of whom you seem to think highly. On that matter, I often said to my great and very dear friend, the Count of Falkenstein [Joseph II] (whom I shall forever miss), that I was preserving the species intact so that, when they were needed, I would have the satisfaction of offering them to Roman Catholic countries for free. Note that the King of Prussia had offered them, for his part, at a price of one ducat apiece. You must think that I take more pleasure in seeing people fight than Mr Freeport does, since you are advising everyone to attack, whereas he just thought it wrong to separate those who are hankering to come to blows.* Thank God your advice has not been followed, at least up to now. If everything of which you spoke were to happen to me, I believe that game of carom-billiards would deprive me of the time and wish to play billiards in the Hermitage. We danced gaily in that spot this winter, as your cousin, Count Starhemberg, will have told you.* In addition, there were theatricals before and after supper, and suppers after which we raced to a masked ball under the pretext of amusing the Alexanders and Constantines.* Everyone was enchanted to be there, myself most of all, and all were vying to have the best costume. Ah well, after all that, go on and try to tell me that the Grand Equerry is wrong when he argues in his way, and with his physic-comic nonsense, that gaiety is very good for imbuing what you call spirit, whereas seriousness, sadness, and especially monotony freeze one to the marrow of one's bones. Do you not find it odd that it is I who tell you this about monotony! But I have something else entirely in my head: I think that the Academies should establish a prize, first of all for the question: *What becomes of honour and valour*—synonyms that are precious, I repeat, to heroic ears—*in the mind of an active citizen* under a government that is suspicious and jealous to the point of prohibiting every distinction? This is despite the fact that nature itself has granted to intelligent people superiority over the stupid, and when courage comes from a sense of physical or mental power. The second prize will be given for the question: *Is there a need for honour and valour?* If there is a need, then this is why emulation should not be prohibited or impeded by its intolerable enemy, equality. I seem already to hear the voice of your son,* crying out, 'No, no, there is no such thing, equality will not come about! It does not exist in nature. I have proven that and shall prove it again at every opportunity I can. The two crosses I wear on my chest, and the wound I sustained, attest to it. My father himself took pleasure in arranging those marks of distinction in the picturesque way that another prince wore them. Joseph II predicted that he would have yet more.* The same thing will happen to me, be certain of that.' Rats have devoured all the titles of Alexander and Caesar, but not their deeds. Every one of us knows those by heart. What the rapacity of the cats of our own day has produced I find it hard to say ... at least not even a mouse has been captured. I have not read more than seventeen pages of the *Works* of the late King of Prussia. Those done, I cannot say why exactly I closed the book and have never opened it again.

We saw the Comte de Ségur arrive, conjuring up the spirit of the court of Louis XIV, in rejuvenated form.* You then found him to be truly enjoyable company during the trip to Tauris. At the moment, Louis Ségur is suffering from a bad case of the national consumption. I do not know whether the air of the Pontine marshes* suits him. The old French knights were well loved, but one really does not know what to make of an active, equal citizen with flat hair, a black tailcoat, a waistcoat, and a riding crop in his hand. Whether the declared enemies of all kings will spark the indignation of all the latter to go against them: that is another question that might generate more than one dissertation.

As for my 50,000 lancers, they are too busy at the moment to go that far. For that reason, as you see, I have not stolen a march on anyone. There was a moment when I rejoiced to see the royal family out of Paris. Their safety, we were told, was owed to 8,000 French gentlemen. This joy proved short-lived, and, since their entourage put up no resistance against the Municipality of Sainte-Menehould,* it is to be supposed that they existed only on paper. If all the knights of France do not mount their steeds at this very moment, I despair of ever seeing them do so. I am very flattered by the trust you show me. You will always find in me the very same good nature that, it seems to me, you admire. I am confident that my grandsons, who at this very moment are jumping about me, will have their fair share of it, too. Alexander is four digits taller than myself, his brother comes up to his shoulder. If you saw them now, I think you would be pleased with them. Farewell, my Prince, rest assured of the continued sincerity of my feelings towards you.

at Peterhof, this 30 June 1791

192. *To Semën Vorontsov*

The Anglo-Prussian alliance spearheaded by Pitt had been a deep concern for Catherine, but the efforts of her ambassador in London, Semën Vorontsov, and of the Whig opposition, led by Charles James Fox, turned public feeling against Pitt. Catherine relishes the evident symbolism of placing the bust of Pitt's rival Charles James Fox among the great statesmen and orators of the past, the Greek Demosthenes (384–322 BC) and the Roman Cicero (106–43 BC). The concluding Anglophile statements were clearly intended for communication back to the Whigs.

Count Vorontsov, Sir, I am writing these lines to ask you to thank on my behalf my Lord Fitzwilliam for having graciously agreed to surrender to me the bust of his friend, Mr Fox, which I shall place in my colonnade in Tsarskoe Selo between Demosthenes and Cicero. This is a real gift for me at this particular moment. Mr Adair has been able to see the pedestal prepared for the bust. I have been aware for a considerable time that my Lord Fitzwilliam, the inheritor of the effects of the Marquess of Buckingham, professes sentiments equal to those Buckingham always espoused in his lifetime for me and my empire. These are the very ones that in the past I found among all old-style Englishmen, and they have inspired in me the esteem and the partiality that I have genuinely enjoyed feeling for that nation and for which others have often reproached me. The talents of my Lord Fitzwilliam, for which I bear esteem, lead me to hope that he and his friends will succeed in their effort to bring about the rebirth of this England of olden days which enabled friendship, of a stable and pragmatic kind, as well as good harmony, between my empire and Great Britain to be regarded as essential. Farewell, stay well and continue to serve me just as you have up until the present.

Catherine
at St Petersburg, this 20 August 1791

193. *To Johann Georg Zimmermann*

In her final letter to Zimmermann, Catherine discusses her attempts to convince Frederick William II of Prussia to arm against Revolutionary France. Recalling the king's intervention to reinstate his sister Wilhelmina and her husband, William V of Orange, in Holland in 1787, Catherine here suggests that he do the same for Louis XVI and Marie Antoinette. Although she had come to mistrust Zimmermann's interest in conspiracy theories surrounding the French Revolution, Catherine, too, had been trying to make sense of events, reading and largely concurring with Edmund Burke's 'Reflections on the Revolution in France' (1790).

Mr Zimmermann, I see from your letter of 2 September that you are as delighted as we are at the preliminaries of peace that have been concluded between Prince Repnin and the grand vizier. I am most delighted too. I thank you for your compliments on the subject. Truly, I had no idea that I would be said to be in my death throes in the month of July, when I was going for walks every morning and evening in the gardens of Tsarskoe Selo, ordinarily joined by a fairly numerous company. Therefore, I presume that this bit of news does not come from Petersburg, but rather that it is forged I know not where in Germany. But then, if it is envy that is forging this news, I am perfectly ignorant of where it makes its abode. I have always held dear the esteem of the English nation, and my prediction for it, I admit, was not in vain. I am quite perfectly in agreement with Edmund Burke's opinion, especially with all that he says about the anarchy in France. There is immortal glory to be acquired in destroying it, and in truth I doubt not that this glory is reserved for the King of Prussia: if he wishes, he can and will do it. And in doing so he will render a very great service to humanity, who will be obliged to him for restoring the obedience and the happiness of all peoples. Besides, of all types of resistance, anarchy is incontestably the smallest. But then, I am of the opinion that with 12,000 or 15,000 men in action, indeed he could not fail to re-establish monarchical government in France as soon as he would like. And he will carry with him the emperor and quite a few other powers and will make them do whatever he likes. But farewell, I am making projects for others, whereas I should mind my own affairs. But it is a vast topic, and it is difficult not to concern oneself with it. The affairs of the King of France are those of all sovereigns, and his offended dignity requires stunning reparation. The King of Prussia obtained the like for his sister, so why should he not obtain it for the descendants of Henry IV and Louis XIV? But enough of these fine things—I must go and dress.

this 16 September 1791

194. *To Grigory Potemkin*

The preliminary peace with the Turks, signed by Prince Repnin on 31 July 1791, paled in importance before a greater worry for Catherine: Potemkin's failing health. Before he could complete the negotiations for a final treaty, he died near Iassy on 5 October.

Dear friend of my heart, Prince Grigory Alexandrovich, I have received your letters from 29 August and 6 September. The first gave me much joy, since I learned that you were better, but the second once again increased my disquiet when I learned that for four days you had had a constant fever and a headache. I pray that God will give you added strength. I do not doubt that as far as work goes, everything will go according to plan. But I know by my own experience what work is like when one is ill.

I am, thank the Lord, well, and the attacks of colic have abated entirely, which I attribute to the girdle and Tokay that you advised me to use. Farewell, my friend, may Christ be with you.

16 September 1791

Platon Alexandrovich thanks you for the greeting and will write to you himself.

195. *To Gustav III of Sweden*

Busy with finishing off her war against the Ottomans, Catherine had no interest in sending her own troops against Revolutionary France, and the other European powers were similarly disinclined to fight. Catherine nonetheless wished to see the monarchical order restored, and she believed that there were two ways to achieve this. The first was an army mustered by the émigré princes of French royal blood like the Comte d'Artois, but, as Catherine mentions, they failed to cooperate with the royal family still in France; Catherine hints that Gustav's old ties to a country that once subsidized him could be influential in this domain. The second option was a coalition of Prussian and Austrian troops, and on 28 and 29 September Catherine also wrote to Frederick William II and Leopold II, respectively, exhorting them to take action.

I am charmed, dearest Brother, to see from the tone that you have assumed in your letter of 13 September that you have entirely returned to the old sentiments that you once professed for me and which Y. M. will always find me ready to reciprocate with most perfect cordiality.

By now you know my inclinations regarding the ties of a political alliance by which I am ready to strengthen those of blood which unite us. Given that these inclinations are rooted in the principles of equality and complete reciprocity, there is no reason to fear that they might fail to lead us to the goal we are setting ourselves. With this assurance, I have not hesitated to share with you my most secret sentiments regarding the affairs of France.

The letter from the King of England, which Your Majesty has communicated to me, is but a copy of the one which that prince wrote to the emperor. It is vague, and the least that one can conclude from it is that one cannot rely on the support of His British Majesty. But what is most vexing in this matter, other than the lack of warmth that the other sovereigns have shown, is the sight of the dissension that seems to reign between the Queen of France and the princes who have taken refuge in Germany. After both being stripped of all authority and all prerogatives, they seem to display the same resentment and the same jealousy of the enjoyment of that authority and those prerogatives, as though they had repossessed them. It hardly occurs to them that they will not manage to restore even a shred, unless they are closely united and operate impeccably and with sincerity.

You might, dearest Brother, have even broader notions on this sad subject than I have, and it may also be that you do not lack the means to preach in the appropriate places the peace and harmony essential to the common good of all. Be that as it may, my intentions and my resolutions are the same, and I am greatly counting on the constancy of yours and on the steps and pleas that I am renewing in the courts of Vienna and Berlin, in order to incite them to act in a way that favours our wishes.

In the course of the winter we shall learn what to expect, and I have not at all lost hope that our benevolent, noble, grand, and equally generous intentions will prevail in the end.

It will be yet another title which I shall add to all those that are dictated to me by the tender and sincere friendship with which I am,

My dear Brother,

Your Majesty's good Sister and Cousin, Friend, and Neighbour,

Catherine

at St Petersburg, this 29 September 1791

196. *To Friedrich Melchior Grimm*

In these final sections of a letter begun on 23 September 1791, Catherine reflects on Potemkin's death. She has lost her most trusted advisor at a difficult time: with the final peace treaty with the Ottoman Empire not yet agreed upon, she signed on 7 October a treaty of alliance with Gustav III, whom she did not trust but whom she hoped to push towards action against France. In the meantime, she sought to encourage the French émigré princes to act too, publicly declaring her support for them as the legitimate upholders of the monarchy.

this 13 October, at two thirty in the morning

Yesterday a terrible blow once again descended on my head. Around six in the afternoon a courier brought me the very sad news that my pupil, my friend, and well-nigh my idol, Prince Potemkin of Tauris, has died after about a month's illness in Moldavia. You cannot fathom my affliction: he combined an excellent heart with rare comprehension and a far from ordinary breadth of mind. His aims were always great and magnanimous. He was exceedingly humane, full of knowledge, and singularly amiable, and his ideas were always new. No man has ever had the gift of witticism and repartee as he did. His military qualities during this war must have been striking, for he never once missed the mark on land or at sea. No one in the world was more indomitable, and he, moreover, had a particular gift for employing people. In a word, he was a statesman able to advise and execute. He was passionately and zealously attached to me. He scolded and got angry when he believed one could do better. With age and experience he was ridding himself of his faults. Three months ago, when he was here, I said to General Zubov that I feared this change because he no longer had his known faults. And now, sadly, has my fear not turned into a prophecy? But his rarest quality was the courage of his heart, mind, and soul, which perfectly distinguished him from the rest of humanity: this meant that we understood one another perfectly, and so we allowed those who understood less to babble at their leisure. I regard Prince Potemkin as a very great man, who achieved not half of what was within his reach.

this 22 October

In your letter of 20 (31) August, you begin by speaking of my peace with the Turks, which has not been made. I sent Lord Factotum to Iassy eight days ago to get it finished as soon as possible, and, as of tomorrow, he will have been on his way for eight days now. Prince Potemkin played a cruel trick on me by dying! The whole burden falls on me: I would have liked you to pray for me. After all, things must go on. Imagine: here I have Prince Viazemsky, who has literally been senile for two years; Count [Ivan] Chernyshev in the navy who, after a fit of apoplexy in the spring, has gone travelling again; and they all are alive, and the man who seemed likely to live the longest dies on me! Well, despite the 600,000 roubles spent this summer on fortifications in Finland, I received news two days ago that a treaty of alliance had been concluded between Gustav III and myself: there he is, in accordance with your wishes, entirely out of the clutches of the Gegu.* The new ally has shamelessly asked to come and show himself here, which is something we are seeking to turn down as humanely as possible. How do you want me to entrust him with troops? He does not know how to lead them. You see that that convention signed at Pillnitz has neither substance nor results.* At the princes' request, I wrote to both of them* in an effort to rouse them. I have had no reply, but I hope that the new legislature will make blunder upon blunder until it forces the king to raise an outcry or to flee, and then we shall see. But the key thing is to bring together the queen and the party of the princes; she must regard this party as the most numerous and the most in favour of royal authority, as it really is; and then she must join with me in making her brother act; and when the latter gets moving, Gu. [Frederick William II] will be obliged to do the same.

Monsieur de Saint-Priest was here, and I am very pleased with him: he is a man of merit who speaks plainly. They were wrong not to follow his advice: it was good. As for Madame de Saint-Priest, she stayed with her brother in Stockholm. My God! At present I am certainly Lady Resource: I am again reduced to training people up for myself, and assuredly the two Zubovs show the most promise. But just think! The elder of the two is not yet twenty-four, and the younger barely twenty. But they are men of wit and understanding: the elder is infinitely knowledgeable and everything admirably falls into place in his brain. He really has a good mind.

I am truly glad that you approve of my conduct towards the descendants of St Louis: I swear to you that I take a fervent interest in them. I like that nobility, those true French knights who are gathered around them. They wrote me a beautiful letter, and I am replying to them. Well, let me tell you that I have always had a soft spot for Milady Malmesbury, even though she is the wife of that meddler Harris.* I like very much the recipe you have composed of female perspicacity, male wit, female gentleness, and male steadfastness.* Well, does everyone not have that? It is all over the streets! I read Monsieur Du Repaire and Monsieur de Miandre's depositions.* You are right that they are two interesting characters, and I might be tempted to do something extraordinary for them.

I am vexed that the signature of the preliminaries for peace prevented Admiral Ushakov from going a bit further and pressing hard after his naval victory. I am sending this letter to Count [Nikolai] Rumiantsev. He will know where to find you. (Forgive me, I thought I had taken a full sheet, and I took only half of one, as I just realized when I turned over.) Since Madame de Bueil's husband signed the letter from the nobility residing at Tournay, which I received the day before yesterday, on 21 October, I believe she too must already be out of France. Your saint* will assuredly be wandering this winter. I see that Mr Schomberg is pleased with the portrait: I hope he will be equally so with my letter, which you have perhaps sent him. At the moment, they say that the Parisian populace is for the king, but so as not to change my opinion every fortnight, I remain steadfast in the party that I have taken and made public. I believe that I am helping the king and France in helping, as I have, the expatriates.

I no longer have the time to read Gibbon,* or anything else. I am very glad that the princes gave you a message for the king and queen. I hope you will work to unite their principles—at least, that is what I am trying to do, too. I do not doubt in the least the princes' sentiments towards me. In my view the emperor has given them nothing but vague words, but there is evidently something unspoken in the cards between the emperor and the queen: I think the latter is contemplating a second flight,* and that is why they are trying to lull everyone to sleep at present. The princes must continue cultivating all the courts; complaints are good for nothing. The queen must be informed that the Jacobin Club is bragging of having suborned Spielmann. It would be very hard for me to pilot the princes' boat from so far away. I am writing to them personally by this courier, and I am also informing Count [Nikolai] Rumiantsev of my intentions. I write you in haste because I have hardly a moment to myself. Farewell. Keep well.

this 23 October 1791

They tell me that the queen does not like the *parlements*, and I say that it was the king who re-established them and that he would be in contradiction with himself if he wanted them to be abolished at present.* Those *parlements* uphold the monarchy, and without them France will be a republic, or the king will become a despot.

197. *To Gustav III of Sweden*

To Catherine's great vexation, Louis XVI accepted the French Constitution of 3 September 1791 (NS), thus appearing to approve the new political order. For their own reasons, all the courts of Europe hesitated to intervene. While making conjectures and planning future action, Catherine and Gustav agreed to withdraw their representatives from Paris: Gustav's representative, Baron Erik Magnus de Staël-Holstein (1749–1802; husband of the famous French writer Germaine de Staël), left on 5 February 1792 (NS), and Catherine's envoy, Ivan Matveevich Simolin (1720–1799), departed two days later.

My dear Brother and Cousin, after receiving Your Majesty's letter of 19 October from Count Stackelberg's courier bearing the treaty of alliance concluded between us, I delayed my response only in expectation of the letter that you told me you wanted to send with Major-General Baron von Pahlen. Since he arrived soon afterward and gave me the two other letters of the 28th of the same month, with which Your Majesty entrusted him for me, I am now capable of discussing the contents of your three letters with you.

I shall begin by expressing, dearest Brother, my satisfaction at seeing the alliance between us and our countries strengthening the ties that naturally bind us to one another. This useful and advantageous undertaking promises us a happy future and will endow our union with more sincerity and rectitude than could usually be found in the actions of

Ferdinand and Isabella, whom Your Majesty mentions in your letter. I am very touched by the protestations of trust and friendship that Your Majesty has given me. You can count on the most perfect reciprocity on my part.

I rejoice, dearest Brother, to see that there is great consistency between our principles and considerations regarding France's affairs. I see that Your Majesty thinks as I do about the discord that might arise or that might exist between the Queen of France and the princes, her brothers-in-law, and about the necessity of working to bring them closer together in their principles and aims, from which neither side should stray for their common good.

The letter that Your Majesty wrote on the subject to the Baron de Breteuil, a copy of which you were so good as to communicate to me, proves so well the need for such a rapprochement that I hope it will have a good effect. The reflections you add on the situation and conduct of Louis XVI are filled with so much nobility and dignity that I can only applaud them, since I am convinced, just as Your Majesty is, that the unhappy monarch did all that he did only because he was forced and without a shade of liberty. For, it would not be reasonable to suppose that he would voluntarily have gone from being the hereditary sovereign of his subjects to the rank of first civil servant and that he would have thus consented to degradation like Louis the Pious—and the latter became a monk, too.

But following an event so totally devoid of any plausible motive, would we not be justified to conclude that the King and Queen of France are contemplating a second flight and that their acceptance of the supposed constitution took place only the better to hide that scheme and to beguile the assassins whose dagger is raised over the royal family, now as it was before?

Upon examination, the conduct of the emperor [Leopold II], from whom I have yet to receive a response, seems equally compatible with this conjecture. Since that prince is now perfectly free and unconstrained by the least fear of a foreign war; since he is spurred into action by multiple interests and on multiple sides; and since he has declared that this is his intention and has invited the other powers to join him, could he all of a sudden and without any known grounds lose sight both of his promises, which the Comte d'Artois claims to have obtained from him, and of his own dignity offended in the person of his sister and of his brother-in-law? Could he lose sight of the infractions that have been made against the Treaty of Westphalia and of the complaints and grievances of so many German princes, whose lands have been encroached upon? Moreover, he has such a legitimate claim to act and such effective means in the presence of his 60,000 troops in the Netherlands. How could he not undertake and execute that which so many combined considerations ought to induce him to do? It would seem that under such circumstances, his inaction can be ascribed only to a desire to temporize, and since we do not know his motives, we can be permitted to suppose that, in consultation with his sister and fearing to endanger her life, which she thinks cannot be saved except by a new flight from the captivity in which the king and she have been held for two years, the emperor thinks that he can perhaps support the execution of this plan by assuming a kind of indifference and resignation towards the fate of that unhappy family, and thus better diminish their guardians' vigilance.

Without exaggerating the solidity of these conjectures, I present them to Your Majesty such as they are, just as they came to my mind. I shall not hide from you either that it had seemed to me that until now the King of Spain [Charles IV] was also inclined to temporize and to negotiate, but according to the latest news from Spain, it seems there is cause to be better pleased with the manner in which that king expressed himself on the occasion of the act of acceptance that was presented to him in the name of the king his cousin; Your Majesty will not have failed to be informed of it by your ministers in Paris and Madrid. The King of Spain has professed aloud that he does not believe that the King of France was physically and morally free when he passed the act. And, really, how can it be believed that one can contradict oneself so much in so short a time without being forced?

It is doubtless to be wished that the Baron de Breteuil's reply to Your Majesty should clarify things sufficiently to reveal the true intentions of the King and Queen of France. The queen has recently written to someone whom she seems to trust 'that she demands that she not be judged without being heard, and that she hopes to justify herself'. These words, combined with those in the King of Spain's letter to Your Majesty and joined with the emperor's conduct, open a broad field for the conjectures to which all the various delays give rise. I hope that the winter, which already seems to have set in throughout our lands, will clarify many things for us. In the meantime, I am preaching, and shall continue to preach, to the French émigrés loyalty and perseverance in the cause of their king and his representatives, and I also hope by those means to support Your Majesty's aims and actions.

The purity of your intentions, dearest Brother, the urgency of the circumstances, and your personal acquaintance of so many years with the Baron de Breteuil certainly give you the right to speak to him as you do in the letter with which you honoured him. But I confess that I am counting more on your agent in Brussels [Axel Fersen] than on the said baron in all that regards the rapprochement that I would like to see occur between the Queen of France and the princes, her brothers-in-law. I consider this rapprochement to be useful chiefly to the cause of the king and queen—for, no matter how one looks at the princes' party, it appears very formidable. It brings together the nobility, the clergy, the *parlements*, and the true Roman Catholics of the Kingdom of France, not to mention the respect and esteem that can be acquired by noble, firm, and persevering conduct, as well as the approval of all classes of people, even among the neutral.

Another substantial reason or consideration ought to sway the queen: it is better for her to have that party with her rather than against her. There is no doubt that if the princes had followed the advice that Your Majesty gave them in the memorandum read at Aix-la-Chapelle, and which suited the circumstances at that time, they would have made more progress than they have at present, and this they were completely entitled to make.* That step even seemed so natural to me that, expecting it to be adopted, I hurried to accredit an envoy to them. Yet we must acknowledge their tact, which hindered them from resolving upon it and which motivated them to seek a solution by other means.

I have just received a reply from the King of Prussia, a copy of which Your Majesty will find attached. You will see from the contents that the king refers us to the emperor's decision. I expect to receive a reply from the latter shortly, and I shall not fail to communicate it to Your Majesty.

I would like very much to be in possession of the secret of sharing the life-giving fire that you are so good as to ascribe to me, so that I might light it in favour of the cause that we support, but thus far all my efforts in Vienna and Berlin have been in vain. It seems to me that great ventures are generally like vessels being launched from the shipyard: the barricades have been broken down, but the vessel moves only when its own weight carries it away. But then it would be futile to try and stop it!

From the memorandum brought by Baron von Pahlen, I see that the mood in Normandy seems highly favourable to the good cause. The number of troops fixed on by the authors of the memorandum is 8,000 men, which they think sufficient to shield their homes. But, as the second detailed memorandum on the same subject concedes, such an undertaking is perforce highly precarious unless it is combined with a general plan of attack. But since such a plan cannot yet be devised, it would be very risky to undertake anything on this score until that time—unless we want to assume that resistance in France would be completely non-existent, something that is not strictly true. It is worthy of Your Majesty's wisdom to do as you propose and to send expert engineering officers to reconnoitre the exact lay of the land in order to act with more certainty when circumstances permit. Present circumstances do not seem to me to favour Your Majesty's proposal that you and I make a joint declaration to the other courts of our intention to act without delay to restore France. First of all, it is doubtful that such a step would induce them to follow us and to make up their minds. But, moreover, there could be great disadvantages for me especially, when I have not yet made peace with the Turks and when it is still impossible for me to foresee the circumstances under which I shall do so. And, quite separately, such a declaration on my part might attract the attention of the King of England's government. Master Pitt* could ask for nothing better, perhaps, than to have such a pretext to resume last year's mobilization, if only to make Parliament give him money. Thus, for all sorts of reasons, it would seem prudent not to burst forth until we are completely capable of doing so; moreover, we would put adversaries on their guard before it is time [to act and to undertake].

As for sending my vessels to Karlshamn,* since it is late in the season and the ports are ready to close, there are absolute obstacles to it. But I thank Your Majesty for the offer of allowing them to winter in that port as a mark of trust that you have given me.

Given this state of affairs and the considerations that I have just presented to Your Majesty, only the following means come to my mind to aid in the cause we have embraced until circumstances further evolve:

(1) To use the winter to work towards a common accord to establish and consolidate cooperation and a positive plan, both between us and with the emperor and the Kings of Prussia, Spain, and Sardinia, and to draw from them precise promises to act at the beginning of spring. Supposing, as is more than probable, that the spirit of subversion will persist in France, that the so-called National Assembly will go from one incongruity to the next, that no one in that country will be able to command or to obey, and that actions will necessarily result that will give all sovereigns more and more cause for complaint and that will thoroughly outrage and provoke them, it will then be the instance and the moment in which to undertake and to execute the planned invasion.

(2) To try to discover the true sentiments and dispositions of the King and Queen of France and to get from the said king a declaration or authorization for what we would undertake in his favour, in order to

allay the scruples of the King of Prussia, who does not wish to serve him against his will. It is true that the unlimited powers that the King of France has given to Monsieur could have replaced such a statement in the eyes of His Prussian Majesty,* but, since he thinks it important, it would be good to satisfy him on the matter by trying to get him as authentic a statement as possible, given the King of France's position.

(3) Far from making any public preparations, it would be good to take advantage of the natural obstacles that the present season sets in our way in order to dupe the Assembly made up of coachmen, lawyers, and prosecutors, and to let them believe, if they so wish, that the speed of mobilization has slowed everywhere. This way, they will take fewer precautions themselves, and we can catch them more off their guard, especially by sea, where they have not failed to obtain very considerable forces, with thirty ships of war ready at Brest, which they can arm within six weeks, since they do not lack sailors. It is true that their officers are deserting en masse. But they can get them for money, and perhaps even from the English, who like the new order of things in France so much that they would provide some in a hurry, for fear of seeing it destroyed.

There you have, dearest Brother, the conduct that prudence urges upon us, in my opinion, until we can see more clearly into the dispositions and resolutions of the other powers. From what you have told me, you feel the same. And I must adhere to it all the more strongly, since a thirty-year reign accompanied by a few successes, of which Your Majesty kindly made such honourable mention in your letter, imposes upon me an obligation of maintaining it. Besides, Your Majesty is convinced, I hope, that my circumspection has never degenerated into timidity, and you can rest assured that if I have not resolved upon any actual active or decisive actions for this cause, which I most certainly regard as that of all kings and which keenly interests me, it is because I see an absolute physical impossibility at present.

In relation to the reply to give to the King of France, when his letter notifying us of the new order of things reaches us, and about which Your Majesty is so good as to consult me, I think that it would be most suitable to follow the example of the King of Spain on this occasion, and to have our ministers say that we cannot be persuaded that the King of France has either the physical or the moral liberty to accept the constitution. We would like to be able to convince ourselves of it, but as long as we do not have that conviction, we cannot respond to the communication that has been made to us.

As for the *declaration*, the plan of which I had transmitted to Your Majesty last summer and which was to be handed over jointly by all the powers at the moment when they had decided to declare themselves, I am of the view that it should be kept until that time, if it is to take place. But recalling our ministers from Paris on the pretext of a leave of absence can be done now, and I am accordingly having orders sent to mine, prescribing nonetheless that he be guided by those that Your Majesty's ambassador will receive. Your Majesty may accordingly act as you deem fitting in this matter.

In deserving the approval and goodness of Your Majesty, Baron von Pahlen has fulfilled one of the most essential parts of the orders that I had given him, and I am grateful to him, as it is a new merit in my eyes. He cannot boast enough of the gracious welcome that Your Majesty gave him and of the continually benevolent manner in which you treated him throughout his entire stay with you. It is a pleasure for me to attribute some of this to the sentiments that Your Majesty professes for me, and which correspond so well with those of true and sincere friendship with which I am,

My dear Brother and Cousin,

Your Majesty's good Sister, Cousin, Friend, Neighbour, and Ally,

Catherine

St Petersburg, 9 November 1791

I beg Your Majesty to pardon the enormous thickness of this letter.

198. *To Gustav III of Sweden*

As the powers of Europe continued to hesitate about a possible intervention in France, Catherine reiterated her belief that the émigré princes must be central to the counter-Revolutionary effort. Meanwhile, the international situation was further troubled by changes in leadership. The Holy Roman Emperor Leopold II of Austria died unexpectedly on 1 March 1792 (NS) and was succeeded by his son, Francis II. Meanwhile, Gustav III held a meeting of the Swedish Estates at Gävle in January–February 1792, but the nobility remained hostile to his absolute rule. Shortly before this letter was written, a military officer shot the king at a masquerade ball on 16 March (NS). Gustav died from his wounds on 29 March (NS).

My dear Brother and Cousin, Count Stackelberg's latest courier brought me Your Majesty's two letters of 23 February and 4 March NS. I am very touched by the obliging manner in which Your Majesty speaks in the first about the conclusion of my peace treaty with Turkey. I in turn send you my compliments on the outcome of the Diet which you have summoned, and I entreat you to be convinced that I take a sincere interest in all that concerns you.

I replied to Your Majesty regarding the plans that you had sent me through Baron von der Pahlen by sharing with you my feelings: namely, that we should wait until we had made sense of the winter's negotiations before acting. I hurried the latter as much as I could, and, seeing that certain courts were stalling endlessly, I proposed a ready-made plan. Without stating his views positively, the King of Prussia referred me to those of the Viennese court. Instead of the decisive answer that I was expecting any day from the latter, a few days ago I received the unexpected news of the emperor's death, an event which, although it does not totally upset the plan, could at least delay its execution.

Then again, I have learned that, rather than join in Your Majesty's and my own pleas that the courts of Vienna and Berlin hurry to act, Spain is advising them to do nothing, for fear of putting the lives of the King and the Queen of France at risk, and to remain calm spectators of our efforts while merely sending us some secret monetary aid. Spain is sticking to the same role itself, and has as a further motive the fear of finding itself attacked by England and of compromising its potential right to the succession of the French monarchy.

In truth, the responses from the courts of Turin and Naples were satisfactory, but they could not but be devised in general terms, given that the other powers have not yet articulated anything precise and positive.

As for the French princes, Your Majesty knows that all I tried to do to put them in a position to act on their own has been destroyed and obliterated, and that even Their Most Christian Majesties [the King and Queen of France] wish it to be so and are working to push them aside and leave them behind with their party, whom I have always considered to be made up of people truly attached to the king and who by dint of their position have an interest in re-establishing his authority. It is scarcely probable that their opinions on this matter could change any time soon. On the contrary, they seem farther than ever from meeting with the princes in the Tuileries. Even the latter, as Your Majesty has very well observed, have not exactly gone down the path they should have taken to facilitate such great projects. At the very least, they were ill served by the circumstances and perhaps by their entourage.

In the plan that I have communicated to Your Majesty, it was indeed a matter of putting those forces in the front lines, but it was understood that they would be seconded by the French, who were said to number 12,000 to 15,000 men. They were then gathered together, but now that they have been scattered here and there, it will be difficult, at the very least, to re-assemble them in such great numbers. And since not one of the European courts has yet made any agreement with us, it seems to me that it would be too much of a risk for Your Majesty's glory and my own to arm and to show ourselves first on the scene without the least assurance in the world of their support.

I am informed that Master Bischoffwerder is in Vienna and that he was sent principally to coordinate the plan of operations to be carried out regarding France. It will not be long before we find out what the new King of Hungary and Bohemia will decide. As we wait on his plans, word has reached me of something that Your Majesty, I think, already knows: that the basis or the pretext will be the breach of the treaties between the German Empire and France. Now, I ask Your Majesty: if they want our aid to this effect, would it not suit our dignity for them to summon us as guarantors of the breached treaties? In addition, I must confide in Your Majesty that I have a perfectly good opinion of the young King of Hungary and Bohemia. He was raised by his uncle [Joseph II], and I assume that he will move more steadily and decisively than his predecessor.

We can definitively arrange our conduct only in accordance with all that I have just said. As soon as all these circumstances have developed, I shall not lose a moment in informing Your Majesty of my decision, which I shall try to contrive in concert with Your Majesty's good intentions, circumstances permitting.

I am, with sentiments of the sincerest friendship and the most distinguished regard,

My dear Brother and Cousin,

Your Majesty's good Sister, Cousin, Friend, Ally, and Neighbour,

Catherine

at St Petersburg, this 7 March 1792

199. *To George III of Great Britain and Ireland*

Catherine asks George III to support the Comte d'Artois's mission to invade the French province of the Vendée, but the British government was not yet willing to commit substantial resources to such an undertaking.

My dear Brother! Convinced that Your Majesty shares the satisfaction that I feel at seeing renewed the ancient ties under whose auspices we began our respective reigns, it is a pleasure for me today to profess to you personally my heartfelt feelings. They will grow with the drafting of the treaty of alliance that Your Majesty proposes to me, and my intentions in this matter perfectly match yours. I have no fear of seeing results delayed by haggling over issues that can so easily be resolved and settled as the interests of our countries and of our respective subjects can, since those interests coincide in all respects and without divergence. Thus, considering this salutary aim, which is so apt to tighten the bonds that will unite us, as already accomplished, I think that I can already allow myself to show Your Majesty that trust which must henceforth accompany those ties on both sides.

There were incontrovertibly fewer compelling reasons for me to intervene in the affairs of France than for the other powers that border that kingdom. With the immense barriers separating me from France, and with a few precautionary measures, I could have calmly watched events unfold. Perhaps even the almost universal exhaustion that would inevitably have been produced by the efforts of some to overturn those barriers and of others to defend them would have offered most attractive opportunities for a policy more exclusive than mine has ever been. But, since I am a friend to order, justice, and the common happiness of humanity, it was only with such pure and disinterested motives that I have sought to draw the attention and efforts of the powers of Europe to the dangers of all kinds that threaten them as a result of the French Revolution. Among the measures that I have always considered and still consider to be the most efficacious and efficient of all is that of forming within France a party that might ultimately prevail over the detestable faction of scoundrels who currently hold sway there. Indeed, without this means, how can one hope to restore a nation of twenty-five million men, alternately led astray by perfidious advice or swept along by the atrocious violence of their current leaders, and therefore how can one hope to ensure the peace and tranquillity of their neighbours?

With this conviction, I tried to enjoin my allies, the Holy Roman Emperor and the King of Prussia, to facilitate, from the start of the last campaign, the entry into France of the princes, the brothers of the too-unfortunate King Louis XVI, along with the body of troops formed around them, by having them act separately and of their own accord. Either because it was incompatible with the circumstances, or perhaps because another seemed preferable, this plan was not followed. But events unfortunately did not justify the plan adopted, which has become another reason for me to persist in my opinion. I shall not conceal from Your Majesty that I have always combined this conviction with the feeling of rightful concern for the fate of a family so cruelly and so horribly oppressed, which still makes me keenly desire to see them restored to the rights and titles that belong to them so legitimately. Moreover, why should I hesitate to express to Your Majesty a feeling which I am persuaded that you harbour in your own heart and that you have so well professed by the so-worthy grief you showed upon learning of the unfortunate Louis XVI's deplorable end!

The brothers of that unhappy monarch, the born defenders of the tender offspring whom he left,* had long since been made aware of Your Majesty's magnanimous character. Encouraged by the latest proof that you have given of it, one of them, the Comte d'Artois, has resolved to go personally to confide to Your Majesty's bosom his wishes, his hopes, and his cares for the most just cause that has ever called for the union of sovereigns to bring about its triumph. He has entrusted me with his intentions and asked for my advice and intercession. I thought it my duty to approve the former and not to refuse the latter, and it is to discharge this obligation that I add my prayers to those that the Comte d'Artois will address to Your Majesty: that you should be so good as to lend him a helping hand from the height of a throne surrounded by the love and zeal of a nation that has always been capable of imitating and often of giving examples of noble generosity. I am not unaware of the rightful limits that must be placed on this impulse by the care that Your Majesty owes to the interests of your peoples. Yet, on this occasion it is a matter, on the one hand, of providing for the dignity of your crown and the safety of your lands, while, on the other, extracting a neighbouring kingdom from an abyss of troubles and confusion so destructive to its own happiness and the general peace. Therefore, it is doubtless right that, when restored by Your Majesty's efforts, France should repay you in proportion to the extent of those efforts and that your subjects should be compensated for the momentary burden that they will bear.

Based on this principle, I flatter myself that, far from finding any indiscretion in the step that I am taking towards you today, Your Majesty will see in it, on the contrary, a new means of attaining the goal that you proclaimed on taking up arms.

Leaving this subject, as well as the cooperation on your aims and plans that Your Majesty has requested from me, to be discussed in more depth by our respective envoys, I shall end my letter by renewing to you my assurances of the highest regard with which I am,

My dear Brother,
Your Majesty's good Sister and Friend,

Catherine
at St Petersburg, 13 April OS 1793

200. *To Prince Charles-Joseph de Ligne*

Getting one's house in order is a motif of the correspondence with de Ligne. After a long hiatus, Catherine resumes the correspondence by returning to their delight in art and gardens. But the French Revolution overshadows these joys and Catherine's letter throughout. A reference to audible cannon-fire conveys the sense of imminent threats to the stable order she hoped her reign would achieve, a disorder that de Ligne would come to know only too well when his properties in France and Belgium were confiscated in 1794. The sale of Partheniza and Nikita, his estates in Crimea, to Platon Zubov may have been out of financial necessity.

Dear Prince, if I have not replied to your last letter these six months, excuse me. I am simply following the famous examples that teach us that, when we are promised that a courier will depart on pressing business in eight or ten days, it's tantamount to saying that you'll wait eight or ten months without anything arriving or being dispatched. All the same, a well-run household still gets the business done. I am reasonably pleased with my own, especially since we are exhausted by festivities and fatigue: firstly because of the peace with the Sublime Porte; secondly because of the marriage of my grandson, Mr Alexander*—this is Psyche united with Love. During these celebrations, we were visited by the ambassador of His Highness the Sultan, whose retinue does little honour to the finances of the Sultan Selim, for they are dressed in rags and, in keeping with the latest fashion, lack the articles of clothing that have been considered till now the most essential for a gentleman. Well, it hardly matters, since they might announce on day one that there is to be a third war. That is no problem: where there's a will there's a way. The Turks are not like Christian powers: they do not normally formulate their plans until late in the season. This gives them time to mull it over and wait for their grapes to ripen. If on his way back from Spain, Baron St Helens had found his overland route cleared in the way that I would have liked* and even, I believe, had proposed, he would not have failed, I think, to pay you a second visit at Belœil. And then, I flatter myself, I would have received from him new reports on the beauties of that charming place. It will soon be unparalleled in your region, in the event that internal discord and war continue to devastate the square miles located between the two seas from the Pyrenees to the Rhine. But, in the end, what is delayed is not lost, if one cares little about time. As for Tsarskoe Selo, which as you say is a place that rightly claims all my fancies, I recently embellished it with a gentle slope, which leads from the colonnade into the garden, and with an open rotunda of thirty-three columns of Siberian marble. From this spot I would like to see my grandsons with their wives and children running on the lawn, once the former have some of the latter. About two or three years ago, in this same Tsarskoe Selo I heard on the sea breezes rounds of cannon-fire such as you hear now from your chateau when you are shooting partridge or sparrows. Our ancient Vaubans* were very far from leaving reputations for genius as celebrated as that of the one who lived under Louis XIV; he alone, up till now, has prevented 300,000 men from entering France, which has neither generals, nor discipline, nor an army. Just try and tell me after that that all men are equal. Oh well, despite our Vaubans, we pulled through in two years. But how happy I would be if I knew that all of those for whom we care the most had [escaped] all the horrible misfortunes to which they have been prey for so long. Well, what can one expect from this hydra with 700 heads as avid for human blood as it is wicked and perfidious? It must be destroyed and never negotiated with. If the war can produce heroes up to the task, and if they are not hindered in their aims by internal politics, then we can hope for success. While I wait, it seems to me that you are correcting very well the style of your subordinates and that this is a way to get rid of stumbling blocks for yourself. The governor-general of Tauris, Count Zubov, will give you the proceeds from the sale of Partheniza and Nikita. I do not know whether he will employ the Israelite who enjoys your trust, or whether he is dead and buried. My taste for antiques and billiards has diminished a bit, and it seems to me that I have no time for anything, other than to tell you that I remain always the same for you, my Prince. Adieu and be well.

C.

this 22 October 1793

201. *To Friedrich Melchior Grimm*

In this opening section of a letter written over three days, Catherine expresses obliquely her horror at the execution of Marie Antoinette on 16 October 1793.

(NS). The British Parliament reopened on the first anniversary of Louis XVI's death, 21 January 1794 (NS); in his opening speech, George III declared Great Britain's intention to fight vigorously against the French Revolution.

this 10 February 1794

You ask what will come of the actions of dirty dogs. The answer is very easy, since you can see for yourself: nothing but the actions of dirty dogs.* You can see that I have received and am reading your documents, which were brought by Tiesenhausen. I cannot answer the first point of the first document: I scarcely open my mouth on the subject any more because ... because I am silenced by subjects that cause pain as profound as the queen's horrible fate makes one feel. But there is no effect without a cause. Only great and terrible truths can guide us through this one. *Basta.* I hope that the King of England's harangue and the opening of his Parliament in January will have relieved your feeling of discouragement. It seems that there is nothing to add to what has been pronounced, and the Parliament's conduct is perfect. All the great houses of England are joining the king's cause, and Mr Pitt's self-interest and his passions seem to be bound up in it. Besides, scoundrels so devoid of sense cannot survive, and when all the regicides have been exterminated, there will be fewer people with an interest in perpetuating the current state of affairs. Now, more than half of those monsters have already perished in one way or another: divine justice makes them perish, mostly by killing one another. This is something very much to be noted, since it is a direct result of their very principles.

As for peace, I hereby challenge you: never have calls for perpetual war—the war that people were shouting for on 21 January this year in Paris—been more timely in disabusing people about the fantasy of peace. Peace—peace is not a crime. They regard crime as a virtue and virtue as a crime. Speak rationally to madmen, if you can! You will drive them into a rage, for they are incapable of following reason. Like you, I have received an anonymous letter twelve pages long, trying to persuade me to send troops to the Rhine. But how can I? If I send small numbers to carry out the plans of dirty dogs, then they will be defeated like the rest. And I cannot send large numbers because I am expecting at any moment to have to deal with the Turks, whom Ainslie and Descorches are riling up. Please distinguish a bit between Milord Ainslie and the English prime minister at the moment: the latter wants the Turks to attack me only if they cannot be prevented from going to war against the court of Vienna, and only in that case is war against Russia being advocated. But Ainslie wants war against Russia no matter what. Descorches is preaching war against both imperial courts at once. Now, the result of this whole mishmash is that I have to be on my guard and that I cannot have my troops marching to far-off countries in large numbers. Besides, you know that last spring I had proposed to send a good number of them to aid the Vendée, or rather the royalists, and that the Comte d'Artois was to be part of the mission, but that over there they did not want to hear of it.

202. *To Holy Roman Emperor Francis II*

With this letter, Catherine requests help from her ally Francis II in fighting the Kosciuszko Uprising in Poland. Her rhetoric both exploits pan-European fear of the French Revolution and hints at the tangibility of that fear for Catherine and her contemporaries. To bolster her request, Catherine enclosed copies of Kosciuszko's declarations as well as a report containing the details of a Polish rebel's clandestine visit to Paris and his success in winning support from the French Revolutionary government. The Russian repression of the uprising was notoriously bloody and concluded with the third and final Partition in 1795.

My dear Brother, Your Imperial Majesty is doubtless already fully informed of the explosion of unrest in Poland that has suddenly engulfed the unhappy kingdom from one end to the other. You similarly cannot be unaware of the rebels' extreme violence and perfidy during and after this unfortunate event. Finding myself obliged to resort to the most vigorous methods and most efficacious measures to put a halt to its dire consequences, I had to call for the support of the King of Prussia, who is as near a neighbour to the Republic as I am and who shares my interest in stifling as soon as possible such a dangerous blaze. He anticipated my request by offering to send into Poland an army of 40,000 men to cooperate with my troops in extinguishing everywhere the newly kindled fire of revolt before it has the chance to grow any stronger. Your Majesty will be even further convinced of the need to combine so many forces and, above all, of the need for speed in their actions, once you have been so good as to glance through the attached papers, which, owing to their authenticity and the reliability of the sources from which I drew them, I thought I must bring to your attention directly. In them, you will see that it is not an ordinary plot, spun with the thoughtlessness and carelessness characteristic of the Poles. Rather, it is a plan that has been conceived and composed with profound villainy by the regicide cult of Jacobins, that is to be faithfully executed by the rebel Kosciuszko, and that encompasses the most unbounded aims. It lays out the principles, the means, and the end. The coordinated vigilance of the generals commanding the allied armies might easily intercept some of the means, such as mutual dispatches of emissaries between the Polish and French rebels, and the provision of monetary assistance on the part of the latter, especially when it is carried in cash. This is a measure which I dare to propose to Your Imperial Majesty's foresight, the effect of which cannot but be very useful to the common cause. It will be very easy for you to make the other courts appreciate and adopt it. The content of the papers just mentioned seemed so important to me that, not satisfied with having communicated them to the King of Prussia, I have also informed the Sovereign Pontiff of the Romans of the danger that threatens in Poland the Church of which he is the head. I have invited him by letter to use spiritual weapons to restrain pious souls and to turn them away from such imminent danger. I flatter myself that Your Imperial Majesty not only will approve of this step, but that you will also be so good as to support it with an analogous one. In seeing our common enemies' persevering tenacity in their sinister conspiracies against the tranquillity and safety of all states, as well as the unanimity of intentions and efforts with which they are marching towards the execution of their atrocious aims, we cannot for our part erect against them a barrier more powerful than the one they must come up against in a sincere and cordial union of our means and our forces, directed towards the single goal of laying low their criminal audacity and putting an end to the agitation it has caused in all of Europe, while leaving aside all the other interests which we shall be at leisure to remedy when calm has been everywhere restored. As a friend, I shall share deeply in what remains of Your Imperial Majesty's concerns on this matter and shall be scrupulously attentive to satisfy them. In renewing to you my assurances on this matter, I add to them truthfully and with pleasure the same friendship and the highest regard with which I shall never cease to be,

My dear Brother,

Your Imperial Majesty's good Sister and faithful Friend and Ally,

Catherine
at St Petersburg, this 27 April OS 1794

203. *To Friedrich Melchior Grimm*

In 1792, Catherine republished her historical drama, 'An Imitation of Shakespeare: A Historical Spectacle without the Usual Theatrical Rules, from the Life of Riurik' (1786), this time with commentary by the historian Ivan Nikitich Boltin (1735–1792). In these final sections of a letter begun on 9 April 1795, she justifies historically Russia's annexation of new territories in the Third Partition of Poland, and continues to proclaim Russia's long-standing and enduring role in European history.

this 13 April, after lunch

I congratulate Count Nikolai Rumiantsev on knowing who Riurik, the first prince of his dynasty in Russia, was. My conjectures thereupon have been printed in the drama of *Riurik* with Boltin's commentaries. Yet, as the Russian proverb says, he who knows best holds all the cards.

To respond to the second question: which people does Nestor call 'Russians'? I think that one might give an answer, but that might demand work that is best avoided in the spring. As for the words inserted between two parentheses (*i Pol'sha tozhe vsiu Rus'*),* I would ask that one not say *Pol'sha*, but rather that *Litva* be substituted for *Pol'sha*, and then it would be correct, and the article of the present letter in which the great Hertzberg's ignorance is whipped* proves it sufficiently. But Poland, of which Krakow was formerly the capital, was a separate country. It was perhaps populated by Slavs too, as their language can prove. I shall give an ignoramus's reply to question 3: in all humility, I have no idea.

I respect the remaining propositions because everyone can make hypotheses. As more and more are made, they obscure or illuminate history in accordance with how luminous they are. But, for myself, I require proofs like those about Lithuania, for instance—see page 1 of this document.* Me, I say: since the Slavs conquered the whole world three times, they must have had weapons, and so one cannot call the Slavs 'a people without weapons'. The harmony between the different provinces, I say, came from how they were conquered three times by the Slavs. The first coming of the Slavs can be dated to the time when Odin,* who came from the Don and who did not have wings to fly to Sweden, was therefore forced to pass through the land between the Don and Sweden. The Swedes made Odin into a god whose dynasty reigned for a long time in Sweden, etc. etc. etc.

Me, I maintain that King Alfred or any other Anglo-Saxon dynasty was Slavic; that even today in England they pay a tribute called *ot sokhi*, of the ploughshare; and that the English know that this tribute was established by the Saxons, who are a Slavic tribe. I read no books nor even flick through any if they are not 300 years old, at least. I learn nothing from any others, and I am up to my neck in conjectures.

this 14 April

I read the hodgepodge of old news, and I endorse the hanging of the Abbé Sieyès.

If Prince Henry becomes King of France as a reward for the shameful and disastrous peace that he has just made his nephew conclude,* one must hope at least that, if he is not himself guillotined, he will hold to account the enemies of his cause. Otherwise we shall say that the great little man is committing and making others commit unpardonable puerilities, and that he and his nephew *have neither faith nor law nor heart.* Look out: that will become the refrain of a song about them.

All that the Marshal de Castries writes is marked with the seal of wisdom.

Of the four attachments contained in the inventory, three were handed over: the one to Monsieur de Lambert, who is not here, will reach him in time.

I congratulate you on breaking off communications with Citizen Necker. Recall the aversion I have always had for that fabricator of starched sentences in which one saw in each line, in big letters, 'Me'.

At last, at last, Whipping-Boy, with a reply forty-eight pages long I have succeeded in sinking to the bottom my review of your documents. Farewell, be well; I am doing the same.

204. *To Friedrich Melchior Grimm*

One of the most renowned painters of late-eighteenth-century France, and Marie Antoinette's favoured portraitist, Louise-Élisabeth Vigée Le Brun (1755–1842) arrived in Russia as an émigrée in 1795. Catherine was unimpressed with Vigée Le Brun's fashionable sentimental style: the painter had to rework the portrait of Catherine's granddaughters described here, replacing the grapes with traditional flowers and covering up the girls' bare arms. Today the painting is in the Hermitage in St Petersburg.

this 8 November [1795]

I received by the last post the bulletin of 18 October, which is more interesting than the previous ones. But listen, please: in the age of

Louis XIV, the French school of painting showed promise of painting nobly and showed signs of combining intelligence with nobility and charm. Along comes Madame Le Brun in August. I return to the city. She claims to be a follower of Angelica Kauffmann, and the latter certainly combines elegance with nobility in all her figures. She does more: all her figures even possess ideal beauty. For a first attempt, Angelica's follower starts painting Grand Duchesses Alexandra and Elena. The former has a noble, engaging face and the bearing of a queen; the latter is a perfect beauty with the look of a goody-two-shoes. Madame Le Brun squats those two figures down on a sofa, twists the younger one's neck, makes them look like two pugs warming themselves in the sun, or, if you prefer, two ugly little Savoyardes with their hair done up like bacchantes with bunches of grapes, and dresses them up in red and violet grosgrain tunics. In a word, it is not only a failed likeness, but the two sisters are so very disfigured that there are people who ask which is the elder and which the younger. Madame Le Brun's supporters praise all that to the skies, but in my opinion it is very bad because in this portrait painting there is neither likeness, nor taste, nor nobility. One must be dumb to fail so completely to capture one's subject, especially with such a subject before one's eyes: one needed to copy Lady Nature, and not to invent monkey poses.

205. *To Grand Duke Paul and Grand Duchess Maria Fedorovna*

In this letter, Catherine aims to coordinate with her son and daughter-in-law their efforts to conclude a marriage between Gustav IV Adolf and Catherine's granddaughter, Alexandra. Just as her early letters to Charles Hanbury-Williams used character portraits and dialogues to negotiate court politics, here, in the last months of her life, Catherine sketches a striking tableau of her conversation with the young king in the midst of intense political intrigue.

this 17 August

They brought me your letters from today, my dear children, when I was at lunch. Yesterday was not without difficulties—I noticed it as you did. The king came into the round room where I was seated. Since I had promised him a response within three days, and yesterday was the deadline, I told him that once he was free of his commitments to the Duke of Mecklenburg, I would listen to what he had to propose. I knew already of the difficulties over religion being thrust forward. He stammered out a few phrases of thanks and assurances of friendship. After that, we talked for a very long time about entirely anodyne matters, whereupon I rose to return to the ballroom. Then, on his feet, he started to tell me that, as a man of honour, he was obliged to tell me that the fundamental laws of Sweden required that the queen be of the same religion as the king, and that this was how the matter had always been until now. I answered that I knew the laws had been intolerant in the early days of Protestantism, but that the late king, his father, had made the bishops themselves issue a law that allowed everyone, and even the king himself, to contract marriages with wives of any religion he found suitable. He answered that it was to be feared that his subjects' minds would turn against him. I retorted that it was up to him to know what he had to do, and I assumed a very serious expression. He then wanted to repeat what he had already said; I fell silent and moved very slowly towards the door. He had tears in his eyes. It is a matter of choosing sides. Everyone would like the marriage to be recognized as their handiwork, and they seem to take pride in preventing others' success, but deep down I think that they would not dare to return home without having concluded the matter, since the [attraction]* is very pronounced. What the duke [Charles, Duke of Södermanland] told my dear son, namely that he had not received a response from us, is true, since he has never allowed the matter to be discussed without adding either Armfelt's head or some other impertinence; he had been told and therefore knew that we would not address those.* Now, note as well that this is the first time I have ever heard that the Mecklenburg marriage was conditional. And how could it have been, when they have prayed for her by name and surname in all the churches as the future queen, and when the betrothal has been celebrated in front of all Sweden? Those people constantly get tangled in their own nets because they mistake their craftiness for skill. The young Kemd [Gustav IV Adolf] seems to have a good and sensitive heart, but he is only 17.

Farewell, I send you my greetings.

206. *To Friedrich Melchior Grimm*

This is Catherine's last letter to Friedrich Melchior Grimm, written just over two weeks before her death of a stroke on 6 November 1796. As she had throughout her life, Catherine seeks to found her actions on statements of principle. As she sends her troops to fight Persia and plans a campaign against Revolutionary France, she contemplates once more the key ideas of honour and glory that had always motivated her.

this 20 October 1796

I received yesterday and the day before yesterday the letters that you sent me through Kolichev and Iakovlev. I have no time to answer them because I have also received some from England and from Persia, which, although highly satisfactory in every respect, nonetheless give me plenty to do. The King of Prussia is arming. What do you think of that? Against whom?—Against me. To please whom?—His friends, the regicides, on whom he cannot count for one moment. One must admit that whoever is giving that prince such perfidious advice is singularly compromising his honour and glory. There is but one path to honour and glory. Whereas I have taken the liberty of proposing it to him, others turn him away from it and entrap him in a maze well beneath his stature. They will reduce him to the most humble servant of the arrogant villains who, in the end, aim at nothing other than his destruction. If, by these armaments, they think that they can deflect me from sending my troops marching under the command of Marshal Suvorov, they are very much mistaken. For I shall, nonetheless, remain armed on all fronts—no exceptions. I am preaching and shall continue to preach the common cause of all kings against the destroyers of thrones and of society, despite all the adherents to the wretched opposing system. And we shall see who gains the upper hand: reason, or the unreason of the perfidious partisans of an execrable system, which by its very nature excludes and tramples upon all sentiments of religion, honour, and glory. That is quite enough in telling you that I have received your letters. Farewell, be well, I have imparted to you what appeared on the tip of my pen. It is good for you to know how I think about and envisage things.

EXPLANATORY NOTES

Letter 1

6 *the flutterer*: presumably referring to herself, Catherine uses the nonsense word 'papiller', probably related to 'papillon' (Fr. 'butterfly') or 'papillote' (Fr. 'curling-paper').

Letter 2

7 *Zerbst*: the young Sophia Augusta's mistake in dating her letter from Zerbst rather than from Russia touchingly suggests a slight case of homesickness.

Letter 5

10 *Explain yourself, Sir*: Shuvalov addresses Catherine as a man, in keeping with the masculine persona she adopted in her secret letters when she was grand duchess.

11 *Prasse*: Johann Moritz Prasse, representative of Saxony at the Russian court. The elector of Saxony was at that time also the King of Poland and therefore Poniatowski's sovereign.

Bernardi: Italian jeweller, who bore messages and carried out commissions for Catherine and Hanbury-Williams.

document: in Catherine's friendly correspondences, she regularly uses 'pancarte' (Fr. 'a placard displaying tariffs') as a humorous word for 'letter'. We employ 'document'.

I am thinking of writing to Ivan Ivanovich: this is the letter to Ivan Shuvalov, the reception of which Catherine narrates at the start of her missive to Hanbury-Williams.

12 *the generosity of my action*: a further attachment contained another letter from Ivan Shuvalov to Catherine, in which he said he would do what he could for Kirill Razumovsky and offered advice on how Razumovsky should behave if he wanted to return to court. This noncommittal reply constituted a refusal to arrange for Razumovsky to remain, which was the very favour Catherine had been seeking.

Letter 6

13 *Lacedaemon*: Sparta (also known as Lacedaemon) was legendary for its citizens' military prowess and absolute devotion to the state.

Letter 8

15 *Prometheus*: a Titan of Greek mythology who defied the gods and gifted fire to mankind, suffering eternal punishment as a result. A byword for altruistic sacrifice.

the Prince: Dashkova's husband, Prince Mikhail Ivanovich Dashkov, was a lieutenant colonel in the Imperial Guards. He died in Poland during the manoeuvres that put Stanislas Poniatowski on the throne.

Letter 9

15 *Counts Skavronsky, Sheremetev, … Korf*: the group of senators named to guard the young Paul was composed of senior statesmen, including Count Martyn Karlovich Skavronsky (1714–1776), nephew of Peter the Great's wife, Catherine I; Count Petr Borisovich Sheremetev (1713–1788), a member of a prominent aristocratic family and grand chamberlain at Peter III's court; and Baron Nikolai Andreevich Korf (1710–1766), Peter III's police director.

Letter 11

17 *Prince Adam*: Poniatowski's cousin, Adam Kazimierz Czartoryski (1734–1823). The Poniatowski family was part of the so-called 'Familia', a powerful, reform-minded political alliance led by the Czartoryski family.

L.W. … Prince George: L.W. stands for Elizaveta Vorontsova, Peter III's mistress. Prince George is Catherine's maternal uncle, Prince Georg Ludwig of Schleswig-Holstein-Gottorf. Catherine's boorish husband, Peter, alienated large swathes of Russian society by, among other things, his long-standing preference for his childhood faith, Lutheranism, and for his compatriots from his native German duchy of Holstein. Catherine won popular support by presenting herself as the defender of the Russian state religion and of Russian political and cultural interests more broadly.

Princess Anne and her children: Anna Leopoldovna (1718–1746), briefly regent for her son Ivan VI (1740–1764), until Empress Elizabeth's coup, at which point Anna and her family were imprisoned; Ivan VI was killed in 1764 during an abortive attempt to liberate him and put him on the throne.

Oranienbaum: imperial residence on the Gulf of Finland, near St Petersburg.

Orlov brothers … following me everywhere: there were five Orlov brothers, all staunch supporters of Catherine throughout her reign: Ivan, Grigory, Aleksei, Fedor, and Vladimir. Catherine's lover, the dashing guardsman Grigory, was the second (not the eldest) brother. The others who participated in the coup were Aleksei and Fedor.

19 *new Winter Palace*: the Winter Palace that we know today, which had recently been built by Empress Elizabeth; the old Winter Palace was a temporary wooden building nearby.

Vice-Chancellor Golitsyn: Prince Alexander Mikhailovich Golitsyn (1723–1807), vice-chancellor under Peter III and then under Catherine until 1775, not to be confused with Prince Alexander Mikhailovich Golitsyn, commander of the Russian army in the First Russo-Turkish War (see Biographical Register, p. 413).

22 *Potemkin*: Catherine's future lover Grigory Potemkin.

Letter 12

24 *Madame Des Houlières*: Antoinette Des Houlières (1638–1694), learned French poet and dramatist, one of the first women to be admitted to scholarly

academies (the Academy of the Ricovrati in Padua and the Academy of Arles). The (slightly modified) couplet that follows is, in fact, from Pierre Corneille's tragedy *Horace* (1640), act 2, scene 3.

Letter 13

29 *the conduct of Queen Christina*: Catherine alludes to Queen Christina of Sweden's decision to abdicate in 1654. D'Alembert was the author of *Reflections and Anecdotes about Christina, Queen of Sweden* (1753).

Letter 14

30 *a day ... with the Lord*: 2 Peter 3:8 (KJV): 'But, beloved, be not ignorant of this one thing, that one day is with the Lord as a thousand years, and a thousand years as one day.'

Jean-Jacques Rousseau's prophecy: 'The Russian Empire will try to subjugate Europe, and will be itself subjugated. The Tartars, its subjects or neighbors, will become its masters and ours: This revolution seems to me inevitable' (Jean-Jacques Rousseau, *The Social Contract* (1762), bk 2, ch. 8, in *The Social Contract and Other Later Political Writings*, ed. and trans. Victor Gourevitch (Cambridge: Cambridge University Press, 1997), 73).

the second volume of Peter the Great: Voltaire's *History of the Russian Empire under Peter the Great*, 2 vols (1759–63).

31 *the General History*: Voltaire's history of the world, which would become the *Essay on the Manners and Spirit of the Nations* (first full edn 1756; final version 1775).

the great Corneille: Catherine alludes to Voltaire's heavily annotated edition of Corneille's works, published in 1764 for the benefit of an impoverished relative of the dramatist.

Letter 15

32 *the business of Courland*: in 1763 Catherine arranged for the reigning Duke of Courland (now in Latvia), Charles of Saxony (1733–1796), to be replaced by the dukedom's exiled ruler, Ernst Johann von Biron (1690–1772), whose loyalties lay with Russia, since he had been a favourite of the late Empress Anna (1693–1740, r. 1730–40).

Letter 16

33 *Nastasia*: on the back of this letter, Madame Geoffrin annotated this name for the benefit of a close friend whom she allowed to read the letter: 'Nastasia, the empress's lady-in-waiting, whom I know well. She was in Paris for a long time.' This was Anastasia Ivanovna Sokolova (1741–1822), ward and possibly illegitimate daughter of Ivan Betskoy.

the naughty General comes to instruct me: at court, Betskoy regularly read literary works aloud to the empress, as she describes here. On the back of this letter, Geoffrin noted: 'The one whom the empress calls "the naughty general" is General Betskoy, her favourite, who is a very amiable man who made several trips to Paris and spent a long time here. He is my friend.'

33 *my knots*: knotting decorative braid with a shuttle was a popular elite handicraft in the eighteenth century.

Letter 17

35 *carousel*: a court spectacle imitating a medieval tournament. Modelled on Louis XIV's Grand Carousel of 1662, Catherine's carousel took place in 1766 and featured four *quadrilles* ('teams'), representing the Slavs, the Romans, the Indians, and the Turks. Catherine herself led the Slavs; the winner of the carousel was another woman, Princess Natalia Golitsyna (1741/4?–1837).

If he were alive … just as: that is, Montesquieu, like d'Alembert, would have refused to come to Russia. D'Alembert frequented Geoffrin's salon and would have been made aware of these comments. Catherine's *Instruction* draws, often verbatim, from Montesquieu's *Spirit of the Laws* (1748) and adapts his ideas to Russia's needs.

36 *another manifesto on such an occasion*: in a previous letter, Catherine had defended a manifesto that she had published on the execution of Vasily Mirovich, an unsuccessful conspirator against her, which had been ridiculed in the European press.

Letter 18

Kalmyk: nomadic people of the northern Caucasus.

37 *Count Orlov*: Catherine's lover, Grigory Orlov.

38 *I shall have … such good friends at home*: although she received the cream of Parisian society, Geoffrin was of bourgeois origin and made her humble simplicity part of her public image. Catherine asserts that she will create a middle class in Russia, flatteringly claiming that its members will resemble Geoffrin.

ne plus ultra: the very best example.

if German roads … very agreeable: Catherine resented d'Alembert's willingness to visit Frederick II in Berlin in 1763, in contrast to his refusal to go to St Petersburg.

Letter 19

39 *Catechism … afraid to complete*: still hoping to draw on d'Alembert's talents as a source for her *Instruction*, Catherine presses him for a 'moral catechism for children' that he had proposed to write. He never completed it, claiming to fear persecution for his largely secular morality.

Letter 20

41 *Jesuits are not allowed*: Peter the Great had banned the Jesuits in 1689, but, when the Society of Jesus was officially disbanded in 1773, Catherine allowed them to remain as educators in formerly Polish territories.

Letter 21

42 *My own experience*: Catherine alludes to her experiences as grand duchess, when she studied to escape the boredom and restrictive atmosphere of the Russian court.

Letter 22

43 *Emp. Elizabeth ... her mother*: Empress Elizabeth's mother was the second wife of Peter the Great, who ruled Russia for two years after his death, as Empress Catherine I (1684–1727, r. 1725–7).

he has sacrificed ... pension: Catherine claims that she would have given d'Alembert far more than the pension he belatedly received from the French government in 1765.

not one principle ... letter: Voltaire's *Pastoral Letter of the Most Reverend Father in the Lord Alexis* (1765) asserts the precedence of secular powers over the Church and celebrates Russia as an example of such an arrangement.

you can burn it: Voltaire did not burn her attachment: he published part of it in his *Letter on Panegyrics* (1767).

44 *Methuselah ... honour*: the longest-lived individual in the Bible, Methuselah lived 969 years (Genesis 5:27). In his previous letter, Voltaire had jokingly complained that Catherine's name came from the Christian rather than the classical tradition: it was therefore less euphonic and less appropriate for poetry.

Minerva: the Roman goddess of wisdom and of warfare, also of art and ideas. Catherine was very frequently represented as Minerva in portraiture, pageantry, and other media.

my patroness: St Catherine of Alexandria.

Antoine Vadé and his speech: Vadé is the fictional author of *Address to the Welches* of 1764, in which Voltaire mocked French frivolity.

Letter 23

Sirven: in his previous letter (in which he referred to Catherine as the Northern Star), Voltaire had implored her help for a new cause: the Sirvens, a Protestant couple from southern France, had been condemned to death in 1764 on charges of killing their mentally handicapped daughter, Élisabeth, supposedly to prevent her from converting to Catholicism. Although Madame Sirven died in exile, Voltaire helped to obtain the revocation of Monsieur Sirven's sentence in 1771.

45 *memorandum ... from an incontrovertible source*: Catherine is alluding to the attachment to Letter 22. The Archbishop of Rostov had virulently opposed Catherine's secularization of Church lands and was consequently imprisoned by the Synod, which included Metropolitan Dimitry of Novgorod.

'In a great empire ... citizens': this text can be found in the final version of Catherine's *Instruction* (1767). See 'Rules Necessary, and of Great

Importance', *The Instructions to the Commissioners for Composing a New Code of Laws*, ch. 20, ¶¶494–6, in *The Documents of Catherine the Great*, ed. W. F. Reddaway (Cambridge: Cambridge University Press, 1931), 289. Voltaire was eager to publicize this preview in Europe and published it in the *Letter on Panegyrics* (1767).

Letter 24

46 *my vague question*: Catherine had sent to Madame Geoffrin a question for d'Alembert: 'Would an accumulation of fine maxims put into practice have a fine and good effect in general?' (*Œuvres et correspondances inédites de d'Alembert* (Paris: Perrin, 1887), p. 244, our translation).

my Academy: the St Petersburg Academy of Sciences, founded by Peter the Great in 1724.

Letter 25

47 *declaration*: Catherine's *Declaration from Her Majesty the Empress of All the Russias to His Majesty the King and the Republic of Poland* (1767), justifying Russia's armed intervention in Poland in terms of civic order and respect for the rights of religious dissidents.

Letter 26

48 *principles ... established*: in the *Instruction*.

Letter 27

the article 'Religious Order': Catherine is referring to the article by Louis de Jaucourt, 'Ordre religieux', in *Encyclopédie, ou Dictionnaire raisonné des sciences, des arts et des métiers*, ed. Denis Diderot and Jean Le Rond d'Alembert, 17 vols (Paris: Briasson, David, Le Breton, Durand, 1751–72), xi. 600 ; 'your king St Louis' is Louis IX of France (1214–1270, r. 1226–70).

49 *Order of Preachers ... Order of Friars Minor*: the Dominicans and Franciscans, respectively.

spoken like Chimène in Le Cid: in a much mocked line in act 3, scene 3, of Pierre Corneille's *Le Cid* (1637), the heroine, Chimène, says: 'One half my life | Has sent the other to the grave; this strife | Binds me to avenge the half I've lost, you see, | Upon that half which yet remains to me' (Pierre Corneille, *Le Cid: A Translation in Rhymed Couplets*, trans. Vincent J. Cheng (Newark: University of Delaware Press, 1987), 78)

the letter on the blind: Denis Diderot's *Letter on the Blind for the Use of Those who can See* (1749), an essay on vision and cognition. Its boldly materialist perspective was controversial and led to Diderot's imprisonment for a few months soon after its publication.

Letter 28

50 *Tsar Ivan Vasil'evich's council*: presumably Ivan the Terrible's Council of a Hundred Chapters (1551).

manifesto that I signed ... last year: Catherine's summons to the Legislative Commission for the Composition of a New Law Code.

51 *one in French ... sent via Schaffhausen*: Voltaire had asked about the two essays that he had submitted for an anonymous essay contest, initiated by Catherine, on the proper extent of peasants' rights to property; neither essay was successful. Schaffhausen is a canton of northern Switzerland.

mottos: submissions to eighteenth-century essay contests were anonymous, but authors included a motto, usually in Latin, at the top to identify their texts.

Letter 29

Jaucourt and his article 'Russia': Louis de Jaucourt's article 'Russia' in the *Encyclopédie* drew heavily on Voltaire's *History of the Russian Empire under Peter the Great*, but was criticized by many, including Diderot and d'Alembert, for its lack of exact knowledge about Russia.

So, then, my friends, create pleasures!: in his letter to the empress of 16 March 1767, Falconet declared himself an Epicurean, advising his fellow man to 'create pleasures'.

52 *debate on posterity*: see Letter 34.

what you call your 'folly': in his letter of 16 March 1767, Falconet spoke of his 'folly', namely his Epicurean philosophy of letting go of sorrows and focusing on pleasant thoughts.

Greuze's The Paralysed Man: Jean-Baptiste Greuze's *The Paralytic, or Filial Piety* (1763) was discussed by Diderot in his *Salon of 1763*; it was acquired by Catherine the Great with the help of Golitsyn and is now in the Hermitage.

Peter the Great fully clothed: Falconet kept Catherine up to date on the progress of his work on the statue of Peter the Great, and they enjoyed joking about the statue and its horse as though they were alive.

Letter 30

53 *a patched coat is good for nothing*: Mark 2:21: 'No man ... seweth a piece of new cloth on an old garment: else the new piece that filled it up taketh away from the old, and the rent is made worse' (KJV).

Letter 32

55 *The refugees*: the French Huguenots, Protestants forced to flee France after Louis XIV's edict of 1685, which revoked their right to practise their religion.

the scholar ... until I am dead: Voltaire published the *Letter on Panegyrics* under the pseudonym of Irénée Alethès (Greek, 'Peaceful Truth-Speaking'), professor of law in the canton of Uri. Located in central Switzerland, this German-speaking canton was the home of the legendary William Tell.

55 *Bélisaire says ... for the likes of me*: in chapter 9 of *Bélisaire*, which Catherine was then translating, Marmontel's hero insists on the need for sovereigns to listen only to the truth, rather than to flatteries.

Letter 33

56 *ideas*: in French.

This is ... in general: in French.

57 *Old man Kudriavtsev*: see Letter 31.

Letter 34

57 *placed your name at Saint-Roch*: Falconet contributed impressive religious statuary to the Church of Saint-Roch in the rue Saint-Honoré, Paris, in the 1750s. As Catherine prophesies in the following passage, some of it did disappear, destroyed during the French Revolution.

Letter 35

59 *works of Greuze ... his better half*: in a letter to Falconet, Diderot advised Catherine to acquire Greuze's works, but said that the artist himself was 'a bad lot' and his wife 'among the most dangerous creatures in the world'.

Van Loo: Louis-Michel Van Loo (1707–1771), who painted a portrait of Diderot in 1767. The Van Loo family were a successful dynasty of painters in eighteenth-century France.

Letter 37

62 *the Inquisition, whose manual I have read*: probably André Morellet's *Abridgement of the Inquisitors' Manual* (1762), which offered an Enlightenment view of the medieval Inquisition.

63 *'What times, what customs!'*: Catherine later used this famous line by Cicero ('O tempora, o mores') as the title of her first comedy (1772).

Letter 38

Tver: city located 110 miles north-west of Moscow, its own principality in the medieval period; it was completely rebuilt in the neoclassical style, including a royal palace, by order of Catherine.

Simbirsk: now Ul'ianovsk, city on the western bank of the Volga below Kazan. It later became famous as Lenin's birthplace.

Bishop of Tver: Gavriil Petrov-Shaposhnikov (1730–1801), Bishop of Tver, later Metropolitan of Novgorod and St Petersburg, man of letters dedicated to Enlightenment ideals such as the struggle against superstition and cruelty.

64 *I. Volkov*: not I. Volkov, but Dmitry Vasil'evich Volkov (1718–1785), head of the College of Manufacturing, a government department responsible for industrial development.

A. Naryshkin: not Catherine's favourite courtier, Lev Naryshkin, but rather Aleksei Vasil'evich Naryshkin (1742–1800), diplomat, delegate to

Catherine's Legislative Commission, and later a member of the Russian Academy.

S. P. Meshchersky: Prince Semën Borisovich Meshchersky (d. 1778), military officer.

Letter 39

69 *Count Vorontsov*: Count Alexander Vorontsov, on his way home to Russia from his posting as ambassador in The Hague, had stopped in Berlin and met the king.

Count Chernyshev: Count Ivan Chernyshev, on his way to become Russian ambassador in London, also stopped in Berlin to meet Frederick.

the war ... those who envy me: Catherine implies that the Ottoman Empire was merely doing the bidding of France in declaring war on Russia.

Letter 40

71 *the mountain ... a mouse*: one of Catherine's favourite idioms, alluding to 'The Mountain in Labour', an Aesopian fable taken up by La Fontaine.

Letter 41

72 *the man ... in plaster*: Voltaire had sent Catherine a porcelain bust of himself.

overgrown children ... for the sake of talking: a stab at the Catholic Church in France, which staunchly opposed the practice of inoculation.

73 *Scotswoman ... The Princess of Babylon*: all comedies or philosophical tales by Voltaire; Catherine herself makes an appearance in the last work on the list.

It was awaiting the manuscript: that is, the manuscript of the French translation of Catherine's *Instruction*.

'Muhammad, close your eyes': a line from Charles-Simon Favart's comedy *Soliman the Second* (1761), act 2, scene 15, uttered by the head eunuch in the sultan's harem as he takes a sip of wine.

74 *this December 1768*: the day is omitted in the original.

Letter 42

75 *ultramontanist cardinals ... the conclave*: ultramontanists were strong supporters of the pope's authority and prerogatives. The conclave of 1769 elected Giovanni Vincenzo Antonio Ganganelli as Pope Clement XIV.

Mr Huber's paintings ... a gift: Huber painted a series of gently comical scenes (known as the *Voltairiade*) of the Patriarch Voltaire going about his daily activities: riding a horse, greeting guests, chatting with peasants, dictating to his secretary while putting on his trousers.

Welche: Voltaire's ironic term for the French.

The advice ... to the young Gallatin: a prominent family of Geneva, the Gallatins were good friends with Voltaire, who recommended sending a 16-year-old member of the family to Riga to study German, Russian, and law, in order to enter Catherine's service.

Letter 43

76 *he who knows things … acts accordingly*: a hint at the Duc de Choiseul.

   my fine colony … souls: between 1764 and 1772, on Catherine's invitation, many thousands of German settlers founded colonies in the Volga region near Saratov and Samara. Catherine's aim was to increase the population and the agricultural productivity of an area historically populated by nomadic groups such as the Kirghiz and the Kalmyks.

77 *the export … price of wheat rise*: from very early in her reign, Catherine saw the grain trade as a key means of earning revenue for Russia.

   Peter the Great … a monastery: the tradition of caring for the mentally ill in monasteries in fact dated from the Middle Ages in Russia.

   the emperor's envoy: the envoy of the Holy Roman Emperor, Joseph II.

   three horsetails: in the Ottoman Empire, a pasha's rank was indicated by the number of horsetails he could exhibit on his standard. Three horsetails indicated the highest rank.

78 *the supper at Sofia that you suggest*: in his letter of 27 May 1769 (NS), Voltaire suggested that Venice and Austria ought to ally themselves with Catherine against the Ottomans and seek territorial gains for themselves. By way of gallantry, Voltaire joked that after taking Bosnia and Serbia, the Holy Roman Emperor, Joseph II, ought to invite himself to dinner with Catherine at Sofia (now the capital of Bulgaria) or at Philippopolis (now Plovdiv, Bulgaria). Since the Catholic Church in Poland opposed the Russian intervention in the name of religious toleration, and therefore sided with the Ottomans against Russia, Catherine joins Voltaire in enjoying the irony of Catholic support for a Muslim empire.

   what befell the young Gallatin: inoculated for smallpox, the neighbour whom Voltaire had wanted to send to Russia was afflicted with blisters in his eyes, threatening his sight.

   a reform … schools in future: Catherine later asked Diderot and Grimm for such a plan.

79 *the Pruth*: a river that today forms part of the Romanian border.

Letter 44

80 *the epitaph … were used*: in his letter of 2 September 1769 (NS), Voltaire imagined travelling to St Petersburg and suggested that, if he happened to die on the journey, his epitaph should read: 'Here lies the admirer of the august Catherine, who had the honour of dying on his way to pay his profound respects to her.'

Letter 45

81 *A colonel … the Turks*: François-Gabriel Le Fournier, Marquis de Wargemont (1734–*c*.1789), officer of the Légion de Soubise, to whom Voltaire had written on 1 May 1769 (NS), discouraging him from entering Turkish service: 'You are too good a Christian and too gallant to side with

the Infidels against the Ladies' (Voltaire, *Correspondence and Related Documents*, ed. Theodore Besterman, 2nd edn, 51 vols (Geneva, Banbury, and Oxford: Voltaire Foundation, 1968–77), xxxiv. 439–40, D15623). Catherine supported the Corsicans resisting French annexation in 1768–9.

somewhere: that is, in Siberia. From the seventeenth century, the Russian state sent political figures, religious dissenters, and criminals into exile in remote Siberia.

a young man … the Aeneid in verse: Vasily Petrovich Petrov (1736–1799), often referred to as Catherine's 'pocket poet'. She was very proud of his translation of the *Aeneid* (published 1770, 1781–6), which nonetheless was much critiqued and parodied by Russian men of letters for its complex and antiquated style.

Letter 46

82 *Levushka*: diminutive of Levshina, used as a nickname.

Tsarskoe Selo: Catherine's favourite palace, located 15 miles outside St Petersburg. She spent the summers there and greatly improved its gardens and park with the addition of English gardens, monuments to her military victories like the Chesme Column, and buildings in the Chinese style.

83 *Miss Molchanova*: Ekaterina Ivanovna Molchanova (1758–1809), one of Levshina's classmates at the Smolnyi Institute.

the little brown children … the white pelerines: the girls at the Smolnyi Institute wore uniforms that were colour coded according to age; Catherine works her way up from the youngest to the oldest.

Letter 47

Port Mahon: the capital of Minorca in the Mediterranean.

84 *the ignorance of the governor of Rumelia*: in his letter of 2 January 1770 (NS), Voltaire wrote that he had once met a Turkish ambassador who had been governor of Rumelia (the Balkan Peninsula) and who had never heard of Greece or Athens. The ambassador was Mehmed Said Pasha, who had visited Paris in 1742.

Most Christian ambassadors: the King of France styled himself the 'Most Christian King'.

those who … deceive themselves: an allusion to the French foreign minister, the Duc de Choiseul, insinuating that he likes to deceive himself, particularly as regards Russia's power.

Letter 48

85 *the English Civil List*: until its abolition in 2011, the Civil List was an annual grant that funded the expenses of the English monarch.

Monsieur Tronchin: François Tronchin (1704–1798), member of a Genevan banking family, sold to Catherine in 1770 a collection of ninety-five paintings, which entered what is now the Hermitage Museum.

85 *Monsieur Huber ... collection to be complete*: Catherine eventually received nine paintings in the *Voltairiade* series. She seems to have turned down one canvas that was a spoof on the Last Supper, with Voltaire in the role of Christ.

86 *The hospodar*: the ruler of Moldavia and Wallachia (now parts of Romania, Moldova, and Ukraine).

Babadag: Romanian town near the Black Sea.

87 *Henri IV ... Mustafa*: Catherine is depicting her own legacy: she imagines herself in the afterlife alongside the eighteenth century's ideal king, Henri IV, and his famously wise advisor. She plans to be as far as possible from her enemy Mustafa, whom she and Voltaire imagine as the antithesis of the enlightened monarch.

spend carnival ... in their damp city: in chapter 26 of Voltaire's *Candide*, the hero meets six dethroned kings, including Ivan VI of Russia, who are attending carnival at Venice.

Letter 49

88 *Isaccea*: town in Romania, on the right bank of the Danube.

the animal ... between two bales of hay: a philosophical problem usually referred to as that of Buridan's donkey: equidistant from two bales of hay or between hay and water, the donkey never moves because he cannot rationally prefer one over the other.

the bostanjis: the Ottoman imperial guards.

Brother Ganganelli ... Avignon nor Benevento: Pope Clement XIV recovered the territories of Avignon and Benevento for the Holy See.

Brother Rezzonico: Pope Clement XIII (1693–1769, r. 1758–69), born Carlo della Torre Rezzonico, was responsible for banning works such as the *Encyclopédie*.

Letter 50

89 *Monsieur Collin's letter*: Charles Jacques Collin (1707–1775), steward to Madame de Pompadour, was a collector of gemstones and amateur gem engraver. Catherine had sent him a set of medallions to replace the model of Falconet's *Pygmalion* (1763), which the sculptor had promised to Collin, but which Catherine wanted. Collin had proposed to her, via Falconet, the purchase of an engraved gemstone (she was an avid collector herself).

Ingermanlandia: the Russian name for the historical Swedish region of Ingria, where St Petersburg is situated.

Letter 51

90 *I found Petersburg ... adorned with marble*: the allusion is to Suetonius' 'Life of Augustus', in his *Lives of the Caesars* (*c*.121), in which Augustus is said to have claimed: 'I found Rome a city of bricks and left it a city of marble.'

I do not like ... the son of the Prince-Bishop: Peter Friedrich Wilhelm (1754–1823), son of Catherine's uncle Friedrich August of Oldenburg, Prince-

Bishop of Lübeck. Mentally ill from his youth, he never was able to rule his hereditary lands.

leather breeches ... for a woman: Catherine alludes to Queen Caroline Matilda of Denmark, who was known to hunt in men's clothing.

To ... Hamburg: the address is in Catherine's hand.

Letter 53

95 *The vizier*: Ivazzade Halil Pasha (1724–1777).

96 '*George Dandin, you asked for it*': the eponymous protagonist of Molière's comedy *George Dandin, or The Confounded Husband* (1668), a foolish bourgeois who suffers greatly for marrying a capricious noblewoman. His self-castigation at the end of the first act, 'You asked for it, you asked for it, George Dandin, you asked for it,' was one of Catherine's favourite phrases. The line's ironic tone, its questioning of the power of the will, and the play's concern with the nature of true nobility all fit Catherine's tastes and preoccupations.

Peter the Great ... the Persians: Peter the Great fought the Great Northern War (1700–21) against the Swedes, with the Ottomans and Poles also involved in the conflict, followed by a Russo-Persian War (1722–3).

the lion's share in the fable: in La Fontaine's fable 'The Heifer, the She-Goat, and the Ewe, in Partnership with the Lion' (1668), the lion takes all four equal shares of the group's takings.

97 *the Isthmian Games*: in Ancient Greece, the Isthmian Games were a sporting event held every two years on the Isthmus of Corinth, which links the Peloponnese to mainland Greece.

Braila ... Kiliya: cities in present-day Romania and Ukraine, respectively.

Letter 54

98 *Nafplio*: a port town on the Peloponnese.

Chios: a Greek island, separated by a narrow strait from the Anatolian mainland, where Chesme is located.

xebec: a type of sailing ship used in the Mediterranean.

Letter 55

100 *Belgorod ... Bender*: these territories are all now in the region of Odessa.

Letter 56

101 *Mr Glebov ... occupied it*: the Russians took Braila, in present-day Romania, on 10 November 1770.

102 *Poti ... ancient Iberia*: Mithridates VI (135–63 BC) was King of Pontus and a legendary conqueror, who fought against the Romans in the region of present-day Georgia, where Poti and the ancient kingdom of Iberia are located.

The Oracle: by Germain-François Poullain de Saint-Foix (1740).

103 *19 toises*: the length is 114 feet.

Letter 57

103   *this 14/3 March 1771*: unusually the NS date is given first in this dateline.

   your Encyclopedia: *Questions on the Encyclopédie* (1770–72), an alphabetical
   dictionary of approximately 440 articles, which constitutes Voltaire's last
   great compendium of his thinking. While a certain number of the articles
   engage with the articles in Diderot and d'Alembert's *Encyclopédie*, the
   work uses the *Encyclopédie* as a vehicle to organize Voltaire's own philosophical ideas and is not a commentary.

104   *the celebration I gave for Prince Henry*: see Letter 56.

   the horrible things ... in Paris: at the fireworks display celebrating the marriage of the future Louis XVI with Marie Antoinette in May 1770, the
   crush of the crowd killed more than 130 people.

   nothing of what he predicted has come true: Catherine is referring to Jean-
   Jacques Rousseau's prediction that Russia would be conquered by the
   Tatars: see Letter 14.

   Salé: a city in Morocco known for its pirates.

   Knight of St John of Jerusalem: a member of the Sovereign Military
   Hospitaller Order of St John of Jerusalem of Rhodes and of Malta.

105   *Count Orlov's deed ... that of Scipio*: the episode in which the Roman general
   Scipio Africanus refused a generous ransom and returned a female prisoner to
   her fiancé was a popular subject in seventeenth- and eighteenth-century opera
   and painting. In 1771, the Roman artist Pompeo Batoni was painting
   a *Continence of Scipio* to a commission from Catherine; another was later commissioned from Joshua Reynolds for Grigory Potemkin (completed in 1789).

   your clockmakers: starting in early 1770, Voltaire was the protector and
   patron of a group of clockmakers, political refugees from Geneva. He
   helped them to set up shop in Ferney and developed a somewhat chimerical plan of trading with China via Russia.

106   *like the old lady ... tell you an anecdote*: the old lady tells her story in chapters 11 and 12 of *Candide* in order to establish a parallel between her situation and that of Candide's beloved, Cunégonde; Catherine tells Peter the
   Great's story to establish a parallel with herself.

   the letter ... King of Denmark: Voltaire's *Epistle to the King of Denmark* (1771)
   congratulated Christian VII on establishing in September 1770 unlimited
   freedom of the press; this freedom was short-lived and was curtailed by 1773.

Letter 58

107   *this 7/26 March 1771*: the date is incorrect. Catherine probably meant '7
   April/26 March': writing the letter on 26 March OS, she slightly miscalculated the corresponding NS date, which would have been 6 April.

Letter 59

108   *the northern powers ... addressed to them*: in 1771, Voltaire addressed epistles
   to Catherine, Christian VII of Denmark, and Gustav III of Sweden.

109 *Master de Tott's ... my resident minister*: by referring to the Baron de Tott as the 'Sieur Tott', she disparagingly lowers his social status to a mere 'master' or artisan; Catherine frequently uses the title 'master' as a sarcastic label. The Russian resident minister in Constantinople, Aleksei Obreskov, was imprisoned by the Ottomans in October 1768 when he refused to promise that Russia would cease interfering in Poland. He was released in 1771 and reached St Petersburg at the end of August.

St Sophia: Hagia Sophia in Constantinople.

your flock: Voltaire's group of clockmakers, whom he supported in Ferney.

Letter 60

110 *this 22 July / 3 August 1771*: Catherine slightly miscalculated the NS date, which should be 2 August.

Temryuk, Achai, and Achuevo: towns on the Taman peninsula on the Sea of Azov.

explored enough for four: see Letter 118 for the origin of this turn of phrase, much used by Catherine.

111 *My ambassador*: Catherine's representative in Poland, Kaspar von Saldern (1711–1786).

Descartes's vortices: the seventeenth-century French philosopher René Descartes (1596–1650) explained planetary motion through the movement of interlocking vortices of tiny particles.

your questions: the *Questions on the Encyclopédie*, see note to Letter 57.

St Helena: a convert to Christianity and mother of the Emperor Constantine, St Helena was believed to have discovered the True Cross.

one or two more Kaffas: occupied in 1771 by the Russians, Kaffa became part of the officially independent khanate of Crimea after the war. It was renamed Feodosia when it was annexed by Russia along with the rest of Crimea in 1783.

I also had ... a few weeks ago: Catherine was thinking about resuming work on legislation and wanted the relevant materials to hand.

112 *Scottish pretender ... Culloden*: the Stuart pretender Charles Edward Stuart, known as Bonnie Prince Charlie (1720–1788), was defeated at the Battle of Culloden on 16 April 1746 (NS).

Letter 61

113 *Lauterbourg ... French army*: in 1744, as the French, led by Adrien-Maurice de Noailles, were advancing into the Netherlands, Habsburg troops marched in behind them and took Lauterbourg on the very eastern border of France.

When Prince Repnin fell ill: in 1771, the disapproval of his superior, Rumiantsev, pushed Repnin to claim illness and leave the army to take the waters in Germany.

113 *Lieutenant-General Essen*: Christoph Friedrich von Essen (1717–1771).

your navy … Paris to Saint-Cloud: Voltaire and Catherine are alluding to Louis-Balthazar Néel's mock travel narrative, *A Journey from Paris to Saint-Cloud by Sea and a Return from Saint-Cloud to Paris by Land* (1748). Since Saint-Cloud is located on the outskirts of Paris, the journey is comically short.

Letter 62

114 *Marshal Saltykov*: the then governor of Moscow, Petr Saltykov.

115 *a Cyrus … an admiral*: a list of Enlightenment heroes: Cyrus the Great (*c.*580–*c.*530 BC), founder of the Persian Achaemenid Empire; Solon (*c.*630–*c.*560 BC), Athenian legislator; Maximilien de Béthune, Duc de Sully (1559–1641), advisor to Henri IV of France; Jean-Baptiste Colbert (1619–1683), French finance minister under Louis XIV; Étienne-François, Duc de Choiseul, who had been France's foreign minister and minister of war and of the navy; and George Anson (1697–1762), who circumnavigated the globe and became head of the British navy during the Seven Years War.

Letter 63

116 *Someone*: the Duc de Choiseul.

Chalcis, Volos, Kavala, Makria Miti, Lokroi: these are all locations on the Greek coast or islands; the last two (modern) names are conjectural— Catherine writes 'Magria' and 'Lurci'.

Letter 64

117 *this 30 January/1 February 1772*: Catherine omitted a 'o': the NS date should be 10 February.

assassination attempt … confederates: the Bar Confederates made a failed attempt to kidnap and murder Stanislas Poniatowski in November 1771. An Italianate surname based on the French word for 'dagger', Poignardini appears repeatedly in Voltaire's writings to designate criminal Jesuits.

118 *author … made an academician*: Pierre-Laurent Buirette, pen name Dormont de Belloy (1727–1775), author of *The Siege of Calais* (1765), was elected to the Académie française in 1771.

Letter 65

119 *Darta's ode … sick man*: The 'Ode to the Confederates of Poland, by Monsieur Darta of Courland', which Voltaire sent to Catherine with his letter of 12 February 1772 (NS), is not generally considered to be Voltaire's work, though Catherine assumes it to be so.

120 *Tronchin's actions … are impeccable*: Catherine purchased ninety-five paintings from the Genevan François Tronchin in 1770 (see Letter 48).

Letter 66

Sumarokov … have heard: Prince Fedor Kozlovsky, the messenger who carried Letter 41, also brought the Patriarch of Ferney a letter from Alexander Sumarokov (see Biographical Register).

121 *St Cyr*: the Maison royale de Saint-Louis, at St Cyr to the west of Paris, was a boarding school for girls opened by Louis XIV's second wife, Madame de Maintenon, in 1686; it served as a model for educational institutions for girls across Europe.

Blaise: possibly from Michel-Jean Sedaine's *Blaise the Cobbler* (1759).

Lady Croupillac: from Voltaire's *Prodigal Son* (1736).

Lawyer Patelin: from David Augustin de Brueys and Jean de Palaprat's *Lawyer Patelin* (1706).

Jasmin: also from Voltaire's *Prodigal Son* (1736).

122 *bad farce … Italian comedy*: i.e. with beatings.

unhappy news from Denmark: in January 1772, Johann Friedrich Struensee and Queen Caroline Matilda were arrested in Denmark. Struensee was a court physician and enlightened reformer, who had essentially taken over the Danish government, and the queen had become his lover. Struensee was executed on 28 April (NS). Catherine was right: Christian VII was mentally ill and was soon declared unfit to rule.

Letter 67

behead … people: Struensee and his collaborator Enevold Brandt (1738–1772) (see Letter 66).

123 *'Whatever … it?'*: in German, a favourite phrase of Catherine's.

the one … his plan: a reference to Antoine de Fériol de Pont-de-Veyle's *The Sleepwalker* (1739), in which the baron is exceptionally proud of his unrealistic plan for a garden.

Letter 68

the Baroness … all possible castles: Voltaire's *Candide*, chapter 1.

124 *carriages … the god Apis*: i.e. by oxen; Apis was an Egyptian god in the shape of a bull.

Mount Haemus: the Balkan Mountains.

Your imprisoned coxcombs: Catherine alludes to the French officers taken prisoner by the Russians when fighting in Poland alongside the Confederates (see Letters 70 and 71).

Letter 69

125 *Baron Pellenberg*: perhaps Hyacinthe-Philippe-Melchior de Villegas, Baron de Pellenberg, son of Jean-François de Villegas, Baron de Hovorst and Pellenberg. He had previously served in the Spanish Walloon Guards and carried to Catherine a recommendation letter from Voltaire, dated 17 August 1772 (NS).

In … his Travels, Mr Pallas: Peter Simon Pallas, *Reise durch verschiedene Provinzen des russischen Reichs*, 3 vols (St Petersburg: Kayserliche Academie der Wissenschaften, 1771–6), ii. 324.

125 *Reasoned and Universal Dictionary ... 2, page 179*: the *Dictionnaire raisonné et universel des animaux, ou Le règne animal*, 4 vols (Paris: C.-J.-B. Bauche, 1759) is attributed not to Brisson, but to François-Alexandre Aubert de La Chesnaye Des Bois. An article about the flamingo can be found on the page Catherine indicates.

Ornithology, volume 6, page 532: Catherine's citation from Mathurin-Jacques Brisson, *Ornithologie, ou Méthode contenant la division des oiseaux en ordres, sections, genres, espèces & leurs variétés*, 6 vols (Paris: C.-J.-B. Bauche, 1760), is correct.

Letter 70

126 *Reis Effendi*: chief secretary of state for foreign affairs in the Ottoman Empire.

Bolgar ... for his son: the settlement of Bolgar, now in Tatarstan, predates Tamerlane by some six centuries. It is still a pilgrimage site for Tatar Muslims today.

a shorter route to come here: Catherine is alluding to Voltaire's hypothetical journey to St Petersburg, which he mentioned regularly in his letters, but which he had no intention of undertaking, just as Catherine had no expectation of receiving him.

127 *the Englishman Jenkins ... 169 years old*: Henry Jenkins, from Yorkshire, supposedly lived from 1501 until 1670.

two Russian comedies: by Catherine herself.

Letter 71

128 *add the names ... on your tombstone*: a reference to the epitaph that d'Alembert proposes for himself at the end of his letter of 31 December 1772 (NS): 'He obtained the freedom of the French prisoners from the immortal Catherine in the name of philosophy and humanity.'

Letter 72

your anger ... Greek and Roman Churches: in his letter of 1 December 1772 (NS), Voltaire expressed annoyance that the two reigning empresses in Europe, Catherine and Maria Theresa, had not made an alliance to take Constantinople and free the women in the sultan's harem.

Aubry: Charles-Louis Aubry (1746–1817), a surveyor whom Voltaire recommended to Catherine on 1 December 1772 (NS).

129 *works of Algarotti ... Greece*: Francesco Algarotti calls the Greeks 'the fathers of the arts and sciences, which we have received from them', in his *Essay on the Question of Why Great Geniuses Appear Together and Flourish at the Same Time*, in *Œuvres du comte Algarotti, traduit de l'italien*, 6 vols (Berlin: G. J. Decker, 1772), iii. 249. It was a very typical eighteenth-century commonplace.

130 *I await ... you promise me*: an edition of Voltaire's tragedy *Les Lois de Minos*, promised in his letter of 13 February 1773 (NS).

Letter 73

spasibo: Russian, 'Thank you'.

Letter 74

131 *the king ... Queen Mother*: the king was Frederick the Great, and the Swedish Queen Mother was Frederick's sister, Louisa Ulrika.

my uncle ... Lübeck: Friedrich August of Schleswig-Holstein-Gottorf, father of Hedwig, the chosen bride.

132 *her mother*: Karolina Henrietta of Hesse-Darmstadt, who was visiting St Petersburg for the marriage of her daughter Wilhelmina when this letter was written.

Letter 75

books of classical costumes ... Cochin: Charles-Nicolas Cochin (1715–1790), an engraver and designer, and famous taste-maker in France, who worked for Louis XV; he had proposed that Catherine subscribe to Michel-François d'André-Bardon's *The Costume of the Ancient Peoples* (1772–4), which she did.

Letter 76

133 *Henri IV ... Henriade*: with his *Henriade* (1728), Voltaire sought to provide a French national epic and a portrayal of the perfect sovereign in Henry IV, who ended civic strife and opposes religious fanaticism. Catherine greatly admired the work, and in her later years repeatedly referred to it as embodying the monarchical ideal to be upheld against the threat posed by the French Revolution.

134 *the Welches*: Voltaire's satirical name for the French.

Letter 78

136 *the Convent*: the Smolnyi Institute for Noble Girls, where amateur theatricals were regularly performed as part of the curriculum (see Letters 64 and 66).

The person you call the apothecary: probably Ivan Betskoy, an authority, among other things, on education. He was close to the Orlov brothers and was therefore viewed with suspicion by Potemkin.

Letter 80

138 *the Diamond Chamber*: the room in the Winter Palace where royal treasures were stored.

Letter 83

141 *O, Mr Potemkin ... best in Europe?*: in French.

Letter 84

142 *a letter ... corrections as necessary*: her rescript authorized Orlov to make expenditures from the treasury of the elite Preobrazhensky Regiment; she

wanted to use his fleet in the Mediterranean to pressure the Ottoman
Empire into concluding a peace treaty on favourable terms for Russia.

142 *the promotion … the Mining College*: the wealthy Nikita Demidov (1724–
1789) and his son Evdokim (d. 1782) were descended from entrepreneurs
promoted by Peter the Great; Catherine awarded them civil ranks in
a ministry founded by the same emperor in 1719, the Mining College.

Bilstein: a functionary in the Chamber of Commerce.

Bibikov … Reinsdorp: all these figures had been rewarded with promotions
by Catherine on 21 April as part of her birthday honours.

Ivan Chernyshev … love at a distance: Ivan Chernyshev was away from the
capital in 1774, so the conversation to which Catherine alludes may date to
1770.

Letter 85

143 *Adieu, my jewel … most delightful*: in French.

Letter 86

The landgravine … knew how to die!: Karolina Henrietta died almost immediately upon her return home from Russia, on 30 March 1774 (NS).

my 46th birthday: Catherine in fact turned 45 on 21 April/2 May 1774.

144 *Mr Thomas*: Sir Thomas Anderson, Catherine's greyhound, a gift from
the English doctor Thomas Dimsdale.

no eccentric will be spared: in the correspondence with Grimm, Catherine
labels as 'eccentrics' members of her social and cultural circles in whom
she appreciates creative and entertaining minds; they include Potemkin,
Voltaire, Huber, and, here, Diderot.

Letter 89

146 *confrontatie*: comparison.

Letter 90

147 *the return and non-return*: in her letter of 14 July 1774, Catherine insisted
that Grimm was free to return to Russia or not, and to stay as long as he
wanted if he did.

what are you going to do … Duc d'Orléans: Louis-Philippe I, duc d'Orléans
(1725–1785), whose service Grimm had entered in 1755, was at the time
not on good terms with the newly acceded Louis XVI.

148 *I have not made a single knot*: see Letter 16.

Mr Heretic … to take the waters: Catherine implies that Grimm, as a less-
than-devout Christian, will go to Hell, where he will discover whether or
not the devils are entertaining. She scolds him for exerting himself so
much and writing such a long letter when ill, suggesting that he will die
and thus go to Hell sooner.

Asclepiuses: in Greek mythology, Asclepius was the god of medicine; he
was the son of Apollo and of a mortal woman, Coronis.

Letter 92

149 *Penza*: city to the south-east of Moscow, which Panin had recently taken back from the rebels.

in the provinces and uezds: an *uezd* was a district or a subdivision of a province.

the treachery of the Bashkirs ... the raids of the Kirghiz: the Bashkirs and the Kirghiz are two Turkic peoples living in the regions of the Urals and Central Asia, from among whom Pugachev had recruited many supporters. Amid the general unrest, the Kirghiz had inflicted several destructive raids on German settlers in the region.

Bukhara: Persian-speaking city in Uzbekistan, located on the Silk Road.

the Irgiz River: a tributary of the Volga.

Schismatics: the Old Believers, who had split from the Russian Orthodox Church after the reforms of Patriarch Nikon in the mid-seventeenth century.

Letter 95

152 *Leo of Catania*: St Leo of Catania was an eighth-century Italian saint; this was a nickname for the courtier Lev Naryshkin, who had helped to host an operatic performance and gala that evening, after which Potemkin fell ill.

sniff a bit of snuff: Catherine enjoyed taking snuff recreationally and believed in its therapeutic power.

Adieu, my love, my heart: in French in the original.

Letter 96

153 *Reply to no. 9*: when writing to Catherine, Grimm followed the frequent eighteenth-century practice of numbering his letters to help both correspondents keep track of potential losses or delays in transmission.

Our Saviour himself ... thereabouts: Mark 2:21 and Matthew 9:16 (see Letter 30).

he agreed to delay his journey ... to come back: Henry returned to Russia for a second visit in April 1776 and departed before Grimm arrived. Grimm reached St Petersburg in September 1776 and stayed until July 1777.

154 *your young monarch*: Louis XVI of France.

the other three ists: it is not clear what other '-ists' Catherine and Grimm were discussing, besides *Encyclopédistes* and economists (Physiocrats).

tests: Catherine uses the German word 'Prüfungen'; the term originally refers to Friedrich Wagner's proofs of religious truths, but Catherine turns it to her own purposes in the correspondence with Grimm.

the young man: Prince Ludwig of Hesse-Darmstadt.

His sister: the Grand Duchess Natalia Alekseevna.

cannot yet speak ... the language: by contrast with Catherine herself, who was proud of having studied hard to learn Russian, telling in her memoirs how she got up in the middle of the night and worked barefoot in her nightgown until she fell ill.

154 *Prince Dolgorukov's arrival on my feast day*: perhaps an allusion to the arrival on 14 November 1773 of Major-General Vasily Dolgorukov, bearing news of Russian victories beyond the Danube; alternatively, Catherine alludes to Vladimir Sergeevich Dolgorukov.

155 *the Marquis Felino … I can buy his paintings*: Catherine did not buy Felino's paintings, and at his death they were sold at auction in Paris.

the author … the article on Russia: the *Philosophical and Political History of the Establishments and Commerce of the Europeans in the Two Indies*, by Guillaume-Thomas Raynal and his collaborators, first published in 1770, was a successful work that included some early analyses of colonialism. From the edition of 1774 onwards, it included an extended section on Russia, mostly written by Diderot.

Have … Mr Baron: in German. Grimm was ennobled by Joseph II in 1772, but was not made a baron until 1777. Catherine is playing with the confusing title: on the one hand, the German word 'Freiherr' means merely 'free nobleman' in the Holy Roman Empire, but on the other hand it translates into English only as 'Baron'. She was delighted to see him assume the title in both its meanings in 1777.

Letter 98

162 *My consent to the coadjutor's marriage*: presumably Catherine's permission for a marriage between her cousin Peter Friedrich Wilhelm of Schleswig-Holstein-Gottorf (1754–1823) and Grand Duchess Natalia Alekseevna's sister, Charlotte of Hesse-Darmstadt (1755–1785). The marriage did not take place, as Peter Friedrich Wilhelm was soon recognized as mentally ill. His hereditary domain, the Prince-Bishopric of Lübeck, was therefore administered from 1777 by Catherine's nephew and ward, Peter Friedrich Ludwig of Schleswig-Holstein-Gottorf.

the Faculty … the Comte d'Artois has belied them: the 'Faculty' is the Faculty of Medicine in Paris; although Catherine's allusion is obscure, it continues her usual mockery of doctors, which she borrowed from literary sources like Molière and *Tristram Shandy*. The wife of the Comte d'Artois, Maria Theresa of Savoy (1756–1805), gave birth in August 1775 to a son, the first Bourbon heir of the next generation and therefore a great relief to the French ruling family.

the treaty between the House of Austria … and the enemy of Christendom: Catherine alludes to a secret treaty of alliance between Austria and the Ottoman Empire, intended to prevent Russia from making conquests during the Russo-Turkish War. The treaty had been concluded in June / July 1771, and Catherine had found out about it within a few months.

Letter 99

163 *the Greek calendar … summer or spring in the winter months*: the Julian calendar (used in Russia until 1918) falls behind by one day every 128 years, whereas the Gregorian calendar (to which most of Europe switched by the mid-eighteenth century) corrects for this error.

the vice-chancellor's brother: Mikhail Mikhailovich Golitsyn (1731–1804), brother of Vice-Chancellor Alexander Mikhailovich Golitsyn (1723–1807; not to be confused with Field Marshal Alexander Mikhailovich Golitsyn).

Letter 100

164 *Your Olympie*: Anne-Germaine Girardot de Vermenoux (1739–1783), a well-to-do widow to whom Jacob Heinrich Meister (1744–1826), Grimm's collaborator and successor as editor of the manuscript periodical, *Literary Correspondence*, was exceptionally devoted. Catherine had read Meister's description of her in the *Literary Correspondence*.

I greatly esteem ... reached the printers: Catherine refuses to allow Grimm to give his friend the Marquis de Castries a copy of her answers to a series of detailed questions about the Russian government and economy that Diderot presented to her during his stay in Russia. She advises Diderot to put the questions and answers in his library, which she had purchased in 1765 and which she received after his death.

the book ... from Emilie's mother: Vladimir Sergeevich Dolgorukov forwarded a copy of Louise d'Épinay's book to Catherine from Germany. D'Épinay was, in fact, the grandmother of Emilie de Bueil (née de Belsunce), later one of Catherine's protégées.

165 *You see them as Diderot sees paintings ... saw all in God*: that is, they see the presence of something marvellous that is not there. Nicolas Malebranche (1638–1715) promoted a theory of causation according to which God is the source of all knowledge and is present and active in every being.

Letter 101

in Holy Week: in German.

166 *the point regarding Jules and his calendar*: Catherine and Grimm had a running joke about the difference between the Julian and the Gregorian calendars; see Letter 99.

167 *I do not have a high opinion of Van Loo's drawing*: the Van Loo family were a successful dynasty of painters in eighteenth-century France. The drawing in question was probably by its most famous member, Carle (1705–1765).

I have received from Ferney ... hung out to dry: Voltaire's *Dialogue of Pegasus and the Old Man* and its accompanying *Notes of Monsieur de Morza* (1774) were republished in 1775 in a collection containing his tragedy *Don Pedro, King of Castile* (1761) and a few other texts. The Jesuit Claude-Adrien Nonnotte (1711–1793) and the journalist Élie Catherine Fréron (1718–1776) were two of Voltaire's adversaries whom he most vociferously attacked in writings like the *Dialogue* and *Notes*.

Letter 103

168 *no one ... with the date*: Catherine's comment is intentionally ironic, since epistolary etiquette required that letters be dated either at the beginning or at the end.

168 *I have not lost hope … economic nonsense*: François Quesnay (1694–1774), doctor to Madame de Pompadour, was the leader of Physiocracy—an abstract, agriculture-based approach to economics.

livres tournois: the *livre tournois* was a unit of account used in French finance.

169 *Prince Orlov … Prince Tiufiakin*: Grigory Orlov, Lev Naryshkin, and Ivan Petrovich Tiufiakin (1740–1804). The Naryshkins were a large, old aristocratic family, so it is hard to identify which other members of the family were in possession of Tom Anderson's descendants.

170 *Emilie's Conversations … translated into Russian*: *Emilie's Conversations* (1774) by Grimm's companion, Louise d'Épinay, were first published in Russian translation in 1784.

the young person's state of health: Catherine alludes to the health of Grand Duchess Natalia Alekseevna.

I shall take ad notam: I shall take note of.

the dowager duchess … they say at Wetzlar: the dowager duchess of Saxony-Weimar was Anna Amalia (1739–1807), an outstanding patron of the arts, whose two sons were being looked after in Paris by Grimm. Wetzlar, in Hesse, was the seat of the Holy Roman Empire's Imperial Supreme Court, and Catherine and Grimm greatly enjoyed mocking the pomposity of its legal jargon.

Vicomte Laval-Montmorency was here: Catherine received Mathieu Paul Louis, Vicomte de Laval-Montmorency (1748–1809), at her court in Moscow on 20 April 1775. Voltaire praises the Montmorency family in his *Henriade* (1728), which Catherine greatly admired; he highlights, in particular, François-Henri de Montmorency (1628–1695), known as Luxembourg, a Marshal of France and a key general under Louis XIV.

Letter 104

171 *Prince Kantemir*: Sergei Dmitrievich Kantemir (1706–1780). His brother Antiokh Dmitrievich Kantemir (1708–1744) was a famous poet and ambassador to England and France.

It came to me from my brother: a third brother, Matvei Dmitrievich Kantemir (1703–1771).

172 *After the natural history of birds of prey, you should enlist Huber*: Jean Huber published in 1784 his *Observations on the Flight of Birds of Prey*.

the forty-seven ineptitudes … were seven years in the making: as she often did, Catherine self-deprecatingly refers to her legislative efforts as 'trifles'. Her manifesto *On the Graces Granted by Her Majesty to the Various Estates, on the Occasion of the Conclusion of the Peace Treaty with the Ottoman Porte* of 17 March 1775, consisted of forty-seven points.

We also have … when we reread them: her Statute for the Administration of the Provinces of the Russian Empire.

173 *scripile*: a comic distortion of the French word for 'scruple', which Catherine has probably drawn from popular theatricals.

a conversation ... the result would be the same: Diderot's *A Philosopher's Conversation with the Wife of Marshal **** appeared in the *Literary Correspondence* in April–May 1775, where Catherine would have read it. In the end neither the philosopher nor the marshal's wife changes opinion, and the atheistic philosopher confesses himself willing to pretend to be a believer in order to maintain order in society. Catherine frequently asserts that no one ever changes opinions by arguing, and she is also perhaps admitting here that she is willing to behave decorously with the French ambassador whether or not his policy is hostile to her.

Letter 106

174 *the holy oil ... with all due respect to it*: see Letter 101.

Platon ... neither could I, just like the others: the sermon that Catherine describes was given by Platon Levshin on 10 July 1775 in the Assumption Cathedral in the Kremlin.

ukases: 'ukase' (or 'ukaz'), meaning a royal edict, has entered the English language from Russian.

175 *like a cow by a new gate ... Table Talk*: 'like a cow at a new gate' is in German in the original. Martin Luther's *Table Talk* is a collection of his sayings compiled and published by his students in 1566.

ma: Italian, 'but', a form of which Catherine was very fond.

176 *The young man*: Prince Ludwig of Hesse-Darmstadt.

Letter 107

leader of the coach drivers: these words are in French.

Letter 108

177 *Annette and Lubin ... comic opera in the world*: in *Annette and Lubin* (1762), a comic opera by Marie-Justine-Benoîte Favart and Jean-Baptiste Lourdet de Santerre, with music by Adolphe Blaise, the shepherd Lubin is busy building a house for himself and his beloved shepherdess Annette.

178 *Prince Orlov's appearance in Paris*: Grigory Orlov arrived in Paris on 14 July 1775 (NS).

his stay will last ... Madame Clotilde: Louis XVI's sister, Marie Clotilde Adélaïde Xavière (1759–1802), married the future king Charles Emmanuel IV of Sardinia (1751–1819) by proxy at Versailles on 21 August 1775 (NS).

the famous inkstand: the Chesme Inkstand.

Letter 109

179 *one of your protégés*: possibly Jean-Bernard Gauthier de Murnan (1748–1796), who left the French army after a duel. Voltaire recommended him to Catherine in October 1774; he served briefly in Russia and later in the American and French Revolutionary Wars.

the Beylerbey of Rumelia: a beylerbey was a provincial governor in the Ottoman Empire; Rumelia was the name for the Balkans when under

Ottoman control. The Beylerbey of Rumelia, Abdülkerim Pasha, travelled to Russia in 1775 as a special envoy from the Ottoman Empire.

179 *Baron Pellenberg*: see Letter 69.

Letter 111

180 *To hear you speak ... would it?*: the letter, entirely French up to this point, switches hereafter to Russian.

181 *If you wish ... never be angry*: in French.

Letter 114

184 *I was not born ... acquainted with it*: in French.

Letter 116

185 *But since the dead ... the living*: Matthew 8:22 and Luke 9:60.

186 *basta*: Italian, 'enough'; another of Catherine's favoured expressions.

on 24 July NS ... destined for you: the planned date of Paul's engagement.

your big, foolish, lanky fellow ... good news: Catherine alludes to Prince Ludwig of Hesse-Darmstadt, who had followed his sister Natalia Alekseevna to Russia in hopes of making a career. Volprecht Hermann Friedrich von Riedesel was a trusted advisor to the prince's father.

Monsieur Laurent ... when he was young: Catherine's writing master, who had also taught her new daughter-in-law Sophia of Württemburg (see Letter 106).

187 *tests*: this word is in German.

Letter 118

188 *God Knows Where*: Catherine repeatedly used 'God Knows Where' in addresses, sending a letter thus addressed to Gustav III in 1780.

189 *'God bless you', ... 'Go to bed'*: in Beaumarchais's *The Barber of Seville* (act 3, scene 5), Figaro's common-sense answers to someone who is sneezing and someone who is yawning.

the political tinkers: people who chatter about politics without understanding it; the expression comes from the Danish–Norwegian playwright Ludvig Holberg's *The Political Tinker* of 1722.

Paisiello's opera ... September: Paisiello's opera *Lucinda e Armidoro* was premiered in October 1777.

Prince Belosel'sky ... King of Sweden: Andrei Belosel'sky was in Stockholm at the same time as Grimm in the summer of 1777.

Svartsjö: residence of Gustav's mother, Louisa Ulrika.

the so-called reigning queen: Gustav's wife, Sophia Magdalena, was less influential than his mother, Louisa Ulrika.

the one in Portugal: Queen Maria I of Portugal.

190 *enough intelligence ... Piron said*: since the French poet and dramatist Alexis Piron (1689–1773) never obtained a seat at the Académie française, he

famously asserted that, in the Académie, 'There are forty of them, but they have wit enough for four.' Catherine's taste for irony is clear in her use of the phrase here, although in some cases it might have suited her well to see her fellow monarchs so lacking in intelligence.

tests: in German, referring to the Lutheran theological proofs that Catherine had to learn from her teacher Friedrich Wagner.

Letter 120

191 *The Lord of Drottningholm*: one of Gustav's pseudonyms, jokingly pretending that he is nothing more than the lord of his summer residence, which was acquired by the Swedish state from Gustav's mother, Louisa Ulrika, in 1777.

my late governess: Élisabeth Cardel.

192 *'circumstances and the conjunctures'*: that is, the international diplomatic situation.

'it will come': Gustav used this phrase to insinuate that one day he would attain Catherine's glorious public stature.

Letter 121

Mr Alexander ... in The Ingénu: in a satirical passage in chapter 9 of Voltaire's *L'ingénu* (1767), the title character travels to Versailles to seek justice from the king, but finds all doors closed to him: unable to see the king, he is sent to the minister Louvois; refused access to Louvois, he is referred to Louvois's assistant Mr Alexander; not allowed to enter Mr Alexander's office, he goes on to Mr Alexander's assistant, who finally sees him.

But ... the young man?: in German.

193 *I take comfort in Bayle ... the thing*: during her years as grand duchess, Catherine read the whole of Pierre Bayle's *Historical and Critical Dictionary* (1697), which was one of Laurence Sterne's sources for mock erudition in *Tristram Shandy*, a novel that Catherine greatly enjoyed and admired. In vol. i, ch. 19, Tristram explains the view of his father, Walter Shandy, that 'there was a strange kind of magic bias, which good or bad names, as he called them, irresistibly impressed upon our characters and conduct'. In his short essay, 'Great Superstition of the Pagans Regarding Names' (1681), Bayle asserted that names have no impact on things.

matadors: a 'matador' is a trump card in certain card games, such as the French *hombre* and the more recent German game *Skat*.

the body mass ... the mind off course: Catherine uses the vocabulary of physics and chemistry to describe her hopes for her grandson: she does not want the passions of the body (the 'mass' of flesh and blood) to impede the progress of the mind (the 'volatile spirits', which were substances that could be evaporated by fire).

the dowager Queen of Sweden: Louisa Ulrika.

193 *the eulogy of Madame Geoffrin*: Antoine Léonard Thomas's *In Memory of Madame Geoffrin*, which Grimm sent to Catherine in November 1777.

God knows that ... all wound up: in German.

Letter 122

194 *macao*: card game popular in the eighteenth century and resembling black-jack.

The pea soups: Catherine's nickname for diplomats.

played a nine: the winning card value in macao.

195 *a large 'A'*: standing for 'Alexander', the name of Catherine's 2-month-old grandson.

the Breteuil dessert service: in 1777, Catherine acquired a magnificent dessert service, encrusted with precious stones and antique cameos, from Jacques-Laure Le Tonnelier de Breteuil (1723–1785), a member of the Order of Malta and a protector of the arts.

Letter 123

196 *Baron*: Grimm was given the title of Baron of the Holy Roman Empire on 29 October 1777 (NS).

They do not entertain me ... they would like to go: 'for it is new' is to be taken ironically: these two sentences sum up the eighteenth century's clichés about letter-writing as spontaneous conversation at a distance.

197 *the hero ... the same name*: St Alexander Nevsky or Alexander the Great; see Letter 121.

my good brother ... penitence: in this case, the 'good brother' whom Catherine avoids naming is George III. During the American Revolutionary War, both sides repeatedly decreed 'days of fasting, humiliation, and prayer'.

a good citizen: Catherine's usual epithet for George III.

As for Franklin ... this way: in February 1778, the American revolutionary Benjamin Franklin concluded an alliance between France and the American colonies.

the 80-year-old elder: Voltaire.

This is a proof ... on the road: in German.

the K. of S.: Gustav III.

make it clear ... only from afar: the French 'Cat(e)au', the equivalent of Kate, was Voltaire's nickname for Catherine in many letters to people other than the empress, including d'Alembert.

the Queen Emp. ... the K. of Prussia: Maria Theresa of Austria and Frederick II of Prussia.

198 *Dona Maria*: Queen Maria I of Portugal, known in Portugal as Maria the Pious.

198 *the national costume ... black and bright red*: Catherine is mocking Gustav III's introduction in 1778 of a national costume, made of local materials and intended to be worn by the nobility and middle class to reduce the excesses of luxury.

that sort of prettiness ... people dispute: see Letter 29.

But, my God, ... doings and dealings?: in German.

My Lord Chatham is a brawler: William Pitt the Elder, 1st Earl of Chatham, who in 1777 argued forcefully for reconciliation with the American colonies.

my marabouts ... true believers: the Ottomans.

shufflers: we translate as 'shuffler' Catherine's German word, 'Paßgänger' ('ambler'), which she uses to describe slow, incompetent government ministers.

Lord Charles Theodore: the Elector Palatine, Charles Theodore (1724–1799), became the Elector of Bavaria on 30 December 1777 (NS), and on 3 January 1778 (NS) he recognized Austria's claims to Lower Bavaria and the Upper Palatinate, leading to the War of the Bavarian Succession (1778–9).

'My good man ... when we are here': the refrain of a French children's song ran 'My good man, my good man, do you know how to play?'

199 *But if only you knew ... a good nose*: this paragraph, in German, relates to Catherine's favoured habit of summing up her accomplishments as empress: at this time, she was intending to produce a manifesto on the subject, reviewing the sixteen years of her reign so far.

Letter 124

Osinovyia roshchi or Eschenbaum: meaning 'aspen grove'.

200 *the article 'Schomberg' ... how far it can go*: the entry in question from Pierre Bayle's *Historical and Critical Dictionary* (1697), 'Schomberg (Charles de)', narrates how Marie de Hautefort (1616–1691), the second wife of Duc Charles de Schomberg (1601–1656), rejected the advances of Louis XIII himself; she was not only exiled from court, but was even accused in print of having later ceded to the attentions of a former tailor.

if I did not provide ... if the opportunity arises: Frederick II was alarmed at the possibility that his sister, Louisa Ulrika, might be exiled for her role in the affair concerning the future Gustav IV's legitimacy. Catherine does not mention Louisa Ulrika in her letters to Frederick from this period.

Count Hamilton: Count Adolf Ludvig Hamilton (1747–1802), chamberlain to Gustav's wife, Sophia Magdalena, was sent to Russia in February 1778, bearing Gustav's congratulations on the birth of Catherine's grandson. He had only recently returned to Sweden at this time. He later joined the group of nobles who opposed Gustav's absolute power.

your new outfit ... easy on the eyes: Catherine, in fact, repeatedly mocked the national costume that Gustav had just introduced; see Letter 123.

200 *I am invariably*: in the interests of informality, Catherine omits the signature that would normally complete this concluding formula.

Letter 125

201 *a pr. of R.*: a Princess of Russia.

202 *Miss Catherine … more quirks than her sisters*: Catherine's granddaughter Ekaterina (Catherine) was not born until 1788, but she indeed turned out to be the most intellectual, independent-minded, and politically active of Paul's six daughters. She married Duke George of Oldenburg (1784–1812) and then William I of Württemberg (1781–1864), but died prematurely in 1819.

by naming them all … ten of them: a mocking allusion to Maria Theresa of Austria, whose eleven daughters' names all began with 'Maria'.

But, my God, … heads out there: in German.

the Raphael loggias … Blackstone: on the Raphael loggias and William Blackstone's *Commentaries on the Laws of England*, see the introduction to Part IV; on Bibiena, see the Biographical Register.

no more wit than a pin: in French, not to be worth 'a pin' is to be worthless.

203 *the confederated priest's lies … to his king*: the Polish Abbé Wiazewicz had revealed to the invading Russians a hidden stash of money belonging to the Confederate leader Michal Kazimierz Oginski (c.1730–1800). Offered refuge in Russia in 1772, Wiazewicz fled instead to France, where he won the patronage of major cultural figures like Stéphanie de Genlis (1746–1830) and Voltaire.

Monsieur Du Busquet … any poems: the cartoons by Giulio Romano were from the art collection of a certain Buscher. Marie-Gabriel-Florent-Auguste de Choiseul-Gouffier's *Picturesque Voyage through Greece* was a much celebrated and richly illustrated piece of travel writing; it was published in parts beginning in 1778. The poem in question was Jean-Antoine Roucher's *The Months* (1779).

Letter 126

204 *get me from the Cramers … from his pen*: Gabriel (1723–1793) and Philibert (1727–1779) Cramer were Voltaire's publishers in Geneva.

the Moroccan ambassador … merchant ships: Muhammad ben Abdelmalek had travelled on a mission from Morocco to Tuscany in 1777 to seek the liberation of north African slaves held there; the Russians provided two ships for him to carry about a hundred people home.

I am like Basile … when I apply them: in Beaumarchais's *The Barber of Seville* (1775), Basile is a foolish music teacher who says that he has 'arranged several little proverbs, with variations' (act 4, scene 1).

The pig's breakfast: we translate as 'pig's breakfast' Catherine's jokey term for a diplomatic mess: 'purée' or 'soupe aux pois' ('mushy peas' or 'pea soup').

Mademoiselle Bertin's judgment … immortality: Marie-Jeanne 'Rose' Bertin (1747–1813) was a fashionable Parisian dressmaker, who counted Marie Antoinette among her clients.

Her brother ... Monsieur Bertin: a cook named Jean Bertin served Potemkin and the Russian court, but he was not Rose Bertin's brother.

I am at present reading what Baron Dalberg has to say: Catherine is probably reading Baron Karl Theodor von Dalberg's *Observations on the Universe* (1777).

the notorious inkstand has arrived: the Chesme Inkstand has finally arrived in St Petersburg.

205 *God bless our inkstand ... helped with it*: in German.

Letter 127

Maltesholm, near Kristianstad in Scania: Maltesholm Castle was the home of Baron Hans Ramel (1724–1799) and is located in Scania, the province on the southern tip of Sweden.

the piteous state ... your brother-in-law: the mentally ill Christian VII of Sweden, the brother of Gustav's wife, Sophia Magdalena.

Prince Ferdinand ... quite another sort: Duke Charles William Ferdinand of Brunswick (1735–1806), reputed to be one of the best generals in Europe.

206 *The weather was diabolical that day*: that is, unlike during Gustav's stay in 1777, the weather—and, Catherine politely implies, the Swedish king's absence—put a damper on festivities in 1778.

Letter 129

208 *the political tinkers*: see note to Letter 118.

Monsignor de Beaumont refused to bury him: Christophe de Beaumont (1703–1781), Archbishop of Paris from 1746 until his death, was responsible for the order not to bury Voltaire in hallowed ground, which came too late to prevent his quiet burial at Sellières.

When Field Marshal Rumiantsev ... a right proper brother: Catherine takes the opportunity to remind Gustav of Russia's military strength, recalling two Russian victories over the Ottomans in July 1770.

you too have two uncles ... there ever were any: Frederick the Great and his brother Henry of Prussia, brothers of Gustav's mother, Louisa Ulrika.

Letter 131

211 *time brings wisdom*: in German (which both correspondents, as descendants of the German princely house of Schleswig-Holstein-Gottorf, would have understood).

your dear uncles go on superb marches: Frederick the Great and his brother Henry were still facing off with the Austrians over Bavaria.

Letter 132

212 *the Roman emperor ... smelled fragrant*: the allusion is to Vitellius (AD 15–69, r. April–December 69). He is quoted by the Roman historian Suetonius as making 'the abominable remark that the odour of a dead enemy was sweet and that of a fellow-citizen sweeter still' (Suetonius, *Lives of the Caesars*,

trans. J. C. Rolfe, 2 vols (Cambridge, MA: Harvard University Press, 1914), ii. 253).

212 *His last oration … two years ago*: on 7 April 1778 (NS), Pitt the Elder's last speech in the House of Lords insisted that the British continue the struggle to retain the American colonies.

213 *As for the sorrows … sincerely*: probably an allusion to the physical ailments of the writer Louise d'Épinay, Grimm's companion, who died of breast cancer in 1783.

   it was illogical … deprived of burial: an allusion to the Church's attempt to prevent Voltaire from receiving a Christian burial owing to his irreverent writings.

   Place de Grève: the site of executions in pre-Revolutionary France, now the Place de l'Hôtel-de-Ville in Paris.

   Up to now … dug up: 106 letters from Voltaire to Catherine survive.

214 *my prince-bishop*: Peter Friedrich Ludwig of Schleswig-Holstein-Gottorf, Catherine's younger cousin and ward.

Letter 133

a C. called N. F.: that is, a castle called New Ferney.

Let us see whether you recall … Academy of Sciences: Catherine's riddle remains hard to decipher today. It is likely that she is alluding to a letter she wrote to Grimm on 14 September 1775 (not included in this volume) from the New Jerusalem Monastery outside Moscow. Her comment about the 'master of the house' is ironic, since in that earlier letter she called the abbot an 'idler' and mocked the monks for having no stories or miracles to tell. She thus creates an analogy between the sacred site, designed as an exact replica of the Church of the Holy Sepulchre in Jerusalem, and her projected shrine to Voltaire, which would have reproduced his home at Ferney.

215 *the bookseller Panckoucke's idea … they were written*: in the end, the first posthumous edition of Voltaire's complete works was edited by Beaumarchais, not by the bookseller Charles-Joseph Panckoucke; it was not arranged chronologically, as Catherine had hoped, but rather by genre.

   but, my God, … an opportune hora: in German, though Catherine throws in the Latin words for 'studies' and 'time' to highlight teasingly her own 'pedantry'.

   The maker of the notorious inkstand: Barnabé Augustin de Mailly.

   came from Rome … sent it to him: Semën Voronstov lived in Italy in 1776–8.

   Mr Shuvalov told me … drew my portrait from it too: presumably Ivan Shuvalov. Catherine's discussion of her grandson's name in Letter 121 makes clear why she would like to see her portrait modelled on that of Alexander the Great. The latter died at the age of 32, whereas Catherine was 49 in 1778.

   Martin Luther's floating, living, and weaving: a joking allusion in German to Luther's translation of Acts 17:28, by means of which Grimm likens Catherine to God in whom 'we live, and move, and have our being'.

When one day I meet Caesar: that is, in the afterlife.

the Chevalier Corberon's negotiations: see Letter 132.

Under Louis XV... suspect only Mignot and company: Catherine is punning on the name of the head of Louis XV's secret diplomatic network, the Comte de Broglie, and the Italian 'imbroglio', meaning 'tangle' or 'fraud'.

216 *the two-faced man's mum ... is treated even worse*: Joseph II, son of Maria Theresa of Austria, is known in Catherine's correspondence as the 'two-faced man' and is here referred to also as the 'little child' (Italian). Catherine's opinion of Joseph changed markedly after their meeting in 1780.

Monsieur Bertin is now my head cook: on Bertin, see Letter 126.

a copy of the trial ... not yet been printed: Catherine sought copies of unpublished classical manuscripts from the Vatican Library; instead she received the records of Anne Boleyn's trial, which are not held in the Vatican.

217 *summa summarum*: Latin, 'the total'.

Letter 134

how much I shared ... the crown prince: the future Gustav IV Adolf of Sweden. The 'bitterness' is an allusion to the continuing rumours that he was illegitimate.

a second tot: the child would be Catherine's second grandson, Constantine.

Letter 135

219 *Lord Constantine ... when he came into the world*: Catherine's grandson Constantine was born on 27 April 1779.

Letter 137

226 *gentlemann*: Catherine uses the English word, spelled with two 'n's, to designate Gustav's son, Gustav Adolf.

227 *the coadjutor*: Peter Friedrich Ludwig of Schleswig-Holstein-Gottorf.

I am off ... leaving pleasant Troezen: Catherine is quoting the opening lines of Racine's tragedy *Phèdre* (1677). The speaker, Hippolytus, repeatedly announces his departure from his home at Troezen throughout the play; when he finally leaves in act 5, he is destroyed by sea monsters at the behest of his father, Theseus.

my chariot ... pulled by griffins: Apollo and Alexander the Great were both traditionally depicted travelling on chariots drawn by griffins.

the Count of Gotland: Gustav himself.

Letter 138

22 April: Catherine gets the date wrong by one day: Frederick's letter is dated 23 April.

Letter 139

229 *Dr Falk ... in the middle of Vienna*: the Jewish Cabalist Samuel Hayyim de Falk (*c*.1710–1782) was reputed to have killed a servant by turning his

head backwards during a rite performed with a black goat, in the company of, among others, Louis-François-Armand de Vignerot Du Plessis (1696–1788), Duc de Richelieu, French ambassador to Vienna, 1725–9.

229 *kibitka*: covered cart or sleigh.

accompany him … to Mitau: the 'countess' is Cagliostro's wife and collaborator, Lorenza Serafina Feliciani (c.1754–1794); Mitau is also known as Jelgava, Latvia.

230 *letters from lawyers in Chartres … erasable*: a lawyer from Chartres, a Monsieur Le Tellier, gave Catherine a manuscript of Voltaire's tragedy *Zulime* (1740), corrected in the author's hand, for which he received a golden medallion, struck on the occasion of the birth of her grandson Alexander. Grimm sent to Catherine the issue of the newspaper *Journal de Paris* of 8 May 1781, in which Le Tellier announced the gift and published his letter to Grimm. As Grimm pointed out, a passage in the letter appears to have been censored and replaced with lines of dots.

why are they … in the tracks of their grandfather: 'they' are Louis XVI of France, whom Catherine here accuses of being as weak-willed and ineffectual as his grandfather, Louis XV.

Lord Brother-in-Law … very soon forgotten too: Louis XVI's brother-in-law, Joseph II, had just effected a complete reversal of his mother, Maria Theresa's, diplomacy by concluding an alliance with Russia.

But, my God, … the young man go his way: in German. The 'good-willed' grandson is again Louis XVI.

I shall add Siberian furs … found in Siberia: Catherine greatly admired the work of the French natural historian Georges-Louis Leclerc de Buffon. On 25 April 1781, she asked Grimm to deliver to Buffon a piece of a supposedly ancient golden chain found on the banks of Irtysh River in Siberia. She claimed that, according to the best Russian artisans, the work was too fine to imitate and 'therefore cannot be of the present time'.

I found the fragment … Mr Grand Cham. explains it: in her letter to Grimm of 14 April (not in this volume), Catherine recounted that she and her court had mocked the Grand Chamberlain Ivan Shuvalov by telling him about the biblical king Nebuchadnezzar, who in his insanity 'did eat grass as oxen' (Daniel 4:33). The grand chamberlain explained the story by claiming to have found biblical commentaries explaining that 'stupefied' and 'ox' are the same word in Hebrew. She is therefore joking that she would make fools of pedants by making them devotees of an ox.

Ma basta per lei: Italian, 'but enough of that'.

I am very sorry … on the same level: in his letter of 6/17 June 1781, Grimm expressed mock alarm that Catherine had called the Spanish Inquisitors 'rogues'.

put my blunders … in the same category: after buying François Tronchin's art collection in 1770, Catherine refused to buy the new collection that he had amassed; Grimm congratulates her on her frugality in that regard, which he contrasts with her generosity in offering aid to cities in the Holy Roman Empire after they were destroyed by fire.

230 *on 28 June ... report up until that day*: Catherine celebrated on 28 June the anniversary of the coup d'état that brought her to the throne in 1762.

231 *Well, Sir, ... been idle?*: in German.

If Mr Haller is happy ... I am too: in January 1781, Grimm forwarded to Catherine a request for funds from Rudolf Emanuel von Haller (1747–1833), a Parisian banker and the son of the Swiss scientist and poet Albrecht von Haller (1708–1777).

Gillet: Nicolas François Gillet (1709–1791), French sculptor. Grimm had petitioned Catherine to ensure that Gillet's pension be paid.

About the fire ... ashes: a fire destroyed the Paris Opéra on 8 June 1781 (NS).

Mr Shuvalov ... the exchange rate: presumably Andrei Petrovich Shuvalov, who returned to Russia from Paris in 1781.

Pope Braschi: Giannangelo Braschi (1717–1799) became Pope Pius VI in 1775.

why did he not go to Prague?: Catherine is alluding to the brother of her current favourite, Alexander Lanskoy; subsequent exchanges between Catherine and Grimm trace the family's efforts to rein in the excesses of this wayward brother on his travels across Europe.

know everything without ever having learned anything: proverbial phrase much used in eighteenth-century France, drawn from Molière's *Les Précieuses ridicules* (*The Affected Ladies*, 1659).

whether it fits ... rhymes or no: in German.

Letter 140

232 *They were inoculated ... other people here*: see Letters 40, 41.

233 *I am not sure ... invitation that you have made them*: on their tour of Europe in 1781–2, Paul and Maria Fedorovna did not visit Sweden.

Letter 141

one should see ... everything: a direct quotation from Prince Charles-Joseph de Ligne, *Coup d'œil sur Belœil* (Belœil: De l'imprimerie du P. Charles De—, 1781), 69.

Letter 142

234 *Pskov*: one of Russia's oldest cities, located near the border with modern Estonia; Catherine had visited in 1780, on a tour inspecting the implementation of her new regulations for provincial administration.

Gdov: also near the Estonian border, it was granted the status of a town in 1780.

Admiral Kempenfelt: Richard Kempenfelt (1718–1782), British rear-admiral, famed for his victory against the French in the Second Battle of Ushant in

1781. Catherine correctly describes his death in a naval accident on 29 August 1782 (NS).

Letter 144

235 *I am opening ... Chesme*: Catherine founded in 1774 a palace and then in 1777 a church on the road from St Petersburg to Tsarskoe Selo, renaming the area in honour of the Russian naval victory at Chesme in 1770. The church became the chapterhouse of the military Order of St George.

you are in danger ... nearly drowned you: in his letter of 2/13 February 1783, Grimm wrote several pages of hyperbolic thanks for a forty-one-page series of letters that he had received from Catherine, comparing the letters to the Flood in the Bible and claiming that his joy at receiving them had induced a 'torrent of tears'.

the first age of the history of Russia ... translated into German for you: Catherine's *Notes Concerning Russian History* remained incomplete. She originally planned to divide them into five periods: the beginning of time to the time of Riurik (862); from Riurik to the Tatar invasion (862–1224); the Tatar yoke (1224–1462); from the end of the Tatar yoke until the accession of Mikhail Fedorovich Romanov (1462–1613); from the accession of the Romanovs to the present day (1613 to the end of the eighteenth century).

236 *Dr Le Clerc and Tutor Levesque*: Nicolas-Gabriel Le Clerc (1726–1798), author of a *Physical, Moral, Civil, and Political History of Russia*, 6 vols (1783–5), and Pierre-Charles Levesque (1736–1812), author of a *History of Russia*, 5 vols (1782).

'Bruder': German, 'brother'.

my lord the Grand Master: Catherine herself was the Grand Master of the order.

237 *the passing of Prince Orlov... before him*: Nikita Panin died on 31 March 1783; Grigory Orlov on 13 April.

as Sir Alexander did with the Gordian knot: allusion to Richard Brompton's *Portrait of Grand Dukes Alexander Pavlovich and Constantine Pavlovich* (1781), in which the young Grand Duke Alexander is represented as his ancient namesake cutting the Gordian knot.

short gallop: in German.

and since ... cope with it all too: in German.

Letter 145

238 *I felt real pain ... letter of 28 March*: the letter brought news of the death of Gustav's second and much loved infant son, Charles Gustav (25 August 1782–23 March 1783 NS).

I hope ... such a significant loss: that is, by having more children, which Gustav did not do.

239 *Prince Golitsyn*: Prince Nikolai Alekseevich Golitsyn (1751–1809), sent by Catherine to bring Gustav her condolences on the death of his mother and her congratulations on the birth of Charles Gustav.

This best of all possible worlds makes us sigh so very much: an allusion to the refrain of Voltaire's *Candide* (1759).

Letter 146

239 *he arrived safely in Åbo ... outside Tavastehus*: Swedish names for the modern Finnish cities of Turku and Hämeenlinna, respectively.

Gosh, mon Ami, ... in front of his troops: in French.

240 *goes to Riga, up the Daugava*: the Daugava or Western Dvina flows through Russia into the Gulf of Riga.

the licornes: a type of cannon.

Akhtiar harbour: also known as Sevastopol.

Adieu, mon Ami, be well: in French.

Zorich was going to come ... the Zanovich business: the brothers Mark and Annibal Zanovich were counterfeiting money on the estate of Catherine's former favourite, Semën Zorich.

Cesvaine: town in Latvia.

Letter 147

241 *so that I can follow ... that often torment me*: in French.

Field Marshal Rumiantsev ... blunders: Rumiantsev was nervously arming in anticipation of the Ottoman response to the annexation of Crimea.

Adieu, mon Ami, ... once and for all?: in French.

Letter 148

one of the worthiest ... of my Academy: Gustav was an honorary member of the St Petersburg Academy of Sciences.

242 *it was agreed by common consent ... since the fourteenth century*: in 1682, Tsar Fedor III (1661–1682) abolished the old Muscovite *mestnichestvo* system for assigning ranks and lands to nobles in accordance with each family's status. He ordered the burning of the genealogical books on the basis of which decisions were made under the former system. These records, however, began to be kept at the end of the fifteenth century, not in the fourteenth.

your arm is giving you trouble: the meeting between the two sovereigns at Fredrikshamn had been delayed when Gustav broke his left arm falling from his horse on 12 June 1783 (NS) (see Letter 146); the continued pain in his arm gave him an excuse for another trip to the continent.

kissel, shchi, and kvas, ... untransportable: *kissel* is a gelatinous dessert or drink made of red berries; *shchi* is cabbage soup; *kvas* is a drink made normally from fermented rye and with a low alcohol content. At the end of this sentence Catherine uses the French neologism 'intransportable'.

drozhki: a low, open carriage.

Letter 149

243 *the death of our metropolitan in Kiev*: Gavriil Kremenetsky (1708–1783), Metropolitan of Kiev from 1770 until his death.

klobuks: a klobuk is a head covering worn by Orthodox clergymen.

eparchies: Orthodox dioceses.

the Synod: Holy Synod was the governing council of the Russian Orthodox Church, established by Peter the Great to replace the patriarchate of Moscow, in effect placing control of the ecclesiastical hierarchy under the ruler.

This will all come to nothing ... my dear friend: in French.

Letter 150

244 *Adieu ... rightly*: in French.

Letter 152

246 *when I was ... grammar*: see Letter 153.

If you should arrive ... by balloon: the brothers Joseph-Michel and Jacques-Etienne Montgolfier carried out the first public demonstration of their invention, the hot air balloon, in 1783.

the testimonial ... new minister: in his letter of 14 April 1784 (NS), de Ligne recommended to Catherine the new French ambassador to Russia, de Ligne's friend Louis-Philippe, Comte de Ségur. Catherine's scepticism about Ségur quickly evaporated after his arrival.

Letter 153

247 *The Queen of Golconda*: *Aline, Queen of Golconda* (1766), a French opera-ballet with a libretto by Michel-Jean Sedaine and music by Pierre-Alexandre Monsigny; it was based on a prose tale of the same name by Stanislas de Boufflers (1761).

When Emilie marries: Emilie de Belsunce, granddaughter of Grimm's companion, Louise d'Épinay, married the Comte de Bueil in 1786.

Give Diderot's widow: after a long illness, Diderot died in Paris on 31 July 1784 (NS).

248 *Cheremis ... Votyaks*: the Cheremis are now called the Mari, a Finno-Ugric people who still today inhabit the area between the Volga and Vyatka rivers in Russia. The Votyaks or Udmurts are an Uralic people who now live mostly between the Kama and Vyatka rivers.

circles: certain territorial divisions of the Holy Roman Empire were known as 'circles'.

As for purchases ... of a certain kind: Catherine had guided and funded Lanskoy in constructing a collection of books, miniatures, precious stones, coins, statues, and prints. It was too painful for her to think of such purchases so soon after his death.

Letter 154

249 *Ostyak*: a Siberian language, now known as Khanty.

249 *I grew weary ... read through*: in German, matching the language of
Zimmermann's book. Laurence Sterne, in *The Life and Opinions of
Tristram Shandy, Gentleman* (1759–67), defines a hobby-horse as 'a ruling
passion'; Catherine read Sterne's novel in German translation and cited it
often in letters to Grimm in the 1780s.

St Anthony, dressed by you: in the Enlightenment spirit of debunking religious myths, Zimmermann described St Anthony the Great's wardrobe as
follows: 'On his bare body he wore a hair shirt, over this a sheepskin cloak,
and on his head a hood. He might well have looked dirty, for he never
washed or cleaned himself, and therefore gave free rein to the little animals that live between skin and hair' (*Ueber die Einsamkeit*, 4 vols (Leipzig:
Weidmanns Erben und Reich, 1784–5), vol. 1, 159) (our translation).

you speak ... about my Prince Orlov: Grigory Orlov had been one of
Zimmermann's patients.

the medallion that you liked: in his letter of 29 March (NS), Zimmermann
mentioned that he had seen the Grigory Orlov medallion in the home of
a German prince and had admired the inscription, 'Russia too has such sons.'

250 *I ... cure it*: presumably by giving him Bestuzhev drops (see Letter 145).

I find in it: that is, in Zimmermann's letter.

Letter 155

Shuvalov ... Russian Academy: Ivan Shuvalov and Alexander Stroganov
were both founder members of the Russian Academy and collaborators on
the dictionary project.

ignorantissimi bambinelli: Italian, 'most ignorant little children', a phrase
from an aria in Giovanni Paisiello's comic opera *The Imaginary Philosophers*
(first performed in St Petersburg in 1779). Catherine used it in her 'Daily
Record of the Society of the Ignorant' (1783), an affectionate satire of the
new Russian Academy that appeared in the academy's journal, the *Interlocutor
of Lovers of the Russian Word* (1783–4).

251 *Sire Factotum ... come*: Alexander Bezborodko and Catherine's other secretaries and officials.

I go out ... I am reconciled: that is, Catherine had now recovered sufficiently from her grief at Lanskoy's death to be able to hold audiences in
her antechamber as usual.

I have been getting up ... At eleven I go to bed: Catherine gives such accounts
of her daily routine very regularly: this description matches almost exactly
the one she sent three months before, on 22 August, but she has added the
squirrel and the monkey.

the toy ambassadors ... beautiful and agreeable location: Catherine refers to
certain foreign ambassadors at her court as her 'pocket ministers' (here
translated as 'toy ambassadors'), implying her ability to guide their opinions by keeping them close to her. Taking them out of their box means
taking them out of their usual court routine for a special trip. In June 1785,
Catherine made a lightning visit to Moscow in the company of the French

and British ambassadors, Louis-Philippe, Comte de Ségur, and Alleyne Fitzherbert, later Baron St Helens. On the way back, they visited Pella, a site on the Neva River, where Catherine intended to build a palace for the young Alexander; the incomplete building was destroyed by Catherine's son Paul after her death.

251 *crib-biters*: a term Catherine uses to refer to hostile foreign observers; it derives from crib-biting, a kind of tic that attacks horses, causing the animal to breathe abnormally while gripping a fence or other object with its teeth. Catherine thereby suggests that the observers in question are carping in an unhealthy and unnecessary manner.

Count Anhalt: Count Friedrich of Anhalt (1732–1794), entered Catherine's service in 1783. In 1785 he was on a three-year tour around Russia. In 1786 he became director-general of the elite military school in St Petersburg, the Noble Cadet Corps.

Zelmira and her boor ... her parents' letters: the subject of this passage is Augusta Karolina of Brunswick-Wolfenbüttel (nicknamed Zelmira), who was married to Frederick of Württemberg, the brother of Grand Duchess Maria Fedorovna. Catherine used Grimm as an intermediary in her negotiations with Zelmira's parents, who for a long time were not willing to believe Augusta's claims that her husband was abusing her. Catherine sent Augusta the letters from her parents on 5 November, after another fight between the spouses; Augusta and her husband then made a temporary agreement to separate.

There is a touching passage ... burst into tears: Catherine was still grieving for Lanskoy.

252 *Mr Thomas's eloquent eulogies*: Antoine-Léonard Thomas (1732–1785), famous for his eulogies of figures such as Marcus Aurelius and Madame Geoffrin.

they just lost a big one: perhaps referring to the death of the head of the Jesuit order in Belarus, Stanislas Czerniewicz, in July 1785.

The German translation ... its master: an allusion to the translation of Catherine's *Notes on Russian History*, published by Friedrich Nicolai in Berlin.

Shchedrin ... my bust for you: Grimm's collection of images of Catherine, presumably including this bust, was lost during the French Revolution.

'What I did, I would do again': Jacques Necker had to resign his post as French comptroller-general in 1781. A quotation from Jacques Necker, *De l'administration des finances de la France*, 3 vols (1784), i. clvi.

Poor people ... with boots: Catherine's phrase for the French, and here more specifically Louis XVI, who was at this time poor both financially and, in Catherine's opinion, intellectually. She contrasts him with Jacques Necker, whom she presents as intellectually stronger and more efficacious than the king, whose refusal to follow Necker's advice had forced the latter to resign in 1781.

252 *he sits there … but how does that help?*: Catherine asserts that Jacques Necker would be more useful if he were restored to his post in government.

Poor people … people of all sorts: this paragraph, cryptically attacking the ineptitude of the French government and its failure to keep Necker in his role as comptroller-general, is in German. Catherine's notion that one could accomplish much even with less than ideal personnel (such as the uneducated officials she often found in Russia) is a frequent refrain in her later writings.

Letter 156

253 *Mr Kalifalkzherston*: the eponymous deceiver in Catherine's anti-Masonic play *The Deceiver* (1785); his characterization clearly recalls Cagliostro.

Letter 157

254 *Medusa heads … adding to their number*: Catherine frequently compares heads of state to heads of Medusa, the female monster who turned people to stone when they looked at her. By this Catherine means that people become stiff and awkward when faced with a regal personage, and she prefers to see people behave less formally and more sociably when they are around her.

255 *You will find … swimming than racing*: Catherine is describing Lev Naryshkin, her friend, courtier, and favourite satirical target. In his official capacity as Grand Equerry, he was responsible for the horses at Catherine's court. Her joking comparison of the horses in his care to the mermaid-like Tritons, who formed the entourage of the classical sea god Poseidon, suggests that he is less than skilled at his job.

I recommend the other one to you: possibly Catherine's new favourite, Alexander Dmitriev-Mamonov.

the journey … eye to smart: de Ligne had been suffering from eye problems earlier in the year.

Monsieur … told me about: in his letter of 15 November 1786 (NS), de Ligne remarked that his father and two tutors had said he would always be a bad lot.

Letter 158

255 *Bacchus*: Bacchus Weynach, an intermediary for many of Catherine's and Grimm's letters.

Letter 159

256 *a letter from Papa Brunswick … my protégée*: 'Papa Brunswick' is Duke Charles William Ferdinand of Brunswick, father of Zelmira (Augusta Karolina), whom Catherine had given refuge from her husband in Koluvere Castle in Estonia (see note to Letter 155).

his ambassador … the Redcoat: the Austrian ambassador was Count Johann Ludwig Joseph von Cobenzl; the Redcoat is Catherine's favourite, Dmitriev-Mamonov.

257 *Ekaterinograd*: intended to be the provincial capital of the Caucasus, the town was not particularly successful and is now the Cossack village of Ekaterinogradskaia.

per la curiosità: Italian 'as a curiosity'.

Monsieur de Ségur's father: Louis-Philippe de Ségur's father, Philippe-Henri (1724–1801), was French minister of war 1780–7.

is called: Catherine's emphasis.

Letter 160

258 *On Solitude*: Catherine wrote the title in German, to match its original language.

Nicolai ... Berlin: Christoph Friedrich Nicolai did publish Catherine's anti-Masonic trilogy in Berlin; see Letters 156, 167.

Letter 161

259 *Kremenchuk*: located on the Dnieper River, today in Poltava Province, Ukraine; it had been a Russian possession from 1667.

the Cathedral of the Assumption: also known as the Dormition Cathedral (Uspensky Sobor) and dedicated to the Virgin, it is one of the grandest churches in the Kremlin complex. Monarchs (including Catherine) were crowned there, and most metropolitans and patriarchs were buried there.

On St Peter's Day ... metropolitan: the news of the clergyman's elevation took him by surprise and was confirmed by the empress in person during the service.

sewed ... a half-arshin: normally black, the klobuk or head covering of an Orthodox metropolitan is white, and the cross is also a sign of rank; an arshin is approximately a yard long. See Letter 149.

260 *Torzhok*: a Russian town in Tver Province, an important post station between St Petersburg and Moscow and famed as a centre of goldwork embroidery.

Letter 163

265 *Fevey*: the comic opera *Fevey* (1786) was set to Catherine's libretto, with music by Vasily Pashkevich.

Hospodar: see Letter 48.

In order not ... the way things are: in French.

266 *but this ... of truth*: in French.

Tor ... Elizavetgrad: Tor (now Slaviansk) and Bakhmut are located in the region of Donetsk. Elizavetgrad was a fortified town in central Ukraine, now called Kropyvnytskyi, founded by the Empress Elizabeth in 1754 to forestall Tatar raids; it was granted city status in 1775.

Peace of Kaynarca: the Treaty of Küçük Kaynarca was signed at the end of the First Russo-Turkish War in July 1774.

267 *if my minister ... the same manner as before*: Iakov Bulgakov was imprisoned in the Seven Towers Fortress on 5 August 1787, which constituted a

declaration of war by the Ottoman Empire. The Ottoman government had used the same method to declare war in 1768, when Aleksei Obreskov was imprisoned there. Catherine accordingly threatens to do the same as before and to inflict defeat on the Ottomans.

Letter 164

269 *At this particular moment … I shall continue*: in French.

Major-General Reck and Commander Tuntsel'man: Ivan Grigor'evich von Reck and Egor Andreevich Tuntsel'man were responsible for defending Kinburn against the Ottomans.

Sarepta: a settlement founded in 1765 south of the city of Tsaritsyn, now Volgograd.

the Gorich brothers: two brothers, both named Ivan Petrovich Gorich, served under Potemkin.

270 *we should make up to the English*: Catherine had no credit stored up with George III, since she had refused a decade earlier to aid the British in the American War of Independence; the British were just at that moment allying themselves with the Prussians (and the United Provinces) in the Triple Alliance to oppose Russia. Yet Catherine astutely expected tensions between Pitt and the king in the conduct of foreign policy to keep Britain on the sidelines.

Their troops … say about this: well aware that France was hobbled by financial and political turmoil, Catherine rightly expected France to fail in its attempt to prevent Prussia and Great Britain from intervening in the Netherlands.

a prime minister … have resigned: Étienne-Charles de Loménie de Brienne was Louis XVI's chief minister, president of the Assembly of Notables, and finance minister in 1787–8; the secretary of war was the father of Louis-Philippe de Ségur, Philippe-Henri, and the secretary of the navy was the Marquis de Castries.

271 *When the manifesto … was issued*: the manifesto was promulgated on 9 September.

MacNob will be pardoned: Potemkin interceded on behalf of Fedor MacNob, a decorated colonel, who was court-martialled after a row with a commanding officer. He served with distinction in the Second Russo-Turkish War and was badly wounded at the siege of Izmail.

Letter 165

273 *for his faith … St Andrew*: Catherine uses here the motto of the order, 'Faith and fidelity', in her wording.

the ship Mary Magdalene: the *Mary Magdalene* was captured by the Ottomans when a storm blew it into the harbour at Constantinople in October 1787.

In exchange … Lombard: Giuliano Lombard was a lieutenant of Maltese origin, who had been taken prisoner by the Ottomans near Khadjibey (now Odessa) in 1787.

273 *the Prince of Hesse-Philippsthal*: Friedrich of Hesse-Philippsthal (1764–1794), princeling from a minor German state, who served in Russia.

Letter 166

274 *the status of Danzig ... confirmed this*: as part of the First Partition of Poland in 1772, Russia annexed territory east of the Daugava (Dvina) and Dnieper, ceding parts of Galicia, Podolia, and Ruthenia to Austria, while Prussia annexed most of the territory known as Royal or West Prussia. Danzig and Thorn, however, remained independent until the Second Partition in 1793.

275 *I have written ... coming here*: Catherine had invited Aleksei and Fedor Orlov to command the Russian fleet that was to sail to the Mediterranean, as they had in the First Russo-Turkish War. In the end, they declined the invitation.

276 *The Glory of Catherine ... rename the ship*: rumours of all kinds were rife, including this false report about the loss of *The Glory of Catherine* (the ship was, in fact, in harbour in Sevastopol). Wary of symbolic damage in the event of a real disaster, Catherine and Potemkin had the ship renamed the *Divine Transfiguration*.

Letter 167

277 *I recall very well ... spoke on my behalf*: in his letter of 4 September 1787 (NS), Zimmermann conveys the delight of an Englishman, Stuart Willis, and a Hanoverian doctor, Wüllen, at encountering Catherine and Joseph II in Crimea, and especially at receiving a smile from Catherine. Zimmermann received this information from Wüllen, whom he had recruited for Russian service.

Pyrmont: Bad Pyrmont is a spa town in Lower Saxony.

all the shamans ... Switzerland: in March 1787, Cagliostro fled England for Switzerland.

Letter 168

278 *Captain Lieutenant Sacken's brave deed*: sent on a mission to Kinburn in May 1788, the Baltic German Johann Reinhold von Osten-Sacken was chased by a much larger Ottoman force into the mouth of the Bug River; to avoid capture, he blew up his own ship, damaging those of his attackers.

279 *we shall have ... Danish ones*: although Denmark declared war on Sweden in support of its ally, Russia, in August 1788, it was forced by the Prussians and the British to back down in September. Catherine ultimately received no support from the Danes.

Letter 169

280 *[17] June 1788*: the day of the month is supplied by the *Berlin Monthly*, where the letter was published.

Letter 170

281 *or to his nation*: Catherine's emphasis.

I have received news … chased away the others: Catherine proudly announces the joint successes of the Prince of Nassau-Siegen and John Paul Jones against the Ottomans in the First Battle of the Liman in the Black Sea on 7 June 1788.

treaty of 1743 … Gustav III: the Treaty of Åbo (7/18 August 1743), which ended the Russo-Swedish War of 1741–3, settled the Swedish crown on Adolf Frederick of Schleswig-Holstein-Gottorf, Catherine's uncle and Gustav's father.

282 *the King of Sweden … recommended him to me*: in a letter of 13 February 1784 (NS), Gustav thanked Catherine for the help that Andrei Razumovsky gave him 'to make a good impression' on his visit to Naples.

Letter 171

Count Apraksin: Count Fedor Matveevich Apraksin (1765–1796).

Aleksiano: Panagioti Pavlovich Aleksiano was a naval officer of Greek origin. He served in both of Catherine's Russo-Turkish Wars. He died of illness only a few weeks after his successes in the two battles of the Liman (mentioned here, and for which he was rewarded—see Catherine's mention of 'the crosses').

the Swedes have attacked Nyslott … war has not been declared: it was rumoured albeit not proven that in the hope of provoking the Russians, the Swedes sent a small party of soldiers, disguised in Russian uniform, into Finland to attack a border town. Gustav then complained publicly of Russian aggression.

This is … banditry: in French.

He who laughs … on our side: in French.

Letter 172

284 *Count Nesselrode*: Catherine was sending Count Wilhelm Karl Nesselrode (1724–1810) to represent her in Berlin, since he had served in Prussia before entering Russian service and would therefore have the insider knowledge necessary for his delicate diplomatic mission.

285 *Spiridov*: Aleksei Grigor'evich Spiridov (1753–1828), the son of Admiral Grigory Spiridov, famous for leadership at the Battle of Chesme; Aleksei too later became an admiral.

Letter 173

Berezan: island in the Dnieper estuary near Ochakov.

Tekelli: Potemkin had sent a general of Serbian origin, Petr Abramovich Tekelli (1720–1793), to lead troops in the Kuban (a region on the Black Sea opposite Crimea).

286 *the King of England is dying … establish concord*: George III fell victim to bouts of porphyria-induced madness in November 1788, creating a political crisis. Catherine supported the regency of the Prince of Wales (the future George IV), proposed by Charles James Fox, because she hoped thereby to remove George III's anti-Russian prime minister, William Pitt the Younger, from power. The king's recovery in February 1789 put an end to these discussions.

287 *like water in steep places*: possibly a recollection of Micah 1:4: 'And the mountains shall be molten under him, and the valleys shall be cleft, as wax before the fire, and as the waters that are poured down a steep place.'

Maximovich: Stepan Petrovich Maximovich, a major-general killed during the siege of Ochakov.

Letter 174

288 *the distress … the king's state of health*: although she had previously been held up as a model of modest domesticity, during the Regency crisis of 1788–9, Queen Charlotte was widely accused of using her husband's illness to grasp at power herself. Catherine's comment may therefore contain a touch of irony.

289 *Mr Elliot's threats*: British diplomat Hugh Elliot prevented Denmark from entering the Russo-Swedish War on the side of their ally, Russia; he acted in the interests of the Triple Alliance between Britain, Prussia, and the United Provinces, designed by William Pitt and aimed against Russia.

it was Catherine II … house of Brandenburg: the Russians briefly occupied Berlin in autumn 1760. It was in fact Catherine's late husband, Peter III, who returned conquered territories to Prussia, but Catherine here implies that, after her coup, she could have opted to re-enter the war on the side of the Austrians. Prussia acquired a large slice of Swedish Pomerania in 1720, at the end of the Great Northern War, in which Peter the Great was victorious.

Letter 175

290 *the Marquis Lucchesini … position from 1762*: Catherine is alluding to the aggressively anti-Russian policy of Prussia at the time. She highlights the irony of Girolamo Lucchesini's participation in this policy, since he was once chamberlain to Catherine's ally Frederick II.

Letter 176

293 *Slizov*: Petr Borisovich Slizov was the Prince of Nassau-Siegen's predecessor as commander of the Russian galley fleet.

Berezovye Islands: islands in the Gulf of Finland between Vyborg Bay and St Petersburg.

Povalishin: Rear-Admiral Illarion Afanas'evich Povalishin (*c.*1739–1799) received the Order of St George, second class, for his role in the Battle of Vyborg Bay.

293 *Khanykov*: Rear-Admiral Petr Ivanovich Khanykov received the Order of St George, third class, and a golden sword for his role in the Battle of Vyborg Bay.

Pushkin: Aleksei Vasil'evich Musin-Pushkin served in the Baltic fleet from 1789.

I ask you to read … destroyed: Catherine included with her letter a more formal account of the outcomes of the battle.

Crown: Robert Crown (1754–1841), a Scotsman in Russian service since 1788.

Pitkäpaasi: an island off the coast of Finland, on the other side of the entrance to Vyborg Bay from the Berezovye Islands.

Kronstadt: fortress and port serving St Petersburg, located on an island in the Gulf of Finland.

Sveaborg: now the Finnish fortress of Suomenlinna in Helsinki.

the naval church … Wonderworker: St Nicholas Naval Cathedral in St Petersburg, built in the eighteenth century as the principal church of the Russian navy.

294 *negotiations … in Reichenbach*: negotiations between the Prussians and the Austrians began at Reichenbach, in Prussian Silesia, on 27 June 1790 (NS) and lasted for a month.

Letter 178

295 *Ushakov and all his subordinates*: see Letter 177.

a receipt … by the Turks: Hussein Pasha and his treasurer were prisoners of war, taken during the capture of Ochakov.

Letter 179

296 *where you were awaiting … 14 July*: Catherine leaves a gap in her text, copying a blank left in de Ligne's dateline. De Ligne was with the Austrian army, waiting for the campaign against the Ottoman Empire to begin. The Convention of Reichenbach brought peace instead—hence Catherine's irony in quoting de Ligne's uncertainty as to whether he was waiting for peace or war.

The Princess of Clary: de Ligne's daughter, Christine (1757–1830).

why have you not … like Belling: the Prussian Wilhelm Sebastian von Belling (1719–1779) obtained a victory at Gabel in August 1778 during the War of the Bavarian Succession, a war that consisted mostly of the Prussians and the Austrians facing off in inaction.

297 *commentaries …You promised me one*: de Ligne's *Memoirs Regarding the Campaigns of Prince Louis of Baden against the Turks and the French in Hungary and on the Rhine* (1787). Margrave Ludwig Wilhelm of Baden-Baden (1655–1707) commanded the troops of the Holy Roman Empire fighting against the Ottoman Empire; his many successes included the defence of Vienna in 1683.

It is clear why Catherine would have been interested in a general known for defeating the very same enemy she was then facing.

297 *My Refuge*: that is, rustic retreat; de Ligne had two such country houses near Vienna.

298 *as Pasha Köprülü did ... a year*: of Albanian origin, the Köprülü family produced several Ottoman grand viziers and pashas in the second half of the seventeenth century. They actively sought to expand the Ottoman Empire into Eastern Europe, but they were repulsed after the Battle of Vienna in 1683. One member of the family, Fazil Mustafa Pasha (1637–1691), was defeated and killed by imperial troops under Margrave Ludwig of Baden-Baden.

since 14 July ... drunk: probably an allusion to the Fête de la Fédération, a Revolutionary festival that took place in Paris on 14 July 1790 (NS).

fable about ... law to the stomach: La Fontaine's version of Aesop's 'The Belly and the Members' is an explicit defence of monarchy; when the limbs rebel and refuse to serve the stomach, they all suffer from lack of nutrition. La Fontaine parallels this situation with the need for all members of society to serve the king for their own good.

great man's letters to his correspondents: the 'great man' is Frederick the Great, whose *Posthumous Works*, including his correspondence, appeared in 1788.

I fell upon ... proven falsehoods: Catherine was irritated by the (numerous) anti-Russian comments in Frederick's writings.

Neither the hundred chariots ... like a parvenu: this cryptic passage is a response to de Ligne's assertion that the Prussians would not be able to sustain a war, but that Catherine, like Alexander the Great, could continue to support both the war and the luxuries of her court.

299 *the Imperturbable One*: de Ligne's nickname for Catherine.

Letter 181

300 *the declarations ... sent here*: the courier is bringing Potemkin a copy of the Convention of Reichenbach.

301 *Hertzberg*: Ewald Friedrich von Hertzberg had been a leading player in Prussian foreign policy in the reigns of Frederick the Great and Frederick William II. His chagrin concerned the Prussian failure to obtain Danzig and Thorn at Reichenbach.

Hertzberg ... in hard cash: in French.

Letter 182

303 *Rumiantsev ... he leaves quickly*: when in 1789 Catherine removed Petr Rumiantsev from his command of part of the Russian army fighting the Ottoman Empire, and gave him a new assignment preparing to fend off a potential attack from Prussia, Rumiantsev took offence and resigned; he took up residence in Iassy until, vexed by his complaints, Catherine firmly ordered him to depart.

the knights: members of the Imperial Order of St Alexander Nevsky.

'*We praise you, O Lord*'... *with instruments*: see Letter 181.

the Metropolitan of Novgorod and Petersburg: Gavriil Petrov-Shaposhnikov, dedicatee of the Russian translation of Marmontel's *Bélisaire* in 1768 (see Letter 38).

Letter 183

304 *the Poles ... military despotism*: under the influence of Prussia, Poland was dismantling its old republican system, which Russia had guaranteed because the need for all legislation to be passed unanimously kept the government weak. The new system, if it had been implemented, would have significantly strengthened the Polish government's capacity to act.

Divan: the privy council of the Ottoman Empire, chaired by the sultan.

Count Starhemberg ... cost of postage: Count von Starhemberg brought to St Petersburg the news of Leopold II's accession.

you have done my finances a good turn: recipients of letters paid the postage; Voltaire frequently complained that the volume of letters he received would impoverish him. Catherine uses the motif sarcastically to contradict the constant rumours that her finances were failing.

Letter 184

307 *The friend ... leave of absence*: this line, granting August von Kotzebue leave of absence from Russian state service, is the only one in the entire letter that replies directly to Zimmermann's missive.

Letter 185

heavy: in German. Catherine often uses the phrase, 'the heavy baggage', to refer to her son, Paul, but here it seems to mean literal baggage.

the people of Grimma: in his rhetoric of praise, Grimm hyperbolically claims to be speaking for the entire Saxon town of Grimma, which both inflates the numerical strength of his adoration for the empress and undercuts it as a provincial attitude.

the scene ... to deal with: in his letter of 29 March/9 April 1791, Grimm imagined a 'political pageant' representing the negotiations, hostile to Russia, between George III and the Prussian ambassador to England from July 1790 to May 1792, Count Sigismund Ehrenreich von Redern (1761–1841). Catherine's proposed counterpart presumably represents herself and Gustav III's representative in the context of negotiations for a Russo-Swedish alliance concluded in October 1791.

on the payroll of the Absolute and the Limited: Catherine suggests that the absolute monarch Friedrich Wilhelm II and the limited monarch George III are subsidizing the French Revolution.

the plan ... partly executed: Grimm proposed counteracting British plans to attack Russia by supporting the opposition in Parliament, which is precisely what Russia successfully did.

308 *'Jean left ... his income'*: the epitaph that the seventeenth-century French fable-writer Jean de La Fontaine wrote for himself.

Mr Mashkov ... compliments: Mashkov is one of Catherine's messengers who carries letters between Paris and St Petersburg.

My third granddaughter: Maria Pavlovna (1786–1859) later married Grand Duke Charles Frederick of Saxe-Weimar-Eisenach.

308 *grandissimo ... ma*: for comic effect, Catherine interjects two words of Italian, meaning 'very great' and 'but', respectively.

the quarrel ... up to you: Grimm was puzzling over how to translate the new title accorded to Potemkin during the voyage to Crimea in 1787: 'Tavrichesky', meaning 'of Tauris'.

Such is my will: an allusion to the concluding phrase of certain French royal orders: 'Car tel est notre (bon) plaisir' ('for that is our (good) will').

Letter 186

310 *strict justice ... only equity*: the article 'Equity' in the *Encyclopédie* explains this distinction, to which Catherine frequently returns. It asserts that justice is 'to reward or to punish in accordance with certain established laws or rules'. But the article recommends equity as 'the will of the prince, which the rules of prudence dispose to correct what can be found in a law of his state [...] when things have been arranged contrary to what the common good requires in the given circumstances' (Denis Diderot and Jean Le Rond d'Alembert (eds), *Encyclopédie, ou Dictionnaire raisonné des sciences, des arts et des métiers*, 17 vols (Paris: Briasson, David, Le Breton, Durand, 1751–72), v. 894 (our translation)).

Letter 188

311 *the exalted allies*: the Triple Alliance of Great Britain, Prussia, and the United Provinces.

312 *and I cannot bear it ... to withstand*: in German.

the Swedenborgish rainbow of ideas: in the *Arcana cœlestia* (1749–56), the Swedish mystic Emanuel Swedenborg discusses the metaphorical and mystical meanings of rainbows.

the whole baggage of children, all six: that is, Catherine's six grandchildren.

and whatever else ... lies the secret: in German; 'Bacchus', 'Factotum', 'pre-occupied', and 'secret' are written in Roman script. Catherine wrote German in a pre-twentieth-century form of handwriting called *Kurrentschrift*.

Letter 189

313 *I fear God ... no other fear*: one of Catherine's favourite catch phrases, taken from the seventeenth-century French dramatist Jean Racine's tragedy *Athalie* (1691).

Letter 190

316 *When your sentimental journey ... read it*: in the letter to which Catherine is responding, Sénac de Meilhan had written that he was planning to write a book about his trip to Russia under the title of *Sentimental Traveller*, in the style of Laurence Sterne's *A Sentimental Journey through France and Italy* (1768). This plan did not come to fruition.

317 *my good universal knowledge of languages*: an allusion to Catherine's work on her *Comparative Dictionary of All Languages and Dialects* (1787–9), in collaboration with the scholar Peter Simon Pallas.

Letter 191

317 *that which has never been copied out ... their talent*: Catherine continues to scold de Ligne for allowing the publication of Letter 183.

the Sibyls: ageless oracles of Greek myth.

318 *a nation that says ... take it*: Catherine alludes to the Hungarians, who had offered her some troops.

Mr Freeport ... come to blows: a character in Voltaire's *The Café, or The Scotswoman* (1760), who in the final scene asks why one would separate people who want to come to blows.

We danced gaily ... told you: see Letter 183.

319 *the Alexanders and Constantines*: in 1791, Catherine had six grandchildren.

your son: Charles-Joseph-Antoine de Ligne (1759–1792), the addressee's son, to whom Catherine awarded in March 1791 the Russian Order of St George for his valour at the capture of Izmail.

Joseph II predicted ... yet more: in his previous letter, de Ligne mentioned Joseph II's promise that he would soon grant to Catherine's former lover and most trusted subordinate, Grigory Potemkin, membership of the Habsburg Order of the Golden Fleece, but he never did.

the Comte de Ségur ... in rejuvenated form: Ségur arrived in Russia in 1785 and left for good in 1789; in March 1791 he was named the French Revolutionary government's envoy to the Holy See.

the air of the Pontine marshes: that is, Italy where Ségur was then Revolutionary France's representative to the Holy See.

320 *their entourage ... Sainte-Menehould*: in 1791, Louis XVI and Marie-Antoinette took flight for Varennes, in an attempt to escape Revolutionary France; members of the municipal government of Sainte-Ménehould recognized the royal family and gave chase.

Letter 196

325 *the Gegu*: George III of Great Britain and Frederick William II of Prussia.

that convention ... results: the Declaration of Pillnitz (27 August 1791 NS), made jointly by Leopold II and Frederick William II, promised to attack

France if Louis XVI were endangered. Neither ruler had much intention of carrying out the threat, but it was sufficient to antagonize the Revolutionaries and to foster the outbreak of the Revolutionary Wars.

325 *I wrote to both of them*: Catherine wrote to Leopold II and Frederick William II on behalf of the French émigré princes, respectively on 28 and 29 September (see Letter 195).

326 *that meddler Harris*: James Harris, 1st Earl of Malmesbury (see the Biographical Register, p. 420).

female perspicacity… male steadfastness: the four qualities are in German.

Monsieur Du Repaire and Monsieur de Miandre's depositions: these figures are unidentified.

Your saint: Nikolai Rumiantsev, whom Grimm dubbed 'St Nicholas'. At this time, Rumiantsev was busy with two important missions entrusted to him by Catherine: serving as an intermediary between the Russian government and the French émigré princes, and finding a bride for Catherine's grandson Alexander.

to read Gibbon: Catherine had been reading Edward Gibbon's masterwork, *The History of the Decline and Fall of the Roman Empire* (1776–88).

327 *something unspoken … a second flight*: no such secret accord between Leopold II and the French royal family existed.

it was the king who re-established them … abolished at present: in 1774, one of Louis XVI's first actions as king was to re-establish the *parlements*, abolished under his predecessor Louis XV. The Revolutionaries definitively abolished them in 1790, and in early 1791 they instated a new judicial system in their place. Catherine wants to see the *parlements* reinstated again, along with the entire *ancien régime*.

Letter 197

330 *There is no doubt … entitled to make*: when Gustav met with the émigré princes at Aix-la-Chapelle in June–July 1791, he insisted that Louis XVI's brother, the Comte de Provence (the future Louis XVIII), who had managed to escape Paris, assume the title of regent. The Comte de Provence formally declared himself regent only after the king's execution in 1793.

331 *Master Pitt*: Catherine uses the title of 'Master' disparagingly.

Karlshamn: a Swedish town on the Baltic.

332 *the true sentiments … in the eyes of His Prussian Majesty*: on 7 July 1791 (NS), Louis XVI had authorized his brothers to negotiate with foreign powers on his behalf, but disagreements raged as to the true extent of the powers granted to the Comte de Provence (known as 'Monsieur') and the Comte d'Artois.

Letter 199

337 *the born defenders … whom he left*: Louis XVI's son, Louis XVII, died in prison at the age of 10 in June 1795.

Letter 200

338 *the marriage of ... Alexander*: on 28 September 1793, Catherine's grandson
Alexander married Princess Louise of Baden (1779–1826), who became
Grand Duchess Elizabeth Alekseevna.

If on his way ... I would have liked: that is, if the Austrians and Prussians had
defeated the French Revolutionaries, allowing Alleyne Fitzherbert to travel
back to England through France under the auspices of a restored monarchy.

339 *Our ancient Vaubans*: Sébastien Le Prestre de Vauban (1633–1707), Marshal
of France, was a military engineer renowned for his expertise in siegecraft
and fortifications.

Letter 201

340 *You ask what will come ... dirty dogs*: in German. The 'dirty dogs' here are
the French Revolutionaries.

Letter 203

343 *i Pol'sha tozhe vsiu Rus'*: Russian, 'And Poland is also all Russian.'
Catherine then suggests replacing the word 'Poland' with the word
'Lithuania', which came fully under Russian control through the Third
Partition of Poland in 1795.

the great Hertzberg's ignorance is whipped: in an earlier passage of this letter,
Catherine criticizes the Prussian government for mismanaging the campaign against the Polish rebels, and for making peace with Revolutionary
France so that they could seek more territory in Poland instead. In the
present passage, she takes aim at her particular bugbear, the key Prussian
government minister, Count Ewald Friedrich von Hertzberg. In referring
to Hertzberg's failures in Poland as his 'ignorance', she is alluding ironically
to his image as a scholar and curator of the Royal Prussian Academy of
Sciences.

see page 1 of this document: at the start of her letter, Catherine noted that
the members of a Lithuanian deputation had danced cheerfully at a ball
she had organized. The goal of these entertainments was to present
Catherine positively to her new subjects in formerly Polish territories.

Odin: the Norse god of rulers, war, wisdom, and poetry.

344 *If Prince Henry ... made his nephew conclude*: Prince Henry of Prussia's
name was circulating at the time as a possible candidate for a restored
French throne. Prussia concluded the Peace of Basel with Revolutionary
France on 25 March/5 April 1795.

Letter 205

346 *attraction*: word illegible in the original.

Armfelt's head ... we would not address those: Duke Charles was seeking the
extradition of Count Gustav Mauritz Armfelt as a condition of the marriage with Alexandra. Sentenced to death in Sweden, Armfelt had taken
refuge in Russia. Catherine rejected the duke's demands.

BIOGRAPHICAL REGISTER

Abdülhamid I (1725–1789) Ottoman sultan from 1774 until his death; brother of Mustafa III.

Adair, Sir Robert (1763–1855) Diplomat and friend of Charles James Fox.

Ainslie, Sir Robert (1729/30–1812) British ambassador to the Ottoman Empire, 1775–93, who, when Russia's commercial treaty with Britain lapsed in 1786, was ordered to press for war between Russia and the Ottomans.

D'Alembert, Jean Le Rond (1717–1783) French mathematician, scientist, permanent secretary of the Académie française from 1772. Co-edited with Denis Diderot the first seven volumes of the *Encyclopédie* (1751–9), the most iconic undertaking of the French Enlightenment, which sought to systemize all of human knowledge.

Alexandra Pavlovna of Russia (1783–1801) Catherine's eldest granddaughter. Catherine cherished the project of marrying her off to Gustav IV Adolf of Sweden, but the plans fell through owing to the Russian refusal to allow Alexandra to convert to Lutheranism. In 1799, she married the younger brother of Emperor Francis II of Austria, Joseph (1776–1847), but died soon after giving birth to a child, who also did not survive.

Alexander I of Russia (1777–1825) Catherine's first and much loved grandson, whose education she oversaw personally and for whose amusement and edification she wrote fairy tales and a history of Russia. He ruled as emperor from March 1801 until his death.

Alexander the Great (356–323 BC) King of Macedonia, conqueror of the Persian Empire, and an important heroic model for Catherine.

Alfred the Great (848/9–899) King of the West Saxons and of the Anglo-Saxons, celebrated in the eighteenth century as an early model of the enlightened ruler, both a legislator and a patron of the arts.

Algarotti, Count Francesco (1712–1764) Venetian-born traveller, friend of Voltaire, and author of numerous works, including essays on aesthetics, a travelogue about Russia, and *Newtonianism for the Ladies* (1737).

Ali Bey al-Kabir of Egypt (1728–1773) An Egyptian slave of Georgian descent, he won his freedom through military prowess. In 1768 he took advantage of the Ottoman forces' concentration on fighting Russia to seek to establish an independent Egyptian sultanate. Catherine praised him to Voltaire and gave him some naval support against the Ottomans.

Apraksin, Stepan Fedorovich (1702–1758) Russian field marshal, who led Russian troops against Prussia at the start of the Seven Years War. He was recalled for retreating immediately after the first Russian victory at Gross Jägerndorf (19 August 1757); although his decision was motivated by supply shortages, Apraksin's enemies at court insinuated to the ailing empress that he had been trying to curry favour with the pro-Prussian grand ducal couple, who would take power when she died. Catherine was accused of a treasonous correspondence with him. He died before the accusations made against him could be decided one way or the other.

Armfelt, Count Gustav Mauritz (1757–1814) Swedish minister and diplomat. One of Gustav III of Sweden's most trusted advisors, he was appointed by the dying king in 1792 as one of the guardians of the under-age Gustav IV Adolf. Disliked by the regent, Charles of Södermanland, he took refuge in Russia from 1794 until 1797. Catherine refused to extradite him to Sweden, even though it was made a condition of the marriage between her granddaughter Alexandra and Gustav IV Adolf, a match she very much desired.

Augustus III of Poland (1696–1763) Elector of Saxony from 1733, he succeeded his father as King of Poland in 1734, despite the opposition of another pretender to the throne, Stanislas Leszczynski (1677–1766). After Augustus's death, Catherine ensured that the Polish throne passed not to his son, Elector Friedrich Christian of Saxony (1722–1763), but rather to Stanislas Poniatowski.

Azor, Francisque (baptized Grigory Alexandrovich Gvadelupsky, 7 April 1778) Catherine's black servant from Guadeloupe. She served as his godmother, naming him in honour of Potemkin. For a time, he played an important role in court entertainments.

Bariatinsky, Fedor Sergeevich (1742–1814) Russian officer and court official, brother of Ivan Sergeevich Bariatinsky. He was a key conspirator in Catherine's coup d'état (1762), and later served as Hofmarschall or steward of Catherine's court from 1778 until her death.

Bariatinsky, Ivan Sergeevich (1740–1811) Russian lieutenant-general, and Russian ambassador in Paris, 1773–85.

Bauer, Friedrich Wilhelm (1731–1783) German-born military officer and engineer, who was responsible for constructing ports, fortifications, and embankments, such as the walls of the Fontanka River and the Griboedov Canal in St Petersburg (which still survive).

Bazhenov, Vasily Ivanovich (1737–1799) Russian architect, trained at the Imperial Academy of Arts in St Petersburg, under the French royal architect Charles de Wailly in Paris, and in Rome.

Belosel'sky, Andrei Mikhailovich (1735–1779) Russian ambassador in Dresden, 1766–77.

Benkendorf, Sofia Ivanovna (née Loewenstern) (d. 1783) Widow of a commandant of Revel (now Tallinn) and governess of the young grand dukes Alexander and Constantine (Catherine's grandsons).

Berg, Maksim Vasil'evich (Magnus Johann von) (d. 1784) Baltic German general who participated in Empress Elizabeth's Russo-Swedish War (1741–3), fought in the Seven Years War, and became one of the leading officers responsible for occupying Crimea in 1771.

Bernis, François-Joachim de Pierre de (1715–1794) Cardinal, member of the Académie française, and French legate in Rome, 1769–91.

Bestuzhev-Riumin, Count Aleksei Petrovich (1693–1766) Russian diplomat and government minister, vice-chancellor of Russia, 1741–4, and chancellor and *ex officio* head of Russian foreign affairs, 1744–58. Initially an opponent of Catherine's marriage to the heir to the Russian throne, he came to see in Catherine the future leader of Russia, and his fall from grace in 1758 almost ruined her. He was also the inventor of a panacea known as 'Bestuzhev drops', of which Catherine was a great promoter.

Betskoy, Ivan Ivanovich (1704–1795) The illegitimate son of a Russian aristocrat, Betskoy spent many years abroad, mostly in Paris, where he belonged to elite social and literary circles, including the salon of Madame Geoffrin. From the start of Catherine's reign through the mid-1770s, Betskoy was her primary advisor on educational affairs; he headed the Imperial Academy of Arts, the Moscow Foundling Home, and St Petersburg's Smolnyi Institute for Noble Girls. The key intermediary for Catherine's correspondence with Geoffrin, he is referred to in those exchanges as the 'naughty General'.

Bezborodko, Count (afterwards Prince) **Alexander Andreevich** (1747–1799) Ukrainian-born civil servant, Catherine's secretary from 1775. A supporter of Catherine's Greek project, he helped her to develop the policy of Armed Neutrality in 1780 and to design the alliance with Austria in 1781. He was effectively chief of Russian foreign affairs from the early 1780s, in which capacity he concluded the advantageous Treaty of Iassy to conclude Catherine's Second Russo-Turkish War. He is known in the correspondence with Grimm as 'Mr Factotum' for his importance in managing Catherine's day-to-day business, such as dispatching letters and couriers.

Bibiena, Carlo Bernardo Giuseppe Galli (1721–1787) Italian artist working in St Petersburg, 1776–8, as a painter of theatrical sets.

Bibikov, Alexander Ilich (1729–1774) Russian general who fought in the Seven Years War and in 1767 served as marshal of the Commission for the Composition of a New Law Code. He fought in Poland against the Bar Confederation from 1771. In November 1773, he was appointed to lead the forces suppressing the Pugachev Rebellion; he died of a fever in Bugulma (now in Tatarstan, Russia) while on this mission.

Bielke, Johanna Dorothea (née von Grothusen) (*c.*1708–1780) A childhood friend of Catherine's mother, the widowed Bielke lived near Hamburg on territory that belonged to Denmark until 1768, when it was given to the German city-state. Catherine met Bielke during her childhood visits to Hamburg; Bielke wrote to the empress on 5 July 1765 (NS), reminding her of their former acquaintance, and Catherine responded positively, beginning a correspondence that lasted until Bielke's death. Frequenting Danish and German elite society, Bielke was a useful contact for Catherine politically, especially in the years leading up to the 1773 exchange of Holstein, when Catherine's son Paul ceded that territory to Denmark. Bielke's proximity to Hamburg as a centre of journalism was also advantageous, and Catherine pressed her (eventually unsuccessfully) to recruit German noblewomen to serve as governesses at court and at the Smolnyi Institute.

Bischoffwerder, Hans Rudolf von (1741–1803) Prussian general who recruited Frederick William II to Rosicrucianism and who was involved in the negotiations between Austria and Prussia during the French Revolution, including those surrounding the Convention of Reichenbach (1790) and the Declaration of Pillnitz (1791).

Bohusz-Siestrzencewicz, Stanislas (1731–1826) Belarusian clergyman, appointed by Catherine as a bishop in the Catholic diocese of Mogilev in 1773, then as archbishop in 1782, when Mogilev became an archdiocese, though papal approval was delayed for two years.

Bouillé, François-Claude-Amour de (1739–1800) Leading French general in the wars against the French Revolution. He organized the royal family's failed flight to Varennes in 1791 and then served in the émigré and British armies against the Republic.

Braganza, João Carlos de, Duke of Lafões (1719–1806) Portuguese nobleman, related to the Portuguese royal family, who travelled widely and visited Russia in 1774.

Branicka, Countess Alexandra Vasil'evna (née Engel'gardt) (1754–1838) Potemkin's niece and sometime lover, who was with her uncle at his death in 1791.

Branicki, Franciszek Ksawery (1730–1819) Polish Great Crown Hetman from 1774, and husband of Potemkin's niece Alexandra Engel'gardt. He entered Russian service after the Second Partition of Poland (1793).

Breteuil, Louis Charles Auguste Le Tonnelier, Baron de (1730–1807) French ambassador to Russia, 1760–3, and then to Sweden; later government minister to Louis XVI. He emigrated to Switzerland in 1789; he was involved in organizing the royal family's flight to Varennes in 1791. He returned to France in 1802.

Broglie, Charles-François, Comte de (1719–1781) French diplomat. He was the head of Louis XV's so-called 'King's Secret', a clandestine diplomatic network run separately from, and often in opposition to, the official foreign ministry of France and whose policies were strongly anti-Russian.

Brompton, Richard (*c*.1734/5–1783) English portraitist, a student of Anton Raphael Mengs, who was much admired by Catherine. After a period of favour with the English royal family, Brompton fell into debt and in 1779 moved to Russia. He painted a well-known portrait of the young grand dukes Alexander and Constantine (1781) and a bust-length portrait of Catherine. He died suddenly in 1783 without finishing the full-length portrait of Catherine on which he was then working.

Browne, George (1698–1792) A native of Limerick, Ireland, he was an officer in the service of the Elector Palatine and then of Russia. He served as governor of Livonia (today part of Latvia and Estonia) from 1762 until his death.

Bruce, Countess Praskovia Alexandrovna (née Rumiantseva) (1729–1786) Sister of Field Marshal Petr Rumiantsev, she was a lady-in-waiting to Catherine and a member of the empress's inner circle.

Buckingham, George Nugent-Temple Grenville, 1st Marquess of (1753–1813) British statesman.

Bueil, Emilie de (née de Belsunce) (1768–1814) Granddaughter of Louise d'Épinay and the subject of her grandmother's famous work on education, *Emilie's Conversations* (1774). After d'Épinay's death in 1783, Friedrich Melchior Grimm looked after the young woman and won Catherine's patronage for her marriage to the military officer Louis Alexandre Auguste, Comte de Bueil. Her children were named after their godmother, Catherine the Great: Catherine-Hélène-Alexandrine (known in the letters as Katinka) and her brother, Catherine-Henri (known in the letters as Cateau).

Buffon, Georges-Louis Leclerc, Comte de (1707–1788) French naturalist, director of the Jardin des plantes in Paris, and author of a *Natural History* (1749–89) in thirty-six volumes, much admired by Catherine. She corresponded briefly with Buffon in the early 1780s.

Bulgakov, Iakov Ivanovich (1743–1809) Russian ambassador to the Ottoman Empire, 1781–9. Imprisoned by the Ottomans at the start of the Second Russo-Turkish War, he was liberated in 1789. He was then ambassador to Poland, 1790–2.

Burigny, Jean Lévesque de (1692–1785) French author of historical and theological works and one of the closest associates of the salon hostess Marie-Thérèse Geoffrin.

Caesar, Gaius Julius (100–44 BC) Roman general and dictator. All later Roman emperors were given the title 'Caesar', and the original Caesar became the archetype of imperial power.

Cagliostro, Count Alessandro (alias of Giuseppe Balsamo) (1743–1795) Italian-born adventurer and mystic, founder of Egyptian Rite Freemasonry. He visited St Petersburg in 1779–80, but Catherine was highly suspicious of Freemasonry as the antithesis of Voltairean rationalism and as a politically dangerous secret association which sought ties to her son Paul. Catherine parodied Cagliostro as the Tartuffe-like swindler Kalifalkzherston in her comedy *The Deceiver* (1785).

Calas, Jean (1698–1762) French Protestant merchant, tortured and broken on the wheel in Toulouse. Voltaire's writings turned the case into a landmark in Enlightenment struggles against religious intolerance and judicial cruelty.

Cardel, Élisabeth (1712–1764) The young Sophia Augusta Fredericka's governess, a French Huguenot who educated her young charge in good manners, letter-writing, and seventeenth-century French literature.

Caroline Matilda of Denmark (1751–1775) Sister of George III of Great Britain and Ireland, Queen of Denmark and Norway, 1766–72. Her husband, Christian VII of Denmark, was mentally ill; Caroline Matilda's affair with his leading minister, Johann Friedrich Struensee, beginning in 1770, led to her divorce and the execution of Struensee in 1772.

Castries, Charles-Eugène-Gabriel de La Croix, Marquis de (1727–1801) French naval minister, 1780–7, and commander in the émigré army during the French Revolution. Long-time friend of Friedrich Melchior Grimm.

Charles I of England (1600–1649) King of England, executed by the victorious Parliamentarians during the English Civil War.

Charles IV of Spain (1748–1819) King of Spain from 1788, he fought against Revolutionary France from 1793 but then formed an alliance with France in 1795. He was forced to abdicate by Napoleon in 1808.

Charles VI of Austria (1685–1740) Holy Roman Emperor, 1711–40, father of Maria Theresa of Austria.

Charles IX of France (1550–1574) King of France from 1560 until his death. Largely governed by his powerful mother Catherine de' Medici, he ruled during the difficult period of the French Wars of Religion, but was nonetheless a patron of the arts, especially of poetry.

Charles, Duke of Södermanland (1748–1818) Brother of Gustav III of Sweden, Freemason, and regent of Sweden during the minority of Gustav IV Adolf, 1792–6. Upon the latter's deposition in 1809, the Duke of Södermanland acceded to the throne as Charles XIII, the last of the Swedish monarchs of the House of Holstein-Gottorf.

Charles-Philippe, Comte d'Artois (afterwards Charles X of France) (1757–1836) The youngest brother of Louis XVI. He visited Russia in 1793 seeking aid for a counter-Revolutionary invasion of France; Catherine received him well and was willing to provide some troops, but expected England to cover the costs and provide the ships to carry the invaders; England refused, and the undertaking was aborted.

Chaumeix, Abraham de (1725–1773) French journalist and polemicist, author of virulent writings against the *Encyclopédie*, which contributed to the ban placed on the enterprise in 1759. Chaumeix escaped the journalistic fracas in Paris by becoming a tutor in Russia from 1763 until his death.

Chernyshev, Count Ivan Grigor'evich (1726–1797) Brother of Zakhar Chernyshev. He was Russian envoy-extraordinary to Great Britain, 1768–70, and vice-president of the Russian Admiralty College from 1769.

Chernyshev, Count Zakhar Grigor'evich (1722–1784) Russian courtier, the object of Catherine's first flirtation as grand duchess. Under Catherine, he served as governor-general of Polotsk and Mogilev, and then from 1782 until his death as commander-in-chief of Moscow.

Chichagov, Vasily Iakovlevich (1726–1809) Russian admiral. He fought in Catherine's First Russo-Turkish War and commanded the Russian fleet in the Baltic during the Russo-Swedish War of 1788–90. He was famous for his success at the Battle of Revel (now Tallinn, 2 May 1790), where the Russians defeated a Swedish fleet more than twice their size.

Choglokov, Naum Nikolaevich (1743–1798) Russian pretender. He volunteered to serve in the Caucasus with the chimerical intention of seizing the Georgian throne. He was arrested after defecting to the Georgians, and the war council in Kazan sentenced him in April 1771 to exile in Siberia, where he remained until the accession of Catherine's son Paul. In a letter of 9

November 1770 (NS), Voltaire conveyed to Catherine demands from merchants in Geneva to whom Choglokov owed payment.

Christian August, Prince of Anhalt-Zerbst (1690–1747) Catherine's father and a military officer in Prussian service. He married Johanna Elisabeth of Schleswig-Holstein-Gottorf in 1727.

Christina of Sweden (1626–1689) Queen regnant of Sweden from 1632 until her abdication in 1654. She was renowned as one of the most educated women of the age, with an interest in religion, philosophy, and mathematics; she recruited distinguished scientists to Stockholm, earning the nickname 'Minerva of the North', a title that would eventually be applied to Catherine herself.

Clement XIV (Giovanni Vincenzo Antonio Ganganelli) (1705–1774) Pope from 1769, best-known for dissolving the Order of the Jesuits in 1773.

Choiseul, Étienne-François, Duc de (1719–1785) French secretary of foreign affairs, 1758–61 and 1766–70; secretary of war, 1761–70; and secretary of the navy, 1761–6. Catherine detested him for his active anti-Russian policy during her reign; she later claimed to have brought about his disgrace in 1770 by feeding information about the failures of his foreign policy to the French government through her correspondence with Voltaire.

Cobenzl, Count Johann Ludwig Joseph von (1753–1809) Austrian ambassador to Russia, 1779–1800.

Collot, Marie-Anne (1748–1821) Étienne-Maurice Falconet's acolyte and daughter-in-law, she was active as an artist and sculptor in her own right. Mentioned as gifted by Denis Diderot in the Salon of 1767, she made busts of Diderot and Dmitry Alekseevich Golitsyn. She accompanied Falconet to St Petersburg, where she completed a bust of Catherine, as well as several medallions. In 1767 she was the first woman elected to the Imperial Academy of Arts. Falconet entrusted her with the task of sculpting the head of Peter the Great for his monument to the emperor, known as the Bronze Horseman.

Constantine Pavlovich (1779–1831) Catherine's second grandson. The Decembrist Uprising in 1825 was an attempt to place him on the Russian throne, but, as governor of Poland, he had renounced the throne to marry a Polish noblewoman, Joanna Grudzinska.

Corberon, Marie Daniel Bourrée de (1748–1810) French diplomat in Russia, 1775–80, and author of a journal of his stay, which is often critical of Catherine.

Corneille, Pierre (1606–1684) One of seventeenth-century France's most famous authors of tragedies, known especially for his version of *Le Cid* (1637).

Dashkova, Princess Ekaterina Romanovna (née Vorontsova) (1743–1810) Russian woman of letters. Born into the prominent aristocratic Vorontsov family, she married Prince Mikhail Ivanovich Dashkov (1736–1764). The young Dashkova was involved in the conspiracy leading to Catherine's coup in 1762. Highly educated, she toured Europe, visiting Voltaire at Ferney and befriending Diderot and Benjamin Franklin in Paris; she lived for some years in Edinburgh while her son was studying at the university there.

Catherine appointed her as president of both the St Petersburg Academy of Sciences (1782) and the newly founded Russian Academy (1783).

Deluc, Jean-André (1727–1817) Genevan naturalist, who resided at Windsor as reader to Queen Charlotte of Great Britain and Ireland from 1773, when he also became a fellow of the Royal Society.

Denis, Marie-Louise (née Mignot) (1712–1790) Voltaire's niece and companion after the death of her husband in 1744. Voltaire's principal heir, she agreed to Catherine's acquisition of his library, sold the château at Ferney, and colluded with the editors of the Kehl edition of Voltaire's complete works to publish Voltaire's correspondence with Catherine.

Descorches, Marie-Louis-Henri, Marquis de Sainte-Croix (1749–1830) French Republican envoy to Istanbul, 1793–5.

Devier, Count Petr Antonovich (1710–1773) Russian general who, during Catherine's coup of 1762, was sent by Peter III to secure Kronstadt and its garrison as a base. He was arrested by Catherine's envoy Admiral Ivan Talyzin, who received the garrison's oath of loyalty to the new empress.

Diderot, Denis (1713–1784) French philosopher and highly original writer who singlehandedly oversaw the *Encyclopédie* to completion after d'Alembert withdrew from the enterprise in 1759, when faced with government censorship. Diderot's resultant financial straits induced him to sell his library, which Catherine purchased in 1765 but left in his care until his death. Diderot paid his debt of gratitude in 1773–4 by visiting St Petersburg, where he met frequently with the empress to discuss a wide range of topics, producing a set of short essays written for these occasions. The letters that Catherine addressed to him have been lost.

Dimitry (Daniil Andreevich Sechenov) (1708–1767*)* Archbishop of Novgorod, 1757–67, and Metropolitan from 1762. Catherine specifically requested that he perform her coronation rites; thereafter she frequently consulted him on ecclesiastical affairs.

Dimsdale, Baron Thomas (1712–1800) English doctor whom Catherine invited to Russia in 1768 to inoculate her and her son against smallpox, a then controversial medical procedure that he promoted through his practice and publications. She used his services to make the practice widespread in Russia. She rewarded him with the title of baron and invited him back in 1781 to inoculate her grandsons, Alexander and Constantine. In 1768, Dimsdale also gave Catherine the two beloved greyhounds often mentioned in the correspondence with Friedrich Melchior Grimm: Sir Thomas and Lady Anderson.

Dmitriev-Mamonov, Count Alexander Matveevich (1758–1803) Catherine's favourite from 1786 until June 1789, when she discovered his infidelity and personally arranged his marriage to her rival, Princess Daria Shcherbatova. Catherine's nickname for him is 'The Redcoat'.

Dolgorukov, Prince Iury Vladimirovich (1740–1830) Russian military officer. He served in the Seven Years War, at the Battle of Chesme, and in the early stages of the Second Russo-Turkish War.

Dolgorukov, Prince Vladimir Sergeevich (1717–1803) Russian representative in Prussia, 1762–86, and intermediary for exchanges between Catherine and Friedrich Melchior Grimm.

Dorat, Claude-Joseph (1734–1780) French poet, playwright, and novelist, whom Catherine disliked.

Eck, Friedrich Matthias von (in Russian, Matvei Matveevich Ek) (1729–1789) Russian civil servant of Swedish descent. Director of St Petersburg's postal service, 1764–89.

Elagin, Ivan Perfil'evich (1725–1794) Russian poet and historian, Catherine's ally at court during her years as grand duchess, and director of the Russian imperial theatres, 1766–79. He was provincial grand master of Russia, subordinated to the English Grand Lodge, but his attempted reforms of Russian Freemasonry failed, and other currents within the movement took over.

Elizabeth of Russia (1709–1761) Daughter of Peter the Great, Empress of Russia from 1741 until her death on Christmas Day 1761. She selected the future Catherine the Great as a bride for her nephew and heir, the future Peter III.

Elliot, Hugh (1752–1830) British diplomat, envoy-extraordinary to the Elector of Bavaria, 1774–6, to Prussia 1777–82, and to Denmark 1783–9. He prevented Denmark from entering the Russo-Swedish War alongside its ally, Russia.

Elphinston, John (1722–1785) Scottish-born rear admiral in Russian service, 1769–71.

Eropkin, Petr Dmitrievich (1724–1805) Russian military officer, who served in the Seven Years War, and senator from 1765. He led the effective suppression of the Moscow Plague Riot in 1771; he later became commander-in-chief of Moscow, 1786–90.

Euler, Leonhard (1707–1783) Influential Swiss mathematician, astronomer, and physicist, based at the Russian Academy of Sciences, 1727–41 and again from 1766, when Catherine won him back from Frederick the Great.

Falconet, Étienne-Maurice (1716–1791) French sculptor patronized by Madame de Pompadour, he was director of sculpture at the Sèvres porcelain factory. Falconet was invited to Russia in 1766 on the recommendation of his friend Diderot. He produced for Catherine the famous monument to Peter the Great, the Bronze Horseman in Senate Square in St Petersburg. Falconet left Russia disillusioned in 1778, four years before his statue was unveiled in 1782.

Felino, François Guillaume Léon Du Tillot, Marquis de (1711–1774) French-born advisor to the Duke of Parma, 1749–71.

Ferdinand II of Aragon (1452–1516) and **Isabella I of Castille** (1451–1504) Spanish monarchs, who, by their marriage, created the union of the two Spanish kingdoms. They were most famous for supporting the explorations of Christopher Columbus and for bringing the Inquisition to Spain.

Fersen, Count Hans Axel von (1755–1810) Swedish intimate of Marie Antoinette, participant in the American Revolutionary War, and an important agent in the attempts to free the French royal family from their captivity during the French Revolution.

Fitzherbert, Alleyne (afterwards Baron St Helens) (1753–1839) British ambassador in St Petersburg, 1783–7, where he failed to obtain a trade agreement with Russia. He was then chief secretary for Ireland, 1787–9 and became an Irish peer, with the title Baron St Helens, in 1791. He returned to St Petersburg as ambassador, 1801–2.

Fitzwilliam, William Wentworth Fitzwilliam, 2nd Earl (peerage of Great Britain) **and 4th Earl** (peerage of Ireland) (1748–1833) British peer and friend of Charles James Fox.

Fox, Charles James (1749–1806) English Whig politician, intent on curbing the authority of the crown, which he viewed as despotic. He thereby earned George III's animosity, further aggravated by his support for American independence. He later extolled the French Revolution against the arguments of his friend Edmund Burke. As foreign secretary in 1782, he sought to improve trade relations with Russia, and in 1791 he proved instrumental in settling tensions between Britain and Russia during Catherine's Second Russo-Turkish War. Catherine expressed her gratitude by placing a bust of Fox in the Cameron Gallery at Tsarskoe Selo, ignoring his radical politics.

Francis II, Holy Roman Emperor (1768–1835) Nephew of Joseph II, he succeeded his father, Leopold II, as Holy Roman Emperor in 1792. Catherine arranged his marriage to Maria Fedorovna's younger sister, Elisabeth, hoping thereby to solidify the alliance between Russia and Austria, but Elisabeth died in childbirth aged only 22. In the wake of the Napoleonic invasion, the Holy Roman Empire was dissolved, and Francis became Emperor Francis I of Austria.

Franklin, Benjamin (1706–1790) American inventor, scientist, journalist, publisher, and statesman. He contributed to drafting the United States Declaration of Independence and the Constitution, and founded the University of Pennsylvania in 1740. He served as diplomatic representative of the colonies in London, 1757–75, and then of the United States in France, 1776–85. He was one of the eighteenth century's biggest celebrities, and collectors' items, from medallions to teacups, were made bearing his image.

Frederick II (the Great) **of Prussia** (1712–1786) King of Prussia from 1740 until his death. Hailed as the paragon of the enlightened monarch, Frederick was one of the century's most celebrated military leaders and a great patron of French culture, corresponding with and inviting to his court writers like Voltaire and d'Alembert, and himself writing extensively in French. His correspondence with Voltaire lasted for more than forty years. Prussia was allied with Russia from 1764 until 1781, when Catherine switched her allegiances to Austria.

Frederick William II of Prussia (1744–1797) Nephew of Frederick the Great, and King of Prussia from his uncle's death in 1786. Catherine was unimpressed with the heir to the throne when he visited St Petersburg in 1780; their differences were not only diplomatic but also philosophical, since Frederick William had a fascination with the occult, which Catherine vehemently opposed. During the years of the French Revolution and Catherine's Second Russo-Turkish War, the two rulers were often at odds, with Prussia seeking to limit Russia's territorial gains while nonetheless aiming to annex as large a portion of Poland as possible.

Frederiks, (afterwards Baron) **Ivan Iur'evich** (1723–1779) Catherine's court banker, whom she made a baron in 1773.

Friedrich August of Schleswig-Holstein-Gottorf (1711–1785) Catherine's maternal uncle, from 1773 Duke of Oldenburg.

Geoffrin, Marie-Thérèse Rodet (1699–1777) French salon hostess and intellectual, who made her house in the rue Saint-Honoré, Paris, one of the most important literary and artistic meeting-places of the day. She acted as a generous mentor to many of her guests, including Stanislas Poniatowski; the visit that Geoffrin paid to her royal 'son' in Poland in 1766 received much attention across Europe, but her decision not to travel on to St Petersburg offended Catherine and caused their correspondence to falter. Catherine corresponded with Geoffrin from 1763 to 1768; Geoffrin's acquaintance with Catherine's mother, Johanna Elisabeth of Anhalt-Zerbst, her friendship and correspondence with Catherine's advisor Ivan Betskoy and her lady-in-waiting Anastasia Sokolova, and her role as a hub for the distribution of information among artistic, literary, and society circles in Paris all attracted Catherine's attention.

George III of Great Britain and Ireland (1738–1820) King from 1760 until his death. When he fell victim to bouts of madness in late 1788, the dissolute Prince of Wales (the future George IV) was proposed as regent. Hoping to remove the prime minister, William Pitt, from power and thus defeat his anti-Russian policies, Catherine strongly supported Charles James Fox and the Prince of Wales as regent.

Georg Ludwig of Schleswig-Holstein-Gottorf (1719–1763) Catherine's maternal uncle, who asked for her hand in marriage but was refused, as the young Sophia had greater things in store for her. He was a close advisor to Catherine's husband, Peter III, but left Russia soon after Catherine's coup in 1762. After his death, Catherine became the guardian of Georg's two young sons, Wilhelm August and Peter Friedrich Ludwig.

Glebov, Fedor Ivanovich (1734–1799) Russian general, who served in the French army during the Seven Years War and under Rumiantsev during Catherine's First Russo-Turkish War. He later became a senator.

Goltz, Count Leopold Heinrich von der (1745–1816) Prussian ambassador in St Petersburg, 1789–94.

Golitsyn, Prince Alexander Mikhailovich (1718–1783) Commanded the Russian First Army against the Ottoman Empire in 1768–9. Relieved of his command for failing to take Khotin, he nonetheless managed to take both Khotin and Iassy before his replacement, Petr Rumiantsev, arrived. He was promoted to field marshal upon his return to St Petersburg.

Golitsyn, Dmitry Alekseevich (1734–1803) In Russian diplomatic service in Paris from 1760, Golitsyn was Russian ambassador there, 1763–8, then in The Hague, 1770–82. Involved in literature and science, a supporter of the Physiocrats, and a friend of Diderot's, Golitsyn served as an intermediary for Catherine's correspondence with Voltaire and helped to arrange Diderot's trip to Russia in 1773–4; Diderot stayed with him at The Hague on his way to and from St Petersburg.

Greig, Sir Samuel (1735–1788) Scottish-born naval officer in Russian service from 1764 until his death. He served under Aleksei Orlov in the Mediterranean during the First Russo-Turkish War, before becoming commander of Kronstadt. He was placed in command of the Russian fleet fighting Sweden in the Baltic in 1788, but he died of illness the same year.

Greuze, Jean-Baptiste (1725–1805) French painter, known especially for his moralistic, sentimental genre paintings.

Grimm, (afterwards Baron) **Friedrich Melchior** (1723–1807) German-born man of letters. The son of a Protestant pastor, he was a tutor in aristocratic households, moved to Paris, and became close to many important figures in the circle of the *philosophes*. He became known to the crowned heads of Europe through his manuscript periodical, the *Correspondance littéraire, philosophique et critique* (known as the *Correspondance littéraire* or *Literary Correspondence*) (1753–90), which was circulated to a highly exclusive group of recipients, including Catherine and Frederick the Great. He was ennobled in the Holy Roman Empire in 1772 and made a baron in 1777. He met Catherine in 1773, when he was part of the entourage of the future Grand Duchess Natalia Alekseevna, and he returned to Russia in 1776–7, when he officially entered Russian service as Catherine's cultural agent in Paris for a stipend of 2,000 roubles annually. In this capacity he served as Catherine's key cultural representative in France, overseeing, for example, the purchase of Voltaire's library.

Gross, Fedor Ivanovich (1729–1796) German-educated Russian diplomat. From 1779 until his death he was Catherine's envoy-extraordinary in Hamburg. He and Johann Georg Zimmermann collaborated to recruit German doctors and other experts to Russian service, mostly in the newly acquired southern provinces, in the 1780s.

Gustav I Vasa of Sweden (1496–1560) Elected King of Sweden in 1523, he freed Sweden from Danish control, established a centralized monarchy, introduced Lutheranism, and founded the Vasa dynasty, the direct line of which ended with the abdication of Queen Christina in 1654.

Gustav II Adolf (the Great) (1594–1632) King of Sweden from 1611 until his death. Known especially as a military commander, he conquered the provinces of Ingria and Karelia (including the present site of St Petersburg) and the Baltic state of Livonia. He died fighting for the Protestants in the Thirty Years War.

Gustav III of Sweden (1746–1792) Catherine's cousin (the son of her maternal uncle), King of Sweden from 1771. In 1772, he orchestrated a coup d'état that restored absolute power to the monarch, depriving the Swedish Diet of its sovereignty and diminishing Catherine's influence. The two rulers commenced a semi-clandestine correspondence after their first face-to-face meeting in 1777, but Catherine constantly evaded Gustav's attempts to lend diplomatic significance to the etiquette-free exchange. He provoked a war with Russia in 1788 in hopes of regaining popular support within Sweden; the war ended with the Treaty of Värälä in 1790 without any territorial changes. Catherine hoped to manipulate him to fight against Revolutionary France, but Gustav was assassinated by a Swedish officer in March 1792.

Gustav IV Adolf of Sweden (1778–1837) Son of Gustav III and his wife, Sophia Magdalena of Denmark, though at the time of his birth he was rumoured to be illegitimate. He became king at the age of 14 upon the assassination of his father in 1792. He visited St Petersburg in 1796, when Catherine hoped to arrange his marriage to her granddaughter Alexandra, but the wedding was broken off on religious grounds, since Gustav Adolf refused to allow his bride to remain Orthodox, insisting that she convert to Lutheranism. He abdicated in 1809 following a coup d'état by army officers dissatisfied with the king's renunciation of Finland, which became Russian territory.

Gyllenborg, Count Henning Adolf (1713–1775) Swedish diplomat, who met the young Sophia Augusta when he was sent on a mission to Hamburg in 1743. Sophia and her mother began a joint correspondence with Gyllenborg, in which Sophia went by the codename of 'the Young Philosopher'. They met again in Russia a year later, at the time of Catherine's betrothal and marriage: distressed to see Catherine immersed entirely in court frivolities, Gyllenborg advised her to educate herself with serious readings, such as Plutarch, Montesquieu, and the life of Cicero. Catherine later credited him with instilling in her the moral and intellectual strength that permitted her later achievements.

Hanbury-Williams, Sir Charles (1708–1759) English member of parliament, diplomat, and well-known Whig satirist. Sent as ambassador to Russia in 1755, he corresponded with, and subsidized the expenses of, the Grand Duchess Catherine from August 1756 through spring 1757; through her he sought to cultivate a pro-British and pro-Prussian party at the Russian court, whereas Empress Elizabeth preferred to support France and Austria as the Seven Years War began. The correspondence with Hanbury-Williams marked Catherine's initiation into international politics: writing with codenames, they used the correspondence to report to and advise one another on their actions at court. These manoeuvres nearly led to Catherine's expulsion from Russia in 1758; Catherine burned her letters during that crisis, but copies were preserved in Hanbury-Williams's letter-books. He left Russia in 1757, suffering from tertiary syphilis, which soon killed him.

Hénault, Charles-Jean-François (1685–1770) French politician, president of the Paris *parlement* (high court), friend of Voltaire, member of the

Académie française, and author of the *New Chronological Abridgement of the History of France, containing the events of our history from Clovis to the death of Louis XIV* (1744).

Henri IV of France (1553–1610) King of Navarre from 1572 until his death, he converted from Protestantism to Catholicism in order to become King of France in 1589, at the end of the French Wars of Religion. His Edict of Nantes, 1598, gave Protestants the right to practise in France; it was revoked by Louis XIV in 1685. Along with his most trusted minister, Maximilien de Béthune, Duc de Sully (1559–1641), 'Good King Henri' represented for the eighteenth century the model of good, tolerant kingship. He was assassinated by a Catholic extremist, François Ravaillac, in 1610.

Henry, Prince of Prussia (1726–1802) Frederick the Great's brother, commander of Prussian troops during the Seven Years War and the War of the Bavarian Succession. Henry visited Russia twice, in 1770–1 and again in 1776. During the first visit, instigated by the prince independently of his brother, the king, Henry pressed Catherine to negotiate the First Partition of Poland (1772). During Henry's second visit, Grand Duchess Natalia Alekseevna died in childbirth, and Henry then escorted Grand Duke Paul to Prussia to bring home his new bride, the future Grand Duchess Maria Fedorovna. Catherine's cordial correspondence with Henry ran parallel to that with Frederick from 1770 until the collapse of the alliance between Russia and Prussia in 1780; it was an alternative means of sending messages to Frederick and of smoothing relations between the allies.

Heraclius (Erekle) **II of Georgia** (1720–1798) Georgian ruler. During Catherine's First Russo-Turkish War, he collaborated with Russia as a Christian power that might help him to prevent the Persians from reclaiming territory in Georgia. By the Treaty of Georgievsk (1783), Georgia formally separated from Persia and became a Russian protectorate. The conflict that followed Heraclius's refusal to return to Persia in 1795 pushed Catherine to undertake the Persian campaign of 1796, which was interrupted by her death.

Hertzberg, Count Ewald Friedrich von (1725–1795) Prussian government minister. Catherine loathed him for his expansionist policies and his opposition to Russian territorial acquisitions.

Huber, Jean (1721–1786) Swiss painter and silhouettist active in Geneva. He created the 'Voltairiade', a series of lovingly humorous depictions of Voltaire going about his daily activities, a number of which were acquired by Catherine.

Igelström, Count Osip Andreevich (Otto Heinrich) (1737–1823) Baltic German military officer, in Russian service from 1756, commander in Crimea, 1784, then governor-general in Simbirsk and Ufa, 1784–90, and in Pskov and Smolensk, 1792–3. As a diplomat, he negotiated on Catherine's behalf the Treaty of Värälä that ended the Russo-Swedish War in 1790, and acted as her representative in Poland in 1794, where he was chased from his post by the Kosciuszko Uprising.

Iusupov, Prince Nikolai Borisovich (1750–1831) Russian nobleman who travelled around Europe to complete his education for several years in the 1770s, becoming an important art collector, director of the imperial theatres, 1791–9, and, under Catherine's son Paul, the director of the Hermitage.

Izmailov, Mikhail L'vovich (d. 1797) Favourite of Peter III.

Johanna Elisabeth, Princess of Anhalt-Zerbst (née Johanna Elisabeth of Schleswig-Holstein-Gottorf) (1712–1760) Catherine's mother and the aunt of Gustav III of Sweden.

Jones, John Paul (1747–1792) Scottish-born naval officer, who fought on the side of the colonists in the American Revolutionary War, before serving briefly in the Russian navy in 1788, until interpersonal intrigues forced him to depart for Western Europe.

Joseph II, Holy Roman Emperor (1741–1790) Holy Roman Emperor from 1765, he ruled jointly with his mother, Maria Theresa, until her death in 1780, when he became sole sovereign of the Habsburg lands. An exemplary but sometimes overambitious Enlightenment monarch, he worked tirelessly to reform his territories, abolishing serfdom, reducing the power of the Catholic Church, granting religious toleration, and instituting a new penal code. In 1781, Joseph and Catherine formed an alliance, which made possible Russia's further expansion to the south in the latter part of Catherine's reign. Joseph visited Russia twice, first meeting Catherine in 1780 and then accompanying her on her journey to Crimea in 1787.

Juigné, Jacques-Gabriel-Louis Le Clerc, Marquis de (1727–1807) French ambassador in St Petersburg, 1775–7.

Kamensky, Count Mikhail Fedotovich (1738–1809) Russian field marshal, who served in both of Catherine's Russo-Turkish wars. In 1806, the elderly general was named commander-in-chief of the Russian armies fighting Napoleon, but he almost immediately resigned his command.

Karolina Henrietta, Landgravine of Hesse-Darmstadt (1721–1774) The mother of Grand Duchess Natalia Alekseevna. Called the 'Great Landgravine' by Goethe, she was an outstanding patroness of writers such as Sophie von La Roche and Johann Gottfried Herder. Like Catherine, she corresponded with Frederick the Great and Grimm, to whose *Literary Correspondence* she subscribed. During Karolina's visit to St Petersburg in 1773, Catherine developed a genuine affection and appreciation for her.

Kauffmann, Angelica (1741–1807) Swiss-born painter and founding member of the Royal Academy of Arts in London, where she lived for sixteen years. After her marriage in 1781 to the Italian painter Antonio Zucchi, she moved permanently to Rome. Catherine became her patron after being introduced to her work by Dashkova.

Keyserlingk, Count Hermann Carl von (1695–1764) Baltic German diplomat, briefly president of the Russian Academy of Sciences in 1733. He was Russian ambassador to Poland, 1733–44, 1749–52, and 1763–4, serving in between as ambassador to Prussia and the Holy Roman Empire.

Kingston, Elizabeth Chudleigh, Duchess of (1721–1788) A scandalous Englishwoman, found guilty of bigamy in 1776. She visited Russia from

August to November 1777. She was received by the empress and greatly enjoyed the city's entertainments.

Kotzebue, August von (1761–1819) Very popular German playwright and friend of Johann Georg Zimmermann; he served as a Russian civil servant from 1781 until 1790. He was murdered by a member of a radical student group, in response to which the German Confederation implemented the repressive Carlsbad Decrees, restricting freedom of speech and association.

Kozitsky, Grigory Vasil'evich (1724/5–1775) Russian writer and translator, Catherine's secretary from 1768 until shortly before his death.

Kozlovsky, Prince Fedor Alekseevich (d. 1770) Russian military officer, writer, translator, and one of the secretaries for Catherine's Legislative Commission. He was killed at the Battle of Chesme.

Koz'min, Sergei Matveevich (1723–1788) Russian translator, Catherine's secretary, 1762–81.

Kruse, Alexander Ivanovich van (1731–1799) Russian admiral of Danish descent. He commanded the *St Eustace* at the Battle of Chesme; he was aboard the ship when it exploded, but managed to survive. He then served in the Russo-Swedish War of 1788–90.

La Barre, François-Jean Lefebvre, Chevalier de (1745–1766) French nobleman, who was tortured and killed on accusations of desecrating the crucifix. In his extensive writings on the subject, Voltaire enlisted La Barre's case in his battles against judicial cruelty and clerical fanaticism.

La Fayette, Gilbert du Motier, Marquis de (1757–1834) French general, who fought for the colonists in the American Revolutionary War and then became a moderate supporter of the French Revolution.

Lafont, Sophie de (née Dubuisson) (1717–1797) French Huguenot, head of the Smolnyi Institute for Noble Girls in St Petersburg from 1764 until her death.

La Harpe, Jean-François de (1739–1803) French writer. He was a disciple of Voltaire but Catherine did not think very highly of him.

Lambert, Henri-Joseph, Marquis de (1738–1808) French military officer, who, through Grimm's intercession, entered Russian service in 1794. In 1795, he went to Prussia on a mission from Catherine to prevent the court at Berlin from making peace with Revolutionary France and to encourage Duke Charles William Ferdinand of Brunswick to lead troops against France instead.

Lanskoy, Alexander Dmitrievich (1758–1784) Catherine's favourite from 1780 until his untimely death. His already sickly constitution was weakened further by a fall from a horse in 1783; he died of a fever on 25 June 1784.

La Rivière, Pierre-Paul Lemercier de (1719–1801) French Physiocrat, who travelled to Russia on Diderot's recommendation and in hopes of guiding Catherine's policies. His arrogant behaviour quickly alienated his imperial hostess, and he was soon sent packing.

La Teyssonnière, Joseph-Marie de (1742–after 1802) Frenchman who travelled to Russia in 1777 and entered Potemkin's service, but he was later sent to Siberia for killing two men in a fight.

Laudon, Generalissimus Gideon Ernst, Baron von (1717–1790) Highly successful Austrian field marshal. He was initially in Russian service, but primarily in that of Austria during the Seven Years War, the War of the Bavarian Succession, and the Second Russo-Turkish War.

Lekain, Henri-Louis (born Henri-Louis Cain) (1729–1778) Successful French tragic actor and protégé of Voltaire.

Leopold II, Holy Roman Emperor (1747–1792) Son of Maria Theresa and brother of Joseph II, an exemplar of enlightened monarchy. He was Grand Duke of Tuscany, 1765–90, and Holy Roman Emperor from 1790 until his untimely death in 1792.

Levshina, Alexandra Petrovna (1757–1782) A member of the founding class of students at the Smolnyi Institute for Noble Girls, which was established by Catherine in 1764. Catherine took a liking to the lively girl and corresponded with her occasionally over several years. After receiving a gold medal upon her graduation in 1776, Levshina was appointed a maid of honour at Catherine's court. In 1780, she married Prince Petr Alexandrovich Cherkassky, but she died two years later, aged only 25.

L'Hôpital, Paul-François de Galluccio, Marquis de (1697–1776) French ambassador to Russia, 1757–60.

Ligne, Prince Charles-Joseph de (1735–1814) Belgian nobleman in Austrian service, sovereign in his native estates, military commander, diplomat, and socialite. He visited Berlin and St Petersburg in 1780 and was a success at Catherine's court, participating in the entertainments in her Hermitage and soon beginning to correspond with the empress. For the first year of Catherine's Second Russo-Turkish War, de Ligne was the Habsburgs' representative at Potemkin's military headquarters. He was better known, however, for his conversation and for dabbling in literature, his writings ranging from descriptions of his garden to military affairs. He later published a heavily edited version of his correspondence with Catherine, correcting especially his own letters and even fabricating new ones that he had never sent.

Louis I, the Pious (or the Fair) (778–840) Holy Roman Emperor, son of Charlemagne. His reign was ravaged by strife between his sons.

Louis XIV of France (1638–1715) King of France from 1643 until his death, known as the Sun King. As consolidator of the French monarchy's absolute power and as a patron of the arts he became the model for monarchs throughout Europe until the end of the *ancien régime*.

Louis XVI of France (1754–1793) King of France from 1774, removed from power and then beheaded by the French Revolutionaries on 21 January 1793 (NS). His death understandably shocked and horrified Catherine.

Louis XVIII of France (1755–1824) Brother of Louis XVI, known as Louis-Stanislas-Xavier, Comte de Provence, until his accession as King of France in 1814.

Louisa Ulrika of Sweden (1720–1782) Sister of Frederick the Great, wife of Adolf Frederick of Sweden (1710–1771), Queen Consort, 1751–71, and mother of Gustav III.

Lucchesini, Girolamo (1751–1825) Prussian diplomat. He was chamberlain to Frederick II of Prussia from 1780, and diplomat under Frederick William II. From October 1788 until 1792, he frequently represented Prussia in Poland, where he actively thwarted Russian influence.

Ludwig, Prince of Hesse-Darmstadt (1753–1830) Brother of Grand Duchess Natalia Alekseevna and later Grand Duke of Hesse from 1806. He was briefly betrothed to Sophia of Württemberg, but the engagement was broken off so that she could marry Catherine's son Paul and become Grand Duchess Maria Fedorovna.

Mailly, Barnabé Augustin de (1732–1793) Parisian goldsmith and enameller, the creator of Catherine's Chesme Inkstand. He followed his masterpiece to Russia and then travelled around the country, accumulating a mineral collection, which he later donated to the French nation.

Malmesbury, James Harris, 1st Earl of (1746–1820) British diplomat, envoy-extraordinary to Russia, 1777–83, where he was accompanied by his wife, Harriet Maria (née Amyand) (1761–1830).

Mansurov, Pavel Dmitrievich (1726–after 1798) Russian lieutenant-general, then senator. He was instrumental in suppressing the Pugachev Rebellion (1773–4).

Marcus Aurelius (121–180) Roman emperor from 161 until his death, and author of a set of Stoic *Meditations* still widely read today. He was revered in the eighteenth century as a model ruler.

Maria I of Portugal (1734–1816) Queen of Portugal, who, as the sole heir of her father, José I (1714–1777), reigned in her own right from 1777, alongside her husband, Pedro III (1717–1786). She was mentally ill, and her son João (1767–1826) acted as regent for much of her reign.

Maria Theresa of Austria (1717–1780) Queen of Bohemia, Hungary, and Croatia, Archduchess of Austria, Holy Roman Empress as the consort of Emperor Francis I, and mother of Holy Roman Emperors Joseph II and Leopold II and of Marie Antoinette of France.

Marie Antoinette of France (1755–1793) Daughter of Maria Theresa of Austria, Queen of France, wife of Louis XVI. She was executed by the French Revolutionary government on 16 October 1793 (NS).

Maria Fedorovna (née Princess Sophia Dorothea of Württemberg) (1759–1828) Second wife of Catherine's son Paul, Grand Duchess of Russia, 1776–96, empress consort, 1796–1801.

Marmontel, Jean-François (1723–1799) French man of letters, sometime lodger in the home of Madame Geoffrin, and d'Alembert's successor as secretary of the Académie française from 1783 until the Academy was closed during the French Revolution. His philosophical novel *Bélisaire*, essentially a how-to guide for enlightened monarchs, was banned by French religious authorities; Catherine joined the several crowned heads (including the future Gustav III of Sweden) in writing letters of support, which Marmontel published. Catherine's gesture of translating *Bélisaire* in the company of her court, and especially of translating chapter 9 on the duties of the sovereign, was a key display of enlightened status and was meant as a pointed contrast with French ineptitude and backwardness.

Menshikov, Prince Petr Alexandrovich (1743–1781) Russian nobleman whom Catherine sent to Sweden to give Gustav III official notification of the birth of her grandson Alexander in December 1777. He was a direct descendant of Prince Alexander Danilovich Menshikov (1673–1729), an intimate advisor to Peter the Great, and chief minister during the reign of Catherine I, 1725–1727.

Mignot, Alexandre Jean, Abbé de Sellières (1725–1790) Voltaire's nephew, who arranged for the Patriarch's burial despite the Church's prohibition. Catherine complained about his meddling in the negotiations for her purchase of Voltaire's library.

Mirabeau, Honoré-Gabriel Riqueti, Comte de (1749–1791) French statesman, orator, and libertine writer. During the French Revolution, he was both president of the Jacobin Club and a secret supporter of the monarchy. After his death on 2 April 1791 (NS), he was the first person to be honoured with burial in the Panthéon, but his remains were removed in 1794.

Morkov, Arkady Ivanovich (1747–1827) Russian ambassador to Sweden, 1783–6, then a leading member in the ministry of foreign affairs in the final years of Catherine's reign. He was made a count of the Holy Roman Empire in 1796.

Münnich, Count Burkhard Christoph von (1683–1767) German-born field marshal, who entered Russian service in 1721 and became famous for his successes against the Ottoman Empire (1735–9), leading the first Russian invasion of Crimea. Exiled to Siberia by Empress Elizabeth, he spent twenty years there before being recalled and rehabilitated by Peter III. Catherine forgave him for supporting her husband and treated him kindly in his final years.

Musin-Pushkin, Count Valentin Platonovich (1735–1804) Russian general. In 1788–9 he commanded the Russian troops in Finland during the Russo-Swedish War.

Mustafa III of the Ottoman Empire (1717–1774) Sultan, 1757–74. He declared war on Russia in 1768 in hopes of checking Russia's growing power in the Caucasus and in Poland; in the event, despite French military advisors and support, the Ottomans lost extensive territory to Russia and were forced to make serious trade and shipping concessions.

Naryshkin, Lev Alexandrovich (1733–1799) Russian courtier. He was appointed to Grand Duke Peter's court in 1751, managing to win the approval of both the grand duke and the grand duchess. A highly amusing and enthusiastic socialite, Naryshkin was a fixture of all Catherine's entertainments at court and one of her favourite satirical targets in her letters and other literary works. She frequently refers to him by his ceremonial court title of grand equerry.

Nassau-Siegen, Charles-Henri-Nicolas-Othon, Prince of (1745–1808) French-born military officer, who circumnavigated the globe with Louis-

Antoine de Bougainville in the 1760s, and served in France and Spain before entering Russian service as a naval captain in 1788. During the Russo-Swedish War of 1788–1790, Nassau-Siegen was successful in the First Battle of Svensksund in August 1789, but suffered a blistering defeat at the Second Battle of Svensksund / Rochensalm in July 1790. Catherine refused his resignation and insisted that he serve until the end of the war, after which he participated in negotiations between Catherine and the émigré princes in Koblenz during the French Revolution.

Natalia Alekseevna (née Wilhelmina Louisa of Hesse-Darmstadt) (1755–1776) First wife of Catherine's son Paul, and Grand Duchess of Russia from 1773 until her death. Catherine quickly grew frustrated with her daughter-in-law's indocility and refusal to learn Russian; the grand duchess's affair with Andrei Razumovsky was well known. She died in childbirth.

Necker, Jacques (1732–1804) Swiss banker, head of French finances from 1777 until 1781, and again in 1788–9 and 1789–90. Catherine admired him initially, but became increasingly disillusioned as he failed to halt the mounting turmoil in France.

Nepliuev, Ivan Ivanovich (1693–1773) Russian diplomat, admiral, and administrator, educated under Peter the Great. Catherine entrusted to him her son during her coup of 1762, and the city of St Petersburg during her absence for her coronation in Moscow in 1762–3.

Nestor (*c*.1056–*c*.1114) Russian hagiographer and author of one of the most important historical sources of the period, the *Primary Chronicle* (1113).

Nevsky, St Alexander (1220/1–1263) Prince of Novgorod, Kiev, and then of Vladimir, who defended Russia against Swedish and German invasion. His decision to combat the West while paying tribute to the Mongol Golden Horde has been seen as a key moment orientating Russia towards the East; he remains an important and popular cultural icon in Russia to this day.

Nicolai, Christoph Friedrich (1733–1811) German writer, bookseller, and leading figure of the Berlin Enlightenment. Catherine very much enjoyed his novel *The Life and Opinions of Master Sebaldus Nothanker* (1773–6), and he became her publisher in Berlin, printing German translations of her anti-Masonic trilogy of 1785–6, her *Notes Concerning Russian History*, and other works for her grandsons.

Noailles, Adrien-Maurice, Duc de (1678–1766) French military officer, commander of the French army during the War of the Austrian Succession.

Nolcken, Baron Johan Fredrik von (1737–1809) Swedish envoy-extraordinary to Russia, 1773–88.

Obreskov, Aleksei Mikhailovich (1718–1787) Russian representative in the Ottoman Empire, 1751–71. His arrest by the Ottoman government in 1768 signalled the start of Catherine's First Russo-Turkish War, and his release was one of her key preconditions for starting peace talks. Once freed in 1771, he participated in the failed peace negotiations at Focşani and Bucharest. He then served as a senator from 1779 until his death.

Olavide y Jáuregui, Pablo Antonio José de (1725–1803) Peruvian-born Spanish reformer who was condemned by the Inquisition in 1778 but escaped to France, where he remained through the French Revolution.

Orlov, Count Fedor Grigor'evich (1741–1796) Younger brother of Grigory and Aleksei Orlov. He served on Catherine's Legislative Commission, before entering military service for the war against the Ottomans; he was aboard the *St Eustace* before it exploded during the Battle of Chesme. On his way back to St Petersburg in 1771, he passed through Geneva without visiting Voltaire. He spent the rest of his life in retirement in Moscow.

Orlov, Prince Grigory Grigor'evich (1734–1783) One of five Orlov brothers, Catherine's favourite and lover from 1761 until 1772; he was a key figure in organizing the coup that brought her to power in 1762. Catherine's pregnancy with their son Aleksei Grigor'evich Bobrinsky, among other causes, prevented her from seizing the throne immediately upon the death of Empress Elizabeth in December 1761. Catherine granted Orlov the title of count, then prince; she regularly refers to him by his position of grand master of the artillery.

Orlov, Count Vladimir Grigor'evich (1743–1831) The youngest of the brothers of Catherine's favourite Grigory Orlov. He was director of the Russian Academy of Sciences, 1766–74.

Orlov-Chesmensky, Count Aleksei Grigor'evich (1737–1807) Brother of Catherine's favourite Grigory Orlov; key conspirator in her coup of 1762, for which he and his brothers were granted the title of count. He is typically held responsible for the death of Catherine's husband, Peter III. Placed in command of the Russian fleet in the Mediterranean during Catherine's First Russo-Turkish War (1768–74), he received the honorary surname 'Chesmensky' as a reward for his brilliant victory at Chesme (24–6 June 1770), where much of the Ottoman navy was wiped out and Russia definitively proved its might in the southern European seas.

Osten, Count Adolph Sigfried von der (1726–1797) Danish diplomat, friend of Stanislas Poniatowski. He was the representative of Denmark in St Petersburg during Elizabeth's reign, and later Danish minister of foreign affairs under Johann Friedrich Struensee (1770–3).

Osterman, Count Ivan Andreevich (1725–1811) Russian vice-chancellor from 1775 until the end of Catherine's reign, and official head of the Russian College of Foreign Affairs. From 1781 onward, his second in command, Alexander Bezborodko, was in reality far more active and influential than he was. He was chancellor in the first year of Paul's reign, but soon retired.

Pahlen (or Paalen), Baron (afterwards Count) Peter Ludwig von der (1745–1826) Russian envoy to Sweden and repeatedly an intermediary for communications between Catherine and Gustav III from 1790 until Gustav's death in 1792.

Paisiello, Giovanni (1740–1816) Italian composer in Catherine's service, 1776–84.

Pallas, Peter Simon (1741–1811) German botanist, zoologist, mineralogist, and geologist, who came to Russia in 1767 on Catherine's invitation. He remained until 1810 and published travelogues and natural-historical descriptions based on his journeys across the country. He co-authored with Catherine her *Comparative Dictionary of All Languages and Dialects* (2 vols, 1787–9).

Panckoucke, Charles-Joseph (1736–1798) Parisian publisher, who initially planned the first posthumous edition of Voltaire's complete works.

Panin, Count Nikita Ivanovich (1718–1783) Russian diplomat and statesman. After serving as a diplomat, particularly in Sweden, 1748–60, Panin was placed in charge of the education of Catherine's son Paul from 1760 until Paul's majority in 1773. De facto head of Russian foreign affairs from 1763 until 1781, Panin advocated a Northern Alliance between Russia, Prussia, Britain, and the other states surrounding the Baltic.

Panin, Count Petr Ivanovich (1721–1789) Russian general and senator, younger brother of Nikita Panin. He retired from active service in 1770, after fighting in Catherine's First Russo-Turkish War, but he returned to lead the forces suppressing the Pugachev Rebellion after the death of Alexander Bibikov in April 1774. He advocated harsh reprisals against those who participated in the uprising; Catherine disliked him as one of her most outspoken critics in Moscow.

Paoli, Pasquale (1725–1807) Leader of the Corsican fight for independence against Genoa and then against France; defeated by the French, he fled to England in 1769. He was buried in Westminster Abbey.

Passek, Petr Bogdanovich (1736–1804) Russian guardsman, then civil servant and nominal president of the Free Economic Society, 1794–7. He was one of the principal conspirators aiming to put Catherine on the throne, and his arrest on 27 June 1762 precipitated the coup; Catherine rewarded him financially and with promotion.

Paul I of Russia (1754–1801) Catherine's only legitimate son and heir. Taken away from Catherine at birth, Paul was raised under the supervision of Empress Elizabeth. Nikita Panin was responsible for his education until 1773, when Paul reached his majority and married Wilhelmina of Hesse-Darmstadt (Grand Duchess Natalia Alekseevna). After her death in childbirth, he married Sophia of Württemberg (Grand Duchess Maria Fedorovna). The relationship between Catherine and her son was always tense, and upon coming to the throne in 1796 Paul attempted to erase his mother's legacy. His obsession with militarism and micromanagement rendered his reign disastrous, and he was assassinated by a conspiracy of noblemen in March 1801.

Peter I (the Great) of Russia (1672–1725) The first Russian ruler to assume the title of emperor (1721), Peter brought about a complete reorientation of Russian culture and policy in the years of his personal rule (1696–1725). He was celebrated by Russian and Western writers such as Voltaire as the creator of a new Russia. Catherine promoted her reign as a continuation and refinement of his Europeanizing policies.

Peter III of Russia (born Karl Peter Ulrich of Holstein-Gottorf) (1728–1762) Emperor of Russia from December 1761 until his death. He was declared heir to the Russian imperial throne by Empress Elizabeth in 1742. His marriage to his cousin, Catherine, in 1745 was an unhappy one: the spouses' interests and habits diverged greatly, and both were unfaithful. After his accession at the end of 1761, Peter's short reign brought about several important reforms, including the release of the nobility from obligatory state service. Nonetheless, he rapidly became unpopular owing to his abrasive manner, his adulation of all things Prussian, his disdain for Russian religion and customs, and his decision to return all Russian conquests after withdrawing from the Seven Years War, planning instead to ally with Prussia to conquer Schleswig. His insults led Catherine to fear that he would send her to a convent and marry his mistress instead; he was killed in mysterious circumstances nine days after Catherine's coup.

Peter Friedrich Ludwig of Oldenburg (1755–1829) Son of Catherine's uncle Georg Ludwig of Schleswig-Holstein-Gottorf, he was Catherine's ward after his father's death in 1763. He became Coadjutor of Lübeck in 1777, and was Prince-Bishop of Lübeck, 1785–1803, regent of the Duchy of Oldenburg, 1785–1823, and Duke of Oldenburg, 1823–9.

Pitt, William (the Elder), **1st Earl of Chatham** (1708–1778) British prime minister, 1766–8, he was highly influential even when out of office.

Pitt, William (the Younger) (1759–1806) Son of Pitt the Elder and prime minister of Great Britain, 1783–1801, and of the United Kingdom, 1804–6. His belligerent anti-Russian policies during Catherine's Second Russo-Turkish War earned her animosity.

Platon (Levshin) (1737–1812) Russian churchman, one of those most in tune with intellectual developments in the West. He was appointed Metropolitan of Moscow in 1775. He delivered a sermon at the celebration of the victory at Chesme, which Voltaire received from Princess Dashkova in her own translation. In 1785, Platon was ordered by Catherine to investigate the publishing activities of the Freemasons.

Poliansky, Vasily Ipat'evich (1742–1800/1) Russian civil servant, whom Catherine funded to travel abroad and who stayed for some time near Voltaire's home in Ferney. He later became the secretary of the Imperial Academy of Arts in St Petersburg, contributed to the composition of Catherine's Provincial Reform of 1775, and served in the provincial government of Mogilev before retiring in 1780 to his estate near Kazan.

Pombal, Sebastião José de Carvalho e Melo, Marquis of (1699–1782) Enlightened leading minister of Portugal under José I; he fell from power upon the accession of José's daughter Maria I in February 1777.

Poniatowski, Stanislas August (1732–1798) Last King of Poland (reigned as Stanislas II August, 1764–95). Descended from an important Polish noble family, he visited Paris in his youth, where he met the famous figures of the Enlightenment: Madame Geoffrin called him her 'son', and he corresponded with Voltaire, who praised his attempts at enlightened reform in Poland. He shared literary and cultural interests with Catherine and became her lover when he was serving as Sir Charles Hanbury-Williams's secretary in St Petersburg in 1755–6. He was with Catherine at the dangerous moment in 1758 when the fall of Bestuzhev-Riumin jeopardized her position; it was he who broke the news of the arrest to her. In 1764, with the help of Frederick II of Prussia, Catherine placed Poniatowski on the Polish throne, where he remained until the Third Partition of Poland in 1795 eliminated his kingdom entirely. He spent the last years of his life in exile in St Petersburg.

Pont-de-Veyle, Antoine de Fériol, Comte de (1697–1774) French playwright, author of *The Sleep-Walker* (1739), which Catherine quotes frequently.

Potemkin, Most Serene Prince Grigory Alexandrovich (1739–1791) Catherine's most celebrated favourite and possibly, secretly, her husband; Catherine procured for him the status of prince of the Holy Roman Empire and bestowed on him the honorary surname of 'Tavrichesky' ('of Tauris', i.e. Crimea). An officer in the Horse Guards, he was rewarded for participation in Catherine's coup. He participated in Catherine's Legislative Commission as Guardian of Exotic Peoples. He fought in the First Russo-Turkish War until, responding to a summons from Catherine, he returned to St Petersburg in early 1774; he and Catherine were lovers by the end of February. Catherine initiated him into the business of state, and he remained a crucial advisor after their romantic relationship ended in 1776. He led the annexation of Crimea in 1783 and spent the rest of his life overseeing the development of Russia's southern provinces; the display of his successes during Catherine's Crimean journey of 1787 generated the proverbial phrase 'Potemkin villages' (meaning a sham or an imposing façade with nothing behind it). He led Russian troops in Catherine's Second Russo-Turkish War; his death in 1791 was a great blow to Catherine, who lost in him both her lifelong companion and her strongest advisor and supporter.

Potemkin, Count Pavel Sergeevich (1743–1796) Grigory Potemkin's cousin, general, head of the branch of the Secret Department investigating the Pugachev Rebellion in Kazan and Orenburg; thereafter he served as Grigory Potemkin's assistant.

Pugachev, Emel'ian Ivanovich (*c.*1742–1775) A Don Cossack, who served in Catherine's First Russo-Turkish War. In August 1773 he initiated the Pugachev Rebellion; he was executed in Moscow on 10 January 1775.

Pushchin, Petr Ivanovich (1723–1812) Russian vice-admiral, who commanded Catherine's flotilla on the journey to Crimea in 1787. Responsible for naval logistics, he was promoted to admiral in 1790.

Razumovsky, Andrei Kirillovich (1752–1836) Russian diplomat, son of Kirill Razumovsky. He was Russian ambassador in Naples from 1777, Copenhagen from 1784, Stockholm from 1786, and Vienna from 1790. A friend of Grand Duke Paul, Razumovsky created a scandal in 1776 when his affair with the late Grand Duchess Natalia Alekseevna was made public.

Razumovsky, Count Kirill Grigor'evich (1728–1803) Brother of Empress Elizabeth's favourite Aleksei Razumovsky. The last hetman of the

Zaporozhian Host, 1750–64, he was Catherine's ally at court when she was Grand Duchess. He was president of the Russian Academy of Sciences, 1746–98, although this role became essentially ceremonial after 1765.

Recke, Elisa von der (1754–1833) Baltic German writer. Catherine admired and ordered the translation into Russian of Recke's *Information on the Infamous Cagliostro's Stay in Mitau in the Year 1779* (1787), in which, as a warning to others, Recke describes her own experience of being deceived by the famous charlatan. She is known also as a diarist and religious poet. Catherine struck up a correspondence with Recke and gave her an estate; Recke visited Catherine in St Petersburg in 1795 despite Russia's annexation earlier that year of the Duchy of Courland, of which Recke's sister Dorothea was the last duchess.

Reinsdorp, Ivan Andreevich (1730–1781) Russian military officer of Danish descent, governor of Orenburg, 1768–81. During the Pugachev Rebellion, the city of Orenburg withstood a lengthy siege under his leadership.

Rennenkampff, Johann Dietrich von (1719–1783) Nobleman from Livonia, member of Catherine's Legislative Commission, and Russian military officer during Catherine's First Russo-Turkish War.

Repnin, Prince Nikolai Vasil'evich (1734–1801) Russian ambassador to Poland, 1764–1768. During Catherine's First Russo-Turkish War, Repnin took Izmail (1770) and played an important role in negotiating the Treaty of Küçük Kaynarca (1774). He then was sent as Russia's envoy-extraordinary to the Ottoman Empire in 1775. In the 1770s and 1780s, he served as governor of Smolensk and then Pskov, and he was a key negotiator of the Peace of Teschen (1779), one of Catherine's major diplomatic victories. In the Second Russo-Turkish War he served under Potemkin. As an administrator and military commander, he played an active role in enforcing the final two partitions of Poland.

Ribbing af Koberg, Baron Carl (1718–1773) Swedish envoy in St Petersburg, 1766–73.

Richelieu, Armand-Emmanuel de Vignerot du Plessis, Duc de (1766–1822) French nobleman, officer and administrator in Russian service. He became duc de Richelieu in 1791. He entered Russian military service in 1790, participating in the siege of Izmail the same year. He returned briefly to France in 1791, only to depart again swiftly for Russia. He played a crucial role in the development of the city of Odessa as governor, 1803–14. His ancestor, Cardinal de Richelieu (1585–1642), played a key role in establishing centralized royal power in France.

Riedesel, Volprecht Hermann Friedrich von (1732–1785) Diplomat and trusted advisor to Karolina Henrietta of Hesse-Darmstadt and her husband, Ludwig IX. Like Friedrich Melchior Grimm, he was a member of Karolina Henrietta's entourage during her visit to Russia in 1773.

Rimsky-Korsakov, Ivan Nikolaevich (1754–1831) Russian officer and courtier. He was Catherine's favourite, 1778–9, whom she nicknamed 'Pyrrhus, King of Epirus', after the ancient military commander.

Rogerson, John (1741–1823) Catherine's Scottish-born court doctor, who worked in Russia, 1766–1816.

Ronsard, Pierre de (1524–1585) Leading figure in French Renaissance poetry and member of the poetic grouping 'La Pléiade', along with Joachim du Bellay.

Rumiantsev, Count Nikolai Petrovich (1754–1826) Russian diplomat, son of Field Marshal Petr Rumiantsev. Friedrich Melchior Grimm accompanied Nikolai and his brother on their Grand Tour to Italy in 1775–6. As Russian ambassador in Frankfurt, 1782–95, he was Catherine's primary intermediary for communications with the émigré princes during the French Revolution.

Rumiantsev-Zadunaisky, Count Petr Alexandrovich (1725–1796) Russian field marshal, who first won renown as a general in the Seven Years War; he played a leading role in the Russo-Turkish War of 1768–74, for which Catherine rewarded him with the honorary surname of 'Zadunaisky' ('Beyond the Danube'). Initially placed in command of the Second Russian Army in the Russo-Turkish War of 1787–92, he was recalled from his command in March 1789. Catherine respected and used his military talents although she had little personal affection for him.

Riurik (d. 879) Legendary Viking prince of Novgorod and founder of the ruling dynasty of Kievan Rus'. As a matter of national pride, debates raged in eighteenth-century Russia about whether the Riurikids were of Germanic or Slavic origin.

Saint-Priest, François-Emmanuel Guignard, Comte de (1735–1821) French ambassador to Constantinople, 1768–85. Catherine awarded him the order of St Andrew the First-Called for his role in negotiating the Treaty of Aynalikavak (1779), which confirmed the independence of Crimea from the Ottoman Empire. Briefly a member of the French government with ties to Necker, he emigrated in 1791 and visited Russia in the same year. Two of his sons settled in Russia.

Saltykov, Ivan Petrovich (1730–1805) Russian military officer, son of Petr Semënovich Saltykov. He participated in the Seven Years War and in both of Catherine's Russo-Turkish Wars. He commanded Russian troops at the end of the Russo-Swedish War.

Saltykov, Nikolai Ivanovich (1736–1816) Russian military officer, courtier, and educator. He fought in the Seven Years War and Catherine's First Russo-Turkish War. He then accompanied Paul and Maria Fedorovna on their European tour in 1781–2, and was entrusted from 1783 with the education of Grand Dukes Alexander and Constantine.

Saltykov, Count Petr Semënovich (1698–1772) Russian field marshal, commander-in-chief of the Russian troops fighting in the Seven Years War, 1759–60, and commander-in-chief of Moscow, 1763–71.

Schah Baham A fictional character in Crébillon *fils*'s libertine novel *The Sofa* (1742). A wilfully ignorant, lazy, and self-satisfied sultan, to whom Catherine enjoys ironically comparing herself.

Scheffer, Count Ulrik (1716–1799) President of Gustav III of Sweden's chancellery, 1772–83.

Schomberg, Count Gottlieb-Ludwig (1726–1796) German military officer in French service, and Friedrich Melchior Grimm's friend and patron.

Sedaine, Michel-Jean (1719–1797) French dramatist patronized by Catherine.

Ségur, Louis-Philippe, Comte de (1753–1830) French ambassador to Russia, 1785–9, where he became one of Catherine's intimates, joined her in producing the *Collection of Plays from the Hermitage* (4 vols, 1788–9), and nearly succeeded in negotiating an alliance, which was disrupted by the French Revolution. His Revolutionary sympathies alienated Catherine, who then refused to correspond with her former friend. His *Memoirs* (1824–6) contain an oft cited account of Catherine and her court.

Selim III (1761–1808) Ottoman sultan, 1789–1807, known as a reformer of Ottoman military and diplomatic structures.

Sénac de Meilhan, Gabriel (1736–1803) French administrator and man of letters. Upon emigrating during the French Revolution, he travelled to Catherine's court in 1791 on the pretext of writing a history of Russia. Catherine expected to find in him a possible intermediary with the émigré princes, but instead discovered a careerist, interested essentially in his own profit-making. She had his *On the Principles and Causes of the Revolution in France* (1790) republished in Russia, and he soon left for Germany, where he authored his most famous work, the epistolary novel *The Émigré* (1797).

Seniavin, Aleksei Naumovich (1716–1797) Russian admiral, responsible for building a new type of ship appropriate for shallow waters, during Catherine's First Russo-Turkish War. Ready and in action by 1771, Seniavin's fleet contributed to the capture of Crimea and defended the Sea of Azov.

Shchedrin, Feodosy Fedorovich (1751–1825) Russian sculptor, trained in Paris.

Shahin Giray (1745–1787) The last Khan of Crimea, who ruled with interruptions from 1777 until the annexation of Crimea in 1783. He visited St Petersburg in 1772.

Shuvalov, Count Alexander Ivanovich (1710–1771) Russian politician, brother of Petr Ivanovich. He was a trusted supporter of Empress Elizabeth from before her coup, head of the Russian secret police, master of the court of Catherine's husband Peter from 1754, member of the Conference at the Imperial Court (imperial council). Catherine deeply disliked him, although she attempted to influence him in favour of Prussia as the Seven Years War began.

Shuvalov, Count Andrei Petrovich (1744–1789) Russian civil servant and French-language poet. He visited Voltaire at Ferney and subsequently corresponded with him, sometimes communicating the letters to Catherine and sending information to Voltaire to complement what she wrote herself. He also contributed to the collective Russian translation of Marmontel's *Bélisaire*.

Shuvalov, Ivan Ivanovich (1727–1797) Russian courtier and favourite of Empress Elizabeth. He was the first rector of Moscow University and president of the Imperial Academy of Arts, and he corresponded with Voltaire. Initially befriended by Catherine as a studious boy serving at court, he established himself as Elizabeth's favourite from 1749, marking the rise of the Shuvalov party's influence. He was a resolute supporter of France, in opposition to Catherine's pro-Prussian position in the mid-1750s. He was grand chamberlain from 1778 and, as a member of the new Russian Academy from 1783, contributed to Princess Dashkova's dictionary project.

Shuvalov, Count Petr Ivanovich (1710–1762) Russian politician, brother of Alexander Ivanovich. He was a trusted supporter of Empress Elizabeth from the time of her coup in 1741, and became a senator and member of the Conference at the Imperial Court.

Sieyès, Emmanuel-Joseph (1748–1836) French churchman and writer. He was the author of the Revolutionary tract *What is the Third Estate?* (1788), in which he argued that the nobility's dominion should be cast off and the common people be given a voice in government appropriate to their numerical superiority.

Skavronskaia, Countess Ekaterina Vasil'evna (née Engel'gardt) (1761–1829) Beloved niece of Grigory Potemkin.

Solms-Sonnenwalde, Count Victor Friedrich von (1730–1783) Prussian ambassador to Russia, 1762–79.

Sophia Magdalena of Sweden (1746–1813) Queen of Sweden, daughter of the Danish king Frederick V, wife of Gustav III of Sweden, and mother of Gustav IV Adolf of Sweden.

Spielmann, Anton von (1738–1813) Austrian statesman.

Spiridov, Grigory Andreevich (1713–1790) Russian admiral and commander of the Russian fleet in the Mediterranean alongside Aleksei Orlov during Catherine's First Russo-Turkish War.

Stackelberg, Count Otto Magnus von (1736–1800) Russian ambassador to Poland, 1772–90, and to Sweden, 1791–3.

Starhemberg, Count Ludwig Joseph von (1762–1833) Austrian diplomat, married to one of Prince Charles-Joseph de Ligne's cousins.

Stedingk, Baron (afterwards Count) **Curt Bogislaus Ludvig Kristoffer von** (1746–1837) Swedish military officer and diplomat. He served in the Royal Swedish Regiment in France until he was recalled to Sweden by Gustav III in 1787, when he fought with distinction in Finland against the Russians. He was then Swedish ambassador to Russia, 1790–1808 and 1809–11.

Strekalov, Stepan Fedorovich (1728–1805) Russian civil servant, in charge of Catherine's personal funds, 1784–92, and also of her court theatre.

Stroganov, Alexander Sergeevich (1733–1811) Russian courtier and important art collector; he was president of the Imperial Academy of Arts, 1800–11.

Struensee, Johann Friedrich (1737–1772) German doctor and reforming chief minister under Christian VII of Denmark. His affair with Queen Caroline Matilda of Denmark became public and led to his fall from power and his execution.

Sumarokov, Alexander Petrovich (1717–1777) Russian neoclassical poet and playwright, who considered himself the founder of Russian classical tragedy. He wrote a letter to his idol, Voltaire, which was delivered alongside Catherine's letter of 17 December 1768 (Letter 41). Sumarokov was so delighted with the reply that he published it in the preface to his tragedy *Dimitry the Pretender* (1771).

Suvorov-Rymniksky, Generalissimus Prince Alexander Vasil'evich (1730–1800) The most famous of Russian generals. He participated in all of Catherine's wars, fighting in Poland and against the Ottomans during her First Russo-Turkish War, playing the key role in taking Ochakov in 1788, earning his title of Count Suvorov-Rymniksky after his victory at Rymnik in September 1789, and brutally repressing the Kosciuszko Uprising in 1794. In 1796, Catherine ordered him to prepare to march against Revolutionary France. After her death, Suvorov suffered the disgrace shared by most individuals who had served Catherine, but in 1799 he was sent on a campaign against Napoleon in Italy that proved successful.

Swedenborg, Emanuel (1688–1772) Swedish mystic, who wrote an extensive biblical commentary, *Arcana cœlestia* (1749–56), and who described his vision of the spiritual world in *Heaven and Hell* (1758).

Talyzin, Ivan Luk'ianovich (1700–1777) Russian admiral. During Catherine's coup in 1762, he took over the fortress of Kronstadt on her behalf and arrested Peter's representative on the island, General Devier. His quick action prevented Peter III from finding a base there, as the former emperor was turned away by the garrison when he tried to escape to the fortress.

Tamerlane (or Timur) (1336–1405) Central Asian military leader, legendary for his bloody conquest of territory stretching from the Caucasus into India and nearly to China.

Todi, Luísa (1753–1833) Portuguese mezzo-soprano who worked in Russia, 1784–8.

Tottleben, Gottlob Curt Heinrich von (1715–1773) Saxon-born military officer. He served in the Russian military during the Seven Years War and in Catherine's First Russo-Turkish War. He was sent on an unsuccessful mission to Georgia during the latter war, and was then transferred to Poland, where he died of illness.

Tott, François, Baron de (1733–1793) French military advisor, sent to the Ottomans by the French government and much mocked in the correspondence between Catherine and Voltaire.

Traetta, Tommaso (1727–1779) Italian composer employed at Catherine's court from 1768 until 1774.

Trousson, Khristian Ivanovich (1742–1813) Military officer born in Koblenz. He entered Russian service as an engineer in 1782 and was wounded in both legs during the storming of Ochakov in December 1788. He later served in Catherine's Persian campaign in 1796 and in the war against Napoleon in 1812.

Trubetskoy, Prince Nikita Iur'evich (1699–1767) Russian field marshal, and procurator general of the Senate, 1740–60.

Turchaninov, Petr Ivanovich (1746–after 1823) Russian civil servant. Initially head of Potemkin's chancellery, in 1783 he became Catherine's secretary responsible for military affairs. He remained one of Catherine's secretaries, with various responsibilities, until her death.

Ushakov, Fedor Fedorovich (1745–1817) Russian naval commander, in charge of the Black Sea fleet during Catherine's Second Russo–Turkish War.

Vasil'chikov, Alexander Semënovich (1740?–1804?) Catherine's favourite from mid-1772 until early 1774, when he was replaced by Grigory Potemkin.

Vergennes, Charles Gravier, Comte de (1717–1787) French minister of foreign affairs, 1774–87.

Viazemsky, Alexander Alekseevich (1727–1793) Russian civil servant. He was procurator general of the Senate from 1764, largely responsible for financial matters in the Russian government. Seriously ill from 1789, he retired in 1792.

Voinovich, Mark Ivanovich (1750–1807) Russian naval commander, in charge of the fleet at Sevastopol at the start of Catherine's Second Russo–Turkish War. He was soon replaced by Fedor Ushakov owing to Potemkin's dissatisfaction with him.

Volkonsky, Mikhail Nikitich (1713–1788) Russian ambassador to Poland, 1757–8 and 1769–71, commander-in-chief and then governor-general of Moscow, 1771–80.

Voltaire (born François-Marie Arouet) (1694–1778) French man of letters. Probably the eighteenth century's most famous European writer, Voltaire wrote prolifically in every genre, producing philosophical tales like *Candide* (1759), histories (including a two-volume *History of the Russian Empire under Peter the Great*, 1759–63), some fifty plays, and some 20,000 letters. However, his greatest legacy lies in his long and vocal struggle against religious fanaticism, superstition, and cruelty of all kinds. Catherine was an avid reader of Voltaire, calling him her 'teacher', and shortly after her accession initiated a correspondence that lasted until his death. Catherine then purchased his library, which is still preserved in its entirety at the Russian National Library in St Petersburg; her plan to build an exact reproduction of his house at Ferney on her estate at Tsarskoe Selo was never fulfilled.

Vorontsov, Count Alexander Romanovich (1741–1805) Russian politician, brother of Ekaterina Dashkova and Semën Vorontsov. He was a senator and member of the Conference at the Imperial Court, Catherine's council, 1787–91.

Vorontsov, Count Semën Romanovich (1744–1832) Russian military officer and diplomat. He fought in Catherine's First Russo–Turkish War, but then made a career in diplomatic service as Russian ambassador in Venice, 1782–4, and then in London, 1784–1806. Critical of Catherine and her favourites, Vorontsov nonetheless served assiduously, winning major diplomatic victories, such as averting an attack on Russia in 1791 by manipulating the British press; he also renewed the commercial treaty between Russia and Great Britain in 1793 and then negotiated collaboration between Russia and Great Britain to fight against the French Revolution.

Vorontsova, Elizaveta Romanovna (1739–1792) Mistress of Peter III, sister of Ekaterina Dashkova and Alexander and Semën Vorontsov.

Wagner, Friedrich (1693–1760) German Lutheran theologian, pastor in Pomerania and then in Hamburg. He instructed the young Sophia Augusta Fredericka in religion; Catherine later claimed to have given him much trouble by arguing during lessons.

Wagnière, Jean-Louis (1739–1802) Voltaire's last and most faithful secretary. He brought Voltaire's library to St Petersburg in 1779, but refused to remain there and returned to Ferney in France.

Weikard, Melchior Adam (1742–1803) German doctor working at the Russian court, 1784–9, and sometime friend of Johann Georg Zimmermann. The two soon quarrelled, apparently over rivalries for Catherine's favour and over Weikard's foiled ambition to obtain a higher-ranking position.

Zavadovsky, Petr Vasil'evich (1738–1812) Russian courtier and civil servant. He was Catherine's secretary and favourite in 1776–7. After their relatively brief romance, Catherine continued to employ Zavadovsky in a range of responsible administrative posts.

Zelmira, nickname of **Augusta Karolina, Princess of Württemberg** (née Princess of Brunswick-Wolfenbüttel) (1764–1788) Augusta was physically abused by her husband, Frederick of Württemberg, the brother of Grand Duchess Maria Fedorovna (briefly employed by Catherine as the governor-general of eastern Finland), to the extent that Catherine took Augusta under her wing and gave her refuge in Koluvere Castle in Estonia from early in 1787. She died at the age of 23 giving birth to a child, presumably that of her guardian, Wilhelm Reinhold von Pohlmann (1727–1795).

Zimmermann, Johann Georg (1728–1795) Swiss-born doctor and man of letters. He was the personal physician in Hanover to George III; consulted on Frederick the Great's final illness, he wrote polemical works about the Prussian king. Catherine initiated a correspondence with him after finding great comfort in his most famous work, *On Solitude* (1784–5), after the death of her beloved favourite Alexander Lanskoy. Zimmermann served as an intermediary for Catherine's interactions with the Berlin book trade, especially with her publisher Christoph Friedrich Nicolai. Zimmermann arranged for positive reviews of her books and articles about Russia to be placed in the German press, and he recruited German doctors for the Russian provinces and military. In his last years, he spoke out virulently against the French Revolution.

Zorich, Semën Gavrilovich (1745–1799) Military officer of Serbian origin. He was Catherine's favourite from June 1777 until May 1778.

Zubov, Platon Alexandrovich (1767–1822) Catherine's last favourite, Platon is believed to have been a negative influence on Catherine in her final years owing to his greed and idleness.

ACKNOWLEDGEMENTS

We would like to thank Judith Luna for her commitment to this volume, Luciana O'Flaherty for her continued support, and Rebecca du Plessis and Rosemary Roberts for copyediting. We are also grateful to the anonymous readers for their feedback.

American Literature

British and Irish Literature

Children's Literature

Classics and Ancient Literature

Colonial Literature

Eastern Literature

European Literature

Gothic Literature

History

Medieval Literature

Oxford English Drama

Philosophy

Poetry

Politics

Religion

The Oxford Shakespeare

A complete list of Oxford World's Classics, including Authors in Context, Oxford English Drama, and the Oxford Shakespeare, is available in the UK from the Marketing Services Department, Oxford University Press, Great Clarendon Street, Oxford OX2 6DP, or visit the website at www.oup.com/uk/worldsclassics.

In the USA, visit www.oup.com/us/owc for a complete title list.

Oxford World's Classics are available from all good bookshops. In case of difficulty, customers in the UK should contact Oxford University Press Bookshop, 116 High Street, Oxford OX1 4BR.

	French Decadent Tales
	Six French Poets of the Nineteenth Century
HONORÉ DE BALZAC	**Cousin Bette**
	Eugénie Grandet
	Père Goriot
	The Wild Ass's Skin
CHARLES BAUDELAIRE	**The Flowers of Evil**
	The Prose Poems and Fanfarlo
DENIS DIDEROT	**Jacques the Fatalist**
	The Nun
ALEXANDRE DUMAS (PÈRE)	**The Black Tulip**
	The Count of Monte Cristo
	Louise de la Vallière
	The Man in the Iron Mask
	La Reine Margot
	The Three Musketeers
	Twenty Years After
	The Vicomte de Bragelonne
ALEXANDRE DUMAS (FILS)	**La Dame aux Camélias**
GUSTAVE FLAUBERT	**Madame Bovary**
	A Sentimental Education
	Three Tales
VICTOR HUGO	**Notre-Dame de Paris**
J.-K. HUYSMANS	**Against Nature**
PIERRE CHODERLOS DE LACLOS	**Les Liaisons dangereuses**
MME DE LAFAYETTE	**The Princesse de Clèves**
GUILLAUME DU LORRIS and JEAN DE MEUN	**The Romance of the Rose**

ÉMILE ZOLA

L'Assommoir
The Belly of Paris
La Bête humaine
The Conquest of Plassans
The Fortune of the Rougons
Germinal
The Kill
The Ladies' Paradise
The Masterpiece
Money
Nana
Pot Luck
Thérèse Raquin